# THE ROUTLEDGE HANDBOOK OF FESTIVALS

In recent times, festivals around the world have grown in number due to the increased recognition of their importance for tourism, branding and economic development. Festivals hold multifaceted roles in society and can be staged to bring positive economic impact, for the competitive advantage they lend a destination or to address social objectives. Studies on festivals have appeared in a wide range of disciplines, and consequently, much of the research available is highly fragmented.

This handbook brings this knowledge together in one volume, offering a comprehensive evaluation of the most current research, debates and controversies surrounding festivals. It is divided into nine sections that cover a wide range of theories, concepts and contexts, such as sustainability, festival marketing and management, the strategic use of festivals and their future.

Featuring a variety of disciplinary, cultural and national perspectives from an international team of authors, this book will be an invaluable resource for students and researchers of event management and will be of interest to scholars in the fields of anthropology, sociology, geography, marketing, management, psychology and economics.

**Judith Mair** is an Associate Professor in the Tourism Discipline Group of the UQ Business School, University of Queensland, Australia.

# THE ROUTLEDGE HANDBOOK OF FESTIVALS

*Edited by Judith Mair*

First published 2019 by Routledge
2 Park Square, Milton Park, Abingdon, Oxon OX14 4RN
605 Third Avenue, New York, NY 10017

*Routledge is an imprint of the Taylor & Francis Group, an informa business*

First issued in paperback 2022

Copyright © 2019 selection and editorial matter, Judith Mair; individual chapters, the contributors

The right of Judith Mair to be identified as the author of the editorial material, and of the authors for their individual chapters, has been asserted in accordance with sections 77 and 78 of the Copyright, Designs and Patents Act 1988.

All rights reserved. No part of this book may be reprinted or reproduced or utilised in any form or by any electronic, mechanical, or other means, now known or hereafter invented, including photocopying and recording, or in any information storage or retrieval system, without permission in writing from the publishers.

Notice:
Product or corporate names may be trademarks or registered trademarks, and are used only for identification and explanation without intent to infringe.

Publisher's Note
The publisher has gone to great lengths to ensure the quality of this reprint but points out that some imperfections in the original copies may be apparent.

*British Library Cataloguing-in-Publication Data*
A catalogue record for this book is available from the British Library

*Library of Congress Cataloging-in-Publication Data*
A catalog record has been requested for this book

ISBN: 978-1-138-73581-1 (hbk)
ISBN: 978-1-03-233899-6 (pbk)
DOI: 10.4324/9781315186320

Typeset in Bembo
by codeMantra

# CONTENTS

Lists of figures — x
List of tables — xi
List of contributors — xii

**PART I**
**Introduction** — 1

1 Introduction — 3
   *Judith Mair*

2 Methodological approaches to festival research — 12
   *Mary Beth Gouthro and Dorothy Fox*

3 The value of festivals — 22
   *Donald Getz, Tommy D. Andersson, John Armbrecht and Erik Lundberg*

4 The meaning of festivals: reconfiguring the semiotic approach — 31
   *Xiaoming Zhang*

**PART II**
**Sustainability** — 41

5 Valuing the impacts of festivals — 43
   *Larry Dwyer and Leo Jago*

6 Festivals and social sustainability — 53
   *Bernadette Quinn*

## Contents

7   Evaluating the sociocultural effects of festivals: developing a comprehensive impact correlation model and its application    62
*Ronnit Wilmersdörffer and Daniela Schlicher*

8   Influencers of environmental sustainability success at festivals    71
*Meegan Jones*

**PART III**
**Festival management**    81

9   Managing festival volunteers: the HELPERS model    83
*Kirsten Holmes, Leonie Lockstone-Binney, Karen A. Smith and Alex Rixon-Booth*

10   The role of harm minimisation to prevent alcohol and drug misuse at outdoor music festivals    92
*Alison Hutton*

11   Social media and the transformation of the festival industry: a typology of festivals and the formation of new markets    102
*Marianna Sigala*

12   The innovation of arts festivals: concepts, approaches and effects    111
*Weibing (Max) Zhao and Weng Si (Clara) Lei*

13   Managing networks of meaning in arts festival productions    120
*Mervi Luonila*

**PART IV**
**Festival marketing**    131

14   Festivals and sponsorship: a strategic marketing approach    133
*Gurhan Aktas and Z. Gokce Sel*

15   Festivals' role in branding a destination: a case study of the Barbaros Strawman Festival in İzmir, Turkey    142
*Reyhan Arslan Ayazlar*

16   Branding cultural events using external reference points: Cervantes and the Festival Internacional Cervantino, Mexico    152
*Daniel Barrera-Fernández, Marco Hernández-Escampa and Antonia Balbuena Vázquez*

17　Festivals and social media: a co-created transformation of attendees
　　and organisers　　163
　　*Marianna Sigala*

## PART V
## Strategic use of festivals　　173

18　Leveraging a festival to build bridges in a divided city　　175
　　*Adrian Devine, Bernadette Quinn and Frances Devine*

19　Extending the exit brand: from Serbia's fortress to
　　Montenegro's coast　　185
　　*Nicholas Wise, Tanja Armenski and Nemanja Davidović*

20　The eventful city in a complex economic, social and political
　　environment: the case of Macau　　194
　　*Ubaldino Sequeira Couto*

21　Protesting @ Auckland Pride: when a community stakeholder
　　becomes alienated　　204
　　*Jared Mackley-Crump*

22　Festivals as devices for enhancing social connectivity and the
　　resilience of rural communities　　214
　　*Michael Mackay, Joanna Fountain and Nicholas Cradock-Henry*

23　Geelong's rousing motoring '*Revival*'　　223
　　*Gary Best*

## PART VI
## Festival experiences　　233

24　Understanding feelings, barriers, and conflicts in festivals and events:
　　the impact upon family QOL　　235
　　*Raphaela Stadler and Allan Jepson*

25　Festivity and attendee experience: a confessional tale of discovery　　244
　　*Vern Biaett*

26　Information and communication technology and the festival experience　　254
　　*Christine M. Van Winkle, Kelly J. Mackay and Elizabeth Halpenny*

27  How do residents experience their own festivals? A qualitative
    approach to meanings and experiences                                263
    *Nídia Brás, Júlio Mendes, Manuela Guerreiro and*
    *Bernardete Dias Sequeira*

28  Feminist politics in the festival space                             273
    *Tasmin Coyle and Louise Platt*

**PART VII**
**Types of festivals**                                                  **283**

29  Food and wine festivals as rural hallmark events                    285
    *Jennifer Laing, Warwick Frost and Melissa Kennedy*

30  Positioning in Montserrat's festivals: music, media, and film       295
    *Joseph Lema, Gracelyn Cassell, and Jerome Agrusa*

31  Music events and festivals: identity and experience                 304
    *Michelle Duffy*

32  Religious and spiritual festivals and events                        313
    *Ruth Dowson*

33  Australia celebrates: an exploration of Australia Day festivals
    and national identity                                               323
    *Leanne White and Elspeth Frew*

**PART VIII**
**Cultural perspectives on festivals**                                  **333**

34  Herding livestock and managing people: the cultural sustainability
    of a harvest festival                                               335
    *Guðrún Helgadóttir*

35  Festivals as products: a framework for analysing traditional
    festivals in Ghana                                                  344
    *Oheneba Akwesi Akyeampong*

36  Tourism pressure as a cultural change factor: the case of the
    Guelaguetza festival, Oaxaca, Mexico                                357
    *Marco Hernández-Escampa and Daniel Barrera-Fernández*

| | | |
|---|---|---|
| 37 | Festivals for sustainable tourism development: a case study of Hadoti region, Rajasthan<br>*Anukrati Sharma* | 366 |
| 38 | Placemaking betwixt and between festivals and daily life<br>*Burcu Kaya Sayari and Tuba Gün* | 374 |
| 39 | A festival of song: developing social capital and safeguarding Australian Aboriginal culture through authentic performance<br>*Candace Kruger* | 384 |

## PART IX
## Festival futures — 395

| | | |
|---|---|---|
| 40 | Virtual reality: the white knight of festival management education?<br>*Philipp Peltz, Olga Junek and Joel de Ross* | 397 |
| 41 | Industry perceptions of potential digital futures for live performance in the staging and consumption of music festivals<br>*Adrian Bossey* | 406 |
| 42 | Utopian futures: Wellington on a Plate and the envisioning of a food festival in Tuscany<br>*Ian Yeoman, Sochea Nhem, Una McMahon-Beattie, Katherine Findlay, Sandra Goh and Sophea Tieng* | 417 |

*Index* — 427

# FIGURES

| | | |
|---|---|---|
| 2.1 | Number of journal articles by year of publication | 13 |
| 3.1 | A two-dimensional illustration of major festival impacts | 23 |
| 3.2 | Three main interdependent perspectives on festival values | 25 |
| 4.1 | Three levels of 'festival' and 'meaning' | 36 |
| 4.2 | New framework for analysis of 'festival-meaning' based on Peirce's terminology | 37 |
| 7.1 | Sociocultural impact cycle | 65 |
| 13.1 | The concept and aims of festival as a product | 121 |
| 13.2 | The network of meanings | 124 |
| 13.3 | Management of the network of meanings | 126 |
| 15.1 | Festival activities | 145 |
| 16.1 | Statue devoted to Don Quixote in Guanajuato | 156 |
| 16.2 | References to Cervantes in Guanajuato | 157 |
| 32.1 | The development of interdisciplinary research into religious and spiritual festivals | 315 |
| 35.1 | Map of Ghana showing major traditional festival towns | 345 |
| 35.2 | Festival-as-a-product framework | 348 |
| 36.1 | *Tehuanas* during the Guelaguetza | 360 |
| 38.1 | The retinue of bride receiving | 381 |
| 42.1 | Food festival scenarios | 419 |

# TABLES

| | | |
|---|---|---|
| 2.1 | Number of articles by journal | 14 |
| 2.2 | Number of articles by festival country | 15 |
| 2.3 | Number of articles by type of festival | 15 |
| 5.1 | Indicative types of benefits and costs of a festival | 48 |
| 8.1 | Festivals implementing reusable materials | 74 |
| 10.1 | Drugs/music genre | 94 |
| 10.2 | Definition of terms under the public health umbrella | 95 |
| 10.3 | Health promotion strategies | 98 |
| 12.1 | Major developments and types of innovation of Macao Arts Festival in different periods | 118 |
| 15.1 | Demographic profile of participants | 146 |
| 15.2 | SWOT analysis – II. Barbaros Strawman Festival, Urla | 147 |
| 16.1 | Chi-squared test 'place of origin' and 'adjectives that best define Guanajuato' | 158 |
| 16.2 | Chi-squared test 'place of origin' and 'most representative character related to the city' | 159 |
| 16.3 | Chi-squared test 'place of origin' and 'number of tourist sites visited during festival days' | 160 |
| 16.4 | Chi-squared test 'adjectives that best define Guanajuato' and 'most representative character related to the city' | 160 |
| 20.1 | Excerpt of Macao's Tourism Work Plan 2017 which are directly related to creating Macao into an eventful city | 198 |
| 27.1 | Profile of respondents | 267 |
| 27.2 | Categories emerging from data grouping | 268 |
| 32.1 | Range of disciplines with research related to religious and spiritual festivals | 314 |
| 35.1 | An overview of the main attributes/facets of *Apuor* festival | 350 |
| 35.2 | An overview of the main attributes/facets of *Adekyem* festival | 352 |

# CONTRIBUTORS

**Jerome (Jerry) Agrusa** is Professor of Travel Industry Management, University of Hawai'i at Mānoa. He has been a faculty member at leading hospitality management programmes in the USA for over 25 years.

**Gurhan Aktas** is currently working as an Associate Professor at Dokuz Eylul University, Turkey, in the Department of Tourism Management. He delivers both undergraduate and postgraduate courses on destination management, tourism geography and tourism marketing, and has several publications on crisis management in tourist destinations, visitor attractions, urban tourism, special events and tourist destinations, and alternative tourism forms.

**Oheneba Akwesi Akyeampong** is a Fulbright Scholar, Senior Lecturer and former Head, Department of Ecotourism, Recreation and Hospitality, School of Natural Resources, University of Energy and Natural Resources, Sunyani, Ghana. His research interests are spatial dynamics of tourism, issues of overnight accommodation, events management and residents' perception and participation in tourism.

**Tommy D. Andersson** is Senior Professor in Tourism and Hospitality Management at University of Gothenburg. He received his PhD in managerial economics and has been interested in economic impact analysis, event management and cost-benefit analysis. Most of his publications are in the area of event research and food tourism research.

**John Armbrecht**, PhD, is Head of the Centre for Tourism and researcher at the School of Business, Economics and Law at the University of Gothenburg, Sweden. He received his PhD in marketing and has mainly published research on experiential and non-use values within areas like cultural tourism, cultural economics and event and festival economics.

**Tanja Armenski** is Assistant Professor at the University of Novi Sad (Serbia) and is contracted with the Tourism and Centre for Education Statistics (Statistics Canada) as an analyst involved in national/international projects. She has published broadly in the areas of destination competitiveness, event management, destination image and consumer satisfaction.

**Reyhan Arslan Ayazlar** received her PhD from Adnan Menderes University in 2015. She is an Assistant Professor in the Department of Hospitality Management at Mugla Sitki Kocman University, Turkey. Her research interests include tourism marketing and tourist behaviour. She has published studies focussing on tourist experience; local residents' role in tourism industry; and alternative tourism types, such as rural tourism, festivals, visiting friends and relatives (VFR) tourism and wildlife. She also has national and international conference papers in Turkish and English.

**Daniel Barrera-Fernández** is a Professor in the Faculty of Architecture of the Autonomous University of Oaxaca (Mexico). He is a delegate of ATLAS (Association for Tourism and Leisure Education and Research) for Mexico, Central America and the Caribbean. His research interests focus on urban and cultural tourism, tourist-historic cities and urban planning in heritage contexts.

**Gary Best** is an Honorary Associate of the La Trobe Business School, La Trobe University, Australia. His research and writing focus on automobility, gastronomy and festival and event management. His most recent publication was 'Cars of futures past: Motorclassica 2016 – The Australian International Concours d'Elegance and Classic Motor Show' in Frost, W. and Laing, J. (eds.) (2018) *Exhibitions, Trade Fairs and Industrial Events*.

**Vern Biaett** is an Assistant Professor of Event Management in the Nido R. Qubein School of Communication, Event & Sport Management Department, at High Point University, North Carolina, USA. Vern researches festivity and attendee behaviour with socially constructed grounded theory research method as well as the estimation of attendance at large festivals and events.

**Adrian Bossey** is a Head of Subject at Falmouth University and former artist manager whose clients included Carter the Unstoppable Sex Machine and Chumbawamba. He has both managed the main stage headline act at Glastonbury Festival and chaired the South West Music Industry Forum. He was Executive Producer for the Academy of Music and Theatre Arts (AMATA) Public Programme and won two Staff Excellence Awards for Outstanding Innovation in Teaching.

**Nídia Brás** holds an MSc in Marketing from the University of Algarve (Portugal). Current research interests include marketing and events management.

**Gracelyn Cassell,** BA (UWI), MA (Lond), and MSc (UWI), worked in the Montserrat Public Library (1982 to 1997); worked at the University of the West Indies (UWI) Main Library, Jamaica (1997–2005); and has been Head of the UWI Open Campus Site in Montserrat (2005–present). She is currently pursuing a doctorate in Cultural Heritage at the University of Birmingham, UK.

**Ubaldino Sequeira Couto** is a Lecturer in Festivals and Events at the Institute for Tourism Studies, Macao, China. His research interests are cultural festivals and events, diaspora communities and motor sport races. He is also keen on studying the role of festivals and events in achieving benefits to society, such as equality and inclusion.

**Tasmin Coyle** works within the arts sector in Liverpool. She completed her MA in International Cultural Arts and Festival Management from Manchester Metropolitan University in 2017. Her main interests are how the arts can provide spaces for debates around feminist politics and how nuances of this can be expressed.

**Nicholas Cradock-Henry** is Senior Scientist, Governance & Policy at Manaaki Whenua Landcare Research, Lincoln, New Zealand. His research is focussed on the human dimensions of global and environmental change, including characterising, assessing and enhancing resilience at multiple scales. His work is policy-oriented and collaborative.

**Nemanja Davidović** is Head of the Department for Cooperation with European, Regional and International Institutions at the European Affairs Fund of AP Vojvodina. He is working as senior consultant on international development aid projects with a focus on tourism and has published in the area of tourism economics.

**Joel de Ross** is a social entrepreneur working in application and game development and virtual/augmented reality. He has spent more than a decade in the entertainment industry as a record label owner, event organiser, promoter, graphic designer, music producer and DJ.

**Adrian Devine** is based at Ulster University, Northern Ireland, and has received two Emerald Literati Network Awards for Excellence for his research into inter-organisational relationships and managing cultural diversity. His current research interests include the social and political impacts of events.

**Frances Devine** is based at Ulster University, Northern Ireland, and lectures in the areas of People Management, Leadership and Tourism Impacts. She is actively involved in researching new trends on talent management in the hospitality and tourism sector, presently focussing on inter-organisational relationships.

**Ruth Dowson** is an experienced events practitioner in strategic development, management and delivery of events. A Senior Lecturer at the UK Centre for Events Management, Dowson's research interests focus on the interplay between events and church. Dowson has also published work on planning and managing events and illegal raves. Dowson is a priest in the Church of England.

**Michelle Duffy** is an Associate Professor in Human Geography at the Centre for Urban and Regional Studies, University of Newcastle, Australia. Her research focusses on the significance of emotional, affective and visceral responses to sound and music in creating notions of identity and belonging in public spaces and public events.

**Larry Dwyer** is Visiting Research Professor, Business School, University of Technology, Sydney; Adjunct Professor, Griffith Institute for Tourism (GIFT), Griffith University, Gold Coast, Australia; and Adjunct Professor, Faculty of Economics, University of Ljubljana, Slovenia. He publishes widely in the areas of tourism economics, management, policy and planning.

## Contributors

**Katherine Findlay** graduated from Victoria University of Wellington with a first-class honours degree in Tourism Management and Marketing. Her research interests include VFR travel, consumer behaviour and food tourism.

**Joanna Fountain** is a Senior Lecturer in Tourism Management at Lincoln University, New Zealand. Her research is focussed on the significance of agri-food and wine tourism, and festivals in enhancing rural resilience, community engagement and consumer/tourist experiences in the face of rapid changes for rural regions.

**Dorothy Fox** is a Senior Academic in Events and Leisure Management at Bournemouth University, England. She is the lead author of the first research methods textbook for event management students, entitled *Doing Events Research: From Theory to Practice*. Her particular area of interest is in the interactions between people and socio-natural environments.

**Elspeth Frew** is an Associate Professor in Tourism Management in the Department of Management and Marketing at La Trobe University, Australia. Her research interest is in cultural tourism, with a particular focus on dark tourism and festival and event management, and she has published several articles in these areas. She has also conducted research into industrial tourism and the relationship between the media and tourism management. Consequently, Elspeth's research is often interdisciplinary since she considers aspects of tourism within the frameworks of psychology, media studies, anthropology and sociology.

**Warwick Frost** is an Associate Professor in the Department of Management, Sport and Tourism at La Trobe University, Australia. His research interests include heritage; events; nature-based attractions; and the interaction between media, popular culture and tourism. Warwick is a co-editor of the Routledge *Advances in Events Research* series.

**Donald Getz** is Professor Emeritus, the University of Calgary, Canada, and is affiliated with Linnaeus University in Sweden. He is the author of numerous articles on events and the books *Event Tourism* (Cognizant, 2013) and *Event Studies* (Routledge; the third edition, 2016, is co-authored with Stephen Page). Professor Getz acts as management consultant to universities, cities and destinations in the fields of tourism and events, and participates in major research and development projects.

**Sandra Goh** is a Lecturer in Events and Tourism, with Auckland University of Technology, New Zealand. She has over 15 years of event management experience. She is fascinated with the past and future of successful events, and sees her future work using scenario planning to manage the life cycle of events.

**Mary Beth Gouthro** is a Senior Academic in Events and Leisure Management at Bournemouth University, England. She is co-author of the first research methods textbook, entitled *Doing Events Research: From Theory to Practice*. Mary Beth has wider research interests in qualitative methods of events research and alternative approaches to event evaluation.

**Manuela Guerreiro** holds a PhD in Economic and Management Sciences (University of Algarve, Portugal) and an MSc in Cultural Management (University of Algarve and Université Paris VIII). She is Auxiliary Professor of Marketing at the Faculty of Economics, University of Algarve (Portugal) and Director of the master's course in marketing management.

Current research interests include marketing and brand management, place image and branding, events marketing and experience marketing. She is also a researcher at the Research Centre for Spatial and Organizational Dynamics (CIEO).

**Tuba Gün** is a PhD candidate in the department of Sociology at Anadolu University, Turkey. She has also been working as a research assistant in the same department since 2011. Her research interests include urban studies, place, cultural heritage, fear of crime and terror. Tuba Gün lives in Eskişehir, Turkey.

**Elizabeth Halpenny**, PhD, is an Associate Professor at the University of Alberta, Canada. She teaches and conducts research in the areas of tourism, marketing, environmental psychology and protected areas management. Elizabeth's research focusses on individuals' interactions with nature environments, tourism experience and environmental stewardship.

**Guðrún Helgadóttir** is Professor, University of South-Eastern Norway, Telemark, Norway, and Department of Rural Tourism, Hólar University College, Iceland. Her fields of research are cultural tourism, event management and heritage tourism. She has a special interest in intangible heritage, the production and reception of cultural practices in the context of tourism. Current research is on equine and equestrian tourism, events and visual arts in the tourism context.

**Marco Hernández-Escampa** is a Professor at the Faculty of Architecture of the Autonomous University of Oaxaca (Mexico). He is a delegate of ATLAS for Mexico, Central America and the Caribbean. His research interests focus on urban anthropology, heritage conservation and tourism in historic cities.

**Kirsten Holmes** is an internationally recognised expert in the study of volunteering, particularly in events, leisure, sport and tourism contexts. She also has expertise in developing sustainable events and festivals, and is the lead author of the Routledge textbook *Events and Sustainability* (2015). Kirsten has taught at universities in Australia and the UK, and conducted research projects across 15 countries. She has published over 60 peer-reviewed papers in leading journals and is regularly invited to work with industry and the government, particularly in the not-for-profit sector.

**Alison Hutton** (University of Newcastle, Australia) has an established research profile focussing on strategies to provide safe and supportive environments for young people during youth events, including outdoor music festivals, and Schoolies. Her research has shown that a combination of strategies such as dry zones, on-site first aid, supportive volunteer presence, free water and pastoral care can support young people to party safely and reduce hospitalisations.

**Leo Jago OAM** is Professor in Hospitality and Events at the University of Surrey and Head of the Department of Hospitality. Before joining Surrey, he was the inaugural Chief Economist for Tourism and General Manager of Tourism Research Australia. In 2016, he was awarded an Order of Australia Medal for services to education and the tourism industry.

**Allan Jepson** is a Senior Lecturer and researcher in event studies at the University of Hertfordshire, UK. Allan's research explores community festivals, events, relationships of power amongst stakeholders, event psychology, well-being, family quality of life (QOL) and more recently arts participation and memory creation amongst the over 70s.

*Contributors*

**Meegan Jones** is an event professional, trainer, consultant and writer focussing her work on developing sustainable management solutions for live events. She is a recognised global leader in sustainability for the sector and is the author of *Sustainable Event Management: A Practical Guide* (three editions). She was engaged to work with the Qatar Supreme Committee for Delivery and Legacy in developing the sustainability strategy for the Qatar 2022 Fédération Internationale de Football Associations (FIFA)) World Cup. She was a sector expert in the global working groups developing the Global Reporting Initiative Event Organizers Sector Supplement and International Organisation for Standardisation ISO 20121. She was project consultant for the United Nations Environment Programme (UNEP) Music & Environment Initiative, and she is Chair of the Sustainable Event Alliance. Meegan is currently working on the Volvo Ocean Race as Sustainability Programme Manager.

**Olga Junek** has been a Lecturer in Tourism and Events Management at Victoria University Australia for 16 years and has recently become an Honorary Fellow there. She is also a Visiting Professor at the Munich University of Applied Sciences. Her research focusses on education, international students and events management.

**Burcu Kaya Sayari** is a PhD candidate and has been a research assistant in Tourism at Anadolu University, Turkey since 2012. She also took sociology and social anthropology courses at the Middle East Technical University ( METU). She worked in the hospitality industry holding supervisory positions prior to joining in academia. Her research interests are space and place, rituals, social memory, heritage and performances. She conducted research about social memory and national identity, and participated in an oral history project about tourism in Turkey. Her current doctoral project examines the Australia and New Zealand Army Corps (ANZAC) Day tradition and heritage tourism in Turkey.

**Melissa Kennedy** is a doctoral researcher in the Community Planning and Development Program at La Trobe University, Australia. Her research focusses on rural creative economies. She is particularly interested in community economies and practices of commoning.

**Candace Kruger** (MA Research, BA Mus, Grad. Dip Ed) is an Arts (Music) and Indigenous Educator. She is an Aboriginal woman and traditional owner of the *Kombumerri* (Gold Coast) and *Ngughi* (Moreton Island) regions, Queensland, Australia. She is the author of *Yugambeh Talga* – Music Traditions of the *Yugambeh* people, and in 2014, she established the *Yugambeh* Youth Choir. This Indigenous youth choir regularly performs in the *Yugambeh* language throughout South-East Queensland and in 2016 was awarded the Queensland Reconciliation Award for Community.

**Jennifer Laing** is an Associate Professor in the Department of Management, Sport and Tourism at La Trobe University, Australia. Her research interests include exploring rural and regional regeneration through tourism and events. Jennifer is a co-editor of the Routledge *Advances in Events Research* series.

**Weng Si (Clara) Lei** is an Assistant Professor at the Institute for Tourism Studies, Macau Special Administrative Region (SAR), China. She received her PhD in International Business from the University of Leeds in the UK. Prior to stepping into academia, Clara worked in the industries for some years and took part mostly in marketing and event management.

**Joseph Lema,** PhD, is a Professor in the Hospitality and Tourism Management programme in the School of Business at Stockton University, New Jersey, USA. Professor Lema is a United States – Association of South East Asian Nations (US-ASEAN) Fulbright Specialist.

**Leonie Lockstone-Binney** is Associate Professor and Associate Dean (Research) at William Angliss Institute and Honorary Professor of Victoria University. Prior to joining William Angliss in June 2015, she was employed at Victoria University as Associate Professor of Event Management and Discipline Head of Tourism, Hospitality and Events. Building on her PhD study of the management of volunteers and paid staff in the cultural tourism sector, Leonie's main area of research expertise since 2000 relates to volunteering, specifically in event and tourism settings.

**Erik Lundberg,** PhD, is a researcher and Lecturer at the Centre for Tourism in the School of Economics, Business and Law at the University of Gothenburg, Sweden. He received his PhD in 2014, in which he described and analysed tourism and event impacts from a sustainable development perspective. He has published in journals such as *Tourism Management, Scandinavian Journal of Hospitality and Tourism Management* and *International Journal of Event and Festival Management*.

**Mervi Luonila** (DMus in Arts Management) conducts her research project 'The network of meanings and management in arts productions' as a Postdoctoral Research Fellow at Sibelius Academy of the University of the Arts Helsinki, Finland. Her research interests are focussed on the management of arts festivals and especially on network management in the festival context.

**Kelly J. MacKay** is Professor and Associate Vice President Research and Innovation (interim), Ryerson University, Toronto, Canada. She has worked extensively with Parks Canada, many destination management organisations (DMOs) and major festivals. Her recent research examines information and communications technology (ICT) influences on tourist behaviour. She employs a variety of methodological approaches, including photo-elicitation, focus groups, surveys and mixed methods.

**Michael Mackay** is a Senior Lecturer in Human Geography at Lincoln University, New Zealand. His research is focussed on regional and small-town regeneration, tourism development in peripheral areas, rural entrepreneurship, amenity migration, community festivals and place identity, and critical qualitative inquiry.

**Jared Mackley-Crump** is an ethnomusicologist lecturing on the Events Management programme at the Auckland University of Technology, New Zealand. His research to date has addressed the development of Pacific festivals in New Zealand and is now expanding to other areas of festivalisation, such as Pride and popular music festivals.

**Una McMahon-Beattie** is Professor and Head of Department for Hospitality and Tourism Management in the Ulster University, UK. Una has published extensively and is the author/co-editor of seven books, including *The Future of Events and Festivals* and *The Future of Food Tourism: Foodies, Experiences, Exclusivity, Visions and Political Capital*.

**Júlio Mendes** holds a PhD in Management (Strategy and Organizational Behaviour) and is a Professor at the Faculty of Economics, University of Algarve (Portugal), where he is also Director of the Master in Tourism Organizations Management and an active member of the board of the PhD programme in Tourism. He is also a research member of the CIEO. His research interests include experiential marketing, quality management and creative tourism.

**Sochea Nhem** is currently a staff member in the Department of Tourism at the Royal University of Phnom Penh in Cambodia. He holds a Master of Tourism Management degree from Victoria University of Wellington in New Zealand, for which he was awarded a New Zealand ASEAN Scholarship by New Zealand Foreign Affairs & Trade. Sochea is passionate about sustainability aspects of tourism futures.

**Philipp Peltz** is the specialisation advisor and Lecturer of the Music Industry programme at Victoria University in Melbourne, Australia. His research focusses on entrepreneurship in the creative industries and the question of how technology influences creative industries, artists and society.

**Louise Platt** is a Senior Lecturer in Festival and Events Management at Manchester Metropolitan University. Her primary research interests are around placemaking and festivity. She is on the committee of the Leisure Studies Association and is a member of the Institute of Place Management.

**Bernadette Quinn** works in the School of Hospitality Management & Tourism at the Dublin Institute of Technology, Ireland. She has written extensively about arts festivals and cultural events, being interested in the roles that they play in transforming places and shaping community and place identities.

**Alex Rixon-Booth** has a strong focus on the benefits of volunteering, which has seen him establish I Need Helpers as a platform supporting episodic tourism volunteering. His strong involvement and unique perspective on volunteer management have been utilised by the major events industry in Australia, setting new benchmarks in the successful planning and delivery of volunteer programmes.

**Daniela Schlicher** holds a PhD from the University of Otago and used to work for the United Nations Office on Drugs and Crime (UNODC) in South-East Asia. She currently teaches tourism and business ethics at EU Business School, Munich, Germany.

**Z. Gokce Sel,** MSc, is currently a PhD candidate at Dokuz Eylul University, Turkey, in the Department of Tourism Management, and works as a Research Assistant at Celal Bayar University. In line with her PhD thesis on event management, she has written several publications on event management, crisis management in tourist destinations and semiotic analysis of events' promotional material.

**Bernadete Dias Sequeira** has a PhD in Sociology and an MSc in Organization and Information Systems, and graduated in Sociology (University of Évora, Portugal). She is an Assistant Professor at the Faculty of Economics, University of Algarve (Portugal). Her current research interests include the sociology of organisations, communication and knowledge, knowledge management and tourism. She is a researcher at the CIEO.

**Anukrati Sharma** is Associate Professor in the Faculty of Commerce and Management, University of Kota, Rajasthan, India. Her doctorate degree is in Tourism Marketing. She has two postgraduate degree specialties: one is Master of International Business and the other is Master of Business Administration. Tourism is her research area.

**Marianna Sigala** is Professor at the University of South Australia. She is a well-published authority in the fields of information technologies and service management in tourism and hospitality. She is currently the co-editor of the *JSTP* and the Editor-In-Chief of the *JHTM*. In 2016, she received the prestigious EuroCHRIE Presidents' Award for her lifetime achievements in tourism and hospitality education.

**Karen A. Smith** is based at Victoria Business School at Victoria University of Wellington in New Zealand. Her expertise is in volunteers and their management, particularly in the tourism and events sectors and more broadly in non-profit organisations in areas as diverse as health, emergency management and conservation. Her work also explores the future of volunteering and charities.

**Raphaela Stadler** is a Senior Lecturer and researcher in Event Studies at University of Hertfordshire, UK. Her areas of expertise include knowledge management/transfer in festival organisations, power, community cultural development and more recently event attendance and family QOL as well as arts participation and memory creation amongst the over 70s.

**Sophea Tieng** is a full-time Lecturer of Sustainable Tourism and Tourism Geography at Saint Paul Institute, Cambodia. Sophea is a consultant on Climate Change and Tourism for the Ministry of Tourism Cambodia. Sophea has several years of experiences in community development and has conducted research on Community-Based Ecotourism in Cambodia to complete a Master's Degree of Tourism Management in New Zealand.

**Christine M. Van Winkle** is an Associate Professor at the University of Manitoba, Canada. She is dedicated to community-based research exploring visitors' experiences in tourism and leisure settings. She uses various methods to undertake theory-driven applied research and is experienced at employing mixed-methods in festival contexts. Most recently, her work has focussed on mobile device use at festivals.

**Antonia Balbuena Vázquez** holds a BA in Anthropology from the University of Granada (Spain) and a PhD in Tourism from the University of Malaga (Spain), where she is a member of the research group 'Tourism and Territory'. Her main field of study is residents' attitudes towards tourism. She has several international publications related to tourism and social impacts.

**Leanne White** is a Senior Lecturer in the College of Business at Victoria University, Melbourne, Australia. Her research interests include national identity, commercial nationalism, popular culture, advertising, destination marketing and cultural tourism. She is the author of more than 50 book chapters and refereed journal articles.

**Ronnit Wilmersdörffer** was born in 1991 in Munich, Germany, and obtained an undergraduate degree in tourism and events management in 2015. She is currently affiliated with the Ludwigs-Maximilians-Universität in Munich, Germany, in the fields of sociology and philosophy

**Nicholas Wise** is a Senior Lecturer in the Faculty of Education, Health and Community at Liverpool John Moores University. His research focusses on social regeneration, community and place image/competitiveness. His current research focusses on social regeneration linked to community change and local impacts in Southern and Eastern Europe.

**Ian Yeoman** is an Associate Professor of Tourism Futures at Victoria University of Wellington, New Zealand. Ian is the co-editor of the *Journal of Tourism Futures* and the author/editor of 18 books, including *Tomorrows Tourist, 2050: Tomorrows Tourism* and *The Future of Events and Festivals*. Ian holds Visiting Professor posts at the European Tourism Futures Institute and Ulster University.

**Xiaoming Zhang** is Associate Professor in the School of Tourism Management at Sun Yat-sen University. He is a Bachelor of Regional and Urban Planning and a Doctor of Human Geography. His main research interests focus on the phenomenological and semiotic study of human experiences in festivals and tourism.

**Weibing (Max) Zhao** obtained his PhD in Tourism Management from the University of Calgary, Canada. He is now an Assistant Professor at the Institute for Tourism Studies, Macao SAR, China. His research interests include destination marketing and management, travel behaviour and experience, pro-poor tourism, entrepreneurship and regional collaboration and partnership.

# PART I

# Introduction

# 1
# INTRODUCTION

*Judith Mair*

Festivals represent a vital part of human society, and they have done so for millennia. The history of festivals is likely to go far back into the past, long before the written history of civilisations began. The desire to mark particular occasions, such as equinoxes, solstices and harvests, with communal expressions of feelings has been around since the Neolithic times (Biaett 2017) and continues to this day. Festivals traditionally allowed respite from hard work and mundane daily life, injecting a certain amount of socialising, relaxation and rejuvenation into what Hobbes argued might otherwise be the solitary, nasty, brutish and short existence of many peoples throughout history. In recent times, the importance and number of festivals has increased, primarily in tandem with the increasing importance placed on festivals (and other events) as opportunities for increased tourism, branding and economic development. Boorstin (1961) refers to these as pseudo-events, but regardless of where you stand on the authenticity and effectiveness of such economically and politically motivated festivals, it is fair to say that they are booming and as such are deserving of significant research attention.

As noted, festivals hold multifaceted roles in society, spanning economic development, tourism benefits, social outcomes and others. Although many festivals have been held for decades or more and celebrate important religious or historic traditions, there are significant economic advantages to be gained from either 're-imagining' them or from generating new festivals. For example, festivals (along with other types of events) can be staged or supported by governments for instrumentalist purposes – to bring positive economic impact, secure jobs and growth, underpin regeneration and catalyse infrastructure development (Getz 2009). Festivals and events are often sought after as part of a destination's tourism product offering, for the competitive advantage that they lend a destination and for the marketing and branding benefits they offer (Jago & Dwyer 2006). Festivals are also often created by governments to address a range of social objectives, such as generating social capital, enhancing community cohesion, strengthening community resilience and encouraging tolerance of diversity (Duffy & Mair 2017). Finally, festivals have other roles, which are often underplayed in comparison to the neo-liberal economic development agenda. These include the opportunity for activism and protest, counterculture and catharsis.

Festivals have been the subject of considerable research, but much of this is highly fragmented, with studies on festivals appearing in a wide range of disciplines, including anthropology, sociology, human and cultural geography, marketing, management, psychology and economics, and the broad field of tourism and hospitality. There have been attempts to bring this disparate knowledge together in review studies, with perhaps the best known being that of Getz (2010). Getz identified three major discourses from his review – a classical discourse, concerning the roles, meanings and impacts of festivals in society and culture; an instrumentalist discourse, where festivals are viewed as tools to be used in economic development, particularly in relation to tourism and place marketing; and an event management discourse, which focussed on the production and marketing of festivals and the management of festival organisations (Getz 2010). Other reviews have taken a discipline-specific approach (see, for example, Cudny 2014 on festivals and geography, Frost 2015 on festivals and anthropology and Dowson in this volume on religious and spiritual festivals). However, the subject is so vast it is difficult to get a sense of the full breadth of knowledge that lies at the heart of festival studies.

The Routledge Handbook of Festivals aims to bring this knowledge together in one volume, presenting an array of chapters that focus on a variety of topics, contexts and methods, thus contributing to our knowledge of festivals around the world.

## Definitions and roles of festivals

Festivals are events which are designed for public participation; they may be either traditional or contemporary in form and celebrate a range of themes. In some senses, festivals appear to defy any neat definition – while Getz (1991) referred to them as public events that celebrate a specific theme, a cultural season or a time of year, he goes on in later work to consider them to be more of a spectrum of ideas (Getz 2010). There are several definitions that are used in order to create a basis for research, ranging from the very broad, 'public themed celebrations that are held regularly' (Wilson, Arshed, Shaw & Pret 2017, p. 196) or 'social activities seen as an expression of social norms and the values of a society' (Chacko & Schaffer 1993, p. 475), to the more specific 'themed public occasions designed to occur for a limited duration that celebrate valued aspects of a community's way of life' (Douglas, Douglas & Derrett 2001, p. 358). It seems appropriate for me as editor of this handbook to examine how festivals can, or should, best be defined.

There are a range of characteristics that make it problematic to define festivals in one brief sentence. Thus, perhaps it is more appropriate to consider the full gamut of dimensions that have relevance to festivals in order to fully comprehend their scale and scope. The most important elements are highlighted. In relation to timing, festivals are almost always **short term** and are usually **recurring** (e.g. Saleh & Ryan 1993; Getz 2008). Another key dimension is that festivals are always open to the public – while there may or may not be an entrance fee or other charge, festivals are generally **publicly accessible** as opposed to closed meetings or events where an invitation is required (e.g. Kim, Uysal & Chen 2001; Wilson et al. 2017). In nature, festivals tend to be **celebratory**, although the specific theme of the celebration varies widely from religious and/or traditional to contemporary and arguably inauthentic (Green 1997; Douglas et al. 2001; Getz 2010; Jordan 2016). Nonetheless, the theme usually relates to an element of **culture**, be that traditional culture (religious or secular) (see, for example, Turner 1974 or Falassi 1987), high culture (such as opera, the arts or gourmet food, for example) or popular culture (such as folk or pop music) (inter alia Picard & Robinson 2006; Crespi-Vallbona & Richards 2007). Festivals are usually **place-based** and often celebrate the history, tradition or culture of a particular place (Hall 1989; Saleh & Ryan 1993; Derrett 2003; Getz 2010; Mair & Duffy 2015). Festivals are also social phenomena (Duffy & Mair 2017), and **communities** are at the centre of festivals, whether that implies place-based notions of communities (which is often the case) or broader communities of interest (De Bres & Davis 2001; Arcodia & Whitford 2006; Moscardo 2007; Jepson & Clarke 2015; Black 2016). Festivals often, although not always, have a **performative** element, with music, songs, dancing, parades or other ways of showcasing a way of life. Finally, the behavioural and affective elements of festivals help to differentiate them. The behavioural dimension of festivals highlights that they are often used to provide **recreation and entertainment** involving interaction and socialising (Jago & Dwyer 2006; Lee, Arcodia & Lee 2012). In relation to the affective dimension, festivals are often considered to relate to **feelings of belonging and sharing**, connection and cohesion (Johnstone 2012; de Geus, Richards & Toepoel 2016; Duffy & Mair 2017).

Therefore, perhaps an appropriate, if lengthy, definition of festivals might be

> short term, recurring, publicly accessible events that usually celebrate and / or perform particular elements of culture that are important to the place in which they are held or the communities which hold them; that provide opportunities for recreation and entertainment; and that give rise to feelings of belonging and sharing.

## Outline of contributions

The handbook is divided into nine sections based on the broad underpinning theories, concepts, contexts and topics of the chapters contained in each section. These are the Introduction, Sustainability, Festival Management, Festival Marketing, the Strategic Use of Festivals, Festival Experiences, Types of Festivals, Cultural Perspectives and the Future of Festivals.

### *Introduction*

This section sets the scene for the handbook. The current Introduction chapter offers some initial thoughts on the definitions and roles of festivals. Following from that, Gouthro and Fox systematically examine recent developments in research in the festival sector literature, providing a detailed investigation of the methods and paradigms that inform research in this field and demonstrating the predominance of quantitative methods (particularly surveys) while at the same time highlighting issues for future festival researchers in relation to big data and ethics. Getz, Andersson, Armbrecht and Lundberg address the conceptual and philosophical issues associated with placing a value on a festival. Their chapter provides a theoretical and practical framework within which value issues can be addressed, using the dimensions of people, the economy and the environment. Finally in this section, Zhang considers the meaning of festivals, proposing a new semiotic approach. Zhang notes that while much research has concentrated on *what* is a festival, a better approach may be to interrogate *how* is a festival [experienced, understood, presented].

### *Sustainability*

This section naturally covers the key fundamental tenets of sustainability – the economic, social and environmental impacts of festivals. Initially, Dwyer and Jago examine the economic evaluation of festivals, highlighting the challenges associated with developing techniques which give accurate results while at the same time being practical for policymakers making decisions on the allocation of scarce resources. This is followed by an analysis of the social sustainability of festivals by Quinn, who points to the ever-increasing importance being placed on the ability of festivals to achieve social goals. Quinn concludes that festival research should examine the processes underpinning social change, taking account of the growing influence of more social science concepts and theories, and utilising more critical enquiry. An additional chapter on social sustainability is provided by Wilmersdörffer and Schlicher, who use a case study of the Wacken Open Air festival to analyse the interdependencies of sociocultural impacts and create a tool to assist in the development of policy for the sociocultural sustainability of festivals. Finally, Jones presents a discussion on the environmental sustainability of festivals; identifies common festival environmental issues and impacts, and how to minimise or mitigate these; and explores opportunities for festivals to contribute positively to environmental sustainability through legacy and education initiatives.

## *Festival management*

The festival management section consists of a mix of practical management information and advice, and more conceptual ideas about the ways in which festivals can view their management models. Holmes, Lockstone-Binney, Smith and Rixon-Booth examine the perennial issues of volunteer management, reporting on a new volunteer management model for recruiting and managing volunteer programmes across a range of festivals which has widely been recognised as an example of best practice in this space. Hutton examines another important contemporary issue for festival managers –alcohol and drug misuse at outdoor music festivals. Hutton demonstrates how harm minimisation and health promotion activities can reduce reliance on the healthcare system and thus reduce the burden on the wider community. Sigala considers how social media are transforming the way that festivals are planned, managed and executed. Sigala's chapter examines changes both in the place/space in which festivals occur and in the way in which a variety of actors now play a role in the initiation of festivals. In their chapter, which uses examples drawn from the Macau Arts Festival, Zhao and Lei investigate festival innovation. As they point out, while novelty is an often-cited festival attendance motivation, little is known about what constitutes novelty or how festivals can be innovative in their development of novel approaches. They conclude that further research is needed to understand innovation in the complex domain of festivals. Finally, Luonila examines networks of meanings in festival production. Luonila's chapter sets out to capture the dimensions of meanings related to the fundamental activities of festival management and to analyse how these dimensions of meanings are reflected in managerial practices and decision-making, and thus can serve as a basis for comprehending the role and the effectiveness of festival stakeholders in festival production.

## *Festival marketing*

Festivals rely on a multitude of stakeholders, and the chapter by Aktas and Sel takes a strategic marketing approach to examine an important festival stakeholder – the sponsors – and highlight a lack of research into festival sponsorship as it relates to festival context, location, scope and participant types. Using a case study of two festivals in Izmir, Turkey, the chapter demonstrates that there are a range of elements that contribute to the success of festival sponsorship. Moving to other forms of marketing, festivals are increasingly being expected to play a role in destination branding by offering an activity to encourage tourist visitation. This is not necessarily the fundamental raison d'être of festivals, and so it is important to

*Introduction*

examine how successful or otherwise such festival marketing can be. Ayazlar examines the role of festivals in destination branding by taking a case study of a Turkish strawman festival, demonstrating clearly that while the festival may not have been started for tourism purposes, it nonetheless offers a unique and distinctive addition to the destination's brand and product offering. However, Ayazlar draws attention to the risks associated with the use of the festival as a marketing tool, particularly those risks associated with loss of authenticity. Barrera-Fernández, Hernández-Escampa and Balbuena Vázquez take a different approach, examining the use of a cultural icon (in this case Cervantes) to promote a destination in Mexico with no apparent connection to Cervantes. In this case, there is no authentic link between the topic of the festival and the destination, yet the festival has led to the production of new tourist attractions and experiences, and to the branding of the destination as relating to Cervantes. Finally, Sigala examines social media and festivals, and adopts a co-creation approach for examining the use and impact of social media on two major festival stakeholders, namely festivalgoers and festival organisers. Sigala demonstrates that social media is having a transformational impact on the festival industry by changing the roles and the functions of these stakeholders to become more collaborative and social.

## *Strategic use of festivals*

As has already been discussed in this chapter, festivals are increasingly being used as instrumental devices for a variety of policy aims relating to economic and social development. Devine, Quinn and Devine use a festival in Northern Ireland as an example of how festivals can be used to bridge divides, in this case a political, cultural and religious divide. Their chapter illustrates how the festival organisers were able to work through obstacles and encourage positive cross-community social interactions. In a similar vein, Wise, Armenski and Davidović use the example of the Exit Festival in Serbia, a highly successful festival that has grown out of protest and struggle, to document the relationship between festivals and the tourism they promote. However, this chapter offers a warning for destinations who fail to adequately work with festival organisers, leading to lost opportunities. Macau is the context for the chapter by Couto, which examines how the political and cultural situation in any given city or country can influence the success or otherwise of festivals. Couto problematises the idea of the eventful city, highlighting concerns over the instrumental use of festivals for boosterist purposes, to the potential detriment of the beneficial social outcomes of festivals. Mackley-Crump takes the example of the Pride Parade in Auckland, New Zealand, and discusses protests against a festival, providing a demonstration of what happens when the strategic use of festivals by municipalities comes into conflict with the communities the festivals are supposed to celebrate. The chapter identifies in particular the implicit tension between corporate and community stakeholders, and critiques of the homonormativity and commercialisation of Pride events. The chapter by Mackay, Fountain and Craddock-Henry focusses on the rural context and on the opportunities festivals create for enhancing social connectivity and resilience within communities. Taking two festivals in New Zealand as case studies, they emphasise the benefits of rural festivals as providing time and space for active citizenship, community collaboration and teamwork while at the same time offering essential economic advantages. Finally in this section, Best takes an autoethnographic approach and introduces the example of the Geelong Revival festival, which focusses on the heritage of Geelong (Australia) as a car-manufacturing city. Best argues that the festival encourages a tangible sense of Geelong's community well-being and social capital as well as its historically significant automotive heritage.

## *Festival experiences*

This section delves into the various ways of investigating, understanding and documenting the experiences associated with festivals as they apply to different stakeholders, including attendees and local residents. Stadler and Jepson examine the impact of festival attendance on family quality of life, highlighting findings about the importance of understanding the family unit (particularly where there are young families) as a particular market segment with specific needs and wants. Significantly, barriers to festival attendance are identified as cost, the potential overstimulation of children and the lack of opportunities provided by festivals for family bonding. Biaett takes a novel approach, using a confessional tale to exemplify experiences of attending festivals in terms of bonding and bridging social capital. The chapter concludes that a combination of collaborative and creative activities, a stimulation of the senses and the arousal of emotions create an atmosphere that can give rise to increased bonding capital and feelings of well-being. In a chapter examining the current state and future implications of ICT integration into festival experiences, Van Winkle, Mackay and Halpenny focus on the use of the internet, mobile devices and social media, investigating the implications of these trends for the festival experience. They suggest that while the topic is receiving research attention, further inter- and transdisciplinary studies are required in order to understand the implications of this dynamic field. Moving away from the attendee to local residents, Brás, Mendes, Guerreiro and Sequeira investigate how local residents experience their own festivals. Using the example of an Islamic festival in a small village in Portugal, the chapter considers both the experiences of residents during the festival and the subsequent meanings that locals attach to the festival. Bras et al. identify three key stages of resident involvement – a sensory experience, a cultural experience and a practical interaction experience. Finally, Coyle and Platt look to feminist politics and experiences to document a critique of festivals in relation to intersectional feminism. Their chapter examines festivals as a space for women, festivals as platforms for feminist politics and feminist festivals as spaces of empowerment, and draws important conclusions about the festivalisation of feminism.

## *Types of festivals*

As identified earlier in this chapter, there is a multitude of different types of festivals that can be studied, each offering its own individual characteristics and contexts. Each of the chapters in this section uses a different type of festival as a basis for discussing a range of issues and challenges. Laing, Frost and Kennedy examine rural food and wine festivals, identifying some of the challenges faced by rural festivals, including lack of resources and expertise to keep the festivals viable in the long-term and attracting tourists to places that are geographically isolated. They conclude that such festivals can indeed bring economic and social benefits, and can bring together diverse stakeholders to collaborate on local food and wine branding. Lema, Cassell and Agrusa take music, media and film festivals in Montserrat as their starting point and use these to discuss the challenges associated with branding and marketing an island destination. Their findings suggest that music, media and literary festivals can support a sense of place for Montserrat and help to communicate the unique cultural underpinnings of the culture. Music festivals are also the focus of the chapter by Duffy, who takes a different approach, examining the relationships between music, identity and experience as mediated by performance. Duffy proposes that music festivals offer important forms of participation that facilitate belonging and identification through representational and experiential processes, and stresses the need for further research in this area. Religious and spiritual events form a large proportion of traditional and historic festivals, and Dowson reviews the literature in this area to come to an understanding as to the current state of knowledge of this field of research. Whilst acknowledging the body of literature that exists from various disciplines, Dowson highlights the silo nature of much of this research and the fact that many festival studies remain uninformed by a large body of research that exists outside the discipline of the individual researcher. Dowson concludes by proposing a series of issues that would benefit from future research in this area. Finally, White and Frew examine the festive aspects of national day celebrations, in this case Australia Day, considering the role that such celebrations play in forging community and national identity. Drawing on ideas from Falassi (1987), they use the rites that occur during festivals (such as the rites of reversal, conspicuous display, conspicuous consumption, drama, exchange and competition) to demonstrate how aspects of national day celebrations could be classified as festivals. They conclude by posing questions around why some celebrations and legacies of Australia Day continue to generate such distinct and unique festive meanings.

## *Cultural perspectives on festivals*

Festivals are intimately connected with culture, whether that be in relation to high culture and the arts, local traditions and heritage, popular culture or ethnic culture. This section provides examples of festivals from different countries, each addressing specific issues that face the festival sector. Helgadottir reports on the cultural sustainability of the *Laufskalarett*, a harvest festival in Iceland that celebrates the gathering of livestock (mostly horses) from summer pastures. Helgadottir outlines a range of changes to the festival that have implications for how it is perceived by the locals who identify with it. These changes include increasing festivalisation of the horse gathering and changes in the lived experience of the community as they participate in their traditional event. Ghana is the location for the chapter by Akyeampong, who presents a discussion on the differences between a traditional festival which has been in place for over 200 years and a newer presentation of a traditional festival that only began in the past decade. Using a festival-as-product framework, the chapter identifies questions around the history and cultural practices at each festival. Moving to Mexico, Hernández-Escampa and Barrera-Fernández document the Guelaguetza Festival and raise questions as to the role of tourism in relation to the pressure on the festival organisers to make changes to the traditional form and practices of the festival. While presenting a critique of the role of tourism in such changes, nonetheless, the authors suggest that paradoxically, the festival appears to represent a compromise between tradition and modernity as long as significant efforts are directed towards preserving what is considered genuine by the local community. Sharma presents an investigation of the role of festivals in sustainable tourism development in Rajasthan, India. Sharma is interested in clarifying the role of festivals in empowering communities and at the same time providing useful solutions for the challenges faced by festival organisers in remote and regional areas. The chapter argues that festivals are a key strategy in promoting those rural places that have suffered from underinvestment for long periods of time. Kaya Sayari and Gun offer an ethnographic investigation of the Water Festival in regional Turkey, drawing on the theoretical perspectives of habitus, doxa and heterotopia. Their conclusions show that for local residents, the boundaries between the festival event and their daily lives are porous, allowing for a reciprocal exchange of roles between insider and outsider, attendee and local. Finally, Kruger investigates the indigenous culture of Australia, using the case study of an Australian Aboriginal youth choir and focussing on the extent to which the *Yugambeh* Language and Song project facilitates the development of social capital and safeguards Aboriginal culture through performances at festivals.

## Future of festivals

The final section of the handbook takes a look at some of the things that may be in store for festivals in the future. Peltz, Junek and de Ross examine virtual reality (VR), with a particular interest in how it can be used to teach the students that are to become the festival organisers and managers of the future. The chapter investigates how VR can be implemented to improve the teaching of festival management skills and highlights some of the challenges for educators and students that arise as a result of using the technology. Bossey takes a look at the potential digital futures for live performances at music festivals, basing his chapter on interviews with key industry personnel. Amongst other trends discussed are livecasts, holograms and networked performances. Immersive futures, such as using VR or working with entirely virtual artistes are also considered, although they appear less popular with the industry stakeholders at present. Finally, Yeoman et al. envision the future of the Wellington on a Plate Festival by drawing parallels with a predicted future scenario for a food festival in Tuscany. Key trends that might inform this future include growing health consciousness and an increased drive towards healthy, sustainable and local food, which may attract a premium. Learnings for the Wellington on a Plate Festival, and for other similar festivals, emphasise the importance of authenticity, community and collaboration.

## Conclusion

This chapter has set the scene for the remainder of the handbook, highlighting the multifaceted nature and role of festivals in our societies. As well as providing some guidance on the definition of festivals, the chapter has identified a range of functions undertaken by festivals, including the maintenance of heritage and tradition, the showcasing of communities, the provision of access to culture of varied types and the economic development imperative which is driving the establishment and extension of many festivals around the world.

The chapter has outlined the various contributions in the handbook and hopefully has whetted the reader's appetite to continue reading.

## References

Arcodia, C. & Whitford, M. (2007). Festival attendance and the development of social capital, *Journal of Convention & Event Tourism, 8*(2), 1–18.

Biaett, V. (2017). Festivity, play, wellbeing… historical and rhetorical relationships: implications for communities. In Phillips, R. & Wong, C. (Eds.), *Handbook of Community Wellbeing Research* (pp. 189–198). Dordrecht, the Netherlands: Springer.

Black, N. (2016). Festival connections: how consistent and innovative connections enable small-scale rural festivals to contribute to socially sustainable communities, *International Journal of Event and Festival Management, 7*(3), 172–187.

Boorstin, D. (1961). *The Image: A Guide to Pseudo-Events in America*, New York, NY: Harper and Row.

Chacko, H. & Schaffer, J. (1993). The evolution of festival: Creole Christmas in New Orleans, *Tourism Management, 14*(6), 471–479.

Crespi-Vallbona, M. & Richards, G. (2007). The meaning of cultural festivals: Stakeholder perspectives in Catalunya, *International Journal of Cultural Policy, 13*(1), 103–122.

Cudny, W. (2014). Festivals as a subject for geographical research, *Geografisk Tidsskrift-Danish Journal of Geography, 114*(2), 132–142.

De Bres, K. & Davis, J. (2001). Celebrating group and place identity: A case study of a new regional festival, *Tourism Geographies – An International Journal of Tourism Space, Place and Environment, 3*(3), 326–337.

De Geus, S., Richards, G. & Toepoel, V. (2016). Conceptualisation and operationalisation of event and festival experiences: Creation of an event experience scale, *Scandinavian Journal of Hospitality and Tourism, 16*(3), 274–296.

Derrett, R. (2003). Making sense of how festivals demonstrate a community's sense of place, *Event Management, 8*(1), 49–58.

Douglas, N., Douglas, N. & Derrett, R. (Eds.). (2001). *Special Interest Tourism: Context and Cases,* Milton, Australia: John Wiley and Sons.

Duffy, M. & Mair, J. (2017). *Festival Encounters: Theoretical Perspectives on Festival Events,* Abingdon, UK: Routledge.

Falassi, A. (1987). *Time Out of Time: Essays on the Festival,* Albuquerque, New Mexico: University of New Mexico Press.

Frost, N. (2015). Anthropology and festivals: Festival ecologies, *Ethnos, 81*(4), 1–15.

Getz, D. (1991). *Festivals, Special Events, and Tourism,* New York, NY: Van Nostrand Reinhold.

Getz, D. (2008). Event tourism: Definition, evolution, and research, *Tourism Management, 29*(3), 403–428.

Getz, D. (2009). Policy for sustainable and responsible festivals and events: Institutionalization of a new paradigm, *Journal of Policy Research in Tourism, Leisure and Events, 1*(1), 61–78.

Getz, D. (2010). The nature and scope of festival studies, *International Journal of Events Management Research, 5*(1), 1–47.

Green, A. (1997), *Folklore: An Encyclopedia of Beliefs, Customs, Tales, Music and Art,* Oxford, UK: Abc-Clio.

Hall, C. M. (1989). The definition and analysis of hallmark tourism events, *GeoJournal, 19*(3), 263–268.

Jago L. & Dwyer, L. (2006). *Economic Evaluation of Special Events: A Practitioners Guide,* Altona, Australia: Common Ground Publishing Pty. Ltd.

Jepson, A. & Clarke, A. (2015), *Exploring Community Festivals and Events,* London, UK and New York, NY: Routledge.

Johnstone, M. (2012). The servicescape: The social dimensions of place, *Journal of Marketing Management, 28*(11–12), 1399–1418.

Jordan, J. (2016). Festivalisation of cultural production, *ENCATC Journal of Cultural Management and Policy, 6*(1), 44–56.

Kim, K., Uysal, M. & Chen, J. S. (2001). Festival visitor motivation from the organizers' points of view, *Event Management, 7*(2), 127–134.

Lee, I. S., Arcodia, C. & Lee, T. J. (2012). Key characteristics of multicultural festivals: A critical review of the literature, *Event Management, 16*(1), 93–101.

Mair, J. & Duffy, M. (2015). Community events and social justice in urban growth areas, *Journal of Policy Research in Tourism, Leisure and Events, 7*(3), 282–298.

Moscardo, G. (2007). Analysing the role of festivals and events in regional development, *Event Management, 11*(1–2), 23–32.

Picard, D. & Robinson, M. (2006). *Festivals, Tourism and Social Change: Remaking Worlds,* Clevedon, UK: Channel View Publications.

Saleh, F. & Ryan, C. (1993). Jazz and knitwear: Factors that attract tourists to festivals, *Tourism Management, 14*(4), 289–297.

Turner, V. (1974). *Dramas, Fields, and Metaphors: Symbolic Action in Human Society,* Ithaca, NY: Cornell University Press.

Wilson, J., Arshed, N., Shaw, E. & Pret, T. (2017). Expanding the domain of festival research: A review and research agenda, *International Journal of Management Reviews, 19*(2), 195–213.

# 2
# METHODOLOGICAL APPROACHES TO FESTIVAL RESEARCH

*Mary Beth Gouthro and Dorothy Fox*

## Introduction

When it was first published in 2014, the book *Doing Events Research: From Theory to Practice* (Fox, Gouthro, Morakabati & Brackstone 2014) was the first service-sector research text to focus on event and festival applications specifically. Up until that point, students studying events- and festival-related courses were typically drawn to the 'sister' courses of tourism, leisure and hospitality that had trusted sources (for example, Smith 2010; Veal 2011) to help shape their understanding and research approach. However, in the recent past, academic discussions and contributions across the festival context continue to grow and mature. The aim of this chapter is to reflect how festival research has advanced in the recent past and to identify the current state of play. Accordingly, academic journal articles in the festival field and the methods of research applied are considered, and an appreciation for trend(s) and void(s) of these contributions is also acknowledged.

Getz's (2010) publication is particularly relevant in capturing the state of play of festival literature at that time. Using ontological mapping, the main concepts and themes were identified. Getz captures the focus of each study under the following 'themes': experiences, meanings and managing events (making up 367 of the 423 submissions), with design themes (14 submissions) and motivations and constraints (57 submissions) making up a smaller number of papers. Academic study of festivals continues to diversify, for example, given the digital age we live in, and through their inductive case study approach of consumers, Hudson and Hudson (2013, p. 221) point out the 'high degree of sophistication' related to the implementation of social media at music festivals. New methods relating to the digital age and its impacts on the festival experience are therefore developing. Adopting a broader scope, the work of Crowther, Bostock and Perry (2015) offers valuable reflection into how the methods of research applied in both events and festivals have evolved. This chapter continues the progress arguing for further depth across paradigms and showing how academic contributions can be enriched, thereby enabling insights into how society and culture may benefit from a broader perspective of the festival context. Finally, the discussion reflects on the value of robust methods and paradigms that can be considered in the future study of festivals, thereby allowing a wider reach in the potential for new knowledge.

Van Niekerk (2017) suggests that 'Event and festival research is often criticized for the lack of rigorous research methods being used and the generalizability of the results' (p. 843).

Previous reviews of published articles include studies on conventions (Lee & Back 2005; Yoo & Weber 2005), business events (Mair 2012) and events (Crowther et al. 2015), but to date there does not appear to be a comparable study of festivals. This chapter therefore begins by systematically capturing and appraising developments in research in the festival-sector literature during the period of 2012–2016.

## Method of journal article analysis

Crowther et al. (2015, p. 99) adopted a purposive sampling strategy known as 'critical case sample' in order to select articles based on their importance in the field of events. For this chapter we are interested in the methodologies, so we sought all papers irrespective of their significance, and hence located as broad a range of festival articles in the social sciences as possible. As Crowther et al. (2015, p. 99) note, 'Wider journals needed to be interrogated, particularly as the journal ranking system is not currently favourable to the dedicated event journals and many scholars understandably seek to publish elsewhere'.

A search was undertaken to locate English-language, peer-reviewed, full-text articles in academic journals to capture a picture over a period of five years from January 2012 to December 2016 with 'event', 'festival', 'tourism', 'travel', 'leisure', 'hospitality', 'marketing' or 'management' in the journal title and containing 'festival' in the abstract. Each article was checked to ensure that it contained empirical data and had some relevance, however broad, to the field of festival research, resulting in 159 articles to be examined in detail. Systematic textual analysis was undertaken to ascertain the type of festival and the country in which the research was undertaken and the research methods employed (Weber 1990).

## Results

### Year of publication

Figure 2.1 illustrates the number of articles in each of the five years of study, demonstrating that since 2012, the number of articles has increased from 25 to 31, 33, 33 and 37 in 2016.

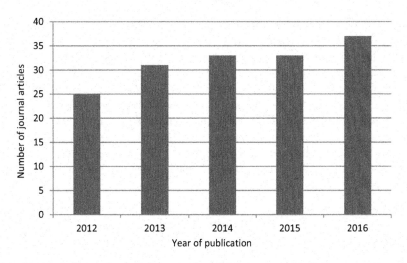

*Figure 2.1* Number of journal articles by year of publication

*Table 2.1* Number of articles by journal

| Journal | Number of articles |
|---|---|
| Event Management | 48 |
| Journal of Convention & Event Tourism | 14 |
| International Journal of Event and Festival Management | 11 |
| Tourism Management | 11 |
| International Journal of Tourism Research | 7 |
| Journal of Travel & Tourism Marketing | 6 |
| Leisure Studies | 6 |
| Journal of Sustainable Tourism | 5 |
| Scandinavian Journal of Hospitality & Tourism | 5 |
| International Journal of Arts Management | 3 |
| Journal of Hospitality Marketing & Management | 3 |
| Journal of Travel Research | 3 |
| Annals of Tourism Research | 3 |

## Journal

A total of 39 journals were located containing an article, of which 19 had published just one article and 6 journals had published only two. Table 2.1 lists the remaining journals, demonstrating that three journals published almost half of the articles, of which the largest number (48) is in *Event Management* (formerly titled *Festival Management and Event Tourism*). This repeats Getz's (2010) study, in which *Event Management* was also the principal journal for festival articles. A further 15 articles in our study are in the *International Journal of Event and Festival Management* and 14 in the *Journal of Convention & Event Tourism*. This rise in publications in specialist event journals is confirmed by the decrease in publications in the *Journal of Travel Research* (from 31 in 2010 to 3 in this study) and *Tourism Management* (from 17 to 11).

## Festival location

The country in which the data were collected was recorded, and in total, festival research has been undertaken in 33 different countries over the five-year period. Of these, 20 countries were represented in only one or two articles, and Table 2.2 shows those countries with three or more publications. The most frequent studies were of festivals in the USA (35) and Australia (18); no doubt reflecting not only the long history of festivals in those countries but also that the articles reviewed were limited to those in the English language. Seven of the researchers undertook their data collection in more than one country. For example, Hudson and Hudson (2013) analysed the use of social media at two music festivals in the USA and one in the UK. Gyimóthy and Larson (2015) carried out a comparative analysis of the management practices of social media using Roskilde Festival in Denmark and the Way Out West and Storsjöyran music festivals in Sweden.

## Type of festival

Many of the studies were undertaken at a single festival (see Table 2.3). The largest group of the particular categories of festivals where data were collected was at cultural and a range of

*Table 2.2* Number of articles by festival country

| Country | Number of articles |
|---|---|
| USA | 35 |
| Australia | 18 |
| China | 13 |
| UK | 12 |
| South Korea | 11 |
| Italy | 8 |
| Finland | 6 |
| South Africa | 5 |
| Sweden | 5 |
| Taiwan | 4 |
| United Arab Emirates | 4 |
| Spain | 3 |
| Turkey | 3 |

*Table 2.3* Number of articles by type of festival

| Type of Festival | Number of articles |
|---|---|
| Cultural and other miscellaneous festivals | 51 |
| Music | 46 |
| Food and drink (including wine) | 23 |
| Film | 7 |
| Arts | 5 |
| Shopping | 5 |
| Multiple festivals | 22 |
| **Total** | **157** |

other miscellaneous festivals (51). The next largest groups were music festivals (46) and food and drink (including wine) festivals (23). However, 22 articles are based on data collected from more than one specific event. For example, Oh and Lee (2012) collected their survey data at an airport in South Korea from domestic tourists, in relation to 17 island festivals held on Jeju. The most visited of these was the Rapeflower Festival with almost three quarters of the respondents aware of it, but less than a quarter who attended it.

## Research participants

The majority of research participants were festival attendees, who were the participants in 90 (56.6%) of the articles reviewed. A variation on this sample group was that of Lei and Zhao (2012) who made statistical comparisons between three groups of respondents in relation to the 2009 Macao Arts Festival. The first group were residents who were attendees that year, the second group were residents who had never attended and the third were also residents but who had attended in previous years but not in 2009.

Other participants included the festival management (for example, Luonila, Suomi & Johansson 2016) who conducted interviews with the managers of three festivals regarding 'Word of Mouth' (WOM) in relation to the festival marketing practices. In some, a broader range of stakeholders are studied; for example, Alonso and Bressan (2013) focussed on the stakeholders on the supply side of a traditional wine festival (The Festa dell'Uva in Impruneta, Italy), and so their participants included 12 owners of local wineries and 5 restaurateurs/hoteliers.

Residents have also been the subjects of festival research (in eight articles), for example, Lei and Zhao (2012) considered the residents to the Macao Arts Festival, as discussed earlier. Festival volunteers were the participants in seven studies; an interesting example is that of Clayton (2016) who undertook a hermeneutic-phenomenological exploration of the volunteers' experiences at UK music festivals.

## Research chronology

With the exception of one paper, all the studies were cross-sectional, that is undertaken in one period of time. The example of a study that was longitudinal was the work of Andersson, Jutbring and Lundberg (2013) who surveyed two different groups of attendees of the Swedish festival 'Way Out West' in 2010 and 2012 and then compared their consumption and ecological footprints.

## Approach and method

'The research approach employed by researchers directly shapes the knowledge generated' (Crowther et al. 2015, p. 94). The majority of studies were quantitative (n = 112; 70.4%), and of these, most used a survey instrument. A typical example is Kruger, Botha and Saayman's (2012) study of information source preferences and associated expenditure of attendees at the Wacky Wine Festival in South Africa. Their self-administered questionnaire was divided into three sections: first demographic data; second 'motivational factors, other festivals attended and media usage' (p. 347); and a third section which was not used in the published study. The motivation section included 22 items, measured on a 5-point Likert scale, where 1 = not at all important through to 5 = extremely important.

Of the remaining studies, 36 were qualitative and the remaining 11 adopted a mixed approach. Alonso and Bressan (2013) used a combination of structured interviews (a mix of telephone and face to face) and a questionnaire, which contained the same questions and then analysed the data using content analysis and word association which were 'used to separate and group different emerging comments and words according to the theme' (p. 317).

## Innovative methodologies

Having identified earlier the principle features of recent festival research studies, we next consider some of the more innovative methods used. As demonstrated earlier and reiterated by Mair and Whitford (2013, p. 4), research into festivals 'continues to escalate exponentially' – offering opportunities for innovative methods as well as new areas of research.

A rare mixed method approach was adopted at the Parkes Elvis Festival (Jonson, Small, Foley & Schlenker 2015). After a questionnaire was completed by 371 festival participants, a memory work study (Haug 1987, cited in Jonson et al. 2015) was conducted to describe the play aspects of the festival. This involved the four Australian researchers, who were all familiar with the singer Elvis Presley but had never attended an Elvis Festival before, writing a memory 'in the third person, in as much detail as possible, and without interpretation … [about] "Play at the Parkes Elvis Festival"' (p. 486). They then met together to read and discuss the memories, identifying 'their shared social understandings and themes' (ibid.) in relation to academic theory. The integration of the two methods is illustrated by this quote from their results:

> When presenting survey participants with the motivational options, [participants] would be... listening, nodding and then when you [would] say "to play and have fun"... people's faces would light up and they'd say, "Oh yeah! To play and have fun. That one [that 'play and have fun' option]! That's what I'm doing!"
>
> *(p. 487)*

An unusual technique was employed by Van Winkle and Falk (2015), who adopted Personal Meaning Mapping (PMM) for their study of two film festivals in the USA. This technique involved the participants being requested to 'write down any ideas, images, words, or thoughts that come to mind when you think about your festival experience' (p. 147). Once analysed, the findings showed that the participants had communicated 'affective and cognitive elements, functional and hedonistic components, and personal, social, cultural, and physical festival experiences' (p. 147).

Another effective, but rarely adopted, qualitative technique was employed as one of three methods of data collection by Kinnunen and Haahti (2015) in their study of cultural festivals in Finland. The Method of Empathy-Based Stories (MEBS) developed by Eskola (1988) is a non-active role-playing technique in which the participant is given a frame story and asked to write a short narrative about it in less than 20 minutes. Frame stories in Kinnunen and Haahti's study included one about a very successful festival in the near future; second, a similar festival in 2027; and third, a festival in 2015 that was 'considered a major disappointment' (p. 255). The data were then analysed using discourse analysis. The authors concluded that MEBS 'served to unfold the significance of the experiences for the cultural festival visitors' (p. 264).

Gyimóthy and Larson (2015) began their study of music festivals, by first undertaking three focus groups and then three in-depth interviews with festival managers including those responsible for the social media and other forms of communication. A second qualitative stage followed in which the organizations' social media communications were analysed using a netnographic approach. A third sequential stage involved a quantitative analysis which, amongst other aspects, measured the frequency of postings and demonstrated the fluctuations during a period of 12 months.

A final interesting example of innovative methodology is the work of Luxford and Dickinson (2015). They incorporated primary data from focus groups of festival consumers and secondary data from nine apps. The latter provided 'base-line knowledge of the current available features and issues with the apps that assisted in the design of a focus group protocol' (p. 37).

## *Methodological trends*

The chapter does not have the scope to delve into a lengthy analytical discussion of the literature in its entirety, yet a main aim of it is to highlight some of the timely themes that surface in these academic discussions. This too can be framed given the current academic climate of neoliberalist ideals (Fletcher, Carnicelli, Lawrence & Snape 2017), and the associated value(s) thereby attached to the creation of certain knowledge. The literature scan discussed earlier clearly shows the predominance of quantitative discussions of research. Whilst the papers that adopt qualitative work are smaller in number, they nonetheless merit similar credit for the new knowledge they create. An example of quantitative festival research that seeks to measure well-being in society, e.g. psychological, social and subjective elements, is that of Ballantyne, Ballantyne and Packer (2014), who apply Confirmatory Factor Analysis to their data. Independent variables, e.g. gender and length of attendance, were subject to a further series of statistical tests: two-way Analyses of Variance (ANOVAs) and 'a stepwise regression analysis as predictors of the composite benefit scale' (Ballantyne et al. 2014, p. 79). The point to illuminate in this is to reiterate the range of statistical tests that festival data are often subject to in research. The study also acknowledges that further qualitative research should be undertaken 'to explore and understand the processes through which music festivals contribute positively to the psychological and social well-being of those who attend' (Ballantyne et al. 2014, p. 81).

Relevant to this, the work of Hudson, Roth, Madden and Hudson (2015) is important in the festival research discussions for several reasons. It combines insight into the relationships between social media and 'festival' brands per se, and how the consumers feel about these interactions. It adopts a quantitative approach to its data collection, which, as shown earlier, is not untypical, and sheds light into some valuable perspectives as a result. It employs a survey instrument that is informed by a 'quota-type sampling scheme' (Hudson et al. 2015). The 'emotion' element of the study adopts a ten-item scale from Thomson, MacInnis and Park (2005) and a scale for Brand Relationship Quality (BRQ) (Fournier 1994; Smit, Bronner & Tolboom 2007 cited in Hudson et al. 2015) and again proves useful in identifying feelings towards the brand by attendees at music festivals. It is equally useful to note that Hudson et al. (2015, p. 74) applied hypotheses testing to the research, supporting notions that 'social media had a direct effect on emotional attachment to the festival, and emotional attachment has a direct effect on word of mouth'. The study, however, found no direct relationship between social media usage and BRQ. In essence, the study validates that 'if marketers wish to build strong brand relationships, they need to incorporate high levels of emotional content in their marketing communications' (Hudson et al. 2015, p. 74). The authors rightfully acknowledge that by way of future research, 'the merits of social media investments' would benefit from further study in varying contexts, e.g. in other countries, cultural contexts and demographic mixes. They do, however, fall short of recommending differing types of methodologies or paradigm concepts that could be applied.

Comparatively, earlier research conducted by Hudson and Hudson (2013) was a qualitative study to examine social media engagement for its role in the consumer decision-making process of festivalgoers. It adopted a case-study methodology and an ethnographic approach to three festivals: Bonnaroo (Tennessee), Lollapalooza (Chicago) and Latitude (Suffolk, UK). Unlike the 2015 work discussed previously, for which S. Hudson and R. Hudson were two of the four authors who contributed to it, their 2013 qualitative study was not published in a high-ranking journal as assessed by the Association of Business Schools (ABS) but rather in a lower-ranked journal. The methods applied in each merit comparing/contrasting for their role in knowledge creation, yet the prevalence of quantitative methods in academic accounts of festival 'insights' in higher-ranking journals is highlighted here. In any case, Hudson and Hudson's study (2013, p. 220) offers comprehensive insight into festival perspectives whereby 'the touch points when consumers are most open to influence have changed, requiring a major adjustment to realign marketers' strategy and budgets with where consumers are actually spending their time'.

A recent case study by Maeng, Jang and Li (2016) argues that the motivational factors applied to festival studies are in need of brand-new measurement scales. Based on a meta-analysis of 46 specific journal contributions, they concluded that 'major festival attendance motivation has been borrowed from studies of tourism motivation' (Maeng et al. 2016, p. 22). New ways of thinking about approaches to festival research are brought to the fore.

## *Philosophical approaches*

Crowther et al. (2015, p. 94) observe 'a general absence of transparency in event articles relating to the authors' philosophical and methodological commitments' whilst at the same time taking on a subjectivist perspective themselves and one where reality is socially constructed. Similarly, Dredge and Whitford (2010) warned that positivist perspectives in 'event' (and thereby by default festival) research 'underpinned by a belief in rational-technical approach to policy-making and implementation' (2010, p. 3) are at risk of falling short in what can be known/informed about knowledge creation in festival research. In that vein, Dredge and Whitford (2010, p. 5) qualify this with 'ours is a post-structural view of the world, where multiple approaches and perspectives are able to co-exist'. That is to say that universal or generalised forms of data/application may not always suit, and contextual circumstances, e.g. location and cultural history have a place in the research frame, and value of knowledge creation.

Fletcher et al. (2017, p. 300) have acknowledged that 'higher education in the UK is increasingly shaped by a culture of audit and quantification' and analogous developments can be observed in other western countries. Such ideals filter into related discussions of knowledge creation, whereby similar trends are observed in this chapter and thus impact on trends in festival research. Indeed 'the social sciences as a whole are threatened by a neoliberal economic discourse which increasingly informs HE strategic management' (Fletcher et al. 2017, p. 294). The related knock-on effect starts to shape some accepted forms of knowledge over others.

## *Priorities for future research*

Getz, Andersson and Carlsen (2010) proposed a framework and priorities for festival management studies. It drew from a cross-cultural comparative study applying the same research instrument at festivals in four different countries, i.e. UK, Sweden, Norway and Australia. In terms of its research methodology, it presents an analysis of variables, first between the management functions of the festivals, e.g. revenues, demographics and stakeholders – in that 'only those differences that were found to be statistically significant at 0.01 or 0.05 levels of probability are included in the analysis of the paper' (Getz et al. 2010, p. 37). We highlight this so that the research instrument in this work is understood for its function and purpose – and ultimately the descriptive nature of the findings. The resulting application of descriptive statistics and thereby lack of alternative paradigms to festival research are furthermore exposed. In Getz et al.'s concluding comments, the possibilities for future research are, however, acknowledged, stating there is a need for 'greater understanding of antecedents and constraints in different [festival] cultures and settings…the social/cultural and environmental outcome research is in need of considerable advancement both methodologically and theoretically' (Getz et al. 2010, p. 55).

There is, however, optimism for future research developments. Yeoman, Robertson, McMahon-Beattie and Musarurwa (2014) provide some thoughts on consumer trends influencing festivals in the future. The trends identified include everyday exceptional, magic nostalgia, leisure upgrade, mobile living, performative leisure, authentic experiences, affluence, ageless society, consuming with ethics and accumulation of social capital. Although new methodological forms of research are not put forward, it does demonstrate the evolution of festivals and events, and remains noteworthy for shaping areas of future festival research.

In the UK, the Arts and Humanities Research Council (AHRC) commissioned a study (Webster & McKay 2016) that gives credence to academic contributions to festival research. The authors compiled a literature review that included perspectives on the impact of academic research on music festivals and recommendations for future research. As they highlight, festivals are used 'as vehicles to educate the public beyond simply music… [and have also] been sites for public engagement and knowledge exchange, academic research and knowledge exchange' (Webster & McKay 2016, p. 20). The report goes on to recommend developments in festival studies that are 'co-produced research between festival organisations and academic researchers' and 'work on new theorisations and critical approaches to festival culture' (Webster & McKay 2016, p. 21). Building on his extensive repertoire of festival research, Getz (2010, p. 20) has suggested that 'most of what we know about festival experiences, and the meanings attached, is drawn from the classical discourse and disciplines of cultural anthropology and sociology'. This shows scope for further insight beyond academic discussions of, for example, economic impacts of festivals.

## Conclusion

This chapter has demonstrated the breadth of festival research undertaken throughout the world in the recent past. It has highlighted the dominance of quantitative methods particularly using surveys to gather data. Nonetheless, we have shown that qualitative methods of research are receiving greater acceptance in a range of journals, and we have presented some of the more pioneering techniques adopted. However, there are challenges ahead in festival research, for example, in relation to data, the requirements for data protection especially in relation to 'big data'. Furthermore, we have not considered the ethics of research, which is an issue of increasing concern to both academics and the participants of their studies. Of equal concern is how the academic community may be influenced by the demands of governmental monitoring and measurements. To this end, it is the hope of the authors that this chapter helps to capture a meaningful account of trends in current festival research.

## References

Alonso, A.D. & Bressan, A. (2013). Stakeholders' perspectives on the evolution and Benefits of a traditional wine festival: The case of the Grape Festival ("Festa dell'Uva") in Impruneta, Italy, *Journal of Convention & Event Tourism*, 14(4), 309–330.

Andersson, T.D., Jutbring, H. & Lundberg, E. (2013). When a music festival goes veggie: Communication and environmental impacts of an innovative food strategy, *International Journal of Event and Festival Management*, 4(3), 224–235.

Ballantyne, J., Ballantyne, R. & Packer, J. (2014). Designing and managing music festival experiences to enhance attendees' psychological and social benefits, *Musicae Scientiae*, 18(1), 65–83.

Clayton, D. (2016). Volunteers' knowledge activities at UK music festivals: A hermeneutic-phenomenological exploration of individuals' experiences, *Journal of Knowledge Management*, 20(1), 162–180.

Crowther, P., Bostock, J. & Perry, J. (2015). Review of established methods in event research, *Event Management*, 19(1), 93–107.

Dredge, D. & Whitford, W. (2010). Policy for sustainable and responsible festivals and events: Institutionalisation of a new paradigm – a response, *Journal of Policy Research in Tourism, Leisure and Events*, 2(1), 1–13.

Fletcher, T., Carnicelli, S., Lawrence, S. & Snape, R. (2017). Reclaiming the 'L' word: Leisure studies and UK higher education in neoliberal times, *Leisure Studies*, *36*(2), 293–304.

Fox, D., Gouthro, M., Morakabati, Y. & Brackstone, J. (2014). *Doing Events Research: From Theory to Practice*. Abingdon, UK: Routledge.

Getz, D. (2010). The nature and scope of festival studies, *International Journal of Event Management Research*, *5*(1), 1–47.

Getz, D., Andersson, T. & Carlsen, J. (2010). Festival management studies: Developing a framework and priorities for comparative cross-cultural research, *International Journal of Event and Festival Management*, *1*(1), 29–59.

Gyimóthy, S. & Larson, M. (2015). Social media cocreation strategies: The 3cs, *Event Management*, *19*(3), 331–348.

Hudson, S. & Hudson, R. (2013). Engaging with consumers using social media: A case study of music festivals, *International Journal of Event and Festival Management*, *4*(3), 206–223.

Hudson, S., Roth, M., Madden, T.J. & Hudson, R. (2015). The effects of social media on emotions, brand relationship quality, and word of mouth: An empirical study of music festival attendees, *Tourism Management*, *47*(April), 68–76.

Jonson, P.T., Small, J. Foley, C. & Schlenker, K. (2015). "All shook up" at the Parkes Elvis festival: The role of play in events, *Event Management*, *19*(4), 479–493.

Kinnunen, M. & Haahti, A. (2015). Experiencing community festivals and events: Insights from Finnish summer festivals. In: Jepson, A. & Clarke, A. (Eds.) *Exploring Community Festivals and Events* (pp. 31–53). London, UK: Routledge.

Kruger, M., Botha, K. & Saayman, M. (2012). Information source preferences and associated expenditure of first-time and repeat visitors at a South African wine festival, *Tourism Analysis*, *17*(3), 343–355.

Lee, M.J. & Back, K. (2005). A review of convention and meeting management research 1990–2003: Identification of statistical methods and subject areas, *Journal of Convention and Event Tourism*, *7*(2), 1–20.

Lei, W. & Zhao, W. (2012). Determinants of arts festival participation: An investigation of Macao residents, *Event Management*, *16*(4), 283–294.

Luonila, M., Suomi, K. & Johansson, M. (2016). Creating a stir: The role of word of mouth in reputation management in the context of festivals, *Scandinavian Journal of Hospitality and Tourism*, *16*(4), 461–483.

Luxford, A. & Dickinson, J. (2015). The role of mobile applications in the consumer experience at music festivals, *Event Management*, *19*(1), 33–46.

Maeng, H.Y., Jang, H.Y. & Li, J.M. (2016). A critical review of the motivational factors for festival attendance based on meta-analysis, *Tourism Management Perspectives*, *17*, 16–25.

Mair, J. (2012). A review of business events literature, *Event Management*, *16*(2), 133–141.

Mair, J. & Whitford, M. (2013). Guest editorial, *International Journal of Event and Festival Management*, *4*(1), 4–5.

Oh, M. & Lee, T.J. (2012). How local festivals affect the destination choice of tourists, *Event Management*, *16*(1), 1–9.

Smith, S.L.J. (2010). *Practical Tourism Research*. Wallingford, UK: Cabi Publishing.

Thomson, M., MacInnis, D.J. & Park, C.W. (2005). The ties that bind: Measuring the strength of consumers' emotional attachments to brands, *Journal of Consumer Psychology*, *15*(1), 77–91.

Van Niekerk, M. (2017). Contemporary issues in events, festivals and destination management, *International Journal of Contemporary Hospitality Management*, *29*(3), 842–847.

Van Winkle, C.M. & Falk, J.H. (2015). Personal meaning mapping at festivals: A useful tool for a challenging context, *Event Management*, *19*(1), 143–150.

Veal, A.J. (2011). *Research Methods for Leisure and Tourism*, 4th ed. Harlow, UK: Pearson Education Ltd.

Weber, R.P. (1990). *Basic Content Analysis*, 2nd ed. Newbury Park, CA: Sage.

Webster, E. & McKay, G. (2016). *From Glyndebourne to Glastonbury: The impact of British Music festivals*. Retrieved from: www.ahrc.ac.uk/documents/project-reports-and-reviews/connected-communities/impact-of-music-festivals/ Accessed 14/06/2018.

Yeoman, I., Robertson, M., McMahon-Beattie, U. & Musarurwa, N. (2014). Scenarios for the future of events and festivals. In: Yeoman, I., Robertson, M., McMahon-Beattie, U., Backer, E. & Smith, K.A. (Eds.), *The Future of Events and Festivals* (pp. 36–50). Oxford, UK: Routledge.

Yoo, J.E. & Weber, K. (2005). Progress in convention tourism research, *Journal of Hospitality & Tourism Research*, *29*(2), 194–210.

# 3
# THE VALUE OF FESTIVALS

*Donald Getz, Tommy D. Andersson, John Armbrecht
and Erik Lundberg*

## Introduction

This chapter addresses the conceptual and philosophical issues associated with placing a value on a festival from many perspectives. The emphasis is placed on providing a theoretical and practical framework within which value issues can be addressed, and further research suggested. Our approach is derived from the edited book *The Value of Events* (Lundberg, Armbrecht, Andersson & Getz 2017). The starting point is definitional, looking at the key terms, then providing a framework for exploring value perspectives. In the concluding section we identify gaps and suggest a research agenda.

## Building a framework

Brown, Getz, Pettersson and Wallstam (2015) carefully examined definitions and usages of 'value' and related terminology. Important synonyms for the noun 'value' include worth, utility, advantage, benefit, profit, merit and usefulness. These suggest how the value of an event might be determined, but raise the questions 'by whom' and 'from whose perspective'? Accordingly, evaluations need to be clear about both the 'subject' and the 'object' of analysis (Andersson & Armbrecht 2017). Valuation is also implicit in discussions of festival impacts, although this requires an indication of whether or not an identified or imputed impact is good, bad or neutral, and from whose perspective.

One meaning of 'value' pertains to a person's or group's values, based on culture and ethics, and influencing what a person becomes and does. In this sense, values determine (at least in part) attitudes towards festivals and influence what a group or society does by way of organising and facilitating (or regulating) planned events. McCarthy, Ondaatje, Laura and Brooks (2004) distinguished between *private* and *public value* and the *extrinsic* and *intrinsic value* dimensions. Intrinsic value is derived from intellectual, emotional and spiritual experiences and relates to the notion that something is valuable in itself. Extrinsic value stems from utility and exchanges that provide tangible benefits or value either to individuals (including social groups and subcultures) or to society as a whole.

Andersson, Armbrecht and Lundberg (2012) have provided a pertinent framework (see Figure 3.1). The vertical axis distinguishes between the intrinsic and extrinsic value

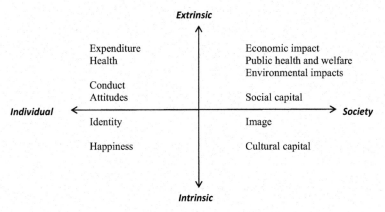

*Figure 3.1* A two-dimensional illustration of major festival impacts
Source: cf. McCarthy et al. 2004; Armbrecht 2009.

perspectives, while the horizontal axis separates individual versus societal values. Note that 'impacts' in this model can be interpreted as potential positive and negative values attributed to festivals.

## *Metrics*

Measurement of intrinsic value is often resisted but can be approached through measures such as willingness to pay valuation, or by relying upon the opinions and attitudes of stakeholders. Indeed, surveys of visitors' and local residents' impact perceptions and attitudes towards events are a standard form of value measurement (e.g. Delamere, Wankel & Hinch 2001; Fredline, Jago & Deery 2003; Small 2007; Woosnam, Van Winkle & An 2013). Claims are often made that culture or the arts do not require justification; therefore festivals should be judged worthwhile without resort to metrics. This is a controversial position to take, especially when the countervailing argument is that culture has major economic impact; in that context, many festivals have conducted economic impact studies.

Logically, both costs and negative impacts should be taken into consideration when assigning worth intrinsically or calculating a quantitative measure of value (see, for example, Deery & Jago 2010 for a comparison of benefits and costs), but this is not always done. Those promoting a festival might be attitudinally 'blind' to costs or any criticism, while impact forecasts and post-event assessments too often ignore externalities such as pollution, security, or inflation; opportunity costs are seldom weighed up. Little is known about long-term cumulative festival and event impacts or the synergistic effects of managed portfolios. The study of whole populations of festivals and events is in its infancy (Andersson, Getz & Mykletun 2013; Getz & Andersson 2016).

To 'prove' an impact requires strong evidence, even experiments, to demonstrate cause and effect, and this is seldom possible. As well, many of the imputed roles of festivals, particularly related to society and culture, are therefore highly subjective.

## *Synergies*

Portfolios of festivals, managed for policy and strategy, present opportunities for synergies and long-term sustainability. Whereas one festival can enhance a city's image or help in its (re)positioning, many festivals can offer greater balance, reduce risk and generate efficiencies. Theory on event portfolios is a relatively new area within event studies, with an early model by Getz (1997) suggesting an event-tourism strategy for destinations and Ziakas (2013) emphasising the potential synergies for destinations.

A 'convergence model' (Getz & Page 2016) demonstrates how value is increased by combinations of event forms and functions. Hallmark Events, defined as permanent, traditional events that become institutions, typically reflect this convergence (Getz & Page 2016). The appeal of these festivals, and the values they create, extend to individuals, groups, society, the economy and culture. By evolution or strategy, festivals and events combining the major domains of economic, symbolic and social exchange with value for individuals achieve much greater power – to attract tourists, appeal to a wider range of resident interests, and possibly to become more sustainable.

## Spatial and temporal considerations

Value perspectives on festivals vary over time and through space, and this is a rather neglected area of research. Benckendorff and Pearce (2012) modelled the stages of experience, namely pre, on-site and post, and the differing psychological experiences of spectators/attendees, performers and participants, and elite participants. Personality, motivation and involvement figure into pre-event experiences, while the on-site experience relates to role theory, identity, liminality, flow and mindfulness. Phenomenological research on festival experiences is therefore a key theory-building methodology (Ziakas & Boukas 2014).

Spatial and temporal issues increase when the discussion turns to portfolios and populations of events. Portfolios are managed for specific purposes, and many managers want to measure return on investment (ROI). As 'assets', festivals should each contribute to the overall ROI of the investors, and they might, over time, lose their asset value or, as Hallmark Events, gain asset value. Whole populations of events are subject to forces of ecological constraints that could enhance or diminish the value of individual festivals over time. Competition for resources is a major influence, including competition for audiences and competition for political support. Too many events in one area could result in serious financial problems for all of them, leading to failures.

## Cross-cultural variations

Very limited research has been cross-cultural in nature. One study by Schneider and Backman (1996) suggests that basic motivations for attending festivals are the same everywhere, and it is certainly logical to assume that both generic social/leisure benefits and festival-specific benefits accrue to people the world over. But this is an area of uncertainty, as religious beliefs, social norms and cultural traditions are bound to have an effect on how festivals are valued from the different perspectives.

## The people perspective

The value of festivals is a well-established theme within the 'classical' sociological and anthropological literature. Getz (2010), in his literature review, identified the following themes: myth, ritual and symbolism; ceremony and celebration; spectacle; *communitas*; host-guest interactions (and the role of the stranger); liminality, the carnivalesque and festivity; authenticity and commodification; pilgrimage; and a considerable amount of political debate

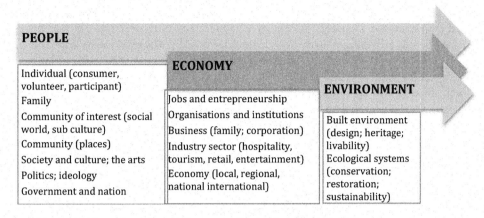

*Figure 3.2* Three main interdependent perspectives on festival values

over impacts and meanings. Landmark works include Van Gennep (1909), Victor Turner (1982) and Falassi (1987). Several books make explicit connections between tourism and the cultural dimensions of festivals (e.g. Long & Robinson 2004).

Value to the individual is the most logical starting point, as most other people perspectives are in some way aggregations. It is largely an area of psychological and social-psychological research, including the nature of the festival experience. Therefore, most of the value is intrinsic in nature. A potential benefit or value proposition is not of real value to the individual, unless they believe it to be so; therefore perception and attitude studies abound – usually regarding perceived impacts or costs and benefits.

The potential intrinsic benefits accrue to individuals directly through attendance (spectator or audience member) or engagement (e.g. volunteer, participant or performer). These are direct use values, but there can also be indirect use value creation when visitors ascribe wider benefits to festivals, such as an appreciation of other experiences at the destination during the festival visit. Perhaps the most studied perspective is satisfaction, as it has marketing implications, and satisfaction is often linked (such as through path mapping) to motivations, anticipated and perceived quality of programme and service, or other variables related to value. Numerous motivation studies have revealed much about the expectations of benefits to be attained, and it is useful to distinguish between those that are generic to events and leisure, such as socialising or escaping from boredom, and those that are specific to the festival (for example de Geus, Richards & Toepoel 2016), such as the entertainment or food. Both seeking and escaping are primary motivational factors.

Value can also accrue to individuals even if they do not attend festivals. Non-use valuation of events (e.g., Andersson et al. 2012; Gration, Raciti, Getz & Andersson 2016; Dwyer & Forsyth in Lundberg et al. 2017) takes into account the fact that people value them for providing choices (this is option value) and because they are perceived to be good for non-personal reasons like community and economic development. Non-use valuation also covers legacy value, being the passing on of traditions or the consideration given to younger generations and their needs. Value for the family is also an emerging line of research.

People form into many social groups, and these can be thought of as communities of interest or identity. The primary values relate to personal and group identity but can also include the legitimation of lifestyle or political positions. Ethnic identification can be included here and in the wider perspective of culture. Numerous ethnic-themed festivals around the world, many related to diaspora, reflect the high value placed by groups on celebration shared with society as a whole.

Many people are engaged in 'serious leisure' (as used by Mackellar 2009, based on the theories of Stebbins 1982) and belong to 'social worlds' (from Unruh 1980) which can mean that a given festival fosters and reinforces personal and social identity. Semiotic or symbolic value is important to communities of interest and identity. 'Iconic' events, in this context, hold symbolic value for those who are highly involved in a given leisure or lifestyle pursuit (on involvement see Kim, Scott & Crompton 1997; for iconic events see Getz & McConnell 2013).

The consumer perspective takes us into the realm of extrinsic valuation, as consumers are those who purchase an experience or product. Accordingly, they are exchanging something of value (money, time, effort) for expected and usually defined benefits, but also for co-created experiences. Measuring consumer satisfaction and future intentions is a very common research approach that can be used as both a marketing evaluation tool and a way to understand more theoretically what people value about the festival experience.

Prebensen (in Lundberg et al. 2017) argued that the key for events and destinations is to create value to attract the customer to visit the event and the destination. In the attempt to attract locals and tourists to visit an event, the event develops, facilitates and communicates potential experience value, i.e. emotional, social and epistemic value. Goolaup and Mossberg (in Lundberg et al. 2017) provided an overview of consumer culture studies and concluded that social value of festivals occurs when an individual associates himself/herself with a specific socio-economic or cultural-ethnic group. Within these consumption communities, there are networks of meanings, values, outlook and lifestyle practices that are shared by specific socio-economic milieus.

The community of place perspective refers to the common interests of people living together, whether whole cities or particular neighbourhoods. The value of festivals in this context is primarily intrinsic in nature, linked to place identity and attachment, pride, community spirit or community development. However, this is easily turned into extrinsic valuation when civic authorities, or politicians, exploit these feelings for other purposes. The 'eventful city' as articulated by Richards and Palmer (2010) refers to the purposeful creation of places in which festivals and events figure prominently, achieving multiple goals. Colombo and Richards (in Lundberg et al. 2017) have argued that Barcelona, as an example, obtained different forms of value from the studied event and, in turn, delivered different types of value to the event, which are important in the 'knowledge economy' or the 'network society'.

Politics and ideology complicate matters greatly, because celebrations of all kinds can be subverted to particular ideological aims. Is the purpose of a festival to foster community development and social integration, or to make certain politicians or parties look like they care? Will dissent on the expenditure or meanings ascribed to festivals be tolerated or repressed? Political discourse on the meanings and effects of festivals is essential. In one school of thought, festivals and rituals bind people together in communities and cultures (Durkheim 1912), while in another they reflect and encourage disagreement and even disputation of the meanings and impacts of events. Wood (in Lundberg et al. 2017) stated that leisure events are inherently political, and therefore the power embedded in practices, messages and commitments must be considered.

The perspective of government and the nation is often directly linked to politics and ideology. However, all governments have a regulatory interest in festivals and events, as well as decisions to make about spending, place marketing or image making, and fostering national pride. Intrinsic values like national pride and feelings of solidarity can easily be exploited by propaganda and manipulation of funding, resulting in extrinsic values coming to the fore. Frew and White (2015), for example, noted that national identity and commemorative events are strongly connected, and they discussed anniversaries and commemorative events in the context of Australian national identity, collective memory and how the significance of these commemorations may change from generation to generation. The potential of events to communicate social messages and influence attitudes and behaviour has been analysed as social marketing through events (Jutbring 2017).

The final people perspective, that of society as a whole, is challenging. Often the values assigned to festivals are group- or place-specific, and debate or conflict can erupt because of differing perspectives on meanings. Many of the purported benefits of festivals, such as social capital formation (e.g. Quinn & Wilks 2013) and social integration (e.g. Packer & Ballantyne 2010), apply to society as a whole and are presumably valued by both residents and government for improving welfare. However, demonstrating how this works is difficult, and the metrics employed (such as crime statistics, networking, or public attitudes) are not likely to be accepted by everyone.

## *Economic perspective*

Largely the realm of extrinsic valuation, the economic perspective often starts with the simplest metric, jobs. Entrepreneurial opportunities can be included here, with the observation that festivals offer many for-profit opportunities. However, festivals generate few direct jobs, and the number of direct and indirect jobs created is only going to be significant when many events and event venues are combined into a large and competitive portfolio that together create a stable upward shift of demand.

Festivals are very important in the mandates of many institutions (i.e. educational, religious, cultural, scientific) and are the *raison d'etre* for many not-for-profit festival organisations. Institutions use festivals and other events for their own purposes, including raising money and keeping members and volunteers active. Training might be important, as festivals also engage numerous volunteers who might benefit from the experience and inherent networking. The very existence of festival organisations is determined by their ability to generate funds, and this ultimately means attracting and satisfying attendees. They often are public service oriented, a fact that places them in a unique social category.

Private companies and corporations benefit from festivals in many ways. Sometimes their involvement is altruistic, but mostly it is part of marketing, sales and branding strategies. Numerous suppliers are partners with festivals, and the entire festival/event sector is often co-dependent with the corporate world, as sponsorship is a major source of funding. This results in a blending of intrinsic and extrinsic valuation that can become quite complex. While economic values are intended to accrue to everyone, individual businesses and corporations gain from their association with festivals through sponsorship and co-branding.

Tourism is the industry sector most closely linked to festivals and events, benefitting from destination image enhancement, animation and tourist expenditure. The relationship between festivals and tourism is sometimes uneasy or unwelcome. Many festivals are not large enough or marketed in a way that appeals to tourist organisations and are therefore ignored. Others can be exploited, and their authenticity can be diminished by over-commercialisation. To the tourism/hospitality industry, festivals have the most tangible value when they attract tourists who otherwise would not come. To hotels, the value is usually measured as bed-nights generated, and preferably in off-peak times.

Local, regional and national economies present different perspectives on value. Many local festivals will have limited or no impact on regional or national economies, with most of the transactions, including tourism, being local or domestic. On the other hand, mega-events hosted by the nation are bound to have many impacts on the local and regional economies of host cities. All too often benefits accrue to external interests, leaving communities and cities with disturbances and debt. One indicator of potential benefits is within the tax regime, namely how much the local economy gets from increased transactions and development; in some countries the nation benefits, but the local economy gets none.

## Environmental perspective

Built-environment includes physical developments, from the scale of a single facility to large-scale urban redevelopment. In many cities this is facilitated through culture-led, or in some places event-led, strategies. The elements of such strategies include design for events (such as festival places), animation programmes and coordinated festival and event portfolios. Heritage buildings can sometimes be adapted to become event venues, or figure in the design of festival spaces. A related concept is the repositioning of cities where cities aim to change the way they are perceived as destinations.

Ecological systems cover nature conservation or restoration, and environmental sustainability issues. These are of concern to all residents and to governments, but the related values ascribed to festivals are seldom studied. These include raising awareness, direct education, social marketing, raising money and acting as role models through the implementation of green and sustainability standards (Andersson et al. 2013). Negative ecological values, revealed through 'footprint analysis', are generated by most events from travel to and from the event, and from accommodation and catering.

## Conclusions

Given the almost innumerable value perspectives that can be taken on festivals, this chapter has focussed on providing a framework for analysis, research and theory development. The most important considerations pertain to intrinsic versus extrinsic approaches, as these reflect quite different philosophies of value and lead to quite different metrics. For intrinsic worth, the opinions or value judgements of stakeholders are most important; quantitative measures are often deemed unnecessary or are actually shunned. Extrinsic valuation generally reflects the instrumental worth of festivals from consumer, corporate and economic development perspectives. This gives rise to quantitative measures, usually expressed in monetary terms, such as direct expenditure or willingness to pay.

The second important consideration is that of scale, from the individual perspective through groups and places all the way to society as a whole. Intrinsic values accruing to and perceived by individuals and family units can also apply at broader levels of aggregation including society as a whole. Also discussed were matters of time and space as they influence value, and synergies that can arise. These aspects of festival valuation deserve greater attention.

Many research gaps remain, mostly to provide evidence on claims made about the benefits of festivals. Even where intrinsic value is ascribed and quantitative measures eschewed, evidence is required on who values festivals, why and under what circumstances. The ledger must also be balanced by considering the costs and negative impacts, many of which fall into the category of 'felt' or 'perceived'.

Perceived value might increase and decrease over time, with (potentially) memorable experiences fading in value, or experiences collectively increasing in value as their experiences provide reinforcing meanings. Researchers can quantify some of these temporal dimensions in several ways, including the monetary value of the travel and time committed to festival tourism (Mortazavi & Heldt in Lundberg et al. 2017). Since all activity has potential opportunity costs, the time and effort devoted to festival experiences can be valued. Looking at longer-term value creation, measures of satisfaction and future intentions are pertinent, and considering festival value in the light of serious leisure, involvement and social-world membership is important.

Researchers have examined perceived impacts of events and attitudes towards them with distance as an independent variable. It appears that the further one is away from a major event the less one perceives negative impacts and this spatial effect might also hold true to valuing the event. For example, do people without easy access to festivals value them in the same ways as those who can take close availability for granted?

The most notable gap pertaining to festival research is within the social and cultural range. Individuals are often asked about their perceptions and attitudes, and data have been collected from many surveys on the motivations and benefits felt by persons. But when the scope of discourse is elevated to that of social and cultural impacts, particularly the issues of 'social capital' and 'cultural capital', the literature is more about opinion than evidence. There is also evident resistance to such claims by economists, politicians and business interests, the people who are most impressed by hard data and 'proof'.

The need for longitudinal research has been identified, with emphasis on cumulative impacts and the dynamics of festivals – singly, in managed portfolios and in whole populations. There is much to be gained by examining how synergies, networks or collaboration among festivals and between festivals and other policy domains can be facilitated. Another area that would benefit from being explored in greater detail, and cross-culturally, is non-use values. Just how do people in different cultural environments value festivals, especially when they are not getting direct use benefits? Additionally, although not specifically addressed in this chapter, the methodology of value measurement is a big concern. Beyond the economic perspective, how intrinsic values are to be considered is problematic. Whose claim of intrinsic value is actually listened to, and is evidence actually provided about attributed benefits of festivals?

Finally, what happens to a festival that loses its popular support or appeal? Does this indicate reduced value to society as a whole? And how do we measure the loss of a failed festival? Many have disappeared without a trace or have been reborn in new locations or with new themes and programmes. Anyone making the argument that festivals hold intrinsic social, cultural or artistic value has to acknowledge that it is neither permanent nor accepted as a given by all concerned parties.

## References

Andersson, T. D., Armbrecht, J. & Lundberg, E. (2012). Estimating use and non-use values of a music festival, *Scandinavian Journal of Hospitality and Tourism*, 12(3), 215–231.

Andersson, T., Armbrecht, J. & Lundberg, E. (2017). The use and non-use values of events: A conceptual framework. In, Lundberg, J. et al. (eds.), *The Value of Events* (pp. 89–104). London: Routledge.

Andersson, T., Getz, D. & Mykletun, R. (2013). Sustainable festival populations: An application of organizational ecology, *Tourism Analysis*, 18(6), 621–634.

Armbrecht, J. (2009). *Att mäta det omätbara*, Lic. Thesis Gothenburg, Sweden: University of Gothenburg.

Benckendorff, P. & Pearce, P. (2012). The psychology of events. In, Page, S. J. & Connell, J. (eds.), *Routledge Handbook of Events* (pp. 165–185). London: Routledge.

Brown, S., Getz, D., Pettersson, R. & Wallstam, M. (2015). Event evaluation: Definitions, concepts and a state of the art review, *International Journal of Event and Festival Management*, 6(2), 135–157.

De Geus, S., Richards, G. & Toepoel, V. (2016). Creation of an event experience scale, *Scandinavian Journal of Hospitality and Tourism*, 16(3), 274–296.

Deery, M. & Jago, L. (2010). Social impacts of events and the role of anti-social behaviour, *International Journal of Event and Festival Management, 1*(1), 8–28.

Delamere, T. A., Wankel, L. M. & Hinch, T. D. (2001). Development of a scale to measure resident attitudes toward the social impacts of community festivals, Part I: Item generation and purification of the measure, *Event Management, 7*(1), 11–24.

Durkheim, E. C. (1912). [1995]. *The Elementary Forms of the Religious Life*, trans. Karen Fields. New York: Free Press.

Falassi, A. (1987). *Time Out of Time: Essays on the Festival*. Albuquerque: University of New Mexico Press.

Fredline, E., Jago, L. & Deery, M. (2003). The development of generic scale to measure the social impacts of events, *Event Management, 8*(1), 23–37.

Frew, E. & White, L. (2015). Commemorative events and national identity: Commemorating death and disaster in Australia, *Event Management, 19*(4), 509–524.

Getz, D. (1997). *Event Management and Event Tourism*. New York: Cognizant.

Getz, D. (2010). The nature and scope of festival studies, *International Journal of Event Management Research, 5*(1), 1–47.

Getz, D. & Andersson, T. (2016). Analyzing whole populations of festivals and events: An application of organizational ecology, *Journal of Policy Research in Tourism, Leisure & Events, 8*(3), 249–273.

Getz, D. & McConnell, A. (2013). Comparing trail runners and mountain bikers' motivation, portfolios, and event-tourist careers, *Journal of Convention and Event Tourism, 15*(1), 69–100.

Getz, D. & Page, S. (2016). *Event Studies* (3d ed.). London: Routledge.

Gration, D., Raciti, M., Getz, D. & Andersson, T. D. (2016). Resident valuation of planned events: An event portfolio pilot study, *Event Management, 20*(4), 607–622.

Jutbring, H. (2017). *Social Marketing through Events*. Gothenburg: BAS.

Kim, S. S., Scott, D. & Crompton, J. L. (1997). An exploration of the relationships among social psychological involvement, behavioral involvement, commitment, and future intentions in the context of birdwatching, *Journal of Leisure Research, 29*(3), 320–341.

Long, P. & Robinson, M. (eds.) (2004). *Festivals and Tourism: Marketing, Management and Evaluation*, Sunderland: Business Education Publishers Ltd.

Lundberg, E., Armbrecht, J., Andersson, T. & Getz, D. (eds.) (2017). *The Value of Events*. London: Routledge.

Mackellar, J. (2009). An examination of serious participants at the Australian Wintersun Festival, *Leisure Studies, 28*(1), 85–104.

McCarthy, K. F., Ondaatje, E. H., Laura, Z. & Brooks, A. C. (2004). *Gifts of the Muse: Reframing the Debate about the Benefits of the Arts*. Santa Monica, CA: RAND.

Packer, J. & Ballantyne, J. (2010). The impact of music festival attendance on young people's psychological and social well-being, *Psychology of Music, 39*(2), 164–181.

Quinn, B. & Wilks, L. (2013). Festival connections: People, place and social capital. In, Richards, G., de Brito, M. & Wilks, L. (eds.), *Exploring the Social Impacts of Events* (pp. 15–30). Abingdon: Routledge.

Richards, G. & Palmer, R. (2010) *Eventful Cities: Cultural Management and Urban Revitalisation*. London: Butterworth-Heinemann.

Schneider, I. E. & Backman, S. J. (1996). Cross-cultural equivalence of festival motivations: A study in Jordan, *Festival Management and Event Tourism, 4*(3/4), 139–144.

Small, K. (2007). Social dimensions of community festivals: An application of factor analysis in the development of the social impact perception (SIP) scale, *Event Management, 11*(1–2), 45–55.

Stebbins, R. A. (1982). Serious leisure: A conceptual statement, *Pacific Sociology Review, 25*(2), 251–272.

Turner, V. (ed.) (1982). *Celebration: Studies in Festivity and Ritual*. Washington DC: Smithsonian Institution Press.

Unruh, D. R. (1980). The nature of social worlds, *Sociological Perspectives, 23*(3), 271–296.

Van Gennep, A. (1909). *The Rites of Passage*. (1960 translation by M. Vizedom and G. Coffee). London: Routledge and Kegan Paul.

Woosnam, K., Van Winkle, C. & An, S. (2013). Confirming the festival social impact attitude scale in the context of a rural Texas cultural festival, *Event Management, 17*(3), 257–270.

Ziakas, V. (2013). *Event Portfolio Planning and Management: A Holistic Approach*. London: Routledge.

Ziakas, V. & Boukas, N. (2014). Contextualizing phenomenology in event management research: Deciphering the meaning of event experiences. *International Journal of Event and Festival Management, 5*(1), 56–73.

# 4
# THE MEANING OF FESTIVALS
## Reconfiguring the semiotic approach

*Xiaoming Zhang*

### Introduction

Contemporary humanities and social studies related to the meaning of festivals are based on two obvious presuppositions. One is that the meaning of festivals is generally recognised through typical expressions, such as that festivals can 'make' meaning (Holloway, Brown & Shipway 2010; Knight, Freeman, Stuart, Griggs & O'Reilly 2014), and meaning can be 'attached to' (Crespi-Vallbona & Richards 2007; Getz 2010), 'identified with' (Versnel 1992) or 'offered by' festivals (Lucas 2014). The other presupposition, which is based on the previous one, is that the meaning of festivals may be classified into various sorts, either according to the social representation system it has its roots in, for example, social meaning (Lewis 1997), cultural meaning (Quinn 2003) and political meaning (Waterman 1998), or according to the relationship between a festival and its host – individual meaning (Stadler, Reid & Fullagar 2013) and group meaning (Getz 2010).

These two presuppositions share two common points. First, both of them view festivals as an object or a complex set of objects, so that festivals can be produced, carried, divided and compounded as a physical object is. Second, both of the presuppositions assume that festivals are made up of components such as special costumes; food; a mascot; a particular colour; a core person who organises the festival; or a particular day, time, place and venue. In short, both the meaning and the components of festivals are divisible and, whether as a whole or as divided elements, festivals can be thought of as symbols. Therefore, the analysis and study of signs – semiotics – is an important approach for studying the meaning of festival. This approach includes Ferdinand de Saussure's structuralism semiology, Charles S. Peirce's pragmatist semiotics and Victor Turner's anthropologic symbolism (symbolic anthropology).

Contemporary studies on the meaning of festivals demonstrate two easily perceivable contradictions, one of which is relevant to the genesis of the meaning. Some argue that a festival 'offers' meaning (Lucas 2014), while others argue that meaning can be 'given to' a festival (Waterman 1998). The second contradiction is relevant to the specific way meaning has been studied in the festival context, and seems to directly correspond with the two positions in the first contradiction. Some people tend to believe that the meaning of festivals is relatively fixed if it is identifiable and explainable, while many others argue that the meaning of festival depends on the festival context (Mewett 1988). This is a reflection of the atmosphere of epistemological relativism that has been very popular in the fields of humanities and social research in recent decades.

However, in the attempt to lay a new foundation for the study of festivals in the coming decades, there is no excuse to turn a blind eye to those obvious or potential disagreements and contradictions in the study of the meaning of festivals. Therefore, contrary to the common practice of directly applying existing theories and concepts, this chapter tries rather to delve into the semiotic study of meaning on a more fundamental level, so as to reconsider the inquiry domain and basic frame of the study, expose any potential deficiencies in contemporary studies and propose directions for possible future improvements in the study of festivals.

## Reconfiguration of the semiotic approach

### Semiosis and holism

Saussure's semiology, which is closely concerned with linguistics, and Peirce's semiotics, which is closely concerned with phaneroscopy (i.e. his independent version of phenomenology) and logic, are the two major generally recognised schools of thought on sign (Cobly 2010, p. 3). Though appearing to be associated with the same archaic Greek term – *semeion* (static and real sign, symbol, icon or mark) (Liddell & Scott 1996, p. 1593), the significances of their names are quite different. Saussure's *semiology* is apparently the blend of *semeion* and *logos*, which means 'interpretation or research on semeion', while Peirce's *semiotics* is actually coined from another Greek word – *semiosis* (signifying, indicating) (Peirce 1955, p. 282), which is used to describe the dynamic signification process instead of the static sign.

Peirce's signification process requires that three elements must be present at the same time, i.e. something to signify, something to be signified, and a way to signify, which correspond, respectively, with the three elements in Peirce's sign system, i.e. *representamen*, *object* (or *designatum*) and *interpretant* (Peirce 1958, p. 343). Originally, these three elements were indivisible. *Representamen* (i.e. the sign itself, including symbols) is usually the easiest element to be identified and used. When it is used, it is destined to connote or interpret in a certain way or rule (the *interpretant*) an idea (the *object*) expressed or indicated by the *representamen*. The signification process, i.e. the semiosis, in which any sign is involved, is more fundamental than the sign itself (or any symbol, icon, index or mark). Logically, semiosis as a whole precedes the three constituent elements of sign, and it requires that each of these three elements must be present at the same time without absence.

The *holism* of sign may be viewed as a 'theoretical common denominator' of the two major contemporary schools of semiotics and also the first point to be considered in introducing any new semiotic frame. The position of *holism* does not completely negate the value of studying an 'objective' sign. After all, according to both Saussure and Peirce, the operation of semiotics cannot be conducted without a keen sense of identification of the 'components' of a sign. Therefore, observation of the objective world should always be a basic requirement for semiotic researchers. Nevertheless, either a two-element dyad constituted by sound-image and concept (or the *signifier* and the *signified* defined by Saussure), or a three-element triad constituted by *representamen*, *object* and *interpretant* (developed by Peirce) starts from the *holism* of sign. Researchers should only divide a sign to explore its constituent characteristics and evolution, instead of taking it for granted from the beginning that in reality these two or three elements can exist independently before they constitute a sign.

From a methodological perspective, Peirce's semiotics has a sounder position on *holism* over Saussure's semiology. Saussure himself has a clear position on *holism*, as his conception of sign originally meant an integrated whole of sound-image and concept in the human language phenomenon connected through mental activities (Saussure 1993, p. 74a). Roland Barthes, the critical heir of Saussure's theory, also clearly pointed out the structural indivisibility of the signifier and the signified (Barthes 1972, pp. 111–112). Regretfully, *holism*, the primary characteristic of a sign system, has been ignored by many researchers interested in semiotics. In fact, research into the meaning of 'festival' conducted by many researchers to date is just research on sign(s) or symbol(s), instead of genuinely *semiologic* or *semiotic* research. This could be an ontological trap that prevents semiotics from contributing more to festival studies.

## Structure and interpretation

Researchers often define a research object based on their own life experience or knowledge needs. This method of investigation can be described as 'structuring the object'. With this method, all information or knowledge is based and focussed on the object, unless the object in question is inherently viewed from the very beginning as a whole, i.e. an all-possible and non-objectified world. Therefore, understanding things based on an individual's own knowledge background and cognition ability suggests that human knowledge is always produced in a certain direction towards a certain object and described as a certain *structure*. The *structure* used here should not be interpreted as a composite constructed from various static components, relations, forms and quantity, but rather as a perspective and an approach to direct the researchers to seek better cognition of the related object without ignoring its holism and to acknowledge that any possible answer will have its own orientation and limitedness.

Both Saussure's dyad frame and Peirce's triad frame are structured research approaches. Due to the orientation and limitedness of individual researchers, knowledge on the object of study derived from structured research, i.e. the so-called *interpretation* in contemporary humanities and social research, might be unlimited. Researchers who want to utilise the analysing power of semiotics always need to have an open mind. As to interpretation or derivative understanding, the two major frameworks relating to signs have some differences but are basically consistent.

First, the earliest series of Saussure's dyad terms include *langue* and *parole*. *Langue*, as a holistic sign of sound-image and concept, is embedded in society, hard to alter and thus is static, while *parole* is the specific speech used in everyday life by any person but influenced by *langue*. However, this dyad cannot explain the historical evolution of language. Although he recognised this in his later years, Saussure had no time to reconfigure his entire thought system and only briefly made some remedy notes relating to the 'historical reality of time' (Saussure 1993, p. 110a). In his *Mythologies*, Roland Barthes gave up the fixed distinction between *langue* and *parole*. The only dyad completely inherited and accepted from Saussure is the holism in a sign of sound-image and concept. Following from the primitive sign system – the language system – Barthes created a secondary sign system – the myth system. The original meaning of 'myth' in ancient Greek (*mythos*) is 'speech' (Liddell & Scott 1996, p. 1151). Barthes specifically pointed out that the myth system, as with the language system, has a dyad structure of the signifier and the signified, and that the *signifier* in the myth system corresponds with the holistic sign in the language system, while the *signified* in the myth system is any potential concept developed from that holistic sign (Barthes 1972). In doing so, Barthes discovered the mechanism of idea, knowledge and ideology, and he further developed this in a three-layered system of signs that consists of *reality*, *denotation* (meta-language) and *connotation* (Barthes 1972). The connotation and reality layers have become a meaning system in social life that can be continuously interpreted and remade, and that is open, changeable and endless.

Second, as noted, Peirce's semiosis has three elements, i.e. *representamen*, *object* and *interpretant*. It is notable that the '*interpretant*' is an equivalent or even a more developed sign (Peirce 1967, p. 798) created by *representamen* in the mind of a human. As a sign, the *interpretant* will be involved in a new triangle of semiosis and derive a new *representamen*. That is to say, every *interpretant* may change to a new *representamen* (Echtner 1999). In Peirce's words, the *interpretant* keeps 'becoming a sign, and so on ad infinitum' (Peirce 1932, p. 303). This is exactly the *unlimited semiosis* emphasised by Umberto Eco (1976, pp. 68–69). The analysis frame of Peirce's semiotics clearly points to the social construction of the meaning of sign, implying that thorough understanding of the meaning of sign may be accessed through structured interpretative analysis of the *holism* of sign, or by considering any conceivable and practical effect that it may have.

A new semiotic approach consisting of *holism*, *structure* and *interpretation* is coming into form and seems to have some theoretical common factors between the two major schools of semiotic systems, which are traditionally viewed as quite different. From a functional perspective, *holism* involves rule setting and general description, while specific operation is carried out through analysis of *structure* and subsequent *interpretation*. *Holism* leads researchers to make keen judgement on and abstraction from reality as a whole. However, operationally, Peirce's triadic sign system might be more suitable than Saussure's dyadic sign system because the triadic sign system not only has a sound philosophic basis – pragmatism – but also enables researchers to take into account social reality.

## Possible relationships between festival and meaning

### *Puzzles in metaphysical entity analysis*

Taking a semiotic approach, researchers investigating the meaning of festivals should first try their best to define the sign as a whole. There are three puzzling questions to be answered. First, is meaning embedded in festivals, i.e. is it a part of the festival which can be observed by examining a distinct component of the festival? Second, is meaning attached to festivals, i.e. connected with festival as an external matter? Third, are there any other sorts of relationships between them?

The first two questions reflect a metaphysic position commonly held in contemporary research into the meaning of festivals, such that a festival is considered to be an *entity*, the meaning is an entity too and all possible relationships between these two entities are the object of research.

We can surely disagree with the view that meaning is embedded 'in' festivals. Obviously, if 'in' describes a constituent and inclusive relation, then all components 'in' a composite entity are essential for such an entity to exist. However, even though people have different answers to question like 'what is a festival' and have not understood or cannot get in touch with the so-called 'meaning', they still can identify the fact that a festival is being held by other people as a mixture of actions in the real world. It is obvious that analysis of an entity based on metaphysics is not applicable in such a case.

Similarly, views that propose that meaning is 'attached to' festivals are quite problematic too. A potential presupposition of such a view is that a festival is an independent occurrence and meaning is another independent occurrence, which can be randomly combined together.

At first glance, this view seems to be completely consistent with the diversified descriptions and understandings of festivals, which were introduced at the beginning of this chapter, and are often highlighted by researchers. However, even though festivals are changeable and dynamic, such views fail to explain why some festivals always have a particular meaning, or some restrained meanings, rather than random or unlimited meanings? What is combining festivals and meaning in certain way or, in other words, in a certain structure? This question cannot be convincingly answered through analysis based on metaphysics. Therefore, it seems appropriate to disregard such metaphysic positions.

## *Phenomenological analysis*

This chapter proposes an important judgement: meaning cannot exist independently. Although we can use the words, meaning cannot be understood without reference to the phenomenon under study. This judgement has its basis in phenomenology, especially related to Edmund Husserl's thought on *objectification (Objektivierung)* (Husserl 1987) of the human conscious experience. Husserl identified the existence of two different meaning-attributing components (Husserl 2001, p. 191), which are inherently rooted in the human consciousness experience. One of the components refers purely to the activity of presentation (objectification) which can produce *intentional meaning*. The other component is the effect or result of objectification, i.e. *filled meaning* – the content constructed and expressed by intentional meaning. Husserl also used pairs of terms *Sinn* (sense) and *Bedeutung* (meaning or significance) (Husserl 1987, p. 28) to describe the genesis of meaning as a whole.

Hence, once a meaning is determined as the object of research, the associated 'genesis of meaning' should also be explored. This may directly lead to two new propositions. One is that, no matter whether intentionally or unintentionally, 'festival' and 'meaning' can be separated; thus the 'meaning' here, without a genesis to rely on, loses its foundation. Another proposition is that such genesis of meaning is highly consistent with the semiosis emphasised by Peirce and that it reflects the genesis of sign elements.

Is it possible that there is a third relationship between 'festival' and 'meaning'? Besides 'embedded in' and 'attached to', there might be another relationship: they are closely connected, even overlapping, they permeate each other or melt into one. This, however, may seem unreasonable, as how can festival and meaning be melted into one?

To answer this question, it is necessary to introduce the thoughts of Martin Heidegger, a phenomenological philosopher. Heidegger, deeply provoked by Husserl, held that meaning is not something primarily expressed as a word or a proposition. For Husserl, meaning 'is that wherein the intelligibility of something maintains itself', and 'structured by fore-having, fore-sight, and fore-conception, is the "upon which" of the project in terms of which something becomes intelligible as something' (Heidegger 1996, p. 142). Though seeming obscure, these two statements have clear layers of meanings. First, meaning does not generate from nothing but always emerges from the existing life background, presenting an existential-practical meaning that appears to some extent in a primitively vague state or, in Husserl's words, presenting a '*Sinn*'. Second, meaning is generated in certain directions or structures, not in a completely random, casual or uncontrollable manner; rather, 'from' or 'as' something. Hence, the context is important. Third, based on the previous two points, the primitive meaning of a thing or an event is all of the possible conscious experiences associated with the thing or event in certain context, i.e. direction or structure, while the implication or semantics directed to by mentioning of 'meaning' in language is just a derivative form of such holistic meaning or conscious experience.

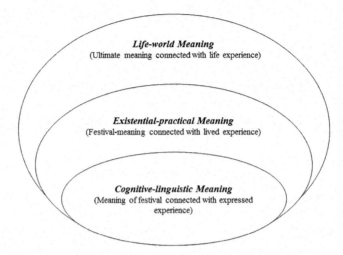

*Figure 4.1* Three levels of 'festival' and 'meaning'

If we consider the third possible relationship between 'festival' and 'meaning' outlined earlier, we can see that this is the only feasible relationship between 'festival' and 'meaning' that can be identified, understood and accepted. The following analysis is conducted with reference to Figure 4.1. On the one hand, when a 'festival' is being experienced in real time and in real life as an ongoing festival, for example, when people are enjoying experiencing all the events and atmosphere of a festival, 'festival' exists in the overall background of *lifeworld* (*Lebenswelt*) (Husserl 1970, p. 103) in a structured *existential-practical* form. It exists, it is present and it is being experienced. This thus presents an unlimited diversity of meanings in a very open 'as...' structure: for example, 'as a medium of cultural memory', 'as a channel of access to social identity' or 'as a place for escaping the self'. On the other hand, when a 'festival' is being thought about or talked about as an objectified festival, for example when someone is asked in an interview by a researcher to say something about a specific festival, as an object being discussed, considered or studied, 'festival' may only present its meaning as a cognitive-linguistic form in a relatively narrower context. In this latter case, the meaning would be better defined as 'implication' or 'semantics'.

In fact, when we are considering the meaning of a festival in the sense of primitive meaning, as the consideration is always focussed on the existence-practice, or 'lived experience', of each individual or group associated with the festival, it may be better to abandon the popular phrase 'the meaning of festivals' at this level and use 'festival-meaning' instead, a new expression with more emphasis on the inseparable connection between them.

## A semiotic illustration of the phenomenological findings

Based on the phenomenological analysis made earlier, the three layers of 'meaning' have been revealed and the concept of *holism* required in semiotics has been interpreted. While *holism* is being interpreted, in fact, '*structure*' and '*interpretation*' are delineated too. The 'festival-meaning' in a semiotic approach can be explicitly explained later based on Peirce's semiotic terminology (Figure 4.2).

## The meaning of festivals

First, '*holism*' indicates an ontological standpoint held by this framework on the object of research and is the logic starting point for all further thinking. Whatever the difference in scale, size and influence of the semiotic whole is, a meaningful sign whole is definitely equivalent to a semiosis in the core of Peirce's system. As for festival research, both 'festival' itself as a sign and some popularly recognised symbols of festival appearing in concrete form may be deemed as a semiotic whole. The key point is that all these symbols must be ontologically taken as a semiotic whole, either as the 'festival-meaning' whole in the existential-practical level or as the lifeworld whole associated with life experience.

Second, '*structure*' indicates the teleological methodology of this framework, which reminds researchers to try to find appropriate and irreducible elements of a sign system. In Peirce's system, as noted previously, such a sign system consists of the three elements: namely, *representamen*, *object* and *interpretant*, and their relationship. Moreover, the genesis of 'structure' is associated with the limitation of cognitive ability and the directivity of cognitive purpose. As for 'festival', the analysis of its structure first requires researchers to identify those basic social sectors involved in the sign system of a festival and their intertwined relationships.

Third, '*interpretation*' indicates an effective approach in semiotic research. Interpretation is, in its most common sense, to translate or to understand something by restating it with different ways. In the continuous process of interpretation, there are some phenomena that can hardly be perceived of and confirmed using common methods, and thereby form concepts, introduce point of views and raise propositions for further study. In the context of festival research, on the one hand, propositions may be put forward on a certain meaning of a festival; on the other hand, other propositions may be put forward on social realities revealed by such meaning. Therefore, it is further understood that the so-called 'meaning of festival' acquired in the cognitive-linguistic level is only one preliminary possibility of interpretation of meaning. As it is highly dependent on everyday language ability, such interpretation can be easily conducted and even be mistaken as the whole content of the meaning of festival.

How can more possibilities be explored? Three possible interpretations can be imagined here (see Figure 4.2).

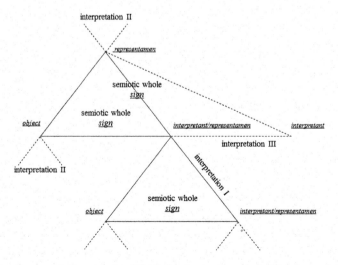

*Figure 4.2* New framework for analysis of 'festival-meaning' based on Peirce's terminology

1   The most direct interpretation approach is to analyse the *interpretant* as emphasised by Peirce ('interpretation I'), i.e. the *interpretant* in the previous semiosis needs to be interpreted by a new semiosis, thus entering into an unlimited semiosis.
2   On the basis of Peirce's *interpretant* analysis, we may expect that the other two elements of the whole, i.e. *representamen* and *object*, are actually involved in some other semiotic whole(s) and thus need to be further interpreted as well; in other words, their different elemental roles in other semiosis need to be interpreted ('interpretation II'). In short, *representamen* and *object* need to be analysed and discussed too. In the context where a specific festival is deemed as a semiotic whole, researchers are required to continue to investigate greater semiosis such as local culture, traditional culture or popular culture. The continuous interpretation of *representamen* and *object*, in addition to the continuous interpretation of *interpretant* (as originally required by Peirce), will finally form a very complicated and expansive landscape of signs. We may imagine that the utmost interpretation of this abstract landscape of signs is actually a holistic process of understanding our society and culture.
3   In social reality it is very likely that the same group of *representamen* and *object* may come from different semiosis, that is to say, are different in *interpretant* only. Then, the researchers need to explore all possibilities of the *interpretant* ('interpretation III'). In consideration of the purposiveness and directivity of structure thinking of human beings, the difference between *interpretants* is expected.

As can be seen from the aforementioned possibilities, interpretation is both complicated and fascinating for research. This may inspire researchers to experimentally and creatively interpret any seemingly simple festival phenomenon. The methodological guarantee is that '*structure*' and '*interpretation*' are specific analyses of the meaning of 'festival' on two different levels in the ontological premise of *holism*.

## Conclusion

This chapter has readdressed the semiotic perspective on the 'meaning of festivals' and explored both pragmatism (Peirce) and phenomenology (Husserl and Heidegger) as philosophical foundations underpinning this perspective. A proposed theoretical framework is summarised later. 'Meaning' itself cannot be separated from any event, including festivals, to exist alone. The primitive 'festival-meaning' is closely connected with various specific existence-practices in the lifeworld background; thus diversified explanation and interpretation are almost unavoidable. Just like reality or lived experience prior to representation and reflection, 'existential-practical' is a more fundamental logic preceding 'cognitive-linguistic'. Therefore, people first acquire on the prelinguistic level the primitive 'festival-meaning', which is not necessarily 'uttered', but thereafter, it becomes possible to get the derivative and 'uttered' 'meaning of festivals' that is connected only with expressed experience by using language at the cognitive and linguistic level. This can explain why, after a lived experience of festival has ended or is recorded in memory, one can keep attributing new meanings to this experience through recall and retrospection. On the one hand, the lifeworld itself keeps accumulating its content, and its connection with the primitive 'festival-meaning' keeps changing. On the other hand, what one is trying to attribute to the festival is actually some derivative implication, as all recall and retrospection present mostly in the form of concepts for thinking or speaking.

In terms of research into the 'meaning of festivals', a primary inquiry manner would be interpretive, open and descriptive questions like '*how* is the meaning of festival' or '*how*' to experience, '*how*' to present, and '*how*' to represent the meaning of festival instead of being limited to metaphysic or linguistic questions such as '*what* is the meaning of festival'.

Taking the new semiotic approach established in this chapter, the two contradictions in the current studies as mentioned at the beginning of the chapter can be explained somewhat here. As to the first contradiction related to the genesis of meaning, the more possible truth might be that festivals do not offer meaning; neither can meaning be given to festivals. Rather, people get primitive and prelinguistic 'festival-meaning' from their lived festival experience in their lifeworld. Once they need to communicate with each other, or even with themselves (such as writing a diary or blog), such communications are very likely expressed in language, and during such expressing process, it is natural that omissions of meaning will occur. Further, even greater omissions might be caused by trying to express meanings using linguistic marks such as numbers, formulae or models. As to the second contradiction, related to the specific way of studying meaning, if only considered from a linguistic perspective, the meaning of 'festival' certainly presents relatively fixed, identifiable and understandable characteristics since it can be spoken or written down. But if we consider the fact that the meaning of 'festival' is generated from a specific existence-practice – the lived festival experience – and that such existence-practice is always embedded in the continuously changing world in the manner of life experience, the meanings of 'festival' certainly could contain unlimited rich interpretations of 'festival-meaning', which may be imagined as ultimate meaning.

The new approach put forward in this chapter is not intended to radically criticise or negate all past and contemporary semiotic analyses on the meaning of festivals but rather to point out two possible directions for improvement. First, this chapter suggests that researchers should pay more attention to exploring the theoretical foundation behind their chosen study methods or tools. Second, this chapter suggests that researchers should not ignore the various disagreements and contradictions that exist, nor should they casually deal with these disagreements and contradictions with an attitude of epistemological relativism. Even though there is arguably no single correct theory in the humanities and social research field, there are surely some theories that can better define the scope and nature of issues studied and thus are much more useful for presenting views that can stand up to challenges.

## References

Barthes, R. (1972). *Mythologies*. New York: The Noonday Press.
Cobly, P. (Ed.). (2010). *The Routledge Companion to Semiotics*. London: Routledge.
Crespi-Vallbona, M. & Richards, G. (2007). The meaning of cultural festivals: Stakeholder perspectives in Catalunya. *International Journal of Cultural Policy*, 13(1), 103–122.
Echtner, C. M. (1999). The semiotic paradigm: Implications for tourism research. *Tourism Management*, 20(1), 47–57.
Eco, U. (1976). *A Theory of Semiotics*. Bloomington: Indiana University Press.
Getz, D. (2010). The nature and scope of festival studies. *International Journal of Event Management Research*, 5(1), 1–47.
Heidegger, M. (1996). *Being and Time*. Albany, NY: State University of New York Press.
Holloway, I., Brown, L. & Shipway, R. (2010). Meaning not measurement: Using ethnography to bring a deeper understanding to the participant experience of festivals and events. *International Journal of Event and Festival Management*, 1(1), 74–85.
Husserl, E. (1987). *Husserliana, Vol.26: Vorlesungen über Bedeutungslehre*. Dordrecht: Martinus Nijhoff.
Husserl, E. (2001). *Logical Investigations, Volume II*. London & New York: Routledge.
Husserl, E. (1970). *The Crisis of European Sciences and Transcendental Phenomenology: An Introduction to Phenomenological Philosophy*. Evanston, IL: Northwestern University Press.
Knight, P., Freeman, I., Stuart, S., Griggs, G. & O'Reilly, N. (2014). Semiotic representations of Olympic mascots revisited: Virtual mascots of the games 2006–2012. *International Journal of Event and Festival Management*, 5(1), 74–92.

Lewis, G. H. (1997). Celebrating Asparagus: Community and the rationally constructed food festival. *The Journal of American Culture, 20*(4), 73–78.

Liddell, H. G. & Scott, R. (1996). *A Greek–English Lexicon*. Oxford: Clarendon Press.

Lucas, M. J. (2014). The organizing practices of a community festival. *Journal of Organizational Ethnography, 3*(2), 275–290.

Mewett, P. G. (1988). Darwin's 'Beercan Regatta': Masculinity, frontier and festival in North Australia. *Social Analysis: The International Journal of Social and Cultural Practice, 23*(August), 3–37.

Peirce, C. S. (1967). *Annotated Catalogue of the Paper of Charles S. Peirce*. Boston: The University of Massachusetts Press.

Peirce, C. S. (1932). *Collected Papers, Vol. 2: Elements of Logic*. Cambridge, MA: Harvard University Press.

Peirce, C. S. (1958). *Collected Papers, Vol.8: Reviews, Correspondence, and Bibliography*. Cambridge, MA: Harvard University Press.

Peirce, C. S. (1955). *Philosophical Writings of Peirce*. New York: Dover Publications, 1955.

Quinn, B. (2003). Symbols, practices and myth-making: Cultural perspectives on the Wexford Festival Opera. *Tourism Geographies, 5*(3), 329–349.

Saussure, F. de. (1993) *Saussure's Third Course of Lectures on General Linguistics (1910–1911)*. Oxford: Pergamon Press.

Stadler, R., Reid, S. & Fullagar, S. (2013). An ethnographic exploration of knowledge practices within the Queensland Music Festival. *International Journal of Event and Festival Management, 4*(2), 90–106.

Versnel, H. S. (1992). The festival for Bona Dea and the Thesmophoria. *Greece and Rome (Second Series), 39*(1), 31–55.

Waterman, S. (1998). Carnivals for elites? The cultural politics of arts festivals. *Progress in Human Geography, 22*(1), 54–74.

# PART II

# Sustainability

# 5
# VALUING THE IMPACTS OF FESTIVALS

*Larry Dwyer and Leo Jago*

## Introduction

Increasingly, economic assessment is used by festival convenors to support access to public funding. Governments are often asked to provide financial support for festivals, including the allocation of substantial funds to provide or upgrade the facilities required to stage them. As a consequence, governments will generally require credible forecasts of the festival impacts and their comprehensive evaluations. Besides the economic impacts, festivals usually generate a range of other benefits such as enhancing the image of a city or region, facilitating cultural awareness, helping to forge community identity and sense of place, enhancing resident recreational opportunities, social networking and civic pride. On the other hand, festivals and events are recognised as potentially generating adverse social impacts such as disruption to local business and community backlash and adverse environmental impacts such as various forms of pollution (Robertson 2013).

## What is a festival?

While different definitions exist (Smith 1990; Getz 2005) we take festivals to be 'themed public occasions designed to occur for a limited duration that celebrate valued aspects of a community's way of life' (Douglas, Douglas & Derrett 2001, p. 358). Typically, they originate within the community in response to a need or desire to celebrate the community's unique identity (Douglas et al. 2001; Wood 2005).

Festivals are of two key types. First there are the very large festivals that are more akin to a mainstream special event where a key purpose is to attract visitors. Glastonbury, which does not really have a local community dimension, is an example of this type of festival. The second type, which reflects the majority of festivals, is where there is a strong community dimension; indeed, most of these festivals are generated from within the community often to celebrate community values. For this category of festival, visitation, and the expenditure such visitation generates, is a secondary benefit. Characteristically, festivals provide important social and recreational opportunities for local communities. They are also associated with additional demand for destination goods and services generating increased sales, jobs, income, investment in infrastructure and economic development opportunities.

Ideally, festivals also foster a greater sense of community co-operation, goodwill, reciprocity, belonging and fellowship (Lee, Arcodia & Lee 2012). Given their relevance to community, regional and even national identity and pride, creative learning and development, celebrating community values, destination image and branding, they form a fundamental component of the tourism development strategy in many destinations (Jago & Dwyer 2006). Whilst these non-economic objectives are more difficult to measure and thus evaluate, they are real and must be considered in determining the overall value of a festival. Since the focus of this chapter is on the economic contribution of festivals, the evaluation of the non-economic contribution falls largely outside the scope and receives less attention in this chapter. This does not, however, suggest that the authors undervalue the importance of the non-economic dimensions.

For the first type of festival mentioned, the economic analysis is exactly the same as for major events. For the second type, the non-economic impacts are likely to be more important than the economic impacts. The challenge for researchers is to provide techniques which give accurate results while at the same time providing practical use for policymakers, who must make decisions on whether allocating resources to support a particular festival is appropriate and, if so, to what extent.

## Evaluation

Given the increasing calls for funds from the generally constrained public purse, it is nowadays essential that the contributions of festivals that draw upon public funds be evaluated. This is done to ensure that their return justifies the public investment compared to the alternate uses of those funds. Justifications for public-sector involvement in planned events include consideration of public good, social equity, return on investment, efficiency, achievement of destination tourism visitation targets, psychic benefits to residents and market failure arguments (Getz 2009).

In general, there is an organisational purpose to evaluation. Evaluation is often driven by internal management requirements (for example, to evaluate against the objectives, evaluate finance and use of resources, audience satisfaction and quality of the continuing planning and management processes). Rather than being an infrequent task for solving problems or generating new ideas; the results of an evaluation can be used to direct the marketing and planning functions; and enable an organisation to continually learn about itself, its environment and ways to improve its performance (Getz 2005). Festival evaluations can inform management processes and procedures for subsequent hosting of events. Festival managers see evaluation as a way of determining success, by reviewing what has been done against the objectives set (whether these are clearly articulated or not), with the aim of feeding results into the planning process for the future. Evaluation is learning from strengths and weaknesses that can be taken into account in future planning and operation. We can identify three basic types of evaluation; formative (pre-event assessment), process (monitoring) and outcome or summative evaluations (post-event), with the latter being the most common (Getz 2005; Robertson 2013).

For an evaluation to be effective, it is critical that the evaluation be undertaken against the objectives that were set for that particular activity. This highlights the need for clear and, if possible, quantifiable objectives to be established at the outset. In the case of the larger festivals, a key objective is often to attract large numbers of visitors to the destination and to maximise the spending in the area that these visitors make. Given this objective, assessing the economic contribution that these major festivals make to the host region becomes a key driver of the festival evaluation. An overview of the different approaches that can be used to perform this type of evaluation will be provided in this chapter.

As indicated earlier, it is necessary to clearly articulate the overall objectives or expectations of the festival if the evaluation is to be in any way effective (O'Sullivan, Pickernell & Senyard 2009). In the case of festivals, objectives may be vague or difficult to quantify. The aims of the Edinburgh festival, for example, are to be 'the most exciting, innovative and accessible festival of the performing arts in the world, and thus promote the cultural, educational and economic well-being of the people of Edinburgh and Scotland' (Williams & Bowdin 2007, p. 193). While some of these aims (the economic) are quantifiable, others are not.

There is widespread agreement that events should be assessed in respect of (at least) their economic, social/cultural and environmental impacts. A popular view is that triple bottom line (TBL) evaluation should be used (e.g. Fredline, Jago & Deery 2003; Getz 2005), although with some exceptions (Wood 2008), the specifics of this balanced approach to festival evaluation and implications for festival planning and operations are seldom articulated. For each of the three dimensions of TBL, possible goals, related policy initiatives and a number of performance measures are suggested. More formal methods are likely to be used in festivals that are run by local authorities. No matter which methods are chosen, it is likely that both quantitative and qualitative data will be required to evaluate performance against the objectives.

## *Attendance*

For many festivals, audience size and attendance are the principal means by which festivals evaluate their success. Accurate and robust measurement of attendance has emerged as a critical factor to ensuring the reliability of event monitoring and evaluation. A major challenge for festivals is to estimate attendance numbers as many of the component activities are not ticketed. Even for those festivals that have a turnstile entry, if not paid tickets, there is the problem in identifying how many sub-events attendees attend. Davies, Coleman and Ramchandani (2010) identify a genuine gap in knowledge about the processes involved in estimating attendance figures at festivals. In any case, participation numbers in themselves are insufficient to value a festival. Not only do numbers tell us nothing about a festival's value or worth to a community, but festivals with similar attendance numbers will have very different impacts (economic, social and environmental).

However, an accurate estimate of attendance at a festival is an essential prerequisite for evaluating the economic contribution of the event. Expenditure data from visitors can be collected via surveys, but unless there is an accurate estimate of the total attendance number, particularly in relation to visitors from outside the host destination, it is not possible to estimate the economic contribution. Even festivals that are largely ticketed often have free components rendering estimates of total attendance numbers problematic. Added to this is the problem that individuals may buy tickets to multiple sub-events, so distinguishing between attendees and attendances is most important.

Much work has been done over the years to estimate crowd numbers at events in general, and festivals in particular (Tyrrell & Ismail 2005), that will reduce the effort required to estimate attendees. Even with more accurate estimates of attendee numbers, it is essential that there are sound estimates of the attendee mix so that the number of visitors to the region can be estimated as it is only the spending by visitors from outside the host region that contributes to the economic contribution of the festival.

## Direct expenditure

A pragmatic approach to measuring economic activity linked to festivals is the Direct Expenditure Approach (DEA). The DEA involves measuring the first-round 'direct' economic expenditures associated with an event, which are injected into the host economy from external sources (Jago & Dwyer 2006). Direct expenditure includes both money spent on the event itself and related expenditure on items such as transport, accommodation, food and beverage, and shopping. In the UK, for example, UK Sport, Event Scotland and Visit Britain, amongst others, endorse the use of the DEA for evaluating events (Davies, Coleman & Ramchandani 2013). The DEA is argued to provide an accessible, cost-effective and practical alternative to multiplier analysis, providing the 'first stage' for modelling the indirect effects of the festival on economic variables such as Gross Domestic Product (GDP) and employment.

DEA provides an indicative assessment of the economic scale of an event. There are, however, several problems with the DEA when applied to larger festivals. No information is given as to the economic impacts of the festival on variables such as GDP and employment, and the same injected expenditure can generate different economic impacts. Most importantly, the DEA ignores resident values in festival assessment.

## Economic impact analysis

Economic impact analysis (EIA) involves estimating the additional expenditure generated by a festival, and then using some form of economic model to estimate how this expenditure affects the destination economy. The economic model identifies and quantifies the linkages between different sectors of the local economy and linkages with other regions. The injected expenditure of visitors and organisers/sponsors stimulates economic activity and creates additional business turnover, employment, value added, household income and government revenue in the host community. The relationship between expenditure and output, income, value added and employment (direct, indirect or induced) can be described by multipliers. The size of the multipliers will depend upon the type of model used to estimate the impacts (Jago & Dwyer 2006).

## Input–output modelling

The standard model used for the economic impact estimation of festivals and special events has been through multipliers derived from input–output (I–O) models. The restrictive assumptions of I–O modelling (fixed technical coefficients, no capacity constraints and consequently no impact of the festival on wages or prices) mean that it fails to capture the industry interactive effects that would be revealed in the use of a more sophisticated model for economic impact assessment, thereby exaggerating the economic impacts (Dwyer, Forsyth & Spurr 2004).

## Computable equilibrium modelling

Computable general equilibrium (CGE) models are designed to capture the complex pattern of price changes, feedback effects and resource constraints which exist in all economies following a demand side shock such as that occasioned by the holding of a festival (Dwyer et al. 2004; Blake 2005). They include more specifications of the behaviour of consumers, producers and investors, thus permitting specific models to be calibrated to actual conditions for a particular festival in a particular economy (Dwyer 2015). In contrast to I–O analysis, which always produces a positive gain to the economy no matter how disastrous the performance of the festival, CGE modelling recognises that price rises due to land, labour and capital constraints may limit the increase in economic activity and may even lead to contractions in economic activity in some sectors or the whole economy. CGE models can also be undertaken using different assumptions, which provides transparency rarely offered by I–O models (Dwyer 2015). However, if no suitable model already exists, it is very expensive to construct a new CGE model, thus limiting its use to the largest contexts.

## Criticism of EIA in festival assessment

EIA is narrow and excludes the wider (social and environmental) costs and benefits of festivals that can be crucial inputs to policy. As indicated earlier, the key objectives for staging many festivals are not economic in focus, and thus EIA provides only a partial perspective to decision makers facing the problem of funding or subsidising a festival. In order for the government to be more comprehensively apprised, the evaluation exercise must transcend a narrow concern with economic issues and embrace the wider range of effects associated with festivals and events (Wood 2005).

A second type of criticism is that, contrary to the standard view, the outcomes of EIA have no direct policy implications. Economic impact studies can only estimate the effect on economic variables such as output, GDP, employment and the like. Since festivals (and society itself) have goals that are not purely economic, EIA alone cannot decide which is the best allocation of public resources in support of festivals (Dwyer, Jago & Forsyth 2016).

Third, EIA neglects community values other than those that are purely economic. EIA regards only expenditure by non-residents (injected expenditure) as relevant to the creation of economic value, treating residents' festival-related expenditure merely as 'transferred expenditure' playing no role in determining economic impacts (Dwyer et al. 2016). This exclusion of resident preferences, including their willingness to pay (WTP) for festival attendance, is generally ignored by theorists and practitioners alike.

## Cost–benefit analysis

Cost–benefit analysis (CBA) can be used to capture, measure, weight and compare all expected present and future benefits of a festival with all its expected present and future costs. As a result of holding a festival, individual firms, consumers and/or workers may be better or worse off as a result of changes in their own consumption, income and level of effort as well as how they are affected by associated government expenditure. Firms can gain (or lose) if there is a change in the level of profits. Consumers gain (or lose) from the holding of the event, and workers can gain from additional wages less any costs of additional effort. Governments may gain through increased tax receipts at existing tax rates, and they will pass these gains on to the community in a number of ways – through tax cuts or additional expenditures which benefit the community – or they may save their gains and pass them on to future generations.

For a festival to be socially acceptable, the sum of the benefits to society (including private and social benefits) must exceed the sum of the costs to society (including private and social costs). 'Value' or 'benefit' is measured by WTP – what people are willing to pay (or give up) to get what an event provides and is estimated by measuring the additional consumer surplus and producer surplus of a given option over the 'do nothing' or 'no event' case (Boardman,

Greenberg, Vining & Weimer 2011). Economic costs are measured by 'opportunity cost' – what people or a society give up by investing capital and employing workers in event-related activities as opposed to the best alternative. The method most often employed to estimate non-use values is Contingent Valuation (CV) whereby value is determined through a survey of peoples' preferences in hypothetical market situations in which people state what they would do in a given situation(s) (Walton, Longo & Dawson 2008; Andersson, Armbrecht & Lundberg 2012). Residents are asked to state their maximum WTP for or, alternatively, their willingness to accept (WTA) specific intangible benefits and costs associated with a festival. Table 5.1 lists indicative types of benefits and costs of holding a festival.

## *Estimating benefits of events*

Unfortunately, many of the benefit items in Table 5.1 are often ignored in festival evaluation. The use of EIA has resulted in the neglect of both surpluses to businesses and surpluses to labour. Techniques exist for estimating these two types of surplus from festival-related net expenditure (Dwyer et al. 2016). Economic techniques can help to estimate ongoing (legacy) benefits to residents from construction of assets for the festival (or festivals), but follow-on benefits to residents resulting from future visitation to the destination (brand benefit) are notoriously difficult to estimate with any precision.

*Table 5.1* Indicative types of benefits and costs of a festival

| Benefits | Costs |
| --- | --- |
| **Payments to festival organisers** (e.g. ticket revenue, sponsorship and advertising revenue and media payments) | **Capital expenditures** on festival-related infrastructure |
| **Consumer surpluses of local households** (derived from attending the event) | **Operating expenditures** (e.g. festival management and staging, security, catering, administration, marketing/promotion) |
| **Consumer surpluses of local households from attending associated off-site events/activities** (e.g. satellite events, public screenings and off-site parties) | **Festival-related costs incurred by government agencies** (e.g. road agencies, police, fire brigade and state emergency services) |
| **Other benefits of local households** (e.g. pride, excitement and satisfaction) | **Social costs** (e.g. disruption to business and resident lifestyles, traffic congestion, crime, litter, noise, crowding, property damage) |
| **Surpluses to destination businesses** (the operating profits of local owners of visitor-related businesses) | **Environmental costs** (e.g. environmental degradation, air/water pollution, carbon footprint) |
| **Surpluses to destination labour** (the net benefits to local labour after compensation for working and tax) | |
| **Follow-on benefits to residents** (resulting from future visitation to the destination) | |
| **Ongoing (legacy) tangible benefits to residents** (from construction of assets for the festival) | |
| **Ongoing (legacy) intangible benefits to residents** (from values experienced, preserved and generated by community) | |

Some outcomes of a festival on a destination are not sufficiently well accepted or measurable to be included in a CBA. These are often referred to as 'intangible' outcomes which vary from one festival to another, depending upon size and type. They include such beneficial items as increased business confidence, enhancement of business management skills, emergent values such as increased community interest in the issues relevant to the festival 'theme' and enhanced destination image. Ongoing benefits from intangible values experienced, preserved and generated by community as a result of the festival are notoriously difficult to measure.

## *Estimating costs*

The cost of employing capital, land and labour for the festival is the value of what those economic resources could have produced in their best alternative use. Governments often allocate resources to support a festival, and whilst festivals are much less likely than other types of events to require new infrastructure, they do require support in other forms, such as policing and security. Many relevant costs can be based on balance sheet figures of government departments and agencies. Any time devoted to festival management issues by public servants has an opportunity cost, estimated with reference to some measure of average wages of public service employees. However, volunteers, who often take leave from their employment to provide services at a festival, would not be included as costs. While their time has an opportunity cost, there is no practical way of putting a value on it.

Estimating the social and environmental costs of festivals poses some difficulties. In each case, the valuation process requires two steps: estimating the amount of physical change (e.g. to recreation areas and amenity, traffic diversion and congestion, and noise), and thence estimating the value associated with that change. Standard methods are available for valuing temporary disruption to resident lifestyles through loss of land uses, traffic congestion, noise and air quality impacts on property values and time lost due to congestion (Boardman et al. 2011). The increased incidence of crime associated with a festival can be estimated from statistics for previous events, as can property damage, accidents and vandalism (Weimer & Vining 2005). Costs of removing litter and cleaning festival sites can also be estimated. The standard economic method of valuing such benefits is WTP or WTA.

The carbon costs of festivals can also be estimated (Collins, Jones & Munday 2009; Andersson et al. 2012). Different festivals have different carbon footprints, and techniques for measuring the carbon footprint of an economic activity are available on the web. It should be noted, however, that valuing such impacts is not always straightforward. There are some festivals that involve preservation of valued environmental resources (e.g. a wilderness area for cross-country skiing), and the value attached to preservation of such areas will include the types of non-user values and measurement approaches identified earlier.

Festivals also have the power to destroy cultural heritage by creating the commoditisation of culture to meet the needs of an increasing number of visitors (Getz 1997; Douglas et al. 2001). Social attitudes can be monitored using community tracking surveys to gauge the trend of support/discontent for a festival over time. More detailed study of the effect of resident perceptions on the measurement of event-related costs and benefits is needed by researchers. In particular, a greater research effort is required to specify 'trade-offs' between particular social outcomes and the associated losses (or gains) by way of the economic contribution of different festivals.

## A hybrid approach

The standard approach to festival evaluation has been for researchers and consultants to estimate the economic impacts and then, alongside these, consider some of the possible wider effects that are not captured in the economic modelling. This has resulted in a less than satisfactory approach to event evaluation since the EIA and the CBA can give conflicting results (Dwyer & Forsyth 2017). Standard EIA and CBA focus on different aspects of the festival evaluation problem. While an EIA of events emphasises the injected expenditure associated with events as the basis for further analysis, a CBA recognises that the consumer surpluses of residents are essential to event evaluation. As noted earlier, EIA modelling treats resident expenditure simply as 'transferred' expenditure which is then ignored. In contrast, by making residents' values central to the assessment, CBA improves the information base for public-sector decision-making, thereby assisting in the assessment of relative funding priorities.

The projected net benefits of a festival represent the 'bottom line' for determining the extent, if any, of support from public funds that is warranted. However, since a CBA cannot measure the level of economic activity generated from the event or the wider flow-on effects on Gross Regional Product and employment, an EIA is required to identify and measure these effects. For larger festivals in particular, CGE modelling would pick up general equilibrium impacts which the partial equilibrium CBA is not capable of detecting. Since neither technique is completely comprehensive, there is a need for an integrated approach to festival evaluation that includes the advantages of each separate approach. Research is currently being undertaken on this issue (Dwyer et al. 2016). The motives for staging festivals are different to major events, and thus the techniques used to evaluate festivals need to reflect this. While many issues relevant to the development of an integrative approach to festival assessment demand further exploration, the dual approach allows the advantages and limitations of each approach to be exposed and the methods refined for future research. This 'dual' approach seems to be particularly relevant to festival evaluation given that festivals typically have different and wider objectives as compared to other types of special events.

In practice, festival organisers, governments, the community and other stakeholders may have to settle for a less than ideal assessment exercise. Conducting a full-scale EIA and/or CBA can be costly and is unnecessary for many festivals, particularly those of small scale. This suggests not only that there are cost limitations to festival evaluation but also that the practicalities of evaluation have to be fully considered in the context of organisation funds. This flags the need for a better understanding of the relationship between events and public policy agendas (Whitford 2009).

## Conclusion

This chapter has attempted to set down some elements of 'best practice' in festival evaluation. Unfortunately, much of the research literature, including special events evaluation, seems uninformed by economic theory. While economic objectives may not be the most important in various festivals held worldwide, and, indeed, for some festivals they are of minimal consideration, they need to be considered explicitly when any form of public subsidy is sought by festival organisers. Economic approaches to valuation can also play an important role in valuing the social and environmental effects of festivals. For smaller festivals, DEA provides an indicative estimate of the festival economic scale without confronting the challenges of developing and using economic models with assumptions subject to debate. However, for the majority of festivals, much more focus is needed to document and measure the non-economic objectives. Economic techniques are available both to estimate larger festival economic impacts and to measure the net benefits to society from festivals taking account of resident and other stakeholder values. Economic techniques can also play an essential role in identifying and measuring the trade-offs between achievement of a festival's economic, social and environmental objectives.

Recently, arguments have been advanced to the effect that the attainment of a sustainable and responsible events sector will require the institutionalisation of a new paradigm, one that employs a TBL approach both to the determination of the worth of events and to evaluation of their impacts (Getz 2009). The key challenges are how to compare values (economic, social and environmental) that seem to be 'incommensurable' and the current underdevelopment and underutilisation of economic approaches to value the wider (economic and non-economic) impacts of festivals. The implications of a 'new evaluation paradigm' should be explored further for the festival context, including its consistency with calls for paradigm change in the wider tourism context (Dwyer 2017).

## References

Andersson T.D., Armbrecht, J. & E. Lundberg (2012). Estimating use and non-use values of a music festival, *Scandinavian Journal of Hospitality and Tourism*, 12(3), 215–231.

Blake, A. (2005). *The Economic Impact of the London 2012 Olympics*. Research report 2005/5. Nottingham: Christel DeHaan Tourism and Travel Research Institute, Nottingham University.

Boardman, A., Greenberg, D., Vining, A. & Weimer, D. (2011). *Cost–Benefit Analysis: Concepts and Practice* (4th ed.). Chicago, IL: Prentice Hall.

Collins, A., Jones, C. & Munday, M. (2009). Assessing the environmental impacts of mega sporting events: Two options? *Tourism Management*, 30(6), 828–837.

Davies, L., Coleman, R. & Ramchandani, G. (2010). Measuring attendance: Issues and implications for estimating the impact of free-to-view sports events, *International Journal of Sports Marketing and Sponsorship*, 12(1), 6–18.

Davies, L, Coleman, R. & Ramchandani, G. (2013). Evaluating event economic impact: Rigour versus reality? *International Journal of Event and Festival Management*, 4(1), 31–42.

Douglas, N., Douglas, N. & Derrett, R. (Eds.). (2001). *Special Interest Tourism: Context and Cases*. Milton, Australia: John Wiley and Sons.

Dwyer, L. (2015). *Computable General Equilibrium Modelling for Tourism Policy – Inputs and Outputs*. Statistics and TSA Issues Paper Series, Madrid: UNWTO.

Dwyer, L. (2017). Saluting while the ship sinks: The necessity for tourism paradigm change. *Journal of Sustainable Tourism*, 26. http://dx.doi.org/10.1080/09669582.2017.1308372.

Dwyer, L., Forsyth, P. & Spurr, R. (2004). Evaluating tourism's economic effects: New and old approaches, *Tourism Management*, 25(3), 307–317.

Dwyer, L. & Forsyth, P. (2017). Event evaluation: Approaches and new challenges. In Lundberg, E., Armbrecht, J., Andersson, T.D. & Getz, D. (eds.) *The Value of Events* (pp. 105–123). London: Routledge.

Dwyer, L., Jago, L. & Forsyth, P. (2016). Economic evaluation of special events: Reconciling economic impact and cost–benefit analysis, *Scandinavian Journal of Hospitality and Tourism*, 16(2), 115–129.

Fredline, L., Jago, L. & Deery, M., (2003). The development of a generic scale to measure the social impacts of events, *Event Management*, 8(1), 23–37.

Getz, D. (2005). *Event Management and Event Tourism* (2nd ed.). New York: Cognizant.

Getz, D. (2009). Policy for sustainable and responsible festivals and events: Institutionalization of a new paradigm, *Journal of Policy Research in Tourism, Leisure and Events*, 1(1), 61–78.

Jago, L. & Dwyer, L. (2006). *Economic Evaluation of Special Events: A Practitioners Guide*. Altona, Australia: Common Ground Publishing Pty. Ltd.

Lee, I.S., Arcodia, C. & Lee, T.J. (2012). Key characteristics of multicultural festivals: A critical review of the literature, *Event Management*, 16(1), 93–101.

O'Sullivan, D., Pickernell, D. & Senyard, J. (2009). Public sector evaluation of festivals and special events, *Journal of Policy Research in Tourism, Leisure and Events*, 1(1), 19–36.

Robertson, M. (2013). *Events and Festivals: Current Trends and Issues*. London: Routledge.
Schlenker, K., Edwards, D.C. & Sheridan, L. (2005). A flexible framework for evaluating the socio-cultural impacts of a small festival, *International Journal of Event Management Research*, 1(1), 66–76.
Tyrrell, B.J. & Ismail, J.A. (2005). A methodology for estimating the attendance and economic impact of an open-gate festival, *Event Management*, 9(3), 111–118.
Walton, H., Longo, A. & Dawson, P. (2008). A contingent valuation of the 2012 London Olympic Games: A regional perspective, *Journal of Sports Economics*, 9(3), 304–317.
Whitford, M. (2009). A framework for the development of event public policy: Facilitating regional development, *Tourism Management*, 30(5), 674–682.
Williams, M. & Bowdin, G. (2007). Festival evaluation: An exploration of seven UK arts festivals, *Managing Leisure*, 12(2–3), 187–203.
Wood, E.H. (2008). An impact evaluation framework: Local government community festivals, *Event Management*, 12(3–4), 171–185.

# 6
# FESTIVALS AND SOCIAL SUSTAINABILITY

*Bernadette Quinn*

## Introduction

Researchers are turning to investigate the social dimensions of festivals in an unprecedented way (Andrews & Leopold 2013; Jepson & Clarke 2015a,b; Roche 2017). Historically, social impacts were a strong preoccupation, but Deery and Jago (2010) argue that this body of work has come of age. The literature can now be seen to be growing in size and developing in its conceptual foundations, methodological underpinnings and research questions. New directions are emerging as researchers negotiate a wide array of theoretical perspectives, concepts and approaches, emanating in fields of study that range from narrow domains like event management through to broader areas of cultural studies, anthropology, human geography and beyond. More critical questions are being asked about the kinds of social change that festivals are associated with (Sharpe 2008), and this is prompting more awareness of the need to fully grasp and articulate the profound social significance of festivals.

However, while the body of work investigating the social dimensions of festivals is hugely interesting and growing strongly, it could, at this point, be said to be quite uneven (Quinn & Wilks 2013) with several disparate realms of enquiry (Ziakas & Costa 2010). Much knowledge seems to have built up along parallel lines with only partial insights shared across disciplinary boundaries. In addition, the terminology employed across the literature to refer to the social dimensions of festivals varies widely to include terms like impact, value, meaning, change, benefit, outcome and several more. Sometimes, the indicators used to denote these dimensions, e.g. cohesion, inclusion, equity, community building and connectivity, are attributed different meanings. Meanwhile, researchers are increasingly asking critical questions about the nature of the contribution that events (Hall 2012) and festivals (Mair & Duffy 2015) make to society. In light of this, this chapter suggests that a useful way forward might be to think about the social dimensions of festivals in terms of sustainability. Sustainability is widely accepted as an important, overarching, conceptual framework within which to analyse all kinds of human development. While it has risen up the festival research agenda in recent years, Pernecky and Luck (2013) suggest that work on sustainability is lagging behind and that more breadth and volume of research is needed. Social sustainability as a specific concept is as yet little applied in festival studies.

The chapter begins by briefly reflecting on developments in the literature on the social dimensions of festivals before reviewing definitions of social sustainability and discussing how festival research might be advanced in light of broader social sustainability debates. While cultural sustainability and its concern for cultural diversity, cultural heritage and cultural vitality (Soini & Birkeland 2014) would add a very useful dimension to this discussion, it is largely excluded as it is simply beyond the scope of this chapter.

## Research into the social dimensions of festivals

As Mair and Duffy (2015) remind us, festivals are predominantly a social phenomenon with the potential to provide a variety of social outcomes. Not surprisingly then, when social questions began to be asked of festivals there was a strong focus on identifying social impacts. Among event management researchers, there was a keen interest to measure such impacts, with Delamere (2001) initiating a strong and clearly identifiable body of ongoing work that uses empirical scales and quantitative tools to measure resident attitudes towards events. Gursoy, Kim and Uysal (2004), following a brief overview of the literature on residents' perceptions of festivals and special events, suggest that they are likely to generate economic benefits for the local community, build community cohesiveness and produce social incentives for residents and businesses. Small (2007), in a study of community festivals specifically, identified six underlying dimensions of the social impacts of community festivals as inconvenience, community identity and cohesion, personal frustration, entertainment and socialisation opportunities, community growth and development, and behavioural consequences, with the latter including underage drinking, delinquent behaviour and vandalism. Deery and Jago (2010) reviewed social impacts, identifying an extensive list of both positive and negative impacts relating to, e.g., employment, living standards, entertainment, socialising, community pride, skills, facilities and infrastructure building in respect of the former; and crime, overcrowding, delinquent behaviour, noise, environmental damage, litter and congestion in terms of the latter. Their summation of the literature found three dominant lines of enquiry: the development of scales to measure social costs and benefits, the influence of residents' perceptions on residents' support for events, and policy recommendations for enhancing social impacts. Social exchange theory, which examines how interaction patterns are influenced by the structure of rewards and costs in a relationship (Molm 1991), was widely employed throughout this body of work.

Concurrently, numerous other researchers less intent on measurement were being inspired by a range of social sciences questions as they undertook studies identifying how festivals can be implicated in developing a sense of community (Reid 2007), place identity and pride in place (De Bres & Davis 2001), a shared sense of belonging and identity (Gibson & Connell 2005; Duffy & Waitt 2011) and social cohesion (Duffy & Waitt 2011). Researchers were also noting that festivals are highly politicised affairs that serve to reproduce social relations along gender, sexual and social class lines (Waterman 1998; Browne 2009), and thus generate contested meanings. Other researchers were problematising processes of commodification (Greenwood 1989) and authenticity (MacLeod 2006; Matheson 2008), while many more were highlighting the ability of festivals to generate economic-related benefits, which feed into positive social and cultural change (e.g. Gibson, Waitt, Walmsey & Connell 2010). This long-standing body of work is very disparate in its conceptual underpinnings and methodological approaches. Perhaps this is partly what led Carlsen, Ali-Knight and Robertson (2007) to argue that the cultural, community and social benefits of major festivals had not yet been systematically studied.

More recently, there has been an increase in researchers investigating social interaction in festival settings using social capital ideas. Arcodia and Whitford (2006) were some of the first to investigate the social interactions between festival attendees using social capital, as was Wilks (2011). Finkel (2010) approached the topic from the standpoint of community residents, while Mykletun (2009) approached it from the perspective of festival organisers. There is now a small but steady stream of studies using social capital to understand festivals (Rao 2001; Finkel 2010; Wilks 2011; Wilks 2013; Black 2016; Wilks & Quinn 2016). As Lundberg, Armbrecht, Andersson, and Getz (2017, p. 5) explain, 'events can be regarded as facilitating and catalysing social interaction and social networks among individuals as well as groups of people', and so they lend themselves to analyses that use social capital ideas. The rise of interest in studying the value of festival and event networks, sometimes in the context of co-creation (e.g. Van der Zee & Olders 2016; Richards & Colombo 2017), has close parallels.

Many festival studies deal with community-run festivals; however, recently there has been a marked rise of interest in expressly studying community festivals (Jepson & Clarke 2015a,b). This recent work shows an intensified interest in investigating how festivals are linked to the creation of identity and community building (Curtis 2011), the development of community resources including volunteers (Whitford & Ruhanen 2013), as well as to social cohesion and inclusion (Chew 2009). Sometimes, these enquiries draw on social capital ideas. In this respect, Pedrana (2015) makes a helpful contribution by distinguishing between social capital in societies and in communities, with the former being comparable to an institution with formal rules and organisation, and the latter characterised by interpersonal and informal networks and relationships. This research is not, however, unproblematic. There is a need to define more clearly what is meant by the term 'community'. Furthermore, the question as to whether the social dimensions of community festivals differ from those of other kinds of festivals remains to be addressed.

There has also been a growing acknowledgement of the need to investigate rural festivals to balance the strong preoccupation with urban festivals (Johansson & Kociatkiewicz 2011; Stevens & Shin 2012; Quinn & Wilks 2017). Gibson, Connell, Waitt and Walmsley (2011) highlight the exceptional importance of festivals to rural communities, emphasising their transformative effect, as well as their role in reflecting the collective identities of place and people. Meanwhile, Ziakas and Costa (2010) briefly synopsised a number of studies showing that rural events produce an array of social values, including building social networks (Rao 2001), strengthening social capital (Derrett 2003; Arcodia & Whitford 2006) and enriching the quality of small-town life (De Bres & Davis 2001; Picard & Robinson 2006). Much potential remains to study urban and rural settings comparatively to see whether and how the social significance of festivals varies accordingly.

All of these interconnected developments bring a more critical studies perspective to the study of festivals, with researchers moving away from asking *if* impacts occur to investigating the processes involved in shaping *how* and *why* they occur (Smith 2009), as well as to what end. This is leading to more probing of the roles that festivals play in reinforcing and reproducing existing social structures and social relations. In some of the recent literature on community festivals, a critical perspective has been adopted to problematise social dimensions like social justice (Mair & Duffy 2015), community engagement (Bostock, Cooper & Roberts 2016) and social networking (Van der Zee & Olders 2016).

At this point, Hinch and Holt's (2017) argument that the concept of place needs to be part of this discussion seems relevant. Several earlier studies have pointed to the role that festivals play in creating place identities, and more recently, place has been shown to be implicated in shaping social capital (Quinn & Wilks 2013). While festivals are always grounded in place, they are strongly shaped by much wider social and material networks and flows of interactivity (Weller 2013). As festival activities unfold, space becomes transformed in ways that disrupt and temporarily suspend social relations (Waitt 2008), alter routine mobilities (Johansson & Kociatkiewicz 2011), modify how spaces are used (Quinn & Wilks 2017) and revalue the symbolic capital of the place (Weller 2013).

While all of these different, often overlapping developments are very constructive in advancing understanding, they are unravelling more complexities that call for comprehensive investigation. In this context, the main suggestion made here is that incorporating the concept of social sustainability into the literature might be a useful development.

## Defining social sustainability

It is 30 years now since the Bruntland Report first introduced and defined the concept of sustainability (World Commission on Environment and Development 1987). Countless researchers and policy writers have turned to the concept in the intervening years to advance developments in all spheres of human activity in the attempt to safeguard, respect and nurture the earth's resources. Sustainability is widely understood to incorporate economic and social as well as environmental dimensions; however, huge complexities exist in trying to interweave these three sets of dimensions together into one concept. Accordingly, there has been a tendency for sustainability to be articulated most often and most obviously in ecological and environmental terms. Certainly, the social dimensions of sustainability have received lesser attention than the other two, although a very sizeable literature on the topic now exists in several fields of study including urban studies, rural studies, geography and sociology. As yet, the term 'social sustainability' tends not to be as well defined or as uniformly understood as environmental sustainability, and this is key topic of discussion in the literature (Griessler & Littig 2005; Dempsey, Bramley, Power & Brown 2009; Eizenberg & Jabareen 2017). There has also been something of a debate as to whether social sustainability is an actual goal in itself or merely a tool to achieve environmental sustainability (Åhman 2013). A number of researchers have identified indicators that define and help to operationalise the concept. McKenzie (2004), for example, pointed to a number of mechanisms, e.g., for fulfilling community needs through community action, collectively identifying its strengths and needs, supporting cultural integration when that is desired by groups and individuals, and supporting political advocacy. Following a review of the urban social sustainability literature, Dempsey et al. (2009) produced an extensive list of factors thought to contribute to social sustainability. These covered areas like education and training, health, quality of life and well-being, employment, fair distribution of income, as well as social inclusion, community, social interaction and cohesion, local democracy and social justice. Åhman (2013), meanwhile, thought it useful to cluster criteria: basic needs and equity, education, quality of life, social capital, social cohesion, integration and diversity, and sense of place. For several researchers, including Knox and Mayer (2013), sustainability is strongly allied to the ideal of 'liveability', with social sustainability relating to social well-being and social equity.

From even this very brief discussion, the definitional problems are clear. There are a great many indicators that include institutional as well as social factors. Some of these are themselves difficult to define. Some, like social capital, are strongly theoretically underpinned as a concept, while others are not. Several seem closely related, while others, like education, seem quite distinct and enormous in their own right. In an attempt to impose some structure and to tackle the 'conceptual chaos' that 'compromises the term's utility', Vallance, Perkins and Dixon (2011, p. 342) have suggested thinking about social sustainability in three ways: as 'development sustainability' – addressing basic needs, the creation of social capital, social justice, etc.; 'bridge sustainability' – behaviour so as to achieve environmental goals; and 'maintenance sustainability' – preserving and sustaining sociocultural characteristics in the face of change. This categorisation groups individual criteria into clusters, but it also helps to focus attention on what stage a societal group is at in respect of social sustainability, given that social processes are dynamic and that social sustainability cannot be understood as a 'one size fits all', fixed idea. In turn, it prompts thinking about what priorities are most relevant and through what vehicles they might be addressed. It links to McKenzie's (2004) understanding of social sustainability as a life-enhancing condition within communities, and a process within communities that can achieve that condition. Eizenberg and Jabareen (2017) propose a new conceptual framework premised first on tackling social sustainability's definitional problems by considering all three pillars of sustainability while trying to define each separately and, second, on foregrounding risk as a key organising concept and focussing on how societies cope with or ignore risks as a determent (though not solely) of social injustices.

## Festivals and social sustainability

Getz (2009) has written that sustainable events are not just those that can endure indefinitely but those that also fulfil important social, cultural, economic and environmental roles that people value. Pernecky and Lück (2013, p. 26) similarly note that 'events are an important means of socio-cultural sustainability and have the potential to promote equality, cultural diversity, inclusion, good community relations, and human rights'. Li, Moore and Smythe (2017, p. 23) argue that in urban areas, community festivals are a means for 'collective action, community building, and multi-literate meaning-making'. However, while sustainability is now a key and growing theme in festival and event studies, there remains a gap in knowledge about what constitutes a sustainable festival (Zifkos 2015). Most of the literature to date deals with the environmental pillar (e.g. Mair & Laing 2012), while very few studies overtly consider 'social sustainability'. Fewer still rigorously interrogate or problematise the concept with reference to festivals as social practices, or situate festivals in the context of the broader social sustainability debates discussed in the preceding section (although see Black 2016). Thus, while a lot is known about the social dimensions of festivals, there still remains an urgent need to address Whitford and Ruhanen's (2013) question about how the benefits arising from festivals contribute more broadly towards sustainable community development.

Finding answers to this admittedly complex question could be advanced by deeper engagement with broader social sustainability debates. Already, even a cursory knowledge of the latter reveals obvious connections and overlaps, with themes and terminology being extremely familiar to festival researchers. One key lesson to be heeded here is that while sustainable development is ultimately change-oriented and has an applied dimension that is critical, if it lacks solid theoretical underpinnings then its effectiveness may be compromised. Much could be gained by drawing on the conceptual resources of this wider literature to more rigorously define and review the terms that populate the festival literature, e.g. community building, sense of community and social cohesion. Such factors are said to be among the benefits that festivals can generate, but more needs to be known about how exactly they are to be recognised, how they relate to each other and how they come to be produced through festival activity. Rather than focussing on the broad array of benefits that festivals can produce it might be more useful to undertake more narrowly focussed, in-depth scrutiny of fewer individual, or clustered, benefits, as in Black (2016).

In a sense, the definitional problems characterising social sustainability are not dissimilar to those associated with the social dimensions of festivals: an unevenness of theoretical underpinnings, a wide variety of sometimes ill-defined criteria and difficulties in translating knowledge into meaningful actions for policymakers and actors on the ground. While more efforts to create helpful, overarching conceptual scaffolding are needed, so too are more efforts needed to translate knowledge into actions, be it to seek to influence individuals or groups to adopt more sustainable practices or to influence government to introduce change. As noted earlier, the festivals literature is moving to be more concerned with the processes of social change, as opposed to identifying the change itself (Smith 2009). Focussing attention on the idea of process, as Vallance et al. (2011) have done, should help link theory and practise in terms of breaking down the enormity of the problem (fostering socially sustainable festivals) into parts, and encouraging enquiries to take account of how scale matters, something that has been infrequently addressed in the festivals literature under study here.

It is important to note that interchange between festival studies and broader social sustainability debates would be mutually constructive. The extensive and long-standing body of research on the social dimensions of festivals attests to the fact that far from being some marginal, trivial activity, festivals are important social practices. They perfectly illustrate Fine's (2012, pp. 117–116) 'focused microgatherings' and 'archetypal form of wispy communities', which constitute the basic building blocks of society and play a pivotal role in organising social life and developing local cultures and identities. Festivals are premised on people willingly coming together and are an example of the 'occasional public' that Wynn (2015, p. 9) associates with 'local actions and greater social forces com(ing) together for bounded periods to engage in cultural work'. Equally, they are an example of a 'third space', the type that people need to be able to access in order to enjoy informal, social interactions that lead to shared experiences, common understandings, a sense of community and an improved sense of social well-being (Knox & Mayer 2013).

## Conclusion

This chapter has briefly reviewed the literature dealing with the social dimensions of festivals. It noted a growing interest in social questions and identified a number of developments in the literature. All of these, it is argued, point to a deepening and broadening of interest in the processes underpinning social change, a growing influence of more social science concepts and theories, and of critical enquiry. While all of these developments are very constructive in advancing understanding, they are also serving to further expose the complexities and the many unknowns that encompass the social significance of festivals. In an attempt to make a contribution, the chapter suggests turning to the under-explored concept of social sustainability. Sustainability is now widely accepted as a worthy conceptual framework of analysis. Yet relative to environmental and economic sustainability, social sustainability is a little used concept. This chapter suggests that a closer interrogation of the concept would be of value in addressing some of the theoretical and conceptual shortcomings in the existing literature and in further encouraging critical enquiry in the field. It might also offer a more systematic means of making more sense of the social dimensions, both negative and positive, that have long been identified in numerous empirical studies. In addition, the evidence emerging from festival studies has much potential to inform evolving understandings of social sustainability in other areas of study. In conclusion, this chapter hopes to encourage festival researchers to tune into broader debates about social sustainability more generally. It offers some suggestions to encourage the integration of the concept into festival studies and advocates that further consideration is given to taking the literature in this direction.

# References

Åhman, H. (2013). Social sustainability: Society at the intersection of development and maintenance. *Local Environment, 18*(10), 1153–1166.

Andrews, H. & Leopold, T. (2013). *Events and the Social Sciences.* Oxon, UK: Routledge.

Arcodia, C. & Whitford, M. (2006). Festival attendance and the development of social capital. *Journal of Convention and Event Tourism, 8*(2), 1–18.

Black, N. (2016). Festival connections: How consistent and innovative connections enable small-scale rural festivals to contribute to socially sustainable communities. *International Journal of Event and Festival Management, 7*(3), 172–187.

Bostock, J., Cooper, R. & Roberts, G. (2016). Rising to the challenge of sustainability: Community events by the community, for the community. In Jepson, A. & Clarke, A. (Eds.), *Managing and Developing Communities, Festivals and Events* (pp. 16–33). London, UK: Palgrave Macmillan.

Browne, K. (2009). Womyn's separatist spaces: Rethinking spaces of difference and exclusion. *Transactions, Institute of British Geographers, 34*(4), 541–556.

Carlsen, J., Ali-Knight, J. & Robertson, M. (2007). Access: A research agenda for Edinburgh festivals. *Event Management, 11*(1–2), 3–11.

Chew, M. M. (2009). Cultural sustainability and heritage tourism: Problems in developing bun festival tourism in Hong Kong. *Journal of Sustainable Development, 2*(3), 34–42.

Curtis, R. (2011). What is Wangaratta to jazz? The (re)creation of place, music and community at the Wangaratta Jazz Festival. In Gibson, C. & Connell, J. (Eds.), *Festival Places: Revitalising Rural Australia* (pp. 280–293). Bristol, UK: Channel View Publications.

De Bres, K. & Davis, J. (2001). Celebrating group and place identity: A case study of a new regional festival. *Tourism Geographies, 3*(3), 326–337.

Deery, M. & Jago, L. (2010). Social impacts of events and the role of anti-social behaviour. *International Journal of Event and Festival Management, 1*(1), 8–28.

Delamere, T. (2001). Development of a scale to measure resident attitudes toward the social impacts of community festivals, Part II. Verification of the scale. *Event Management, 7*(1), 25–38.

Dempsey, N., Bramley, G., Power, S. & Brown, C. (2009). The social dimension of sustainable development: Defining urban social sustainability, *Sustainable Development, 19*(5), 289–300.

Derrett, R. (2003). Making sense of how festivals demonstrate a community's sense of place. *Event Management, 8*(1), 49–58.

Duffy, M. & Waitt, G. (2011). Rural festivals and processes of belonging. In Gibson, C. & Connell, J. (Eds.), *Festival Places: Revitalising Rural Australia* (pp. 44–59). Clevedon, UK: Channel View Press.

Eizenberg, E. & Jabareen, Y. (2017). Social sustainability: A new conceptual framework. *Sustainability, 9*(1), 68–73.

Fine, G. A. (2012). *Tiny Publics: A Theory of Group Action and Culture.* New York, NY: Russell Sage Foundation.

Finkel, R. (2010). "Dancing around the ring of fire": Social capital, tourism resistance, and gender dichotomies at up Helly Aa in Lerwick, Shetland. *Event Management, 14*(4), 275–285.

Getz, D. (2009). Policy for sustainable and responsible festivals and events: Institutionalization of a new paradigm. *Journal of Policy Research in Tourism, Leisure and Events, 1*(1), 61–78.

Gibson, C. & Connell, J. (2005). *Music and Tourism.* Clevedon, UK: Channel View Publications.

Gibson, C., Waitt, G., Walmsley, J., & Connell, J. (2010). Cultural festivals and economic development in nonmetropolitan Australia. *Journal of Planning Education and Research, 29*(3), 280–293.

Gibson, C., Connell, J., Waitt, G. & Walmsey, B. (2011). The extent and significance of rural festivals. In Gibson, C. & Connell, J. (Eds.), *Festival Places: Revitalising Rural Australia* (pp. 3–24). Bristol, UK: Channel View Publications.

Greenwood, D. J. (1989). Culture by the pound: An anthropological perspective on tourism as cultural commoditization. In V. L. Smith (Ed.), *Hosts and Guests. The Anthropology of Tourism* (pp. 171–185). Philadelphia: University of Pennsylvania Press.

Griessler, E. & Littig, B. (2005). Social sustainability: A catchword between political pragmatism and social theory. *International Journal for Sustainable Development, 8*(1/2), 65–79.

Gursoy, D., Kim, K. & Uysal, M. (2004). Perceived impacts of festivals and special events by organizers: An extension and validation. *Tourism Management, 25*(2), 171–181.

Hall, C. M. (2012). Sustainable mega-events: Beyond the myth of balanced approaches to mega-event sustainability. *Event Management, 16*(2), 119–131.

Hinch, T. & Holt, N. L. (2017). Sustaining places and participatory sport tourism events. *Journal of Sustainable Tourism*, 25(8), 1084–1099.

Jepson, A. & Clarke, A. (2015a). *Managing and Developing Community Festivals and Events*. Oxon, UK: Routledge.

Jepson, A. & Clarke, A. (2015b). *Exploring Community Festivals and Events*. Oxon, UK: Routledge.

Johansson, M. & Kociatkiewicz, J. (2011). City festivals: Creativity and control in staged urban experiences. *European Urban and Regional Studies*, 18(4), 392–405.

Knox, P. L. & Mayer, H. (2013). *Small Town Sustainability: Economic, Social and Environmental Innovation*. Basel, Switzerland: Birkhäusen Verlag GmbH.

Li, J., Moore, D. & Smythe, S. (2017). Voices from the "heart": Understanding a community-engaged festival in Vancouver's downtown eastside. *Journal of Contemporary Ethnography*, 1–17. doi.org/10.1177/0891241617696808.

Lundberg, E., Armbrecht, J., Andersson, T. D. & Getz, D. (2017). *The Value of Events*. Oxon, UK: Routledge.

MacLeod, N. (2006). The placeless festival: Identity and place in the post-modern festival. In Picard, D. & Robinson, M. (Eds.), *Festivals, Tourism and Social Change: Remaking Worlds*. Clevedon, UK: Channel View Publications.

Mair, J. & Laing, J. (2012). The greening of music festivals: Motivations, barriers and outcomes. Applying the Mair and Jago model. *Journal of Sustainable Tourism*, 20 (5), 683–700.

Mair, J. & Duffy. M. (2015). Community events and social justice in urban growth areas. *Journal of Policy Research in Tourism, Leisure and Events*, 7(3), 282–298.

Mair, J. & Laing, J. (2012). The greening of music festivals: Motivations, barriers and outcomes. Applying the Mair and Jago model. *Journal of Sustainable Tourism*, 20(5), 683–700.

Matheson, C. M. (2008). Music, emotion and authenticity: A study of Celtic music festival consumers. *Journal of Tourism and Cultural Change*, 6(1), 57–74.

McKenzie, S. (2004). *Social Sustainability: Towards some Definitions*. Hawke Research Institute Working Paper Series No 27. Magill, Adelaide, South Australia: Hawke Research Institute, University of South Australia.

Molm, L. D. (1991). Social exchange: Satisfaction in power-dependence relations. *American Sociological Review*, 56(4), 475–493.

Mykletun, R. J. (2009). Celebration of extreme playfulness: Ekstremsportveko at Voss. *Scandinavian Journal of Hospitality and Tourism*, 9(2/3), 146–176.

Pedrana, M. (2015). New and old tourism traditions: The case of Skieda in Livigno, Italian Alps. In Jepson, A. & Clarke, A. (Eds.), *Managing and Developing Communities, Festivals and Events* (pp. 66–78). Oxon, UK: Routledge.

Pernecky, T. & Luck, M. (2013). *Events, Society and Sustainability: Critical and Contemporary Approaches*. Oxon, UK: Routledge.

Picard, D. & Robinson, M. (2006). *Festivals, Tourism and Social Change: Remaking Worlds*. Clevedon, UK: Channel View Publications.

Quinn, B. & Wilks, L. (2013). Festival connections: People, place and social capital. In Richards, G., de Brito, M. P. & Wilks, L. (Eds.), *Exploring the Social Impacts of Events* (pp. 15–30). Abingdon, Oxon, UK: Routledge.

Quinn, B. & Wilks, L. (2017). Festival heterotopias: Spatial and temporal transformations in two small-scale settlements. *Journal of Rural Studies*, 53(July), 35–44.

Rao, V. (2001). Celebrations as social investments: Festival expenditures, unit price variation and social status in rural India. *Journal of Development Studies*, 38(1), 71–97.

Reid, S. (2007). Identifying social consequences of rural festivals. *Event Management*, 11(1–2), 89–98.

Richards, G. & Colombo, A. (2017). Creating network value: The Barcelona Sónar Festival as a global events hub. In Lundberg, E., Armbrecht, J., Andersson, T. D. & Getz, D. (Eds.), *The Value of Events* (pp. 73–86). Oxon, UK: Routledge.

Roche, M. (2017). *Mega Events and Social Change. Spectacle, Legacy and Public Culture*. Manchester: Manchester University Press.

Sharpe, E. K. (2008). Festivals and social change: Intersections of pleasure and politics at a community music festival. *Leisure Sciences*, 30(3), 217–234.

Small, K. (2007). Social dimensions of community festivals: An application of factor analysis in the development of the social impact perception (SIP) scale. *Event Management*, 11(1–2), 45–55.

Smith, A. (2009). Theorising the relationship between major sport events and social sustainability. *Journal of Sport and Tourism*, *14*(2–3), 109–120.

Soini, K. & Birkeland, I. (2014). Exploring the scientific discourse on cultural sustainability. *Geoforum*, *51*(January), 213–223.

Stevens, Q. & Shin, H. (2012). Urban festivals and local social space. *Planning Practice and Research*, *29*(1), 1–20.

Vallance, S. Perkins, H. C. & Dixon, J. E. (2011). What is social sustainability? A clarification of concepts. *Geoforum*, *42*(3), 342–348.

van der Zee E. & Olders P. (2016). Events: Cause or consequence of community involvement. In Jepson, A. & Clarke, A. (Eds.), *Managing and Developing Communities, Festivals and Events* (pp. 120–129). London, UK: Palgrave Macmillan.

Waitt, G. (2008). Urban festivals: Geographies of hype, helplessness and hope. *Geography Compass*, *2*(2), 513–537.

Waterman, S. (1998). Carnivals for elites? The cultural politics of arts festivals. *Progress in Human Geography*, *22*(1), 54–74.

Weller, S. (2013). Consuming the city: Public fashion festivals and the participatory economies of urban spaces in Melbourne, Australia. *Urban Studies*, *50*(14), 2853–2868.

Whitford, M. & Ruhanen, L. (2013). Indigenous festivals and community development: A sociocultural analysis of an Australian indigenous festival. *Event Management*, *17*(1), 49–61.

Wilks, L. (2011). Bridging and bonding: Social capital at music festivals. *Journal of Policy Research in Tourism, Leisure and Events*, *3*(3), 281–297.

Wilks, L. (2013). The special challenges of marketing the arts festival. In Biggs, M. & Karlsson, H. (Eds). *The Routledge Companion to Arts Marketing* (pp. 334–343). Abingdon, UK: Routledge.

Wilks, L., & Quinn, B. (2016). Linking social capital, cultural capital and heterotopia at the folk festival. *Journal of Comparative Research in Anthropology and Sociology*, *7*(1), 23.

World Commission on Environment and Development (WCED). (1987). Report of the World Commission on Environment and Development: Our Common Future. Available online: www.un-documents.net/our-common-future.pdf. Accessed 14/06/2018.

Wynn, J. R. (2015). *Music/City: American Festivals and Placemaking in Austin, Nashville, and Newport*. Chicago, IL: University of Chicago Press.

Ziakas, V. & Costa, C. (2010). "Between theatre and sport" in a rural event: Evolving unity and community development from the inside-out. *Journal of Sport and Tourism*, *15*(1), 7–26.

Zifkos, G. (2015). Sustainability everywhere: Problematising the "sustainable festival" phenomenon. *Tourism Planning and Development*, *12*(1), 6–19.

# 7
# EVALUATING THE SOCIOCULTURAL EFFECTS OF FESTIVALS

Developing a comprehensive impact correlation model and its application

*Ronnit Wilmersdörffer and Daniela Schlicher*

## Introduction

Over the past decade, the analysis of sociocultural impacts of festivals and festival tourism has been increasingly considered in tourism and events research (Crespi-Vallbona & Richards 2007; Getz 2010; Mair & Whitford 2013). However, as a review of the existing literature reveals, this particular strand of research is still in its infancy. While the economic impacts of festivals have been subject to research since the 1980s (see, for example, Gartner & Holecek 1983; Ritchie 1984), the study of sociocultural effects is a more recent phenomenon. Equally, as Zifkos (2015) pointed out, sociocultural aspects have usually been neglected within the sustainability policy and planning of festivals, with emphasis being placed on economic aspects instead (Crespi-Vallbona & Richards 2007; Brown & Trimboli 2011). This shortcoming needs to be addressed given the well-documented importance of community support for the – not least economic – sustainability of events and event tourism (see, for example, Gursoy & Kendall 2006). In this chapter, the authors develop a tool based on available research to analyse the interdependencies of sociocultural impacts and thereby enable the development of policy for the sociocultural sustainability of festivals. A short case study serves to demonstrate the practical applicability of the model.

## Literature review

Literature on the sociocultural dimension of festivals draws on the existing body of research within the field of tourism and events. Despite its slightly longer history, the area of sociocultural impact analysis within tourism and events is characterised by a certain vagueness; in search for a clear definition of sociocultural impacts, one is frequently confronted with fuzzy terminology or mere listings of individual effects (Fredline, Jago & Deery 2003; Small, Edwards & Sheridan 2005; Small 2008). One of the more comprehensive definitions is given by Teo (1994) for whom sociocultural impacts are the ways in which tourism is contributing to changes in the value systems, morals and their conduct, individual behaviour, family relationships, collective lifestyles, creative expressions, traditional ceremonies and community organisation.

*(p. 126)*

Sociocultural impacts are usually categorised into social costs and benefits. While the latter refers to issues such as community pride, improvements to the social infrastructure, preservation of local traditions, image effects and a positive self-perception of community members, the former includes the well-known community disruptors of congestion, noise pollution or vandalism (Ritchie 1984; Dwyer, Mellor, Mistilis & Mules 2000; Delamere, Wankel & Hinch 2001; Fredline et al. 2003; Small et al. 2005). The commodification of culture (King & Stewart 1996) or social relationships (Tucker 2003), as well as intra-community conflicts, may also be considered as social costs. Leier (2006) and Gibson and Connell (2012) further identify the issue of gentrification as a negative consequence of hallmark events due to their effect on (particularly property) prices and the resulting displacement of residents. While local property owners and landlords would certainly benefit from such a development, hallmark events may thus contribute to an increasing social divide within the host community.

For approximately a decade, the term *sociocultural capital* has increasingly been gaining popularity to describe potential community benefits of events. Sociocultural capital refers to an enhanced awareness of community resources and their optimised utilisation; more efficient or valuable cooperative structures within a community (Arcodia & Whitford 2005, cited in Lassila, Lindroth & Rantanen 2013), community pride and stability (Fredline et al. 2003), as well as inclusion, trust, networks and solidarity within a community (Quinn & Wilks 2013). Particularly relevant to the area of festivals and festival tourism are the factors of *bonding and bridging social capital*, which refer to an enhancement of communication and understanding between previously divided groups and social strata within the community or between hosts and guests (see, for example, Fisher 2004; Sam & Berry 2010; Lassila et al. 2013; Quinn & Wilks 2013). Such a divide may first appear unsurpassable in the context of traditional, rural host communities and their 'alien' visitors attending a subculture festival (Gibson & Connell 2012).

The mobilisation and deployment of sociocultural capital has been identified as a highly significant – if not the most important (Mykletun 2009) – factor in ensuring the long-term success of festivals (Gursoy & Kendall 2006; Kania 2013). The (perceived) value of sociocultural benefits may, in fact, surpass the value community members attach to tangible and monetary benefits accruing from the festival or event (Gursoy, Kim & Uysal 2004; Gibson & Connell 2012; Andersson & Lundberg 2013), ultimately giving rise to the host community's enthusiasm and support for, or otherwise resistance to, the festival. The current trend among festival organisers towards attempts to create *community pride* within host communities may be attributed to this insight (Gibson & Connell 2012).

Attempts to measure community perceptions of a festival's sociocultural impacts abound, despite the difficulties to quantify the 'soft' factor due to the need to measure the impacts indirectly via community attitudes and perceptions of change (Pasanen, Taskinen & Mikkonen 2009; Wilks 2013). This requirement of indirect quantification has therefore given rise to divergent research designs, limiting the compatibility, reliability and generalisability of results (De Grosbois 2009; Pasanen et al. 2009; Robertson, Rogers & Leask 2009; Wood 2009). Depending on the factors and items analysed, the choice of stakeholders included in the analysis and the timing chosen for the surveys, studies of the sociocultural dimension tend to yield very different results.

In an attempt to measure the 'soft' factor, Andersson and Lundberg (2013) transferred Lindberg und Johnson's (1997) *contingent valuation method* from tourism to a festival context. The host community's attitude is determined by attaching monetary values to perceived impacts: the *willingness to pay* or *willingness to accept* certain sociocultural effects. Among the most influential scales developed to measure sociocultural impacts of festivals are Delamere's (Delamere et al. 2001) Festival Social Impact Attitude Scale (FSIAS) and Small's (2008; Small and Edwards 2003) Social Impact Perception Scale (SIP), each with their own lists of items and factors. While the FSIAS encompasses the unique factors of community costs and benefits, as well as individual benefits, the SIP proposes six factors relating to community sociocultural capital and individual costs and benefits. As observed by Woosnam, Jiang, Van Winkle, Kim and Maruyama (2016), the FSIAS has regained popularity among researchers in recent years. However, the SIP's added value lies in its applicability before and after the festival, while the FSIAS is used to analyse residents' projected attitudes before the event. Additional scales to measure sociocultural effects of festivals and special events were put forward by Fredline et al. (2003), Wood (2006) and Kim, Jun, Walker & Drane (2015), among others. In order to increase the validity of results, Wood (2009) has called for a standardised, as well as flexible and adaptable, scale to reflect the uniqueness of each community and event.

Adding to the complexity at hand, a sound framework for analysing the sociocultural effects of festivals must take into account the various independent variables shaping the host community's perception – the term 'host community' being misleading in itself, given its heterogeneous nature (Picard & Robinson 2006). Researchers therefore need to consider the external factors shaping the subjective perceptions of individuals, the sum of which translates into the 'host community'. These factors range from the availability of information (Kwon & Vogt 2010) and media effects (Weaver & Lawton 2013) to destination image, economic opportunities and host-guest ratio (Gibson & Connell 2012).

## A tool to inform sociocultural sustainability policy

Based on the literature review at hand, the cyclic impact model depicted in Figure 7.1 provides an overview of the different facets of sociocultural impacts explored. Using *change in attitude* (as a proxy for behaviour) as the ultimate reference mark for the sociocultural impact of a festival, the model highlights a chain, or cycle, of cause and effect between all occurrences of sociocultural impacts.

The model highlights the circular and interdependent nature of manifested sociocultural impacts occurring in a festival-hosting community, residents' perception and evaluation of the impacts, proactive and reactive measures taken to address the impacts, and residents' attitude and behaviour towards the festival.

*Manifested Impacts* refer to physical, destination, community and cultural impacts. *Physical Impacts* are physical changes to the site of the event. *Destination Impacts* constitute changes to the external perception or awareness of the geographical space associated with the event as a touristic destination and thereby to its touristic value. *Community Impacts* are changes to the social cohesion within the host community resulting from internal interactions related to the planning, organisation and/or execution of the event. *Cultural Impacts,* finally, are changes to the host community's cultural identity resulting from interactions with festival visitors.

*Impact Perception* refers to factors where locals may perceive changes to a previous status quo in their lives or in the life of the community resulting from the festival. An individual assessment – or impact evaluation – of occurrence, relevance and intensity of manifest impacts form the basis for a catalogue of overall positive or negative experiences and perceptions

## Sociocultural effects of festivals

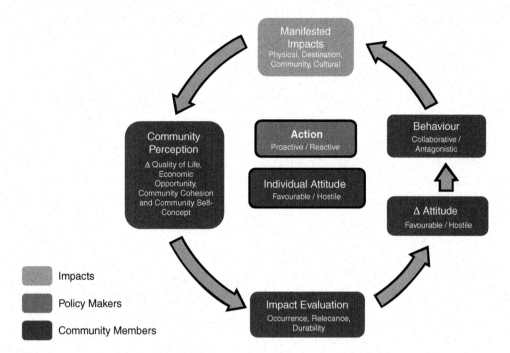

*Figure 7.1* Sociocultural impact cycle

Source: Adapted after Teo 1994; King & Stewart 1996; Dwyer et al. 2000; Fredline et al. 2003; Fisher 2004; Small et al. 2005; Small 2008; DeGrosbois 2009; Sam & Berry 2010; Lassila et al. 2013; Quinn & Wilks 2013; Kim et al. 2015.

relating to the festival. Opinions on the sum of positive and negative impacts from each perceived area of impact give rise to residents' *Attitude* towards the festival. The thus formed attitude, in turn, becomes manifest in the *Behaviour* displayed by the host community towards the festival's organisers and visitors. The manifestation of this behaviour – collaborative or otherwise – can constitute an asset or an existential threat to a festival, making the host community an extremely powerful stakeholder. The individual attitude of members of the host community therefore constitutes a pivotal factor in assessing sociocultural sustainability.

Proactive and/or reactive measures taken to address those impacts influence both the manifestation of impacts as well as residents' perceptions of the impacts. Such measures include impact management and action by public-sector organisations, festival organisers, Non-Governmental Organisations (NGOs) and community members. By assessing expectable negative impacts in advance or already manifested impacts and taking corresponding action, the factual occurrence – or at least intensity – of those impacts can be contained, improving the support of and reducing the pushback from the host community. Similarly, positive impacts can be enhanced by according policy, creating a stronger positive experience in some areas for the host community. This is invaluable, as it can be used to compensate in the personal assessment for negative impacts that are difficult or impossible to alleviate.

The influence of the individual attitude, too, is by no means limited to manifestation of behaviour. Much rather, it must be acknowledged and taken into consideration in every link of the impact chain. Each member of the host community brings her individual attitude and expectations into the assessment of occurrence, relevance and intensity of festival externalities. They even affect the very manifestation of those sociocultural impacts that are causally related to the host community's behaviour (*Community Impacts* and *Cultural Impacts*).

While the individual attitude and expectations prior to the very first festival cycle are largely dependent on intrinsic factors, in the following years these will be largely congruent to the changes in attitude effected throughout the previous festival cycle.

The importance, impact and interplay of impacts, perceptions, attitudes and measures will be demonstrated on the example of the Wacken Open Air (W:O:A) festival.

## Case study

The W:O:A is Europe's largest heavy-metal festival, taking place annually in a small village in Northern Germany. While today it is known for its exceptional convergence between the village and the festival (Hinrichs 2011), it actually faced a real threat of being shut down by the local community in the past (Schöwe 2009). A comprehensive case study of the festival was conducted as part of an undergraduate thesis submitted at the International School of Management; extracts of this case study are applied here to illustrate the journey of the change in attitude of the Wacken host community through effective policy. The study used descriptive data collection and relied primarily on secondary sources: a host of in-depth stakeholder interviews from various publications and media outlets, newspaper articles, documentaries, elements of popular culture, anecdote collections and academic publications about the W:O:A. All combined, these offer a relatively comprehensive picture of the sociocultural impacts and their influence on the success of the festival. For the purpose of this chapter however, we shall merely identify key stages of the festival development and develop one area of impact in each stage to illustrate the applicability of the impact cycle model.

The first stage in the existence of the W:O:A can suitably be described as *phase of insignificance*. The festival started out as an all-weekend metal party organised by four local youths in 1990. Between that year and 1995, visitor numbers never exceeded 5,000 people (ICS Festival Service GmbH 2017), and as the event took place in a secluded gravel pit near the village, the early years of the W:O:A went by most of the local community completely unnoticed. Accordingly, no conscious policy or measures for sociocultural sustainability were implemented during this initial time. Nonetheless, *community impacts* started to become manifest from the very beginning. Even the formation of the team of organisers from within the village community constitutes an increase in interaction within the community, intensifying with the increasing number of other community members becoming involved in the organisation and realisation of the first festival cycles. Beside volunteering activity, we can already observe a heightened awareness and sourcing of community expertise and resources at this stage: tasks and responsibilities related to the festival were delegated in accordance with skill sets available in the volunteering body. Examples for this are Mathias Venhor, who as electrician was put in charge of the festival's power supply, or the farmer Uwe Trede, who supplied his field as camping grounds and volunteered as a security guard (Schöwe 2009). Until 1993, the festival was thus executed solely on the basis of community volunteering (Schöwe 2009) and through this involvement also gained supporters within the village community. This was to prove critical in the following period of negotiation that resulted from heightened awareness for the festival due to increasingly perceptible sociocultural impacts.

The second stage we shall refer to as the *phase of negotiation*. The period of negotiation began in 1996, when visitor numbers unexpectedly doubled in comparison to the previous year, taking by surprise locals and organisers alike. The lack of necessary crowd management systems led to a series of widely perceived adverse *physical impacts*, when 10,000 festival visitors first notably exceeded the local infrastructure's carrying capacity (ICS 2017): miles of traffic jams, hours spent queuing for groceries, heaps of rubbish and vandalised front gardens were effects that were felt intensely and unfavourably by the unprepared locals (Kunkel 2009). This resulted in a village council's decision to deny the organisers the use of the public gravel pit in 1997, forcing them to move the event site to a private property instead. The same chaotic situation as in 1996 reoccurred when visitor numbers jumped again by nearly 100 percent to 18,000 persons in 1998 (ICS 2017). Combined with increasing issues of noise pollution, the pushback from the local community was so strong that the village council considered banning the festival altogether. 'However, the organisers worked tirelessly to eliminate the grievances and thus earned the village community's respect', current mayor Alex Kunkel said in an interview about the development of W:O:A (2009, p. 89). The measure of a clearance task force patrolling the village during the festival not only got rid of the pollution problem but also worked to decrease the perceived gravity of the problem by locals. Kunkel added that since then, the streets of the village were never as impeccable as on the Monday following the festival (Kunkel 2009). The passing nature of the nuisance, combined with a relative improvement to the original state, increased the tolerance of the locals towards short-term negative *physical impacts*. The proactive stance of the organisers towards also solving *perceived* problems contributed heavily towards eliminating many sources of resistance, as illustrated by the case of one local man who was convinced the noise pollution was detrimental to his heart condition. The organisers offered him a short holiday for the duration of the festival which became obsolete when in the following year, the same individual attempted to take the money without actually taking a holiday (Trede 2009).

The final stage, here referred to as the *phase of consensus*, began in 2000: the changes in the behaviour of the locals soon began to affect the visitors' festival experience and public perception. It was not long before the original Unique Selling Proposition (USP) of the festival as 'a party by metalheads for metalheads' was complemented by a reputation for its special atmosphere that was in large part down to the participation of the host community (Hinrichs 2011). Hinrichs describes this dynamic as a perceived merging of the village Wacken and the W:O:A festival into a consolidated unit. We shall use this phase to examine *cultural impacts*: the changes in attitude of the locals altered not only how they encountered visitors but also the locals' openness to engaging with visitors altogether. Hinrichs (2011) describes how locals invite visitors on their properties to get to know them and consequently form friendships. Another result of this openness is the extraordinary atmosphere of trust between locals and festival visitors. One example for this is the instance of a barman lending money to some random festival visitor – never to be seen again, his colleagues assumed at the time – and was sought out by the same visitor the following year to settle the debt (Hinrichs 2011). In fact, the openness is not only limited to the interaction between villagers and members of the metal subculture, but it also extends to interactions with strangers as a whole: while a minority of the villagers still consider them an invasion to their homely idyll, most locals are excited about the opportunity for intercultural exchanges and experiences (Hinrichs 2011).

Cultural exchange in this case goes both ways. One example of cultural transfer is the integration of the local voluntary fire brigade's brass band, which was introduced to the festival in 2000 and has since been accepted and celebrated with enthusiasm by the festival visitors as an element of indigenous Wackenese culture. A great deal of cultural adaptation can also be observed on part of the locals: the village and its inhabitants decorate themselves with symbolism typical of the metal scene. The *Wacken Skull*, an apparently occult buffalo skull, is omnipresent as emblem of the W:O:A on the houses and T-shirts of both locals and visitors. The 'Wacken Salutation' used by visitors to express their delight over their visit to the festival[1] is seconded or even initiated by many locals. This behaviour can be considered a temporary acculturation on part of the locals, suggesting some manifestation of a demonstration effect, albeit without the usually associated loss of identity.

In this exact balance between cultural adaptability and preservation of identity lies the secret to the festival's sociocultural success. The negotiation of this fine line is also represented in policy, as can be illustrated using the example of the fire brigade's brass band: on the one hand, the band is an iconic part of the W:O:A. The band members enjoy the attention of the fans and the media throughout the festival (*Wacken – ein Dorf sieht schwarz* 2012), and are happy to adapt their set list to the lowered standards of the raving metal fans. At the same time, their festival performance is clearly distinguished from their usual social role and standing; rather than performing under their official name, they adopt the stage name *Wacken Firefighters* and wear T-shirts in place of their usual uniforms. That way, the band can at the same time participate in and contribute to the extraordinary festival atmosphere and retain the dignity and prestige of their sociocultural standing in the community. A similar approach to the festival by other parts of the host community is illustrated in the regional documentary *Full Metal Village* (2006). It shows the exceptional circumstances of the W:O:A exactly as what they are: namely exceptional, a diversion from the remaining 51 weeks a year in which rural idyll, farming, choir practice and coffee parties dominate the lives of the community members. The perpetuity of these routines, the stable connection to the community and its traditions, is what allows for the participation in the festival happening without existential fear, loss of identity or self-abandonment. And this, in turn, is the key to the special dynamic the W:O:A is famous for today.

The W:O:A is a particularly interesting case with regard to sociocultural impacts; the development of its meaning within the community illustrates the interdependencies between attitude, behaviour, impact manifestation, perception, and policy. It also gives a clear idea of the role this plays in the long-term economic success of the festival. It also allows the conclusion that resolution of all negative impact manifestations is by no means required to produce a positive attitude amongst the host community as long as other aspects are experienced as sufficiently rewarding. The policy and measures taken by the organisers to contain negative impact, resolve conflict and enhance economic and emotional participation can be taken as a didactic play in how to increase the host community's support for a festival.

## Conclusion

The importance of sociocultural impacts on the success of festivals has experienced increased attention within the academic community in recent years. Most research conducted to this point, however, has taken a purely empirical, non-analytical approach to the subject which does not sufficiently reflect the complexity or the relevance of the matter. The impact cycle developed in this chapter has proved a useful tool to understand and describe the interconnected sociocultural impacts of a festival. A development of this approach may include additional external factors, and adding examples of preventive and reactive policy and measures, to give a more comprehensive basis for action for practical application.

## Note

1  The exclamation 'Wacköööööön!' accompanied by the devil horns gesture.

## References

Andersson, T. & Lundberg, E. (2013). Commensurability and sustainability: Triple impact assessment of a tourism event. *Tourism Management*, *37*(August), 99–109.

Brown, S. & Trimboli, D. (2011). The real 'worth' of festivals: Challenges for measuring socio-cultural impacts. *Asia Pacific Journal of Arts and Cultural Management*, *8*(2), 616–629.

Crespi-Vallbona, M. & Richards, G. (2007). The meaning of cultural festivals: Measuring stakeholder perspectives in Catalunya. *International Journal of Cultural Policy, 13*(1), 103–122.

DeGrosbois, D. (2009). Assessing the socio-cultural impact of special events: Frameworks, methods and challenges. *Journal of Tourism Challenges and Trends, 2*(2), 39–52.

Delamere, T. A., Wankel, L. M. & Hinch, T. D. (2001). Development of a scale to measure resident attitudes toward the social impacts of community festivals. Part I: Item generation and purification of the measure. *Event Management, 7*(1), 11–24.

Dwyer, L., Mellor, R., Mistilis, N. & Mules, T. (2000). A framework for assessing 'tangible' and 'intangible' impacts of events and conventions. *Event Management, 6*(3), 175–189.

Fisher, D. (2004). The demonstration effect revisited. *Annals of Tourism Research, 31*(2), 428–446.

Fredline, L., Jago, L. & Deery, M. (2003). The development of a generic scale to measure the social impacts of events. *Event Management, 8*(1), 23–37.

Full Metal Village. (2006). DVD recording, Berlin: Flying Moon.

Gartner, W. C. & Holecek, D. F. (1983). Economic impact of an annual tourism industry Exposition. *Annals of Tourism Research, 10*(2), 199–212.

Getz, D. (2010). The nature and scope of festival studies. *International Journal of Event Management Research, 5*(1), 1–47.

Gibson, C. & Connell, J. (2012). *Music Festivals and Regional Development in Australia.* Burlington, VT: Ashgate.

Gursoy, D. & Kendall K. W. (2006). Hosting mega events: Modelling locals' support. *Annals of Tourism Research, 33*(3), 603–623.

Gursoy, D., Kim, K. & Uysal, M. (2004). Perceived impacts of festivals and special events by organisers: An extension and validation. *Tourism Management, 25*(1), 171–181.

Hinrichs, P. (2011). *Wacken. Ein Dorf wird Metropole und Marke.* Göttingen: Cuvillier.

ICS Festival Service GmbH. (2017). *Wacken Open Air – History.* Retrieved from: www.wacken.com/de/festivalinfo/history/ Accessed 09/01/2018.

Kania, L. (2013). Social capital in the metropolis BrabantStad: Exploring the role of a community event in developing social capital. In Richards, G. DeBrito, M. P. & Wilks, L. (Eds.), *Exploring the Social Impacts of Events* (pp. 45–56). Abingdon, UK: Routledge.

Kim, W., Jun, H. M., Walker, M., & Drane, D. (2015). Evaluating the perceived social impacts of hosting large-scale sport tourism events: Scale development and validation. *Tourism Management, 48,* 21–32.

King, D. & Stewart, W. (1996). Ecotourism and commodification: Protecting people and places. *Biodiversity and Conversation, 5*(3), 293–305.

Kunkel, A. (2009). Interview. In Schöwe, A. (Ed.), *Wacken Roll. Das größte Heavy Metal Festival der Welt* (88–93). Höfen, Austria: Koch International GmbH.

Kwon, J. & Vogt, C. (2010). Identifying the role of cognitive, affective, and behavioural components in understanding residents' attitudes towards place marketing. *Journal of Travel Research, 49*(4), 423–435.

Lassila, S., Lindroth, K. & Rantanen, T., (2013). Events as a contributor to social capital. In Richards, G. DeBrito, M. P. & Wilks, L. (Eds.), *Exploring the Social Impacts of Events* (31–42). Abingdon, UK: Routledge.

Leier, K. D. (2006). *Impacts of Hosting a Major Event on Annual Events and Festivals,* Master thesis. Library and Archives Canada, University of Waterloo.

Lindberg, K. & Johnson, R. L. (1997). The economic values of tourism's social impact. *Annals of Tourism Research, 24*(1), 90–116.

Mair, J. & Whitford, M. (2013). An exploration of events research: Event topics, themes and emerging trends. *International Journal of Event and Festival Management, 4*(1), 6–13.

Mykletun, R. J. (2009). Celebration of extreme playfulness: Ekstremsportveko at Voss. *Scandinavian Journal of Tourism and Hospitality, 9*(2–3), 146–176.

Pasanen, K., Taskinen, H. & Mikkonen, J. (2009). Impacts of cultural events in Eastern Finland – Development of a Finnish event evaluation tool. *Scandinavian Journal of Hospitality and Tourism, 9*(2–3), 112–129.

Picard, D. & Robinson, M. (2006). Remaking worlds: Festivals, tourism and change. In Picard, D. & Robinson, M. (Eds.), *Festivals, Tourism and Social Change* (1–31). Clevedon, UK: Channel View Publications.

Quinn, B. & Wilks, L. (2013). Festival connections: People, place and social capital. In Richards, G. DeBrito, M. P. & Wilks, L. (Eds.), *Exploring the Social Impacts of Events* (15–30). Abingdon, UK: Routledge.

Ritchie, J. (1984). Assessing the impact of hallmark events: Conceptual and research issues. *Journal of Travel Research, 22*(1), 2–11.

Robertson, M., Rogers, P. & Leask, A. (2009). Progressing socio-cultural impact evaluation for festivals. *Journal of Policy Research in Tourism, Leisure and Events, 1*(2), 156–169.

Sam, D. L. & Berry, J. W. (2010). Acculturation: When individuals and groups of different cultural backgrounds meet. *Perspectives on Psychological Science, 5*(4), 462–481.

Schöwe, A. (2009). Die Historie des WOA. In Schöwe, A. (Ed.), *Wacken Roll. Das größte Heavy Metal Festival der Welt* (17–50). Höfen, Austria: Koch International GmbH.

Small, K. (2008). Social dimensions of community festivals: An application of factor analysis in the development of the social perception (SIP) scale. *Event Management, 11*(1–2), 45–55.

Small, K. & Edwards, D. (2003). Evaluating the socio-cultural impacts of a festival on a host community: A case study of the Australian festival of the book. In Griffin, T. & Harris, R. (Eds.), *Proceedings of the 9th Annual Conference of the Asia Pacific Tourism Association* (580–593). Sydney, Australia: School of Leisure, Sport and Tourism, University of Technology Sydney.

Small, K., Edwards, D. & Sheridan, L. (2005). A flexible framework for evaluating the socio-cultural impacts of a (small) festival. *International Journal of Event Management Research, 1*(1), 66–77.

Teo, P. (1994). Assessing socio-cultural impacts: The case of Singapore. *Tourism Management, 15*(2), 126–136.

Trede, U. (2009). Interview. In Schöwe, A. (Ed.), *Wacken Roll. Das größte Heavy Metal Festival der Welt* (72–75). Höfen, Austria: Koch International GmbH.

Tucker, H. (2003). *Living with Tourism: Negotiating Identities in a Turkish Village*. Abingdon, UK: Routledge.

Wacken – ein Dorf sieht Schwarz. (2012, December). *Heavy Metal Spektakel auf grüner Wiese*. Television program, NDR, Hamburg.

Weaver, D. B., & Lawton, L. J. (2013). Resident perceptions of a contentious tourism event. *Tourism Management, 37*, 165–175.

Wilks, L. (2013). Introduction. In Richards, G. DeBrito, M. P. & Wilks, L. (Eds.), *Exploring the Social Impacts of Events* (1–12). Abingdon, UK: Routledge.

Wood, E. (2006). Measuring the social impacts of local authority events: A pilot study for a civic pride scale. *International Journal of Nonprofit Voluntary Sector Marketing, 11*(3), 165–179.

Wood, E. (2009). An impact evaluation framework: Local government community festivals. *Event Management, 12*(3–4), 171–185.

Woosnam, K. M., Jiang, J., Van Winkle, C., Kim, H. & Maruyama, N. E. (2016). Explaining festival impacts on a hosting community through motivations to attend. *Event Management, 20*(1), 11–25.

Zifkos, G. (2015). Sustainability everywhere: Problematising the 'sustainable festival' phenomenon. *Tourism Planning & Development, 12*(1), 6–19.

# 8
# INFLUENCERS OF ENVIRONMENTAL SUSTAINABILITY SUCCESS AT FESTIVALS

*Meegan Jones*

## Introduction

Throughout the ages, festivals have been intimately entwined with the environment. Communities have come together to celebrate harvests and signify changes of seasons. However, in the modern age, and until recently, many festivals have been a reflection of a consumption-focussed society – leaving legacies of irresponsible resource use, environmental degradation, disruption to habitats, discarded waste, and immeasurable greenhouse gas (GHG) emissions (Jones 2017). Fortunately, as we progress towards sustainable development, festivals are now coming full circle back to our environmental roots. These days, regardless of their purpose, festivals acknowledging their connection with or impact on the environment is *de rigueur*.

Achieving environmental sustainability in a global sense means maintaining our ability to continue to develop and improve our society throughout future generations – and doing this within the Earth's carrying capacity (WCED 1988). The Earth can only provide so much, and we must stay within those limits in order to comfortably endure – to be sustainable. Inherent in this state of environmental sustainability is living in harmony with natural environments and ecosystems. I believe that we need to be protecting wilderness and only extracting resources that can replenish themselves, rather than exploiting and degrading our natural environment leading to its annihilation. As a global community, we are on this journey towards sustainability together. Nations, cities, industries and individuals are striving to play their part in creating an inclusive, fair and environmentally responsible world (ICLEI 2017).

The festival sector is in a unique position to take a dual role in the story of the environment and challenges facing it in the 21st century (Mair & Laing 2012). First, organisers must commit to running environmentally responsible festivals, by avoiding or reducing negative impacts and wherever possible, positively contributing to enhancing the environment and developing innovative sustainability solutions (Jones 2017). Second, organisers have enviable access to people in the form of patrons and attendees, which gives them the chance to use this public power to inform, engage and inspire others to action (Sharpe 2008; Mair & Laing 2012).

Throughout my time as an events sustainability consultant, I have built a considerable store of knowledge and expertise, which I will share in this chapter. I will identify common festival environmental issues and impacts such as site/venue environmental management, resource consumption, sanitation, water use, waste, transport, catering, energy supply and GHGs. I will also explore opportunities for festivals to contribute positively to environmental sustainability – through legacy programmes or through leveraging festival operations and logistics to engage attendees in environmental initiatives.

## Sustainability

A 'sustainable event' can be viewed as one that fulfils the social, cultural, economic and environmental roles that people value (Getz 2009). Environmental management is one of these foundations of sustainability, alongside concerns for social/cultural and economic impacts (Raj & Musgrave 2009). There are many adaptions and interpretations of what sustainability actually means for a festival (Henderson 2011). Whilst some festival leaders simply consider sustainability to be the longevity and financial survival of the festival (Ensor, Robertson & Ali-Knight 2011), issues of environmental management are most often key issues for consideration (Jones 2017).

However, the pillars of sustainability – environmental, social/cultural and economic – are inextricably linked. Where there may be an environmental impact, investigating more deeply will likely reveal sociocultural and economic concerns. When reviewing the economic (financial) viability or feasibility of a festival, the non-financial costs must be included in the assessment to get a truly balanced 'triple-bottom-line' assessment (Getz 2009). For the festival manager wanting to produce an environmentally responsible event, embracing the concept of 'spending well' will help to ensure they are not complicit in negative environmental or socio-economic impacts through their purchasing choices. Economic sustainability in this sense will mean expenditure that does not contribute to resource depletion and environmental degradation back along the supply chain, and which is fair and just for the workers and communities affected by production (Jones 2017). To bring us to a state of 'sustainability' all aspects must be considered (Jones 2010).

### *Environmental management*

Festivals are usually held in outdoor settings, or a combination of indoor and outdoor settings. Some sites may be 'green' or 'brown' field, where all infrastructure and services need to be brought in temporarily. Other festival sites may have a combination of permanent infrastructure such as power, road and car park services, staging, amenities, water supply and effluent management. In some circumstances the management of various environmental impacts will lie firmly with the festival management; in other cases the venue or site owner will assume responsibility. For example, purchasing may be a shared responsibility between the festival owner, catering contractor and venue/site management.

Regardless of who takes responsibility for management of environmental impacts, all stakeholders should reflect on the festival's overall environmental performance. The issues of concern are likely to be

- resource use (depletion and unsustainable exploitation of resources, wastefulness, use of hazardous materials, sustainable sources);
- solid and gaseous emissions to air (pollution, particulates, GHGs, airborne litter, dust);
- solid and liquid emissions to land (litter, waste management, toxic residue, landfill leachate, resource recovery);
- solid and liquid emissions to water (waste water, waterborne litter, chemical releases, landfill leachate to ground water);

- sound and light pollution (disrupting neighbourhood amenity, and disruption to wildlife);
- terrestrial surface protection, sediment and erosion;
- water flow/diversion;
- marine environment protection (riparian zone, turbidity, underwater noise);
- protection of local biodiversity (flora and fauna);
- protection of local archaeological and heritage assets in the natural setting.

From a festival production viewpoint, these can be summarised as relating to site environment, materials, catering, waste, water (including amenities), transport and energy (Jones 2017). Each will now be discussed in turn (see also Jones 2017 for more details on each issue).

## Site and local environment

Protecting the immediate natural environment is of course a major priority, and every festival should conduct an environmental impact assessment and prepare their environmental management plan (EMP). In many cases, this will actually be required by local authorities in order to gain the relevant licences to proceed. Issues to consider are protecting the marine and riparian zone environments from liquid waste and not damaging local water quality, as well as considering whether festivals should draw from local water sources. Light and noise pollution are also a concern both to local residents and to wildlife. The use of chemicals and other hazardous substances and materials need to be identified and management plans put in place, such as the use of spill kits. Protecting surfaces from physical impact of footfall, vehicles and infrastructure installation must be addressed. Solid waste management, especially materials which can be airborne or get into waterways, is especially important.

## Suppliers

Each and every material and product used to produce a festival has its own production and manufacture backstory. When considering the environmental performance of a festival, the impacts of these products, materials and catering ingredients must also be reviewed. A festival is a sum of its parts, and therefore suppliers must also be environmentally responsible to support the festival's environmental ambitions (Henderson 2011). Often purchasing will be done by those contracted to service or participate in the festival, but regardless of who is making the actual purchase, if it is for the festival, and especially if it is a visible item, stakeholders will place the responsibility for environmental impacts of that purchasing with the festival.

Environmental impacts come all along the supply chain – extraction (mining or agricultural) processes, transport, treatment or processing of materials, manufacturing or production processes, energy and water intensity, packaging and waste, and use and disposal (Genovese, Acquaye, Figueroa & Koh 2017). Supply chain traceability is increasing, and credible 'eco-labels' set criteria for various materials sectors. For example, Trace and Trust is a sustainable food-sourcing programme in the USA (www.traceandtrust.com). To manage environmentally sustainable purchasing, festival organisers should develop a Sustainable Procurement Policy that will set the 'must take' and 'preferential' criteria for typically purchased items. This, along with creating a Supplier Code of Conduct, can help to influence or control sourcing decisions made on behalf of the festivals (Dooley & Augustin-Behravesh 2016).

Table 8.1 Festivals implementing reusable materials

| Festival | Innovation | Website |
| --- | --- | --- |
| Bonnaroo, USA | Reusable steel containers | www.bonnaroo.com |
| Treefort, USA | Reusable steel containers | www.treefortmusicfest.com |
| Woodford Folk Festival, Australia | Reusable steel containers | www.woodfordfolkfestival.com |
| Glastonbury, UK | Reusable steel containers | www.glastonburyfestivals.co.uk |
| Latitude, UK | Reusable plastic cups | www.latitudefestival.com |
| La Route du Rock, France | Reusable plastic cups | www.laroutedurock.com |
| Splore, New Zealand | Reusable plastic cups | www.splore.net |

## Waste (resource recovery)

Waste is one of the most visible impacts and is often thought of as a festival's biggest impact (Moore 2012). The aims for any festival manager focussing on waste and resource recovery should be to avoid waste creation in the first place, prevent littering, recovering 'waste' resources rather than sending to landfill, and using systems that will encourage participation and positive behaviour by traders, workforce and attendees (Jones 2017).

At festivals, waste will occur back of house, during the build and break of the festival, from food and beverage (Institute of Sustainable Futures 2017), and disposable food and beverage service-ware (Verdonk, Chiveralls & Dawson 2017). Waste is also created by attendees, with campsite waste being a major contributor (A Greener Festival 2017; Jones 2017). Festivals that have adequate bin allocation, participatory recycling collection systems, clear signage and thoughtful communications will be the most successful in their efforts (Cierjacks, Behr & Kowarik 2012; Gilmour, Alcorn & Moore 2013; Jones 2017; Verdonk et al. 2017).

Reducing waste is the first step, and avoiding disposable service-ware is key. Table 8.1 illustrates some best practice examples (Jones 2017).

## Energy

Energy supply is an operational necessity for most festivals. Often using mains power or mobile diesel generators, energy will be a significant line item in a festival's GHG emissions inventory. Ultimately, organisers want to reduce total energy demand and maximise renewable sources (Powerful Thinking 2017). Festivals are the perfect platform to showcase innovative renewable energy solutions. Mobile solar power, hybrid generators, hydrogen fuel cell lighting towers and interactive energy generation such as pedal power or kinetic energy are making frequent appearances at festivals (Fleming, Marchini & Maughan 2014; Powerful Thinking 2017).

Energy efficiency for festivals can mean using energy-efficient equipment and lighting. Operational intervention, such as not placing glass front fridges in full sun, will also lead to efficiency. Catering and food service outlets should use gas for cooking rather than electricity-hungry heating elements (Live Performance Australia 2013). Finally, switching off and powering down, not only of equipment but also of generators, is essential. Generators are commonly overspecified and underutilised, leading to wasted fuel and avoidable GHG emissions (Fleming et al. 2014).

## Transport

Moving people and production assets might be the largest GHG impact of a festival. Certainly if air travel is involved, then this will very likely be the case (Bottrill, Lye, Boykoff &

Liverman 2007; Bottrill, Papageorgiou & Jones 2009). It is also worth noting that freight, electricity and biodegradable waste being sent to landfill also contribute to a festival's carbon footprint. The key to reducing transport impact (and consequential fuel use and GHG emissions) is to source equipment and materials as locally as possible. Renewable fuels, fuel-efficient vehicles and even electric vehicles are also solutions. Reducing waste and waste water volumes will also reduce their transport impacts. Other ways that festivals can reduce their GHG emissions include encouraging festivalgoers to travel by public transport, car sharing or active travel methods such as cycling and walking; providing shuttle buses to ensure that the travel dots are connected; and charging for car parking to dampen enthusiasm for travelling by car (although car sharing and full cars could be rewarded with reduced parking fees).

## *Water and amenities*

For those in water-scarce regions, water conservation should be a top priority. Water scarcity, water quality, volume of water used or conserved, the way water is delivered to the site, waste water disposal and protection of waterways are all key water issues for festivals (Tracada 2016; Jones 2017). Festivals can have a significant negative impact on the availability of water locally. Boom Festival, whose setting is next to a lake in an arid area of Portugal, takes its water conservation and reuse very seriously. They have installed reedbed filtration systems, which then return perfectly clean water back to nature. Festivals can also cut their use of water by using low flush volume, or water-free toilets, such as compost toilets, the innovative straw bale urinal concept from L'Uritonnoir (uritonnoir.com). Ideally festivals should aim to collect grey water, treat it on-site and reuse it either for toilet flushing or irrigation post-festival for site remediation, as has been done by IeperFest in Belgium. Finally, festivals held in water-scarce regions will also likely have to manage dust. In this case, using an organic (not chemical) additive to water before spraying for dust suppression significantly reduces the number of times spraying is needed (Jones 2017).

## Setting up for success

Festival producers want to find the issues and solve problems. This approach is beneficial for the surface-level challenges such as fixing up the recycling, managing effluent and powering the event. Festival sustainability management is, however, moving past this ad hoc and reactionary approach to one that is more strategic and longer view (Pelham 2011; Jones 2017). The good news is that many festivals are successfully managing their environmental impacts and authentically and effectively communicating their endeavours.

In the author's analysis of a huge number of festivals across the world (Jones 2010; 2017), and from conclusions drawn by academic research (Getz 2009; Mair & Laing 2012; Yuan 2013; Van Berkel 2014; de Brito & Terzieva 2016), the environmental management success of leading festivals can be distilled to common traits – leadership and commitment, an inspired and capable team, systems, a fertile ground, stakeholder participation and involving and inspiring festivalgoers.

The following festivals are examples of best practice that will be referred to in the next section of this chapter:

Roskilde in Denmark – www.roskilde-festival.dk/more/sustainability
Shambala in the UK – www.shambalafestival.org/essential-info/sustainability
Bonnaroo in the USA – www.bonnaroo.com/experience/sustainability

Boom in Portugal – www.boomfestival.org/boom2018/vision/our-principles/
IeperFest in Belgium – www.ieperfest.com/green-policy
Tollwood in Germany – www.tollwood.de/en/mensch-und-umwelt
DGTL in the Netherlands – www.dgtl.nl/revolution/about-revolution
Northside in Denmark – www.northside.dk/culture/124
Øyafestivalen in Norway – www.oyafestivalen.no/en/environment/environment/
Lightning in a Bottle in the USA – www.lightninginabottle.org/ethos-page

## Leadership and commitment

All have remarkable vision and commitment to sustainability from the top. A bold mission and a fierce commitment to environmental sustainability by festival leadership are critical to success (Ludema, Laszlo & Lynch 2012). This can come in the form of the personal values of the Festival Director or other senior management, or the organisational values and policies of those festivals part of a larger corporate group (Van Berkel 2014). If a festival's top management does not have an awe-inspiring environmental sustainability vision, then a shift in culture and attitudes within the festival team may need to be orchestrated. IeperFest is an excellent example of this in practice. The personal commitment to a vegan lifestyle by the Festival Director has pushed this principle through the festival since its inception in 1992. They continue to excel in many facets of environmental management still (Jones 2017).

## Inspired and capable team

Having a team of committed individuals whose personal values align with the environmental sustainability values of the festival is essential (Mair & Laing 2012). The existence of an 'eco-champion', whether formally assigned or not, can drive festival teams towards effective environmental management (Mair & Jago 2010). Festivals with comprehensive and successful environmental sustainability programmes often have a specialist environmental/sustainability project manager, and they also develop interdepartmental working groups focussing on sustainability management (de Brito & Terzieva 2016). Boom's Andre Soares has been a relentless driver and leader in environmental sustainability programmes at this Portugal-based festival. His passion and drive fuels their programme (Jones 2017).

## Systems

Alongside leadership and team commitment, must come relevant policies, objectives, goals and action plans to give the focus to the vision. Implementing ISO 20121: Event Sustainability Management Systems is one pathway to formalising the (environmental) sustainability management strategy for a festival. It is particularly beneficial for those with ongoing editions of a festival, for groups that organise multiple festivals or for festival management teams likely to have staff turnover (Cumming & Pelham 2011; Jones 2010).

## A fertile ground

The type of organisation that owns or manages the festival, the site in which it is held, and the expectations of stakeholders all set the context in which a festival is operating (Pernecky 2015) These factors influence the attitude to environmental management, the sense of urgency and expectation, and indeed whether solutions are possible locally. Destinations that are adopting sustainable development principles and whose municipalities and citizens embrace environmental sustainability will be more likely to be the hosts of festivals that are also embracing these values (Jones 2017). 'Sustainable event-ready' destinations will have solutions, services and supplies to enable effective environmental management of festivals. This might include excellent urban connectivity and active travel, power supply from renewable sources, abundant locally sourced food and beverage, and a waste management ecosystem with a focus on resource recovery (Bigwood, Simons, Sethaputra & Ching 2017).

## *Stakeholder participation and contribution*

Managing environmental sustainability successfully means engaging and involving stakeholders – attendees, local community, supply chain, regulators and industry peers (Yuan 2013). When reviewing potential environmental issues for management, it is important to review stakeholder concerns and, in fact, engage the contribution of those stakeholders who may be integral to the issue (ISO 20121 2012). They might include regulators, subcontractors, the venue, stallholders, waste contractors and festival attendees. Smart festival managers are drawing on stakeholders to be part of the solution. Roskilde Festival works with catering and merchandise suppliers to provide sustainable solutions – this has included the creation of a Roskilde-branded wine and ethically-branded merchandise (Jones 2010).

## *Involving and inspiring festivalgoers*

Festivals successful in their sustainability endeavours actively pursue the festivalgoer in bringing to life every aspect of the festival, including their environmental programmes. They offer multiple routes for expression and involvement. If a festival wants to generate environmental value and leave lasting impressions with festivalgoers, then they must carefully design settings and opportunities which set the stage for enlightening, eye-opening and value-adjusting experiences (Yuan 2013; de Brito & Terzieva 2016).

Festivals offer many touchpoints including the practicalities of attendance, the programming and the environmental messaging. For example, through encouraging them to take action to minimise the impacts of their festival attendance, such as the way they travel or amount of stuff they bring and then potentially discard, attendees can be encouraged to participate in composting and recycling, or reusable beverage container programmes. They can be exposed to environmental issues, ideas and concepts via programme content, art, performance and other expression.

Incentivising and rewarding festivalgoers for participating in environmental programmes are seen at many festivals. Global Inheritance (USA) has their TRASHed Recycling Store, which encourages recycling in exchange for points. These points allow holders to purchase items or experiences at the festival (www.globalinheritance.org/recycling-programs/). DGTL in the Netherlands has instigated a sustainability currency 'ECO Coin'. Festivalgoers earn an ECO coin through each sustainable action they carry out – attending a workshop to learn about sustainable food production, participating in a recycling programme, purchasing a meal from an organic trader, arriving by public transport or cycling to the festival.

Researchers and project initiators have recognised that changing attendee attitudes and consumption and disposal habits is going to be key to addressing this modern challenge facing festivals (Henderson & Musgrave 2014; Love Your Tent 2017).

## Using the festival for good

Festivals are often a much-anticipated happening in a community's calendar and can act as a magnet, drawing people together. This sense of being 'in it together' can be harnessed to improve the environmental performance of a festival (Rogers & Anastasiadou 2011). With feelings of freedom, fun and a sense of solidarity and community, openness can make festivalgoers receptive to new ideas and experiences (Gration, Arcodia, Raciti & Stokes 2011). Festival managers can craft settings and scenarios to not only have festivalgoers actively participate in their environmental initiatives but also leave a lasting and positive impression with them (de Brito & Terzieva 2016). Using the environmental credentials of a festival for promotional purposes also enhances reputation, offers an avenue for competitive advantage and offers a way to demonstrate to stakeholders your intentions and results. Communicating these efforts publicly can also help differentiate your festival and build the brand (Henderson 2011; Tinnish & Mangal 2012).

Festivals are often touted as powerful vehicles for change. They can also use their platform to agitate for environmental campaigns and throw their support behind various calls to action (Sharpe 2008). However, there is a huge gap between the supposition that festivals are change-vehicles and proof they are achieving these lofty ambitions (Brown & Getz 2015). This is probably because there is also a considerable gap between what people say they believe in and how they act (Castro, Garrido, Reis & Menezes 2009; Maio 2011). This is something to consider when embarking on a change-making programme aimed at improved environmental behaviour by festivalgoers.

In his book *Changeology*, Robinson (2012) investigates the keys to successful change within organisations. Facts and figures or slogans don't inspire people to action. Rather, telling stories and making it relatable is what will inspire action. Convenience can also be a motivator (Osbaldiston & Schott 2012). If you want to change the way attendees interact with the festival environment, make the actions you want them to take simple and convenient.

## Conclusion

This chapter is just the tip of the iceberg in what can be an enormously inspiring and valuable journey of environmental discovery. Luckily, those festival professionals already in the sector are tuning into the importance of environmentally responsible festival management, and we are also turning out cohorts of event management graduates into the industry with a passion for and skills in environmental management. My suggestions for taking this forward include remembering to share successes and lessons learned, linking with neighbouring festivals to develop solutions and supporting local innovator and suppliers. Environmental management of festivals is not a competitive sport!

## References

A Greener Festival (2017). *Waste Management*. Available online. www.agreenerfestival.com/waste-management/. Accessed May 2017.

Bigwood, G., Simons, R., Sethaputra, P. & Ching, J. (2017) *Sustainable Destination Management Trends and Insights: A Pathway to a Brighter Future*. Report. GDS Index. Available online. www.gds-index.com. Accessed May 2017.

Bottrill, C., Lye, G., Boykoff, M. & Liverman, D. (2007). *First Step: UK Music Industry Greenhouse Gas Emissions for 2007*. London, UK: Oxford University Environmental Change Institute.

Bottrill, C., Papageorgiou, S. & Jones, M. (2009) *Jam Packed Part 1: Audience Travel Emissions from Festivals*. London, UK: Julies Bicycle.

Brown, S., Getz, D., Pettersson, R. & Wallstam, M. (2015). Event evaluation: Definitions, concepts and a state of the art review. *International Journal of Event and Festival Management*, 6(2), 135–157.

Castro, P., Garrido, M., Reis, E. & Menezes, J. (2009). Ambivalence and conservation behaviour: An exploratory study on the recycling of metal cans. *Journal of Environmental Psychology*, 29(1), 24–33.

Cierjacks, A., Behr, F. & Kowarik, I. (2012). Operational performance indicators for litter management at festivals in semi-natural landscapes. *Ecological Indicators*, 13(1), 328–337.

Cumming, P. & Pelham, F. (2011). *Making Events More Sustainable, A Guide to BS 8901*. London, UK: British Standards Institution.

de Brito, M. & Terzieva, L. (2016). Key elements for designing a strategy to generate social and environmental value: A comparative study of festivals. *Research in Hospitality Management*, 6(1), 51–59.

Dooley, D. & Augustin-Behravesh, S. (2016). Social influence and similarities in supplier codes of conduct. *Proceedings, Academy of Management* (Meeting Abstract Supplement) January, 1677.

Ensor, J., Robertson, M. & Ali-Knight, J. (2011). Eliciting the dynamics of leading a sustainable event: Key informant responses. *Event Management*, 15(4), 315–327.

Fleming, P. Marchini, B. & Maughan, C. (2014). Electricity related GHG emissions at off-grid, outdoor events. *Carbon Management*, 5(1), 55–65.

Genovese, A., Acquaye, A.A., Figueroa, A. & Koh, S.C. (2017). Sustainable supply chain management and the transition towards a circular economy: Evidence and some applications. *Omega, The International Journal of Management Science*, 6(B), 344–357.

Getz, D. (2009). Policy for sustainable and responsible festivals and events: Institutionalization of a new paradigm. *Journal of Policy Research in Tourism, Leisure and Events*, 1(1), 61–78.

Gilmour, P., Alcorn, J. & Moore, G. (2013). *Build It and They Will Recycle*. Report. Available online. www.sustainable. unimelb.edu.au/sites/default/files/docs/MSSI-Report_Build-it-and-they-will-Recycle_2013_full.pdf. Accessed August 2017.

Gration. D, Arcodia, C. Raciti, M. & Stokes, R. (2011). The blended festivalscape and its sustainability at nonurban festivals. *Event Management*, 15(4), 343–360.

Henderson, S. (2011). The development of competitive advantage through sustainable event management. *Worldwide Hospitality and Tourism Themes*, 3(3), 245–257.

Henderson, S. & Musgrave, J. (2014). Changing audience behaviour: Festival goers and throwaway tents. *International Journal of Event and Festival Management*, 5(3), 247–262.

ICLEI (2017). *Local Governments for Sustainability*. Available online. www.iclei.org. Accessed May 2017.

ISO 20121 (2012). *Event Sustainability Management Systems: Requirements with Guidance for Use*. International Standards Organisation. Available online. www.iso.org/standard/54552.html. Accessed August 2017.

Johnson, C. (2017). The Powerful Thinking Guide 2017, Smart Energy for Festivals and Events, *Powerful Thinking*. Available online. www.powerful-thinking.org.uk. Accessed August 2017.

Jones, M. (2010). *Sustainable Event Management: A Practical Guide* (1st Ed). Didcot, UK: Taylor and Francis.

Jones, M. (2017). *Sustainable Event Management: A Practical Guide* (3rd Ed). Didcot, UK: Taylor and Francis.

Institute of Sustainable Futures (2017). *Love Food Hate Waste: Food Festivals and Farmers Markets*. Available online. http://foodstallsavers.org.au/wp-content/uploads/2017/01/Yamba-Festival-trial-report-FINAL-v1.0.pdf Accessed 14/06/2018.

Love Your Tent – Available online. www.loveyourtent.com/. Accessed May 2017.

Ludema, J., Laszlo, C. & Lynch, K. (2012). Embedding sustainability: How the field of organization development and change can help companies harness the next big competitive advantage. In Shani, A.B., Pasmore, W.A. & Woodman, R.W. (Eds.), *Research in Organizational Change and Development* (pp. 265–299). Bingley, UK: Emerald Group Publishing Limited.

Maio, G.R. (2011). *Don't Mind the Gap Between Values and Action*. Common Cause Breifing. Available online. www.valuesandframes.org. Accessed August 2017.

Mair, J. & Jago, L. (2010). The development of a conceptual model of greening in the business events tourism sector. *Journal of Sustainable Tourism*, 18(1), 77–94.

Mair, J. & Laing, J. (2012). The greening of music festivals: motivations, barriers and outcomes: Applying the Mair and Jago model. *Journal of Sustainable Tourism*, 20(5), 683–700.

Moore, T. (2012). *Audience Attitudes on the Environmental Impact of Events. Report. Bucks New University and a Greener Festival.* Available online. www.agreenerfestival.com/wp-content/uploads/pdfs/Bucks-AGF_AUDIENCE_RESEARCH_2012.pdf. Accessed June 2017.

Osbaldiston, R. & Schott, J. (2012). Environmental sustainability and behavioral science: Meta-analysis of pro-environmental behavior. *Environment and Behavior, 44*(2), 257–299.

Pelham, F. (2011). Will sustainability change the business model of the event industry? *Worldwide Hospitality and Tourism Themes, 3*(3), 187–192.

Pernecky, T. (2015). Sustainable leadership in event management. *Event Management, 19*(1), 109–121.

Raj, R. & Musgrave, J. (2009). *Event Management and Sustainability.* Oxfordshire, UK: CAB International.

Robinson, L. (2012). *Changeology. How to Enable Groups, Communities and Societies to Do Things They've Never Done Before.* Cambridge, UK: Green Books.

Rogers, P. & Anastasiadou, C. (2011). Community involvement, in festivals: Exploring ways of finding increasing local participation. *Event Management, 15*(4), 387–399.

Tinnish, S. & Mangal, S. (2012). Sustainable event marketing in the MICE industry: A theoretical framework. *Journal of Convention & Event Tourism, 13*(4), 227–249.

Tracada, E. (2016), Music festivals: How are people encouraged to be mindful in their uses of finite resources and not waste water? Where does water go after use? In Charlesworth, S. (Ed.), Proceedings of the Water Efficiency Conference 2016, 7–9 September, Coventry, UK: WATEF Network/University of Bath.

Sharpe, E. K. (2008). Festivals and social change: Intersections of pleasure and politics at a community music festival. *Leisure Sciences, 30*(2), 217–234.

Van Berkel, F. (2014). *Researching Environmental Sustainability at Music Festivals: A Dutch Case.* Cardiff, UK and Nijmegen, the Netherlands: Cardiff University & Radboud University.

Verdonk, S. Chiveralls, K. & Dawson, D. (2017). Getting wasted at WOMADelaide: The effect of signage on waste disposal. *Sustainability, 9*(3), 344.

WCED Brundtland Commission. (1987). Our common future. *World Commission on Environment and Development.* New York, USA: United Nations.

Yuan, Y. (2013). Adding environmental sustainability to the management of event tourism. *International Journal of Culture, Tourism and Hospitality Research, 7*(2), 175–183.

# PART III
# Festival management

# 9
# MANAGING FESTIVAL VOLUNTEERS
## The HELPERS model

*Kirsten Holmes, Leonie Lockstone-Binney, Karen A. Smith and Alex Rixon-Booth*

### Introduction

Festivals are highly dependent on volunteers. Community festivals are frequently entirely organised and run by volunteers, and major international festivals rely on large numbers of volunteers to steward events, host artists and provide a range of behind-the-scenes support. Volunteering has positive outcomes for the volunteers, the festival organisation, festival attendees and participants, and communities more generally (Holmes & Smith 2009). For the volunteer, helping at a festival is a means of becoming an insider, gaining greater access than an audience member – to meet artists, be a part of the festival team and to augment the festival experience. Volunteers can also enhance the visitor experience of those attending festivals (Jensen & Buckley 2011). However, there are also personal costs for the volunteer involved in festival volunteering (e.g. Holmes & Smith 2009) and there are barriers to an individual's ability to volunteer, and financial costs for the festival organisation associated with recruiting, managing, training and rewarding volunteers.

This chapter critically examines the small body of literature on festival volunteers to examine the ways in which they can be organised. It then goes on to explore and detail a new volunteer management model for recruiting and managing volunteer programmes across a range of festivals and events developed by the Australian company I Need Helpers (INH). The model in question, the HELPERS model represents a **H**ub for **E**vents **L**ooking to **P**rocure **E**ngage **R**etain and **S**upport volunteers. It represents an evolution of the 'outsourcing' model of volunteering recruitment (Smith & Lockstone 2009) in that HELPERS represents the contracting out to INH of all aspects of volunteer management, from recruitment through to operational management and post-event engagement, with INH working closely with the festival organiser across the event cycle to ensure, wherever possible, the seamless integration of the volunteer programme with all other functional components of festival management.

### Research to date on festival volunteers

The majority of research on event volunteering has focussed on sporting events, particularly large-scale events (Smith, Baum, Holmes & Lockstone-Binney 2014), with relatively scant attention paid to festival volunteering, or, indeed, volunteering at other types of events. Researchers have captured a range of types and scales of festival, including music (Clayton 2016), film (Love, Sherman & Olding 2012), beer (Ragsdell & Jepson 2014), science (Jensen & Buckley 2011) and religious festivals (Gallarza, Arteaga & Gil-Saura 2012), amongst others.

Volunteers are an important part of the not-for-profit festival business model, holding a significant role in terms of stakeholder power and influence, and involving many more volunteers than public or private-sector events (Andersson & Getz 2009). Jæger and Olsen (2017) discuss the commodification of the volunteer experience; however, an issue rarely addressed is the ethics of involving of volunteers in private or profit-making event organisations.

In a festival context, the term 'volunteer' is typically used for operational staff who primarily deliver the event. However, in volunteer-led festivals, where there may be no paid staff, community members in organisational and governance roles are crucial to the very existence of the event. Many community festivals would struggle financially without governance and operational volunteers (Rogers & Anastasiadou 2011). Yet, volunteer support can be a challenge; in a study of festivals in Australia, Norway, Sweden and the UK, just over a third of festival organisers reported a lack of volunteers, or difficulty in keeping them, as a major threat to their event, and this threat was greatest for not-for-profit festivals (Carlsen & Andersson 2011). Frost and Laing (2015) also highlight the challenges faced by festival organisers in rural communities, where issues included difficulties in finding new committee members, and burnout of committee volunteers, linked to the increasingly onerous regulatory and administrative burden of managing and staging events.

Motivation has been a dominant focus of festival volunteering studies, as it has been with event volunteering research more widely (Smith et al. 2014), with motivation increasingly being linked to retention of festival volunteers (e.g. Bachman, Norman, Hopkins & Brookover 2016; Elstad 2003). A second research theme has been volunteering experiences (e.g. Campbell 2009; Clayton 2016), with experiences and satisfaction also being related to future volunteering intentions (Bachman, Backman & Norman 2014; Lee, Alexander & Kim 2013). This focus on the re-engagement of volunteers stems from the reoccurring nature of many festivals where building a pool of volunteers who return to the event can reduce resource-intensive recruitment efforts with securing new volunteers.

Event volunteers are the archetypal episodic volunteer, one that seeks short-term or one-off experiences. However, various studies suggest event volunteers are not homogenous (e.g. Bachman et al. 2014; Handy, Brodeur & Cnaan 2006). Festival organisers cannot assume that all episodic volunteers are motivated by the same reasons or want to be involved in similar ways.

Many festivals focus on recruiting individuals or groups from their local community as their volunteer pool (Laing & Mair 2015) and informal approaches to selection and screening dominate (Smith & Lockstone 2009). Festivals can also draw volunteers from a wider geographical area, such as the solo female 'grey nomad' travellers in Campbell's study (2009) who were regular volunteers at Australia's National Folk Festival. However, Rogers and Anastasiadou (2011) note that when outsiders are brought in as volunteers, some potential community benefits of a festival are lost. The proportion of local (compared to non-local) volunteers can therefore be used as an indicator of a festival's level of community involvement (Rogers & Anastasiadou 2011). Students have also been recognised as an important group of festival volunteers, primarily motivated by instrumental reasons, such as gaining work experience for future employment (Jensen & Buckley 2011).

Other studies have focussed on supporting volunteers as festival managers, for example, through mentoring schemes (Hede & Rentschler 2007), knowledge management and sharing of volunteer organisers (Ragsdell & Jepson 2014) and operational volunteers (Clayton 2016), and operational challenges such as scheduling volunteers and training (Gordon & Erkut 2005).

## Organising festival volunteers

Organisers are concerned with how to source volunteers and how to keep them, particularly for recurring festivals. Festivals use a range of models for managing their volunteers depending on their scale, budget and whether they are a one-off or recurring festival (Holmes, Hughes, Mair & Carlsen 2015). Many festivals are organised entirely by volunteers. All-volunteer festivals typically use a *membership management* model (Meijs & Hoogstad 2001) for organising their volunteers. This model involves using a bottom-up approach to designing and assigning volunteer roles (Meijs & Hoogstad 2001), which seeks to assign volunteer roles on the basis of the volunteers' skills and interests.

The reliance of community festivals on volunteers raises questions about the long-term sustainability of the event if the main event organisers are unable or unwilling to continue in their role (Holmes & Ali-Knight 2017). For example, Casino Beef Week is an agricultural festival in New South Wales, Australia, which claims to be Australia's longest-running volunteer run event (NCMC Casino Beef Week 2017). However, in 2007, with insufficient volunteers to run the event, the organising committee chose to cancel it. The volunteer organisers were experiencing burnout, due to the workload falling to fewer people (Preez 2007). The decision to cancel encouraged new volunteers to become involved, and the festival was reinvigorated for 2008 (O'Neill 2007). However, the new volunteer committee also chose to employ a paid professional festival organiser to assist with future festivals (Derrett 2009).

Major festivals with substantial budgets and large numbers of volunteers tend to adopt the *programme management* approach for organising their volunteers, which involves treating the volunteers largely as unpaid staff, replicating typical human resource management processes (Holmes & Smith 2009). The volunteer programme is normally managed in-house by either a paid or voluntary coordinator. The festival organiser will need to first identify how many volunteers are needed and in which roles. Next, they need to develop descriptions for each of these roles, then recruit, select and possibly train the volunteers.

An alternative model for festivals is to *outsource* their volunteer requirements (Smith & Lockstone 2009). Festival organisers recruit local community or special interest groups who then recruit volunteers from among their members. The volunteers can be directly managed by the festival organisers, or their group can be given responsibility for a specific task which they manage among themselves, e.g. a local Rotary club running the car park. Typically, the group will be given a donation by the festival organisers as a recognition of their contribution, rather than rewarding individual volunteers. The advantage for the festival organisers is that they save time and funds on recruiting and managing the volunteers. The disadvantage is the loss of direct control, which is less of a risk when the tasks to be fulfilled are relatively unskilled and simple in nature.

Destinations can also establish a dedicated pool of trained and experienced event volunteers. This mirrors the commercial companies that supply festival staff such as stewards but is typically run by government. To date this practice has been relatively rare, and these pools have usually been formed as part of the volunteer legacies of mega-events, such as the

Manchester Commonwealth Games (Nichols & Ralston 2012). However, festivals can make use of such pools in their volunteer recruitment, and large recurring festivals could establish their own pool with other similar festivals within the same location.

## Methods

This chapter uses a case-study research design to examine the development of a new model for sourcing and organising festival volunteers, the **H**ub for **E**vents **L**ooking to **P**rocure **E**ngage **R**etain and **S**upport volunteers model, referred to as HELPERS hereafter. Case studies are particularly useful for examining why and how contemporary, real-life phenomena occur (Yin 2009) and have been a commonly used method in festival studies research.

Case studies typically involve the collection of multiple forms of evidence (Yin 2009). This research employed a mixture of data sources and data types to provide a complete picture of the phenomenon under study (Yin 2009). The INH HELPERS model was selected as a unique case offering a novel approach to recruiting, training and managing a festival volunteer programme. The defining elements of the model are examined in reference to one particular event that INH managed over a two-year period, the Virgin Australia Melbourne Fashion Festival (VAMFF), hereafter referred to as the Festival. INH's engagement with the staging of the Festival in 2015 is the particular focus of this case study. The Festival is Australia's largest consumer-focussed fashion event, featuring 'world-class runway shows featuring Australia's established and emerging designers, state-of-the-art production, beauty workshops, retail events, industry seminars, forums, live entertainment' (VAMFF 2018). Informing the case study were secondary sources including the Volunteer Program Growth and Development Report prepared by INH for festival management, together with personal reflections of INH's Director, who is a co-author of the current chapter. These data generated a case-study report (Yin 2009), which provides a detailed analysis of the volunteer programme, how it operates and its distinctive features. The following section details the case-study findings in reference to the HELPERS model as applied to the 2015 Festival.

## Case study: I Need Helpers

INH was established in 2010 in recognition that there was scope to develop an event volunteering management platform for temporal events of varying sizes, allowing these events to tap into an existing base of experienced event volunteers. INH, through its HELPERS model, provides staff and volunteer management consulting; on-site management and coordination of festival and event management programmes; and access to a custom-built rostering platform, the INH Volunteer Management System (VMS), which will be described in further detail later.

INH has worked with a range of small- and large-scale events (INH 2017). Within the Australian major events sector, these include Melbourne Food & Wine Festival and L'Étape Australia by Le Tour de France (New South Wales) and Vivid Sydney. Their portfolio also includes a number of internationally recognised events where INH has held the exclusive volunteer management Partner/Supplier rights to manage the volunteer programmes.

Turning to examine the HELPERS model, discussion will elaborate INH's approach as a full service provider across the cycle of the Festival from application process, on-site management through to post-event reporting. In 2015, INH coordinated 890 individual volunteer shifts at the Festival, accounting for 6,949 volunteer hours contributed by

279 volunteers across 16 venues before and during the event held from 14 to 22 March. Volunteers contributed on average 25 hours to the Festival (INH 2015).

The HELPERS model is underpinned by each customised technologies developed by the INH team to support volunteer management. At the time of the Festival, INH had approximately 2,000 students registered on its volunteer database, 'INH Opportunities', as expressing interest in event volunteering opportunities (INH 2015). Students have been a particular source for INH, and the organisation has worked closely to establish relationships with vocational education and higher education providers, mostly in Melbourne and Sydney. This model benefits not only from the increasing push towards episodic volunteering but also the mandating of volunteering in many higher education degree programmes (Handy et al. 2010). The database integrates with INH's cloud-based and automated VMS. For the Festival, the VMS was used to 'capture applicants' details, manage the shortlisting process, record briefing attendance, manage rostering and commentary, generate required documentation reports and allow for automated scheduled SMS notification during event operations' (INH 2015, p. 8).

Applicants, if not already on the INH Opportunities database, were required to create a profile prior to completing a Festival Application Form. This allowed INH to track the involvement of each volunteer at the Festival (e.g. number of shifts completed) and monitor any other opportunities volunteers undertook with INH throughout the year to assess their suitability for future placements. For applicants not familiar with the Opportunities database, INH created a series of How-to-Guides to familiarise them with the platform.

Applications for the 2015 Festival volunteering programme were launched in November 2014, with the application period open for one month. In total, 822 applications were received (INH 2015). The demographic profile of applicants was mostly female (93.3%), commonly aged between 21 and 23 years (35.2%). Not surprising given the heavily student-focussed approach to recruitment, the majority of applicants indicated that 'skill and career development' was their key motivation for volunteering (INH 2015).

To assist in reducing attrition and ensuring appropriate placement of potential volunteers, INH staff conducted one-on-one 5-minute interviews with 500 applicants over a two-week period in January 2015. Applicants were notified of their interview time through the Opportunities platform, and an automated SMS was sent to each candidate on the morning of their interview containing a relevant location map and contact information. Resulting in part from the interview process, only 50 candidates who were deemed successful subsequently withdrew or failed to attend their allocated shifts (INH 2015).

Pre-Festival volunteers were recruited to assist in a number of roles including supporting the Festival campaign launch (December 2014), volunteer interview support (January 2015) and volunteer briefing support (March 2015). During the Festival, volunteers assisted in a number of roles including but not limited to Backstage Manager Assistant, Production Runner, Event Stylist Assistant, Office Support, Back of House Runner and Front of House Usher. INH created 85 unique position descriptions for volunteers reflective of their event role and venue location (INH 2015).

Two pre-Festival briefing sessions were held in early March 2015 in the lead-up to the Festival. These were scheduled for the early evening (6–8 pm) to accommodate commitments volunteers might have had during business hours and were well attended by 222 volunteers (INH 2015). These sessions covered an overview of the Festival programme, customer service basics, communication protocols and reasonable expectations associated with volunteering at the event. In addition, a comprehensive Volunteer Handbook was prepared for volunteers, which outlined expected standards on behaviour. This was supplemented by the volunteer's individual position description, which was available on the Opportunities platform.

During Festival time, technology continued to be used to engage the volunteers. Volunteers again received SMS notifications for every shift, outlining their shift time, venue location and contact details for their on-site coordinator (a role to be discussed in further detail). The SMS functionality also allowed for any urgent messages or last-minute changes to be communicated to on-site volunteers and Festival management. All volunteers signed in and out for each shift by way of the VMS, which was accessed by on-site staff via their mobile phones. At the conclusion of each shift, volunteers received a personalised email requesting their feedback on that particular shift (e.g. the in-depth on-site briefing provided, suitability of the tasks allocated), allowing INH to collect accurate data throughout the Festival, not just at one point in time, e.g. a post-event survey.

Volunteers were also encouraged to engage with the Festival via technology and social media platforms to build retention and gratification. On the Opportunities platform, volunteers were able to post pictures and status updates for sharing with their fellow volunteers, which were moderated by INH. INH coordinators also uploaded photos to the INH Facebook page and tagged with them the first name of the volunteer, which allowed for further sharing amongst followers.

As a full service provider, another key element of the HELPERS model is INH's deep engagement with the festival organiser at all stages of the event cycle and their on-site management of volunteers. INH worked closely with all Festival Project Managers, production staff and the management team in the lead-up, during and after the event. A Volunteer Management Guide was developed by INH and circulated to all Project Managers and internal management staff that would be interacting with volunteers during the Festival. Additionally, INH circulated the volunteer profile information (age bracket, gender and key motivations) to all Project Managers to provide them with an informed understanding of who the volunteer cohort were and why they were choosing to engage with 2015 Festival. Production Managers were engaged as contractors themselves to the Festival to plan and oversee a specific show as part of the 2015 programme.

Festival volunteer requirements were captured via a Volunteer Resource Requirements template that allowed Project Managers to populate the requested positions and shifts for their assigned events. Once volunteer rosters were drafted, an online portal was circulated to Project Managers which provided them with the ability to view live roster reports, monitor allocated resourcing and keep track of which volunteers were on-site at any given time.

Supporting the volunteers and liaising with Festival staff, INH had three volunteer coordinators servicing the 2015 Festival. A coordinator was on-site for each volunteer shift to manage sign-in and sign-out, ensuring up-to-date monitoring of volunteer attendance. Additionally, these staff were responsible for briefing volunteers at the commencement of each shift and distributing on-site accreditation passes, which were date specific (volunteers were able to retain these as mementos post-shift). Other coordinator duties included responsibility for ensuring volunteers' on-site safety, break management and entering a commentary in the VMS on all the volunteers that they had dealt with during their shift, information which was intended to be reviewed if candidates sought future involvement with the Festival.

Post-event, INH's VMS allowed volunteers to download a Certificate of Appreciation (signed by the Festival CEO), a 'Certified Hours' document detailing the hours they had contributed to the Festival and a Reference Letter for any mandated study requirements or for their CV. Hours contributed by the volunteers were labelled INH points, which could be exchanged for attendance at future networking events and also strengthened the volunteer's profile on the Opportunities platform for consideration for future volunteering opportunities. The volunteer with the most INH points was also profiled on the Opportunities platform.

INH administered a survey to both volunteers and Project Managers post-event to collect a range of data to inform future planning for the Festival. Forty-three per cent of volunteers completed the survey, with a higher response rate for the Project Manager survey (71%) (INH 2015). On a 5-point scale, volunteer respondents assessed their 'overall involvement with the Festival' positively with a rating of 4.3. Overwhelmingly, 98% indicated they were interested in registering their availability for next year's Festival. In the case of the Project Managers, all (100%) found the live roster updates to be 'convenient to access and useful' and also agreed that the Volunteer Management Guide 'provided them and/or their on-site team with the proper guidance when interacting with volunteers' (INH 2015).

## Discussion

The case highlights the key distinctive features of the HELPERS volunteer management model. First, although there are variants (e.g. consultancy to existing Festival management programmes), in the case of the 2015 Festival, the HELPERS model provided contracted full service support, with INH managing all aspects of the volunteer programme, from recruitment to on-site coordination of volunteers and post-Festival volunteer recognition. This represents an extension of the recognised *outsourcing* model (Smith & Lockstone, 2009), which has typically been applied by festival management to outsource an ancillary component of festival operations to a third party, usually a community group. Interestingly, the HELPERS model also encompasses elements of the *programme management* model (Holmes & Smith 2009), with INH developing tailored volunteer position descriptions based on the Festival's requirements for each role and venue. Indeed, INH relies on close engagement with Festival staff, with in the case of the 2015 Festival, Production Managers being their key liaison point.

The HELPERS model integrates technology solutions (VMS and Opportunities platform) to streamline and support the management process. These technologies extend beyond existing Australian volunteer platforms such as GoVolunteer and SeekVolunteer, which essentially act as matching sites, to connect potential volunteers to volunteer-involving organisations. In the case of the 2015 Festival, volunteers received SMS notifications regarding their shift times and were able to log on to the Opportunities platform to track their hours volunteered, whilst Festival management received live updates on volunteer rosters, enabling monitoring of potential shortfalls. Monitoring volunteering activity in real time allows greater insight into the volunteer experience across the Festival's duration, supplemented by the data collected from volunteers at the end of every shift, allowing for multiple data collection points rather than relying on one retrospective post-event survey. Finally, the HELPERS model has greatly benefited by tapping into vocational and higher education students as a source of potential volunteers, cognisant that many of these programmes are now mandating volunteering as part of their course requirements.

## Conclusions

In their exploration of the future of event volunteering, Lockstone-Binney, Baum, Smith and Holmes (2014) envisaged the continued need for volunteers at event and festivals. Factors influencing future volunteering included demographic changes, increased choice and time pressures, information and communication technology developments, the growth of corporate or employee volunteering, and the increasing diversity of volunteering engagements. A number of future forms of volunteering were proposed, including the development of the outsourced model discussed here.

The HELPERS model offers a one-stop shop of festival and event volunteering expertise, and reduces the duplication of effort and resources of festivals trying to each separately recruit volunteers, leading to increased professionalism of festival volunteer management. Indeed, the HELPERS model has been recognised as best practice and the learnings from it shared at several tourism and volunteering conferences within Australia.

Since 2015, the INH team has focussed on refining the systems and technology to support internal volunteer programmes throughout Australia. INH now grants access to volunteer-involving organisations to tap into the scheduling platform, mobile applications and automated services (i.e., automated calls and SMS reminders) as well as a shared database between all organisations to manage their own volunteer programme. The model continues to evolve and to expand the services it provides to festival organisers.

The review of the HELPERS model offers some directions for future research. For example, the model could be used to support other forms of episodic volunteering such as spontaneous volunteering. The HELPERS model also shows the value of digital technology in assisting festival organisers, however big the volunteer programme may be, alongside the possibility of involving virtual festival volunteers in, for example, website development and marketing. The HELPERS platform allows for tracking of volunteer activity, which might allow for a greater understanding of the festival volunteer experience. Being able to recruit and retain satisfied volunteers is at the heart of any festival volunteer programme.

## References

Andersson, T. & Getz, D. (2009). Festival ownership: differences between public, non-profit and private festivals in Sweden. *Scandinavian Journal of Hospitality and Tourism, 9*(2/3), 249–265.

Bachman, J., Norman, W., Hopkins, C. & Brookover, R. (2016). Examining the role of self-concept theory on motivation, satisfaction, and intent to return of music festival volunteers. *Event Management, 20*(1), 41–52.

Bachman, J. R., Backman, K. F. & Norman, W. C. (2014). A segmentation of volunteers at the 2013 Austin City Limits Music Festival: Insights and future directions. *Journal of Convention and Event Tourism, 15*(4), 298–315.

Campbell, A. (2009). The importance of being valued: Solo 'grey nomads' as volunteers at the National Folk Festival. *Annals of Leisure Research, 12*(3–4), 277–294.

Carlsen, J. & Andersson, T. D. (2011). Strategic SWOT analysis of public, private and not-for-profit festival organisations. *International Journal of Event and Festival Management, 2*(1), 83–97.

Clayton, D. (2016). Volunteers' knowledge activities at UK music festivals: A hermeneutic-phenomenological exploration of individuals' experiences. *Journal of Knowledge Management, 20*(1), 162–180.

Derrett, R. (2009). How festivals nurture resilience in regional communities. In Ali-Knight, J. Robertson, M., Fyall, A. & Ladkin, A. (Eds.), *International Perspectives of Festivals and Events* (pp. 107–124). London: Elsevier.

Elstad, B. (2003). Continuance commitment and reasons to quit: A study of volunteers at a jazz festival. *Event Management, 8*(2), 99–108.

Frost, W. & Laing, J. (2015). Avoiding burnout: The succession planning, governance and resourcing of rural tourism festivals. *Journal of Sustainable Tourism, 23*(8–9), 1298–1317.

Gallarza, M. G., Arteaga, F. & Gil-Saura, I. (2012). The value of volunteering in special events: A longitudinal study. *Annals of Tourism Research, 40*(January), 105–131.

Gordon, L. & Erkut, E. (2005). The 'sound' science of scheduling. *OR-MS Today, 32*(2), 32–35.

Handy, F., Brodeur, N. & Cnaan, R. (2006). Summer on the island: Episodic volunteering. *Voluntary Action, 7*(3), 31–46.

Handy, F., Hustinx, L., Kang, C., Cnaan, R., Brudney, J. L., Holmes, K., Kassam, M., Meijs, L., Pessi, A., Ranade, B., Yamauchi, N. & Zrinscak, S. (2010). A cross-cultural examination of student volunteering: Is it all about resumé building? *Nonprofit and Voluntary Sector Quarterly, 39*(3), 498–523.

Hede, A.-M. & Rentschler, R. (2007). Mentoring volunteer festival managers: Evaluation of a pilot scheme in regional Australia. *Managing Leisure, 12*(2–3), 157–170.

Holmes, K. & Ali-Knight, J. (2017). The event and festival life-cycle: Developing a new model for a new context. *International Journal of Contemporary Hospitality Management, 29*(3), 986–1004.

Holmes, K., Hughes, M., Mair, J. & Carlsen, J. (2015). *Events and Sustainability*. Abingdon: Routledge.

Holmes, K. & Smith, K. A. (2009). *Managing Volunteers Within Tourism*. Oxford: Butterworth-Heinemann.

I Need Helpers (INH). (2015). *Volunteer Program Growth and Development Report*. Melbourne: INH.

I Need Helpers (INH). (2017). *Staff & Volunteer Management System (VMS)*. Retrieved from https://ineedhelpers.com/vms/.

Jæger, K. & Olsen, K. (2017). On commodification: volunteer experiences in festivals, *Journal of Tourism and Cultural Change*, 15(5), 407-421.

Jensen, E. & Buckley, N. (2011). *The Role of University Student Volunteers in Festival-Based Public Engagement*. Bristol: The University of Cambridge and National Co-ordinating Centre for Public Engagement.

Laing, J. & Mair, J. (2015). Music festivals and social inclusion – the festival organizers' perspective. *Leisure Sciences, 37*(3), 252–268.

Lee, K.-H., Alexander, A. C. & Kim, D.-Y. (2013). Motivational factors affecting volunteer intention in local events in the United States. *Journal of Convention & Event Tourism, 14*(4), 271–292.

Lockstone-Binney, L., Baum, T., Smith, K. A. & Holmes, K. (2014). Exploring future forms of volunteering. In Yeoman, I., Robertson, M., McMahon-Beattie, U., Backer, E. & Smith K. A. (Eds.), *The Future of Events and Festivals* (pp. 175–186). London and New York: Routledge.

Love, G., Sherman, K. & Olding, R. (2012). Will they stay or will they go? A study of volunteer retention at film/music festivals in the southwest United States. *Event Management, 16*(4), 269–281.

Meijs, L. & Hoogstad, E. (2001). New ways of managing volunteers: Combining membership management and programme management. *Voluntary Action, 3*(3), 41–61.

NCMC Casino Beef Week (2017). *NCMC Casino Beef Week*. Retrieved from www.casinobeefweek.com.au.

Nichols, G. & Ralston, R. (2012). Lessons from the volunteering legacy of the 2002 Commonwealth Games. *Urban Studies, 49*(1), 165–180.

O'Neill, E. (2007, July). Casino Beef Week set for comeback. *Northern Star*. Retrieved from www.northernstar.com.au/news/apn-casino-beef-week-set-for/13573/.

Preez, R. (2007). *Beef Week Cancelled*. Retrieved from www.abc.net.au/site-archive/rural/nsw/content/2006/s1838984.htm.

Ragsdell, G. & Jepson, A. (2014). Knowledge sharing: Insights from Campaign for Real Ale (CAMRA) festival volunteers. *International Journal of Event and Festival Management, 5*(3), 279–296.

Rogers, P. & Anastasiadou, C. (2011), Community involvement in festivals: Exploring ways of increasing local participation. *Event Management, 15*(4), 387–399.

Smith, K., Baum, T., Holmes, K. & Lockstone-Binney, L. (2014). Introduction to event volunteering. In Smith, K., Lockstone-Binney, L., Holmes, K. & Baum, T. (Eds.), *Event Volunteering: International Perspectives on the Event Volunteering Experience* (pp. 1–15). London: Routledge.

Smith, K. A. & Lockstone, L. (2009). Involving and keeping event volunteers: Management insights from cultural festivals. In Baum, T,. Deery, M., Hanlon, C., Lockstone, L. & Smith, K. (Eds.), *People and Work in Events and Conventions: A Research Perspective* (pp. 154–167). Wallingford: CAB International.

Virgin Australia Melbourne Fashion Festival. (VAMFF). (2018). *About Us*. Retrieved from https://vamff.com.au/about-us/.

Yin, R. (2009). *Case Study Research*. Thousand Oaks: Sage Publications.

# 10
# THE ROLE OF HARM MINIMISATION TO PREVENT ALCOHOL AND DRUG MISUSE AT OUTDOOR MUSIC FESTIVALS

*Alison Hutton*

## Introduction

The outdoor music festival (OMF) is a unique social event where music is the central theme. As OMFs have grown in popularity, so too has the amount of recorded patient presentation rates, highlighting the impact that OMFs have on the health and safety outcomes for the audience. A range of site environmental conditions (for example, temperature, humidity, high audience density levels and the presence of drugs and alcohol) also result in a higher number of patient presentation rates (Milsten, Maguire, Bissell & Seaman 2002; Hutton, Ranse, Verdonk, Ullah & Arbon 2014; Westrol et al. 2016). As event knowledge evolves, public health strategies and policies become increasingly important in supporting the safety of the audience, event staff and others attending OMFs. It is critical, therefore, that health promotion strategies and public health information are integral to the planning of any mass gathering to minimise public health risk, support harm reduction and provide opportunities for the promotion of healthy behaviours in the local population. Given the popularity of OMFs with young people globally, health promotion and protection efforts should be directed towards the prevention and minimisation of harm to this population.

## Outdoor music festivals

OMFs are unique events that are for the most part bounded, ticketed and where alcohol is served. The genres at OMFs include hard rock, electronic, house music, world music and anything and everything in between. OMFs frequently have a higher incidence of injuries and illnesses when compared with similar scale events (Raineri & Earl 2005; Hutton et al. 2014). In addition to this, OMFs are identified as having a higher transport to hospital rate than other similar events due to the combination of drugs and alcohol consumed by the audience and the population predominantly being young people aged 18–30 (Hutton et al. 2014).

In Australia a significant proportion of young adults are injured, incarcerated and at increased risk of sexual and physical violence due to alcohol and drug use. Alcohol consumption usually peaks in young adulthood (18–25 years of age), with over half of young people engaging in binge-drinking behaviour (Arnett 2006). Research has shown that at social events, alcohol contributes to increased risk for adverse consequences among young people (Kamel Boulos, Brewer, Karimkhani, Butler & Dellavalle 2014). Young people may feel less inhibited by normal constraints and embrace potential anonymity, doing things in groups they might otherwise not do (Hutton, Savage, Ranse, Finnell & Kub 2015). This is likely to be the case in other countries too.

Many case studies of mass-gathering music events have been conducted to understand what injuries and illnesses occur at these events and to ensure ways in which these can be prevented (Milsten et al. 2002; Krul, Blankers & Girbes 2011; Westrol et al. 2017). Hutton and colleagues (2014) documented the number and types of injuries and illnesses for 4,950 young people presenting for medical assistance at 26 OMFs. In line with most mass-gathering events, Hutton et al. found that the majority of presentations were minor, preventable injuries (n = 1,377; 27.7%) and illnesses (n = 2,766; 55.9%), with drug and alcohol use associated with higher presentation rates and transport to hospital rate. Westrol et al. (2017) also found that the programme played a role in the incidence of higher patient presentations at OMF.

An easy response would be to argue that these programmes need more medical resources (such as on-site care). However, instead of relying on a single approach to health response, harm reduction and health promotion can be used in conjunction with on-site services to promote health at these events. In Europe, this mix is used effectively, with on-site medical services seen as just one component of an organised public health response (Munn, Lund, Colby & Turris 2016).

## Alcohol and drug use

Patterns of alcohol and drug use have long been associated with certain types of mass gatherings and as significant contributors to increased patterns of morbidity and mortality (Hutton et al. 2014). The use of drugs and alcohol leads to other crowd behaviours such as 'moshing,' (jumping up and down with the intent of bumping into others) and the 'circle of death' (the audience creating a circle, and on the command of the performer rushing in towards each other with the intent to collide). These also contribute to an increase in injuries (Raineri & Earl 2005). For event organisers, the provision and consumption of alcohol at events creates the greatest risk (Institute of Alcohol Studies 2015). The presence of alcohol at events also increases the workload of on-site care and emergency services (Hutton et al. 2014; Institute of Alcohol Studies 2015).

Even though it is an illegal activity, drugs are commonly used in combination with alcohol consumption at OMF. Evidence of drug usage at these events can be found in presentations to on-site care (Hutton et al. 2014; Munn et al. 2016) and media reports of illness and death at these events. In 2016 in Australia, five deaths were reported and many were hospitalised due to drug overdoses (News 2016). In the UK, a British teenager died of a fatal over dose after ingesting 'left over' drugs she had shared with her friends (Daily Mail 2017).

The way in which drugs are viewed in wider society, however, restricts the implementation of harm minimisation strategies in relation to OMF events. Policing methods can be ineffective and, in some cases, may increase harm. For example, young people who are scared of being caught with drugs by police during searches at entry points to or within the OMF event site have been known to ingest all their drugs at one time to avoid getting caught by police with fatal consequences (Daily Mail 2017).

Club drugs such as methylenedioxymethamphetamine (MDMA), cocaine (coke) and amphetamines (speed) are closely linked to dance music and electronic music festivals

*Table 10.1* Drugs/music genre

| | |
|---|---|
| Dance/rave house | Ecstasy, speed tobacco alcohol solvents, cannabis inhalants, amyl nitrite, cocaine, LSD, benzodiazepines and ketamine |
| Grunge | Cannabis and amphetamines |
| Rap music | Crack and illicit drugs |
| Metal | Alcohol, tobacco and cannabis, and any illicit drugs |

*Source:* Adapted from Lim et al. (2008).

(Van Havere, Vanderplasschen, Lammertyn, Broekaert & Bellis 2011). The most commonly reported drug taken at OMF is cannabis. Van Havere et al. (2011) found that 44% of OMF goers took cannabis, followed by MDMA (19%) and cocaine (11%). The music genre also plays a part in determining what types of drugs are likely to be consumed (see Table 10.1).

OMFs such as Shambhala in Canada have had established drug testing for years. This includes education and 'amnesty bins' for safe disposal (Munn et al. 2016). Dr David Caldicott, an advocate of pill testing at OMF, claims that pill testing is an opportunity to discuss the inherent risk of drugs with festivalgoers who then have an opportunity to ask questions and receive information on tips for staying safe (News 2016).

## Harm minimisation

Excessive drinking and the ingestion of drugs by young people at OMFs is a serious public health issue. We need to think more broadly than targeting the individual in a paternalistic way and expecting them to comply (Hutton et al. 2015). Young people need to be actively engaged in choices that affect their health. Smith, Louis and Tarrant (2017) state that preventative health messages are more likely to be effective for young people in specific contexts. The event environment of an OMF is an appropriate place to engage young people in practices that can minimise harm with non-medical initiatives that ensure the continued health of attendees at that event (Munn et al. 2016). See Table 10.2 for definitions of the terms in use in public health.

Health promotion and the provision of public health information should be at the core of any planned event to minimise public health risk and to provide opportunities for the promotion of healthy behaviours (Isla, Endericks & Barbeschi 2016). For example, at all events, the ability to wash hands and have running water is essential. Identifying and agreeing on what public health information is needed for a mass-gathering audience is key. Information sharing between emergency departments, on-site care providers, police, local authorities and the event organisers can develop more targeted and effective strategies for tackling a range of problems (Institute of Alcohol Studies 2015). Second, there should be agreement about how to communicate this information. A developed understanding of audience behaviour will provide critical information for mass-gathering event planners, risk managers and emergency medical service personnel, enabling them to predict and plan to minimise risk of injury or illness (Hutton, Brown & Verdonk 2013). In turn, this can result in reduced patient presentations and reduced health service use. For the event designer, understanding audience motivation and subsequent behaviour enables the event design to be modified and settings and programmes adapted as a response to observable audience behaviour proactively in real time (Brown & Hutton 2013).

The event environment is a space where health promotion and primary healthcare strategies can be applied to reduce levels of excessive or risky drinking, ingestion of illicit

*Table 10.2* Definition of terms under the public health umbrella

| | |
|---|---|
| Public health | Organised measures to prevent disease, promote health, and prolong life among the population. Activities aim to provide conditions in which people can be healthy and focus on entire populations, not on individuals. |
| Health promotion | The process of enabling people to increase control over and improve their health. Moves beyond a focus on individual behaviour towards a wide range of social and environmental interactions. |
| Illness/injury prevention | Averting the occurrence of illness/injury and halting the progression from its early, unrecognised stage to a more severe one. |
| Harm reduction | Any programme or policy designed to reduce behaviour-related harm without requiring the cessation of the behaviour itself. |

*Source:* Reproduced with permission (Munn et al. 2016, p. 229).

substances and the subsequent behaviours and injuries related to such use. The principles of the Ottawa Charter will be applied to the event environment of the OMF to develop further understanding of how primary healthcare and harm minimisation principles can be enacted in this space. Furthermore, to how positive intervention in the event site can be used to support and enable young people to attend festivals safely.

## *The Ottawa Charter*

Distinct frameworks, approaches and ideological underpinnings can shape health promotion and harm minimisation initiatives. The Ottawa Charter, a primary healthcare framework, is useful in determining harm minimisation strategies for OMFs (Hutton, Zannettino & Cusack 2012). Even though the Ottawa Charter was established in 1986 (World Health Organization (WHO) 1986), it still provides an opportunity for researchers and policymakers to think outside the square when developing health promotion and harm minimisation strategies for young people at OMF events (Baum 2007; Ward & Verrinder 2008). The interface between OMF events and the wider community will be examined to address the underlying structural factors that may contribute to the safety of attendees at these events (see also Hutton, Zannettino & Cusack 2012).

The Ottawa Charter originated from the first international conference of health promotion in Ottawa, Canada (WHO 1986). The Charter comprises five strategies which address broader determinates of health. Importantly, this Charter seeks to shift the focus from the individual to one that considers the individual within the community and the wider environment, such as an event. The five strategies are:

1 Building public policy.
2 Creating supportive environments.
3 Strengthening community action.
4 Developing personal skill.
5 Reorientating strategies (WHO 1986).

Together, these strategies can address factors that affect health at both the individual and community levels, encompassing a wider settings approach. This framework is widely applicable in a range of settings. As a temporary community, OMFs are particularly vulnerable to health-related issues (Arbon 2005), for example minor problems such as twisted ankles, abrasions and headaches as well as the major issues of drug and alcohol including nausea, inebriation, agitation, dehydration and unconsciousness (Hutton et al. 2014).

## *Building public policy*

As the Ottawa Charter focusses on the interests of both the audience and the wider community, the goal is to work together in an effort to foster a safe, supportive environment for event goers. Current efforts include 'crowd care' and on-site medical teams, and at some events, like 'Groovin the Moo™,' a safe space (a 'chill out zone') is provided for audience members to disconnect from the event for a while (Headspace 2017). However, these harm minimisation strategies are set in isolation, whereas a combined approach can be used between the community, young people and the event management team to explore issues around enabling a safe supportive environment for all. This combined effort not only fosters collaboration in assessing risks but also fosters the development of frameworks to reduce harm (Hutton et al. 2012). This approach encourages all parties to have a voice, representing the motivations of all groups, and if agreed upon can increase community spirit both within and outside the event.

Alcohol plays a significant role in the culture of many Western countries, and drinking is commonly associated with relaxation, celebration and having fun (Alcohol and Rehabilitation Foundation 2011). Instead of relying on individual levels of responsibility for safe drinking, it is important to focus on the relationship between alcohol misuse and the experience of enjoyment. Creating policies that value and support young people's choices involves identifying strategies that relate to managing community events with a high youth attendance (Hutton et al. 2012). Current policies generally focus on curtailing the activities of individuals and do little to reduce the burden on the wider community. The creation and adaptability of a single multi-organisational response that includes police, event managers and on-site care providers would enable better communication and coordination between all parties, and sends one clear message to event goers.

An important outcome of a single policy is the opportunity for consistency in the incident and health-related documentation at OMF, leading to the collection of more evidence-based data that informs and supports the management and development of strategies supporting intoxicated audience members. Consistency – and the increased amount of data – will assist in the evaluation of harm minimisation approaches at OMFs and provide a more reliable analysis of the effectiveness of policies on the health and safety of audience members at these events. This approach also assists in maintaining good collaborative practice amongst all participating organisations (Hutton et al. 2012).

## *Creating supportive environments*

Creating supportive environments deals with the inextricable links between people and their environments (Ward & Verrinder 2008). These environments are important as they ensure that the place where young people live and interact is safe and enjoyable. The event management team works across organisational boundaries at both the state and community levels at the site of the OMF. This cross-boundary approach provides a community environment rather than just an event space, within which young people can participate in safely.

Building safe supportive environments is about the environment that surrounds the OMF, which in itself is a community. This strategy focusses on the need to respect the local community's needs pre, during and after the event, whilst also ensuring that the community structures do not impact on the event. For example, a large world music festival held in the parklands of an Australian city experienced a sudden upsurge in presentations of respiratory distress related to allergies and asthma. The event health service rapidly depleted its on-site stocks of medication and equipment and needed support from the local ambulance authority to respond effectively. Following review and evaluation of the event it became apparent that the local government routinely mowed grass throughout the venue a few days before as part of its preparation of the site; creating a dusty environment and stirring up pollens and other irritants. This created a health hazard for those in attendance. Post-event, stakeholders met to discuss this incident, and this policy was reviewed and altered for subsequent years (Goodwin Veenema, Arbon & Hutton 2018).

## *Strengthening community action*

The heart of strengthening community action is giving people a say in decisions that affect them in their community. This includes both the permanent community and the temporary one, such as an OMF. Recently Green Music Australia announced #plasticfreejuly announcing that events should be plastic free as post event the ground is littered with plastic which ends up in landfill and is harmful to the environment (Music Feeds 2017).

What is missing from this initiative is all stakeholders who work within and around the event coming together to determine how this initiative could take place. For example, if people were to bring their own bottles, could they still buy drinks in plastic containers at the event? What measures will be put in place to ensure that these bottles are not thrown or used in a harmful way? Have police and on-site medical care been included in this conversation?

In Germany Rheinkultur (an OMF featuring classical and jazz music) has introduced a similar initiative. At the event, you buy your own cup for 2 euros on top of the costs of your first alcoholic drink. This initiative aims to encourage the audience to reuse and return cups during the event. At the recycle station, audience members have the opportunity of donating the 2 euros to a charity. This initiative resonated with the audience with most attendees donate their money to charity. This encourages recycling, keeping the event green and safe, saving money and being involved in charity (Rheinkultur 2017). However, initiatives such as this also impact on the health of attendees. The main types of injury presentations at OMFs are superficial lacerations, followed by sprain or strains on lower limbs, many of which are caused by uneven surfaces and litter on the ground (Hutton et al. 2014). Recycling initiatives such as these can reduce these injuries and thereby decrease the number of patient presentations at OMF events.

It takes many groups to make a successful event, and understanding the role and responsibility of all parties involved is a good place to start. Through such understandings, each organisation learns about each other's roles and responsibility, and what each other's idea of collaboration is. There is an opportunity for all groups to work together to champion and enact policy change to support harm minimisation practices. As well as the opportunity for collaboration, it is also important to acknowledge and respect the boundaries and limitations of each other's role. These considerations contribute to opportunities for formal evaluation of the event, which in turn will inform the future knowledge and skill development for both the event management group and the wider community.

Another group that may benefit is local community members who gain new skills or attitudes by participating in the OMF event in some way. For example, keeping the community informed about the event and how it may affect them for a short period of time via radio or community forums. In this way, community members can make an informed decision about the activities that are included in the event and how they would like to be involved during the event timeframe. In addition, a mass-gathering event is an opportunity to reinforce health behaviours amongst the resident and attending population. For example 'Pit Stop for Men' (at motor races) is a health programme that aims to engage men of all ages in their health by likening areas of the body to parts in a car: for example checking for fuel additives is a measure of alcohol consumption, and measuring the waist circumference is called a chassis check (Pit Stop Health Check Evaluation 2010). These types of health promotion activities can impact positively on social cohesion, which can create opportunities to facilitate healthy behaviours in the wider population (Harrison & Gilgunn-Jones 2015).

## *Developing personal skills*

Empowerment through knowledge and skills suggests the need to use the event as an opportunity to build and develop the skills and knowledge of those involved. In the context of OMFs this includes all stakeholders in the planning.

Helping young people develop their knowledge and skills around health behaviours whilst at the event is another aspect of developing personal skill. These messages need to be empowering rather than pejorative, to assist the attendee to make informed choices whilst they are at the event. Hutton et al. (2012) found that content-specific messages worked at Adelaide Schoolies festival. Many young people presented to on-site care with foot and ankle injuries due to wearing flip-flops at events. A simple slogan posted online ('if you want to dance 'till you drop don't wear flip flops') resonated with the younger audience, reducing foot injuries at future events (Hutton, Cusack, Zannettino, Shaefer & Arbon 2013).

## *Reorientating health services*

The last aspect of the Ottawa Charter is reorientating health services, with the aim of reorientating mindsets. Part of event organisation involves working with the local health service and/or on-site care to proactively prepare for events. Yet the notion of shifting the mindset of the wider community is so they can see the *potential* for providing a safe supportive environment at these events (Hutton et al. 2012). For example, instead of curtailing the activities of young people during the event, it may be more beneficial for the community to be proactive in creating a safe supportive environment for young people pre, during and post event through providing free public transport and water stations

*Table 10.3* Health promotion strategies

| Planning/health promotion strategies | Public health/harm reduction/health promotion |
|---|---|
| Handwashing with soap | Public health |
| Running water in bathrooms | Public health |
| Free water | Public health |
| Shade | Public health |
| Handwashing reminders | Health promotion |
| Look after your mates messages | Health promotion |
| Information about safe sex | Health promotion |
| Chill-out rooms/alcohol-free zones | Harm minimisation |
| Crowd care | Harm minimisation |
| Pill testing | Harm minimisation |
| Distribution of condoms | Harm minimisation |

outside and inside the event. Community members such as restaurateurs, short-term accommodation owners and retailers can play a vital role in safeguarding an event. It is a fundamental feature of good practice to listen to their concerns and involve them in any planning and preparation that happens in their local community (Baum 2007). A shift in community attitude about an event can have a positive impact of the overall communities' perspective. Instead of seeing it as a public nuisance, the perspective may shift to a whole of community celebration, in turn creating a safer more supportive environment for young people (Table 10.3).

## Discussion

OMFs have received relatively little research attention despite being key sites for alcohol and drug use among young people internationally (Dilkes-Frayne 2016). The way in which current health services are set up during OMFs privileges a reliance on existing healthcare systems without taking into account how harm minimisation and health promotion activities can lessen the need for these services, thus reducing the burden on the wider community. Reducing harm in this cohort because of the risk-taking behaviours, such as driving under the influence, drug consumption, sexual behaviour and violence, that have been seen at celebratory events could have far-reaching impacts (Smith & Rosenthal 1997; Zinkiewicz, Davey & Curd 1999).

Events such as OMFs rely on the premise of 'just in time' on-site care, with a focus on crisis and emergency management. On-site care gives event managers a sense of safety and is vitally important to participants' well-being. However, the presence of on-site care does not curtail patrons drinking at risky levels (Hutton et al. 2015). Prevention is socially and economically cheaper, and event organisers and community members need to be prepared to invest the time necessary to develop and strengthen preventative strategies (Baum 2007). There is a real opportunity for festivals to be used to promote health for the audience members and the wider community. The event environment is a specific space where health promotion and primary healthcare strategies can be applied to reduce levels of excessive drinking, ingestion of illicit substances and the subsequent behaviours and injuries related to such use.

Mass gatherings, such as OMFs, are a unique opportunity to promote the health of young people. These interventions are cost-effective in improving morbidity and mortality. In addition, they are an opportunity to platform and implement public health, harm minimisation and health promotion interventions through access and engagement with communities, reinforcing social norms, generating investment in health and stimulating partnerships to improve overall health outcomes.

## References

Alcohol and Rehabilitation Foundation (2011). *Annual Alcohol Poll: Community Attitudes and Behaviours.* Deakin ACT: AER Foundation Ltd.

Arbon, P. (2005). Planning medical coverage for mass gatherings in Australia: What we already know. *Journal of Emergency Nursing, 31*(4), 346–350.

Goodwin Veenema, T., Arbon, P. & Hutton, A. (2018). Chapter 5, Emergency medical consequence planning for special events, mass gatherings, and mass casualty incidents. In Veneema, T. (Ed.), *Disaster Nursing and Emergency Preparedness*, 4th edn. New York, USA: Springer Publishing.

Arnett, J. (2006). Emerging adulthood: Understanding the new way of coming of age. In Arnett, J. & Tanner, J. L. (Eds.), *Emerging Adults in America: Coming of Age in the 21st Century* (3–19). Washington, DC: American Psychology Association.

Baum, F. (2007). Health for all now! Reviving the spirit of Alma Ata in the twenty-first century: An introduction to the Alma Arta Declaration. *Social Medicine, 2*(1), 34–41.

Brown, S. & Hutton, A. (2013). Developments in the real-time evaluation of audience behaviour at planned events. *International Journal of Event and Festival Management, 4*(1), 43–55.

Daily Mail (2017). Teenager took fatal quantity of MDMA. Available at: www.dailymail.co.uk/news/article-4235674/Teenager-took-fatal-quantity-MDMA-queue-O2.html. Accessed 24/03/2017.

Dilkes-Frayne, E. (2016). Drugs at the campsite: Socio-spatial relations and drug use at music festivals. *International Journal of Drug Policy, 33*(July), 27–35.

Harrison, H. & Gilgunn-Jones, E. (2015). *Public Information and Health Promotion, Public Health for Mass Gatherings: Key Considerations*. Madrid: World Health Organisation.

Headspace (2017). Groovin The Moo 2017 – headspace Help Desk is back! Available at: www.headspace.org.au/news/new-news-blog-post-15/. Accessed 4/06/2017.

Hutton, A., Brown, S. & Verdonk, N. (2013). Exploring culture: Audience predispositions and consequent effect on audience behaviour in a mass gathering setting. *Prehospital Disaster Medicine, 28*(3), 292–297.

Hutton, A., Cusack, L., Zannettino, L., Shaefer, S. & Arbon, P. (2013). What are school leavers' priorities for festival preparation? *Australian Journal of Primary Health Care, 21*(2), 249–253.

Hutton. A., Ranse. J., Verdonk, N., Ullah, S. & Arbon, P. (2014). Understanding the characteristics of patient presentations of young people at outdoor music festivals. *Prehospital Disaster Medicine, 29*(2), 1–7.

Hutton, A., Savage, C., Ranse, J., Finnel, D. & Kub, J. (2015). The use of Haddon's matrix to plan for injury and illness prevention at outdoor music festivals. *Prehospital and Disaster Medicine, 30*(2), 175–183.

Hutton, A., Zannettino, L. & Cusack, L. (2012). Building public policy Australian journal of primary health. *Australian Journal of Primary Health, 18*(2), 96–100.

Institute of Alcohol Studies (2015). Alcohol's impact on emergency services. London, UK: Institute of Alcohol Studies.

Isla, N., Endericks, T. & Barbeschi, M. (2016). *Contextual Issues and Risk Assessments Public Health for Mass Gatherings: Key Considerations*. Madrid: World Health Organisation.

Kamel Boulos, M., Brewer, A., Karimkhani, C., Butler, D. & Dellavalle, R. (2014). Mobile health apps: State of the art, concerns, regulatory control and certification. *Online Journal of Public Health Informatics, 5*(3) e229, 1–23.

Krul, J., Blankers, M. & Girbes, A. R. J. (2011). Substance-related health problems during rave parties in the Netherlands (1997–2008). *PLoS ONE, 6*(12), e29620.

Milsten, A. M., Maguire, B. J., Bissell, R. A. & Seaman, K. G. (2002). Mass-gathering medical care: A review of the literature. *Prehospital Disaster Medicine, 17*(3), 151–162.

Munn, B., Lund, A., Colby, C. & Turris, S. (2016). Observed benefits to on-site medical services during an annual 5-day electronic dance music event with harm reduction services. *Prehospital Disaster Medicine, 31*(2), 228–234.

Music Feeds (2017). Killing Heidi & Bernard Fanning join calls for no disposable plastic bottles at Gigs & Festivals. Available at: http://musicfeeds.com.au/news/killing-heidi-bernard-fanning-join-calls-no-disposable-plastic-bottles-gigs-festivals/. Accessed 06/12/2017.

News (2016). As Australian authorities prevent pill testing, the US is quietly telling festivalgoers all about their drugs. Available at: www.news.com.au/lifestyle/health/health-problems/as-australian-authorities-prevent-pill-testing-the-us-is-quietly-telling-festivalgoers-all-about-their-drugs/news-story/a60026bba04507883d402d2428d4fef3. Accessed 06/12/2017.

Pit Stop Health Check Evaluation (2010). http://www.centralwestgippslandpcp.com/projects/projects pitstop/ Accessed 14/06/2018.

Raineri, A. & Earl, C. (2005). Crowd management for outdoor music festivals. *Journal of Occupational Health and Safety - Australia & New Zealand, 21*(3), 205–216.

Rheinkultur (2017). https://de.wikipedia.org/wiki/Rheinkultur. Accessed 06/12/2017.

Smith, J., Louis, W. & Tarrant, M. (2017). University students' social identity and health behaviours. In Mavor, K. I. Platow, T. & Bizumic, B. (Eds.), *Self and Social Identity in Learning and Educational Contexts*. Abingdon, Oxon: Routledge Psychology Press.

Smith, A. & Rosenthal, D. (1997). Sex, alcohol and drugs: Young people's experience of Schoolies week. *Australian and New Zealand Journal of Public Health, 21*(2), 175–180.

Van Havere, T., Vanderplasschen, W., Lammertyn, J., Broekaert, E. & Bellis, M. (2011). Drug use and nightlife: More than just dance music. *Substance Abuse Treatment, Prevention, and Policy, 6*(18), 6–18.

Ward, B. & Verrinder, G. (2008). Young people and alcohol misuse: How can nurses use the Ottawa Charter for health promotion. *The Australian Journal of Advanced Nursing, 25*(2), 114–119.

Westrol, M., Koneru, S., McIntyre, N., Caruso, A., Arshad, F. & Merlin, M. (2017). Music genre as a predictor of resource utilization at outdoor music concerts. *Prehospital and Disaster Medicine*, February. doi:10.1017/S1049023X17000085.

World Health Organization WHO (1986). The Ottawa Charter for health promotion. Available at: www.who.int/healthpromotion/conferences/previous/ottawa/en/. Accessed 06/12/2017.

Zinkiewicz, L., Davey, J. & Curd, D. (1999). Sin beyond surfers? Young people's risky behaviour during Schoolies Week in three Queensland regions. *Drug and Alcohol Review, 18*(3), 279–285.

# 11

# SOCIAL MEDIA AND THE TRANSFORMATION OF THE FESTIVAL INDUSTRY

A typology of festivals and the formation of new markets

*Marianna Sigala*

### Introduction

Technological advances and the social media (SM) revolution are transforming all industries, and the festival sector is no exception. Increasingly, festival organizers are exploiting SM to market their festivals and distribute festival content (Pasanen & Konu 2016). SM are increasingly used by festival organizers for partially or fully digitizing festivals (e.g. online streaming and virtual festivals). Similarly, festivalgoers demand but also expect to use SM for sharing their festival experiences and interacting with festival communities (MacKay, Van Winkle, Halpenny & Barbe 2016; Morey, Bengry-Howell, Griffin, Szmigin & Riley 2016).

However, the impact of SM on the festival industry is not only instrumental in terms of simply serving the functional needs of the industry by providing the technological tools for digitizing existing festival operations. Instead, SM are also a transformational driver by restructuring the festival industry, supporting the formation of new 'competitors' and festival products, as well as transforming the role and the function of traditional festival stakeholders. SM are converting attendees from passive festival viewers to active co-creators and co-marketers of their festival experiences. SM empower attendees and other festival stakeholders to assume and undertake festival organization practices, to initiate and drive festivals and ultimately, become festival micro-entrepreneurs. Peer-to-peer marketplaces and platforms (e.g. www.meetup.com, www.kickstarter.com) – empowering users to co-create and/or co-fund projects and ventures – expand the role of attendees and stakeholders to festival co-funders and co-entrepreneurs.

These fundamental disruptions of technology and SM are recognized in the tourism literature (Sigala & Gretzel 2018). Sigala (2018) has also recently advocated that the technologies have transformed tourism management and marketing from a static and utilitarian sense to a transformative conceptualization whereby tourism markets and actors both shape and are shaped by technology. Unfortunately, research and literature in the festival field has not yet caught up with this technological revolution. Although there are an increasing number of studies looking at the use of SM by festival demand and supply, research has failed to investigate so far the transformational power of SM in shaping and driving the formation of new festival products, markets, and competitors. Instead, festival research has mainly focused on discussing the functional and instrumental role of technologies on 'existing' and traditional festival stakeholders and products (e.g. Hoksbergen & Insch 2016). Moreover, research has failed to examine the entrepreneurial impact of SM on the festival industry demonstrated by the increasing number of user-generated and crowdfunded festivals.

To address these gaps, this chapter aims to discuss the transformational role and impact of SM on the festival industry.

## Social media and the digitization of festivals

SM are platforms enabling users to meet, network, socialize, collaborate, store, share, and distribute information and resources. In the festival context, SM provide a common online space where users can gather in order to either host a virtual festival and/or to broadcast online a traditional festival to a mass international audience. Digital broadcasting overcomes space and time constraints, and so it can significantly increase festival 'attendance' by allowing anyone on the globe with an internet connection to attend and participate in an online broadcast festival. SM also represent a 'free', two-way communication medium that not only efficiently distributes content but also empowers online users to interact with each other, the content itself, and the content creators. By doing this, an online festival community is created whereby online festivalgoers create and consume festival content as well as share and discuss it by interacting with other festival stakeholders (Hede & Kellett 2012; Hoksbergen & Insch 2016). Through their online engagement with festival content, creators, and online users, online festivalgoers can personalize and actively participate in the co-creation of their (online) festival experiences.

SM affect the type and the nature of festivals in two fundamental ways: 1) the place/space whereby the festival takes place and/or is distributed, and 2) the actors and the way in which the actors are involved in festival practices, i.e. initiating the festival and/or (passive or active) role in festival practices.

## The place/space of festivals

### *Festivals enabled and supported by SM: traditional, hybrid, and virtual festivals*

SM provide the digital platform and space whereby one can either broadcast festivals and/or host virtual festivals as well. However, festival research has not discussed yet the role and the impact of SM on the types of festivals based on the location whereby they are hosted and distributed. Zanger (2014) developed an event typology according to the degree of intensity that events integrate with SM for digitizing their practices. This typology is also adapted here for identifying the types of festivals enabled and supported by SM. In this vein, the following types of SM 'enabled' festivals can be identified (from the most to the least integrated with SM): 1) virtual festivals (festivals totally held online), 2) hybrid festivals (online festivals with offline activities, e.g. red carpet events or traditional festivals streamed online), and 3) traditional festivals with a complementary use of SM for promotion. Overall, SM can be used as platforms for streaming and sharing videos and other content of both traditional and virtual festivals before, during, and after the festival.

SM are increasingly used for live streaming the performance of traditional festivals (e.g. Dekmantel in the Netherlands, Notting Hill Carnival, and The Social in Maidstone). Live streaming is claimed to help festivals to expand, internationalize, and diversify their audience reach with limited costs; engage and interact with festival audience (e.g. online polls, competitions, communications, share of content); increase festival exposure and attract future attendees; and better control and manage the sponsored content in terms of when, how often, and who views the sponsored content. Festival organizers and/or artists also post video performances on SM platforms such as SoundCloud, YouTube, Spotify, Facebook Live, and BE-AT.TV. Such videos enable attendees to relive, share, and reflect on their experiences; interact with others and debate what they have learned from their festival participation; and/or use videos as a festival memory and souvenir. Sometimes, users can also curate their own 'festival favourites' playlists, which can be a mix-and-match of their preferred pieces and festival moments. Before the festival, SM and streaming can be used for broadcasting pre-festival playlists in order to announce festival lineup and program, enhance festival promotion, get attendees into the mood and reinforce the festival atmosphere, and reduce purchase risk and increase ticket sales by giving an example of what the festivals are about. Anecdotal evidence (Reidy 2016) shows that the streaming of festivals increases both the festival prestige and ticket sales.

Internet advances have also fueled the rise of many (online) virtual festivals (Robehmed 2013). Music and film online festivals in particular are booming, due to the digital nature of their festival 'product' and experience. In online festivals, the organizers distribute and share the festival content online to an international audience without time zones and place constraints. Attendees of online festivals can also 'attend' the festival performance; participate in festival activities; and become part of, interact with, and network with the festival community from the convenience of their armchair. Moreover, the mobility and connectivity afforded by the smart phones allow the online festivalgoers to be continuously connected and updated with the festival happenings and community. In other words, the SM create a new type of festivalgoer, i.e. the 'always on' festival co-creator.

Some film festivals are held entirely online. This was pioneered in the 1990s by the Webdance Film Festival (http://webdancefilmfestival.com/). Usually, films are shown for a certain amount of time, and viewers can vote on the films they have watched. Other film festival activities such as the red carpet, behind the scenes, greenroom interviews, and viewers' contests also take place online. Nowadays, websites (e.g. https://filmfreeway.com/festivals and https://festhome.com/) also list online film festivals alongside traditional film festivals. This might imply that film festivalgoers may consider traditional and online film festivals as equally substitutable and comparable experiences. However, primary research is needed to verify whether, for whom, and to what extend this is true.

## *The actors initiating (SM-supported or virtual) festivals: firm-driven vs customer-driven festivals*

Online festivals can be initiated and organized by any actor, including traditional festival organizers, online start-up companies, the traditional mass media, and artists themselves.

For traditional festival organizers, one of the key issues is to address the challenges raised by the SM and the digital festivals to their business model and to the attractiveness of traditional film festivals. The traditional Tribeca film festival in New York has created an online film festival with features that redefine the type of online film festivals and at the same time do not jeopardize, but instead reinforce the image and appeal of its traditional film festival.

Instead of buying an 'online pass', users reserve free tickets for any of the six feature films offered online via the Tribeca (Online) Streaming Room (https://tribecafilm.com/festival/tribecanow). Films have three to five screening windows, and the number of '"seats' per window is limited, i.e. there are limited virtual seats that online users have to reserve – just like at the regular festival. Tribeca also offers live streaming of certain events taking place at the traditional festival – including the opening press conference, the award show and the red carpet. The online screenings are only one part of the Tribeca (Online) Film Festival. Attendees online and offline can take advantage of the revamped Tribeca website to engage in conversations with the directors and Tribeca staff. The Filmmaker Feed (www.tribecafilm.com/tribecaonline/filmmaker-feed/) is Tribeca's way of letting festivalgoers connect with the filmmakers. Each filmmaker page includes the official trailer for their film, embedded Twitter and Facebook streams, and access to other SM links. This aggregation of social channels for a specific film or filmmaker further increases and supports the engagement of online users with the festival community. The website also allows the online audience to ask questions of filmmakers or Tribeca programmers while also engaging with the overall online community.

Some traditional festivals have also used SM as a platform for hosting a parallel festival or an extension of the festival on the Internet in order to enhance the festival promotion and/or engage more with the attendees. The Burning Man festival has created BURN2 (www.burn2.org), which is an extension of the traditional festival and its community in the Second Life platform. Festivalgoers create their avatars in Second Life in order to attend and participate in the online festival activities as well as interact with other avatars and other stakeholders of the festival community.

Online start-up companies or SM platforms are also initiating new festivals. For example, mixify.com streams existing music festivals and one-off concerts, but it also hosts its own digital music festivals attracting numerous online viewers (e.g. a digital event in 2013 drew 70,000 virtual attendees from 143 different countries) (Robehmed 2013). Mixify incorporates the social aspects of sites like Turntable.fm by allowing fans to 'hype' favorite parts of the mix, chat to DJs, while they perform and interact with other online users.

The traditional mass media is also embracing online festivals. MTV has launched a 24-hour online-only music festival (Live Music Day Festival) that featured more than 50 artists. Festival performances were accompanied by fans' picks, while the fans were also able to customize their experience by selecting only the artists they wanted to watch (Cubarrubia 2013b). Another example is Comedy Central, a Twitter-based comedy festival (Cubarrubia 2013a). During a whole week, comics and directors (including famous artists such as Mel Brooks, Carl Reiner, and Amy Schumer) led #Comedyfest with tweeted jokes containing the festival's hashtag and clips of routines, roundtables, and discussion panels shared through the new video platform Vine. The organizers viewed the online festival as a great way to connect with the festival fans, who are quickly adopting this new media and direct approaches in festival participation. The organizers have also developed a free application 'CC: Stand-Up' (financially supported by ads) that allows users to find new comedians based on what they or their friends have been watching. This application enables the users to personalize their online festival experience and actively interact with the online audience.

Finally, artists themselves are getting in on the act. For example, founded in 2011 by working artists, the Art of Brooklyn Film Festival (AoBFF, www.theartofbrooklyn.org) is the only independent, international festival in the world devoted entirely to Brooklyn's vibrant film and media scene. AoBFF only screens work by Brooklyn-born, Brooklyn-based, and Brooklyn-centric filmmakers. AoBFF is also the only indie film festival to build and program its own video-on-demand streaming platform: Brooklyn On Demand (www.brooklynondemand.com), where it broadcasts festival favorites, original series, and more, both online and on a Roku channel with over 10,000 subscribers, alongside Netflix, Hulu, and Amazon Prime. AoBFF is a creative hub, online platform, and showcase for independent film- and media makers in Brooklyn and around the world.

Research in the area of virtual festivals is still lacking, and so these examples raise many questions to be answered by future studies. Topics for future research include strategies for addressing competition and challenges posed by online festivals, defining and understanding the online festival experience, and identifying and segmenting the market for online festivals.

## Actors' involvement in festival practices

### User-generated festivals

The aforementioned examples of online festivals also show that by using SM, any actor (e.g. attendees, artists, communities) can have access to networking, communication, and content distribution tools for designing, hosting, broadcasting, promoting, and distributing festival (content) as well as building a community around a festival. In fact, the festivalgoer can also be one of the actors empowered by the SM to design, fund, and host his/her own (online) festival. The idea of festivalgoers becoming entrepreneurs by driving and organizing festivals is not surprising, and it is supported by several practical examples and preliminary research findings.

From a practical and industry point of view, there are several SM and web service companies providing people with the technological platforms and tools to generate, promote, implement, and fund their events. These include social networks where users can organize and promote their own events (e.g. www.meetup.com); online intermediaries, such as LiveOnDemand (www.liveondemand.com/) or www.eventful.com, that provide useful platforms to empower anyone to pitch and implement their own event; web-based software companies (e.g. www.eventbrite.com and www.eventful.com) which enable any user to get access to free set-up and other business services (such as setting up a webpage for promoting an event and an online booking and payment tools for enabling online ticket sales); and crowdfunding platforms which enable peer-to-peer financing or micro-financing, such as www.Indiegogo.com and www.kickstarter.com. Any user can use these platforms for raising money creating their own festival.

From a research point of view, preliminary findings provide evidence of the ability of SM to support user-generated events. Research shows that by enabling the rapid spread of ideas and user-generated content, SM have given rise to new forms of social movements (Castells 2009) and possibilities for organizing activism (Bennett & Segerberg 2012). Many studies document examples of the power of SM to promote and organize collective action and enhance political empowerment (Segerberg & Bennett 2011; Shirky 2011). Some studies also mention the booming phenomenon of tourism-related events that are created, organized, held, and promoted entirely by the users by using SM (Brown, Getz, Pettersson & Wallstam 2015; Hartmann 2012). In this vein, the SM empower the festivalgoers to be converted from value co-creators to festival micro-entrepreneurs. Events completely generated by users and promoted through SM have not only been growing during the past decade; they have also become more formal, organized, and specialized in certain subjects (Lee & Tyrrell 2012; Shirky 2011).

However, research has not examined yet user-generated tourism events and specifically, festivals. Thus, there are still numerous issues that are worth further and in-depth investigation. Future research can examine the motivation and profile of actors using SM to generate festivals, the consequences for festival entrepreneurship of using SM in this way, the use of the various platforms mentioned earlier (such as crowdfunding) to generate and finance festivals, and the relationship between festivals and grassroots social movements and activism.

## User involvement in festival practices

The previous discussion on the impact of SM on festivals also demonstrates that the nature of the festival is not only influenced by which actor initiates and drives it but also by which other actors are involved and how they are enabled to (actively or passively) participate in the festival practices. Online film festivals can allow goers to simply passively view films online, or they may also allow festivalgoers to actively engage in festival practices by voting on films, sharing comments, asking questions to and interacting with others, such as filmmakers, actors, and judges. Gyimóthy and Larson (2015) highlighted the need to involve many and various festival actors (e.g. festival patrons, offerings, organizers, artists) in the use of SM in festival practices. This is because festivals have a multi-relational context, and so they need to exploit the multi-actor network interactions afforded by SM rather than the dyadic communication models. The way firms can use SM to actively integrate customers into their business operations is well documented in the literature (Sigala 2018; Sigala & Gretzel 2018). To achieve this, firms have to exploit the social and networking capabilities of SM in order to convert all their operations into 'social' functions as follows: open or user-driven product innovation, social marketing and public relations (e.g. online referrals, customer reviews, favorites' lists, influencer marketing), social sales (e.g. recommendation systems based on customers' online purchases, customer reviews of festivals, and artists influencing online sales), social service (e.g. peer-to-peer online support, user- or community-discussion forums), and social production (co-creation of experiences).

Generally, to measure actor involvement in festival practices one would need to consider the following dimensions (Sigala 2012):

- the active or passive role of the actor, for example: actors viewing festivals vs sharing and discussing festival content; or festival operators collecting market research by using available online data (e.g. published festivalgoers' preferences and profiles) vs asking goers to purposefully share and discuss their festival experiences or answer an online poll;
- the number of business functions in which actors are involved;
- the degree of actor involvement in every business function. Actors can be involved in all or some of the following new product development (NPD) stages: ideation, idea evaluation, product testing and prototyping, product launch, and promotion.

Indeed, industry publications reviewing event technology providers (Solaris 2017) provide evidence that there are numerous SM solutions available in the market. These SM technological solutions enable festival organizers to develop web-based and mobile applications for empowering festival actors to participate in all festival functions, from social marketing and social ticketing to mix-and-match customized applications supporting the development of festival communities whereby festivalgoers create their online social profiles for finding, meeting, networking, interacting with and sharing festival experiences with other actors (e.g. other festivalgoers, artists, organizers, local community).

On the other hand, the few existing studies in festival technology (e.g. Gyimóthy & Larson 2015; Hudson & Hudson 2013) do not use festival operations for categorizing the use of SM but instead use the categories of pre-, during, and after the festival. Similar to the benefits sought by tourists when using SM for supporting their tourism experiences (Sigala 2017; Sigala & Gretzel 2018), festivalgoers use SM at every stage of their festival experience, in order to: anticipate and plan their pre-festival experiences, activities, and trip; co-create festival experiences (on-site or online) by participating in online discussions with artists or goers, answering and voting to online polls, generating and posting festival content; and store and share post-festival experiences for memories, reflection, learning, and referrals. Flinn and Frew (2013) suggest that SM can benefit both the organizers and the attendees as lived experiences can be constantly captured, displayed, retold, and relived across numerous SM networks. Hence, festival operators need to integrate SM in all the phases and operations of their festival production and consumption.

Lanier and Hampton (2008) have diverged from the previous approaches by adopting a different perspective for measuring attendee participation in festivals. Specifically, they have identified three types of customer participation in a festival experiences based on the degree of attendee control over the resources (i.e. time, money, and energy) associated with the market offering (from lower to higher degrees of control). The first type of participation is *co-optation*, defined as the process in which customers assume duties traditionally performed by producers, such as self-service technologies for online sales and marketing. The second type is *co-production*, conceived as the process whereby customers participate in the design and/or production of the offering. Finally, the third type is *co-creation*, defined as the process in which 'customers extend or alter the product beyond its original and/or intended form, use, and/or meaning'. Research (Lanier & Hampton 2008) shows that in their search for new ways to sustain their fantasy engagement experience, festivalgoers move from a lower to a higher level of involvement once they perceive that they have reached the peak of the activity and engagement level with the festival organizers. Findings also revealed that participants differed in their ability and/or desire to move through the stages of involvement (Lanier & Hampton 2008).

Overall, from a festival organizer perspective, SM integration is conceptualized from a business operations/functional approach. From a demand perspective, festivalgoers see the use of SM as a co-creation opportunity to enhance and enrich their decision-making and experiences during the whole journey of their festival experience (before, during, and after the festival). SM use for increasing attendee participation in festival experiences is highly recommended because research shows that greater customer engagement in co-creation can lead to higher brand loyalty, repeat sales, positive feedback and referrals, and customer satisfaction (Sigala 2012; 2018). However, research is required to refine and test these relations within the festival context in order to specify which type and level of engagement is more effective and appropriate for each of the various festival actors. Indeed, not all attendees are able and willing to co-create (Lanier & Hampton 2008). Therefore, research should investigate which actors to involve in co-creation and in what type of festival practice as well as what actors' capabilities, motivations/rewards, knowledge, and training need to be provided in order to support and ensure that actors are capable and willing to get involved in co-creation.

Research is also lacking in relation to our knowledge about the level and the type of industry take-up and use of SM for transforming their festival practices and operations. Recently, Pasanen and Konu (2016) surveyed the perceptions and the use of SM by Finnish Festival organizers for engaging their attendees in product innovation. The benefits of involving festivalgoers and stakeholders in festival innovation have been discussed in the literature (e.g. van Limburg 2008). Nevertheless, the findings (Pasanen and Konu 2016) revealed that although the festival organizers are aware of the benefits of using SM for enriching the product innovation processes, they mainly use SM for enabling their festivalgoers to participate only in the first and the last stages of NPD (i.e. product ideation and new festival marketing). The limited industry exploitation of SM for product innovation is not surprising and similar to research showing a low level of SM exploitation for innovation processes in the tourism sector (Sigala 2012). Hence, it becomes clear that the festival industry needs to be informed and educated on how and why to use SM. This can be better achieved by sharing and disseminating best practices providing useful practical examples.

## Conclusions

Technological advances and specifically the SM revolution are transforming the festival industry by forming new products and markets and restructuring the industry by introducing new players to operate and shape the festival sector. Although the adoption of SM is continuously increasing both on the demand and supply sides, the festival literature has failed to examine this transformational impact of SM. This chapter creates a typology for discussing the impact of SM on the festival industry. The typology identifies various types of festivals based on two dimensions: the place/space whereby the festivals happen and are distributed, and the actors initiating and being involved in festival practices.

The challenges imposed by these two new developments in the festival industry are discussed. In sum, traditional festivals and operators are currently being challenged by virtual festivals, even if the former are now integrating SM to digitize their practices. However, research has neither described nor understood the type of these new festival experiences and the new markets being emerged. Are digitized or virtual festivals a substitute or a necessary complementary product sought and expected by festivalgoers? Are online festivalgoers a new festival market or an existing one that has been transformed? More research is required to answer such critical and important questions. Moreover, virtual festival experiences seem to create not only a new product but also a new festival market and experience. Simultaneously, the SM revolution is empowering existing players (e.g. festivalgoers) as well as new players (e.g. crowdfunding platforms, peer-to-peer marketplaces, technology providers, and mass media) to penetrate the festival industry by generating and implementing new types of festivals. The SM are fueling the (micro-) entrepreneurship in the festival sector, but limited research has examined its implications on the industry and the festival stakeholders.

The chapter identifies and discusses all these theoretical and practical implications of the typology by providing numerous real cases and practical guidelines for the industry, as well as by identifying numerous questions for directing future research. However, change is the only constant in the technology and the festival field. Furthermore, the festival actors are continuously and dynamically shaped, but they also shape the festival industry, products, and markets. To that end, research is urgently required to interpret the implications of these industry and technological trends and challenges. Research and innovative thinking is also required to drive and lead research-based and informed transformation in the festival industry.

## References

Bennett, W. L. & Segerberg, A. (2012). The logic of connective action: Digital media and the personalization of contentious politics. *Information, Communication & Society, 15*(5), 739–768.

Brown, S., Getz, D., Pettersson, R. & Wallstam, M. (2015). Event evaluation: Definitions, concepts and a state of the art review. *International Journal of Event and Festival Management, 6*(2), 135–157.

Castells, M. (2009). *Communication Power.* Oxford, UK: Oxford University Press.

Cubarrubia, R. J. (2013a). Comedy central launches comedy festival on Twitter. Available at: www.rollingstone.com/movies/news/comedy-central-launches-comedy-festival-on-twitter-20130422 [accessed on 6 January 2018].

Cubarrubia, R. J. (2013b). MTV launches online music festival with sister channels. Available at: www.rollingstone.com/music/news/mtv-launches-online-music-festival-with-sister-channels-20130605 [accessed on 5 January 2018].

Flinn, J. & Frew, M. (2013). Glastonbury: Managing the mystification of festivity. *Leisure Studies*, *33*(4), 418–433.

Gyimóthy, S. & Larson, M. (2015). Social media cocreation strategies: The 3Cs. *Event Management*, *19*(3), 331–348.

Hartmann, D. (2012). User generated events. In C. Zanger (Ed.), *Erfolg Mit Nachhaltigen Eventkonzepten* (pp. 23–36), Berlin: Gabler Verlag.

Hede, A. M., & Kellett, P. (2012). Building online brand communities: Exploring the benefits, challenges and risks in the Australian event sector. *Journal of Vacation Marketing*, *18*(3), 239-250.

Hoksbergen, E. & Insch, A. (2016). Facebook as a platform for co-creating music festival experiences: The case of New Zealand's Rhythm and Vines New Year's Eve festival. *International Journal of Event and Festival Management*, *7*(2), 84–99.

Hudson, S. & Hudson, R. (2013). Engaging with consumers using social media: A case study of music festivals. *International Journal of Event and Festival Management*, *4*(3), 206–223.

Lanier, C. & Hampton, R. (2008). Consumer participation and experiential marketing: Understanding the relationship between co-creation and the fantasy life cycle. Symposia summary of the understanding the role of co-creation in fantasy and fun. In A. Y. Lee and D. Soman (Eds.), *Advances in Consumer Research* (Vol. 35, pp. 45–48), Duluth, MN: Association for Consumer Research.

Lee, W. & Tyrrell, T. J. (2012). Arizona meeting planners' use of social networking media. In M. Sigala, E. Christou, and U. Gretzel, (Eds.), *Social Media in Travel, Tourism and Hospitality: Theory, Practice and Cases* (pp. 121–132), Ashgate Publishing: Surrey, England.

MacKay, K., Van Winkle, C., Halpenny, E. & Barbe, D. (2016). Social Media Use in Festival and Daily Life Contexts. 2016 TTRA Canada conference.

Morey, Y., Bengry-Howell, A., Griffin, C., Szmigin, I. & Riley, S. (2016). Festivals 2.0: Consuming, producing and participating in the extended festival experience. In A. Bennett, J. Taylor, and I. Woodward (Eds.) *The Festivalization of Culture*, (pp. 251–263), Abingdon: Routledge.

Pasanen, K. & Konu, H. (2016). Use of social media for new service development by finish event and festival organizers. *Event Management*, *20*(3), 313–325.

Reidy, T. (2016). No mud but all the music: Fans flock to watch festivals online. Available at www.theguardian.com/culture/2016/aug/13/live-streaming-festivals-notting-hill-carnival [accessed on 2 January 2018].

Robehmed, N. (2013). Online music festivals: The future of EDM? Available at www.forbes.com/sites/natalierobehmed/2013/03/25/online-festivals-the-future-of-edm/#20bfdd5f60a6 [accessed on 6 January 2018].

Segerberg, A. & Bennett, W. L. (2011). Social media and the organization of collective action: Using Twitter to explore the ecologies of two climate change protests. *The Communication Review*, *14*(3), 197–215.

Shirky, C. (2011). The political power of social media. *Foreign Affairs*, *90*(1), 28–41.

Sigala, M. (2012). Social networks and customer involvement in New Service Development (NSD): The case of www.mystarbucksidea.com. *International Journal of Contemporary Hospitality Management*, *24*(7), 966–990.

Sigala, M. (2017). Social media and the co-creation of tourism experiences. In M. Sotiriadis and D. Gursoy (Eds.) *Managing and Marketing Tourism Experiences: Issues, Challenges and Approaches*. London: Emerald Publishing.

Sigala, M. (2018). New technologies in tourism: From multi-disciplinary to anti-disciplinary advances and trajectories. *Tourism Management Perspectives* https://doi.org/10.1016/j.tmp.2017.12.003.

Sigala, M. & Gretzel, U. (2018). *Advances in Social Media for Travel, Tourism and Hospitality: New Perspectives, Practice and Cases*. Abingdon: Routledge.

Solaris, J. (2017). 30 #Eventtech Startups to Watch This Spring. Available at www.eventmanagerblog.com/30-eventtech-startups [accessed on 6 January 2018].

van Limburg, B. (2008). Innovation in pop festivals by cocreation. *Event Management*, *12*(2), 105–117.

Zanger, C. (2014). *Ein überblick Zu Events Im Zeitalter von Social Media [An Overview of Events in the Age of Social Media]*. Springer: Berlin, Germany.

# 12
# THE INNOVATION OF ARTS FESTIVALS
## Concepts, approaches and effects

*Weibing (Max) Zhao and Weng Si (Clara) Lei*

## Introduction

Hosting festivals is now commonly used as a promising strategy to market a destination to interested visitors and achieve various socio-economic goals amongst local population. However, fierce competition and programme rigidity have resulted in declining popularity for many long-established festivals. Numerous studies have consistently revealed the utmost significance of "novelty" for a festival to maintain its competitiveness (e.g. Crompton & McKay 1997; Nicholson & Pearce 2001; Van Zyl & Botha 2003), but what constitutes "novelty" and how to programme or co-create "novelty" are not yet adequately explored in the literature. Evidence regarding to what extent programme novelty and management innovation could affect festival attendees' motivation, behaviours and experience is scarce as well (Carlsen, Andersson, Ali, Jaeger & Taylor 2010; Hjalager 2009). A possible reason for such a major omission is that any innovation takes time to bring about perceptible changes, thus inherently requiring a longitudinal research design, whereas extant festival studies are predominantly cross-sectional.

This study represents one of the initial attempts to address these emerging research issues. Given the obvious diversity of festivals and to ensure the depth of discussion, this chapter will focus on arts festivals only, a type of event that is quickly gaining in importance across the globe. In addition to a concise review and integration of the concepts and approaches in relation to innovation in arts festivals, a case study of Macao Arts Festival is also presented. This annual festival has had a history of almost thirty years and to date remains one of the most welcomed events in the eyes of local residents. As elaborated in a later section, this festival has gone through a few distinct stages of development, and innovative planning and management practices have been playing a critical role in that process. Therefore, it provides a suitable context for understanding the effects of innovation in rejuvenating the life cycle of a festival.

## Literature review

### *The concept of innovation*

Despite the increasing recognition of the significance of innovation, it is difficult to come up with a universally accepted definition for the concept of innovation as there are numerous in the literature which are given in various fields, at different levels and on a broad continuum in terms of scope (e.g. Baregheh, Rowley & Sambrook 2009; Morrar 2014). An important demarcation line can be drawn between goods and service products, although technical and service characteristics both be present in any given product. Innovations in manufacturing sectors most commonly take the form of technological advancements and/or applications (for example, a novel device). The output can be measured or detected by referring to changes in productivity and other perceptible indicators, thus making it relatively easy to plan, manage and evaluate innovative initiatives. In contrast, service products are more characterised by intangibility. Their production and consumption usually take place simultaneously, which means that the service delivery process itself could be a major part of the value sought by customers (Gallouj & Weinstein 1997). Standardisation rarely applies to service products because the service experience is co-created through the interaction of service providers and customers, and the evaluation of the quality (or service experience) could be highly subjective. These "fuzzy" properties of service products have considerably constrained the study of innovative activities in service sectors (Morrar 2014). Therefore, although recent decades have witnessed explosive growth of theoretical and empirical analyses concerning innovation (e.g. Anderson, De Dreu & Nijstad 2004; Baregheh et al. 2009), they are predominantly based on industrial goods and cannot be readily adapted to the service context.

Other than seeking to coin an integrative definition for the concept of innovation, a more functional approach is to develop a typology that can help identify the various forms of innovation practices (Hsieh, Chiu, Wei, Yen & Cheng 2013; Oke 2007). One notable example in this regard is to distinguish between product and process innovation. The former is limited to the outcome of a process, which is a product (good or service). The product could be totally new or have significantly improved characteristics or intended uses. By comparison, process innovation centres on the implementation of a new or significantly improved production or delivery method. This dichotomy requires three general strategies for examining and pursuing innovations as innovations can be generated by working with the final product, its production/delivery method or both. With reference to the degree of impact, an innovation can also be labelled either as "radical" or "incremental" (Ettlie, Bridges & O'Keefe 1984). A radical innovation is disruptive in nature since it could reshape the structure of the market, create new markets or render existing products obsolete, while the changes brought about by an incremental one to the product and market are largely partial, gradual enhancement or upgrading (Ettlie et al. 1984). Regardless of the differences, these two kinds of innovation are actually closely interrelated. On the one hand, radical innovation is more often than not preceded by a series of incremental innovations that form the necessary foundation to fuel any future breakthroughs. On the other hand, the competitive advantage as established by radical innovation will sooner or later dwindle to nil if the innovation is adequately diffused to or imitated by followers. Therefore, although radical innovation can advance a product into a new era, subsequent incremental innovations are still required in order to maintain the competitiveness before the advent of another radical innovation.

Gallouj and Weinstein (1997) depict a service product as a set of vectors of characteristics and competences that are linked, namely the vector of technical characteristics, the vector of service provider's competences, the vector of client's competences and the vector of final characteristics. Considering the competences of the service provider and the client in the delivery of service is deemed crucial in that the final characteristics of the service product are greatly determined by the interaction of the two players (Gallouj & Weinstein 1997). Following the aforementioned conceptualisation, innovation is defined as any change affecting one or more elements of one or more vectors of characteristics or of competences.

Six modes of innovation in the service sectors have been specified, namely radical innovation, improvement innovation, incremental innovation, ad hoc innovation, recombinative innovation and formalisation innovation (Gallouj & Weinstein 1997).

The aforementioned innovation typologies just represent a very small sample of the pool in the literature, and the authors believe that even more are being developed or to be developed. Further, not all types of innovations are equally important at all times; the key is that an effective innovator should be able to choose suitable types of innovation at the right time. In addition, to pursue innovation is inherently a risk-taking behaviour, and success never can be guaranteed (Brown & Osborne 2013). What is worse is that the effect of innovations, especially major ones, does take time to emerge. Under the pressure of achieving various short-term objectives, many decision makers tend to be conservative with respect to innovation investment. To overcome these barriers, it is important to create an environment conducive to innovation at the firm or organisation level.

## Festival innovation

The festivals sector has experienced phenomenal growth around the world in the past several decades. It also has successfully attracted considerable attention from the academic community and quickly risen as a distinct field of study. The vitality of this new economy, as manifested by the boom of festivals being held and increasingly higher degree of programme diversity and quality, suggests that there exists significant potential to explore the power of innovation. However, it is somewhat surprising that research on innovations in festivals remains sporadic and highly fragmented. The following literature review is not intended to be all-inclusive, but rather to draw the reader's attention to some noteworthy conceptual and theoretical developments or applications.

Carlsen et al. (2010) viewed festival innovation as a process of knowledge generation, transformation and exploitation by the festival organisation in collaboration with various stakeholders involved in the entire festival value chain, including programming, financial planning, marketing and service provision. Accordingly, a festival can be innovated by addressing areas such as festival management and processes, festival outputs or programme, services and experiences, market innovation, funding and festival participants. In virtue of the innovation experience of three festivals, Carlsen et al. (2010) found that despite the rising recognition of the importance of innovation for performance and sustainability amongst festival managers, imitation is still a common strategy; innovations that could provide the unique selling point and basis for differentiation and competitive advantage are comparatively lacking.

MacKellar (2006) proposed a holistic typology of innovation specific to the field of festivals, which is composed of product innovation, process innovation, organisational innovation, management innovation, production innovation, commercial/marketing innovation and social innovation. The inclusion of social innovation is particularly interesting as the term transcends the sphere of the festival and emphasises its potential role in contributing to broader social and cultural development. The evidence from a regional festival in Australia presented by MacKellar (2006) demonstrates that social capital was built up as the festival established new relationships and strengthened existing ties amongst the community. Social innovations occurring out of the networks included a new sense of place, new regional products to celebrate and showcase, enhanced community pride, new forms of interaction, improved community participation, new sources of interaction and entertainment, increased sense of ownership, and development and promotion of a cultural image.

Larson (2011), in her investigation of three Sweden festivals, identified two different innovation processes: institutionalised and emergent. The former is most frequently seen in the execution of repetitive tasks (e.g. organising a recurring festival). It is common sense that every time a task is performed, knowledge and experience will be gained, either consciously or unconsciously. Self-learning makes sure that only effective ways of performing the task will be kept in future and ineffective ways discontinued or incrementally refined. As the knowledge and experience accumulated suffice, the motivation for learning and adopting new practices inevitably declines. Therefore, Larson (2011) cautioned that a recurring festival might become "routinised" or "institutionalised" and thus require reinventing now and then. Introducing novel tasks is obviously a viable strategy to stimulate the emergence of innovation, especially radical innovation.

The significance of networks in generating innovations was elaborated upon by Larson (2009), who advocated a network perspective in researching the renewal of festivals. This study argued that festival innovation is a highly cooperative endeavour because it involves many stakeholders with varying interests, such as the organiser, audience, government, media, sponsors, suppliers and community residents. The inter-organisational network as formed by these actors is not static. To the contrary, it is fairly open and dynamic, thus encouraging the establishment of new partnerships and interactions. It is in that process that new ideas and creative solutions are created. Similarly, Hjalager (2009) applied the innovation systems approach to tracking the evolution and impacts of a festival in Denmark. An innovation system was broadly defined as the totality of factors from varied domains (e.g. social, cultural, economic, institutional and regulatory environments) that influence the development, diffusion and use of innovation. The concept suggests that the collaborative and interactive processes among the factors might contain important information regarding the driving forces and mechanisms of innovation (Hjalager 2009). The empirical analyses revealed that a festival itself can form or be the core of an innovation system that plays a central role in establishing links not only within its own value chain but also with other innovation systems.

Paleo and Wijnberg (2008) investigated the organisational output innovativeness of a Dutch music festival. In this study, the output of the festival was represented by its line-up in a given year, and innovativeness was indicated by novelty. Innovativeness could appear at three progressive levels: novelty to the festival, novelty to the industry and novelty to the world. Two aggregate measures, namely the Referent Innovativeness Index and Classification Innovativeness Index were constructed to operationalise the variable of novelty (Paleo & Wijnberg 2008). Despite the narrow scope and overt simplification of this study in defining and measuring innovativeness, it is recognised as one of the initial attempts to address the challenging task of measurement and evaluation in the domain of festivals. Unlike most of other studies that simply document individual innovations or count the number, the approach as developed by Paleo and Wijnberg (2008) further considers the quality of each innovation. In addition, the indices greatly facilitate comparisons across years and with other festivals.

Overall, festival innovation as a research topic has been limited. There is obviously a need to gain more inspiration from the wider general innovation literature, and in so doing, adaptations are required in order to accommodate the particularities of festivals. It seems that festival researchers commonly equate festivals with the product of a firm; as such, their enquiries have excessively drawn on the innovation theories, models and methods oriented to firms. However, organising festivals is most often a temporary, collaborative task; the supplier is not a single entity but a loosely formed alliance. This chapter will consider the Macau Arts Festival as just such a loose alliance of stakeholders and will consider the development of innovations over the history of the festival.

## The case of Macao Arts Festival

Macao Arts Festival was established in 1988. It had been governed and managed by the Portuguese government until 1999, when Macao was returned to China as a special administrative region. In its history of almost three decades, it has been always fully supported and funded by the government. The changes of the two governments as well as the development of information technology in the new millennium have marked a few distinctive periods of the Macao Arts Festival. Innovation and resulting novelty are important catalysts behind the festival development. Three distinctive periods of the Macao Arts Festival are recognised, and the major innovative actions of each period are examined in order to identify the festival's successful trajectory. This case study used multiple sources of information, including the festival programmes, brochures and leaflets, website contents and newspaper and magazine articles spanning the history of the festival. Finally, the authors gathered direct observational data when attending the festival.

## 1989–1999: a decade of exploration

The first Macao Arts Festival was held in March 1989. As outlined by the former Macao governor Carlos Montez Melancia, it was intended to enhance the cultural life of Macao citizens, with three specific goals: 1. to facilitate the relationship between government and cultural organisations, 2. to enhance collaboration amongst cultural organisations in Macao, and 3. to showcase the works of local cultural organisations and encourage local citizens to participate in art and cultural activities.

After the first year, the organisation of the festival was restructured. Clarifying roles and responsibilities led to the temporary termination of the festival for two years. Later, as commissioned by the governor, the festival was governed and managed by the Cultural Institute of Macao. This new organiser extended the festival to incorporate artists from Mainland China in order to facilitate collaboration with local artists. In the following years, exchange and collaboration were widened with artists coming from Asia, Europe and North America.

In 1995, the Macao Municipal Council was invited to co-organise the sixth Macao Arts Festival together with the Cultural Institute of Macao. Residents' participation was encouraged and enhanced through co-organisation in the following years. The festival went through organisational changes to explore options to better attract residents' interest and improve accessibility. The first "made in Macao" drama was staged in 1997, together with the introduction of drama performed in Patuá. Patuá is spoken by the local Macanese community and is a Portuguese-based creole language with roots from Cantonese and Malay. On February 20, 2009, the new edition of the United Nations Educational, Scientific and Cultural Organisation (UNESCO)'s Atlas of the World's Languages in Danger classified Patuá as a "critically endangered" language. The year of 1997 marked a milestone for the festival development. It showcased the uniqueness of the festival in promoting and conserving local culture, particularly the endangered language of Patuá. The 10th anniversary of the Macao Arts Festival was in 1999. Moreover, 1999 was also a historic year for Macao, when the city was returned to China and had a change of government administration. The official organiser of the Macao Arts Festival, the Cultural Institute of Macao, has changed its name to the Cultural Affairs Bureau after Macao's handover to China. Nevertheless, the organiser has maintained its roles and responsibilities to manage and promote the festival.

## 2000–2010: a decade of development

The 11th Macao Arts Festival was the first festival organised after the change of government in 1999, known as the Macao Handover. The goal, to safeguard the unique "East meets West" culture of the festival, was maintained by holding a mixture of shows and activities representing both Chinese and Portuguese communities. In 2000, with the change of the government and chief of the Cultural Affairs Bureau, the festival continued its development and strengthened its original elements, such as encouraging residents' participation, promoting community theatre and conserving the endangered language by showing Patois Drama. In 2001, the first original musical was created and staged in the festival. In addition, a Chinese Movie Week and a painting exhibition were organised as part of the festival programme. All these new additions to the festival were very well received and welcomed by the city. The local media reported on the festival as innovative, special and dynamic. Furthermore, workshops and masterclasses were organised to initiate art education to the city.

The festival's presence was further extended to local residents in 2003. An Open Air Art Fair was organised for the first time. Local artists and handcrafters were recruited by the Cultural Affairs Bureau to take part in the art fair, held in one of the most important landmarks of the city – the Senado Square. This square, called Largo do Senado in Portuguese, is part of the UNESCO Historic Centre of Macao World Heritage Site. "Audience friendly" was the approach of the festival as emphasised by the chief of the organisation. The festival was full of family-oriented programmes and appeared as a carnival for the residents. More new elements and innovative ideas were continuously introduced in the following years. Besides reaching out to local residents, the Macao Arts Festival started to target overseas audiences by producing promotional materials in three languages, Chinese, Portuguese and English, from 2002. Materials had been available only in Chinese and Portuguese in the previous years.

The Historic Centre of Macao was inscribed in the UNESCO Heritage List in 2005, showcasing the meeting of aesthetic, cultural, religious, architectural and technological influences from East and West. This Historic Centre became the venue for the Outdoor Performance Art Showcase, introduced in the year of 2006, which took a different theme each year. Resident participation increased substantially through this innovative initiative. Another result of hosting art performances in the sites within the Historic Centre of Macao was revitalisation. For example, after hosting part of the art festival in 2005, local and visitor numbers at the Lou Kau Mansion (a historic building) have increased significantly.

The festival was staged every March since its inauguration in 1988. However, it was changed to May in 2007 in order not to overlap with Hong Kong Arts Festival and recruit wider audiences in the region. In addition to the festival schedule changes, multimedia shows were introduced in 2007 together with Chinese Opera performed by trained local children. Workshops and selected performances were staged in local schools' halls. These all show that the Macao Arts Festival has been striving hard over the years to innovate and introduce new elements to the festival in order to incorporate art into the whole community, from local neighbourhoods to local schools.

## 2010–2017: the new era

The well-developed positioning of the festival in the past decade has built up a solid foundation for the festival to pursue further innovations. With the new festival director on board in 2001, another wave of innovation and event novelty has been implemented in the festival. Efforts have been steered to art education and nurturing local artists to help them engage in the creative industries. The outreach programme, first introduced in 2004, has been revamped and is more structured than it was in previous years. This now includes talks, workshops, post-conference/-show discussions, pre-concert talks and a festival corner that is a space for performers and artists to meet with amateur artists and local citizens.

In relation to the aim of nurturing local artists, half of the festival programmes have been specially created and staged by local talents. The festival has been serving as a springboard for the local art community to showcase their abilities and talents ever since. Furthermore, the seeds of art education have been sown among the younger generation: more family-oriented programmes to target parents and young children, and shows and outreach programmes suitable for teenagers are being organised and are sometimes staged in local schools. The responses of citizens to those family-oriented programmes have been very positive. Tickets for family-oriented programmes have always sold out during the first day of ticket selling.

Besides art education, the festival organiser has continued to promote the Historic Centre of Macao via hosting the Macao Arts Festival. More sites were included to stage festival programmes, such as Dom Pedro V Theatre, Mandarin's House, Ruins of St. Paul's, St. Dominic's Church, Casa Garden and others. The audiovisual mapping show on the Ruins of St. Paul's, a newly introduced element of the festival, earned enormous reputation not only locally but in the region as well.

Finally, in addition to the programme innovation, the marketing of the festival has been intensified by using online social media and oversea TV media. TV commercials have been in place locally in the past decade and were extended to Hong Kong in 2011. A Facebook Fanpage was also established in 2011. Currently, there are more than eleven thousand followers of the Facebook Fanpage. Regular updates about the festival programmes are found in the Fanpage.

## Discussion and implications

A summary of major developments is presented in Table 12.1. The type of innovation for each major development is also specified in reference to Mackellar's (2006) typology. This shows that the festival has exhibited all the types of innovation over its history, and the most frequently occurring type is product innovation. Unlike many other festivals, and even in its third decade, the Macao Arts Festival has not become rigid; rather, it is still actively seeking to renew its programme. Another notable finding is that some major developments can be related to more than one type of innovation. For instance, staging shows at the sites of the Historic Centre of Macao not only can make these world heritage sites and their cultural value better known (an effect of social innovation), but also helps attract audiences to watch the shows in an unique setting (an effect of marketing). Furthermore, it appears that organisational and management innovation only occurred in the first period of the festival's development. On the one hand, this result suggests that the government must have been feeling generally satisfied with the way the festival was organised and managed by the Cultural Affairs Bureau (formerly Cultural Institute of Macao); hence, organisational and management changes were either considered unnecessary or less urgent. On the other hand, a lack of organisational and management innovation may have restricted the festival's ability to assimilate new ideas. Indeed, being a government department itself, the organiser has the greatest possible freedom in its decision-making, and its authority has never truly been questioned or challenged by other stakeholders. Although there is no doubt about the professionalism of the Cultural Affairs Bureau, it might arguably have put undue emphasis on arts and culture-related goals, to the detriment of the potential of the festival to generate some

Table 12.1 Major developments and types of innovation of Macao Arts Festival in different periods

| Periods | Major developments | Types of innovation |
|---|---|---|
| Exploration (1989–1999) | Exploring organisational functions and possible path for development | Organisational innovation, management innovation |
| | Introducing "made in Macao" dramas | Product innovation |
| | Encouraging interregional collaboration and exchange | Management innovation, product innovation |
| Development (2000–2010) | Organising Open Air Art Fair and Outdoor Performance Art Showcase | Product innovation, service innovation |
| | Promoting the Historic Centre of Macao by staging shows at various sites | Social innovation, marketing innovation |
| | Starting to target overseas audiences | Marketing innovation |
| | Rescheduling the festival | Production innovation |
| New era (2010–2017) | Promoting art education and nurturing local artists to engage in creative industries | Social innovation |
| | Launching programmes targeting children and teenagers | Product innovation, marketing innovation |
| | Developing well-structured outreach programmes | Product innovation, service innovation |
| | Marketing the festival via social media | Marketing innovation, service innovation |

broader impacts. For example, event tourism is currently undervalued, yet as Macao endeavours to lessen its overdependency on gaming revenue, leisure tourism has arisen as a strategic growth point of the economy. However, the Cultural Affairs Bureau has not as yet formulated any specific strategic plan to take advantage of the festival for tourism development. It would seem worthy of consideration to involve the destination management organisation of Macao, namely Macao Government Tourism Office, in the organisation of the festival.

As discussed by Carlsen et al. (2010), the possible areas of festival innovation include festival management and processes, festival outputs or programme, services and experiences, market innovation, funding and festival participants. In the case of Macao Arts Festival, funding is the only one that has not undergone any significant change. This is because the festival has been organised and fully funded by the government. Although sponsors are always welcome, they can never exert any influence on the not-for-profit nature of the festival. Thanks to the sustained boom of the gaming sector, Macao's economic growth has been robust in the past two decades, and the accumulated budget surplus is substantial. Therefore, the government is able to maintain strong support to the continual expansion of the festival. The pricing has been very reasonable, without compromising the quality of programmes. Nevertheless, in recent years, there has arisen a concern amongst the local society regarding the government's fiscal transparency and accountability for the use of public funds, which may result in some new arrangements in the area of funding.

In contrast to the suggestions from Lawson (2009) and Hjalager (2009), neither the network perspective nor the innovation systems approach has been helpful in explaining the mechanisms by which innovations take place in the Macao Arts Festival. The major developments of the festival mostly originated from the organiser and were substantially shaped by the vision of the chief in charge. With resources and authority highly centralised at the Cultural Affairs Bureau, the ability of the festival's network to facilitate interactions is actually fairly weak. If the network is to become another important source of innovation, introducing more flexibility to the network structure would be necessary.

Whilst this chapter has focussed on a particular case study, the Macao Arts Festival, nonetheless, it is likely that elements of the innovative approach taken in Macao will resonate with other festivals elsewhere. However, the finding that some of the existing literature in festival innovation has not helped our understanding in this case suggests that alternative approaches may be useful in future research. For example, since festivals are time-limited, perhaps innovation in project management will provide useful avenues for research. In addition, future research should examine areas that have been neglected to date, such as innovation risk management and performance evaluation.

## References

Anderson, N., De Dreu, C. K. W. & Nijstad, B. A. (2004). The reutilisation of innovation research: a constructively critical review of the state-of-the-science. *Journal of Organisational Behavior, 25*(2), 147–173.

Baregheh, A., Rowley, J. & Sambrook, S. (2009). Towards a multidisciplinary definition of innovation. *Management Decision, 47*(8), 1323–1339.

Brown, L. & Osborne, S. P. (2013). Risk and innovation: Towards a framework for risk governance in public services. *Public Management Review, 15*(2), 186–208.

Carlsen, J., Andersson, T. D., Ali Knight, J., Jaeger, K. & Taylor, R. (2010). Festival management innovation and failure. *International Journal of Event and Festival Management, 1*(2), 120–131.

Crompton, J. L. & McKay, S. L. (1997). Motives of visitors attending festival events. *Annals of Tourism Research, 24*(2), 425–439.

Ettlie, J. E., Bridges, W. P. & O'Keefe, R. D. (1984). Organization strategy and structural differences for radical versus incremental innovation. *Management Science, 30*(6), 682–695.

Gallouj, F., & Weinstein, O. (1997). Innovation in services. *Research Policy, 26*(4–5), 537–556.

Hjalager, A.-M. (2009). Cultural tourism innovation systems – The Roskilde Festival. *Scandinavian Journal of Hospitality and Tourism, 9*(2–3), 266–287.

Hsieh, J.-K., Chiu, H.-C., Wei, C.-P., Yen, H. R. & Cheng, Y.-C. (2013). A practical perspective on the classification of service innovations. *Journal of Services Marketing, 27*(5), 371–384.

Larson, M. (2009). Festival innovation: Complex and dynamic network interaction. *Scandinavian Journal of Hospitality and Tourism, 9*(2–3), 288–307.

Larson, M. (2011). Innovation and creativity in festival organisations. *Journal of Hospitality Marketing & Management, 20*(3–4), 287–310.

Mackellar, J. (2006). An integrated view of innovation emerging from a regional festival. *International Journal of Event Management Research, 2*(1), 37–48.

Morrar, R. (2014). Innovation in services: A literature review. *Technology Innovation Management Review, 4*(4), 6–14.

Nicholson, R. E. & Pearce, D. G. (2001). Why do people attend events: A comparative analysis of visitor motivations at four South Island events. *Journal of Travel Research, 39*(4), 449–460.

Oke, A. (2007). Innovation types and innovation management practices in service companies. *International Journal of Operations & Production Management, 27*(6), 564–587.

Paleo, I. O. & Wijnberg, N. M. (2008). Organisational output innovativeness: A theoretical exploration, illustrated by a case of a popular music festival. *Creativity and Innovation Management, 17*(1), 3–13.

Van Zyl, C. & Botha, C. (2003). Motivational factors of local residents to attend the Aardklop National Arts Festival. *Event Management, 8*(4), 213–222.

# 13

# MANAGING NETWORKS OF MEANING IN ARTS FESTIVAL PRODUCTIONS

*Mervi Luonila*

### Introduction

Festivals and events form a substantial part of contemporary culture (Jordan 2016; Richards 2015; Yeoman, Robertson, McMahon-Beattie, Backer & Smith 2015). In light of the temporary and fleeting nature of consumption culture, festivals are a means of producing spectacular and immersive art (Jordan 2016) and of reframing consumption as a social activity (Négrier 2015). Festivals have become a popular means for individuals to consume and to experience culture, wherein the emphasis is placed on holistic experiences and the surrounding community and lifestyle (Bennett, Taylor & Woodward 2014; Holbrook & Hirschman 1982; Pine & Gilmore 1999). As a result of this rapidly growing 'festivalisation' of culture, festivals currently serve to produce culture and function as platforms of cultural production, distribution and consumption to a greater extent than ever before (Bennett et al. 2014; Négrier 2015; Richards 2015). In this discourse, festivals are not merely traditional practices but also extend to those sponsored by arts and cultural institutions. This occurs, for example, when arts organisations package and publicise their programmes in the form of festivals as an example of 'festival fever' (Négrier, Bonet & Guérin 2013); having said that, festivals have both directly and indirectly come to play a multifaceted role in contemporary society through their social, cultural and economic contributions (Getz 2012a; Luonila 2016a; Richards 2015).

In discussing the concept of 'festival management', the core questions are related to how audiences and other stakeholders experience and participate in these artistic endeavours (Jordan 2016; Négrier 2015) and how the prevalent development of festivals is reflected in managerial practices within this manifold branch of the arts. The literature on festival management has provided evidence of the networked structures for producing festivals and has placed emphasis on a variety of social elements of festivals, such as the resulting relationships and interactions (e.g. Getz, Andersson & Larson 2007).

The purpose of this chapter is to analyse and to conceptualise the management of arts festivals. Following previous literature on the networked production of festival structures (e.g. Andersson & Getz 2008; Getz et al. 2007; Izzo, Bonetti & Masiello 2012), the discussion of the present chapter focusses on the networked production of arts festivals. Drawing from Getz (2012a), festivals create and are attached to varied dimensions of meanings (DOMs) related to their fundamental activities. The aims of this chapter are to capture these DOMs and to analyse how varied DOMs are reflected in managerial practices and decision-making (see Luonila 2016a). This approach can enable greater understanding of the networked production structures of festivals and serve as a basis for comprehending the role and the effectiveness of festival stakeholders in festival production as well as the changing relationships in production networks.

This chapter first discusses the festival as a product and briefly exemplifies a framework for evaluating its produced networks. Second, the network of festivals and the network of DOMs are defined. Third, the discussion turns towards managerial aspects by emphasising the essential characteristics of network management in festival context. Finally, the chapter concludes by providing a conceptual basis for analysing the management of festival networks and DOMs.

## Conceptual approach: festivals as a product

In this study, festivals are considered to be a short-term, recurring and project-based way to organise a variety of artistic contents for manifold audiences (Luonila 2016a). Accordingly, arts festivals are organisations which produce a setting that *enables* cultural and holistic arts (festival) experiences, hence promoting a sense of community and celebration outside of ordinary life (Jordan 2016; Morgan 2008; see also Chong 2010). This is the basis for the creation of the festival-specific *product*, which can be comprehended as artistic content, as well as essential services designed according to a festival's mission at the festivalscape (Gration, Arcodia, Raciti & Stokes 2011). The artistic content produced in events series (Orosa Paleo & Wijnberg 2006) is positioned as the core of the product (Luonila 2016a). Hence, festivals can be considered to be product-driven productions whose contents are associated as the result of creative act (see Colbert 2007). In line with the literature on the performing arts (e.g. Kotler & Scheff 1997), in this chapter, festivals are acknowledged as products to be consumed in an act of interpretation at a particular time and place as long as the 'performance' takes place (see Figure 13.1; Lampel, Lant & Shamsie 2000; Orosa Paleo & Wijnberg 2006).

Figure 13.1 illustrates festival product and outlines the conceptual approach of this chapter (see also Luonila 2017).

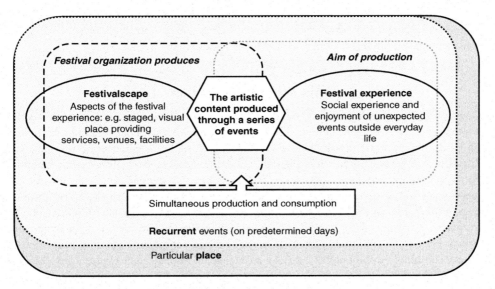

*Figure 13.1* The concept and aims of festival as a product
Source: Luonila 2016a, 82.

## Networks of festivals

The ephemeral nature of festivals influences their economy and resourcing (e.g. Frey & Vautraves-Busenhart 2003), which are also notably reflective of their organisation and management (Johansson 2008). Based on a general understanding of the project organisation (Larson & Wikström 2007), the year-round activities of festivals are managed by scarce organisational arrangements, whereas the number of actors involved and intertwined in the production of festivalscape and contents escalates significantly near the execution of the festival (see Hanlon & Jago 2014). This cyclical process might be seen as a result of the resources required by a festival form in terms of arts contents as well as economic and knowledge capital (e.g. Andersson & Getz 2007; 2008; Getz & Andersson 2010; Johansson 2008). This requirement represents a challenge for festival management, as the management must combine the essential capital and networks that would enable festival production and provide the aspired festival experience. The needs for material and immaterial resources and the temporal nature of the festival influence the production environments of festivals, which are presented in the literature as networked entities consisting of various stakeholder groups and co-producers (e.g. Getz et al. 2007; Johansson 2008; Larson 2002). The stakeholders of festivals, such as the festival organisers, the media industry, local trade and industry, sponsors, public authorities and involved associations and clubs (Getz et al. 2007), create a platform for production (Luonila 2016b; Luonila & Johansson 2016). In this platform stakeholders take on multiple, multifaceted roles as regulators, facilitators, co-producers, suppliers, collaborators and audience members, thus forming the salient basis for festival production (Getz et al. 2007; Larson 2002; see also Robertson, Rogers & Leask 2009).

Therefore, the production structure of festivals might also be seen as a kind of ecosystem that combines public and private sectors as well as market and policy logics (Jordan 2016; Moeran & Strangaard Pedersen 2011). A variety of goals and aims are clearly held by each stakeholder, yet these may also overlap and blur in the face of the demand to provide certain desired outcomes (Getz 2012b). In this sense, the networked production environment is in charge of conducting the fundamental functions of festivals, which are reflective of a complex assembly of actors and interests; such intertwined interests can present challenges for the management of festival productions (e.g. Andersson & Getz 2008; Getz 2015; Getz, Andersson & Carlsen 2010; Getz et al. 2007; Larson 2002; 2009).

## The network of meanings

Getz (2015, 20) states that festivals 'facilitate social and economic exchanges, promise highly desired experiences, embody cultural differences, communicate symbolic meanings and nourish both individual and group identity'. In the context of this argument and the previous discussion, the festival product is a concrete tool in the meaning-based negotiations (Luonila 2016a) that involve economic, social and symbolic exchanges between festival and network actors (Getz 2015). At a concrete level, these meanings may be those associated with the specific target markets of business partners, for instance, who use festivals as valuable leveraging tools for attaining certain ends, or host destinations, which seek to use festivals to develop image and attractiveness or an opportunity to enhance one's cultural capital through artistic experience. From a consumptive point of view, this is a recent evolution that can be explained by changes in the relationship between culture and society as a consequence of changing trends of social relations in the network society (Richards 2015; Yeoman et al. 2015). In that context, festivals have come to serve a variety of interests and aims while simultaneously producing spectacular and immersive arts contents (Jordan 2016) and experiences for a wide range of audiences.

In cultural policy discourse, festivals can also be defined as 'Swiss army knives' that are expected to be in agile, flexible and cost-effective form yet also fulfil manifold cultural, social and economic objectives at once (Négrier et al. 2013). This approach appears to also be true in taking a closer look at the recent evolution of 'festivalisation': festivals have become an alternative to the building-based arts productions with permanent staff (Jordan 2016) and therefore are an economically attractive way of producing arts (Luonila 2016a). Meanwhile, in the sponsorship discourse, festivals are often framed as an attractive accompaniment to marketing activities or as valuable cooperating platforms that can serve as outlets for business partners and others to obtain greater economic success; thus, festivals are now framed as leveraging tools for enhancing business opportunities and effectiveness (see Luonila 2016b).

In the aforementioned examples, festivals are framed as the vehicles of stakeholder objectives and are therefore instrumentalised for the purposes of stakeholders in their own networks. However, taking into account the closer look of the relationship between host destinations and festivals, collaboration can be framed more in terms of their social ramifications. The meanings of festivals are *shared* between a festival's organisation and host destination. Festivals produce value for host cities via intangible influences (e.g. create brand value and attractiveness) and have concrete economic dimensions (e.g. create cash flows or job opportunities). Thus, as mentioned, festivals are flexible and cost-effective ways of producing arts for citizens. In this context, public authorities are seen as the most influential stakeholder and enabler of festival productions (e.g. Luonila & Johansson 2015). However, as a result of this exchange, festivals are imbedded in and based on the locality where they take place: the role of volunteers or the ease of access to events represents multilevel influences that impact the social and cultural values of host destinations (Crespi-Vallbona & Richards 2007). As Elbe and others (2006) have noticed, festivals may benefit from stakeholder support but also contribute to such networks, strengthening public authority, for example. This process might be exemplified by the fundamental activities of festival production and consumption, which are, in many ways, valuable for host regions, as festival organisations often partner with local actors in the public, private and third-party sectors. Hence, festival-producing actions at the operational level can enhance the vitality of a city or host destination and can comprehensively affect the direction of regional development (Crespi-Vallbona & Richards 2007; Luonila & Johansson 2015).

From these perspectives, festivals are clearly vehicles that reflect identities and lifestyles and that promote valuable collaboration across communities and businesses (e.g. Bennett et al. 2014). This discussion has highlighted the varied DOMs that are attached to festivals and some of their cultural, social and economic properties (Getz 2012a), which ultimately influence meaning-based negotiations (Luonila 2016a; 2017). In production networks, the purposes of festivals and stakeholders are twofold: festivals are a way of creating added value for stakeholders, and stakeholders are enablers of festivals, producing festivals that respond to their own strategic goals. In this context, festivals contribute towards the value-creation networks of stakeholders, wherein festivals are positioned as one means of value creation (Luonila 2017). The basis for this lies in the network architecture designed and generated by festivals according to their mission; the aim of the festival-driven 'node' is thus to seek opportunities for value co-creation (see also Thorelli 1986).

However, as Johansson (2008) and Elbe, Axelsson and Hallén (2006) discuss, either the individual or the organisational levels can become the focus of festivals and separately considered because of the nature of social relationships in networked production structures. The mobilisation of resources is one indication of a festival's legitimacy and is linked with the values of respective stakeholders (Elbe et al. 2006; Larson, Getz & Pastras 2015). In

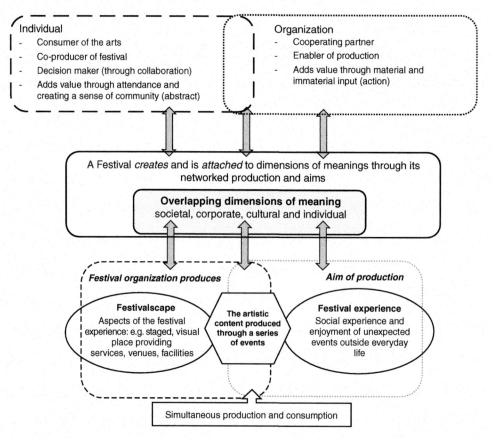

*Figure 13.2* The network of meanings
Source: Luonila 2016a, 94.

meaning-based negotiations, festivals represent opportunities for stakeholders to carry out their strategic goals but also must answer to the desired means of arts consumptions; the framing of this consumptive strategy is imperative in gaining the acceptance and the trust of stakeholders (Larson et al. 2015). The mission of a festival and the nature of a festival as a product influence the overall structure and form of collaboration with stakeholders. Hence, the legitimacy of the festival might be seen as a consequence of DOMs at both individual and organisational levels, considering that festivals are active and agile and renew society according to stakeholder interests (see also Larson et al. 2015).

Figure 13.2 shows the framework for the network of meanings imbued in festivals.

## Managing the network of festivals

In the business management literature, networks and the creation of inter-organisational relationships have been examined in recent decades as a way of enhancing the efficiency of businesses and enabling value co-creation (Håkansson & Snehota 1995). According to Halinen and Törnroos (2005, 1286), 'networks are often viewed as embedded in different spatial, social, political, technological and market structures' that result from 'a game with the partner-specific communication' (Grandori & Soda 1995, p. 195) in which the game pieces are material and immaterial resources (e.g. Håkansson & Snehota 1995). In these context-dependent constructions, informal social and cultural factors, in addition to the autonomy and the decision-making capabilities of each party and hierarchical structures (e.g. Möller, Rajala & Svahn 2005), are found to influence the roles, tasks, functions and causal power of management (Tsoukas 1994; see also Carlsen, Andersson, Ali-Knight, Jaeger & Taylor 2010; Lampel et al. 2000; Luonila & Johansson 2016). These can represent challenges to practical management tasks (i.e. controlling, implementing and developing activities towards a common goal) (e.g. Campbell & Craig 2005). An emphasis on the autonomy and the vastness of hierarchies might lead networks to be seen as *unmanageable*. However, Järvensivu and Möller (2009) disagree: 'management tasks, derived from general management functions and contingent upon networks, differ according to network type' (p. 654). Accordingly, in these constructions, the roles that different actors can adopt 'depend on their resources and capabilities' (Järvensivu & Möller 2009, 654; see also Becker 1974; 1982).

In connecting this network approach to the festival context, the related arguments found might be similar. The relationships and cooperation between the festival organisation and the stakeholders, as well as opportunities for interaction among stakeholders, are crucial elements for guaranteeing festival production and for obtaining resources; also, such collaborations are required to maintain the vitality and the innovativeness of festivals (see, e.g., Carlsen et al. 2010; Getz & Andersson 2010; Larson 2009; Luonila 2016b). The economic and knowledge resources essential for festival-specific production define the unique networks of each festival (Luonila 2016b). As Larson (e.g. 2009) exemplifies, the interaction between the parties involved in networked productions is key for developing events and innovations. According to Johansson (2008), the resources are in relation to each other, and thus, they are constituted by organising. As framed by this author, 'one element creates another' (p. 140). In this sense, the interactions within these social constructions define the uniqueness of the created networks (see Halinen & Törnroos 2005) and of the processes and dynamics that operate within their range of interests (Larson 2002), thereby characterising the network-specific managerial attributes (Luonila & Johansson 2016; Luonila, Suomi & Johansson 2016).

An understanding of the means of co-producing and co-creating festivals, both in terms of designing festivalscape and experiences, requires an understanding of the relationships and interactions that occur in the context of festivals (Larson 2002; 2009). From a strategic management perspective, as Robertson et al. (2009) explain, the presence of a complex set of actors results in contested meanings besides the pursued outcomes of cultural festivals. Larson (2002) exemplifies this by stating that in networked festival production, varied interests, conflicts and power relations define the management of the festival context. The festival embodies the goals of both involved and detached stakeholders as well as other multifaceted objectives, wherein the connections between values, procedural dynamics and outcomes are not linear but dynamically relate to one another over time via intertwined factors (Larson 2002). To manage such relationships, it is necessary to comprehend the interactions with and between parties. This places the manager at the core of such interaction: the manager holds the key role of managing and maintaining activities that are beneficial for the goals of actors who subsequently interact on the networked production platform (Luonila & Johansson 2016).

## Managing the network of meanings

Festivals can be defined in terms of their production of a network of meanings; the resulting networked structures for producing meaning stem from meaning-based negotiations and form the resources of festival production (see Johansson 2008; Luonila 2016a; 2017). In this sense, co-production and co-creation of meaning interact in order to generate the festival products (Larson 2009). As stated by Johansson (2008), the key is to get the resources 'to talk', meaning that the resources 'become a resource by being part of network of relations' (Johansson 2008, 136).

In the festival context, notions of network management are related to a manager's ability to frame, activate, mobilise and synthesise the activities of a festival, imperative for the successful production of the festival (Järvensivu & Möller 2009; Luonila 2016b; see also Ritter, Wilkinson & Johnston 2004). Such orchestration is dependent on the ability to assert influence over stakeholders and to promote *valuable collaborations* (Luonila 2017). In the case of arts festivals, the core component of such festivals rests in their symbolic and cultural meanings, and the production itself widely reflects on social and economic meanings. According to Robertson et al. (2009) and Hede (2007), the identification of the meanings created by and attached to festivals should be a major focus, as should discerning how the festival as an artistic product might serve the varied interests of stakeholders.

In this respect, effective interaction with the audience and other stakeholders is emphasised during festival production, as this enhances the manager's ability to assess both the manageable and unmanageable factors in production processes (Luonila et al. 2016). At a practical level, stakeholder interests in collaborating across a variety of production levels, as well as during various production phases, might be concreted as instrumental (activity), idealistic (commitment) or affective (emotional) interests (Elbe et al. 2006). These interests define the positions of stakeholders in the festivals' networks and characterise the network interfaces in the stakeholders' networks that enable value-creating collaborations.

In this sense, the role of active interactions within the stakeholder network cannot be underestimated. Strategically, the interaction enables the identification of possible forms of collaboration with the aim of creating 'nodes' of value (Luonila 2016a). Accordingly,

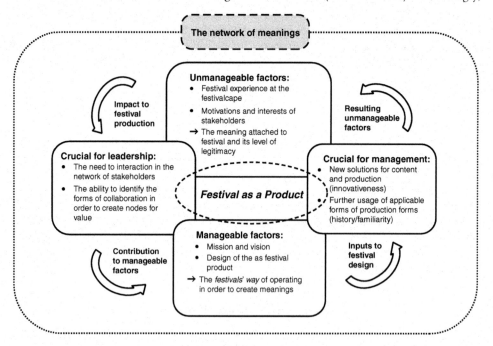

*Figure 13.3* Management of the network of meanings
Source: Luonila 2016a, 111.

interactions may be seen as a crucial tool in engendering innovation or in implementing existent production forms. This analysis contributes towards a greater understanding of the unmanageable aspects of festivals: the festival experience and the motivations and interests of stakeholders elucidate the vulnerability of festivals in light of antagonistic influences stemming from the economic climate, cultural trends and audience demands (Newbold, Jordan, Bianchini & Maughan 2015), a fragile, project-based method of producing art for audiences (Figure 13.3).

## Conclusions

The conceptual basis of this chapter is that festivals can be defined as a multifaceted platform for value co-creation that enables the exchange of the varied cultural, social and economic meanings attached to them as a reflection of their legitimacy (e.g. Getz 2012a; Larson et al. 2015; Luonila 2017). Bearing this in mind, it is argued herein that these DOMs create a basis for the formation of networked structures for producing festivals. These structures can be seen as the result of meaning-based negotiations conducted by the festival that occur on the festival production platform, wherein collaborations aim to produce value and to generate practices with *shared meanings* and relations (see also Luonila & Johansson 2016; Orosa Paleo & Wijnberg 2006). Festival management in this sense involves the management of the network of meanings and of the resources that enable the legitimacy of a festival.

Thus, the active interaction with production networks is an essential component of the management of festivals. These interactions must be understood in order to critically enhance our comprehension of stakeholders and how they 'may place a different value on a particular impact than another' (Robertson et al. 2009, 161). While this chapter has focussed on networks and network management, the cultural, artistic and symbolic dimensions of values represent a critical framework for understanding the management of arts festivals. Therefore, the unique festival product is a strategic tool in meaning-based negotiations (Luonila 2016a), and the management of arts festivals must presume leadership that comprehends diverse topics, such as the nature of art in addition to having sound managerial capabilities (Becker 1982; Bourdieu 1993; DiMaggio & Hirsch 1976) and understanding the logic of art's economy (Caves 2000; Ginsburgh & Thorsby 2006). Leadership can then foster building networks through managing relationships and interactions with and between the involved parties in order to promote valuable collaboration opportunities. To enable the festival-led orchestration of such processes, the clear mission and the ability of management to create a culture of 'collective things' and to enhance a festival's legitimacy thereby enables the formation of a valuable network of nodes across a production platform that allows for successful resourcing (see Luonila 2016a).

More in-depth research at the individual and organisational levels is needed in regard to the meaning of artistic content for stakeholders. In addition, other aspects of festivals for further study are the meanings given to relationships and the opportunities for collaboration at the production platform. Further analysis should also be based on the consumption approach to shed greater light on wider changes in the field of 'festivalised culture'.

## References

Andersson, T. & Getz, D. (2007). Resource dependency, costs and revenues of a street festival. *Tourism Economics, 13*(1), 143–162.
Andersson, T. D. & Getz. D. (2008). Stakeholder management strategies of festivals. *Journal of Convention and Event Tourism, 9*(3), 199–220.
Becker, H. S. (1974). Art as collective action. *American Sociological Review, 39*(6), 767–776.

Becker, H. S. (1982). *Art Worlds*. Berkeley: University of California Press.
Bennett, A., Taylor, J. & Woodward, I. (eds.) (2014). *The Festivalization of Culture*. Farnham, Surrey: Ashgate.
Bourdieu, P. (1993). *The Field of Cultural Production*. Oxford: Polity Press.
Campbell, D. & Craig, T. (2005). *Organisations and the Business Environment*. (2nd ed.). Oxford: Elsevier.
Carlsen, J., Andersson, T.D., Ali-Knight, J., Jaeger K. & Taylor, R. (2010). Festival management innovation and failure. *International Journal of Event and Festival Management*, 1(2), 120–131.
Caves, R. (2000). *Creative Industries: Contracts between Arts and Commerce*. Cambridge, MA: Harvard University Press.
Chong, D. (2010). *Arts Management*. (2nd ed.). Abingdon, Oxon: Routledge.
Colbert, F. (2007). *Marketing Culture and the Arts*. (3rd ed.). Canada: HEC Montreal.
Crespi-Vallbona, M. & Richards, G. (2007). The meaning of cultural festivals: Stakeholder perspectives in Catalunya. *International Journal of Cultural Policy*, 13(1), 103–122.
DiMaggio, P. & Hirsch, P. (1976). Production organizations in the arts. *The American Behavior-al Scientist*, 9(6), 735–749.
Elbe, J., Axelsson, B. & Hallén, L. (2006). Mobilizing marginal resources for public events. *Event Management*, 10(2–3), 175–183.
Frey, B.S. & Vautraves-Busenhart, I. (2003). Special exhibitions and festivals: Culture booming path to glory. In Frey, B.S. (Ed.), *Arts and Economics: Analysis & Cultural Policy* (2nd ed., pp. 67–93). Germany: Springer-Verlag.Getz, D. (2012a). *Event Studies. Theory, Research and Policy for Planned Events*. 2nd ed. Abingdon: Routledge.
Getz, D. (2012b). Event studies. In Page, S.J. & Connell, J. (eds.), *The Routledge Handbook of Events* (pp. 27–46). Abingdon, Oxon: Routledge.
Getz, D. (2015). The forms and functions of planned events. In Yeoman, I., Robertson, M., McMahon-Battie, U., Backer, E. & Smith, K.A., (eds.), *The Future of Events and Festivals* (pp. 20–35). Abingdon: Routledge.
Getz, D. & Andersson, T.D. (2010). Festival stakeholders: Exploring relationships and dependency through a four-country comparison. *Journal of Hospitality & Tourism Research*, 34(4), 531–556.
Getz, D., Andersson, T.D. & Carlsen, J. (2010). Festival management studies: Developing a framework and priorities for comparative cross-cultural research. *International Journal of Event and Festival Management*, 1(1), 29–59.
Getz, D., Andersson, T.D. & Larson, M. (2007). Festival stakeholder roles: Concepts and case studies. *Event Management*, 10(2/3), 103–122.
Ginsburgh, V.A. & Thorsby, D. (2006). *Handbook of the Economics of Art and Culture*, Vol. 1. Amsterdam. The Netherlands: Elsevier.
Grandori, A. & Soda, G. 1995. Inter-firm networks: Antecedents, mechanisms and forms. *Organization Studies*, 16(2), 183–214.
Gration, D., Arcodia, C., Raciti, M. & Stokes, R. (2011). The blended festivalscape and its sustainability at nonurban festivals. *Event Management*, 15(4), 343–359.
Halinen, A. & Törnroos, J.-Å. (2005). Using case methods in the study of contemporary business networks. *Journal of Business Research*, 58(9), 1285–1297.
Hanlon, C. & Jago, L. (2014). Staffing for successful events: Having the right skill in the right place at the right time. In Page, S.J. & Connell, J. (eds.), *The Routledge Handbook of Events* (pp. 304–315). Abingdon, Oxon: Routledge.
Hede, A.-M. (2007). Managing special events in the new era of the triple bottom line. *Event Management*, 11(1–2), 13–22.
Holbrook, M.B. & Hirschman, E.C. (1982). The experiential aspects of consumption: Consumer fantasies, feelings, and fun. *Journal of Consumer Research*, 9(2), 132–140.
Håkansson, H. & Snehota, I. (1995). *Developing Relationships in Business Networks*. London: Routledge.
Izzo, F., Bonetti, E. & Masiello, B. (2012). Strong ties within cultural organization event networks and local development in tale of three festivals. *Event Management*, 16(3), 223–244.
Johansson, M. (2008). *Engaging Resources for Cultural Events: A Performative Perspective*. Stockholm: The Economic Research Institute, SSE. (Published PhD thesis).
Jordan, J. (2016). Festivalisation of cultural production. *ENCATC Journal of Cultural Management and Policy*, 6(1), 44–56.
Järvensivu, T. & Möller, K. (2009). Metatheory of network management: A contingency perspective. *Industrial Marketing Management*, 38(6), 654–661.
Kotler, P. & Scheff, J. (1997). *Standing Room Only: Strategies for Marketing the Performing Arts*. Boston, MA: Harvard Business Review Press.

Lampel, J., Lant, T. & Shamsie, J. (2000). Balancing act: Learning from organizing practices in cultural industries. *Organization Science, 11*(3), 263–269.

Larson, M. (2002). A political approach to relationships marketing: Case study of Storsjöyran festival. *The International Journal of Tourism Research, 4*(2), 119–143.

Larson, M. (2009). Festival innovation: Complex and dynamic network interaction. *Scandinavian Journal of Hospitality and Tourism, 9*(2–3), 288–307.

Larson, M., Getz, D. & Pastras, P. (2015). The legitimacy of festivals and their stakeholders: Concepts and propositions. *Event Management, 19*(2), 159–174.

Larson, M. & Wikström, E. (2007). Relational interaction processes in project networks: The consent and negotiation perspectives. *Scandinavian Journal of Management, 23*(3), 327–352.

Luonila, M. (2016a). The network of meanings and management in the festival production: Case studies of Finnish arts festivals. Sibelius Academy of the University of the Arts Helsinki (Arts Management). Studia Musica 70.

Luonila, M. (2016b). Sponsorship thinking: A creator for collaborative undertakings in the festival context. *Event Management, 22*(2), 267–284.

Luonila, M. (2017). The network of meanings in arts festival productions: The managerial approach. In Johansson, T. & Luonila, M. (eds.), *Making Sense of Arts Management. Research, Cases and Practices* (pp. 82–91). Sibelius Academy Publications 11. Helsinki: Unigrafia.

Luonila, M. & Johansson, T. (2015). The role of festivals and events in the regional development of cities: Cases of two Finnish cities. *Event Management, 19*(2), 211–226.

Luonila, M. & Johansson, T. (2016). Reasons for networking in institutionalized music productions: Case studies of an opera house and a music festival. *International Journal of Arts Management, 18*(3), 50–66.

Luonila, M., Suomi, K. & Johansson, M. (2016). Creating a stir: The role of word of mouth in reputation management in the context of festivals. *Scandinavian Journal of Hospitality & Tourism, 16*(4), 461–483.

Moeran, B. & Strangaard Pedersen, J. (2011). Introduction. In Moeran, B. & Strandgaard Pedersen, J. (eds.), *Negotiation Values in the Creative Industries: Fairs, Festivals and Competitive Events* (pp. 1–35). Cambridge, UK: Cambridge University Press.

Morgan, M. (2008). What makes a good festival? Understanding the event experience. *Event Management, 12*(2), 81–93.

Möller, K., Rajala, A. & Svahn, S. (2005). Strategic business nets: Their type and management. *Journal of Business Research, 58*(9), 1274–1284.

Négrier, E. (2015). Festivalisation: Patterns and limits. In Newbold, C., Maughan, C., Jordan, J. & Bianchini, F. (eds.), *Focus on Festivals. Contemporary European Case Studies and Perspectives* (pp. 18–27). Oxford: Goodfellow.

Négrier, E., Bonet, L. & Guérin, M. (eds.) (2013). *Music Festivals, a Changing World: An International Comparison*. Paris: Michel de Maule.

Newbold, C., Jordan, J., Bianchini, F. & Maughan, C. (eds.) (2015). *Focus on Festivals: Contemporary European Case-Studies and Perspectives*. Oxford: Goodfellow.

Orosa Paleo, I. & Wijnberg, N.M. (2006). Classification of popular music festivals: A typology of festivals and inquiry into their role in construction of music genres. *International Journal of Arts Management, 8*(2), 50–81.

Pine, J. & Gilmore, J. (1999). *The Experience Economy: Work Is Theater & Every Business a Stage*. Boston, MA: Harvard Business School Press.

Richards, G. (2015). Festivals in the network society. In Newbold, C., Maughan, C., Jordan, J. & Bianchini, F. (eds.), *Focus on Festivals: Contemporary European Case Studies and Perspectives* (pp. 245–254). Oxford: Goodfellow.

Ritter, T., Wilkinson, I.F. & Johnston. W.J. (2004). Managing in complex business networks. *Industrial Marketing Management, 33*(3), 175–183.

Robertson, M., Rogers, P. & Leask, A. (2009). Progressing socio-cultural impact evaluation for festivals. *Journal of Policy Research in Tourism, Leisure and Events, 1*(2), 156–169.

Thorelli, H. B. (1986). Networks: between markets and hierarchies. *Strategic Management Journal, 7*(1), 37–51.

Tsoukas, H. (1994). What is management? An outline of a metatheory. *British Journal of Management, 5*(4), 289–301.

Yeoman, I., Robertson, M., McMahon-Beattie, U., Backer, E. & Smith, K.A. (2015). *The Future of Event and Festivals*. Abingdon: Routledge.

# PART IV
# Festival marketing

# 14
# FESTIVALS AND SPONSORSHIP
## A strategic marketing approach

*Gurhan Aktas and Z. Gokce Sel*

## Introduction

Getz (2005) defines festivals as *'themed, public celebrations'* (p. 21). This straightforward and three-word definition underlines three components of festivals: a festival should be themed, people should gather in specific festival locations and venues, and the participating public should either observe or become a part of festival celebrations. All these components require a series of managerial tasks to be initiated and implemented by festival-organising bodies. Such tasks range from preparing a strategic festival plan to the hiring and training of employees and volunteers. Other components include assessing environmental impacts of a festival and marketing it to potential participants. As a result, the organisers responsible for staging and managing festivals rely on both monetary and non-monetary resources in order to fulfil their tasks and aims. While a number of resources, such as the public authorities' support and income generated from participants, can help organising bodies to disburse some of the costs, sponsorship often becomes a crucial constituent of festival budgets and plans. Therefore, identifying potential sponsors, preparing sponsorship proposals and managing ongoing relationships with sponsors for repeating festivals are among the essential responsibilities for anyone associated with the organisation and marketing of festivals.

This chapter focusses on the concept of sponsorship by private organisations in festival management and marketing. To this end, the concept of festival sponsorship, sponsorship benefits for both festival organisers and sponsors, types of sponsorships and the process of festival sponsorship arrangements are discussed from a strategic marketing perspective. The chapter concludes with a case study investigating the sponsorship arrangements of the Izmir Culture and Art Foundation (ICAF), which has been organising the International Izmir Festival and the Izmir European Jazz Festival for more than 20 years.

## Sponsorship in festivals

From a marketing perspective, sponsorship is a monetary and/or non-monetary contribution by organisations to an activity in exchange for access to potential target markets associated with the activity (Meenaghan 1991). Most private organisations use sponsorship as an opportunity to communicate with their potential and existing customers. Hence, the need to synchronise their sponsoring activities with their broader integrated marketing efforts. The organisation responsible for the realisation of the sponsored activity, in the meantime, strives for compatibility between the activity and its sponsors, while the overall aim is usually to cover costs and benefit from non-monetary assistance and support in organising and planning the activity.

Festivals can be ideal platforms for sponsoring organisations to build, communicate and/or strengthen their corporate and brand images among the participating public as well as a broader audience reached through broadcasting and media coverage. Posts shared by festival participants, festival organisers and sponsors in social media accounts can further increase the effectiveness of sponsorship-related marketing efforts with regard to reaching the targeted markets. Although the impact of sponsorship as a marketing tool is, undoubtedly, determined by the scope, aim and target market of the festival sponsored, in addition to the nature of sponsorship arrangement, it is often considered as a cheaper promotion opportunity in comparison to advertisements on TV channels and in newspapers or magazines (Allen, O'Toole, Harris, & McDonnell 2011).

Another advantage of festivals as a marketing medium is associated with their atmosphere and environment. As mentioned earlier, festivals bring people together for celebrations, which, to a certain extent, lead to the participating public perceiving festivals as socialising events with pleasant and memorable recreational experiences. This, as a result, provides opportunities for sponsors to communicate their marketing messages to target markets in festive environments, where the negative environmental factors influencing the conception of the message are minimised, and the message visibility is strengthened through the concentration of people within the physical boundaries of a festival organisation. Such outcomes of sponsorship directly depend on the successful management and implementation of a festival without major adversity or crisis experienced or not dealt with in a timely manner by the organisers.

As *'themed'* celebrations, festivals also offer opportunities for selective marketing. As opposed to marketing to masses, festivals are mostly comprised of audiences sharing similarities in needs, interests and, at times, demographic characteristics. In other words, sponsors can design and adjust their marketing messages according to the characteristics of a homogenous target market attracted by a festival (Hutabarat & Gayatri 2014). While a soft drink company may prefer to sponsor an electronic music festival simply because the expected audience would consist of young people, a company producing sports outfits, for similar reasons, may opt for the sponsorship of a sports festival. Even if there is little congruence between a sponsoring company's business and the theme of a festival, some organisations envisage sponsorship as a social responsibility project. Sponsoring a culture festival, for example, would enable a company to portray itself as an organisation investing in and/or supporting the cultural values and the community development of its target markets. In fact, the overall benefits of sponsorship vary according to both what organisations aim to achieve with their sponsorship arrangements and what opportunities are made available to sponsors by festival organisers. Branding, creating public awareness, launching new products/services, incentivising employees, demonstrating corporate responsibility, encouraging brand loyalty, practising sales promotion and stimulating sales can all be attempted by festival sponsors (Finkel 2010; Richards & Palmer 2010).

The marketing benefits of sponsorship are not only limited to the opportunities available for sponsors. Festival organisers, too, can benefit from these sponsorship arrangements. In addition to the obvious benefits of monetary and non-monetary contributions by sponsors, festival organisers can engage in joint promotion campaigns with their sponsors, whose expertise and knowledge may help festival organisers increase the effectiveness of marketing efforts. If sponsors are engaged in new and innovative ways of communicating with target markets during a festival, organisers may benefit from improved experience for participants (Masterman & Wood 2005). In the case of sponsors circulating a festival programme to their well-established database, festival organisers would be reaching a vast number of people with no extra cost on their marketing budget. Such advantages of sponsorship can be valuable especially if sponsors have strong and positive corporate and brand images among target markets. In other words, festival organisers can enhance the image and credibility of a festival through the inclusion of leading brands and companies as sponsors (Raj & Musgrave 2009).

With a snowball effect, strong sponsors may induce other organisations to consider sponsorship, easing the efforts of festival organisers in search of new sponsors. The only obstacle would be the elimination of competitor companies from the list of potential sponsors, as it is unlikely that competing brands would consider sponsoring the same festival. In fact, competing companies may choose to sponsor competing festivals as a counterattack strategy. In such cases, more established festivals would be expected to gain the support of a leading company in the market. However, sponsors trying to differentiate themselves from their competition may look to other types of events, if their main competitor is already strongly associated with a specific festival in order to diminish the risk of being perceived as an imitator by target markets. Thus, organisers are forced to engage in thorough analysis and evaluation of the ideal and potential sponsors for a particular festival.

## Sponsorship process and sponsor types

Festivals range from local to international events, while the theme could be anything from culture to religion and from sports to agriculture. The overall aims and objectives of staging a festival, its programme, the experience of its management team, the structure of the leading organiser, the number of stakeholders involved in operation, the duration of the festival, the number of locations and venues used, and the number of participants expected to attend would all determine the total budget required, hence the sponsorship needed for that specific festival. Sponsorship, therefore, is a crucial component of a festival's financial management as well as of its marketing. The primary goal of organisers should be to prepare a festival budget and to clarify what resources, including sponsor contributions, are available or required to cover expenses (Richards & Palmer 2010). In order to seek sponsors, a festival should craft a carefully worded sponsorship proposal, including introductions to the festival, its organisers, it objectives and its proposed programme.

Another important piece of information to be provided in sponsorship proposals is the number and characteristics of people expected to participate in a festival. Since private organisations predominantly use sponsorships to reach potential market segments, the detailed information provided on participating people would help them to judge the potential of the festival as a marketing medium. Repeating festivals can benefit from statistics collected from previous years, while the organisers of a new festival can refer to public interest in festivals held in their locality, although organisers should take care not to infer too much from such data. If organisers can enrich the participation information by specifying, at least, the demographic characteristics of participants and their motivations for attendance, sponsors can then rely on such information to determine the overlaps between their target segments and festival participants (Masterman 2004).

Following the identification of objectives, programme and target markets, festival organisers should determine their policies on sponsorship benefits and types in line with their budget requirements. An example set of benefits, which can be presented to potential sponsors by organisers, gleaned from the existing literature, should include use of sponsor information and logos; placement of sponsor billboards or banners in the venue; space for direct sales by sponsors; provision of VIP tickets to the sponsor; inclusion of the sponsor in festival publicity; visible presence of sponsor executives during the festival, perhaps in opening or closing ceremonies; naming of awards and prizes after sponsors; privileged backstage access for sponsors; opportunities to interact with participants as their target market; and initiating joint marketing activities with other festival stakeholders (Allen et al. 2011; Andersson & Getz 2007; Anderton 2011; Masterman & Wood 2005; O'Hagan & Harvey 2000; Shone & Parry 2004).

Organisers also need to decide what benefits would be available for what type of sponsorship arrangements. The easiest classification of sponsors is to categorise them as major and minor sponsors according to their level of contribution (Copeland, Frisby & McCarville 1996). While a single company may prefer to be the sole sponsor of a festival, the different sponsor types would be determined according to the managerial and operational costs of the festival. Although sponsorship arrangements are often made on an ad hoc basis for most local festivals, it is important to form guidelines and regulations on sponsorship types and benefits for the successful management of sponsor relationships for repeating festivals.

In practice, the most widespread distinction between different sponsor types is based on the nature of the contribution, which may be in monetary and non-monetary forms (Richards & Palmer 2010). Sponsors are often asked to pay a certain fee in return for the rights to specific benefits and privileges. For festivals, where monetary contribution expected from individual companies presents variations, organisers could use a hierarchical approach as in bronze, silver and gold sponsorship alternatives. Such an arrangement would range from a limited set of benefits offered to bronze sponsors to the most extensive set of benefits for gold ones (Copeland et al. 1996). In addition to a hierarchical approach, Geldard and Sinclair (2002) identify three other types in sponsorship strategies. The first one of these is sole sponsorship, whereby a single organisation becomes the official sponsor of a festival. In a pyramid structure, sponsors are categorised in the same way as the hierarchical approach, but at the top of the pyramid there would be a limited number of main sponsors. The final strategy, called a level-playing field, denotes each sponsor negotiating a separate deal suiting their needs, without compatibility between different sponsorship arrangements.

Non-monetary support, in the meantime, would relate to sponsors providing their products and services free of charge. Examples of this kind of support would include sponsors offering catering facilities and services, give-away products to participants, and complimentary accommodation for festival organisers and their guests. Although such offers do not relieve festival budgets in the same way that direct income generated from fee-paying sponsors does, they could be of great help in the facilitation and management of various operational tasks and in the reduction of costs involved in running these tasks.

Once the sponsorship types and associated benefits are identified, organisers can then start approaching potential sponsors with proposals. For repeating festivals, the initial efforts should be directed towards renewing the agreements of previous sponsors. For new sponsors, target market congruence between a festival and its sponsors becomes a crucial factor to be considered by both parties (Cornwell, Humphreys, Maguire, Weeks & Tellegen 2006). Here, any information provided on the characteristics of participants could help potential sponsors to evaluate whether their target segments are expected to attend a festival and whether the festival could present an ideal setting for the achievement of sponsors' marketing objectives. In addition to target market congruence, festival organisers should also consider if there are certain restrictions and regulations prohibiting specific types of organisations, such as tobacco or alcohol manufacturers to become sponsors. The theme of a festival could also limit potential sponsors. Organisers of a culture and arts festival, for example, may refuse contributions from private-sector organisations, if their board members are against the idea of such organisations' commercial interests in the festival (Finkel 2010).

Organisers should also eliminate any potential sponsor companies which have negative images amongst targeted festival participants. In some cases, major sponsors may also have an impact on the selection of other sponsors, as they may have concerns over their brand being mentioned alongside smaller and lesser-known organisations. Organisations may request alterations to sponsorship arrangements or may demand further information on the festival, its participants and other sponsors. Therefore, festival organisers should manage the negotiation process carefully and should take all necessary precautions in order not to cause any misunderstanding about the festival, its benefits, sponsorship costs and payment terms. This is especially important as the finalised agreement will establish the grounds of an ongoing relationship between both parties in the future (Masterman 2004). An important point to bear in mind is the fact that most local and regional festivals are run by non-profit organisations and may lack professional staff. Therefore, sponsorship arrangements may be also outsourced to professional event agencies and consultant companies (Giannoulakis 2014).

Attention must always be paid to the timing of negotiations, whether the sponsorship arrangements are being handled by the festival organiser itself or any third-party organisations. The importance of timing relates to two factors. First, festival organisers may need to align expenses with income generated from all sources as far in advance as possible so that they can finalise their programme and start working on its implementation. Second, private organisations determine their annual marketing-related expenses during specific budget-planning periods. This may require organisers to approach sponsors a year before a festival, so that they can allocate specific amounts from their marketing budget to the festival. Last-minute sponsorships are difficult to achieve and diminish the bargaining power of organisers (Allen et al. 2011).

Following the selection of sponsors, the procedure continues with the signing of a sponsorship agreement and the ongoing management of sponsor relations during and after a festival. The agreement prepared in contemplation of legal procedures and in mutual recognition should protect the rights of both sponsors and organisers. The clauses on the requirements of the sponsorship, how each party would fulfil its responsibilities and the terms of payment and provision of services should be clearly stated and approved by both parties (Masterman 2004). It is, therefore, important that organisers maintain constant contact with their sponsors, try to correspond to their requests and help them fulfil their expectations of the festival (Shone & Parry 2004). Organisers should take into consideration that the long-term success of their festival relies heavily on securing financial resources, hence developing and managing good relations with their existing and potential sponsors. They should try to understand the needs and expectations of each sponsor and should attempt to develop relations on the grounds of commitment and trust.

## Case study: the international Izmir Festival and the Izmir European Jazz Festival

The Izmir Foundation for Culture, Arts and Education (IKSEV) was established in 1985 in Izmir, the third biggest city of Turkey. As a non-profit organisation, the aim of IKSEV is to support, develop, research and protect culture and arts. The foundation was established under the leadership of the executive chairman of the Eczacibasi Group, currently embracing 48 companies throughout the country in a variety of sectors ranging from pharmaceuticals to construction. The Group is the main sponsor of the two annual festivals organised by IKSEV in Izmir. The International Izmir Festival, its programme often extending throughout the summer months, was first introduced in 1985 and includes concerts and performances in all genres of music and arts. In previous years, worldwide artists, bands and orchestras, such as Elton John, Ray Charles, the Moscow Symphonic Orchestra and the New York City Ballet Company, have performed during the festival. The Izmir European Jazz Festival, also organised within a month period between June and July of each year, was first organised in 1993 with the aim of bringing international and national jazz artists and bands together with their fans and jazz lovers. Both festivals use various concert halls and venues across the city. The most famous of which, being the amphitheatre at the ancient Roman City of Ephesus, often used for leading events such as opening and closing performances.

In order to learn from the foundation's 32 years of experience in organising culture and arts festivals in Izmir, an in-depth semi-structured interview was arranged with the current head of the Board of Directors, Filiz Sarper, who is also a board member of the European Festivals Association. The topics discussed during the interview covered all aspects of sponsorship in relation to these festivals. Findings highlight the difficulties associated with sponsoring festivals but also provide important lessons for festivals seeking sponsorship.

First, despite the fact that IKSEV attempts to cover some of its costs through ticket sales, it depends heavily on third-party contributions. This is because the foundation aims to keep ticket prices affordable in order to reach wider audiences. Also, a series of performances like those on offer, in numerous locations and with international artists and groups, necessitates a significant amount of financial investment. The foundation has observed that while ticket sales cover 20 per cent to 30 per cent of all expenses, third-party contributions are required for the remaining 70 per cent to 80 per cent. Since there are public funds and grants available for culture and arts events in the country, IKSEV applies for various grants, including those offered on a national scale by the Promotion Fund and the ones offered by local and regional authorities such as the Izmir Development Agency and the Municipality of Izmir. Further, the foundation has also developed good relations with the official representatives of various countries in Turkey, which are approached for sponsorship of special concerts and performances by artists from the concerned countries. In 2017, for example, the Embassy of Spain, the Consulate of Italy and the Consulate of Poland all became sponsors of the International Izmir Festival.

For private-sector sponsors, IKSEV develops a sponsorship proposal that is distributed among existing and potential sponsors every year and for both festivals. The main and official sponsor of both events has always been the Eczacibasi Group, whose contribution is often shaped according to the budget deficits between the financial requirements of a festival and the income sources finalised for a specific year's programme. The remaining categories of sponsorship are partners, contributors and service providers. Partners include public authorities providing grants to the festivals and the international governmental representatives of countries sponsoring specific concerts and performances. Private-sector companies who choose to sponsor a specific concert or performance scheduled within the festivals are also referred to as partners. The monetary contribution of partners is larger than from contributors, but the exact amount varies according to the requirements of the concert/performance selected for sponsorship. Private partners (only two in 2017 for the Izmir European Jazz Festival) are offered the full festival programme during sponsorship negotiations and can decide which concert/performance to sponsor following their own assessment of individual events and their likely impacts on fulfilling the intentions in sponsorship. Contributors are then offered a set of benefits according to specific predetermined fee. Both partners and contributors benefit from their logos being placed in publications and on the websites of the festivals, and from various event-related privileges such as free and VIP tickets. Partners, however, gain further advantages including their logos being used on tickets, on the posters of the concert/performance they are sponsoring, in email messages send to around 2,500 people registered into IKSEV databank and on IKSEV's social media accounts currently followed by around 25,000 people. In 2016, IKSEV estimated that its promotional material reached around 3 million people, while 700,000 people watched the concerts/performances of the International Izmir Festival. Finally, service providers offer non-monetary sponsorship and benefit from their company logos being used in festival brochures and programme booklets. Two hotels offering complimentary accommodation to the artists and guests and a publishing company producing all written material of the festival were examples of service providers for the Izmir European Jazz Festival in 2017.

The only obstacles in sponsorship arrangements mentioned were in regard to encouraging local private companies based around Izmir to consider sponsorship, likely due to the ongoing economic crises in recent years. Despite the international scope of both festivals, the majority of the audience consists of people residing in Izmir, with the exception of small groups of enthusiasts following the programmes of particular artists and art companies. The locality of these festivals and the competition from festivals in other metropolitan areas of the country may be the reasons for this – since the festivals organised in Istanbul have a greater potential to reach wider audiences than those in Izmir, they receive priority in sponsorship alternatives by most private organisations.

## Conclusion

Festivals are organised by public, non-profit or private organisations and may require sponsorship from different types of organisations. Urriolagoitia and Planellas (2007) state the most common benefit that private organisations expect from their sponsorship arrangements is to enhance or change their corporate image and reputation. Clearly, various other aims could also be listed according to the scope and nature of the festival sponsored, and the marketing objectives identified for a specific organisation considering sponsorship as a marketing medium. Whatever the purpose of involvement is, sponsorship relates to either monetary or non-monetary investment and hence requires thorough planning and management to be executed by both parties. While sponsorship is a crucial factor in the long-term success of festivals, it could offer cheaper and valid opportunities to sponsor companies in reaching their marketing goals in comparison to other traditional forms of advertisement.

Despite the emerging research on events in the existing literature, there is still a lack of research focussing on sponsoring festivals in general. However, there seems to be a concentration of sponsorship research on specific festival types. The first group of these research looks into sponsorship at music and arts festivals. In his study, Anderton (2011) investigated the history of music festivals in Britain and noted that sponsorship has evolved from ad hoc efforts with aims of community development to a professional activity, where commercial interests are more evident. While Rowley and Williams (2008), Choi, Tsuji, Hutchinson and Bouchet (2011), and Hutabarat and Gayatri (2014) studied participant attitudes towards music festivals' sponsors and their products, Cummings (2008) examined the commercialisation of festival spaces through sponsorship from the perspective of participants with primary data collected at a music festival in Australia. The commercialisation of festival spaces was also investigated from the perspectives of festival organisers by Finkel (2010), who suggested that local people and arts enthusiasts feel alienated with the increase in sponsors' involvement at arts events. Oakes (2003) analyses the demographic characteristics of different music festivals' participants and compares them with the target markets of sponsors. Alexandris, Douka, Bakaloumi and Tsasousi (2008) compare a folklore dancing festival with two different sports events with regard to the events' influence on sponsorship awareness and suggest that the demographic characteristics of spectators may become an influential factor in sponsorship awareness.

The second group of sponsorship research focusses on sports festivals. Dees, Bennett and Tsuji (2006), for example, assess consumers' affective and behavioural responses to commercial sponsors at a state sports festival and support the argument that participants demonstrating high levels of involvement with a festival are more likely to develop awareness and positive purchase behaviour towards its sponsors. Henseler, Wilson and de Vreede (2009) discuss the impact of corporate sponsors' brand images and associations on the image of sports festivals, while Kuzma, Shanklin and McCally (1992), in one of the earliest research on festival sponsorship, elaborated upon how the corporate sponsors of a sports festival integrate their sponsoring activities into overall marketing efforts and campaigns.

In their research comparing five different festival types (music, arts, sports, market, and themed festivals), Andersson, Getz, Mykletun, Jaeger and Dolles (2013) investigate the factors influencing the amounts and sources of sponsorship revenues through the analysis of primary data obtained from 260 festival managers in Australia, Norway, Sweden, and UK. The authors suggest that while arts festivals are sponsored more by state and national grants, corporate sponsors favour market and sports festivals mainly due to target market congruence. The research also indicates that the amounts and sources of monetary sponsorship are strongly influenced by the size of a festival in terms of participant numbers and the professionalism of an organising body.

The limited amount of research suggests that there is still a need to study sponsorship within the context of festivals in different locations, at different scopes and with diversified participant types and festival themes. Differences between the sponsorship arrangements of private and non-profit organisers, the measurement of sponsorship effectiveness from the perspectives of both sponsors and organisers, and the impact of sponsors on festivals' image and reputation are only a couple of suggestions for further research in the field.

# References

Alexandris, K., Douka, S., Bakaloumi, S. & Tsasousi, E. (2008). The influence of spectators' attitudes on sponsorship awareness: A study in three different leisure events. *Managing Leisure, 13*(1), 1–12.

Allen, J., O'Toole, W., Harris, R. & McDonnell, I. (2011). *Festival and Special Event Management* (5th ed.). Milton, Australia: John Wiley and Sons.

Andersson, T. & Getz, D. (2007). Resource dependency, costs and revenues of a street festival. *Tourism Economics, 13*(1), 143–162.

Andersson, T.D., Getz, D., Mykletun, J., Jaeger, K. & Dolles, H. (2013). Factors influencing grant and sponsorship revenue for festivals. *Event Management, 17*(3), 195–212.

Anderton, C. (2011). Music festival sponsorship: Between commerce and carnival. *Arts Marketing: An International Journal, 1*(2), 145–158.

Choi, J., Tsuji, Y., Hutchinson, M. & Bouchet, A. (2011). An investigation of sponsorship implications within a state sports festival: The case of the Florida Sunshine State Games. *International Journal of Sports Marketing and Sponsorship, 12*(2), 7–22.

Copeland, R., Frisby, W. & McCarville, R. (1996). Understanding the sport sponsorship process from a corporate perspective. *Journal of Sport Management, 10*(1), 32–48.

Cornwell, T.B., Humphreys, M.S., Maguire, A.M., Weeks, C.S. & Tellegen, C.L. (2006). Sponsorship-linked marketing: The role of articulation in memory. *Journal of Consumer Research, 33*(3), 312–321.

Cummings, J. (2008). Trade mark registered: Sponsorship within the Australian indie music festival scene. *Continuum, 22*(5), 675–685.

Dees, W., Bennett, G. & Tsuji, Y. (2006). Attitudes toward sponsorship at a state sports festival. *Event Management, 10*(2–3), 89–101.

Finkel, R. (2010). Re-imaging arts festivals through a corporate lens: A case study of business sponsorship at the Henley Festival. *Managing Leisure, 15*(4), 237–250.

Geldard, E. & Sinclair, L. (2002). *The Sponsorship Manual: Sponsorship Made Easy*. Victoria, Australia: Sponsorship Unit.

Getz, D. (2005). *Event Management and Event Tourism* (2nd ed.). New York, USA: Cognizant.

Henseler, J., Wilson, B. & de Vreede, D. (2009). Can sponsorship be harmful for events? Investigating the transfer of associations from sponsors to events. *International Journal of Sports Marketing & Sponsorship, 10*(3), 47–54.

Hutabarat, P. & Gayatri, G. (2014). The Influence of sponsor-event congruence in sponsorship of music festival. *The South East Asian Journal of Management, 8*(1), 47.

Giannoulakis, C. (2014). Sponsorship of non-profit sporting events: The case of the Well-Being Festival. *Sport Marketing Quarterly, 23*(4), 244.

Kuzma, J.R., Shanklin, W.L. & McCally, J.F. (1992). Make corporate sponsorship more effective with promotional support. *Journal of Promotion Management, 1*(3), 95–103.

Masterman, G.R. (2004). A Strategic Approach for the Use of Sponsorship in The Events Industry: In Search of a Return on Investment In Yeoman, I., Robertson, M., Ali-Knight, J., Drummond, S. & McMahon-Beattie, U. (Eds.), *Festival and Events Management: An International Arts and Cultural Perspective* pp. 261–272). Oxford, UK: Elsevier.

Masterman, G. & Wood, E.H. (2005). *Innovative Marketing Communications: Strategies for the Events Industry*. Oxford, UK: Elsevier.

Meenaghan, T. (1991). The role of sponsorship in the marketing communications mix. *International Journal of Advertising, 10*(1), 35–47.

Oakes, S. (2003). Demographic and sponsorship considerations for jazz and classical music festivals. *Service Industries Journal, 23*(3), 165–178.

O'Hagan, J. & Harvey, D. (2000). Why do companies sponsor arts events? Some evidence and a proposed classification. *Journal of Cultural Economics, 24*(3), 205–224.

Raj, R. & Musgrave, J. (2009). *Event Management and Sustainability*. Oxford, UK: CAB International.

Richards, G. & Palmer, R. (2010). *Eventful Cities*. Oxford, UK: Elsevier.

Rowley, J. & Williams, C. (2008). The impact of brand sponsorship of music festivals. *Marketing Intelligence & Planning, 26*(7), 781–792.

Shone, A. & Parry, B. (2004). *Successful Event Management: A Practical Handbook* (2nd ed.). London, UK: Thomson.

Urriolagoitia, L. & Planellas, M. (2007). Sponsorship relationships as strategic alliances: A life cycle model approach. *Business Horizons, 50*(2), 157–166.

# 15
# FESTIVALS' ROLE IN BRANDING A DESTINATION
## A case study of the Barbaros Strawman Festival in İzmir, Turkey

*Reyhan Arslan Ayazlar*

### Introduction

Tourists' changing expectations and behaviours push destination managers to launch new and different products in the tourism market. Cities must explore new ways to differentiate themselves from their competitors (Zetiu & Bertea 2015). In this context, destination branding has become an important way to get a competitive advantage over rival destinations (Crockett & Wood 1999). However, the question of how destinations may become distinct from their competitors remains on the agenda. Culture and cultural events are good tools to answer this question.

The use of local culture in destination branding can serve as a good method of communicating the destination's and the community's unique characteristics (Walker 2010). Cultural events have recently made progress as destination attractions, particularly where the destinations are naturally and spontaneously related to the events. An event held in the destination may differentiate the place in the competitive market. Therefore, events play an important role in branding the destination (Zetiu & Bertea 2015). Destination managers have begun to use cultural events, such as traditional rituals of a community, in order to revitalise their economy, develop their image (Getz 1991; McCartney & Osti 2007) and attract visitors (Hall 1992; Zetiu & Bertea 2015). Hosting special events such as festivals can be beneficial not only for short-term targets to revitalise the region's economy but also in the longer term for building a destination brand (Yu, Wang & Seo 2010).

This chapter investigates the value and applicability for a specific festival organisation of taking a destination branding approach, using a case study of the Barbaros Strawman Festival held in Urla-İzmir in Turkey. Understanding the role of thematic festivals for destination branding may help organisers to promote and make a brand for the destination.

### Destination branding and festivals

A brand is identified as 'a name, term, design, symbol, or any other feature that identifies one sellers' good or service as distinct from those of other sellers' by the American Marketing Association (AMA 2017). Brand is also defined as 'a cluster of functional and emotional values that promise a unique and welcome experience between a buyer and a seller" (Dinnie 2008, p. 14). Branding means "what differentiates you and makes you special' (Milligan 1995, p. 39). Even if the brand theory is related to products and companies, it is also undoubtedly important for services (Mossberg & Getz 2006). Branding was first applied to destinations in the late 1990s (Taşçı & Kozak 2006). Destination branding involves the active management of a city's components such as tourism, culture, history, lifestyle and fashion (Zetiu & Bertea 2015). According to place-branding theory, places compete with each other for a series of valuable resources (Blichfeldt & Halkier 2014). Place branding, in this sense, is identified as the efforts of any place to position itself in competition with any rival destinations (Avraham & Ketter 2008).

Destination branding is identified as 'the process used to develop a unique identity and personality that is different from all competitive destinations' (Morrison & Anderson 2002, 17). Destination branding is seen as the most powerful existing weapon for Destination Marketing Organisations (DMOs) (Morgan, Pritchard & Piggott 2002). It is identified by Blain, Levy and Brent Ritchie (2005, p. 337) as

> a set of marketing activities that (1) support the creation of a name, symbol, logo, word, mark or the other graphic that readily identifies and differentiates a destination (2) consistently convey the expectations of a memorable travel experience that is uniquely associated with the destination that (3) serve to consolidate and reinforce the emotional connection between the visitor and the destination and that (4) reduces consumers search costs and perceived risk.

Destination branding has benefits in terms of attracting tourists curious to learn about a place's culture and history (Dinnie 2008, p. 17) as well as reinforcing the reputation and image of a place (Pike 2004, p. 77).

The intangibility and heterogeneity of tourism products and limited resources make a difference in the operation of branding in this industry (Cai 2002; De Chernatony & Riley 1999). A destination can build a brand with slogans, images and even special events (Dimanche 2002; Kotler & Gertner 2002). According to Boyne and Hall (2004) there has been a trend towards promoting regions with actual activities rather than places. According to Dimanche (2007), events have the potential to meet the experiential needs of visitors. Events also have an important role in creating and/or maintaining awareness of the destination. Therefore, events may be used to establish a bond between the destination and the tourists leading to destination branding in the tourists' mind. They can be used as a marketing campaign for the destination and as a destination-branding strategy (Jago, Chalip, Brown, Mules & Ali 2003).

Special events have the ability to create and/or enlarge destination brand (Chalip & Costa 2005). There is a symbiotic relationship between events and city brands. This relationship attracts many tourists. Thus, events may be used as a marketing strategy in order to improve destination brand (Yu, Wang & Seo 2010). Special events have the power to build a positive attitude in individuals' minds. For example, Kaplanidou and Vogt (2007) developed a model which showed the effect of event image on destination image. Jun and Lee (2008) found that if Korean students were exposed to more special events in Germany, they developed positive attitudes towards Germany. Yu, Wang and Seo (2010) report that World EXPO 2010, a mega event held in Shanghai, played a significant role in influencing tourists' attitudes towards the event brand as well as the city brand. Therefore, events may not only be seen as a financial resource of the destination but can also represent destination-branding values (Trost, Klaric &

Ruzic 2012). Where this is the case, festivals may be a strategic resource to reduce some of the challenges of destination branding.

Festivals have been described as public events that celebrate a specific theme, a culture, a season or a time of year (Getz 1991; Kim, Uysal & Chen 2001). Festivals attract tourists because they are an opportunity for visitors to share traditional community attributes. Sharing these traditions can positively impact tourists in terms of their visiting decision (Cooper, Fletcher, Fyall, Gilbert & Wanhill 2005). Festivals provide a unique part of a place. Thus, tourists may experience a special part of a culture different from their own (Saleh & Ryan 1993). According to Mossberg and Getz (2006, p. 310) 'attaching a place name to a festival with a generic theme at once brands it by product category and distinguishes it by locale'. Both major and minor festivals are important events to promote a destination and attract tourists.

Esu and Arrey (2009, p. 184) define cultural festival branding as

> a set of marketing activities involved in differentiating a cultural festival from competing festivals by use of name, marks, words, symbols, products or services etc. thereby building a positive image of the festival in the minds of the consumers and ultimately influencing consumer choice.

If destination managers use cultural festivals for branding, the positive attributes of cultural festival branding will be transferred to the destination. In other words, festivals as a brand may increase tourist visitation and, in turn, the competitiveness of the destination (Esu & Arrey 2009).

In order for a cultural festival to become a successful element of a destination brand, there are a number of environmental factors that should be considered. Besides physical attributes such as ambience, infrastructure and facilities, interactional attributes are also related to cultural festival branding. Residents' attitude towards events in their region is one of the interactional attributes of a cultural festival (Esu & Arrey 2009). Therefore, this study reports on the results of research investigating host community attitudes towards a cultural festival in order to provide a vision to destination managers of İzmir regarding the perspectives of Barbaros Strawman Festival and the experiences of the host community. The method chosen was a SWOT analysis, which shows the strengths, weaknesses, opportunities and threats of an organisation, situation and decision-making for events (Popa 2010). A situation analysis such as SWOT may be useful to obtain detailed understanding of an event's environment (Allen, O'Toole, McDonnell & Harris 2005). SWOT analysis is an approach used in the preliminary stages of decision-making and strategic planning of various kinds of applications (Bartol & Martin 1991). Kotler and Gertner (2004, p. 46) state that SWOT analysis presents a process to monitor the environmental factors relevant to the development of a destination brand.

Many studies have investigated festivals' role in destination branding using SWOT analysis. For example, Jolliffe, Bui and Nguyen (2009) investigated the first Buon Ma Thuot Coffee Festival in Daklak province, interviewing the stakeholders of the region and employing a SWOT analysis. Karadakis, Kaplanidou and Karlis (2010) interviewed the administrators of the Athens Olympic Games using a SWOT analysis to examine future strategy planning and event leveraging. DosSantos and Campos (2013) discussed the destination-branding process of Cape Verde using a SWOT analysis. Duran (2013) performed a SWOT analysis in order to identify the current position of International Troia Festival. Finally, Vladi (2014) conducted a SWOT analysis on tourism development strategies in Albania. Thus, this method and the research results that emerge will present the host community's views and feelings about hosting Barbaros Strawman Festival.

## Case study: Barbaros Strawman Festival

Barbaros Strawman Festival was held in 19–21 May 2017 in Urla county of İzmir province, South-West Turkey.'*Oyuk*' is the local name of '*Korkuluk* (Strawman)' in Turkish. The owners of the festival, BuKöyDer (West Urla Villages Associations), organised it as a thematic festival. Besides BuKöyDer, both local authorities and sponsors supported the organisation. Barbaros Village is located the west of İzmir province around 20 km from Urla and 50 km from İzmir. The village is also very close to popular touristic destinations such as Çeşme and Alaçatı.

Barbaros is an old Turkish village. There are windmills, wells and ponds in the village. Agriculture is the main source of income of villagers. Many wild animals come to the farms; therefore, traditionally, villagers built strawmen to protect their farms from the wild animals. This is why strawmen are very popular in the village.

The strawman culture has started to disappear because of the decline of agricultural activities in the village. BuKöyDer has tried to refresh this culture and send strawmen back to the farms with this festival. In this way, the association also aims to publicise the Barbaros Village culture including local foods and clothing, such as the local headscarf of women called '*boru*'. There are patchwork workshops, activities making strawmen with kids, a female choir performance, a documentary about Barbaros and various competitions, such as best strawman, local cooking, best garden, milking and water extraction at the festival (Figure 15.1). There are also some exhibitions, such as Bonsai trees, patchworks, photographs, figures made from felt and wedding chests. BuKöyDer has also published a book called 'From Sıradam to Barbaros' which contains narratives about Barbaros. All kinds of tangible heritage in the village have been used for this festival.

*Figure 15.1* Festival activities
Source: Author.

Barbaros Village, which has a population of only 300, created 400 strawmen for this festival. These strawmen continue to be on display after the festival. The festival hosted 6,000 festivalgoers in 2016 and around 10,000 were expected to attend in 2017.

## Methodology

Qualitative methods were used to obtain data directly from residents. In-depth semi-structured interviews were conducted during the festival, and direct observation was also carried out, as a way to complement the data collection. In addition, the festival brochure was used as a secondary source of information, thus providing multiple sources of data (Yin 1989). Accordingly, this triangulation helps to ensure the credibility of the research, important when using qualitative methods.

Sixteen residents were selected for interview, representing both those who actively contributed in the festival by having a stall and those who did not contribute actively. Interviews were conducted by the researcher and lasted 15–25 minutes. The interviews were informal, and the researcher took notes as the interviews progressed, as well as documenting observations about the festival and the interviewees. During the three-day festival, the researcher spent approximately 24 hours in total in attendance collecting data. Verbatim transcripts of each interview were produced and reread at the conclusion of the data collection process, along with researcher observations and specific comments of other attendees.

## Findings

Descriptive characteristics of participants were first determined. Accordingly, the majority of participants were female, married, middle-aged and well-educated. The majority of participants were stallholders during the festival (Table 15.1).

*Table 15.1* Demographic profile of participants

| No | Gender | Age | Marital status | Education level | Attendance feature |
| --- | --- | --- | --- | --- | --- |
| 1 | F | 56 | Married | Graduate | Jewellery stall |
| 2 | F | 42 | Married | Graduate | Jewellery stall |
| 3 | F | 42 | Married | Graduate | Handicraft stall |
| 4 | F | 16 | Single | High school | Handicraft stall |
| 5 | F | 41 | Single | High school | Food stall |
| 6 | F | 57 | Married | Primary school graduate | Food stall |
| 7 | F | 60 | Married | Primary school graduate | No stall |
| 8 | F | 85 | Married | Primary school graduate | No stall |
| 9 | M | 47 | Married | Graduate | Food stall |
| 10 | F | 72 | Married | Primary school graduate | Food stall |
| 11 | M | 50 | Married | Primary school graduate | Food and jewellery stall |
| 12 | M | 34 | Married | Master's degree | Jewellery stall |
| 13 | M | 63 | Married | High school | Food stall |
| 14 | F | 36 | Single | Master's degree | Handicraft stall |
| 15 | F | 60 | Married | High school | No stall |
| 16 | M | 45 | Married | Doctor of philosophy | No stall |

Analysis of the data suggests that in the opinion of local people, the festival has a number of strengths. In particular, having a strong theme is one of the advantages of this festival. One cannot find any products that do not match the theme since other types of products are forbidden by the organisers. There are also no hawkers in the festival area. The hospitable nature of residents also adds to the authenticity of the festival. In addition, the festival location is very strategic. Those travelling to the touristic destinations of İzmir can easily drop by the village. İzmir is the third biggest city in Turkey. A particular strength of this festival is the fact that local residents have increasingly been integrated into the festival plans and programme by the organisers, and there is transparency in the management of the festival. Finally, the festival has also the power to educate festivalgoers, especially children, about a village life that may be disappearing with declining agriculture in the region (full details of the SWOT analysis are shown in Table 15.2).

Besides the strengths, there are some critical weaknesses that impede the development of festival in the village. Villagers collectively volunteer to clean the area before and after the

*Table 15.2* SWOT analysis – II. Barbaros Strawman Festival, Urla

| Strengths | Opportunities |
|---|---|
| - Location of the festival (near to touristic destinations, close to İzmir province which is the third biggest city in Turkey, close to historic places) | - To be able to get support from local authorities |
| | - High profile among festivalgoers in comparison with other festivals in the area |
| | - Expand the recognition and familiarity of İzmir province in general |
| - Thematic festival | |
| - The higher education level of Barbaros Village | - Very close to İzmir High Technology University |
| - Organisation structure | - On the way to Alaçatı and Çeşme |
| - Secure and clean village | |
| - Hospitable residents | |
| - Cheap prices in comparison with other festivals close to Barbaros Village | |
| - No hawkers in festival | |
| - Forbidden to sell products that are not handmade | |
| - Residents support the theme of festival | |
| - Consider residents' involvement in the planning of the event (along winter season) | |
| - Restore the ties between farmers and their farm with strawmen | |
| - Educate festivalgoers, especially children, about village life | |

| Weaknesses | Threats |
|---|---|
| - Poor conditions of toilets in festival area | - Dilution of theme |
| - Parking problems | - Trying to sell something out of theme, not handmade products |
| - Lack of foreign-language expertise to communicate with oversees visitors | - Because they earn money from the festival, villagers may not go back to the farms |
| - Transportation problems | |
| - Limited support from local authorities | - The other festivals held in İzmir (in very close destinations to Barbaros Village, for example, Alaçatı and Çeşme) |
| - No publicity in İzmir province and local newspapers | |
| | - Residents' lack of awareness of negative tourism impacts |

festival, and although there are no hygienic and/or cleaning problems with the festival, residents stated that the poor conditions of toilets and parking area are weaknesses of the festival. There is also a lack of transportation from İzmir. More bus services from Urla and Izmir city centre would be beneficial for both residents and visitors. Another identified weakness of the festival is the lack of publicity about the festival. There is no news about the festival in local newspapers, and the organisers have to create their own publicity with a website and social media.

Public awareness of the village is impressive. Therefore, residents support the festival for their villages' publicity. However, if the festival starts to become more crowded, deviates from its aim and theme or disrupts the authentic life of the village, then residents will no longer want the festival. This is the most important threat of this festival for residents. Additionally, there are a large number of festivals held very close to Barbaros Village, such as Alaçatı Herb Festival, Love 360 Festival in Çeşme and the Germiyan Festival. These kinds of festivals near Barbaros Village may become a competitive threat for them. Another potential threat is that the Strawman Festival and Barbaros Village may start to resemble Alaçatı or Çeşme where the success of their festivals has meant more crowds, higher prices and a more touristic destination. However, residents do not feel that this is likely. Given that Barbaros is inland, and therefore has no access to the sea, residents do not anticipate significant tourist development in their village. Perhaps, because tourism and its impacts are in exploration level in the village (see Butler's 1980 tourism area life cycle model), residents are not aware of the possible negative impacts of tourism.

There are also some opportunities that could be used to improve the festival. According to the residents, the profile of festivalgoers at the Strawman Festival is different from the other festivals held near Barbaros Village. Strawman Festival attendees come to the festival area with their private car, and as such they are deliberate travellers to the festival, who are likely to want to maintain the festival and its theme. There may also be opportunities in relation to regional destination marketing. If the festival is added to the marketing campaigns of İzmir, the festival may expand and even reach international size. However, this is not what local residents want. Another opportunity of the festival is the advantage of collaboration between the organisers, local authorities and local residents. The residents fully support this festival and are even willing to host festivalgoers in their homes. Finally, the village is also very close to İzmir High Technology University, and so there are opportunities to get support from the students and academics and get advice about the festival and its organisation.

## Conclusion

Barbaros Strawman Festival is a special themed cultural event in Turkey. Although organisers initially intended to encourage farmers to return to their fields and revitalise agriculture in the village, this festival has a definitely secondary aim which is to publicise the area as a tourism product. Therefore, this festival should be seen as a tool for destination branding. The Barbaros Strawman Festival helps to differentiate the village from their festival competitors.

Destination managers should recognise that the Barbaros Strawman Festival is a distinctive organisation reflecting the unique characteristics of both the culture of the host community and attributes of the destination brand. Destination managers should consider the positive impacts of festivals on destination-branding campaigns. However, there is a risk for cultural events. If the festival is transformed into a show, this situation may mask the intrinsic meanings behind the event and, in turn, destroy the authenticity of culture (Getz 1998). If a brand lacks authenticity the destination may come up against the risk of corruption of the brand over time (Wang 1999), because authenticity is vital in order to establish a bond between brand and culture of a destination (Walker 2010).

There are some strengths and opportunities of the festival. In particular, this festival contributes to the publicity of the village and the province of İzmir. It also enlivens the village, provides transculturation, educates festivalgoers about the traditional culture of the village and creates a source of income as well. As Chwe (1998) states, festivals provide both social and economical incentives to residents to involve in the community. There are also some opportunities in order to develop the festival, such as taking support from local authorities, benefiting from the proximity of expertise at İzmir High Technology University and being located on the way to Alaçatı and Çeşme, better-known destinations.

However, besides the positive aspects of the festival, some weaknesses and threats were determined. The most recognised weaknesses are operational issues such as parking, transport and toilets. In terms of threats, the most important was seen to be a dilution of the traditional theme of the festival, should the festival grow. However, residents are not aware of the negative impacts of tourism. Increasing traffic congestion and pressure on local services are the basic problems most frequently reported by residents in the literature (Gursoy, Kyungmi & Uysal 2004; Jurowski, Uysal & Williams 1997; Tosun 2002). Likewise, this study also revealed that residents are concerned about the crowding and concomitant sense of alienation in the village.

There are some limitations in this research. This study considered only residents, thus excluding the other stakeholders of festival. Participant numbers were also limited. Therefore, these research findings cannot be generalised to all festivals. Future research may extend the participant portfolio and number with a quantitative technique. Further, as destination branding is about how consumers perceive the destination in their mind (Kaplanidou & Vogt 2003), future research may investigate the perceptions of festivalgoers with regard to destination branding. Finally, a comparison could also be made with other festivals near Barbaros Village and their impacts on the publicity of İzmir in general.

## References

Allen, J., O'Toole, W., McDonnell, L. & Harris, R. (2005). *Festival and Event Management*. Milton: John Wiley and Sons Australia Ltd.
AMA (2017). Brand Definition. Accessed Place: www.ama.org/resources/pages/dictionary.aspx?d Letter=B. Accessed 07/07/2017.
Avraham, E. & Ketter, E. (2008). *Media Strategies for Marketing Places in Crisis*. Oxford: Butterworth-Heinemann.
Bartol, K. M. & Martin, D. C. (1991). *Management*. New York: McGraw Hill.
Blain, C., Levy, S. E. & Ritchie, J. R. B. (2005). Destination branding insights and practices from destination management organization, *Journal of Travel Research*, 43(4), 328–338.
Blichfeldt, B. S. & Halkier, H. (2014). Mussels, tourism and community development: A case study of place branding through food festivals in rural North Jutland, Denmark, *European Planning Studies*, 22(8), 1587–1603.
Boyne, S. & Hall, D. (2004). Place promotion through food and tourism: Rural branding and the role of websites, *Place Branding*, 1(1), 80–92.
Butler, R. W. (1980). The concept of the tourist area life-cycle of evolution: Implications for management of resources, *Canadian Geographer*, 24(1), 5–12.
Cai, L. A. (2002). Cooperative branding for rural destinations, *Annals of Tourism Research*, 29(3), 720–742.
Chalip, L. & Costa, C. (2005). Sport event tourism and the destination brand: Towards a general theory, *Sport in Society*, 8(2), 218–237.
Chwe, M. S. Y. (1998). Culture, circles and commercials: Publicity, common knowledge and social coordination, *Rationality and Society*, 10(1), 47–75.

Cooper, C., Fletcher, J., Fyall, A., Gilbert, D. & Wanhill, S. (2005). *Tourism: Principles and Practice* (3rd. edition). Madrid: Prentice Hall.

Crockett, S. R. & Wood, L. J. (1999). Brand Western Australia: A totally integrated approach to destination branding, *Journal of Vacation Marketing, 5*(3), 276–289.

De Chernatony, L. & Riley, F. D. O. (1999). Experts' views about defining services brands and the principles of services branding, *Journal of Business Research, 46*(2), 181–192.

Dimanche, F. (2002). The contribution of special events to destination brand equity. In Wöber, K. W. (Ed.) City *Tourism 2002: Proceedings of European Cities Tourism's International Conference* (pp. 73–80). Vienna: Springer

Dimanche, F. (2007). Strategic development of tourism through events. The UNWTO Conference "Creating competitive advantage for your destination: An International Conference on Destination Management", 7–9 February Budapest, Hungary.

Dinnie, K. (2008). *Nation Branding: Concepts, Issues, Practice.* Burlington, MA: Butterworth-Heinemann.

DosSantos, E. R. M. & Campo, M. L. R. (2013). Destination branding: A reflective analysis of brand Cape Verde, *Place Branding and Public Diplomacy, 10*(1), 87–102.

Duran, E. (2013). A SWOT analysis on sustainability of festivals: The case of International Troia Festival, *The Journal of International Social Research, 6*(28), 72–80.

Esu, B. B. & Arrey, V. M.-E. (2009). Branding cultural festival as a destination attraction: A case study of Calabar Carnival Festival, *International Business Research, 2*(3), 182–192.

Getz, D. (1991). Assessing the economic impacts of festivals and events: Research issues, *Journal of Applied Recreation Research, 16*(1), 61–77.

Getz, D. (1998). Event tourism and the authenticity dilemma. In Theobald, W. (Ed.), *Global Tourism* (2nd ed., pp. 409–427). Oxford: Butterworth-Heinemann.

Gursoy, D., Kyungmi, K. & Uysal, M. (2004). Perceived impacts of festivals and special events by organizers: An extension and validation, *Tourism Management, 25*(2), 171–181.

Hall, C. M. (1992). *Hallmark Tourist Events: Impacts, Management and Planning.* London: Belhaven Press.

Jago, L., Chalip, L., Brown, G., Mules, T. & Ali, S. (2003). Building events into destination branding: Insights from experts, *Event Management, 8*(1), 3–14.

Jolliffe, L., Bui, H. T. & Nguyen, H. T. (2009). The Buon Ma Thout Coffee Festival, Vietnam: Opportunity for tourism? In Ali-Knight, J., Robertson, M., Fyall, A. & Ladkin, A. (Eds.) *International Perspectives of Festivals and Events: Paradigms of Analysis*, USA: Elsevier Press, Chapter 8, pp. 125–137.

Jun, J. W. & Lee, H. D. (2008). Impacts of events on the brand Germany: Perspectives from younger Korean consumers, *Event Management, 11*(3), 145–153.

Jurowski, C., Uysal, M. & Williams, R. D. (1997). A theoretical analysis of host community resident recreations to tourism, *Journal of Travel Research, 36*(2), 3–11.

Kaplanidou, K. & Vogt, C. (2003). *Destination Branding: Concept and Measurement*, Working Paper Michigan State University – Michigan State University, Department of Park, Recreation and Tourism Resources, August.

Kaplanidou, K. & Vogt, C. (2007). The interrelationship between sport event and destination image and sport tourists' behaviors, *Journal of Sport & Tourism, 12*(3–4), 183–206.

Karadakis, K., Kaplanidou, K. & Karlis, G. (2010). Event leveraging of mega sport events: A SWOT analysis approach, *International Journal of Event and Festival Management, 1*(3), 170–185.

Kim, K., Uysal, M. & Chen, J. (2001). Festival visitor motivation from the organizers' point of view, *Event Management, 7*(2), 127–134.

Kotler, P. & Gertner, D. (2002). Country as brand, product, and beyond: A place marketing and brand management perspective, *Journal of Brand Management, 9*(4–5), 249–261.

Kotler, P. & Gertner, D. (2004). Country as brand, product and beyond: A place marketing and brand management perspective. In Morgan, N., Pritchard, A. and Pride, R. (Eds.) *Destination Branding: Creating the Unique Destination Proposition.* Massachusetts: Elsevier Butterworth-Heinemann.

McCartney, G. & Osti, L. (2007). From cultural events to sport events: A case study of cultural authenticity in the Dragon Boat Races, *Journal of Sport & Tourism, 12*(1), 25–40.

Milligan, J. W. (1995). Are banks ready for product branding? *United States Banker, 105*(4), 39–41.

Morgan, N., Pritchard, A. & Piggott, R. (2002). New Zealand, 100% pure: The creation of a powerful niche destination brand, *Journal of Brand Management, 9*(4–5), 335–354.

Morrison, A. M. & Anderson, D. J. (2002). Destination branding, Paper presented at the *Missouri Association of Convention and Visitor Bureaus Annual Meeting*, June 10. Missouri, USA.

Mossberg, L. & Getz, D. (2006). Stakeholder influences on the ownership and management of festival brands, *Scandinavian Journal of Hospitality and Tourism*, *6*(4), 308–326.

Pike, S. (2004). *Destination Marketing Organizations*. United Kingdom: Elsevier.

Popa, N. V. (2010). Romanian universities SWOT analysis, latest trends on engineering education, www.wseas.us/e-library/conferences/2010/Corfu/EDUCATION/EDUCATION-39.pdf pp. 233–236. Accessed 21/12/2017.

Saleh, F. & Ryan, C. (1993). Jazz and knitwear: Factors that attract tourists to festivals, *Tourism Management*, *14*(4), 289–297.

Taşçı, A. D. A. & Kozak, M. (2006). Destination brands vs destination images: Do we know what we mean? *Journal of Vacation Marketing*, *12*(4), 299–317.

Tosun, C. (2002). Host perceptions of impacts: A comparative tourism study, *Annals of Tourism Research*, *29*(1), 231–245.

Trost, K., Klaric, S. & Ruzic, M. D. (2012). Events as a framework for tourist destination branding: Case studies of two cultural events in Croatia, *TURIZAM*, *16*(2), 65–77.

Vladi, E. (2014). Tourism development strategies, SWOT analysis and improvement of Albania's image, *European Journal of Sustainable Development*, *3*(1), 167–178.

Walker, M. (2010). Cities as creative spaces for cultural tourism: A plea for the consideration of history, *Pasos – Revista de Turismo y Patrimonio Cultural*, *8*(3), 17–26.

Wang, N. (1999). Rethinking authenticity in tourism experience, *Annual of Tourism Research*, *26*(2), 349–370.

Yin, R. K. (1989). *Case Study Research: Design and Methods*. Newbury Park, CA: Sage.

Yu, L., Wang, C. & Seo, J. (2010). Mega event and destination brand: 2010 Shanghai Expo, *International Journal of Event and Festival Management*, *3*(1), 46–65.

Zetiu, A.-M. & Bertea, P. (2015). How a tourist destination may become a brand by means of events: A case study on Iasi as a candidate for European Cultural Capital 2021. In Pascariu, G. C., Tiganasu, R., Incaltarau, C. & Simionov, L. M. (Eds.) The Conference Proceeding of *Regional Development and Integration* (pp. 387–403). Editura University: Bucharest.

# 16
# BRANDING CULTURAL EVENTS USING EXTERNAL REFERENCE POINTS
## Cervantes and the Festival Internacional Cervantino, Mexico

*Daniel Barrera-Fernández, Marco Hernández-Escampa and Antonia Balbuena Vázquez*

### Introduction

Festivals and cultural events are an important part of the rising trend towards cultural tourism, not least because they motivate repeat visits, something particularly difficult for cultural tourism attractions. Furthermore, the wide benefits of events make them rival in importance with built heritage and cultural facilities since they are more flexible than some types of facilities, they normally cost less, they have stronger impact in the short term and they help differentiate urban spaces. In addition to these reasons, there is increasing interest in hosting cultural events thanks to their positive contribution to local marketing strategies.

Tourists make intense and short-term use of a very limited number of heritage assets and cultural attractions, including material and non-material ones. The reason is to be found in the fact that tourist experience in cities is measured in days and hours, even in minutes in the case of cultural attractions or seconds in particular sites. In addition, cultural tourists do not often repeat their visit to the same place, and therefore they are continuously looking for new attractions (Ben-Dalia, Collins-Kreiner & Churchman 2013). As a result of this, a process of selection of cultural assets takes place since only a few buildings and only a small number of social representations are able to be adapted to the tourist visit. The main difference between the selection of cultural assets made for locals and the one made for tourists is that in the second case, only a small choice is made among the largest, most spectacular and unique resources.

As Gunay (2008) points out, the tourist use of local culture and heritage can serve to reinforce local identity. However, when interest from the tourism industry is exclusively economic, the values of showcasing the culture and legacy of a social group are lost and only the most relevant elements of culture are promoted for tourists, always with the aim of achieving the maximum economic profit. As a result, when the selection of heritage assets and cultural representations made by and for tourists and locals differ significantly, conflict can arise not only in the choice of resources but also in their interpretation and use. This situation occurs especially when locals and visitors are from very different cultural backgrounds or when relatively recent cultural representations are considered (Ashworth & Larkham 1994).

This chapter will present a case study of the Festival Internacional Cervantino in Guanajuato, Mexico, to demonstrate how a city can use an event based on a character that has no factual or historical links to the city as part of its branding strategy. In this case, Cervantes and Don Quixote ended up inserted in the collective identity, contributing a new component to the traditional social representation about the city.

## Background

### Cultural selection and the role of events in city marketing and in the creation of a city's brand

In the global context, cities become an image to be transmitted to local residents and potential tourists and investors (Llovet Rodríguez 2011). The creation of new events and attractions, the improvement of the public services and urban landscapes, and the increase in local promotion brought about by cultural tourism assist with the dissemination of a new city image. In many cases, thanks to being the host of cultural events, a city starts to develop links with values widely considered as positive such as cosmopolitanism and tolerance. In the construction of that image, a city makes use of all available resources, seeking both differentiation and association with the most successful models of the global economy.

In order to create a seductive image that brings the desired status, a few elements are usually selected to design logos and mottos, which can be material, such as built heritage, infrastructures or iconic architecture (Law 1996; Maitland 2010). Nevertheless, in order to be competitive, non-material assets also play a leading role, such as identity referents, attractive ways of life and cultural values, since they help differentiating cities that were traditionally represented by similar buildings or urban spaces. Heritage also helps to differentiate cities, giving them authenticity, connection to the place and to local history (Burtenshaw, Bateman & Ashworth 1991; Heritage Counts 2012). To do so, a focus on a topic or a historical period is created, with which the city as a whole is then identified. As a result, a more intense heritage selection process can arise, which can make local people feel unrepresented. Uniformity is sought to reinforce the principles of authenticity and singularity, and to differentiate between similar cities. In the process, however, complexity is reduced to the simple idea that is to be transmitted to visitors. Simplification particularly affects historic centres, which, as symbolic of the city's identity, are transformed into an icon of the whole city to clearly respond to the projected image.

Where it is focussed on non-material aspects, city marketing makes use of values transmitted by culture, which go beyond their function as attractions to the city and contribute to make public spaces vibrant (Rifkin 2001). According to Zukin (1996), culture suggests a brand's coherence and consistency and strengthens local uniqueness, and promoting a city as 'cultural' creates less opposition than other values such as multiculturalism (Kavaratzis 2005), currently contested in certain places.

When designing marketing strategies, many cities decide to promote themselves through a brand. Creating a brand is useful to strengthen a city's external image, and it is one of the most influential factors at the time of choosing a destination (Correia, Kozak & Ferradeira 2011). Moreover, a brand gives a certain order and coherence to the complex reality of a city, making it easier to 'read' the place. In order to decide which brand best suits a city, normally a topic is chosen. Public administration, cultural institutions and businesses tend to be involved in the choice of the topic, but it is necessary to include citizens' participation to make the brand long lasting (Lichrou, O'Malley & Patterson 2010), since branding through a topic without the agreement of local people would generate an imposed identity. Although branding has proven as a powerful way to differentiate relatively similar cities from each other and as a source of collective identity, it entails the risk of reducing local society to a few messages easily embraceable by visitors, leaving aside the variety and contradictions of local culture (Eshuis & Edwards 2013).

In some events that are held periodically, the event brand value is more powerful than that of the city itself, as in the case of European Capital of Culture, where the brand has eclipsed individual hosting cities. In other cases, the event brand and the city brand feed each other. The case of the 1992 Olympic Games in Barcelona is considered successful in this sense (Richards & Wilson 2007). In order to develop a successful co-branding between the event and the city, events become the creators of meanings and the core of the city's image, and they dominate the city's public life (Richards & Palmer 2010). The case of Guanajuato and the Festival Internacional Cervantino can be considered as co-branding, since the cultural identity of the city is now intrinsically linked with the festival. The link of Guanajuato with Cervantes has gone beyond tourism-related sources and has become omnipresent in public spaces and in the perception of locals and visitors about the city.

## Guanajuato and the Festival Internacional Cervantino

### Guanajuato

The city of Guanajuato, capital of the state of the same name, is located in central Mexico, 360 km north from Mexico City. It is a semi-arid area. The city has 184,239 inhabitants (Instituto Nacional de Geografía y Estadística 2016) and is the sixth-largest city in number of inhabitants in the state. Focussing on the history of the city, the remains of pre-Hispanic origin are relatively scarce in the site. It was not until colonial times that the discovery of the mineral wealth of its mountains led to a stable urban settlement. Mining gave great splendour to the city, which became the world's largest producer of silver during the 18th century. Mining remains a relevant activity in the local economy, although its previous preponderance has been surpassed by other sectors such as tourism, public administration and the university (García 2007).

The prosperity brought by mining left an important legacy in Guanajuato in the form of monuments, which today are the most recognisable icons of the city, including the *Basílica Colegiata de Nuestra Señora de Guanajuato* and the churches of *La Valenciana, La Compañía* and *San Roque*. Apart from mining, another important historical fact was the participation of Guanajuato in the Mexican independence, symbolised in the *Alhóndiga de Granaditas*, where an important battle occurred. This rich heritage of the silver mines along with the technological innovations that were produced and the quality of its monuments resulted in the inclusion of Guanajuato in UNESCO's World Heritage List in 1988.

### Festival Internacional Cervantino

As mentioned, the economy of Guanajuato has diversified in recent decades, and tourism, especially cultural tourism, is an important source of income. In 2015, over 2.2 million people visited the city (around 795,000 of them stayed overnight) and spent over 6.3 million pesos in the local economy (US$330,000) (Guanajuato State Government 2015). The main attraction of the city in terms of number of visitors and external impact is the Festival Internacional

Cervantino. In 2016, 478,710 people attended the festival (Guanajuato State Government 2016). It takes place every year and is currently considered one of the most important cultural events in Latin America. In this chapter, the 2015 festival has been used as a case study. More than 400 activities took place, including concerts, performances, theatre and exhibitions in both open-air and indoor venues. Outdoor activities are free and aimed at a wider audience, while those held indoors are focussed on new artistic trends and a more specialised audience. Although most of the activities take place in the centre of the city, in recent years there has been an effort to extend the activities to neighbourhoods of the periphery and to other municipalities of the state (Barrera-Fernández & Hernández-Escampa 2017a).

The origins of the festival go back to 1953 with the performance of the *Entremeses of Cervantes* organised by Enrique Ruelas. The success was immediate and was repeated every year until the festival was formally established in 1972 (Noticiero del Servicio Exterior Mexicano 2013). Many cities around the world have traditionally represented the works of Miguel de Cervantes, but the case of Guanajuato is particular because over the years it became a city centred on the figure of the author, despite having no historical connection with him. The success of the first performances drew attention to Cervantes, and the formal establishment of the festival only reinforced it. As a result, Cervantes is today represented in the most symbolic places of the city through sculptures, statues and urban art in general and street names. In addition, a museum devoted to Don Quixote and related works was opened. Furthermore, conferences are regularly held, books are presented and diverse activities are organised on topics related to the author by the university and the city council. As a result, the wide acceptance of the Guanajuato-Cervantes binomial was recognised with the rebranding of the city as '*Capital Cervantina de América*' (America's Capital associated with Cervantes) (Figure 16.1).

The urban presence of Cervantes in the streets of Guanajuato rivals in importance that of the city's most famous son: the world-famous muralist Diego Rivera. Another prominent character of the city is Pípila, a hero of Mexican independence, who is represented in a large statue crowning a hill and facing the city centre. However, other famous characters related to the city, such as the writer Jorge Ibargüengoitia, do not have the same urban presence and are not as well known by either locals or visitors.

With regard to the organisation of the Festival Internacional Cervantino, the Department of Foreign Affairs, the Department of Tourism and the National Institute of Fine Arts were responsible when it was initially set up (Guanajuato State Government 2008). The first festivals were not held in the historic centre, but in the Cata mining site, in the suburbs, in recognition of the historical importance that mining had in Guanajuato. In 1976, four years after the official establishment of the festival, a federal decree decided upon the organisational structure that has been maintained to this day with only minor changes. The federal government took charge of the organisation, and the president of the republic directly elects the president of the committee (Diario Oficial de la Federación 1976). Today, representatives of all levels of government participate in the organisation: the National Council for Culture and Arts at the federal level, the State of Guanajuato's Institute for Culture at the state level and the City Council of Guanajuato at the local level. The University of Guanajuato also participates in the organisation (Festival Internacional Cervantino 2015).

As can be seen in this brief contextual discussion, the main theme of the Festival Internacional Cervantino is based on a figure that is completely alien to the city but has nonetheless ended up inserted in the collective identity, contributing a new component to the traditional social representation around mining. This is what makes this case study particularly interesting.

*Figure 16.1* Statue devoted to Don Quixote in Guanajuato
Source: The authors.

## Methods

The co-branding of Guanajuato-Cervantes is widely accepted and is encouraged in the tourism industry. This co-branding has its core representation in the Festival Internacional Cervantino, but it has also appeared in other parts of the city's branding, as happens in many cases of identification of a city with an author, such as Salzburg with Mozart (Ashworth 2005), Stratford-upon-Avon with Shakespeare (Herstein & Berger 2014) and Malaga with Picasso (Barrera-Fernández & Hernández-Escampa 2017b). However, these examples have a historical, biographical or artistic relationship between the city and the artist. What makes the case of Guanajuato special is the lack of that direct connection. The objective of the research was to analyse the impact of the Festival Internacional Cervantino and related cultural and tourism strategies in the consolidation of the co-branding of Guanajuato-Cervantes. To address this objective, a mixed methodology was developed based on fieldwork to identify where the references to Cervantes are located and what type they are. Questionnaires were presented to visitors and locals, and written sources from the official tourist administration were analysed.

## Cultural events using reference points

Questionnaires were presented to attendees at the Festival Internacional Cervantino during the 2015 festival. In all, 206 questionnaires were collected (31% from residents in Guanajuato City, 23% from people living in other localities in the state, 32% from people from other Mexican states and 13% from people from abroad). Fieldwork was undertaken to identify the urban presence of Cervantes-related references. References to the author himself, to his works, especially to Don Quixote and to the Festival Internacional Cervantino, were included. Photographs of these spaces were also taken, and the result was presented in a map, identifying sculptures, public art, street names and cultural buildings (Figure 16.2).

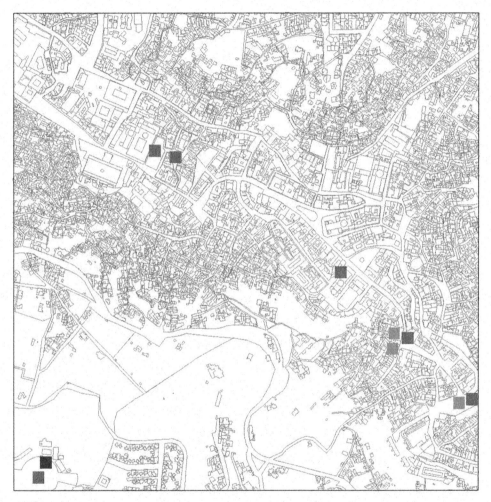

■ Cultural buildings (Quixote Museum, Cervantes Theatre and Cervantine Library)
■ Statues and sculptures
■ Street names

*Figure 16.2* References to Cervantes in Guanajuato
Source: The authors.

Written sources from the official tourist administration include tourist profile surveys to the festival (Guanajuato State Government 2014; Guanajuato State Government 2015, Guanajuato State Government 2016) and official reports (Festival Internacional Cervantino 2015; Guanajuato State Government 2008; Noticiero del Servicio Exterior Mexicano 2013). This information was useful to ascertain the official discourse around the identification of Guanajuato with Cervantes and to identify the venues of the festival's performances, organisation and changes in management and particular initiatives from different editions.

## Findings

When asked about the adjectives that best define Guanajuato, 'associated with Cervantes' was the most popular response (30%), followed by 'colonial' (27%), 'cultural' and 'historic' with the same share of 13.6% and finally 'modern' (9%) and 'cosmopolitan' (6%). Among the most relevant characters related to the city, Diego Rivera was the most recognised one (46%), followed by Cervantes (27%) and Pípila (23%), and considerably further behind was Jorge Ibargüengoitia (2%). In relation to the number of places of interest visited, 57% of respondents visited 1 to 4 selected tourist sites and 43% visited between 5 and 8 places of interest during their stay in Guanajuato.

Additionally, a series of analyses were made on the previous data using cross tables and chi-squared tests. When associating 'place of origin' and 'adjectives that best define Guanajuato', it was found that 63% people from Guanajuato City defined their city as colonial. People from other cities in Guanajuato better agreed with its description as associated with Cervantes (54%), visitors from other Mexican states thought that Guanajuato is mostly associated with Cervantes (30%) and foreign people answered that the city is best defined as cultural (30%) and associated with Cervantes (26%). A chi-squared test reinforced the suggestion that the origin of visitors leads them to choose different adjectives to describe Guanajuato (Table 16.1).

The main difference was between local people, for whom the city is mostly colonial, and visitors, for whom the city is mostly associated with Cervantes. The explanation likely relates to the deeper knowledge and experience of the architecture and the history of the city experienced by locals all year long, for whom the Festival Internacional Cervantino and other Cervantes-related cultural facilities and events are only some of the many activities that happen in their city. On the other hand, most of attendees to the festival come from other states in Mexico, and for them Internet and the social media play a key role in organising their journey (Guanajuato State Government 2016). As a result, it is relevant to analyse the discourses issued by these media as generators of meanings and expectations for attendees to the festival. For example, eight hashtags were promoted from official accounts, such as #ViviendoElCervantino, #PostalCervantina and #SelfieCervantino, all of them

*Table 16.1* Chi-squared test 'place of origin' and 'adjectives that best define Guanajuato'

|  | Value | gl | Asymptotic significance (bilateral) |
|---|---|---|---|
| Pearson's chi-squared | 86.417 | 15 | .000 |
| Likelihood ratio | 95.869 | 15 | .000 |
| Linear-by-linear association | 25.718 | 1 | .000 |
| No. of valid cases | 206 | | |

encouraging attendees to share their personal experience during their visit (Guanajuato State Government 2016). Another source of promotion of the co-branding Guanajuato-Cervantes is the official discourse around the festival, where it states that

> The Festival Internacional Cervantino was born 40 years ago as a result of a singular artistic experience: the staging of the Cervantes Entremeses. These works of Cervantes marked the cultural vocation of Guanajuato. The spirit of the Spanish Golden Century with all its festive and reformist power took the streets and squares of Guanajuato and settled deeply in its inhabitants.
>
> *(Festival Internacional Cervantino 2015, p. 2)*

In conclusion, both the official discourse and dissemination initiatives through social media appear to have an impact on attendees from outside the city, who are more exposed to these sources and have a weaker knowledge and experience of the city.

When seeking relationships between 'place of origin' and 'most representative character', it was found that 50% people from Guanajuato City chose Diego Rivera, people from other cities in Guanajuato considered Diego Rivera (43%) and Cervantes (37%) as the most relevant characters related to the city. Visitors from other Mexican states opted for Diego Rivera (40%) and Cervantes (33%), while people from abroad answered that the most relevant character is Diego Rivera (63%). A chi-squared test reinforced the proposal that the origin of visitors leads them to consider different characters as being linked to the city (Table 16.2).

Interestingly, despite the co-branding efforts, Diego Rivera was widely accepted as the most representative character related to the city among all visitors independently of their origin. Cervantes was only relevant for people from other cities in Guanajuato and other Mexican states. As in the previous analysis, those are the people most exposed to the official discourse, social media and TV coverage about the festival, which is mostly broadcast in Spanish, and therefore the presence of Cervantes is more visible for them. Foreign attendees mostly spoke English, and Cervantes may not have such relevance as Diego Rivera in their cultural background. Local people, unsurprisingly, also considered other characters such as Pípila and Jorge Ibargüengoitia, taking into account their deeper knowledge of the city's history and culture.

When seeking relationships between 'place of origin' and 'number of tourist sites visited during festival days', it was found that 88% people from Guanajuato City and 71% visitors from other cities in the state visited between 1 and 4 sites. However, 72% people from other Mexican states and 71% foreign tourists visited between 5 and 8 places of interest. A chi-squared test reinforced the hypothesis that the visitors' origin is linked to the number of places they visit, with people from other Mexican states and from abroad more likely to visit more places (Table 16.3).

*Table 16.2* Chi-squared test 'place of origin' and 'most representative character related to the city'

|  | Value | gl | Asymptotic significance (bilateral) |
| --- | --- | --- | --- |
| Pearson's chi-squared | 29.450 | 9 | .001 |
| Likelihood ratio | 37.325 | 9 | .000 |
| Linear-by-linear association | 2.784 | 1 | .095 |
| No. of valid cases | 204 | | |

*Table 16.3* Chi-squared test 'place of origin' and 'number of tourist sites visited during festival days'

|  | Value | gl | Asymptotic significance (bilateral) |
|---|---|---|---|
| Pearson's chi-squared | 58.645 | 3 | .000 |
| Likelihood ratio | 62.863 | 3 | .000 |
| Linear-by-linear association | 51.755 | 1 | .000 |
| No. of valid cases | 206 | | |

*Table 16.4* Chi-squared test 'adjectives that best define Guanajuato' and 'most representative character related to the city'

|  | Value | gl | Asymptotic significance (bilateral) |
|---|---|---|---|
| Pearson's chi-squared | 92.411 | 15 | .000 |
| Likelihood ratio | 89.050 | 15 | .000 |
| Linear-by-linear association | .458 | 1 | .498 |
| No. of valid cases | 204 | | |

As might be expected, people from Guanajuato City and other localities in the state visit monuments and tourist sites in the city on a regular basis, and they take advantage of their promenade in the city to visit or revisit only some of them. On the other hand, for people from other Mexican states and from abroad the festival is an occasion not only for attending performances but also for getting to know the rich heritage and culture of the city.

Finally, when examining the relationship between 'adjectives that best define Guanajuato' and 'most representative character related to the city', 38% people that chose Cervantes think that Guanajuato is a cultural city and 44% of people that selected Pípila believe that Guanajuato is mostly a colonial city (Table 16.4).

This analysis is closely related to the meanings associated to the city. It is possible that those people that are aware of the importance of Cervantes are also sensitive to other cultural values of the city, taking into account that Cervantes is acknowledged as the most important writer in the Spanish language. Likewise, people aware of the importance of Pípila (noting that Pípila was a hero of the Mexican Independence War) may also be sensitive to Guanajuato's importance in colonial times thanks to silver mining and its outstanding monuments.

## Conclusions

The Festival Internacional Cervantino is an effective creator of meanings and expectations for people visiting Guanajuato and as the main promoter of the co-branding Guanajuato-Cervantes. This is especially relevant for Mexican visitors, who are the main receivers of the official discourse broadcast through the festival's webpage and advertisements, TV and social media.

The co-branding between Guanajuato-Cervantes has now been consolidated to the point that it has become materialised in the urban scene in the form of a number of cultural facilities, street names, sculptures and public art. Thus, the selection of heritage and cultural manifestations made for and by tourists nowadays includes a repertoire of Cervantes-related places of interest, all of which were created very recently and can be considered as a production of new tourist attractions from a resource that is actually alien to the city.

As this research demonstrates, cultural events have broad potential as a source of differentiation for cities that share similar features. In addition, the research has added to the field a new case study that shows the capacity of cultural events to create new motivations and attractions. In the case of Guanajuato, its importance as a colonial and mining city is widely acknowledged, including by UNESCO's World Heritage List. However, these features are shared with other localities in the region that also promote themselves as cultural tourism destinations, such as Zacatecas and San Miguel de Allende. Due to the vast array of performances, the Festival Internacional Cervantino has contributed to highlight the city of Guanajuato as a main cultural destination. Besides the positive role of the event itself, there has been a successful theming process, implying the association of Cervantes with the city even when no true historic links exist. This way, the Festival Internacional Cervantino effectively contributes the distinction factor that the city needs to maintain its competitiveness.

## References

Ashworth, G. J. (2005). Place branding a useful approach to place management. *Journal of Economics*, 8(16), 45–56.

Ashworth, G. J. & Larkham, P. J. (1994). *Building a New Heritage: Tourism, Culture and Identity in the New Europe*. London, UK: Routledge.

Barrera-Fernández, D. & Hernández-Escampa, M. (2017a). Events and placemaking: The case of the Festival Internacional Cervantino in Guanajuato, Mexico. *International Journal of Event and Festival Management*, 8(1), 24–38.

Barrera-Fernández, D. & Hernández-Escampa, M. (2017b). Malaga vs Picasso. Re-branding a city through non-material heritage. In Albert, M. T., Bandarin F. & Roders, A. P. (Eds.) *Going Beyond. Perceptions of Sustainability in Heritage Studies*, 5(2) Heritage Studies Series, in press.

Ben-Dalia, S., Collins-Kreiner, N. & Churchman, A. (2013). Evaluation of an urban tourism destination. *Tourism Geographies: An International Journal of Tourism Space, Place and Environment*, 15(2), 233–249.

Burtenshaw, D., Bateman, M. & Ashworth, G. J. (1991). *The European City: A Western Perspective*. London, UK: David Fulton Publishers.

Correia, A., Kozak, M. & Ferradeira, J. (2011). Impact of culture on tourist decision-making styles. *International Journal of Tourism Research*, 13(5), 433–446.

Diario Oficial de la Federación. (1976, March). Decreto por el que se crea el Comité Organizador del Festival Internacional Cervantino. Retrieved from www.dof.gob.mx/nota_detalle.php?codigo=4842765&fecha=16/03/1976/. Accessed 08/01/2018.

Eshuis, J. & Edwards, A. (2013). Branding the city: The democratic legitimacy of a new mode of governance. *Urban Studies*, 50(5), 1066–1082.

Festival Internacional Cervantino. (2015). *Festival Internacional Cervantino ¿Un ejemplo a seguir?* Press presentation.

García, A. H. A. (2007). Interventions in the historical center of the city of Guanajuato – Mexico. *City & Time*, 3(1), 15–23.

Guanajuato State Government. (2008, October). *Resultados del Festival Internacional Cervantino*. Retrieved from www.observatorioturistico.org/cenDoc/199FESTIVAL%20INTERNACIONAL%20CERVANTINO%202008.pdf. Accessed 08/01/2018.

Guanajuato State Government. (2014, October). *Perfil del Visitante, Festival Internacional Cervantino 2014*. Retrieved from www.observatorioturistico.org/cenDoc/552ad-Perfil-FIC-2014_OT.pdf. Accessed 08/01/2018.

Guanajuato State Government. (2015, October). *Perfil del Visitante, Festival Internacional Cervantino 2015*. Retrieved from www.observatorioturistico.org/cenDoc/01d3d-Perfil-FIC-2015_OT.pdf. Accessed 08/01/2018.

Guanajuato State Government. (2016, October). *Perfil del Visitante, Festival Internacional Cervantino 2016*. Retrieved from www.observatorioturistico.org/cenDoc/4e553-Perfil-FIC-2016_OT.pdf. Accessed 08/01/2018.

Gunay, Z. (2008). Neoliberal urbanism and sustainability of cultural heritage, *44th ISOCARP Congress*. Dalian, 19–23 September 2008.

Heritage Counts. (2012). English Heritage 2012. England, Tenth Anniversary Edition. Retrieved from http://hc.english-heritage.org.uk. Accessed 08/01/2018.

Herstein, R. & Berger, R. (2014). Cities for sale: How cities can attract tourists by creating events. *The Marketing Review*, *14*(2), 131–144.

Instituto Nacional de Geografía y Estadística. (2016, July). *Cuéntame- Información por entidad Guanajuato*. Retrieved from http://cuentame.inegi.org.mx/monografias/informacion/Gto/Poblacion/default.aspx?tema=ME&e=11/. Accessed 08/01/2018.

Kavaratzis, M. (2005). Branding the city through culture and entertainment, *AESOP 2005 Conference*. Vienna, 13–18 July 2005.

Law, C. M. (1996). *Urban Tourism: Attracting Visitors to Large Cities*, London, UK: Mansell Publishing Limited.

Lichrou, M., O'Malley, L. & Patterson, M. (2010). Narratives of a tourism destination: Local particularities and their implications for place marketing and branding. *Place Branding and Public Diplomacy*, *6*(2), 134–144.

Llovet Rodríguez, C. (2011). La estrategia comunicativa y de marca de la candidatura de Madrid a los Juegos Olímpicos de 2016, *Actas ICONO 14- n° 8. II Congreso de Ciudades Creativas*, Madrid, 26 October 2011.

Maitland, R. (2010). Everyday life as a creative experience in cities. *International Journal of Culture, Tourism and Hospitality Research*, *4*(3), 176–185.

Noticiero del Servicio Exterior Mexicano (2013). *Edición del Festival Internacional Cervantino de Guanajuato*, press presentation.

Richards, G. & Palmer, R. (2010). *Eventful Cities: Cultural Management and Urban Revitalization*. Amsterdam, NL: Elsevier.

Richards, G. & Wilson, J. (2007). Creativities in tourism development. In Richards, G. and Wilson, J. (Eds.), *Tourism, Creativity and Development*. London: Routledge, 255–288.

Zukin, S. (1996). *The Cultures of Cities*. Oxford, UK: Blackwell Publishing.

Rifkin, J. (2001). *The age of access: The new culture of hypercapitalism*. New York, USA: Penguin.

# 17
# FESTIVALS AND SOCIAL MEDIA
## A co-created transformation of attendees and organisers

*Marianna Sigala*

### Introduction

Social media (SM) enrich tourism experiences by transforming the way people search, create, share and discuss information and converting them into co-designers, co-producers, co-marketers and co-distributors of tourism offerings (Sigala 2017; Sigala & Gretzel 2018). The festival sector is no exception. Festival operators adopt SM not only to increase their effectiveness (Inversini & Sykes 2013; Pasanen & Konu 2016) but also to appeal to new attendees who expect to use SM for accessing festival services and information; interacting with, sharing and discussing their experiences with various festival stakeholders (e.g. organisers, artists, local communities and other attendees); and co-designing and co-creating their festival experiences (Lee, Xiong & Hu 2012; MacKay, Barbe, Van Winkle & Halpenny 2017; Morey, Bengry-Howell, Griffin, Szmigin & Riley 2016). SM are compatible with the nature of festivals as a way to socialise, entertain and contribute to the self-development of attendees.

SM in festivals have attracted very few studies focussing on the marketing and co-creation of festival experiences (Csiszár 2016; Gyimóthy & Larson 2015; Hoksbergen, Insch & Insch 2016; Hudson & Hudson 2013). Hence, no systematic research exists investigating how SM are transforming the operations of festival operators as well as the behaviour, decision-making and experiences of attendees. To address these gaps, this chapter adopts a co-creation approach for examining the use and impact of SM on both attendees and organisers.

### Social media and festival experiences: a co-creation approach

Festivals are places that unite people with similar interests, ideas and values to celebrate together and share common experiences. It is this shared collective experience as part of the festival 'product' and its compatibility with SM functionality that make festivals a relevant context for SM. SM enable attendees to interact, share and influence each other's experiences (Gyimóthy & Larson 2015) as well as build festival communities (Hede & Kellett 2012). The following SM features support the formation and quality of festival experiences and the benefits that attendees get (Sigala 2018b):

- **Sharing** of multimedia content with an international audience.
- **(Virtual) Presence**: the 'always on' attendee and his perception that 'everyone is watching him' creates the (online) festival atmosphere and reinforces the motivation

(or addiction) to use SM in order to maintain and build relations, self-promotion and impression management.
- **Conversations**: online dialogues and interactions significantly impact the co-construction of travel content and meaning, which in turn influence the way tourists select, interpret and evaluate their experiences.
- **Identity**: attendees create their SM profile which is used for networking with others and/or for building/promoting their idealisedself.
- **Relationships**: socialising, networking, interactions and sharing resources through SM help attendees develop and maintain social bonds and relations with others and feel that they belong in a community.
- **Groups**: SM users create and join groups, as interactions/collaborations are facilitated and strengthen when they happen within groups.

Few studies show the influence of SM on festival experiences. Networking websites, blogs and forums enable attendees to achieve socio-psychological benefits (such as social capital development and feelings of involvement), which in turn foster feelings of social group belonging and intentions for repeat festival visitation (Gyimóthy & Larson 2015). People increasingly use SM in all stages of their festival experiences (Hudson & Hudson 2013) in order to interact with others, share common experience and engage with festival activities (Flinn & Frew 2013), which in turn generates them social, ludic and symbolic value and meaning (Gyimóthy 2013). SM support and foster tribal gathering in festivals, as attendees can better connect to each other and develop bonds based on their common interest and exchanges (Gyimóthy & Jensen 2014). In summary, the properties of SM (networking, sharing, collaboration, community and dialogues) enable attendees to co-create experiences by generating values of belonging (creating and participating in communities), bonding (communicating, sharing, collaborating), detaching (insulation and territoriality by creating one's space online for passive self-consumption of festival content), communing (fun-making, trusting, embracing), connecting (helping, relating, confiding/sharing) and amiability (acknowledging, advising, conversing) (Rihova 2013).

These examples are compatible with and within the theoretical frames of the experience economy co-creation, and service dominant logic (SDL), whose applicability in the festival context is advocated (e.g. Gyimóthy & Larson 2015; Hayes & MacLeod 2007; van Limburg 2008). These overlapping perspectives recognise that festival experiences are not created to be sold, i.e. value-in-exchange (Vargo & Lusch 2004), but they are co-created through the active participation and interactions of the various festival actors (e.g. attendees, artists, operators, communities, sponsors). Attendees gain value not through purchasing but through festival 'consumption'/living (value-in-use) and by immersing themselves into the sociocultural festival context (value-in-context), which in turn brings them meaning and self-enhancement. Value is not embedded in offerings; instead, customers have to co-create and make meaning out of it via the consumption and co-production of experiences (Firat & Dholakia 2006) as well as the interpretation of experiences that are facilitated and fuelled through SM interactions. As Prahalad and Ramaswamy (2004, p. 14) state, '*the personal meaning derived from the co-creation experience is what determines the value to the individual*'. Hence, attendees do not seek to 'buy' experiences but meanings, and so, to make their festival appealing and meaningful, festival organisers need to facilitate meaning-making co-creation processes amongst all the festival stakeholders.

Csiszár (2016) showed how interactions within an online festival community enabled attendees to co-create values and meanings of their festival experiences. This also influenced how the organiser formed the official festival message and promotion strategy. The findings confirmed the impact of online social interactions and communities on experience cocreation by influencing the attendees' meaning-making and the interpretation processes of the festival's 'intended' messages/values. Hence, the dialectic and networking properties of SM expand festivals from isolated events in a specific venue, to a 'time and space boundless networked gathering' facilitating value co-creation through meaning-making mechanisms. Consequently, to better manage the festival's intended messages/meanings, organisers also need to manage, monitor and moderate these online interactions.

The co-creation paradigm also emphasises that festival organisers have to migrate from a mindset of creating value for festivalgoers to co-creating value with them by seeing them as an empowered partner rather than a passive attendee (Gyimóthy & Jensen 2014). Gyimóthy and Larson (2015, p. 346) described three SM practices for engaging attendees into value co-creation: *customer insourcing* (i.e. recruiting lead users to distribute information, communicating for the purpose of service recovery, and posting and boosting positive user-generated content), *crowdsourcing* (i.e. fostering involvement to generate innovative suggestions, identify problems and suggest solutions/ideas) and *community consolidation* (i.e. facilitating the tribal community dynamics and contributing to the collective experience by posting and sharing UGC).

Based on Grönroos's (2008) framework, it is proposed that SM support and enrich value co-creation in festival at three spheres:

- The supplier sphere: festival organisers integrating SM into their festival operations.
- The customer sphere: attendees integrating SM into their festival journey stages.
- The encounter sphere: any interaction between attendees and organisers at any touchpoint (offline/online, mobile), allowing value co-creation through resource exchange and integration (e.g. knowledge, monetary, cultural and social resources); SM provide the engagement platforms (i.e. blogs, communities, social networks) whereby the festivalgoers and operators can meet, network and interact.

## Social media and attendees

Attendees are transformed from passive value takers to active value makers, and the SM revolution is further empowering them to become co-marketers, co-designers, co-producers and co-creators of festival experiences. By using SM, attendees can better satisfy their motivations for attending festivals (e.g. to learn, network, contribute and share common experiences, have fun, experience thrill and novelty, belong and be in a community).

### SM and attendee decision-making

Hudson and Hudson (2013) analysed the impact of SM on the decision-making of attendees by demonstrating a heightened engagement in the pre-purchase search and the post-purchase evaluation stages. Instead of the traditional sequential purchase funnel, there is an extended evaluation stage comparing offers with multiple information sources; moreover, after the purchase, attendees build and maintain an open-ended relationship with brands by sharing experiences and joining brand communities. Indeed, attendees seek and use festival information from a variety of online sources rather than a single SM to compare and supplement information at different times during their festival journey (Becker, Iter, Naaman & Gravano 2012). Attendees also use multiple SM at different purchase stages (MacKay et al. 2017) because SM possess different features and live period of updated content, e.g. most trends on Twitter last for one week. Research needs to examine whether and how attendees use and place different importance and credibility on various SM (not just Facebook and Twitter but also other SM, such as Snapchat or Instagram) at different stages of their purchase process.

## SM and festival experiences

### The positive impact of SM on festival experiences: a value co-creation approach

Many (Gyimóthy 2013; Lee et al. 2012; Morey et al. 2016) focus on the attendees' use of SM as an interactive space for sharing and co-creating experiences, interacting and communicating with others, creating and participating in festival communities. These online 'tribes' of attendees (in which the presence and contributions of artists play a major role) also help attendees to build a group around the festival and then nurture social connections and a sense of community with likeminded peers located across geographic or temporal divides (Gyimóthy 2013).

SM significantly influence the festival experiences. Attendees use Twitter as a platform of self-expression, discussion and co-creation of meanings and values (Duguay 2016). According to Hoksbergen et al. (2016), the use of Facebook in a music festival enhanced the music experience (seeing favourite bands/performers, new band/performers and being inspired by the music), the festival experience (festival atmosphere and being in a stimulating, peaceful and/ or different environment), the social experience (being with friends/family, meeting new people, being around people with similar interests and getting to know friends on a deeper level) and the separation experience (trying new/adventurous things, food, activities and staying overnight). Thus, attendees reported gaining five types of value (Hoksbergen et al. 2016): functional value (obtaining and providing festival information, purchasing tickets online), social value (identifying and networking with others, achieving self-impression by sharing selfies/content), emotional value (triggering memories and sensations of the festival atmosphere, creating excitement), interactive value (communication and collaboration) and aesthetic value (viewing and enjoying photos/videos).

Motivations for sharing and discussing electronic Word of Mouth (eWOM) include memorable festival experiences (Semrad & Rivera 2016), and the combination of positive event image and participant satisfaction (Prado-Gascó, Calabuig, Añó Sanz, Núñez-Pomar & Crespo Hervás 2017). As eWOM can significantly influence festival demand, organisers need to assure the memorability of their experiences and monitor the online festival image. Attendees use SM at all festival stages to anticipate, co-produce and (re-)consume their festival experiences, and to expand the time horizon and location of the co-creation of their festival experiences beyond the festival site and timing (Gyimóthy & Larson 2015). Thus, using SM to support and monitor attendee interactions after the festival is also equally important for festival organisers.

Similar to tourism studies (e.g. Wang, Xiang & Fesenmaier 2016), festival research (van Winkle et al. 2017) has also revealed that attendee use of SM can be attributed to habit theory and the spillover of technology use from daily life to unique leisure/tourism contexts. Hence, 'addicted' SM users and the millennials seem to be both early and heavy users of SM at festivals. However, further research is required to unravel the specific technographic profile of attendees (e.g. festival motivations, needs and expectations of attendees using SM for various reasons, e.g. content creation, sharing, networking) and their use of different SM tools (MacKay et al. 2017). As attendee participation in festivals also differs temporally

(Gyimóthy & Larson 2015), organisers need to adopt different tactics in various SM in order to stimulate full customer engagement across all SM and during the whole festival journey.

## *The negative impact of SM on festival experiences: a value co-destruction approach*

The dark side of SM use at festivals also needs to be recognised, but research has failed to examine so far its negative impacts on festival co-creation processes and experiences. This is a major gap as research in tourism has already revealed that the pathological or addicted use of SM while traveling can have detrimental effects on tourism experiences (Sigala 2017). Value co-creation processes do not always lead to positive value creation for all the actors, and this is because value co-creation and co-destruction can simultaneously take place (Sigala 2018a). Posting a selfie with an artist or a video of a festival performance can enhance attendee ego and festival experiences, as this increases their online identity and impression. Favourable online festival content may also positively influence the festival image and online promotion. However, these online practices can negatively affect artists (e.g. image making, copyright concerns of content distribution).

Research is urgently required to unravel these contradictory effects of SM use on festival experiences. On the one hand, sharing of festival content manifests the experiences and reactions of the users; creates a feeling of camaraderie; fosters community bonding; and triggers collective excitement, togetherness and emotions generated by attendees experiencing together. On the other hand, instead of connecting, mobile use of SM can cut people off from each other and from their social context, distract attention of the user and diminish the emotional purchase of live events (Hutchins 2016). Mobile phone usage can strengthen social ties within the circle of friends and family, but at the expense of interaction with those who are physically present, which in turn creates 'bounded solidarity' (Ling 2008). As the power of live performances is built on the heightened emotions and sensory engagement generated by the collective focus of a crowd, this 'bounded solidarity' and disregard of what is going around felt by people who experience live festivals through their phone cameras can have detrimental effects on the festival atmosphere, the individual and the collective festival experiences. Constant use of SM can also erode the quality of attendees' focus and festival experience by distracting them and disturbing others wishing to stay offline.

Mindful SM use is required so that it does not negatively affect users' mental, physical, social and psychological well-being (Sigala 2018a). Technology suppliers and festival organisers also suggest that temporary forced disengagement from SM may be beneficial. Apple has registered a patent (Ghosal 2016) that prohibits phone cameras from recording footage in designated areas. Yondr (www.overyondr.com) provides a technological solution to festival venues wishing to have a phone-free space, showing people how they experience more powerful moments by staying away from habitual online checking and sharing. Nevertheless, creating and sharing content online has also become part of the festival experience, and some attendees demand it otherwise they are dissatisfied by not being connected. Future research needs to answer how much content people can afford to record and share before they get disconnected from their immediate environment/companions and fail to experience and share live performances with the ones next to them. Such findings can help festival organisers and attendees alike in designing their festivalscapes, experiences, SM applications and strategies.

Duguay (2016) also found a contradictory SM experience impact: Twitter software simultaneously constrained and enabled the attendees to pursue different co-creation processes that, in turn, resulted in conflicting value outcomes. Twitter's features of visibility, connections, messages and #tags empowered the attendees of WorldPride to self-express and promote the festival's values. This helped the attendees to develop collective connections, nurture an online festival community and achieve the festival aims, i.e. form counterpublics and challenges to the assumed heterosexuality of public space. However, Twitter's algorithm and platform constrained the attendees' expressions and online posts through standardised and datafiable tweets, while it also allowed other actors (i.e. politicians, celebrities and advertisers) to post tweets of self-promotional and banal content. Because the Tweeter algorithm gives more visibility to the latter actors due to their huge online network, this meant that the visibility of attendees' posts was significantly 'hidden'. Overall, the WorldPride Twitter community did not lead online discourses or form counterpublics challenging heteronormativity. Hence, to better understand the SM experience impact, research needs to examine how SM algorithms/functionalities influence actor interactions, co-creation processes and outcomes.

## Social media and festival marketing

By using SM for digitising business operations, festival organisers can increase the Return on Investment (ROI) of all their festival marketing functions. However, the business benefits of SM are not confined to their instrumental and functionalistic roles. The social and the networking capabilities of SM also enable the organisers to transform their operations to more 'social' functions by empowering their attendees to actively participate in festival operations. In doing this, organisers increase their effectiveness and address demand expectations (Sigala 2018b).

There are four major ways to exploit SM for digitising and socialising festival marketing practices. First, organisers can embed SM functionality and applications into the festival website: e.g. include SM share buttons, create guest books, blogs and discussion boards enabling users to create, discuss and share festival content, thus nurturing a festival community. Second, organisers can create SM profiles of the festival for promotion and community building using existing popular SM platforms and SM platforms specialising in festivals (e.g. www.conferize.com/the-chocolate-festival). A third option is to use the new festival intermediaries that provide online and SM web services/software such as online sales, SM marketing and CRM software (e.g. www.eventbrite.com.au/ and http://losangeles.eventful.com/events/spring-festival-gala-/E0-001-107642979-4). Finally, organisers can develop a mobile SM application. There are numerous festival mobile app developers (e.g. www.a2zinc.net/, https://evenium.com and www.core-apps.com/).

These four practices should be complimentary and used synergistically rather than exclusively. This is because the 'always connected' attendees use multiple sources of platforms, devices and information to identify a festival, share festival information and engage with its community. The proliferation of online channels and the customers' expectations to access 'services on the go' at any place, time and device require the adoption of a multi-distribution strategy that provides multiple touchpoints and ways of accessing information and services, and engaging with and interacting with the festival stakeholders/community. However, studies have only examined the mainstream SM (e.g. Facebook, Twitter) overlooking both the features, benefits and the use of other SM platforms and the need to develop an orchestrated multiple SM channel strategy.

The aforementioned SM channels are called owned media, as firms can 'own' and control them. Festival organisers should also be aware of, monitor and manage what is called earned media, referring to SM networks and/or content created and owned by other actors (e.g. artists, attendees, journalists, critics, communities), but which can promote the festival (e.g. YouTube channels, artists' blogs or attendee-created communities). These earned media are equally important because of their significant influence on various factors such as attendee behaviour and decision-making, brand reputation, relationship management and sales. However, research has not yet investigated how festival organisers should monitor, participate and direct conversations and content in earned media (e.g. customer listening, reputation monitoring, and communication and public relation strategies).

Arguably, too much research attention has examined organisers' SM use for marketing and customer engagement practices, with fewer studies looking at the use/benefits of SM for other operations such as New Product Development (NPD), market research, crisis management and community building. Numerous studies (e.g. Gyimóthy 2013; Hede & Kellett 2012; Hudson & Hudson 2013; Lee et al. 2012; Semrad & Rivera 2016; Zanger 2014) examine the SM use for a range of marketing practices, including event promotion and brand awareness; attracting, communicating and engaging with attendees; sales; building a festival community; and nurturing/maintaining relations. Several studies (Lee et al. 2012; Zanger 2014) emphasise the use of SM for providing services before, during and after the festival. However, findings (MacKay et al. 2017) reveal that the organisers use SM more before, less during and only in a limited way after the festival, which represents lost opportunities. SM marketing can also satisfy the festival 'sponsors' and build better sponsorship relations, as sponsors get more promotion for their sponsorship.

To date, no studies have examined SM use for festival sponsorship, crowdfunding, volunteering and impacts management. Despite the widely recognised SM use for involving tourists in NPD (e.g. Sigala 2012), fewer studies investigate this in events (Zanger 2014) and only one study (Pasanen & Konu 2016) examines SM use for festival innovation. Devine, Boluk and Devine (2017) discuss the use of Twitter for festival brand reputation management during and after a crisis, and De Lira et al. (2017) are one of the first to use big data for conducting market research in festivals. Hence, more diverse and advanced research is required to better inform the use of SM in festival operations. Research needs to progress from descriptive studies to more explanatory research investigating the effectiveness and the factors influencing the success and benefits of SM strategies. Research should also adopt new research methodologies (e.g. big data), approaches and disciplines, and make use of the huge amount of online market intelligence and customer data.

A SM marketing strategy should also aim at the different festival stages (Hede & Kellett 2012). Before the festival, SM use should focus on promotion, awareness and customer attraction. During the festival, the aims focus on information sharing and enhancement of attendee experience, while after the festival the major aim is on sustaining loyalty and maintaining presence. Organisers should also think about differentiating the type of SM used across the festival stages, and the type (e.g. conversational, promotional, informational, community building) and purpose (e.g. information provision, relationship building, customer service) of content communicated (MacKay et al. 2017; Semrad & Rivera 2016).

Overall, festival organisers need to adopt a multifunctional, a multichannel and a more strategic approach to SM exploitation that adopts practices, business aims and content to the various festival stages and SM. The SM strategy should match the 5 Ws (audience (who), time/festival stage (when), content/service (what), SM platform (where) and purpose/business aim (why)). The SM strategy should:

- provide the right information and the right service to the right person at the right time and place and for the right reason/purpose;
- attract, engage, retain, learn from and relate with customers (i.e. social CRM, Sigala 2018b);

- actively engage attendees into business practices as value co-creators;
- promote, brand and collect attendee feedback and user-generated content about the festival and its impacts;
- use big data for better understanding and satisfying attendees and markets.

## Conclusions

SM are fundamentally changing the way festivals are created, promoted, implemented and managed. At a basic level, SM have been instrumental in addressing the information search, communication, promotional and other functional needs of the attendees and organisers. However, SM is also having a transformational impact on the festival industry by changing the roles, practices and functions of its stakeholders. SM facilitate, empower and support attendees and organisers to become value and experience co-creators with more 'social' business functions. Festival management and marketing is also being transformed from being static and utilitarian (whereby technologies are tools) to a transformative conceptualisation whereby festival markets and actors both shape and are shaped by the technology (Sigala 2018a).

Research shows that the industry is lagging behind in adopting sophisticated practices for fully exploiting SM. Research investigating SM in festivals is also still in its infancy. Advanced research needs to inform industry strategies and understand attendee behaviour to co-create festival value and eliminate value co-destruction. Research should move from descriptive studies explaining the current use of SM to more explanatory, prescriptive and predictive research that can provide useful guidelines on how SM should be more effectively exploited by festival organisers, attendees, destination managers and policymakers alike.

## References

Becker, H., Iter, D., Naaman, M. & Gravano, L. (2012). Identifying content for planned events across social media sites. In *Proceedings from WSDM '12: The Fifth ACM International Conference on Web Search and Data Mining*, ACM, New York, NY, pp. 533–542.

Csiszár, S. (2016). *An Exploratory Research on Co-Creation in a Festival's Virtual Community*. Master Thesis, Aalborg University, Copenhagen.

de Lira, V. M., Macdonald, C., Ounis, I., Perego, R., Renso, C. & Times, V. C. (2017). Exploring social media for event attendance. In *The 2017 IEEE/ACM International Conference on Advances in Social Networks Analysis and Mining (ASONAM)*, Sydney, Australia, 31 July–3 August, 2017, pp. 447–450.

Devine, A., Boluk, K. & Devine, F. (2017). Managing social media during a crisis: A Conundrum for event managers. *Event Management*, 21(4), 375–389.

Duguay, S. (2016). Constructing public space |"Legit Can't Wait for# Toronto# WorldPride!": Investigating the Twitter public of a large-scale LGBTQ festival. *International Journal of Communication*, 10, 274–298.

Fırat, A. F. & Dholakia, N. (2006). Theoretical and philosophical implications of postmodern debates: Some challenges to modern marketing. *Marketing Theory*, 6(2), 123–162.

Flinn, J. & Frew, M. (2013). Glastonbury: Managing the mystification of festivity. *Leisure Studies*, 33(4), 418–433.

Ghosal, A. (2016). Apple patents a way to stop you from recording video at concerts. Available at https://thenextweb.com/apple/2016/06/30/apple-patents-way-stop-recording-video-concerts/#gref. Accessed on 3 January 2018.

Grönroos, C. (2008). Service logic revisited: Who creates value? And who co-creates? *European Business Review*, 20(4), 298–314.

Gyimóthy, S. (2013). Symbolic convergence and tourism social media. In Munar, A. M., Gyimóthy, G. & Cai, L. (Eds.), *Tourism Social Media: Transformations in Identity, Community and Culture* (pp. 55–71). Bingley: Emerald Group Publishing Limited.

Gyimóthy, S. & Jensen, M. T. (2014). Re-enchanting the orange feeling in the festival community. In Knudsen, B. T., Christensen, D. R. & Blenker, P. (Eds.), *Enterprising Initiatives in the Experience Economy: Transforming Social Worlds* (pp. 262–273). Abingdon: Routledge.

Gyimóthy, S. & Larson, M. (2015). Social media cocreation strategies: The 3Cs. *Event Management*, 19(3), 331–348.

Hayes, D. & MacLeod, N. (2007). Packaging places: Designing heritage trails using an experience economy perspective to maximise visitor engagement. *Journal of Vacation Marketing*, 13(1), 45–58.

Hede, A. M. & Kellett, P. (2012). Building online brand communities exploring the benefits, challenges and risks in the Australian event sector. *Journal of Vacation Marketing*, 18(3), 239–250.

Hoksbergen, E., Insch, A. & Insch, A. (2016). Facebook as a platform for co-creating music festival experiences: The case of New Zealand's Rhythm and Vines New Year's Eve festival. *International Journal of Event and Festival Management*, 7(2), 84–99.

Hudson, S. & Hudson, R. (2013). Engaging with consumers using social media: A case study of music festivals. *International Journal of Event and Festival Management*, 4(3), 206–223.

Hutchins, B. (2016). There's a time to put down the smartphone, seriously. https://theconversation.com/theres-a-time-to-put-down-the-smartphone-seriously-62699. Accessed on 3 January 2018.

Inversini, A. & Sykes, E. (2013). An investigation into the use of social media marketing and measuring its effectiveness in the events industry. In Xiang Z., Tussyadiah I. (Eds.), *Information and Communication Technologies in Tourism 2014* (pp. 131–144). Cham: Springer.

Lee, W., Xiong, L. & Hu, C. (2012). The effect of Facebook users' arousal and valence on intention to go to the festival: Applying an extension of the technology acceptance model. *International Journal and Hospitality Management*, 31(3), 819–827.

Ling, R. (2008). *New Tech, New Ties. How Mobile Communication Is Reshaping Social Cohesion*. Boston, MA: MIT Press.

MacKay, K., Barbe, D., Van Winkle, C. M. & Halpenny, E. (2017). Social media activity in a festival context: Temporal and content analysis. *International Journal of Contemporary Hospitality Management*, 29(2), 669–689.

Morey, Y., Bengry-Howell, A., Griffin, C., Szmigin, I. & Riley, S. (2016). Festivals 2.0: Consuming, producing and participating in the extended festival experience. In Bennet, A., Taylor, J. & Woodward, I. (Eds.), *The Festivalization of Culture* (pp. 251–273). Abingdon: Routledge.

Pasanen, K. & Konu, H. (2016). Use of social media for new service development by Finnish event and festival organizers. *Event Management*, 20(3), 313–325.

Prado-Gascó, V., Calabuig M. F., Añó Sanz, V., Núñez-Pomar, J. & Crespo Hervás, J. (2017). To post or not to post: Social media sharing and sporting event performance. *Psychology & Marketing*, 34(11), 995–1003.

Prahalad, C. K. & Ramaswamy, V. (2004). Co-creation experiences: The next practice in value creation. *Journal of Interactive Marketing*, 18(3), 5–14.

Rihova, I. (2013). *Customer-to-Customer Co-creation of Value in the Context of Festivals*. Doctoral dissertation, Bournemouth University.

Semrad, K. J. & Rivera, M. (2016). Advancing the 5E's in festival experience for the Gen Y framework in the context of eWOM. *Journal of Destination Marketing & Management*, 7, 58–67.

Sigala, M. (2012). Social media and crisis management in tourism: Applications and implications for research. *Information Technology and Tourism*, 13(4), 269–283.

Sigala, M. (2017). Social media and the co-creation of tourism experiences. In Sotiriadis, M. and Gursoy, D. (Eds.), *Managing and Marketing Tourism Experiences: Issues, Challenges and Approaches*. Emerald Publishing.

Sigala, M. (2018a). New technologies in tourism: From multi-disciplinary to anti-disciplinary advances and trajectories. *Tourism Management Perspectives*, 25, 151–155.

Sigala, M. (2018b). Social customer relationship management: Approaches, applications and implications in tourism and hospitality. *International Journal of Contemporary Hospitality Management*,

Sigala, M. & Gretzel, U. (2018). *Advances in Social Media for Travel, Tourism and Hospitality: New Perspectives, Practice and Cases*. Abingdon: Routledge.

van Limburg, B. (2008). Innovation in pop festivals by cocreation. *Event Management*, 12(2), 105–117.

Van Winkle, C. M., Barbe, D., MacKay, K. & Halpenny, E. (2017). Mobile device use at festivals: The role of habit. In Inversini, A. & Schegg, R. (Eds.), Proceedings of ENTER 2016 conference. Bilbao, Spain. February 2–5, 2016.

Vargo, S. & Lusch, R. (2004). Evolving to a new dominant logic for marketing. *Journal of Marketing*, *68*(1), 1–17.

Wang, D., Xiang, Z. & Fesenmaier, D. R. (2016). Smartphone use in everyday life and travel. *Journal of Travel Research*, *55*(1), 52–63.

Zanger, C. (2014). *Ein áberblick Zu Events Im Zeitalter von Social Media [An Overview of Events in the Age of Social Media]*. Berlin: Springer.

# PART V

# Strategic use of festivals

# 18

# LEVERAGING A FESTIVAL TO BUILD BRIDGES IN A DIVIDED CITY

*Adrian Devine, Bernadette Quinn and Frances Devine*

## Introduction

Events are communal celebrations, and because they bring people together they have the potential to create positive social outcomes for individuals and communities. In recent times this potential has received more attention from those bidding for and hosting events; however, despite all the well-intentioned rhetoric surrounding the social case for events there remains a sense that these outcomes are hoped for and desirable as opposed to being expected and planned for (Foley, McGillivary & McPherson 2012). This is in line with Smith's (2012) argument that the social impacts are sometimes lazily citied by host cities to justify events when promised economic impacts have not materialised. To counter this and maximise the positive social benefits, pre-event planning and investment is required. This links to what Chalip (2004) refers to as event leveraging whereby governments (central and local), event organisers and other stakeholders agree on their social objectives at the earliest stage and plan how to achieve these. This chapter will discuss social leveraging in the context of Fleadh Cheoil, an annual festival which celebrates Irish culture through traditional dance, music and song. In particular, the focus will be on the 2013 edition of the festival, which was hosted by Derry/Londonderry, a politically and culturally divided city (McDermott, Nic Craith & Strani 2015). The chapter will discuss how the organisers of the Fleadh Cheoil strategically used the event to break down political barriers and open up the city both socially and physically.

## Festivals, events and social outcomes

Traditionally the social impacts of festival and events and their measurement have been overshadowed by the economic agenda. In more recent years, however, the social outcomes of festivals and events have been recognised by policymakers, and there is increasing pressure on organisers to include social outcomes in their business case. According to Wilks (2011) these impacts can occur at a personal or community level. At a personal level, this impact could be as simple as a shared experience at a music festival. For some, however, this simple encounter can take on added meaning because it can assuage feelings of alienation and social isolation experienced in some of the most challenging community circumstances

(Foley et al. 2012). This links into Smith's (2012) argument that festivals and events can provide a shared mission and help build cohesive communities by allowing new or excluded members to feel part of a collective identity. Smith goes on to state that even if some people are not interested in the events themselves, these occasions encourage reflection on the future direction of a place amongst the communities that live there and this can provide the basis for community development.

The development of community pride and subjective feelings of hope and renewed achievement are other commonly cited social outcomes of festivals and events (Misener & Mason 2006; Wood 2006; Foley et al. 2012; Quinn & Wilks 2013). According to Devine, Devine and Carruthers (2016), festivals and events also have the power to bring communities together by challenging stereotypes and changing perceptions. They discuss Féile an Phobail and how the organisers of this community festival incorporated a series of political debates into the programme which contributed to the peace process in Northern Ireland by encouraging cross-community dialogue. Boland, Murtagh and Shirlow (2016) in another study of an event in Northern Ireland, the UK City of Culture Derry-Londonderry 2013, found evidence of 'transformative change' in city image, civic pride and enhanced community relations. These studies lend support to Duffy and Mair's (2015) argument that festivals can be used to increase tolerance and understanding of community diversity.

## *Leveraging for social outcomes*

There is much evidence in the literature to that festivals and events can generate positive social outcomes for host communities. However, as Smith (2010, p. 163) notes, positive outcomes may not happen automatically; rather, initiatives need to be formulated and implemented to effect lasting benefits. The process of shaping events to produce specific, desirable outcomes that endure beyond the lifetime of the event is encapsulated in the term leveraging. According to Chalip (2004, p. 228) leveraging refers to 'those activities that need to be undertaken around the event itself, which seek to maximise the long-term benefits from events'. For Weed and Dowse (2009, p. 13) leveraging implies a much more proactive approach to capitalising on opportunities 'which differs from impact in that the latter relates to simply measuring outcomes'. Leveraging is thus inherently strategic. While the significance of leveraging is increasingly recognised and studies on the topic are growing, it remains under-researched (Quinn & Wilks 2013), especially with respect to domains beyond the economic. An aspect particularly in need of research is the strategic actions that event organisers can take to achieve effective leveraging.

For Karadakis, Kaplanidou and Karlis (2010), an important starting point in this process is to undertake a SWOT (strengths, weaknesses, opportunities, threats) analysis of the host location. Undertaking and learning from a SWOT analysis lays a strong basis for planning and can 'assist all stakeholders involved in the bidding, preparation, delivery and post-games management to target and prepare much more efficiently with the long-term needs of the host city' (Karadakis et al. 2010, p. 182). Jago, Dwyer, Lipman, Van Lill and Vorster (2010) echo this holistic outlook, arguing that if benefits are to be long term, then the preparation for, and construction of, the event and associated facilities must be viewed as part of a long-term development strategy.

Writing in the context of sports events, O'Brien and Chalip (2008) very usefully develop a strategic framework premised upon identifying and exploiting the resources presented by hosting events. Thinking first from an economic perspective, they begin by conceiving of the event itself as a resource which offers opportunities to achieve a number of strategic objectives through identifiable means. So, for example, an event might represent an opportunity to attract visitors, which can generate revenue, especially if there is a determined effort to increase length of stay and encourage visitor spending.

Thinking specifically about social outcomes, Smith (2010, p. 163) picks up on the inherent sociability that events engender and recommends capitalising on 'the goodwill, civic engagement and publicity that major events can generate'. In similar vein, O'Brien and Chalip (2008) identify liminality, and the *communitas* that can ensue, as an opportunity to be strategically exploited to achieve positive social outcomes. In his discussions of liminality, Turner (1982, p. 50) describes *communitas* as an 'alternative and more liberated way to be socially human'. Festivals, and events more generally, are associated with *communitas* as their extraordinary nature can encourage people to step out of their everyday routines into settings characterised by goodwill and civic engagement. In turn, the ambience generated can represent an opportunity for enhanced communication and community bonding (Howell 2013). For Falassi (1987), *communitas* is associated with an increased sense of equality amongst community members, and as Turner (1982) explains, this sense of equality and the inclusivity of *communitas* contrasts with the exclusionary tendencies of the social structures that give sense and order to everyday life. It thus affords the opportunity for change to be effected during the event.

Therefore, if identified as resources, the enhanced social interaction and sense of *communitas* generated by events represent potential to underpin event leveraging strategies designed to achieve social, and perhaps other, outcomes. However, to date, little research has been undertaken to investigate if and how event organisers think about their events in this way. Certainly, there is a general understanding that in order to succeed, events need to acquire the support of their host communities. Foley et al. (2012) briefly reviewed a number of studies that critique events on the basis of failing to facilitate meaningful engagement for local populations, while Chalip (2004) argues that effective leveraging is best served by providing networking opportunities among key event stakeholders. However, much remains to be learned about how event organisations leverage social outcomes.

The remainder of this chapter will discuss how the organisers of the Fleadh Cheoil planned and managed to leverage positive social outcomes from this particular festival when it was hosted by Derry/Londonderry in 2013. It begins by setting the context and providing some background information both on this festival and, perhaps more importantly, on the host city, Derry-Londonderry.

## Context

Fleadh Cheoil is an annual festival run by Comhaltas Ceoltoiri Eireann in celebration of Irish culture through traditional dance, music and song. The first Fleadh Cheoil took place in 1951, and it has grown to become Europe's largest music and traditional arts festival. Its seven-day programme attracts thousands of visitors, and its economic impact is the main reason why Irish towns and cities are so keen to bid for the right to hold this festival. In 2013 Derry/Londonderry, Northern Ireland's second largest city, hosted the Fleadh Cheoil as part of its 2013 UK City of Culture programme. This was the first time the festival was held in Northern Ireland which is made up of the six counties which were partitioned from the rest of the island in 1921 and became part of the UK. It was this partition that ultimately led to the 'Troubles' in Northern Ireland between 1968 and 1998 as the Protestant, Unionist and Loyalist (PUL) community wanted to remain part of the UK, while the Catholic, Republican and Nationalist (CRN) community wanted independence.

Derry/Londonderry was one of the epicentres of violence during the 'Troubles'. There has been substantial media focus on major atrocities such as Bloody Sunday, but this was only one of many horrific incidents. In total, there were 244 fatal incidents during the 'Troubles' in the Derry/Londonderry council area which equates to a death rate of 1.74 per 1000 of the population (Cost of the Troubles Survey 1995, cited in Derry City Council 2014, p. 45). A peace agreement was signed in 1998 (the Good Friday Agreement), but the 'Troubles' created a legacy of fear, distrust and suspicion between the CRN and the PUL communities. Indeed, 20 years on from the Good Friday Agreement, Derry/Londonderry is still very much a divided city. During the 'Troubles' there was a significant population shift within the city with the majority of the PUL community leaving the Cityside and moving across the River Foyle to the Waterside of the city. As a result of this population shift, the majority of the people in the city now live in segregated areas, i.e. CRN and PUL. This segregation extends beyond housing. With the exception of one school, the young people in the city are educated in segregated schools. Social and leisure activity is also significantly influenced by lines of segregation established in hswome and school. In fact, for many the first sustained contact with 'the other side' may only come at third-level education or first employment experiences.

Derry/Londonderry is thus a culturally divided place. McDermott et al. (2015) discuss how culture within the city constitutes a political issue which is often used to differentiate communities. In the past, cultural expression has often been the cause of conflict within the city, a notable example being the annual Apprentice Boys Parade. For the PUL community their cultural identity is linked to their sense of Britishness, while for the Nationalist community their identity markers evolve around Irish traditions. Shirlow et al. (2005) observed a common perception amongst the PUL community in Derry/Londonderry that their culture heritage was in decline and a tendency to accuse the local council of favouring Irish culture whilst denigrating their British culture. Unsurprisingly, when it was announced that Derry/Londonderry would host the Fleadh Cheoil in 2013 many within the minority PUL community looked upon the decision with contempt. The Fleadh Cheoil has always been strongly associated with Irish national identity, so for the Unionists this festival was another sign of CRN dominance within the city. This was the complex and difficult context within which the organisers of the Fleadh Cheoil sought to use the event to break down barriers and promote inclusivity.

## Methodology

This research adopted a qualitative approach and mixed empirical methods in the form of in-depth interviews and focus groups. Critical case sampling, a form of purposive sampling, was used to select the interviewees. In order to gain an insight into the Fleadh Cheoil 2013 the authors conducted an in-depth interview with the Manager of An Gaelaras (the lead partner). During this interview, the manager discussed the partnership that was formed with the Londonderry Bands Forum during the planning stages. This prompted the authors to interview the Coordinator of the Londonderry Bands Forum. The Director of St Columb's Park House Peace and Reconciliation Centre was also interviewed as it was felt that his experience of working with both the Nationalist and the PUL communities would leave him well placed to comment on the impact of the Fleadh Cheoil. To elicit as much information as possible from these interviews the authors combined the general interview guide approach with an open-ended approach. In conjunction with local community officers, the authors also organised six focus groups with 58 members of the local community who differed by age, sex, occupation and religion. These focus groups encouraged local residents to discuss their experiences during the Fleadh Cheoil and to explain how they felt the festival affected those living in their neighbourhoods. All of the data were analysed using thematic analysis, and the main findings are discussed in the following.

## Discussion

According to Chalip (2004) if the social benefits of an event are to be effectively leveraged they must be incorporated into the event strategic planning process. When Derry/Londonderry, a politically and culturally divided city, won the right to host the Fleadh Cheoil, one of the strategic objectives adopted by the Fleadh Cheoil na hEireann Executive Committee was to make the 2013 Fleadh inclusive of the entire community in the city. The lead partner in delivering the festival was An Gaelaras, an organisation established in 1984 to promote the Irish language and culture within the city and surrounding area. An initial point of note is that the decision to bid for the Fleadh was part of a pre-existing strategy to encourage social cohesion in the city. The Manager of An Gaelaras explained that hosting the Fleadh was a 'natural follow on' and an opportunity to continue pursuing this objective on a larger scale. Having secured the bid to host the Fleadh, the festival was thus understood as an opportunity to be exploited (O'Brien & Chalip 2008) and as part of a long-term strategy (Jago et al. 2010). At the outset, An Gaelaras met with various groups representing the PUL community in order to design a programme of activities which facilitated, enabled and encouraged the participation of the PUL community. This was not an easy process as the Manager of An Gaelaras explained:

> One of the strategic objectives of the Fleadh Cheoil was that we would make it an inclusive event. So we met with North West Cultural Partnership and the Waterside Neighbourhood Partnership – but neither of them were overly enthused about it. But at one of the meetings we did meet with the Chair of Londonderry Bands Forum who was more open to idea of working with us.

The Londonderry Bands Forum was established in October 2010 to represent loyalist marching bands in the city. During the interview with the Coordinator of the Londonderry Bands Forum he discussed how all 14 PUL neighbourhoods in Derry/Londonderry have a marching band. These bands are held in high esteem within their respective communities as the music they play is seen as an expression of their Protestant culture and British identity. It should be noted that on occasions, marching bands have become involved in political demonstrations and protests, and Ramsey (2011, p. 2) describes how 'this sometimes led them into confrontation with the CRN community'. In this context, and given that the Fleadh Cheoil was a celebration of 'Irish' culture coupled with the fact that the Manager of An Gaelaras was a former CRN politician, it was understandable that the members of the Londonderry Bands Forum had mixed feelings about collaborating with An Gaelaras:

> When we went to the first meeting there was a lot of suspicion because some of the people involved in the Fleadh Cheoil committee were very much politically orientated. We were also suspicious of their motives – do they need us in order to get a

grant/money? But once we arrived at the state of the art cultural offices we soon realised they were miles ahead of us on anything we were doing and they genuinely wanted us to be involved in the festival.

*(Coordinator, Londonderry Bands Forum)*

From a PUL perspective, feelings of scepticism and mistrust gradually began to dissipate as they realised that the Fleadh Cheoil could provide them with a unique opportunity to display positive aspects of their culture. Admittedly, the first few meetings were 'heated' as both parties were encouraged to express their concerns. However, both sides persisted, encouraged perhaps by the extraordinary 'once-off' context provided by the event and the enhanced communication that this can engender (Howell 2013). In the long term, thrashing out their differences was vital as it helped to remove some of 'political baggage' that could have later created a deadlock. It also helped to build up trust and respect between the two organisations, something which Devine et al. (2016) described as critical in a collaborative setting:

The meetings were very straight talking. As a former CRN Mayor of the city I would have had a very strong republican image and they (the band members) would have regarded me as the 'enemy'. Likewise some of them had strong loyalist backgrounds but we managed to overcome this.

*(Manager, An Gaelaras)*

What really came out of the Fleadh was trust – that is how it worked – we realised straight away when speaking with Gerry (Manager of An Gaelaras) that it was never tokenism. We knew what the Fleadh Cheoil was about and they knew what the bands forum was about.

*(Director of St Columb's Park House Peace and Reconciliation Centre)*

Muir (2011) discusses the importance of leadership and how individuals can bring groups from a divided community together. In the case of Fleadh Cheoil the friendship that developed between the Manager of An Gaelaras and the Coordinator of the Londonderry Bands Forum proved invaluable. These two individuals were the driving force during the formative stages of the partnership and key to strategically leveraging the social impacts beyond the festival:

Gerry O Hara (Manager, An Gaelaras) was very good privately – behind the scenes encouraging the members of the community to come and sell the idea of an inclusive Fleadh Cheoil. He made us realise its potential and how it could be mutually beneficial.

*(Coordinator, Londonderry Bands Forum)*

After these initial meetings, An Gaelaras formed a very strong working relationship with the Londonderry Bands Forum. Significantly, representatives from the PUL community were invited to sit on a number of organising subcommittees to help develop the Fleadh Cheoil engagement programme. This ensured that the Bands Forum would be able to offer input on the planning and that they were in a position to address any concerns raised from within the PUL community.

As discussed earlier in this chapter, the 'Troubles' had left Derry/Londonderry a segregated city, with the majority of the Protestants leaving the Cityside and moving across the River Foyle to the Waterside. During the planning stages it was agreed that in order to make Fleadh Cheoil 2013 inclusive it would have to be physically staged in both sides of the city. Accordingly, venues were located in both the Waterside and the Cityside. Perhaps even more significantly, four loyalist bands took part in the official programme, including a performance on one of the main stages at Ebrington Square. McDermott et al. (2015) described this as a 'symbolic gesture', but as the following quotes would suggest, it was more than a gesture, serving to open up the city physically:

> It was notable that during the days when our band were playing there was a lot of PUL people from the Waterside over watching giving them legitimacy and a reason to come out and watch rather than say it was an event for the other community.
> (Director of St Columb's Park House Peace and Reconciliation Centre)

> The fact that four loyalist bands played at the Fleadh was crucial as it opened the door for member s of the PUL community to come over to the cityside and enjoy the event.
> (Coordinator, Londonderry Bands Forum)

More generally, events and activities like this created new opportunities for social engagement, enabling the sense of *communitas* (Turner 1982) to emerge. The data showed that the Fleadh encouraged residents to move around parts of the city that are perceived to be closed off to them on religious grounds. The Manager of An Gaelaras told of extensive anecdotal evidence showing how bands' performances encouraged people from PUL communities to socialise in CRN districts of the city. For some residents, specifically some band members, this meant revisiting parts of their city lost to them for decades because of conflict. Cross-city movements like these, and the heightened social relations that they fostered, were intentionally stimulated by programming decisions taken in respect of where and when events were scheduled, in line with the objective of encouraging inclusivity.

Another important intervention taken by the Fleadh Cheoil organising committee was to place restrictions on the flying of flags in order to make this a festival for 'everyone'. While this may have seemed a rather draconian measure, the organisers were aware that flags like the tricolour (the Irish Flag) would have been off-putting and intimidating to members of the PUL community. This is because, as Nic Craith (2013) has discussed, cultural symbols like flags and murals are used by both CRN and PUL groups in Northern Ireland to mark their territories. Preemptive measures like this were important in encouraging inclusion and participation from across the different communities in the city. This was just one of the many actions taken by the Fleadh Cheoil organisers to exploit the 'atmosphere of potentials' (Pløger 2010, p. 853) that festivals represent in an attempt to tackle social divisions in the city. In using the festival to subvert social norms (Bakhtin 1968), the individuals from both communities who acted as leaders were taking risks. The Manager of An Gaelaras, for example, spoke of programming the PSNI (Police Service of Northern Ireland) Pipe Band to perform in one of the city's main civic squares, without any knowledge of how the performance would be received by the public. However, the rewards that accompanied the risk-taking were clearly communicated in the 'community focus groups' data:

> There was a lot of people form the PUL community who attended the Fleadh Cheoil. I know from my contacts through the Women's Group that they had a ball.
> (Greater Shantallow Area Focus Group)

> Our band (The Irish Street Band) took part in the Fleadh Cheoil and it was so nice to see them involved.... both sides celebrating together.
>
> *(Irish Street Focus Group)*

> During the Fleadh Cheoil I saw people in Fountain Street (PUL) sitting outside their homes enjoying the music.... there was so much positivity and goodwill in the city at that time.
>
> *(Outerwest Focus Group)*

These quotes support Quinn and Wilks' (2013) argument that festival settings foster social connections. However, for a divided city like Derry/Londonderry this has added significance because the Fleadh Cheoil allowed people from the CRN and PUL communities to widen their social circles beyond traditional communal barriers and realise that it does not always have to be a case of 'us and them'. Long et al. (2004) suggest that festivals may also provide opportunities for cross-cultural understanding. This was certainly the case with the Fleadh Cheoil 2013 when culture provided participants with a shared focus and interest which transcended prevailing perceptions of difference and division.

Earlier it was noted that the organisers of the Fleadh Cheoil, when bidding for the event in 2012, saw it as an opportunity to pursue their objective of building bridges between communities in the city. In the event's aftermath, they took steps to maintain and strengthen the good will, social engagement and enhanced community relations generated. A key undertaking was the establishment of the Droichead project, 'droichead' being an Irish word meaning 'bridge'. A cross-community project, Droichead is designed to promote inclusivity and awareness of cultural diversity. As the lead partner, An Gaelaras, in conjunction with the Londonderry Bands Forum, developed a number of initiatives, the most notable being a Learning Resource Pack for schools. This pack included a 15-minute film which told the story of engagement between An Gaelaras and the Londonderry Bands Forum during the Fleadh Cheoil. The pack also included tasks which were designed to encourage students to discuss the film and how this festival challenged stereotypes, changed perceptions and encouraged dialogue, diversity and inclusion in Derry/Londonderry. When it was launched this learning resource was well received by the schools in the city and surrounding area, and at the time of writing it is still being taught as part the Global Citizenship Curriculum (Key Stage 3). In 2017 the Droichead project remained ongoing.

## Conclusion

The Fleadh Cheoil hosted in Derry/Londonderry in 2013 had a clear objective of tackling the social divides that continue to characterise the city post conflict. An Gaelaras, the lead organising partner, already had a pre-existing strategy to promote cultural awareness and encourage cross-community activities in the city. Bidding to host the Fleadh was viewed as an opportunity to further advance this strategy. While the organisers may not have had a formal leveraging plan in place, the study has identified a range of outcomes. These include a clear intent to leverage positive social outcomes through the festival; an approach that was distinguished by traits that included clear and simple strategic thinking that was operationalised before, during and after the festival; strong leadership; a commitment to cross-community dialogue, networking and partnership; persistence in the face of obstacles; and risk-taking. The study further identified a range of proactive steps taken by the organisers to avail of the once-off and extraordinary context created by the festival. Availing of the good will and civic pride in the city engendered through the festival, and tapping into the relative neutrality of music and arts, the organisers managed to work through obstacles and encourage positive cross-community social interactions. The relationships built during the festival continue through the auspices of the Droichead project established specifically to further the advances made during the Fleadh.

## References

Bakhtin, M. M. (1968). The role of games in Rabelais. *Yale French Studies*, (41), 124-132.

Boland, P., Murtagh, B. & Shirlow, P. (2016). Fashioning a city of culture: 'Life and place changing' or '12 month party'? *International Journal of Cultural Policy*, http://dx.doi.org/10.1080/10286632.2016.1231181.

Chalip, L. (2004). Beyond impact: A general model for event leverage. In Ritchie, B. & Adair, D. (Eds.), *Sport Tourism-Interrelationships, Impacts and Issues* (pp. 54–69). Clevedon: Channel View Publications.

Derry City Council. (2014). *Good Relations Strategy 2014/15–16/17*. Londonderry: Derry City Council.

Devine, A. & Devine, F. (2011). Planning and developing tourism within a public sector quagmire: Lessons from and for small countries. *Tourism Management*, 32(6), 1253–1261.

Devine, A., Devine, F. & Carruthers, C. (2016). Developing a community festival admits civil unrest. In Jepson, A. & Clarke, A. (Eds.), *Planning, Design and Management of Community Festivals and Events* (pp. 165–179). London: Palgrave.

Duffy, M. & Mair, J. (2015). Festivals and sense of community in places of transition: The Yakkerboo Festival, an Australian case study. In Jepson, A. & Clarke, A. (Eds.), *Exploring Community Festivals and Events* (pp. 54–65). London: Routledge.

Falassi, A. (1987). Festival: Definition and morphology. In Falassi, A. (Ed.), *Time Out of Time: Essays on the Festival* (pp. 1–10). Albuquerque: The University of New Mexico Press.

Foley, M., McGillivary, D. & McPherson, G. (2012). *Event Policy: From Theory to Strategy*. London: Routledge.

Howell, F.C. (2013). Sense of place, heterotopia, and community: Performing land and folding time in the Badalisc Festival of Northern Italy. *Folklore*, 124, 45–63. Jago, L., Dwyer, L., Lipman, G., Van Lill, D. & Vorster, S. (2010). Optimising the potential of mega-events: An overview. *International Journal of Event and Festival Management*, 1(3), 220–237.

Karadakis, K., Kaplanidou, K. & Karlis, G. (2010). Event leveraging of mega sport events: A SWOT analysis approach. *International Journal of Event and Festival Management*, 1(3), 170–185.

Long, P., & Robinson, M. (Eds.). (2004). *Festivals and tourism: Marketing, management and evaluation*. Sunderland, UK: Business Education Publishers.

McDermott, P., Nic Craith, M. & Strani, K. (2015). Public space, collective memory and intercultural dialogue in a (UK) city of culture. *Identities: Global Studies in Culture and Power*, 2(1), 1–12.

Misener, L. & Mason, D. (2006). Creating community networks: Can sporting events offer meaningful sources of social capital? *Managing Leisure*, 11(1), 39–56.

Muir, J. (2011). Bridging and linking in a divided society: A social capital case study from Northern Ireland. *Urban Studies*, 48(5), 959–976.

Nic Craith, M. (2013). Living heritage and religious traditions: Reinterpreting Columba/Colmcille in the UK city of culture. *Anthropological Journal of European Cultures*, 22(1), 42–58.

O'Brien, D. & Chalip, L. (2008). Sport events and strategic leveraging: Pushing towards the triple bottom line. In Woodside, A. & Martin, D. (Eds.), *Tourism Management: Analysis, Behaviour & Strategy* (pp. 122–133). Wallingford, Oxon: CABI.

Pløger, J. (2010). Presence-experiences: The eventalisation of city space. *Environment and Planning: Society and Space*, 28(5), 848–866.

Quinn, B. & Wilks, L. (2013). Festival connections: People, place and social capital. In Richards, G. de Brito, M.P. & Wilks, L. (Eds.), *Exploring the Social Impacts of Events* (pp. 15–30). Oxon: Routledge.

Ramsey, G. (2011). Band practice: Class, taste and identity in Ulster Loyalist Flute Bands. *Ethnomusicology Ireland*, 1, 1–20.

Shirlow, P., Graham, B., McMullan, A., Murtagh, B., Robinson, G. & Southern, N. (2005). Population change and social inclusion study Derry/Londonderry. Retrieved from http://cain.ulst.ac.uk/issues/population/popchangederry05.pdf. Accessed 14 June 2017.

Smith, A. (2010). Leveraging benefits from major events: Maximising opportunities for peripheral urban areas. *Managing Leisure, 15*(3), 161-180.

Smith, A. (2012). *Events and Urban Regeneration: The Strategic Use of Events to Revitalise Cities.* London: Routledge.

Turner, V. (1982). *From Ritual to Theatre: The Human Seriousness of Play.* New York: PAJ Publications.

Weed, M. & Dowse, S. (2009) A missed opportunity waiting to happen? The social legacy potential of the London 2012 Paralympic Games. *Journal of Policy Research in Tourism, Leisure and Events, 1*(2), 170–174.

Wilks, L. (2011). Bridging and bonding: Social capital at music festivals, *Journal of Policy Research in Tourism, Leisure and Events, 3*(3), 281–297.

Wood, E. (2006). Measuring the social impacts of local authority events: A pilot study for a civic pride scale. *International Journal of Nonprofit Voluntary Sector Marketing, 11*(3), 165–179.

# 19
# EXTENDING THE EXIT BRAND
## From Serbia's fortress to Montenegro's coast

*Nicholas Wise, Tanja Armenski and Nemanja Davidović*

### Introduction

Throughout the 1990s, the Western Balkans was a region of geopolitical dispute as the former Republic of Yugoslavia was violently fragmented by a turbulent war. Focusing on Serbia, the war negatively affected the country's national image and deterred international visitors, causing the country to rapidly stagnate. In Novi Sad, images of destroyed infrastructure, bombings and international interventions were conveyed to global audiences through the media. Conflict left Novi Sad city and much of Serbia in a state of despair, thus deterring visitors. International audiences consumed negative images of Serbia as a country with much violence and political corruption, thereby projecting fearful imaginations and left the country isolated. In 2000 a youth-led movement began in Novi Sad as a response to the atrocities in Serbia throughout the 1990s. The Exit Movement, which led to the Exit Festival, was organised by students from the University of Novi Sad. During this time, youths gathered to protest against the policies of then Serbian president, Slobodan Milošević (see Rogel 2004). The Exit Festival has become synonymous with Novi Sad, Serbia, and has gained further international recognition being awarded 'Best Major European Festival' in 2013. The Exit brand was extended with the commencement of the Sea Dance Festival in 2014 (and soon after was awarded 'Best Mid-Sized European Festival' in 2015). The Sea Dance Festival became an instant success, despite the foundations of the Exit Movement being one based on narratives of struggle, protest and democracy. It is the successful relationship between these two festivals, held in neighbouring countries, and the possible lost opportunities for Serbian tourism as a result, that form the focus of this chapter.

Since Exit's origin in 2000, the festival has attracted more than 2 million people from around the world, and it continues to convey messages of social democracy pertinent to contemporary global issues and struggles (ExitFest 2017). What started as a passive political protest has evolved into one of the most popular annual music festivals in Europe. Considered by many to be one of the festival's most unique attributes, the event is held in the Petrovaradin Fortress. The venue is a medieval fortress, a historical structure symbolising local history and heritage, but is more recently renowned for the contemporary festival. For Serbia, the growth of the Exit Festival was deemed significant towards generating tourism in the northern autonomous Vojvodina Region of the country.

This chapter builds on previous research assessing festivals and tourism in Serbia alongside critical discussions of destination/event branding and festival expansion. The next section will offer some conceptual insight on festival brands and event tourism before looking at the Exit Festival and the Sea Dance Festival as an extension of festival branding and success. Official web pages, newspapers and media outlets offer insights that complement observations to inform the section on the Exit brand and the 'Exit Adventure' before leading into a critical discussion of Serbia's lost tourism opportunity; the concluding remarks section will reflect on key points and future research directions.

## Festival branding, destination branding and event tourism

As a destination, Serbia was negatively impacted by negative connotations of war from the 1990s, and by the early to mid-2000s, the Exit Festival played a role in transforming the image of Serbia as a destination (Wise, Flinn & Mulec 2015). Researchers assessing tourism and destination branding have focussed on destination marketing and development (Govers & Go 2009; Kozak & Baloglu 2011; Morgan, Pritchard & Pride 2010). In this case, it is the festival brand that has been most successful. In a competitive business environment, a strong brand is seen as a company's greatest asset (Aaker 1996). Brands also help consumers gain awareness of a product, based on associations, quality, loyalty and experiences, in an attempt to differentiate a product from its competitors (see Keller 2003; Parent, Eskerud & Hanstad 2012). Psychologically, brands are associations, and we frame associations with places based on recognisable features, particular events or various points in a place's history (Bassols 2016; Govers 2011; Kim & Perdue 2011; Morgan et al. 2010; Qu, Kim & Im 2011; Wise 2011).

Destination branding is tied to how a place/destination marketed and promoted, and to informing visitors about a place/destination offering (Çakmak & Issac 2012; Govers, Go & Kumar 2007; Kozak & Baloglu 2011). Corporations use branding to attract customers, using and creating recognisable logos that people associate with products. Likewise, destination branding, according to Kladou, Kavaratzis, Rigopoulou and Salonika (2016), refers to naming or developing recognisable logos or taglines, or creating associations. Beritelli and Laesser (2016) add that particular logos can help detail particular experiences to help visitors identify a destination. In this case, Exit has not only become synonymous with Novi Sad and Serbia, but arguably it is the Exit brand that motivates festivalgoers to visit Serbia. Gladden, Irwin and Sutton (2001) proposed three antecedents to branding (which are team-related, organisation-related and market-related) in the field of sports management, whereas event/festivals and tourism relate to experience-induced awareness and associations through branding specific to the acts involved (and this concerns the Serbian destination organisers and the (European) festival market in this case). Govers (2011, p. 227) further argues that destination branding 'should be about creating an overarching brand strategy or competitive identity that reflects a particular nation's, city's or region's history' (see also Baker 2012; Dinnie 2015). Research on destination branding is well established in the tourism marketing (e.g. Baker 2012; Govers & Go 2009; Kladou et al. 2016) and destination development literature (e.g. Bassols 2016; Dinnie 2015; Zenker & Jacobsen 2015); however, more work concerning festivals and branding is necessary to conceptually and practically consider this more focussed niche within the tourism and events literature.

Attracting festivalgoers helps enhance a destination niche, event tourism (Getz 2013; Getz & Page 2016), and also leads to creative place development (Waitt & Gibson 2009; Wise 2016). According to Getz and Page (2016, p. 597), one of the core propositions of event tourism is 'events can create positive images for the destination and help brand or re-position cities'. However, when places are known for violence in recent history, such negative associations can be burdensome. Therefore, a focus on youth culture or the appeal of festivals helps develop a nascent brand to attract people to a destination and use events as drivers to promote tourism (see Wise et al. 2015). The challenge arises when a destination struggles to develop a tourism agenda and promote its destination, and then a popular festival attract tourists, meaning that tourism and destination managers need to get involved in event and festival management. If the national, regional and local tourism managers/planners do not work with the event, the event itself (as this chapter argues) is solely what is supplied to consumers and visitors. Visitor demand is then linked to the brand, and such influence of the event itself overtakes what additional features a destination might have to offer—making it difficult to destination managers to manage tourism and visitor mobility. This is discussed as the 'Exit Adventure', the emergence of the Sea Dance Festival, and ExitTrip.

## The rise of exit and the new 'Exit Adventure'

As mentioned, the Exit Movement was a political demonstration—messages across Serbia in 2000 were *otpor* (resistance and the people's movement against the Milošević regime) and *gotov je* (a slogan used to refer to the end of Milošević's rule). The Exit Movement aimed to bring people together using the power of music and to encourage people to vote in the upcoming election (Wise et al. 2015). People in Serbia often referred to the movement as the beginning of the end of Slobodan Milošević's rule, and 10 days after the first Exit Movement the first democratic government was established in Serbia. Whether or not the Exit Movement, in fact, contributed to domestic change in Serbia's political scene is debatable; however, the festival encouraged and generated social cohesion among youths. If we consider the impact of the event, its legacy links to the new opening of Serbia. Event organisers continued promoting sociopolitical messages pertinent to ongoing contemporary issues, regionally and globally (such as human trafficking, integration and voting). Furthermore, event organisers recognised the importance of making up for the 'lost decade' of the 1990s that youths in Serbia missed, so they can now experience popular international artists and meet more international visitors. Research on the Exit Festival exists looking at the setting/venue of the event in the Petrovaradin Fortress (Besermenji, Pivac & Wallrabenstein 2009); host/guest interactions (Zakić, Ivkov-Džigurski & Ćurčić 2009); culture and entrepreneurship (Dušica 2011); and politics, youths and city/country image (Wise et al. 2015).

Promoted as a festival with a message held in a fortress which combines popular culture and heritage, in recent years the Exit Festival has become a missed opportunity for Serbia to further (and fully) sell itself as a destination. In view of the success and the growth of popular consumer products, increased demand, rising profit margins and the ability to expand operations, the Exit Festival organisers saw an opportunity to add additional days and extend their brand. The Sea Dance Festival in Montenegro in its first three years has occurred in the days following Exit in Serbia—and is promoted as part of the 'Exit Adventure'. Held at Jaz Beach (near Budva, Montenegro), the Sea Dance Festival channels myriads of young people through Serbia to Montenegro. However, Exit's growth and success has arguably outsold Serbian tourism, with the 'Exit Adventure' suggesting that young people should carry on to the next festival on Montenegro's beachfront as opposed to encouraging festivalgoers to explore the sights, attractions and highlights of Serbia's Vojvodina Region. Moreover, the role of the media in promoting Exit (and now Sea Dance) fuels imaginations of Serbia as a destination specifically for summer music and the land of Exit.

The media has played a key role in promoting the Exit Festival. However, one of the challenges is while the media promotes Exit, they do it to help brand the destination and improve the negative image of Serbia as a war-torn country. Yet it was the festival, as opposed to the destination, that gained media and international recognition, with MTV expressing interest in 2004 to sign a deal with Exit to promote the festival beyond the Balkans (BBC 2004). This would be the main turning point towards establishing (and promoting) the Exit brand, but the negative legacies of war in conflict in Serbia and the immediate region were still fresh in the imaginations of people from outside the region. There was a need for western journalists to travel to Serbia and tell the story of the current situation and Exit to change how people perceived Serbia to promote the destination and the event. For instance, The Independent (2005) noted,'

> after NATO bombed Novi Sad in 1999, the youth of Serbia were ready to retaliate with a 100-day protest party. Exit was born, bringing in musicians and DJs, holding parties on the river, around the castle [sic] and on boats.'

This article was written as Exit began to see more success and benefits from MTV. Years later the narrative and negative imaginations of war began to fade: 'New look of Serbia: magical music event helps dispel the memories of war as country's youth celebrates' (Birmingham Evening Mail 2009). The new destination brand of Serbia began to transition towards representing Serbia as a festival destination, and this was assisted by romanticised images of the event destination: 'Exit is perched high and majestic above the river Danube in its historical fortress; about as far from humdrum as my imagination will stretch' (The Evening Standard-London 2007 'Both the wide range of music genres performed at the Exit Festival and the location in the 17th-century Petrovaradin Fortress in Novi Sad have contributed to the rise in popularity of the event. The four-day festival is now recognised as one of Europe's biggest' (The People-Ulster Edition 2011).

The Irish Times (2001) described the event as one 'held in the 18th century [sic] Petrovaradin fortress overlooking the Danube in Novi Sad, Serbia…these days EXIT draws music fans from all over Europe for its hedonistic atmosphere and idiosyncratic line-up'. As the festival's popularity increased, destination elements were often overshadowed by the event's popularity, although the uniqueness of the venue was a destination feature regularly acknowledged:

> 'The year was the 11th EXIT festival and the madness in a historic fort on the banks of the Danube has grown to such international acclaim, it now attracts headliners such as Placebo, Missey Elliott, The Chemical Brothers, LCD Soundsystem and Mika.
> *(Liverpool Echo 2010)*

> Exit gives concert-goers the unique opportunity of exploring underground passages while checking out headliners Duran, New Order, Plan B and Guns 'n' Roses. The 18th-century [sic] Petrovaradin Fortress in Novi Sad, where Exit is held, offers superb acoustics that allow bands to perform simultaneously without any sound interference.
> *(The Toronto Star 2012)*

While these quotes are only a snapshot of how the media portrays the event, such quotes were common and suggest that the focus is put solely on the event, with little coverage portraying the appeal of the destination beyond the Petrovaradin Fortress venue. While destination marketers and managers cannot always influence how journalists and media outlets promote the festival, they can use these as frameworks of reference to build the destination appeal alongside the event. ExitFest (2017) builds on the promotion of the newspapers stating: 'Exit is an award-winning music festival. It is held annually at the Petrovaradin Fortress in the city of Novi Sad (Serbia), which is considered by many as one of the best festival venues in the world'. The challenge is making the appeal of the destination relate to the audience of festivalgoers if they want to capture them as tourist before or after the event.

The economic impacts of events can vary depending on the destination. Larger cities have continuous business throughout the year, so they can expect hotel receipts to be consistent. Smaller or lesser-known destinations that host one key hallmark event each year may only see a short-term economic spike and may have to depend on the financial impact of the event for the year. A challenge then for destination managers is to give festivalgoers a reason to stay three or four days before or after an event—ideally to extend the impact of the event to nine to eleven days. It may not be achievable for a destination to host several major events or festivals throughout the year, but they can promote the destination in a way that highlights the success of the destination during the event, and they can showcase the quaintness and appeal of the destination when the event is not happening.

Hennessey, Yun, MacDonald and MacEachern (2010, pp. 218–219) note, 'given the ever-expanding number of tourism destinations and the increased supply of products and services, the competition for visitors is intense and bound to become more so in the future'. It is therefore common to assume that destinations are competing against each other. However, what is less common is a destination competing against a local event that is now helping influence attendee mobility patterns. With the discussion concerning the impact and influence of Exit, the organisers now promote the 'Exit Adventure' as '2 FESTIVALS, 2 COUNTRIES, 2 SPECTACULAR LOCATIONS…1 UNFORGETABLE ADVENTURE!' (ExitFest 2017). With the growth and rapid popularity of Exit, this allowed the festival organisers to extend the brand to a new location. The success was perhaps quicker than tourism planners and managers may have anticipated, but with the Exit Festival playing a key role in attracting youth from around the world to Serbia each summer, this allows them to control not only the marketing and promotion but also influence mobility.

The festival organisers are also taking their own lead on promoting the image of the destination based on the unique venues, in bold the state on the office website: 'FROM THE MAGICAL FORTRESS TO THE BEST EUROPEAN BEACH!' (ExitFest 2017). The destination image features of the Exit Festival were assembled around the unique and aesthetic venue: the Petrovaradin Fortress (see Wise & Mulec 2015) which contributes to the destination brand and the event appeal. Thus the 'Exit Adventure' is arguably weakening the ability of destination managers to capture festivalgoers now that attendees can purchase a festival package. As promoted via the official website,'

> EXIT Festival, combined with its seaside sister Sea Dance Festival, makes for a world's most unique festival package which has become the best festival holiday on the planet that spans over 10 days! This amazing package combines two award-winning festivals at two spectacular locations in two neighbouring countries, which proved to be a successful formula that attracts over 270,000 people each year […] to the magical Petrovaradin Fortress in Serbia, then continue their Adventure to the turquoise sandy Jaz Beach in Montenegro'.

*(ExitFest 2017)*

In addition to the destination appeal of both festival locations, the website also notes,'

> EXIT Adventure has been acknowledged among festivals as the best value for the money by The Guardian and many other leading media. Compared to other major festivals, tickets are traditionally more affordable for the very competitive and diverse lineup. Accommodation, food and beverage prices in this region are also much lower compared to other European countries'.
>
> (ExitFest 2017)

In addition, to assist festivalgoers with travel planning, Exit has created a tourist service (called ExitTrip) to book a range of accommodations and arrange flights to various airports across the region. While much of this chapter is concerned with tourist demand, Exit is also controlling the supply side which takes away opportunities for local tourism providers in Serbia.

## Serbia's lost opportunity

It is important that destination marketers and managers develop a brand that will define a place and work with event organisers to ensure the destination benefits from the popular festival and the festival benefits from the destination. In being critical of the case of the Exit Festival, it can be argued that destination marketers could have done more to highlight the destination of Novi Sad, Vojvodina and Serbia as the Exit Festival grew in popularity and influence. Mulec and Wise's (2013) work (conducted 2010–2012) assessed the destination competitiveness of Serbia's Vojvodina Region. Destination management indicators were among the weakest findings, and while the majority of creative resources also needed improvement, they found that the 'quality and originality of festivals' was the most competitive creative resource in their survey of regional tourism experts (Mulec & Wise 2013). While regional experts did recognise the potential then, in 2013 the Exit Festival reached a European milestone being awarded the 'Best Major European Festival'. This status showed that in only 13 years, Exit went from a local grassroots movement in a destination recovering from war and political uncertainty to being the host of a festival that had emerged among the European music festival landscape.

Building on the success of the festival, instead of Serbia embracing this recognition, Exit Festival organisers then extended the Exit brand by promoting the 'Exit Adventure' and developing the Sea Dance Festival in neighbouring (but still distant) Montenegro. A new festival that commenced only in 2014 was also soon recognised with Sea Dance being awarded the 'Best Mid-Sized European Festival' in 2015. With the rising popularity of music festivals across Europe and the extension of festival brands, this creates challenges for destination managers. The example of Serbia is one of lost opportunities, where the chance to build the success of a festival into the development of a destination to promote subsequent tourism opportunities saw the Exit Festival influence the mobility of festivalgoers. While destination marketers in Serbia did promote Exit, the extent to which Exit promoted Serbia is debatable. Wise and Mulec (2015) analysed media content surrounding representations of Exit and found that despite the attempt to speak to the appeal of the destination, it was the uniqueness of Exit's venue, the Petrovaradin Fortress, that highlighted that attributes of the destination. Little else was found in terms of promoting Serbia and Vojvodina as a destination beyond the event. Media presentations were matched with findings from surveys collected at the Exit Festival with the majority of participants only spending time in Serbia for the duration of the event and not knowing about subsequent tourism opportunities in the region.

In most cases, domestic travel through Serbia was between Belgrade and Novi Sad (because of Belgrade's airport).

In order to improve Serbia's competitive position and to sustain it, both destination managers, local business owners and investors need to better consider longer-term planning. Dwyer, Duc Pham, Forsyth and Spurr (2014) highlight the need to focus on expenditure yield rather than visitor numbers, which has also recently been identified as the appropriate objective of Destination Marketing Organisations (DMOs) when marketing from both domestic and international tourism—which can then be applied to festival management using the same approach. In order to provide sustainable visitor yields, tourism operators should create theme-based products and shift promotion on the emotional benefits—which is one of the benefits of events and festivals. To achieve this there needs to be better networking and collaboration between public- and private-sector stakeholders to improve the overall performance of Serbia's tourism, events and leisure industries. Local tourism managers and stakeholders involved with tourism in Serbia need to do much more to present and showcase, or make visitors aware of supplemental tourism opportunities to festival attendees. According to Getz, Andersson and Carlsen (2010), there is a need for tourism planners to better know the festival audience and relate to their travel demands beyond the event. There is a need to better capture tourists before and after the event, but this might be able to be achieved if destination managers in Novi Sad, Vojvodina and Serbia work closely with ExitTrip and Exit organisers to form a stronger event-tourism partnership.

## Conclusions

Once an established brand begins to promote itself and expand, it begins working like a corporate entity that builds strength. Because Serbia was recovering from a negative image, the Exit Festival offered something different, and at first, interpretations were suggesting it was playing a role in regenerating the image of Novi Sad and Serbia (Wise et al. 2015). However, the challenge presented in this chapter is that the destination itself (Novi Sad—Vojvodina—Serbia) was not able to fully capture the potential of the event to present other unique features of the destination. Instead, Exit grew as a brand and now has established the presence of another festival in Montenegro and harnesses its own image and power to create the 'Exit Adventure' and offer a festival package that directs event goers from one place directly to the next. Festivalgoers need to travel between Novi Sad and Budva, so other towns in Serbia may capture some of these tourists as they travel between. Nevertheless, it is the appeal of the sea in Montenegro or the opportunity to traverse Bosnia and Herzegovina that appears to be most attractive. Thus some of the possibilities to capture these event goers in other Serbian destinations might be considered a lost opportunity.

This chapter of the handbook presents an overview and critique of Serbia's lost opportunity given the ability of Exit to build on their own popularity and expand to another festival in another event location. Some of the insights presented from various media outlets and official tourism websites provide an overview of how an event or destination is perceived, allowing for academic inquiry, reflection and critique. More in-depth research is needed from several perspectives. Foremost, the consumer base of festivalgoers who attend both events should be assessed to better understand their interests and travel desires. This could help destination mangers in Serbia better promote places to capture festivalgoers before the Exit Festival or on route to Montenegro. From previous research at the Exit Festival, it was found that many were not aware of tourism opportunities or their main reason for visiting Serbia was to attend the Exit Festival (Bjeljac & Lović 2011; Zakić et al. 2009). Therefore, working with local and regional tourism stakeholders to promote their destinations during the event further and via popular social media platforms may help with reaching the target audience of Exit Festival attendees or those partaking in the 'Exit Adventure'.

Both festival and tourism managers must assume proactive leadership roles in a rapidly changing industry. Ongoing work is continuing to assess Serbian competitiveness as an events and festival destination, but to better secure and facilitate investments and continue building a festival base image, the Serbian tourism industry needs to be explicitly identified by wider stakeholder groups as a key economic sector, supported by a clear vision and strong leadership. Productivity increases in tourism will require a more highly skilled tourism workforce, but a workforce that can also cater to the festival industry and seek ways to capture and maintain festivalgoers as tourists.

## References

Aaker, D.A. (1996). *Building Strong Brands*. New York: The Free Press.
Baker, B. (2012). *Destination Branding for Small Cities*. Portland: Creative Leap Books.
Bassols, N. (2016). Branding and promoting a country amidst a long-term conflict: The case of Colombia. *Journal of Destination Marketing & Management*, 5(4), 314–324.
BBC. (2004). MTV to sign deal with Serbian festival on music promotion. *BBC Summary of World Broadcasts*, 29 June 2004.
Beritelli, P. & Laesser, C. (2016). Destination logo recognition and implications for intentional destination branding by DMOs: A case for saving money. *Journal of Destination Marketing & Management*, DOI: https://doi.org/10.1016/j.jdmm.2016.08.010.
Besermenji, S., Pivac, T. & Wallrabenstein, K. (2009). Significance of the authentic ambience of the Petrovaradin Fortress on the attractiveness of Exit Festival. *Geographica Pannonica*, 13(2), 66–74.
Birmingham Evening Mail. (2009). New look of Serbia; Magical music event helps dispel the memories: of war as country's youth celebrates: The Great Escape. *Birmingham Evening Mail*, 22 July 2009.
Bjeljac, Z. & Lović, S. (2011). Demographic analysis of foreign visitors to the Exit Festival, Novi Sad. *Journal of the Geographical Institute 'Jovan Cvijić' SASA*, 61(2), 97–108.
Çakmak, E. & Issac, R. (2012). What destination marketers can learn from their visitors' blogs: An image analysis of Bethlehem, Palestine. *Journal of Destination Marketing & Management*, 1(1–2), 124–133.
Dinnie, K. (2015). *Nation Branding: Concepts, Issues, Practice*. London: Routledge.
Dušica, D. (2011). Preduzetništvo u kulturi-studija slučaja muzičkog festival. *Kultura*, 130, 350–366.
Dwyer, L. Duc Pham, T. Forsyth, P. & Spurr, R. (2014). Destination marketing of Australia: Return on investment. *Journal of Travel Research*, 53(3), 281–295.
ExitFest. (2017). Exit Adventure. Retrieved from www.exitfest.org/en/exit-adventure. Accessed 21 November 2017.
Getz, D. (2013). *Event Tourism*. Putnam Valley, NY: Cognizant.
Getz, D., Andersson, T. & Carlsen, J. (2010). Festival management studies: Developing a framework and priorities for comparative and cross-cultural research. *International Journal of Event and Festival Management*, 1(1), 29–59.
Getz, D. & Page, S.J. (2016). Progress and prospects for event tourism research. *Tourism Management*, 52(February), 593–631.
Govers, R. (2011). From place marketing to place branding and back. *Place Branding and Public Diplomacy*, 7(4), 227–231.
Govers, F. & Go, F. (2009). *Place Branding: Glocal, Virtual and Physical Identities*. Basingstoke: Palgrave Macmillan.
Govers, R., Go, F.M. & Kumar, K. (2007). Promoting tourism destination image. *Journal of Travel Research*, 46(1), 15–23.
Gladden, J.M., Irwin, R.L. & Sutton, W.A. (2001). Managing North American major professional sports team in the new millennium: A focus on building brand equity. *Journal of Sport Management*, 15(4), 297–317.
Hennessey, S.M., Yun, D., MacDonald, R. & MacEachern, M. (2010). The effects of advertising awareness and media form on travel intensions. *Journal of Hospitality Marketing and Management*, 19(3), 217–243.

Keller, K. (2003). Brand synthesis: The multidimensionality of brand knowledge. *Journal of Consumer Research*, 29(4), 595–600.

Kim, D. & Perdue, R.R. (2011). The influence of image on destination attractiveness. *Journal of Travel and Tourism Marketing*, 28(3), 225–239.

Kladou, S., Kavaratzis, M., Rigopoulou, I. & Salonika, E. (2016). The role of brand elements in destination branding. *Journal of Destination Marketing & Management*, DOI: https://doi.org/10.1016/j.jdmm.2016.06.011.

Kozak, M. & Baloglu, S. (2011). *Managing and Marketing Tourist Destinations*. London: Routledge.

Liverpool Daily Echo. (2010). A musical revolution; Ben Rossington uncovers Serbia's best kept secret. *Liverpool Daily Echo*, 26 October 2010.

Morgan, N., Pritchard, A. & Pride, R. (2010). *Destination Branding: Creating the Unique Destination Proposition*. Oxford: Elsevier Butterworth-Heinemann.

Mulec, I. & Wise, N. (2013). Indicating the competitiveness of Serbia's Vojvodina region as an emerging tourism destination. *Tourism Management Perspectives*, 8, 68–79.

Parent, M.M., Eskerud, L. & Hanstad, D.V. (2012). Brand creation in international recurring sports events. *Sport Management Review*, 15(2), 145–159.

Qu, H., Kim, L.H. & Im, H.H. (2011). A model of destination branding: Integrating the concepts of the branding and destination image. *Tourism Management*, 32(3), 465–476.

Rogel, C. (2004). *The Breakup of Yugoslavia and Its Aftermath*. Westport, CT: Greenwood Press.

The Evening Standard-London. (2007). I'm just a festival fanatic; One aficionado thinks nothing of blowing a week's wages on a music weekend in Serbia; Where to hear the music this summer. *The Evening Standard (London)*, 11 July 2007.

The Independent. (2005). Rock & Pop: How young Serbs rocked the castle. *The Independent (London)*, 15 July 2005.

The Irish Times. (2008). Striking a chord. *The Irish Times*, Travel Section, 22 March 2008.

The People-Ulster Edition. (2011). HEAD FOR EXIT: Serbia's best music festival offers song, sun and blue Danube. *The People (Ulster Edition)*, 29 May 2011.

The Toronto Star. (2012). Rock, shock and 100 tons of splat! *The Toronto Star*, Travel Section, 26 May 2012.

Waitt, G. & Gibson, C. (2009). Creative small cities: Rethinking the creative economy in place. *Urban studies*, 46(5/6), 1223–1246.

Wise, N. (2011). Post-war tourism and the imaginative geographies of Bosnia and Herzegovina, and Croatia. *European Journal of Tourism Research*, 4(1), 5–24.

Wise, N. (2016). Outlining triple bottom line contexts in urban tourism regeneration. *Cities*, 53(April), 30–34.

Wise, N., Flinn, J. & Mulec, I. (2015). Exit Festival: Contesting political pasts, impacts on youth culture and regenerating the image of Serbia and Novi Sad. In Pernecky, T. & Moufakkir, O. (Eds.), *Ideological, Social and Cultural Aspects of Events* (pp. 60–73). Wallingford, UK: CABI.

Wise, N. & Mulec, I. (2015). Aesthetic awareness and spectacle: Communicated images of Novi Sad, the Exit Festival and the event venue Petrovaradin Fortress. *Tourism Review International*, 19(4), 193–205.

Zakić, L., Ivkov-Džigurski, A. & Ćurčić, N. (2009). Interaction of foreign visitors of the Exit Music Festival with domestic visitors and local population. *Geographica Pannonica*, 13(3), 97–104.

Zenker, S. & Jacobsen, B. (2015). *Inter-regional Place Branding: Best Practices, Challenges and Solutions*. Berlin: Springer.

# 20
# THE EVENTFUL CITY IN A COMPLEX ECONOMIC, SOCIAL AND POLITICAL ENVIRONMENT
## The case of Macau

*Ubaldino Sequeira Couto*

### Introduction

Macao is the first and last European colony in Asia (Cheng 1999). Throughout its 442 years of Portuguese rule, Macao had undergone dramatic changes from a quaint, quiet fishing village to a thriving centre of sea trade and, in the 1990s, from a declining economy in the shadows of Hong Kong's prosperity to the gaming capital of the world today, with receipts long surpassing that of Las Vegas (Vong 2008). Macao is just under 31 km$^2$, with a population increased from 513,400 in 2006 to 644,900 in 2016 (DSEC 2017), thanks to immigrant investor programmes and human resources demand brought forth by the prosperous economy, making Macao the most densely populated in the world. The transformation of Macao following the handover from Portuguese rule to Chinese administration on 20 December 1999 has been unprecedented, all of which is attributed to the deregulation of the gaming licences in 2002, just three years following the handover, in the hope of restoring the economy. The economic issues were caused by the aftermath of the Asian financial crisis in the late 1990s, a negative destination image, the effects of death cases brought by the SARS (Severe Acute Respiratory Syndrome) outbreak in neighbouring cities and a declining economy caused by many factories in the manufacturing industry moving to mainland China, among many other reasons. This transformation has affected Macao in three main aspects: the economy, the political environment and the societal life in general.

As it will be discussed in the following sections, Macao has a complex environment with economic and sociopolitical issues. This chapter problematises the situation of Macao, presents the concept of the eventful city as a potential strategy and discusses how being eventful is vital to not only mitigate the effects resulting from having an economy based on one single sector dependent on a single market, but to boost the positive social goals that festivals and events bring. It contributes to the understanding of festivals and events as a catalyst of change, particularly from a socio-economic perspective. The views expressed in this chapter are relevant to other destinations which are developing the gaming industry, particularly if these destinations are over-reliant on gaming or gaming receipts and are heavily dependent on a single or only a few source markets.

## Economic, social and political environment of Macao

Comparing the principal economic indicators during the decade from 2006 to 2016, Gross Domestic Product (GDP) per capita in real terms rose from USD29,755 to USD69,372, the unemployment rate dropped from 3.8% to 1.9% and tourist arrivals rose from just under 22 million to 30.9 million per year. Gaming tax revenues relative to the total tax revenues received by the Macao government have risen from 48.4% in 1999 to 76.4% in 2016. The economic prosperity brought by the gaming industry has obviously created multiple benefits for residents in Macao. For example, the government has introduced policies to alleviate the effects of inflation felt by residents, such as the wealth-partaking scheme, which has run for ten years already, whereby the government gives each Macao resident a one-off cash payment of up to MOP9,000 every year and health coupons that can be used in medical establishments up to a value of MOP600 (USD1 is approximately MOP8). Because of its reliance on the gaming revenues, public spending on destination marketing and organising touristic festivals and events has also been generous. The singular economy and dependency of gaming revenues, which in turn rely on China as the main source market, puts Macao in an unfavourable position.

Although Macao enjoys a high degree of autonomy, its economic survival is largely dependent on the gaming receipts, which are, in turn, heavily reliant on the primary source market of mainland China. When President Xi Jinping came into power, he promised to put an end into China's long and serious problems in corruption. One of his promises was to stop money laundering and scare high-ranking officials, in particular, in order to discourage corruption. Coupled with unfavourable global financial conditions, this had dramatic effects on Macao's gaming receipts over recent years, from a 2014 high of MOP353.6 billion to MOP233.0 billion in 2015 – a drop of 34.1% – although the gaming sector is slowly recovering (DSEC 2017). Figures from the tourism sector also show reductions, although they are not as drastic; it is believed, however, the drop in tourist numbers was not due to China's anti-corruption initiatives, but rather due to Macao and Hong Kong being unstable and unfavourable tourist destinations for mainland Chinese following political incidents in Hong Kong. This was essentially a wake-up call for Macao as the tourism industry, which is largely fuelled by the gaming sector, is extremely sensitive to Beijing policies, global economic environment and regional political situation.

Not only have these incidents had serious implications for Macao's economy as the previous discussion shows, but the strategic direction of Macao's economy also takes its toll by having a narrow range of possibilities (Sheng & Zhao 2016). Although Macao has little say in how the long-term economic strategy is laid out due to lack of possibilities and overarching decisions by the central government in Beijing, recent policy directions from Beijing had placed Macao in a very favourable and strategic position. Macao has assumed the role of a 'one centre, one platform' in China's Belt and Road Initiative (Huang 2016). The 'one centre' refers to the positioning of Macao as the World Centre of Tourism and Leisure, a strategic direction bestowed during the twelfth five-year plan in 2011 (Vong 2016). The 'one platform' is a more recent strategic direction to utilise Macao as a platform between China and Portuguese-speaking countries in commercial and trade cooperation. A very important cornerstone of this positioning is to build Macao into a 'City of Events' where the government, through its involvement in different sectors such as sports, culture and tourism, as well as trade and commerce, initiates and supports festivals and events, particularly those which are related to the Portuguese-speaking diasporas.

Macao has a 'one country, two systems' legal framework that gives Macao a high degree of autonomy in how the city is run. In fact, the Basic Law of Macao has specific articles that encourage the practice of, and safeguard the freedom of Macao residents to engage in, activities related to religion and culture (República Popular da China 1993). Although there were a number of conflicts between the Portuguese and Chinese during the Portuguese administration (Cheng 1999), the relationship to date has been generally positive (Hao 2011). In his reviews about social problems in Macao, Hao (2005, 2011) notes the Portuguese influence still has a prominent position in society following the handover to Chinese administration but is likely to be neutralised due to younger generations of different ethnicities being acculturated. However, Macao still enjoys its advantageous platform between Chinese and Portuguese-speaking countries in trade and cultural exchange.

Recent research suggests that the solution is for Macao to reinvent itself in order to mitigate problems that arise from having only an economy based on one single sector and overdependence on a single or only a few source markets. Such research was conducted as early as the mid-2000s, shortly following the deregulation of the gaming legislation, when there were recommendations to develop Macao's gaming industry by incorporating Chinese and/or Portuguese themes in its casino businesses (Gu 2004). Adopting an urban planning perspective, Wan and Pinheiro (2014) recommend a series of solutions to ensure sustainable tourism planning such as diversifying Macao's tourist offerings, transparent planning missions and involving residents in the planning process. More recently, Sheng and Zhao (2016) recommend that Macao adopts a diversification strategy, such as utilising its United Nations Educational, Scientific and Cultural Organisation (UNESCO) World Heritage properties as well as festivals and events, in order to prepare itself for the economic downturn caused by the eventual saturation in the gaming business.

Greenwood and Dwyer (2017) suggest Macao should adopt a creative city strategy by incorporating essential attributes to mitigate threats to ensure the sustainability of its economy through realising its strategic positioning. They observe that creative cities are competitive, thriving and innovative, liveable, environmentally and socially aware, inclusive, distinctive identity and shared vision of governance. Created in 2004, the UNESCO Creative Cities Network aims to unite the different sectors of the society to commit into sharing best practices and developing partnerships (UNESCO 2015). It has been argued that modern destinations must develop themselves into creative cities that embrace characteristics of today such as technology in order to capitalise and maximise modern consumer behaviour (see Landry 2008). In a recent study conducted in Macao about community support for festivals, and the resulting tourism brought forth by these events, Li and Wan (2017) show that the community is generally positive. However, this is dependent on residents being informed of the wider benefits these festivities bring to the community, festival tourists and residents developing an emotional solidarity, and the community being involved in the festival development. These findings are largely consistent with the current understanding in event studies (Getz & Page 2016).

## Macao: an eventful city

Coupled with issues such seasonality and cities failing to create a unique proposition for place branding, as well as the shift of global citizens seeking rich experience, cities often find it difficult to differentiate one from another based on their conventional touristic offerings. Cities turn to their innate resources – festivals and events – by offering a series of festivities all year round, creating a unique, difficult to replicate and culturally rich experience; this is the eventful city (Richards & Palmer 2010). In a recent study in Romania (Richards & Rotariu 2015), an eventful city strategy created a number of positive impacts, including community pride, cultural enrichment and economic benefits. Premier Asian cities like Seoul, Hong Kong and Singapore have used an eventful city strategy as one of their destination marketing efforts. Cities like Tokyo, with its hosting of the Olympics in 2020, appear to be following suit. In addition, destination marketing efforts by regional cities in Asia seem to be promoting their destinations' unique event propositions. For example, Lantern Festivals in Taiwan, Boryeong Mud Festival in South Korea, matsuris in Japan, Songkran in Thailand, the Feast of the Black Nazarene in the Philippines, the Bun Festival in Hong Kong and Chinese New Year in China are all common sights on tourism brochures and posters, travel websites and travel fairs.

The Macao tourist board launched its strategic global marketing campaign 'Experience Macao' a few years ago, but in recent years further emphasised the initiative with a particular focus on Macao's festivals and events, branding it 'Experience Macao Event Style', showcasing the variety of festivities all year round. Clearly, this shows Macao's commitment and adoption of a long-term branding strategy that moves Macao away from the gaming-laden destination image by creating an eventful city on offer to tourists and residents. The tourist board also teamed up with the region's most respected English newspaper, Hong Kong's South China Morning Post, creating a series of special advertorials to promote Macao's eventful city elements. In fact, one would immediately notice the marketing efforts on festivals and events when browsing websites on Macao tourism (see, for example, http://whatson.macaotourism.gov.mo, http://en.macaotourism.gov.mo or www.scmp.com/topics/experience-macao).

Destinations are able to adopt an event portfolio approach to realise the eventful city strategy (Getz 2007). An event portfolio is a synergised effort to capitalise the benefits of multiple events, strategically spread across a period of time in a destination, rather than to focus on the outcomes brought by a single event (Ziakas 2014). These benefits include balancing different stakeholder interests, maximising the value of events by leveraging multiple events appealing to various market segments based on specific environmental factors, efficient use of local resources, and building towards a sustainable community led by harnessing the benefits of festivals and events (Ziakas 2010). Chalip (2006) shows that through leveraging sport events, the community is able to build social networks, address social issues and strengthen community involvement in events. Ziakas and Costa (2011a) propose a multidisciplinary research framework to understand further how to make use of event portfolios; specifically, they note that an event portfolio is potentially a flexible multipurpose development tool for a host community. In another study by the same authors (Ziakas & Costa 2011b), they observe that events share similar symbolic meanings; an event portfolio approach creates synergy among different types of events by capitalising on economic, sport, tourism and social development objectives.

The Macao strategic tourism planning – and by extension, the embedded event tourism strategy – is led by the local tourist board. Unfortunately, a detailed plan is not accessible by the general public, but a copy of the presentation slides and press release of the annual presentation by the tourist board is available (Macao Government Tourism Office 2017). According to this, the Macao government will

> 'make continuous efforts to develop a diversity of tourism products, organize events and festivals, enhance destination promotion, follow up with law amendments, optimize industry service quality, optimize incentive system, strengthen multipartite cooperation

mechanism and actively engage in international organizations, to enable steady progress in various tasks for the long-term development of Macao's tourism industry.'

(2017, p. 70)

This shows the government's commitment to develop Macao into an eventful city, which is further evident by the breakdown of their aims and objectives into major focal points. Table 20.1 shows an excerpt of these objectives which are directly related to creating Macao into an eventful city.

These objectives appear to support the event portfolio approach to adopting an eventful city strategy in Macao. Festival and event participants contribute not only to the 'event economy' but also to different sectors, such as retail, lodging and entertainment. Therefore, there are also efforts to strengthen and diversify existing tourism products in order to complement the festival and event calendar and to create synergy among different sectors within the overarching 'tourism industry'. One of the recent successes is the designation of Macao as a member of the UNESCO Creative Cities Network in the field of gastronomy. It is, however, unclear whether and to what degree events play a role in Macao's plans to become the World Centre of Tourism and Leisure. Discussions on eventful city strategy call for destinations to adopt a strong and emphasised focus on developing events so as to maximise resources use. The breakdown of tourism budget is unavailable; hence, it is unclear how much the eventful city strategy is costing the taxpayers. Nevertheless, the financial resources and commitment put into tourism must be significant. In Macao, given the substantial tax revenues from gaming receipts, the strong dependency on the tourism economy and also the urgency of diversifying Macao's tourism, the budget for 2017 is MOP1,443,507,900 (equivalent to USD180.4 million).

From these discussions, it is absolutely essential for Macao to move away from its huge and singular dependency from the gaming industry. Due to land shortage and lack of other natural resources, it is impractical for Macao to explore other industries to sustain Macao's economy, so it seems that investing in tourism is the only realistic alternative. Under the umbrella term 'tourism industry', it appears that adopting a festivals and events strategy is most probable given Macao's unique cultural heritage and rich variety of associated

*Table 20.1* Excerpt of Macao's Tourism Work Plan 2017 which are directly related to creating Macao into an eventful city

Focal Point 1: Develop a diversity of tourism products, evaluate event effectiveness and initiate new projects

- Finalise the Macao Tourism Industry Development Master Plan
- Research on effectiveness of mega events and tourism products
- Refurbishment of the Macao Grand Prix Museum
- Creating Macao into a 'City of Events' by organising, supporting and diversifying festivals and events

Focal Point 3: Unleash synergistic effects, enhance destination promotion

- Continuous cooperation with other government departments to unleash synergised effects of activities and events
- Continuous development of smart tourism
- New promotional video 'Experience Macao Your Own Style – Events' to be released in worldwide marketing efforts

*Source:* Macao Government Tourism Office (2017).

activities. Adopting an eventful city strategy ensures Macao a unique destination proposition in order to attract the tourist dollar. Ideally, an event portfolio approach is a careful, calculated and managed process. However, the current tourism development efforts by the local tourist board appear to be somewhat uncoordinated. An eventful city strategy will only be successful if different stakeholder needs are managed appropriately along with a coordinated consumption of resources in order to capitalise the positive effects brought by festivals and events.

Although the majority of major events held in Macao are led and organised by the government, it has been undergoing a series of initiatives to synergise festivals and events efforts. First, the government has undergone a major overhaul to better align festivals and events with the appropriate government departments. For instance, the Lusofonia Festival, which celebrates its 20th edition in 2017, used to be organised by the Civic and Municipal Affairs Bureau. It is now organised by the Cultural Affairs Bureau along with other cultural events such as the Macao Arts Festival and the Macao International Music Festival. This involved restructuring the government departments, creating new divisions and mobilising civil servants across major areas of the government. Second, the government has introduced different events, with various degrees of success, in order to diversity Macao's event offerings such as the Macao Light Festival and Parade for Celebration of the Chinese New Year. Third, the government has also renamed certain events to be more inclusive so as to allow more opportunities for different groups; for example, the carnival-like parade that celebrates Macao's handover to Chinese sovereign has now been renamed from 'Parade through Macao, Latin City' to 'Macau International Parade' to welcome different groups to participate instead of only performers of Latin heritage. Fourth, the government has been bundling events to synergise and complement event offerings. The Macau Food Festival was rescheduled a few years ago and prolonged to coincide the period of the Macao Grand Prix. Fifth, the government has been greatly supporting festival and event efforts led by the community, such as diaspora festivals, religious events and folklore festivals, as well as business events led both by the government and by the private sector.

The 'City of Events' concept is only viable when the ties and bonds within the society of Macao are strengthened, unified and working together towards the same goal. The next section of the chapter illustrates examples of festivals and events that not only survive but thrive in Macao, under a complex economic, social and political environment. Finally, the chapter concludes by a discussion of essential elements to make these festivals and events thrive in Macao.

## Festivals and events support an inclusive society

The Lusofonia Festival celebrates the heritage of Portuguese-speaking communities in Macao. Now in its twentieth year, the festival is one of the most anticipated festivals of the year. The festival is similar to a fun fair with stalls managed by different Portuguese-speaking groups showcasing their food, arts and craft as well as music and other aspects of their heritage. There are also traditional Portuguese games, children's activities, cultural performances and band shows. A smaller version of the festival that celebrates solely the Portuguese heritage in Macao – namely the Portuguese and Eurasians communities – is the Arraial de São João which is smaller in scale as there are only a handful of community groups as opposed to the Lusofonia one which is represented by ten ethnic groups. Although the Lusofonia Festival is organised by the government, the individual performers and ethnic groups are members of the public who participate in the festival upon the organiser's invitation. Funding was minimal, and in many cases, they had to meet costs and resources on their own. Both of these festivals attract a huge following by the Portuguese-speaking communities in Macao, their friends and families, as well as members of the general population who are ethnically Chinese.

Unlike some postcolonial destinations whereby the relationship between the colony and the native country can be negative, such resentment is largely absent in Macao. The Portuguese-speaking communities have been embraced by all levels of the society. This might argue for the case of the success and popularity of both Lusofonia and São João festivals. However, another prominent ethnic group in Macao, the Filipinos, also organise their diaspora festivals in Macao, occupying public space and sharing public resources, such as funding and urban space, as well as creating problems, such as crowding and congestion. There seems to be no resentment of any sort from the wider community; this shows that society embraces festivals and events organised by different ethnic groups.

The Sinulog Festival, held on the third Sunday of January, involves a church activity, a procession and dance performances. It is a festival originating from Cebu in the Philippines and celebrating the adoption of Christianity as the nation's religion. The majority of Filipinos in Macao are labour workers, mostly as frontline staff in the hospitality industry or domestic workers. Like their Portuguese counterparts, this festival is also popular among residents, and when tourists come across these festivals, they are highly attracted too. These events are attractive by nature because of their colour and pageantry, but also symbolically, in terms of the residents' recognition and respect of the contributions and presence of these ethnic groups in Macao. This is a concerted effort that is successful as a result of the community's acceptance, the government's support in resources and private sector's tolerance for impacts caused to their businesses.

## Festivals and events safeguard intangible cultural heritage

In Macao, a number of festivals and events have been inscribed onto the Inventory of Intangible Cultural Heritage, a formal recognition of their significance to Macao's cultural landscape protected by law (Intangible Cultural Heritage 2017). These festivities vary from traditional Chinese festivals to Catholic processions, beliefs and customs of folklore deities to stage performances of Patuá, a nearly extinct creole spoken by Eurasians in Macao.

Festivals and events encompass all domains of the UNESCO Intangible Cultural Heritage (http://ich.unesco.org):

- oral traditions and expressions, including language as a vehicle of the intangible cultural heritage
- performing arts
- social practices, rituals and festive events
- knowledge and practices concerning nature and the universe
- traditional craftsmanship.

The formal inscription of these elements is protected by the law, which not only safeguards their survival but also ensures the education and passing on of the festivals to younger generations. In today's modern societies when the younger generations are generally less religious and culturally different, thanks to the effects of globalisation, institutionalising traditional festivals means that the obligation of ensuring the continuity of the festivals now falls on the government. Although it is uncertain whether or such continuity will mean the festivals are still celebrated authentically in the future, this formal recognition should ensure the festivals do not become extinct. Nonetheless, concerted efforts must be made by different stakeholders to ensure that these festivals have the resources to continue, younger generations are educated and the festivals stay within, organised and for the community, as opposed to becoming just another touristic show.

## Festivals and events enrich the tourist experience

Similar to major discourses in festivals and events research (Getz & Page 2016; Mair & Whitford 2013), festivals and tourism are inseparable. Tourism brings both positive and negative impacts to festivals and their host communities, and this notion is no different in the context of Macao's festival scene. Festivals build social capital (Arcodia & Whitford 2006) by encouraging dialogue between members of the community as well as across members of different communities. The Portuguese influence in Macao has been profound, leaving behind a legacy of both built and intangible heritage. Many of these buildings, along with those of Chinese descent to mark Macao's maritime past, were inscribed on the UNESCO World Heritage List in 2005. Festivals and events complement touristic offering in Macao by offering alternatives and additions to usual attractions as well as livening up built heritage. For instance, the Macao Light Festival is celebrated across many heritage structures and is designed to give life to these otherwise 'dead' heritage buildings. Cultural performances like the Drunken Dragon dance ritual and traditional Portuguese folk dances are also often on show at cultural sites to enrich and enliven historical structures.

Festivals like the International Parade bring tourists closer to the community by offering a highly interactive, rich and intensive experience. Catholic processions bring tourists to the medieval past of Macao being the oldest European colony in Asia and a glimpse of 'western' religious rituals. Many events are celebrated like a carnival, such as the Macao Grand Prix, which offers an immensely exciting experience related to Macao's colonial past to tourists rather unique in Asia. Likewise, diaspora festivals such as the Lusofonia Festival, Arraial de São João and Sinulog Festival emphasise Macao's multiculturalism and offer a rich diversity of unusual touristic offering in Asia. Traditional Chinese community festivals bring tourists closer to community life, particularly ancient times when Macao consisted of many villages, and each of these villages was dedicated to a different Taoist deity. Festivals dedicated to art and music give tourists a flavour of local and international artists and products, and the Food Festival allows tourists to sample different Macanese foods in one place. With Macao's recent designation as a UNESCO Creative City in the field of gastronomy, the number of festivals and events dedicated to its food will almost certainly increase and further enrich the tourist experience.

## Conclusions

Macao has an uncertain future due to its very complex economic, social and political environment. Developing Macao as an eventful city through the event portfolio approach appears to be a reasonable strategy to ensure its high dependency on gaming is mitigated and to rely on its innate diversity of festivals and events. Potentially, Macao could have major social problems brought forth by postcolonial issues and host-guest conflicts. Diaspora festivals and events organised by ethnic groups can sometimes be met with hostility and challenges. Events taking up public space and causing widespread inconveniences such as Catholic processions, Feast of the Drunken Dragon and the Macao International Parade could be met with opposition. Given the size of Macao and the sheer volume of tourists received annually, the relationship between the host community and tourists could well be negative. However, these are not usually seen in Macao. Instead, the city is harmonious and eventful, with many activities happening all year round.

It is important that the policymakers do not take this peace and tranquillity for granted. It is important to manage stakeholder needs and continuously monitor them along the different stages of stakeholder and event lifecycle (Andersson & Getz 2008). It is important that the government, as it leads tourism development in Macao, must have an institutionalised and transparent tourism master plan. If an eventful city strategy is used, it is imperative to properly assess and manage its viability and its process must be monitored and carefully planned. It should not be a coincidental or initiated in an ad hoc manner. In Macao, the lesson learnt to build towards an eventful city is to have strong commitment of resources by different stakeholders, particularly the necessary finances, strong government leadership, coordination and support, as well as the unreserved support, shared vision and tolerance by the community.

## References

Andersson, T. D. & Getz, D. (2008). Stakeholder management strategies of festivals. *Journal of Convention & Event Tourism, 9*(3), 199–220.

Arcodia, C. & Whitford, M. (2006). Festival attendance and the development of social capital. *Journal of Convention & Event Tourism, 8*(2), 1–18.

Chalip, L. (2006). Towards social leverage of sport events. *Journal of Sport & Tourism, 11*(2), 109–127.

Cheng, C. M. B. (1999). *Macau: A Cultural Janus*. Hong Kong: Hong Kong University Press.

DSEC. (2017). *Yearbook of Statistics 2016*. Retrieved from Macao: www.dsec.gov.mo/. Accessed 18/12/2017.

Getz, D. (2007). *Event Studies: Theory, Research and Policy for Planned Events*. London: Elsevier Butterworth-Heinemann.

Getz, D. & Page, S. J. (2016). Progress in tourism management: Progress and prospects for event tourism research. *Tourism Management, 52*, 593–631.

Greenwood, V. A. & Dwyer, L. (2017). Reinventing Macau tourism: Gambling on creativity? *Current Issues in Tourism, 20*(6), 580–602.

Gu, Z. (2004). Macau gaming: Copying the Las Vegas style or creating a Macau model? *Asia Pacific Journal of Tourism Research, 9*(1), 89–96.

Hao, Z. (2005). Social problems in Macau. *China Perspectives, 62*(November–December), 44–54.

Hao, Z. (2011). *Macau: History and Society*. Hong Kong: Hong Kong University Press.

Huang, Y. (2016). Understanding China's belt & road initiative: Motivation, framework and assessment. *China Economic Review, 40*(Supplement C), 314–321.

Intangible Cultural Heritage. (2017). *Annual Press Conference*. Retrieved from www.culturalheritage.mo/en/detail/2264. Accessed 18/12/2017.

Landry, C. (2008). *The Creative City: A Toolkit for Urban Innovators*. Abingdon, Oxon: Earthscan.

Li, X. & Wan, Y. K. P. (2017). Residents' support for festivals: Integration of emotional solidarity. *Journal of Sustainable Tourism, 25*(4), 517–535.

Macao Government Tourism Office. (2017). *Annual Press Conference*. Retrieved from http://industry.macaotourism.gov.mo/en/page/content.php?page_id=200. Accessed 18/12/2017.

Mair, J. & Whitford, M. (2013). An exploration of events research: Event topics, themes and emerging trends. *International Journal of Event and Festival Management, 4*(1), 6–30.

República Popular da China. (1993). *Lei Básica da Região Administrativa Especial de Macau de República Popular da China*. Macau: Conselho Consultivo da Lei Básica da Região Administrativa Especial de Macau de República Popular da China.

Richards, G. & Palmer, R. (2010). *Eventful Cities: Cultural Management and Urban Revitalisation*. London: Butterworth-Heinemann.

Richards, G. & Rotariu, I. (2015). Developing the eventful city in Sibiu, Romania. *International Journal of Tourism Cities, 1*(2), 89–102.

Sheng, L. & Zhao, W. (2016). Strategic Destination management in the face of foreign competition: The case of Macao SAR. *Journal of Travel & Tourism Marketing, 33*(2), 263–278.

UNESCO. (2015). *What Is the Creative Cities Network?* Retrieved from https://en.unesco.org/creative-cities/. Accessed 18/12/2017.

Vong, F. (2008). Changes in residents' gambling attitudes and perceived impacts at the fifth anniversary of Macao's Gaming deregulation. *Journal of Travel Research, 47*(3), 388–397.

Vong, F. (2016). Application of cultural tourist typology in a gaming destination – Macao. *Current Issues in Tourism, 19*(9), 949–965.

Wan, P. Y. K. & Pinheiro, F. V. (2014). Macau's Tourism planning approach and its shortcomings: A case study. *International Journal of Hospitality & Tourism Administration, 15*(1), 78–102.

Ziakas, V. (2010). Understanding an event portfolio: The uncovering of interrelationships, synergies, and leveraging opportunities. *Journal of Policy Research in Tourism, Leisure and Events, 2*(2), 144–164.

Ziakas, V. (2014). *Event Portfolio Planning and Management: A Holistic Approach*. Abingdon, Oxon: Routledge.

Ziakas, V. & Costa, C. A. (2011a). Event portfolio and multi-purpose development: Establishing the conceptual grounds. *Sport Management Review, 14*(4), 409–423. doi:https://doi.org/10.1016/j.smr.2010.09.003.

Ziakas, V. & Costa, C. A. (2011b). The use of an event portfolio in regional community and tourism development: Creating Synergy between sport and cultural events. *Journal of Sport & Tourism, 16*(2), 149–175. doi:10.1080/14775085.2011.568091.

# 21
# PROTESTING @ AUCKLAND PRIDE

## When a community stakeholder becomes alienated

*Jared Mackley-Crump*

In 2015, the Police and Corrections departments were given permission to march in the Pride Parade. In response, activist group No Pride in Prisons staged a protest against the history of mistreatment of transgendered people by these organisations. Additionally, another group staged a number of paint-splash attacks on a corporate sponsor, claiming Pride had been commodified. In the aftermath a polarising debate emerged in online queer community forums, one which perfectly encapsulated the bind that Pride organisers found themselves in: the high cost of Pride necessitates the creation of strategic and politically pragmatic relationships with sponsors; in doing so, members of the queer community had become alienated from processes of Pride celebration.

This chapter presents a netnographic case study of the protests, providing a pertinent demonstration of what happens when municipalities' strategic use of festivals comes into conflict with the communities being festivalised. It synthesises key ideas from event management and queer theory discourses: the implicit tension between corporate and community stakeholders, and critiques of the heteronormativity and commercialisation of Pride events.

### Introduction

In 2015, in Auckland, New Zealand, the country's Police and Corrections Department (who operate state-run prisons) were given permission to march in the city's recently inaugurated Pride Parade. In response, a small group of activists disrupted the Parade, protesting against a history of mistreatment of transgendered people by these organisations. Additionally, another group staged a number of graffiti attacks on a Parade sponsor, highlighting the perceived commodification of the event. In the aftermath, a vociferous and polarising debate emerged in queer community forums. This debate encapsulated the bind that Pride organisers found themselves in: the Parade's high costs necessitate the sourcing of income and sponsorship; in doing so, some members of the queer community (or perhaps more appropriately, communities) had become alienated from the celebration of Pride.

This chapter presents a case study of the protests, providing a pertinent demonstration of what happens when the strategic use of festivals by municipalities comes into conflict with the communities the festivals are supposed to celebrate. It synthesises key ideas from event management and queer theory discourses: the implicit tension between corporate and community stakeholders, and critiques of the homonormativity and commercialisation of Pride events (and queer culture more broadly). I argue that in spite of the recognised necessity of sponsors in the contemporary events environment, the communities being festivalised must remain central to stakeholder management, for without community support, the sustainability of events is ultimately threatened. I begin by providing an overview of key literature and the method employed. I then move on to the context of Auckland's Pride Parade before outlining the protests that took place. Finally, I present illustrative examples of community reaction before offering some concluding remarks.

## Literature review

From an event management perspective, this is a case study centred on stakeholders, and tensions between these parties that lead to what Allen, O'Toole, Harris and McDonnell (2012, p. 64) would categorise as an example of negative social impacts, via community alienation. This tension is driven by increasing competition between municipalities to be known as 'eventful cities' (Richards & Palmer 2010) by using event portfolio strategies to drive economic development (Antchak 2016). These priorities can cause friction when not aligned with community expectations.

This is a dominant theme in event stakeholder research: tension inevitably arises between heterogeneous stakeholder groups, and deft relationship management skills become a key measure of successful event managers (Getz & Andersson 2009). Larson and Wikström (2001), for example, demonstrated that stakeholder relationships can be understood as consensus or conflictive, where inconsistent goals or stakeholders working to achieve their goals at the expense of others can lead to tension, distrust, and ultimately, can risk event sustainability. Larson (2002) furthered this, proposing the concept of 'political market squares' to illustrate how stakeholders interact politically to achieve their goals. Indeed, as Getz (2012, p. 116) recognises, power is a crucial issue: as events become larger, more complex and institutionalised (or professionalised), organisations rely more and more on external stakeholders for sustainability (p. 280). Achieving consensus with such diverse interests is fraught with difficulties, although strategies are often proposed (e.g. Moital, Jackson & Le Couillard 2013; Reid 2011).

Andersson and Getz (2008) zero in on the key source of stakeholder tension: to become financially sustainable, trade-offs are required. Sustainability involves attracting powerful and resource-rich supporters; in doing so, while mitigating existential threats, event organisers are likely to lose some autonomy. Ultimately, the needs and goals of community stakeholders – who Tiew, Holmes and de Bussy (2015) propose have neither asset, resource nor network/referral power – can become compromised. Quinn's (2006) study of well-established arts festivals demonstrates this well. The organisers' desire to grow the events as tourist attractions, enhancing their attractiveness to state and corporate sponsors, began to undermine the links to and support of local communities. Higgins-Desbiolles (2016) concluded likewise from an indigenous festival context that tension arose because communities value events in vastly different ways than those stakeholders driven by economic and tourism imperatives. These values, as George (2015) found, are centred around the degree to which communities feel events reflect (or not) their identity, and thus these stakeholders should be incorporated into planning and design processes to ensure congruence.

Building on this, recent research has also begun to problematise stakeholders being categorised into monolithic units. Instead, there is much heterogeneity *within* stakeholder groups. Lau, Milne and Chui (2017) highlight this well in their study of the 2011 Rugby World Cup, and how the 'host community' was conceived narrowly. In exploring the event's social impacts on the Chinese community in New Zealand, they show that not only was there a desire by community members to be involved, but that the measured impacts occurred outside of any strategy by planners to engage with diverse communities. They argue that migrant communities should have been considered unique stakeholder groups, and nuanced engagement strategies created. The point is thus made that a more holistic approach is needed to account for the complexity of subcommunities within communities, which may be based around ethnicity, or gender, or reflect a multiplicity of other perspectives (Deery, Jago & Fredline 2013). These points are especially salient here. Problems arose at Auckland Pride because of a belief that queer communities can be considered homogeneous, and not enough consideration was given to the vast social, economic and ideological differences that exist.

Within queer studies, these differences are accentuated. Early theorists highlighted a mainstream culture 'riddled' with heteronormativity, privileging and centring heterosexuality as normative (e.g. Berlant & Warner 1995, p. 349). In doing so, queer became a reactive category, positioning queerness in opposition to heteronormative markers. However, in creating this dualism, these theorists failed to account for true diversity (e.g. Spargo 2000). The result was homonormativity, the privileging of educated, middle-class, white, masculine, gay males as idealised representations of queer acceptability. With increasing tolerance, integration was achieved though the consumptive power of the so-called 'pink dollar' and queer identities and bodies made respectable by processes of gentrification and urban development (e.g. Mattson 2014). The imperative to be 'Proud' has been reimagined as civic pride, and this has, in turn, led to the exclusion of 'shameful' queer identities in the normalisation and commodification of queer spaces (e.g. Bell & Binnie 2004).

In this context, Pride festivals, as public representations of queer space, have been particularly criticised as perpetuating homonormativity and commodification. Both Browne (2007) and Ammaturo (2016), for example, position Pride events as sites of tension, where a disruption of heteronormativity is desired but ultimately denied; it is the heteronormative political and economic apparatuses, after all, that provide these events with crucial support. Pride is thus depoliticised through co-option into city-led event strategies and transformed into spectacle; safe, respectable homonormative queerness dominates. The key issue arising from this is one of dependency, and the risk 'goal displacement', where the interests of sponsors take precedence over festivalised communities. As a critique, Taylor (2016) discusses the emergence of 'gay shame' festivals, where, while still employing narratives of celebration, these smaller community-led events subvert both hetero- and homonormativity. In doing so, they illustrate the privileged homonormative forces that dominate mainstream queer spaces (see also Bailey (2013), who discusses race and queer spaces).

## Method

The method employed for this research is one that combines a case-study approach – a long narrative compiled from various sources in order to illustrate contemporary issues and phenomena (Remenyi 2012) – with additional insight from what has become known as 'netnography'. This method evolved spontaneously. As a member of the communities involved, I initially observed the protests and their aftermath with concern about the detrimental and polarising impacts they were having on community discussion; something publicly expressed at the time (Mackley-Crump 2015). As an emerging event management academic,

I observed with fascination the 'real world' case study playing out in our backyard. Sensing its value as a teaching resource, I began to collect media reports and examples of the discussion that was taking place on social media, primarily Facebook comments posted in local queer community pages, like the Pride Festival page and local queer media.

This observation of media and social media forms the centre of the netnographic method, one gaining increasing currency (e.g. Li & Wood 2016; Whitford & Dunn 2014). Netnography was first proposed by Robert Kozinets (2002), who argued that it is simply an extension of the flexible ethnographic approach, 'replacing information gleamed online for the information gleamed in the field' (p. 62). As a qualitative approach, netnography employs key strengths of content-analysis methodologies, using thematic identification techniques to uncover meaning from data collected. Additionally, netnography is suitable for investigating possibly sensitive topics, as it enables the researcher to gain insight into actions and feelings in an unobtrusive way (Morgan 2008).

This is true of the data collected here, which was obtained without making my presence known (I did not add to discussions, merely observed them taking place). In terms of reliability – a key concern raised by Kozinets and others (e.g. Mkono 2013) – the data collected primarily came from Facebook, where anonymous commenting is hard to achieve (due to the number of steps necessary in establishing a profile). Additionally, the forums on which the conversations occurred are directed at the queer communities in Auckland. They are small, self-regulating and frequently contain discussion between posters who demonstrably know each other offline. This is true of the discussions presented here, and it seems likely therefore that the data collected are a valid representation of reactions to the protests. This raises a final pertinent point. Morgan (2008) asserts that the netnographic method is not designed to generate a sample that can be generalised across entire populations. This is also true here. It is not intended to be read as a definitive account of the protests and subsequent reaction. Rather, it is a richly detailed account that allows us to reflect on critical event management issues.

## Pride in Auckland

As its largest cosmopolitan centre, it is unsurprising that Auckland has historically been and remains the centre of gay community and culture in New Zealand (Herkt 2013). The origins of Pride parades there can be contextualised within the post-Stonewall, queer liberation era of Pride protests, which started in New York and Los Angeles in 1970, before spreading to other global cities and evolving into hybridised protest-celebration events (D'Emilio 2013). 1980s queer New Zealand was marked by two key experiences, one global and the other local. As elsewhere, the AIDS epidemic began to have a range of impacts, although its full devastation was limited by comparatively low infection rates (Dickson, Lee, Foster & Saxton 2015). The hard-fought law reform of 1986, decriminalising homosexual acts between consenting men, marked a turning point in the sociopolitical acceptance of queer identities within the New Zealand state and eventually by broader society.

These two experiences created a desire to establish an event to celebrate progress and visibility, and it was within this broader environment that the Hero events began, first with a party in 1991, before becoming the Hero Parade (and accompanying festival) a few years later. While publicly popular, Hero maintained an antagonistic relationship with Auckland City Council and, with subsequent mayors refusing to support or help finance the event, this ultimately lead to its demise in 2001 (Johnston & Waitt 2015). Over the next decade, queer community leaders continued to agitate for the return of Hero. This was given a significant boost in 2010, when Auckland's seven existing city and district councils were amalgamated into one 'super city'. As part of this, a number of 'council-controlled organisations' (CCOs) were established. One of these, Auckland Tourism, Events and Economic Development (ATEED), brought together these distinct areas into one organisation and, employing an 'eventful city' strategy (Richards and Palmer 2010), began aggressively bidding to host a range of major profile-building events that would complement a portfolio of local events (Antchak 2016). The goal was to make Auckland a 'global events destination' that would drive local and national growth, as well as social outcomes (ATEED 2013, p. 3).

After a number of public meetings, and with support from key local and central government figures, an Auckland Pride Festival Trust was established. They were able to capitalise on ATEED's strategy and argue that a global events destination was one that portrayed a queer-friendly image. A business case put forward the positive tourism and economic figures that could be achieved by initiating a high-profile Pride festival, and thus, with key details in place, it was publicly announced that an inaugural Pride festival would be held in February 2013 and supported by the council via ATEED (Tasman-Jones 2012).

It is important to highlight ATEED's role in managing the return/establishment of Pride. It prioritised from the outset an approach that was driven by their event strategy. Structure for the festival's governance and organisation was quickly formalised. In addition, sponsorship was expected to cover over 50% of event costs (Tasman-Jones 2012). Indeed, in the aftermath of the 2015 protests, Megan Cunningham-Evans, co-Chair of the festival trust, pointed out that Pride 'takes money and I don't know how to get around that. We need commercial relationships, without them Pride would just not be possible' (GayNZ.com 2015b). This reality immediately established the possibility of conflict between the priorities of commercial event management practices and the queer communities; it took only two years to surface.

## Pride and protest collide

The incidents that took place in 2015 were driven by two groups. Although similarly motivated, the actions were carried out separately and directed at distinct targets. Unravelling these separate protest actions makes this clear and helps to paint a more complete picture.

In 2014, the local University of Auckland staged an inaugural 'Pride Week' on campus. In response, a group of queer activists established 'Petty and Vindictive' with the explicit intention of trying to radicalise the event. Although ultimately failing, members of this group went on to form the two groups at the centre of the Pride 2015 protests: No Pride in Prisons, and Queers Against Injustice. No Pride in Prisons (hereafter NPIP) was established with the broad aim of prison abolition, and it remains an active lobbying organisation to this day (see www.noprideinprisons.org.nz). Their actions at Pride were primarily focussed on its opposition to the participation of the New Zealand Police and Corrections departments, who they charge with an ongoing history of mistreatment of the queer communities, especially transgendered people (GayNZ.com 2015a). Queers Against Injustice (hereafter QAI), by contrast, were less formally organised and have not been active since 2015. Their actions focussed solely around concerns about 'pinkwashing', the commercialisation of Pride by corporate sponsorship and interests.

QAI were first to strike. As part of its sponsorship, ANZ bank had decorated four ATM machines in central Auckland, relabelling them 'GAYTMs' for the duration of Pride. Two days before the Parade, the GAYTM on Ponsonby Road, along the Parade route, was vandalised. Although QAI later stated they had left a poster at the scene explaining the protest, the paint colour was identified as white and the attack labelled homophobic in press reports (e.g. ONE News 2015; Suckling 2015). The GAYTM was cleaned up, police notified, and no further action occurred.

On Saturday 21 February, the Pride Parade began its march down Ponsonby Road at 7.30 pm. As the Parade got underway, led by the Police and followed by Corrections, a small group of NPIP members jumped over event fencing and onto the Parade route, carrying a large NPIP banner, and attempted to disrupt the flow of the event. A video of the incident shows event security, organisers and Police quickly moving in to remove protesters, achieved after a disruption of only about one minute.[1] The scuffle continued off the Parade route,[2] and one protestor was eventually taken to hospital with a disputed fractured/broken arm.

In the context of the larger event the protest was a momentary incursion at best and did not ever threaten the Parade. The legitimacy of the violence experienced, and the claims and counterclaims that followed are not of central concern to the analysis here. Rather, it is the politics of the protest actions and the public discussion that took place in the aftermath. This discussion quickly became polarised and was fanned by a number of reports and contradictory eyewitness accounts that emerged (e.g. Oates 2015).

Additionally, in the midst of the growing vitriol, QAI released a statement about its attack on the GAYTM. Their central allegation noted that

> we object to the representation of queer identity in terms of consumptive and wealthy citizens…reduc[ing] the queer subject to a bourgeois, cis-gender, white, male subject… We sought to draw attention to the lack of representation of bodies that counter the racist, classist and cis-biased nature of Pride.
>
> *(Queers Against Injustice 2015)*

Despite the overall festival having concluded, the group carried out another attack on Monday 23 February, splashing pink paint on the ANZ bank branch in Ponsonby, on two police stations and two further ANZ bank ATMs. Statements left at the scene this time left no room for confusion about the rationale for the attacks (Newton 2015). After this time, QAI conducted no further actions.

## Online reaction

The online reaction was swift, especially to the protest actions by NPIP. It was, perhaps, inflamed by public statements made by Parade organisers, who did not acknowledge the issues raised and instead attacked the actions of the protestors. Parade director Richard Taki, equating progress with his position as a married gay man, focussed on the amount of hours worked by volunteers and claimed that protesters had 'made a mockery' of this (GayNZ. com 2015c). Ironically, he also stated that the parade was about 'community… [and] us being supportive of each other' (GayNZ.com 2015c).

Supportive is not a word that describes the general tone of online reactions. It should be acknowledged that a reasonable number of commenters engaged in largely civil discussion, and some commenters and replies were incredibly lengthy and detailed. However, the discussion quickly polarised around two extreme positions, with a large number of argumentative repeat commenters, and conflicting accounts from people who claimed to have been at the scene of the protests.

Comments on the Facebook page of GayNZ.com, under the posting of the eyewitness account by Oates (2015), demonstrate this polarisation well. Critical of the protest, a self-identified trans woman commented that 'the Parade is a celebration of all our communities not a soapbox to push political, religious or racial agendas.' Comments like this were met with opposing views, such as one commenter who noted,

> there's nothing more mainstream than siding with the apparatuses of the State and victim blaming members of your own community. Or aren't they part of your community? Is it that you've got what you wanted and the Trans community are now expendable?

Another commenter, sarcastically, summarised the thread well:

> 'I hate that this woman got hurt, but how dare she interrupt our fun time. This is for US' – the majority of what I've seen from most people here. Yeah, god, what an inclusive and welcoming community. You're all extremely brave for Standing Up For Yourselves and throwing more vulnerable queer people under the bus. You should be proud.

Similar positions, albeit more aggressively, were put forward when GayNZ.com posted their story about NPIP public statements (2015a). A commenter, who identified as a trans person of colour, put it bluntly: 'ya'll can continue being thrilled that some of us are…still dying and being incarcerated … go ahead. Enjoy your fucking glitter.' Just as bluntly, someone else noted that, 'they brought shame to a fun day out and again like the weirdos who threw paint on an ATM have successfully given the LGBT community a bad name,' thereby also reflecting on the QAI protest. Someone else asserted that 'this amateurish group doesn't need even more exposure for there [sic] confused ideas.'

And on the festival's Facebook page, posters demonstrated the same polarisation. Compare, for example, a well-known trans artist's comment ('Amazed at the amount of ignorance from what I thought was an understanding part of society') with a gay man who contributed to multiple threads of discussion ('Sad that a couple of thugs try and ruin the Auckland Pride Parade Festival. Well done everyone … who put on a wonderful show').

The QAI protests received less attention overall, and the commentary was far more critical than supportive. When GayNZ.com posted a story on Facebook about the second graffiti attacks, for example, they received comments like 'grow up you wankers and protest something with value instead of a company that has your rights in mind' and 'they have a point. Capitalism doesn't coincide with civil rights' were fairly typical of the polarisation. Interestingly, the critiques included comments like 'obviously have never been on a committee to help organise a community event. Events like this don't happen without sponsorship' and 'let's be honest if they didn't bankroll us everyone would complain no one supports us, yet they support us and it's capitalism.' This can be read as a tacit approval, or at least recognition, of the convergence of events and sponsorship that the contemporary events environment makes necessary, and is also something that the literature is beginning to explore (e.g. Close & Lacey 2014)

## Concluding discussion

The themes visible in online commentary show that while some tried to discuss the protests within a broader historical, sociopolitical and economic context, others viewed the disruption as an affront to the fought-for freedoms and social change that has occurred since prior civic hostility towards Hero. In other words, to their perceived right to view Pride as a depoliticised celebratory spectacle (Browne 2007). While many have benefited greatly from acceptance, this celebratory-progress narrative works against the original impetus of Pride, and both protests were attempting to point out that for some queer people, social acceptance and mobility is not their reality.

This case study demonstrates how divisive the politics of identity can become. Most often referred to as a community, the reality is that the queer communities are as stratified on the basis of race, gender, class, education and consumptive power as the societies of which they are a part (if not more so, given the communities' diverse sexual identities). For event organisers, this makes trying to achieve consensus difficult: identity and cultural politics are deeply personal, and it can be hard to navigate these issues objectively. The economic importance of sponsorship along with perceptions that this represents the commodification of these identities adds an additional layer of tension, something visible in Pride events across the world.

Ultimately, it falls to event organisers to manage diverse stakeholders. In failing to first recognise the tensions within its community stakeholders, and then adequately address those concerns after the protests raised them, Pride management was forced to reckon with the negative fallout from assuming the 'host community' was homogeneous. To their credit, this lesson appears to have been learnt, and a more queer-diverse range of voices have been sought in subsequent years, and in the granting of applications to march in the parade (Furley 2017; GayNZ.com 2015d). This reinforces the argument put forward here: 'host community' – indeed all stakeholder groups – should be viewed as heterogeneous; no single voice should be assumed to speak on behalf of a stakeholder, and a diversity of voices should be sought out and incorporated into processes of festivalisation. In this sense, ideally, a range of voices, issues and concerns can be brought to the attention of event organisers and realistic, acceptable outcomes negotiated. At the very least, discussion occurs, stakeholders feel heard, and organisers become aware of issues that may threaten to disrupt their events.

## Notes

1 Available at www.youtube.com/watch?v=GJS5_mc1ILY.
2 Available at www.youtube.com/watch?v=IJXr-JdynBM.

## References

Allen, J., O'Toole, W., Harris, R., & McDonnell, I. (2012). *Festival and Special Event Management*, Milton, Australia: John Wiley & Sons.

Ammaturo, F. (2016). Spaces of Pride: A visual ethnography of gay Pride parades in Italy and the United Kingdom. *Social Movement Studies*, 15(1), 19–40.

Andersson, T. & Getz, D. (2008). Stakeholder management strategies of festivals. *Journal of Convention & Event Tourism*, 9(3), 199–220.

Antchak, V. (2016). *Event Portfolio Design: Exploring Strategic Approaches to Major Events in New Zealand*. (Unpublished doctoral thesis). Auckland University of Technology, New Zealand.

ATEED. (2013). Auckland's major events strategy. Available from: www.aucklandnz.com/sites/build_auckland/files/media-library/documents/MajorEventsStrategy_1.pdf. Accessed 14 July 2017.

Bailey, M. (2013). *Butch Queens up in Pumps: Gender, Performance and Ballroom Culture in Detroit*. Ann Arbor, MI: University of Michigan Press.

Bell, D. & Binnie, J. (2004). Authenticating queer space: Citizenship, urbanism and governance. *Urban Studies*, 41(9), 1807–1820.

Berlant, L. & Warner, M. (1995). What does Queer theory teach us about X? *Publications of the Modern Language Association*, 110(3), 343–349.

Browne, K. (2007). A party with politics? (Re)making LGBTQ Pride spaces in Dublin and Brighton. *Social & Cultural Geography*, 8(1), 63–87.

Close, A. & Lacey, R. (2014). How the anticipation can be as great as the experience: Explaining event sponsorship exhibit outcomes via affective forecasting. *Journal of Current Issues & Research in Advertising, 35*(2), 209–224.

Deery, M., Jago, L. & Fredline, L., (2013). Rethinking social impacts of tourism research: A new research agenda. *Tourism Management, 33*(1), 64–73.

Dickson, N., Lee, B., Foster, T. & Saxton, P. (2015). The first 30 years of HIV in New Zealand: Review of the epidemiology. *The New Zealand Medical Journal, 126*(1426), 31–48.

D'Emilio, J. (2013). Gay politics, gay community: San Francisco's experience. In De Milio, J (Ed.), *Making Trouble: Essays on Gay History, Politics, and the University* (pp. 74–95). London, England: Routledge.

Furley, T. (2017, February 2). Corrections not welcome at Auckland Pride Parade. *Radio New Zealand*. Available from: www.radionz.co.nz/news/national/323603/corrections-not-welcome-at-auckland-pride-parade. Accessed 28 July 2017.

GayNZ.com (2015a, February 23). Statement: No Pride in prisons explains. *GayNZ.com*. Available from: www.gaynz.com/articles/publish/5/article_16503.php. Accessed 23 Feb 2015.

GayNZ.com (2015b, February 22). Co-chair refutes allegations against Pride. *GayNZ.com*. Available from: http://gaynz.com/articles/publish/2/article_16501.php. Accessed 23 Feb 2015.

GayNZ.com (2015c, February 22). Parade director disappointed by protest. *GayNZ.com*. Available from: www.gaynz.com/articles/publish/2/article_16498.php. Accessed 23 Feb 2015.

GayNZ.com (2015d, November 14). Pride board members apologise to protesters. *GayNZ.com*. Available from: www.gaynz.com/articles/publish/2/article_17542.php. Accessed 2 June 2016.

George, J. (2015). Examining the cultural value of festivals: Considerations of creative destruction and creative enhancement within the rural environment. *International Journal of Event and Festival Management, 6*(2), 122–134.

Getz, D. (2012). *Event Studies: Theory, Research and Policy for Planned Events*. London, England: Routledge.

Getz, D. & Andersson, T. (2009). Sustainable festivals: On becoming an institution. *Event Management, 12*(1), 1–17.

Herkt, D. (2013, January 25). Queen City: A secret history of Auckland. *Public Address*. Available from https://publicaddress.net/speaker/queen-city/. Accessed 13 July 2017.

Higgins-Desbiolles, F. (2016). Sustaining spirit: A review and analysis of an urban Indigenous Australian cultural festival. *Journal of Sustainable Tourism, 24*(8–9), 1280–1297.

Johnston, L. & Waitt, G. (2015). The spatial politics of Gay Pride parades and festivals: Emotional activism. In Paternotte, D. and Tremblay, M. (Eds.), *The Ashgate Research Companion to Lesbian and Gay Activism* (pp. 105–120). London, England: Routledge.

Kozinets, R. (2002). The field behind the screen: Using netnography for marketing research in online communities. *Journal of Marketing Research, 39*(1), 61–72.

Larson, M. (2002). A political approach to relationship marketing: Case study of the Storsjoyran Festival. *International Journal of Tourism Research, 4*(2), 119–143.

Larson, M. & Wikström, E. (2001). Organising events: Managing conflict and consensus in a political market square. *Event Management, 7*(1), 3–22.

Lau, C., Milne, S. & Chui, R. C. F. (2017). Redefining stakeholder relationships in mega events: New Zealand Chinese and the Rugby World Cup. *Journal of Convention & Event Tourism, 18*(2), 75–99.

Li, Y.-N. & Wood, E. H. (2016). Music festival motivation in China: Free the mind. *Leisure Studies, 35*(3), 332–351.

Mackley-Crump, J. (2015, February 26). Conversations we need to have. *GayNZ.com*. Available from: http://gaynz.com/articles/publish/45/article_16533.php. Accessed 26 Feb 2015.

Mattson, G. (2014). Style and the value of gay nightlife: Homonormative placemaking in San Francisco. *Urban Studies, 52*(16), 3144–3159.

Mkono, M. (2013). Using net-based ethnography (Netnography) to understand the staging and marketing of "authentic African" dining experiences to tourists at Victoria Falls. *Journal of Hospitality & Tourism Research, 37*(2), 184-198.

Moital, I., Jackson, C. & Le Couillard, J. (2013). Using scenarios to investigate stakeholders' views on the future of a sporting event. *Event Management, 17*(4), 439–452.

Morgan, M. (2008). What makes a good festival? Understanding the event experience. *Event Management, 12*(2), 81–93.

Newton, K. (2015, February 25). Group protests ANZ 'pinkwashing'. *Radio New Zealand*. Available from: www.radionz.co.nz/news/national/266921/group-protests-'pinkwashing'. Accessed 12 July 2017.

Oates, S. (2015, February 23). A witness account of the Pride protest. *GayNZ.com*. Available from: http://gaynz.com/articles/publish/45/article_16512.php. Accessed 24 Feb 2015.

ONE News (2015, February 21). Gay community rallies together in Auckland after vandalism. *ONE News*. Available from: www.tvnz.co.nz/one-news/new-zealand/gay-community-rallies-together-in-auckland-after-vandalism-6239114.html. Accessed 12 July 2017.

Queers Against Injustice. (2015). Political statement regarding 'vandalism' of GAYTM. *GayNZ.com*. Available from: https://hashtag500words.com/2015/02/21/political-statement-regarding-vandalism-of-gaytm/. Accessed 12 July 2017.

Quinn, B. (2006). Problematising 'festival tourism': Arts festivals and sustainable development in Ireland. *Journal of Sustainable Tourism, 14*(3), 288–306.

Reid, S. (2011). Event stakeholder management: Developing sustainable rural event practices. *International Journal of Event and Festival Management, 2*(1), 20–36.

Remenyi, D. (2012). *Case Study Research*. Reading, England: Academic Publishing International.

Richards, G. & Palmer, R. (2010). *Eventful Cities: Cultural Management and Urban Revitalisation*. Oxford, England: Elsevier.

Spargo, T. (2000). *Foucault and Queer Theory*. Sydney, Australia: Allen & Unwin.

Suckling, L. (2015, February 20). GAYTM attack 'like a punch in the face'. *New Zealand Herald*. Available from: www.nzherald.co.nz/lifestyle/news/article.cfm?c_id=6&objectid=11405088 Accessed 12 July 2017.

Tasman-Jones, J. (2012, June 12). Gay Pride parade to return to Auckland. *Stuff.co.nz*. Available from: www.stuff.co.nz/national/7093175/Gay-pride-parade-to-return-to-Auckland. Accessed 12 July 2017.

Taylor, J. (2016). Festivalizing sexualities: Discourses of 'Pride', counter-discourses of 'shame'. In J. Taylor and I. Woodward, (Eds.), *The Festivalization of Culture* (pp. 27–48). London, England: Routledge.

Tiew, F., Holmes, K. & de Bussy, N. (2015). Tourism events and the nature of stakeholder power. *Event Management, 19*(4), 525–541.

Whitford, M. & Dunn, A. (2014). Papua New Guinea's indigenous cultural festivals: Cultural tragedy or triumph? *Event Management, 18*(3), 265–283.

(NB: www.gaynz.com closed in early 2017. At press time, its content is being transferred to the Lesbian and Gay Archives of New Zealand (LAGANZ), hosted in the Alexander Turnbull Library at the National Library of New Zealand, but currently no web-accessible versions of these references exist. Digitised copies of the stories were made by the author, and are available on request.)

# 22
# FESTIVALS AS DEVICES FOR ENHANCING SOCIAL CONNECTIVITY AND THE RESILIENCE OF RURAL COMMUNITIES

*Michael Mackay, Joanna Fountain and Nicholas Cradock-Henry*

## Introduction

Rural communities in New Zealand have had a long association with festivals and events. Agricultural and pastoral shows (known colloquially as 'A&P' shows) – with their displays of farm machinery and animals, and competitions for farm-based prowess, from wood chopping and sheep shearing, to home preserves and baking – have been an annual highlight for many rural communities since the early 20th century (Phillips 2008). Since the 1990s, however, rural festivals in New Zealand have proliferated and diversified in content and audience (Fountain & Mackay 2017; Higham & Ritchie 2001). Nowadays many small towns invest in and host an annual portfolio of events, rather than focussing on a single community celebration. While A&P shows remain important occasions for many rural communities, they now jostle for space in an increasingly crowded rural festival marketplace.

In this chapter we examine the social value and utility of rural festivals. We focus particularly on the opportunities these events create for enhancing social connectivity and resilience within communities, and speak to calls for research that contributes to the development of an advanced understanding of the social dimensions of festivals and their value and role in community building and rural development (Black 2016; Wilson, Arshed, Shaw & Pret 2017). We define rural festivals as 'themed, public celebrations' (Getz 2007, p. 31) that are held regularly but infrequently (often scheduled annually), and which are firmly anchored in a specific rural locality (Wilson et al. 2017). We interpret a 'resilient rural community' as one that is socially cohesive, connected and communicative, and where residents share a strong sense of identity and belonging, and ultimately care about each other and their locale (Aldrich & Meyer 2015; Berkes & Ross 2013; Maclean, Cuthill & Ross 2014; Magis 2010; Scott 2013).

Our chapter relies on findings of a study of two community festivals held in the rural township of Akaroa (South Island, New Zealand). The first – 'Akaroa French Fest' – is an annual two-day event that celebrates the town's European settlement history, especially elements of its French heritage (Fountain & Mackay 2017). The second event is the 'Akaroa Harvest Festival'. This festival provides a setting for local food and beverage producers to publicise and sell their goods to locals and visitors to the town, while simultaneously raising funds for community causes. While both festivals include the usual spectacle and fun associated with community celebrations, and have underlying economic objectives, our argument here is that they each make a valuable contribution to the resilience of this rural community. They achieve this by providing time and space for active citizenship, community collaboration and teamwork, particularly for those involved in the organisational activities leading up to the event. They also enable residents to develop new skills and intra- and extra-community connections that may be drawn on in times of crisis and change.

## Festivals, social connectivity and resilient rural communities

Over the past two decades the 'resilience renaissance' has led to a proliferation of research programmes and papers exploring resilience; its characteristics and the extent to which it can be measured (Adger 2000; Aldrich & Meyer 2015; Magis 2010; Steiner & Markantonio 2014; Walker, Hollings, Carpenter & Kinzig 2004). The term 'community resilience' generally refers to 'the collective ability of a neighbourhood or geographically defined area to deal with stressors and efficiently resume the rhythms of daily life through cooperation following shocks' (Aldrich & Meyer 2015, p. 255). Resilience research commonly focusses on disaster risk reduction and the capacity of communities to 'bounce back' from immediate shocks such as earthquakes or other hazard events; however, there is also a growing interest in how communities respond to slower-onset change processes (Steiner & Markantonio 2014). In the early resilience literature, the focus was almost exclusively on natural and mixed human-natural systems (Carpenter, Walker, Anderies & Abel 2001; Walker et al. 2004). In response to calls for a 'social turn' in resilience research, more recent attention has been paid to place, attachment, social justice and livelihoods, much of it focussed on rural communities (e.g., Brown 2014; Pomeroy 2015; Scott 2013).

An important goal for research on community resilience has been to characterise the 'attributes' of resilient communities. For example, in work on community resilience and natural hazards, awareness of hazards, the ability to cope with them, positive expectations regarding the effectiveness of mitigation actions, articulating problems, trust, empowerment and participation in community affairs are signposted as key attributes to enhance individuals' resilience (Paton 2013; Thornley, Ball, Signal, Lawson-Te Aho & Rawson 2015). Resilience is fostered at the level of community through collective action, as individuals socialise, develop trusting relationships, recreate, work and solve problems *together* (Adger 2003; Aldrich 2011; Cradock-Henry, Greenhalgh, Brown & Sinner 2017; Paton 2013). Other studies have identified similar characteristic features of resilient communities: vision, leadership and trust; the development of social connections/networks and information and knowledge sharing via these networks; and collaborative and social learning (Maclean et al. 2014; Matarrita-Cascante & Trejos 2013). Berkes and Ross (2013) have sought to synthesise the different perspectives on resilience. Locating their integrated approach in an understanding of complex adaptive systems, they emphasise the ways in which agency *and* the capacity for self-organising invigorate social strengths and agency to help realise resilience (Berkes & Ross 2013).

Particularly important in the context of this chapter are studies of resilient communities that emphasise the importance of social connectivity, and the various relationships that *bind individuals and communities together*, which can be drawn on in particularly challenging times (Adger 2000; Aldrich & Meyer 2015; Magis 2010). Thus, Aldrich and Meyer (2015), pioneers in this field, call for community leaders and planners to extend their activities and investments beyond preparing for and responding to disaster events through 'hard' infrastructure improvements (e.g. roads, communications) – the norm – to investing also in 'softer' social initiatives that connect people to each other and strengthen social relations. They review a selection of policies and programmes from around the world that have deepened, or created new, social networks and community cohesion and trust, and identify social events as key opportunities for this to occur.

While not explicitly discussed by Aldrich and Meyer (2015), some researchers have identified festivals as providing important opportunities for extending and building the social connections so critical to community resilience. Arcodia and Whitford (2007), Moscardo (2007) and Black (2016) argue that festivals provide the time and the space needed to deepen the connections people have with each other, including participating in the organisational processes leading up to the event.

Derrett (2008) is one of only a handful of scholars who has explicitly examined the links between festivals and community resilience. Derrett (2008) studied four community festivals in the Northern Rivers region of New South Wales, Australia, to understand how local events and the associated community interactions foster relationships that ultimately build community resilience. She posits that festivals nourish resilience by 'unleashing' relationships within and beyond the locale, thus enhancing the community's overall sense of connectivity (Derrett 2008, p. v). While acknowledging the role of festivals in the development of social connections, Derrett (2008) draws attention to a wider set of outcomes that also help to nourish resilience, including the development of a shared sense of place and community and social identity. Such positive outcomes are possible, she argues, when the designs of events are inclusive and 'provide a vehicle for communities to host visitors and share such activities as representations of communally agreed values, interests and aspirations', thereby providing 'a distinctive identifier of place and people' (2008, p. v).

Derrett (2008) found that festival stakeholders cited community resilience as an important festival goal, and that 'what is learned from the experience of designing and delivering a festival ensures that the community is better placed to deal with the management of risks associated not only with event management, but broader community challenges' (2008, p. v). This conclusion finds support in other festival research literature. Whilst not specifically looking at the concept of resilience, Gibson and Stewart's (2009) study of rural Australian festivals found that nearly half of the festival organisers contacted believed their festival had helped the community cope with a severe and long-running drought, by lifting residents' spirits, bringing people together and building community networks. Similarly, the National Country Music Muster, which was held in a field near Gympie (New South Wales, Australia) between 1982 and 2006, also contributed to the community's resilience by drawing upon existing, traditional 'country capital' whilst also creating new community capital, thus increasing the capacity of the community to cope with rural change and to assert its identity (Edwards 2012; see also Sanders, Laing & Frost 2015).

This argument points to the connections people have not only with each other but also with the places they live and around which they develop their sense of identity. As noted by Magis (2010), people-place connections play an important role in the building of strong and resilient communities. A connection to a particular place often impels individuals to engage in discussions about the future of their town or region (also see Maclean et al. 2014). Community festivals are one arena where such active agency takes place by providing opportunities for people to express a particular version of place, heritage and culture through which community pride, connectedness and belonging are reinforced. Similarly, festivals provide a place – a moment in time and space – to display and celebrate personal heritage and connection to a locale (de Bres & Davis 2001; Duffy & Waitt 2011; Gibson, Connell,

Waitt & Walmsley 2011). However, as de Bres and Davis (2001) acknowledge, community festivals may not only reinforce existing place and personal identities, but they can provide the opportunity and space to challenge such constructions (e.g., Chalip 2006; Clarke & Jepson 2011; Paradis 2002; Quinn 2006). As noted by Fountain and Mackay (2017), while some constituents of a rural community may appreciate and support a local festival, the theme and focus may not resonate with all and, in some cases, may become the catalyst for friction particularly when the festival is important to the identity of only some sections of the community. A further warning comes from Black (2016) who suggests that the hosting of multiple events and festivals in a community may create silos and frictions as separate networks form around specific agendas. In this situation, the potential of the festival to act as a catalyst for community resilience diminishes.

## A methodological note

To explore the links between rural festivals, social connectedness and community resilience we carried out research in Akaroa, a small rural community on the South Island of New Zealand, which each year plays host to two key community festivals – Akaroa Heritage Festival (known as 'French Fest') and the Akaroa Harvest Festival. Semi-structured interviews of between 30 and 90 minutes with festival stakeholders ($n = 27$) were the primary data collection method. Interviews were audio-recorded and transcribed verbatim, prior to manual thematic content analysis by each researcher separately. The themes were discussed, revised and refined collaboratively ensuring credibility of the results and a high level of investigator triangulation (Wallendorf & Belk 1989). Periods of participant observation in the town, including attendance at both of the festivals in question, added to our understanding of the festivals and the broader research setting, including the town and its festival spaces, and helped to inspire and develop new interview questions. Finally, an analysis of historical and contemporary documentary sources including a simplified content analysis of the local newspaper, the Akaroa Mail, as well as reviews of printed and electronic promotional material, supplemented our understanding. The results of this analysis of interviews, documentary analysis and personal observations in the township, culminated in the following assessment of the role festivals in the enhancement of community resilience.

## Community resilience through festivity: insights from Akaroa

The small rural township of Akaroa (permanent population around 700) is a community that hosts thousands of international and domestic visitors every year. The settlement is located in the picturesque Akaroa Harbour on Banks Peninsula, 75 kilometres from the South Island's largest city, Christchurch. For many decades, tourists arrived in the town by road; however over the last six years, and in response to the 2011 Canterbury earthquakes, which damaged Canterbury's main port of Lyttelton, tens of thousands of cruise ship visitors have arrived annually, presenting both opportunities and challenges for the community (Carroll 2017; Cropp 2017). It could be argued that the community's festivals have ensured a degree of stability for the town in the face of considerable change.

Akaroa is steeped in Maori and European settlement history, including a short period of French settlement in the 1840s, which has long been a central plank of the area's promotional activities. This region is renowned also for its composite of natural amenities, including steep ocean cliffs and sheltered bays, rolling farmland and wildlife habitat. The traditional Māori name for Banks Peninsula: Te Pataka o Rakaihautū – the storehouse of the chieftain

Rakaihautū – recognises the abundance of food from the land and sea found in the region; a quality reflected nowadays in the area's emerging reputation as a premium producer of wine, fresh produce, preserves, cheeses and olive oil. These elements of the region's place identity and heritage are celebrated and animated through two community festivals: 'French Fest' and the Akaroa Harvest Festival.

## Akaroa French Fest

Akaroa has commemorated the French heritage of the township through a relatively large-scale community festival for the past 25 years (Fountain & Mackay 2017). While the name and content of the festival have changed over this period, the focus on the 'French Connection' has remained strong, as has the network of stakeholders brought together to organise the weekend event, most notably through the Akaroa Heritage Festival Committee (AHFC). As is the case for festival committees in many small towns, membership is voluntary and changes as residents arrive and leave the district and as 'new blood' replaces older members who retire. Despite this churn, there are committee members who have been involved since its inception and who see themselves as guardians and disseminators of institutional knowledge to new members. Interviewees stressed the importance of newcomers joining the committee, bringing new skills, ideas, energy and enthusiasm. While the festival occurs over one weekend biennially, the AHFC convenes meetings monthly, providing regular opportunities to build and strengthen local connections and advance the festival agenda, by providing a forum to share knowledge and discuss community issues and personal news. In this way, committee meetings fulfil an important social role, particularly for some retired members who find the work gratifying, and new residents who use the meeting to socialise and embed themselves in community life.

A notable inclusion in the AHFC over the past decade has been Christchurch City Council representatives (the governing authority of Banks Peninsula). Increasing bureaucratic requirements, and costs, around festivals resulted in AHFC members agreeing to divest much of the organisation – and funding – of French Fest to the council events team. While the presence of the events team reduced the burden on time and resources, AHFC members acknowledged that having council representatives at meetings somewhat limited the role of local people and, by extension, the chance for them to engage in a meaningful way in the Festival's organisation. This was most notable in the planning of a significantly upscaled 2015 festival, which marked the 175th anniversary of the arrival of the first French settlers to the district. At the same time, AHFC members were mindful of the absolute need for Council support and resourcing and hoped the relationships they were nurturing with Council staff would endure beyond 2015, when the council withdrew from their on-the-ground organisational role (whilst still supporting the event in other ways). In looking forward to the 2017 festival, some AHFC members expressed hope that this new arrangement would provide opportunities to revitalise the event with greater community input, thereby enabling greater community engagement and strengthening community ties. As one respondent explained,

> Now that the council are pulling out it seems there has been a bit of a reawakening and we've got a larger group of people in Akaroa back on the committee than I've seen for a while.

French Fest also provides opportunities for the wider community to interact and connect with each other, particularly on the weekend of the celebration. The event has three main platforms for social interaction: 1) a Friday night street party primarily held for locals; 2) a re-enactment of the historical French landing on the first morning of the festival; and 3) a market day that takes place at the recreation ground over the remainder of the weekend, comprising stalls, French-themed games, food, drink and music. The landing re-enactment is an important expression of cultural identity for many locals, particularly those with an ancestral connection to the early settlers. The re-enactment was characterised by many interviewees as the device that galvanises the community's shared sense of identity – achieved through this form of storytelling – and has the added benefit of buttressing the town's French notoriety and place-promotion 'brand'. In recent years, the re-enactment has also been the catalyst for the formation of new partnerships in the community, such as a new relationship with local Māori representatives who joined AHFC and actively participated (for the first time) in the 2015 re-enactment. This is not a trivial outcome: one local Māori representative suggested the re-enactment ceremony was the impetus for her people to connect meaningfully with residents of Akaroa township.

The street party and market day provide a very different platform for community members to make and maintain social connections, either through direct involvement in the planning of particular activities or events, or through attending and communally celebrating positive elements of community life. One interviewee explained that the festival was a much-anticipated chance to 'go into carnival mode' and enjoy the company of visitors and other residents and friends from the district, some of whom they seldom saw during the calendar year. One interviewee said he could not imagine life in the town without the festival – echoing the sentiments of others about the embeddedness and importance of the occasion in the everyday lives of many residents. This is not to say that the French motif strikes a chord with all members of the community; one respondent thought the 'Frenchness' of the festival was overdone and that other local cultural markers could be celebrated. These debates over the meaning of the festival arise in the community newspaper every year, usually just prior to and after the event. While seemingly divisive, they play an important role in the building of resilience, by provoking critical – but crucial – reflexive conversations about local change and continuity, and provide opportunities for positive transformation that reflect and speak to a broader set of community aspirations.

## Akaroa Harvest Festival

The Akaroa Harvest Festival is a much smaller event than French Fest, and more recent in origin, being in its fifth year of operation in 2017 and hosting an estimated 500–800 visitors. The impetus for this festival emerged out of an existing community network of small-scale farmers/food processors who met weekly during the summer months at the Akaroa farmers market. It took the initiative of one key individual, however, and initial support from the ADP, for the Akaroa Harvest Festival to be established to celebrate 'Akaroa's bounty' (Santamaria 2017). As with French Fest, this event continues to evolve with time, and the stakeholders involved in its organisation have changed. Yet there is never a shortage of enthusiastic stakeholder-volunteers on the day; as one stallholder explained, 'whether it is just emptying the bins or whether they just love standing on the gate and talking to people … there's somebody out there for every job'.

The purpose of the event remains true to its origins; it is an opportunity for small producers to display and showcase the region's multifaceted local foodscape and to share their stories in an environment of family fun and community celebration. The festival comes to life with music and food-themed activities, such as a highly competitive cake-baking auction that raises money for local charitable causes. Stakeholders are proud of the charitable contribution this festival makes to the community, as evidenced by posters displayed in shop windows thanking the community for this support and publicising the amount raised for local causes. As one stakeholder said of the cake auction, 'the community is amazing at being quite giving and so it's a bit of fun and usually really well run and people put a lot of effort into the cakes'.

While hosting visitors and residents is an important element of the festival, the event also has a local small business orientation. A goal of the stakeholders is for the event to strengthen links between the region's food and beverage producers, who share their connection with Banks Peninsula through the production and/or processing of fresh local produce and an ethos around sustainable, artisanal production. As one organiser explained, 'It is absolutely a celebration of the great food and wine in the area and ... it would be fuelling those food and wine related businesses as well through profile'. The festival also provides local producers with a platform to display and 'advertise' their produce so that they might develop new relationships with local and Christchurch restauranteurs and extend their business reach.

Akaroa producers view these connections as crucial to the future viability of their businesses and want to increase this element of the festival, a strategy extended in the 2017 event with the showcasing of some well-known Canterbury-based chefs, who cooked taster-sized dishes for sale on the day. This network was extended and strengthened with the launch of the *Akaroa and the Bays Food and Wine Guide* at the 2017 festival, which highlights the area's gastronomic delights, including produce outlets and award-winning producers, and ultimately seeks to (re)define the area as a 'foodies paradise influenced by its sea side location and Mediterranean climate'.

## Conclusion

At the most general level, rural festivals are social events that bring local people together to celebrate and/or commemorate selected aspects of community life, while also displaying and reinforcing a particular sense of place (Fountain & Mackay 2017). The proliferation of rural festivals in recent decades provides sound evidence of their increasing social and economic significance. In the current chapter, we have focussed in particular on the *social* significance of rural festivals, emphasising how they provide an arena for celebration, community collaboration and the creation and strengthening of local and external relationships, while providing also a forum for the development of new skills, expressions of creativity and civic engagement. While some of this activity plays out during the day(s) of a festival, our research has shown that the ongoing process of planning and organising a festival is perhaps more significant to the goal of building camaraderie and connections, and ultimately enhancing community resilience (Arcodia & Whitford 2007; Black 2016; Moscardo 2007).

In the case study presented here, it is through committee meetings (where they assume roles and responsibilities) and associated interactions with local authorities and funders that festival stakeholders develop a sense of purpose and belonging. Here there are opportunities to demonstrate and share existing talents, while developing new capacities and learning new skills, an essential element of community resilience (Maclean et al. 2014). Other elements of the earlier discussion draw parallels with central debates in the community resilience literature. As noted earlier, Aldrich and Meyer (2015) have stressed the need to take seriously and invest in the 'softer' infrastructure and associated initiatives that connect people to each other and help to build social capital. Our research suggests that rural festivals are 'soft devices' that provide opportunities for the enhancement of social connectivity and other 'resilience attributes' (Maclean et al. 2014; Magis 2010; Matarrita-Cascante & Trejos 2013).

This research has revealed also the role of pride and passion for Akaroa, its people and products, in motivating continuing involvement and commitment to these festivals (Maclean et al. 2014). A strong sense of place and place attachment provides individuals with the impetus to participate in the shaping of their environment and the future of their town or region, including its cultural landscape, and a commitment to remaining in a region.

## References

Adger, W.N. (2000). Social and ecological resilience: Are the related? *Progress in Human Geography*, 24(3), 347–364.

Adger, W.N. (2003). Social capital, collective action, and adaptation to climate change. *Economic Geography*, 79(4), 387–404.

Aldrich, D.P. (2011). The power of people: Social capital's role in recovery from the 1995 Kobe earthquake. *Natural Hazards*, 56(3), 595–611.

Aldrich, D.P. & Meyer, M.A. (2015). Social capital and community resilience. *American Behavioral Scientist*, 59(2), 254–269.

Arcodia, C. & Whitford, M. (2007). Festival attendance and the development of social capital. *Journal of Convention & Event Tourism*, 8(2), 1–18.

Berkes, F. & Ross, H. (2013). Community resilience: Toward an integrated approach. *Society and Natural Resources*, 26(1), 5–20.

Black, N. (2016). Festival connections: How consistent and innovative connections enable small-scale rural festivals to contribute to socially sustainable communities. *International Journal of Event and Festival Management*, 7(3), 172–187.

Brown, K. (2014). Global environmental change I: A social turn for resilience? *Progress in Human Geography*, 38(1), 107–117.

Carpenter, S., Walker, B., Anderies, J.M. & Abel, N. (2001). From metaphor to measurement: Resilience of what to what? *Ecosystems*, 4(8), 765–781.

Carroll, J. (2017). *Akaroa Dubbed Tack-aroa After Cruise Ship Boom*, Stuff News 2 January, www.stuff.co.nz/national/88042520/akaroa-dubbed-tackaroa-after-cruise-ship-boom. Accessed 7 July 2017.

Chalip, L. (2006). Towards social leverage of sport events. *Journal of Sport and Tourism*, 11(2), 109–127.

Clarke, A. & Jepson, A. (2011). Power and hegemony within a community festival. *International Journal of Event and Festival Management*, 2(1), 7–19.

Cradock-Henry, N.A., Greenhalgh, S., Brown, P. & Sinner, J. (2017). Factors influencing successful collaboration for freshwater management in Aotearoa, New Zealand. *Ecology and Society*, 22(2), 14–32.

Cropp, A. (2017). *Akaroa Voted Top Cruise Port in New Zealand and Australia*, Stuff News 27 July, www.stuff.co.nz/business/95144111/akaroa-voted-top-cruise-port-in-new-zealand-and-australia. Accessed 7 July 2017.

De Bres, K. & Davis, J. (2001). Celebrating group and place identity: A case study of a new regional festival. *Tourism Geographies*, 3(3), 326–337.

Derrett, R. (2008). *Regional Festivals: Nourishing Community Resilience: The Nature and Role of Cultural Festivals in Northern Rivers NSW Communities*. PhD thesis. Southern Cross University, Lismore.

Duffy, M. & Waitt, G. (2011). Rural festivals and processes of belonging. In Gibson, C. & Connell, J. (eds.), *Festival Places: Revitalising Rural Australia*. Channel View Publishing, Bristol, pp. 44–57.

Edwards, R. (2012). Gympie's country music Muster: Creating a cultural economy from a local tradition. *Journal of Rural Studies*, 28(4), 517–527.

Fountain, J. & Mackay, M. (2017). Creating an eventful rural place: Akaroa's French Festival. *International Journal of Event and Festival Management*, 8(1), 84–98.

Getz, D. (2007). *Event Studies Theory, Research and Policy for Planned Events*. Butterworth-Heinemann, Oxford.

Gibson, C., Connell, J., Waitt, G. & Walmsley, J. (2011). The extent and significance of rural festivals. In Gibson, C. & Connell, J. (eds.), *Festival Places: Revitalising Rural Australia*. Channel View Publishing, Bristol, pp. 3–24.

Gibson, C. & Stewart, A. (2009). *Reinventing Rural Places: The Extent and Impact of Festivals in Rural and Regional Australia*. University of Wollongong, New South Wales.

Higham, J. & Ritchie, B. (2001). The evolution of festivals and other events in rural southern New Zealand. *Event Management*, 7(1), 39–49.

Maclean, K., Cuthill, M. & Ross, H. (2014). Six attributes of social resilience. *Journal of Environmental Planning and Management*, 57(1), 144–156.

Magis, K. (2010). Community resilience: An indicator of social sustainability. *Society and Natural Resources*, 23(5), 401–416.

Matarrita-Cascante, D. & Trejos, B. (2013). Community resilience in resource-dependent communities: A comparative case study. *Environment and Planning A*, 45, 1387–1402.

Moscardo, G. (2007). Analysing the role of festivals and events in regional development. *Event Management*, 11(1–2), 23–32.

Paradis, T.W. (2002). The political economy of theme development in small urban places: The case of Roswell, New Mexico. *Tourism Geographies*, 4(1), 22–43.

Paton, D. (2013). Disaster resilient communities: Developing and testing an all-hazards theory. *Journal of Integrated Disaster Risk Management*, 3(1), 1–17.

Phillips, J. (2008). *Shows and Field Days – A & P Societies and Shows*. Te Ara – the Encyclopedia of New Zealand www.TeAra.govt.nz/en/shows-and-field-days/page-1. Accessed 26 July 2017.

Pomeroy, A. (2015). Resilience of family farming 1984–2014: Case studies from two sheep/beef hill country districts of New Zealand. *New Zealand Geographer*, 71(3), 146–158.

Quinn, B. (2006). Changing festival places: Insights from Galway. *Social and Cultural Geography*, 6(2), 237–252.

Sanders, D., Laing, J. & Frost, W. (2015). Exploring the role and importance of post-disaster events in rural communities. *Journal of Rural Studies*, 41, 82–94.

Santamaria, A. (2017). *Banks Peninsula: Akaroa's Bounty*. New Zealand Herald, 28 May, www.nzherald.co.nz/travel/news/article.cfm?c_id=7&objectid=11865788. Accessed 28 July 2017.

Scott, M. (2013). Resilience: A conceptual lens for rural studies? *Geography Compass*, 7(9), 597–610.

Steiner, A. & Markantonio, M. (2014). Unpacking community resilience through capacity to change. *Community Development Journal*, 49(3), 407–425.

Thornley, L., Ball, J., Signal, L., Lawson-Te Aho, K. & Rawson, E. (2015). Building community resilience: Learning from the Canterbury earthquakes. *Ko'tuitui: New Zealand Journal of Social Sciences Online*, 10(1), 23–35.

Walker, B., Holling, C.S., Carpenter, S.R. & Kinzig, A. (2004). Resilience, adaptability and transformability in social–ecological systems. *Ecology and Society*, 9(2), 5.

Wallendorf, M. & Belk, R.W. (1989). Assessing trustworthiness in naturalistic consumer research, *Interpretive Consumer Research* 15, 149–175.

Wilson, J., Arshed, N., Shaw, E. & Pret, T. (2017). Expanding the domain of festival research: A review and research agenda. *International Journal of Management Reviews*, 19(2). 195–213.

# 23
# GEELONG'S ROUSING MOTORING *REVIVAL*

*Gary Best*

## Introduction

Geelong, the second largest city in the Australian state of Victoria, is situated on scenic Corio Bay about an hour's drive from Melbourne, the state's capital. The traditional owners of the land are the indigenous Wathaurong People who called the bay 'Jillong' and the surrounding land 'Corayo', but new settlers inverted the names that became the City of Geelong and Corio Bay.

By 1850 Geelong was one of Australia's six main sea ports (Blainey 1966, p. 136) and major discoveries of gold in Ballarat and Bendigo in 1851 brought further prosperity (Blainey 1966, p. 141). Whilst Geelong was situated on Corio Bay with access to potential transport for the gold, Melbourne interests misrepresented the actual distance and claimed that the city was closer to Port Phillip Bay, so Melbourne became Victoria's state capital, thereby resulting in Geelong being termed 'Sleepy Hollow' well into the next century.

Geelong's history of events since that time was initially framed by the annual agricultural 'Geelong Show' and then through its foundation membership of the Victorian Football Association as the Geelong Football Club in 1877. Thirty-nine years later 'Gala Day' entered the annual calendar of Geelong events and included a parade acknowledging its broad range of annual achievements; this was later refocussed as primarily a fundraiser for the Geelong Hospital's Annual Appeal.

Seismic shocks have profoundly affected Geelong's long-term employment sector in the recent past. Geelong's major industrial heritage began with Ford USA announcing that its Australian operation would be based in Geelong beginning in 1925, and ended with closure of that plant in 2016. Shell Australia opened its refinery in 1954 and is still operating as Viva Energy Australia after acquisition by Swiss chemical company Vitol in 2014. Alcoa began Geelong aluminium smelter operations in 1963 but also closed in 2014.

Despite the impacts of the Ford and Alcoa closures, there is resilience in Geelong and that is most evident in the development and expansion of its festivals portfolio. Embedded in the expansion is the strategic focus on festivals as a means of engaging the local community through the consolidation of the existing suite of festivals as well as new initiatives to attract visitation and tourism to both the City of Geelong and the nearby Bellarine Peninsula region.

One such initiative has resulted in the installation of five new works of public art that are elements in the revitalisation of central Geelong. It could certainly be argued that such City expenditure on public art could be channelled more effectively into low-cost housing or employment initiatives, for example, but reinvigorating public spaces with sculptural art sends a strong and inclusive message that such spaces are meant to be enjoyed and shared by all, even though the artists' abstract sculptural forms may challenge some observers. One of the Geelong Council's recent linking strategies is a new Arts and Culture Trail app that maps a route around the top cultural landmarks of Geelong (McQuillan 2017). A sculpture at the corner of Cunningham St. and Western Beach Road, and very close to the *Revival* site, is titled 'Rescue' and is comprised of seven abstract 'ships'. McQuillan (p. 32) observed the sculpture is 'symbolic of the seven continents being pulled from the sea in an act of rescue', but there was to be no 'immediate rescue' of the next two Geelong proposals.

In the *Geelong Advertiser* editorial titled 'Tourist drawcard needs support' (Houlihan 2017) both a proposed Convention Centre adjacent to Deakin University's Geelong city campus and an adventure park on the waterfront were 'shelved' due to lack of state funding. 'Rescuing' Geelong was also a focus for former Geelong Mayor and paparazzo Darryn Lyons, who also saw Geelong's then neglected waterfront as ripe for reinvention. Squires (2016) had earlier observed in the *Geelong Advertiser* that Lyons's proposals for a gigantic floating Christmas tree viewable from space and a huge 'ice-castle'-themed cruise ship pier proved a little too rich for Geelong Council appetites.

Fowles (2017) reported that there have been other recent proposals and developments, including a new $100 million City of Geelong Headquarters, the luxury apartment complexes 'Miramar' ($35 million) and 'The Mercer' ($45 million), NDIA (National Disability Insurance Scheme) Headquarters ($120 million) and WorkSafe Headquarters ($120 million), and further proposals budgeted at $300 million. Two more modest offerings were the park-side café in the new $45.5 million of the Geelong Library's 'Dome' building and a new accredited farmer's market in Geelong West's Pakington Street precinct. Geelong, it seemed, was still abuzz with good vibrations despite the loss of Ford.

## Reinvigorating the *Geelong Revival Motoring Festival*

Moscardo (2007) observed that in the realm of community development there are three major interrelated constructs: social capital, community capacity and community well-being, and whilst the significant development discussed earlier indicates major investment and expenditure, social capital and community well-being are also local government imperatives. The City of Geelong is proud and supportive of one major annual automotive initiative. The three-day *Geelong Revival Motoring Festival* is located on Geelong's palm-fringed waterfront precinct and promoted as 'Australia's Largest Classic Motoring Festival'.

The roots of the *Revival* can be traced to the speed trials, or 'sprints', that began along the waterfront in 1956 and continued until their ostensible reinvention as the *Geelong Revival* in 1978. Grant's detailed study *The History of the Geelong Speed Trials 1956–1985* (1986) is a remarkable record of participant recollections, media coverage, organising committees, competitors, awards, and competitor cars and motorcycles. It can be convincingly argued thirty-one years later that the current *Revival* is an equally memorable experience, offering car races, classic motor show, trade expo, vintage caravans, national vintage fashion awards and vintage boats.

The *Revival* also offers the benefits of social inclusion through spectating, event participation, experiencing the local automotive legacy (Ford vehicles are always very well represented) and the residual community pride in that legacy. The *Revival* also provides a strong sense of engagement in an annual experience that both nurtures and consolidates a located optimism and exhilaration – albeit only for three days a year – in a regional city that continues to face a range of challenging and ongoing economic impacts. Needless to say, details of all the preceding automotive event content and the promises of more to come have been provided on *Facebook, Twitter* and *Instagram*, and at *http://geelongrevival.com.au/wp/*.

## Engaging with the *Revival* – an autoethnographic approach

Having been born in Geelong, and with a father whose entire career was with the Ford Motor Company of Australia (first in Geelong, then in Melbourne), it seems only fair to declare if not a vested interest then certainly a personal engagement with the focus of this research. Such engagement, however, necessitates a methodology that both permits and validates the authorial participant gaze and 'voice' to further illuminate the research context and setting, and autoethnography can achieve just that.

Breathnach (2006) addressed the nature and forms of the relationship between concepts of authenticity and the consumption of heritage attractions, and concluded that 'The heritage industry peddles an incomplete, inauthentic representation. Individuals' experience of the past in this context is also, therefore, inauthentic' (p. 115). Such a critique is, in a very challenging yet obvious way, really only stating that obvious – the past is just that, and any attempts at recreation frequently focus on foregrounding the most attractive and less challenging constructs of what once was. Holloway observed, however, that 'ethnographers start by 'experiencing' the social world of participants before systematic enquiry and examination can begin' (2010, p. 76), whilst Anderson and Austin investigated what they referred to as 'auto-ethnography' in the context of leisure studies and called for 'a broader academic space for auto-ethnographical integration of the self in qualitative leisure research' (2012, p. 131). Mackellar investigated participant observation at events, observing that it is 'suited to many aspects of event research, where a need or desire exists to explore aspects of audience behaviour, but it is especially useful where on-site surveying techniques are inappropriate' (2013, p. 57).

A final assertion by Holloway on the inductive approach was that 'researchers do not usually begin the research process with a theory, but with curiosity' (2010, p. 77) and just such curiosity was what attracted me to my first *Geelong Revival* in 2015.

## Geelong Revival Motoring Festival 2016

On Thursday, May 23, 2013 Ford Australia president Bob Graziano announced that Ford's Broadmeadows (Melbourne) and Geelong plants would close in October, 2016, putting more than 1000 jobs at risk (ABC News 2013). Geelong had always been a 'Ford' town but that's not to suggest that the usual Ford/GMH/Chrysler rivalries were not in evidence. An earlier closure in Geelong in 2012 had been that of 'The Ford Discovery Centre' after thirteen years as one of Geelong's 'premier attractions'. The Discovery Centre had displayed a range of Ford vehicles as well as providing related interactive engagement.

Ford Geelong's closure, coincidentally, took place just prior to the *2016 Geelong Revival*, but there was nothing maudlin about that Saturday's festivities, nor any evidence of animosity – such as targeted protests – at the *Revival*. It was almost as though the throng attending were determined to participate to the fullest despite the reality of significant unemployment for ex-Ford employees on the horizon. Sharpe, citing Waterman (1998), observed that 'Festivals are meant to be fun and joyous' (2008, p. 219), and in 2016 there was abundant evidence of both.

Whilst De Bres and Davis proposed that 'Festivals can perform a very useful community service, by enhancing both group and place identity' (2001, p. 327), Derrett suggested that 'Festivals can reflect the dynamic value systems of individuals united by the same customs, images, collective memory, habits and experiences' (2003, p. 51). Both perspectives focus on the potential of festivals to nurture beneficial outcomes relating specifically to both the festival location itself as well as benefits accrued through attending and participating.

The cover of the 76-page *Geelong Revival Motoring Festival 2016 Official Event Program* drew attention to the Festival's sixty years of operation and promised to deliver 'Twice the Action at Australia's Largest Classic Motoring Festival!' Two welcomes were extended to visitors on page 7, the first from the Honourable John Uren, Victoria's Minister for Tourism and Major Events, and the second from Nicholas Heath, the Event's Director.

Minister Uren observed in the *Program* that

> World-class events like the Geelong *Revival* Motoring Festival attract visitors from all over Australia and the world, and that's a big win for nearby businesses. Victoria has something for everyone and the best of everything. That's why visitors from all over the world have us high on their list of travel destinations. The local area is no exception.
> (Geelong Revival Motoring Festival 2016, p. 7)

It has taken quite some time for Geelong to shake off its 'Sleepy Hollow' epithet, but Uren's 'something for everyone and the best of everything' resonates throughout the many sub-events within the *Revival* as well as the overall festival.

The term 'revival' suggests a past phenomenon, experience or object being newly invested with a contemporary energy and thus taking the form of a reawakening or return, examples being neoclassical and neo-Gothic architecture. Frequently embedded in such phenomena are nostalgic yearnings (possibly constructed and/or imagined) for what once was. Chase and Shaw proposed three conditions for nostalgia: (i) a secular and linear sense of time, (ii) the failed present and (iii) evidence of the past (1989, p. 4), and Margalit's assertion was that nostalgia distorts past reality and idealises its object whilst locating it in a time or purity and innocence (2011, p. 273). Both Chase and Shaw, and Margalit discuss the frequently uncritical and selective approach to the past employed in a range of museum contexts, and whilst the *Revival* is far removed from such curation and regulation its counterpoint is a much more relaxed approach to operation, one that does not distance the past but rather makes it live through a display of cherished vehicles and significant owner and participant enthusiasm.

McClinchey and Carmichael (2010) discussed what they termed 'The Multi-dimensions of Sense of Place in Cultural Festival Visitor Experiences'. Their model certainly has utility in applied terms for understanding (i) a 'Nostalgic sense of place and experiences' (including the neighbourhood's physical and social setting, the Festival's physical and social setting, and the collective domain), and (ii) a 'Potential sense of place and experiences' in both personal and collective domains (pp. 63–72).

In the personal domain, 'Neighbourhood Physical and Social Setting' is the first of three foci in 'Nostalgic Sense of Place and Experiences'. For the Festival the direct bayside beach location offers both views across Corio Bay and of the recent developments on the foreshore, including apartment blocks, restaurants and some mixed-use buildings. One significant extant building is the 'Sailors' Rest' (1913) that provided accommodation for seamen ashore until 1986. Its electric sign dates from 1926 and is believed to be the oldest remaining electric sign in Victoria. The nostalgic component is further evoked by the historical beachfront, which offered both small boat and ferry rides, including one that had my late uncle, William 'Bill' Watts, known locally as 'Bill the Boatman', as proprietor. Despite some development, much of the original 19th- and early 20th-century planting remains in the form of mature Cyprus trees that provide shade for those inclined to picnic.

Further along the beach from the Festival space is the Eastern Beach Reserve with its remarkably intact 1930s red-brick restaurant and changing rooms building as well as a large swimming area enclosed by a similarly 1930s Art Deco – and shark-proof – boardwalk. There is also a smaller pool for younger children learning to swim, your author being one of those who qualified many summers ago. This is also the site where the *Geelong Revival Motoring Festival* quarter-mile sprints are run, with the *Revival Hill Climb* conducted further into Eastern Park.

The second focus is that of the Festival's physical and social setting, but in light of the immediately preceding discussion it becomes apparent that the Festival operates in a space effectively aligning both McClinchey and Carmichael's first and second sets of conditions. The third focus, however, is about anticipating future place experiences, and on the basis of 2015 and 2016 authorial participation in the Festival such anticipation is already firmly in place. Unless major changes to the current event format are afoot it seems reasonable to expect the next Festival will utilise its tried-and-true approach but possibly with some fresh automotive content and themed experiences.

McClinchey and Carmichael's third focus is the collective domain, which interrogates both physical and social space through neighbourhood and festival scales. Beginning with the neighbourhood scale and physical space, issues such as gentrification, public spaces, built heritage and green spaces all are very much in evidence and have already been discussed. The concept and construct of gentrification, however, is particularly relevant here and can be illuminated by a slight detour to a slightly more 'prestigious' revival.

Mid-September in the United Kingdom sees 'The Revival' staged annually as one event of three days of The Festival of Speed at Goodwood Manor, West Sussex, an event first dating from 1993. A period dress code consists of 'tweeds and trilbies for men, furs and frocks for the ladies', and whilst modern cars are not permitted on the circuit on race days, the selection of cars is always engagingly eclectic with both prestige and more prosaic marques on display. Goodwood celebrates both 'the halcyon days of motor racing and 1940s, '50s and '60s glamour' and is informed by very specific period chic, in terms of both fashion and the automotive experience. However, its location is a privately owned estate that counterpoints the public spaces of the Geelong *Revival*.

The Geelong *Revival's* premise is equally inclusive and has similarly themed experiences but without Goodwood's admission costs or exclusivity. Geelong's scale is also much more modest in comparison, but the participant enthusiasm is, nevertheless, both tangible and contagious. Gyimóthy investigated the term 'amateur spectators' and concluded that accurately characterising the diverse visitor profile justified further research. Her findings offered an expanded terminology identifying 'casual observers, connoisseurs and experimentalists' (2009, p. 177). On the basis of my observations each cohort was well represented at both 2015 and 2016 *Revivals*: those who were casually enjoying the breadth of the display, those who were connoisseurs and enjoying the vehicles but not displaying their own, and the experimentalists for whom it may have been their first visit and were keen to absorb the *Revival* riches.

In terms of period dress, both 2015 and 2016 Geelong *Revivals* offered the National Vintage Fashion Awards where 'Old world glamour comes to life'. Lexi DeRock, creator of 'Yankee Sweetheart Beauty Parlour', author of *Decades of Style: A Step-By-Step Hair and*

*Makeup Guide – 60s and 70s* (2011) and beauty partner of the 2016 *Revival*, observed in the Official Event Program that 'there is something for everyone in vintage fashion and it's a fantastic way to stand out from the crowd while looking totally glamorous' (2016, pp. 14–15). Needless to say, female fashion has also informed the automotive experience almost from its inception in terms of both inherent and applied design, a phenomenon discussed by Marling, who noted that 'In the late 1950s, in an effort to appeal to female buyers, the design chief at General Motors actually hired a group of women to produce a fashion show of feminized models for the 1959 season' (1994, p. 136). Best also explored the 'glamorous intersection' of fashion and automobility, observing that 'fashion, style and automobile classics endure' (2014, p. 47).

Getz proposed that 'From the visitor's perspective, special events present the opportunity to participate in a collective experience which is distinct from everyday life. And because they occur infrequently, or are different each time, novelty is assured' (1989, p. 125). In the case of the Geelong *Revival* each year has provided a distinctive experience, particularly in the case of vehicles displayed, although prior to the formal *Revival*, the primary form of the event was the Geelong Speed Trials. The Geelong Speed Trials 2003 catalogue's 'Welcome' message from Geelong mayor Barbara Abley drew attention to a celebration of Ford's 100th Anniversary and Ford's then important role in Geelong's booming economy.

McClinchey and Carmichael's personal domain includes both the aforementioned present place experiences as well as 'two temporal dimensions to sense of place: (i) a reflective state or nostalgia for past place experiences, and (ii) an anticipatory state or the potential for future place experiences' (2010, p. 63). The 'reflective state' was primarily constituted of nostalgic impulses and responses stimulated by the vehicles displayed; the display location, with its historic foreshore of parkland, bay and built heritage; the broadcast music that privileged rock and roll despite the vehicular display reflecting a much broader historical spectrum; and the women's period clothing that also mainly manifested a 1950s rock and roll vibe. These last two elements suggest two Geelong retail experiences that could also linked in a broader sense to the *Revival's* embedded nostalgia.

Mawby (2014) reported on the saving and refurbishing of North Geelong's Federal Woollen Mills that were transformed 'from derelict to desirable' and are now home to the Geelong Vintage Market. The Mills were considered an 'icon of Geelong's industrial past' but had been neglected for years and fallen into significant disrepair. The Vintage Market now specialises in 'retro chic', but that term depends, of course, on the eye of the canny beholder.

Sinnott (2017) also observed in a *Geelong Advertiser* article that there is 'A vinyl revival sweeping the Geelong region with new figures showing that the phonographic phoenix is rising from the digital ashes'. Independent retailers propose current sales indicate that 2017 will be the best year for record sales in the last thirty years with enthusiasts of all ages choosing music created by the needle in the groove over all other music media forms. Just as the cars of the *Revival* evoke the alluring automobility of the not-too-distant past, other popular cultural trends in architecture, home décor and appliances, such as record players with 45rpm singles and 33rpm albums, both celebrate and consolidate the nostalgic appeal of the stylus and the vinyl.

The most tangible and popular 2016 *Revival* experience in terms of both observed crowd engagement and authorial engagement was the Classic Motorshow sponsored by Shannons. Known primarily for classic car auctions and insurance, as of September 2017 Shannons were offering the prize of a Goodwood Revival UK Tour to those obtaining an insurance quote, further consolidating their commitment to the local classic car experience as well as their own suite of products and services.

The *Revival's* annual Classic Motorshow is something of an endearing grab bag of festival/event elements, and, unlike most classic car shows and displays, the sequence of vehicles on display is a consequence of arrival time rather than marque order. The photograph on pages 16 and 17 of the 2016 Official Event Program records just such an eclectic line-up, which includes a 1937/38 Ford Model Y sedan, two late 1960s Ford Cortina GTs, a 1955 Plymouth Plaza, a 1956 Dodge Custom Royal and a 1971 Valiant Charger R/T.

Despite the somewhat breathless prose of the 2016 Event Program suggesting perhaps a sense of Pebble Beach, California's famed Concours d'Elegance in the *Revival's* Geelong beachside location, there is genuine engagement evident in both spectator enthusiasm and owners' pride. It may be a modest event compared to the rest of the world as, in most instances, the vehicles have been driven to the *Revival* rather than trailered, and when displayed they are rarely roped off, thereby permitting proximity for the spectator. The *Revival* Program suggested, 'Get up close and personal with some truly unique cars, chat with the owners, and revel in the magnificent sight that is the Classic Motorshow' (2016, p. 17). Saleh and Ryan proposed that 'If a festival is to succeed in its economic or social objectives, it must offer an experience which its clientele finds attractive' (1993, p. 291), and for me, the next component of the *Revival* to be discussed did just that.

Adjacent to the automotive display was a temporary caravan park that must have evoked vivid memories for all those who have ever holidayed on wheels. Once a very common sight on summer roads, the caravan was the home away from home and precluded the expense of accommodation costs and restaurant meals. There is evidence to suggest that the caravan now faces competition from cheaper airfares, bargain package deals and the ease of finding new locations rather than relying on the annual holiday at the beach, or in the bush. Googling 'Geelong caravan parks' finds fifteen caravan parks listed for Geelong and the nearby Bellarine Peninsula, suggesting that there may be something of a caravan revival underway. The 2016 *Revival*, however, offered a delightfully nostalgic opportunity to revisit caravan constructs that had more to do with nostalgic imaginings than actually towing a caravan around from site to site.

The 'caravan park' at the *Revival*, however, was on a discrete site across a busy road from the motoring *Revival* vehicles. This setting effectively framed the caravan display as well evoking a faux-campsite intimacy. Most caravans had a period vehicle in close proximity or in some cases hitched to the tow-car. One striking pair was a blue and white EJ Holden station wagon with a caravan in the same colour scheme, and whilst the caravan exteriors were compelling, the interiors were spectacular. Each one was immaculate with more than a few set up for morning or afternoon tea, appearing as though an historical expert in the field, or a time-traveling aunt or uncle, had been technical adviser for the displays.

There was more than a whiff of nostalgia evident at the caravan 'park', and open boot-lids on cars and tailgates on station wagons (period Holdens and Fords, of course) revealed collections of period LP albums, magazines, music memorabilia (The Beatles in particular), cigarette advertising, old soft drink bottles, jigsaw puzzles and so on. Such enthusiasm and extraordinary attention to detail comfortably fits Stebbin's construct of 'serious leisure', where serious leisure is 'the systematic pursuit of amateur, hobbyist or volunteer activity, sufficiently interesting for the participant to find a leisure career' (1997, p. 17), no doubt a dream come true for 'exhibitors' for whom the past resonates more vividly and comfortably than a challenging and potentially less appealing present and future.

A loud broadcast announcement from amongst the display vehicles across the road reminded the throng in attendance that the National Vintage Fashion Awards parade was about to begin, so Eastern Beach Road was crossed and a position in reasonable proximity to the stage was claimed.

The 2016 Official Event Program describes the awards as 'Old world glamour comes to life' and for each of the entrants that was certainly the case, given that they were, political correctness notwithstanding, 'darling dolls, pin-up beauties and dapper dudes' (2016, p. 14). Represented were golfers, matrons, models, 1950s glamour pusses, demure misses, army and air force gals, and gangsters and their molls. A late 1960s fashion plate with a beehive hairdo in a pink mini dress, white-framed sunglasses, a white shoulder bag, white patent leather boots and a QANTAS carry-on bag that indicated she'd be up, up, and away in no time at all, and blitzing the competition on the way.

## Conclusion

*The Geelong Revival Motoring Festival 2016* provided me with an opportunity to engage autoethnographically (Anderson & Austin 2012; Breathnach 2006; Holloway 2010; and MacKellar 2013) with an event that manifested a tangible sense of Geelong's community well-being and social capital (Moscardo 2007) as well its historically significant automotive heritage. Whilst the focus of the *Revival* was primarily automotive there was further evidence of a multidimensional dynamic operating in terms of both a sense of place and the constructed event experience. This duality was consistent with McClinchey and Carmichael's research findings on cultural festival visitor experiences that positively identified with both a nostalgic sense of place as well as a potential sense of place beyond the event experience in both personal and collective domains (2010). Geelong, it seems, continues to consolidate a winning event experience.

## References

ABC News (2013). Ford closure sends shockwave through manufacturing industry. Available online at: www.abc.net.au/news/2013-05-23/ford-closure-sends-shockwaves through manufacturing-industry/4708584. Accessed: 5 June, 2017.

Anderson, L. and Austin, M. (2012). Auto-ethnography in leisure studies. *Leisure Studies*, *31*(2), 131–146.

Best, G. (2014). Glamorous intersection: Ralph Lauren's classic cars at the Musée, and the fashioning of automotive style. In Williams, K.M., Laing, J. & Frost, W. (eds.) *Fashion, Design and Events* (58-70). London: Routledge.

Blainey, G. (1966). *The Tyranny of Distance*. Melbourne: Sun Books.

Breathnach, T. (2006). Looking for the real me: Locating the self in heritage tourism. *Journal of Heritage Tourism*, *1*(2), 100–120.

Chase, M. and Shaw, C. (1989). Introduction. In Shaw, C. and Chase, M. (eds.) *The Imagined Past: History and Nostalgia* (1-18). Manchester: Manchester University Press.

De Bres, K. & Davis, J. (2001). Celebrating group and place identity: A case study of a New Regional Festival. *Tourism Geographies*, *3*(3), 326–337.

DeRock, L. (2011). *Decades of Style: A Step-By-Step Hair & Makeup Guide – 60s & 70s*. Paris, France: Editions D' Empiria.

Derrett, R. (2003). Making sense of how festivals demonstrate a community's sense of place. *Event Management*, *8*(1), 49–58.

Fowles, S. (2017). City's bold high-rise bid, *Geelong Advertiser*, September 16, p. 7.

*Geelong Revival Motoring Festival 2016 Official Event Program* (no publication or printing information included).

Getz, D. (1989). Special events: Defining the product. *Tourism Management*, *10*(2), 125–137.

Grant, G. (1986). *The History of the Geelong Speed Trials 1956–1985*. Geelong: List Print Nominees Pty. Ltd.

Gyimóthy, S. (2009). Casual observers, connoisseurs and experimentalists: A conceptual exploration of niche festival visitors. *Scandinavian Journal of Hospitality and Tourism*, 9(2–3), 177–205.

Holloway, I. (2010). Meaning, not measurement: Using ethnography to bring a deeper understanding to the participant experience of festivals and events. *International Journal of Event and Festival Management*, 1(1), 74–85.

Houlihan, L. (2017). Tourist drawcard needs support, *Geelong Advertiser*, September 16, p. 29.

MacKellar, J. (2013). Participant observation at events: Theory, practice and potential. *International Journal of Event and Festival Management*, 4(1), 56–65.

Margalit, A. (2011). Nostalgia. *Psychoanalytic Dialogues*, 21(3), 271–280.

Marling, K. (1994). *As Seen on TV: The Visual Culture of Everyday Life in the 1950s*. Cambridge, MA: Harvard University Press.

Mawby, N. (2014). Geelong's Federal Woollen Mills to go from derelict to desirable, *Geelong Advertiser*, December 17. www.geelongadvertiser.com.au/realestate/geelongs-federal-woollen-mills-to-go-from-derelict-to-desirable/news-story/4f5406b26f740b684fa7edba9ceef94e. Accessed: 4 June, 2017.

McClinchey, K. & Carmichael, B. (2010). The role and meaning of place in cultural festival visitor experiences. In Morgan, M., Lugosi, P. & Ritchie, J.R.B. (eds.) *The Tourism and Leisure Experience: Consumer and Managerial Perspective* (pp. 59–39). Channel View Publications: Bristol.

McQuillan, M. (2017). Beautiful works give city shapely transformation. *Geelong Advertiser*. September 16, p. 32.

Moscardo, G. (2007). Analyzing the role of festivals and events in regional development. *Event Management*, 11(1–2), 23–32.

Saleh, F. & Ryan, C. (1993). Jazz and knitwear: Factors that attract tourists to festivals. *Tourism Management*, 14(4), 289–297.

Sharpe, E. (2008). Festivals and social change: Intersections of pleasure and politics at a community music festival. *Leisure Sciences*, 30(3), 217–234.

Sinnott, A. (2017). Geelong retailers say 2017 is set to be a big one for vinyl records, *Geelong Advertiser*, January 7. www.geelongadvertiser.com.au/entertainment/geelong-retailers-say-2017-is-set-to-be-a-big-one-for-vinyl-records/news-story/2793cac6a2063ff9c01ea8c0e86238e4. Accessed: May 8, 2017.

Squires, M. (2016). Geelong mayor Darryn Lyons' 10 maddest moments. April 12. www.geelongadvertiser.com.au/news/city-hall/geelong-mayor-darryn-lyons-10-maddest-moments/news-story/2e55715f4572bd10fa134730882bc92a. Accessed: May 8, 2017.

Stebbins, R. (1997). Casual leisure: A conceptual statement. *Leisure Studies*, 16(1), 1–25.

# PART VI

# Festival experiences

# 24
# UNDERSTANDING FEELINGS, BARRIERS, AND CONFLICTS IN FESTIVALS AND EVENTS

## The impact upon family QOL

*Raphaela Stadler and Allan Jepson*

### Introduction

Attending festivals as a family can foster bonding, belonging, and happiness, and has the potential to enhance the family's quality of life (QOL) over time (Jepson & Stadler 2017). Time and space, money, rest, and health and happiness have been identified as frame conditions for QOL (Stadler & Jepson 2017), which – if positive – can improve a family's ability to attend festivals. In order to enhance a family's QOL through festival attendance festival programmes need to be tailored to families' specific needs and expectations. For example, they need to be safe, affordable, and offer activities that contain dimensions of 'play' that can be interpreted as meaningful to all members of the family.

In this chapter we explore feelings, barriers and family conflict that might arise if the family's needs and expectations are not met, and hence their ability to attend festivals becomes limited. Our chapter begins with a brief discussion surrounding the literature on families and festivals, including family time, motivations for attending festivals, and the role of children in the decision-making process as well as the potential positive and negative impacts of festival attendance upon family QOL. We then present our methods for data collection and analysis and move on to a discussion of three major themes around the question of *how has family QOL changed as a result of attending festivals and events?* (Jepson & Stadler 2017). This chapter specifically focusses on the potential negative impacts upon the family's QOL through (1) barriers to entry due to high ticket prices, (2) conflicts arising within the family due to overstimulated children, and (3) a lack of opportunities for family bonding. We conclude our chapter with a set of practical recommendations for families, festival organisers, and other stakeholders.

### Families and family time

Modern family structures and relationships are undergoing rapid change; they are vastly different to what was understood to be a nuclear family of two parents and their children (Murdock 1949) during the 1950s–1980s. Many reasons can be attributed to these changes such as the postponement of family formation or fewer child births per family. The average

age of first childbirth in women within Organisation for Economic Cooperation and Development (OECD) countries is highest in the UK at 30 years of age, despite the UK having the highest percentage of teenage motherhood in OECD countries (OECD 2011). The main reason for this is that educational attainment in women has risen, leading to an increased desire and likelihood to fulfil their career aspirations. Further important factors in the changing nature of the family structure can be seen in the increase in cohabitation rather than marriage, and higher divorce rates leading to an increase in the number of sole parents or reconstituted families (OECD 2011).

As a result of the ongoing changes to family structure, this chapter adopts Poston et al.'s (2003, p. 139) definition of a family: 'A family includes the people who think of themselves as part of the family, whether related by blood or marriage or not, and who support and care for each other on a regular basis'. Poston et al.'s (2003) study is valuable as it recognised the importance of the extended family, and the conditions needed to ensure a healthy family such as spending time together, clarifying roles for the adults, respecting each other's individuality, offering unconditional love and support, and having open and honest communication.

Whilst family structures have changed, it is perhaps more important to look at the relationships within the family and how these impact upon its overall QOL; one of the key determining factors in all relationships is the amount of time one has to spend with others or in this case 'family time'.

## Family motivations to attend festivals

Motivations for attending festivals and events have been widely explored within event studies and event management. The most popular reasons for attendance are cited as bonding between attendees, fostering socialisation and family togetherness (e.g., Crompton & McKay 1997; Lee, Lee, & Wicks 2004; Nicholson & Pearce 2001; Tomljenovic et al. 2001; Uysal et al. 1993), but limited studies have investigated the long-term social benefits of festival attendance which enhance well-being and QOL.

As discussed earlier, the role of children within the family has changed and increased in importance over recent decades; this has been recognised since the mid- to late 1980s, with a steady increase in family-centred service delivery influenced in part by the continuing marketisation of popular children's characters from television programmes. This proliferation has led to the creation of many theme parks orientated towards younger children, such as Sesame Place, Philadelphia, USA; Nickelodeon Universe, Minnesota, USA; J-World, Tokyo, Japan; Moomin Theme Park, Tokyo Metropolitan area, Japan; Thomasland, Drayton Manor Park, Staffordshire, UK; Peppa Pig World, Paultons Park, Hampshire, UK; Hello Kitty Secret Garden, Drusillas Park, East Sussex, UK; and, more recently, Shrek's Adventure, London, UK.

Service delivery is thereby characterised by family choices, a family strengths perspective and further recognition of the family as a support unit to all its members (Poston et al. 2003).

Research has demonstrated that a family day out is about much more than just satisfying adults, and that actually children's satisfaction comes above the needs of parents. Robinson (2008), for example, argues that happy and satisfied children should result in happy and satisfied parents, guardians, or carers. When attending festivals as a family, 'happy children' have been identified as the most important factor enhancing the family's happiness overall (Stadler & Jepson 2017). This is particularly the case when parents get a chance to watch their children have fun or learn new things and gain new skills (Robinson 2008). However, although many festivals, attractions, and other sites appear to be 'family friendly', it is not always clear what this means and what should/should not be included on site (Light 1996). Successful family attractions, such as the ones mentioned earlier, create memorable experiences and appeal to all age ranges. Key to success is thereby a combination of enriching educational and/or cultural experiences that are realised through parents (e.g. nostalgic memories) AND children (new, present-day memories). Family togetherness, socialisation and resultant bonding can therefore be seen as the most important motivational influence for families attending festivals and events.

The ways in which families make decisions (e.g. about which festival to attend) involve a subtle yet complex and dynamic set of processes in which children can exert a decisive influence. Harbaugh et al. (2003) found that 'at age 7, children's choices about consumption goods show clear evidence of rationality, though also many inconsistencies. By age 11, choices by children [...] are as rational as choices by adults'. Harbaugh et al. (2003) further showed in another experiment that children display good bargaining skills as early as 7 years of age. Gram (2007) examined the children's role in family decision making concerning holidays and found that parents thought their children had some impact on the decisions made, while children thought they had quite a high level of impact. Parents have 'the decisive vote', but they do take children's wishes and prior experiences into account, both directly and indirectly, especially as children get older and therefore become better informed. A range of strategies are thereby employed, such as pestering, bargaining, compromising, or persuasion, but ultimately, as Gram (2007, p. 27) stresses, supportive parents engage their children in discussions as they want to have 'quality time with their children' as well as 'peaceful and stress-free holiday time, without conflict'.

In relation to events and festivals, Foster and Robinson (2010) looked at motivational factors influencing families to attend events and also found that children are considered a very important factor during the decision-making process. It is not necessarily the novelty or uniqueness of the event, but rather an opportunity to spend quality time with children or, in other words, 'family togetherness' (p. 124) that determines which event to attend. Again, this is closely related to the concept of happy children equals happy parents (Robinson 2008).

## Festival attendance and the impact upon family QOL

QOL has been a much-debated topic amongst social scientists in recent years (for a brief overview, see George 2006). Plagnol and Scott (2009) highlight that subjective indicators, such as life satisfaction and happiness, are commonly used to evaluate people's QOL. They go on to say that for most people, the concept of QOL changes over the life course. Rapley (2003, p. 67) stresses a similar concern when he says, '[...] the relative importance of various aspects of life may differ at any given moment for each of us, and the relative importance of specific matters may change over a lifetime'. Health is regarded as the most important element of QOL throughout one's life, but it changes dramatically the older we get; other aspects, such as money, employment, family and friends, and home comforts, take on a more or less important role in determining QOL over the life course. Not surprisingly, Plagnol and Scott (2009, p. 11) found that both men and women 'were more likely to mention family as an important aspect of their quality of life five or more years after the birth of their first child'. We therefore take forward Poston et al.'s (2003, p. 139) definition of family QOL, which – in contrast to individual QOL – 'considers all family members in terms of what it takes for them to have a good life and their "aggregated" perspective'.

It is widely argued that social/personal relationships and opportunities to participate in leisure activities are both crucial elements of QOL (Rapley 2003). Cummins (1996), Lloyd and Auld (2002), and Brajša-Žganec et al. (2011) highlight the importance of leisure activities contributing to well-being/QOL but acknowledge that the interrelationship between these two elements is rather complex. Participating in leisure activities with family or other people with whom one has more intimate relationships can enhance the family's overall QOL through any one or a combination of building and maintaining social relationships, creating positive memories, feeling positive emotions, and sharing symbols, identities, and meanings. Whilst family time and spending time together is an important factor, Agate et al. (2009) argued that it is not necessarily the amount of time that families spend together engaging in leisure activities, but rather how meaningful the experiences are to individual family members as well as the family as a whole that is important.

To summarise, research so far has mainly focussed on the positive impact of festival attendance (and other family leisure activities) upon an individual's and, to some extent, the family's QOL. We take a more critical look at festival attendance and family QOL, and argue that whilst the positive experiences tend to be far greater than the negative ones, family QOL does not automatically change in a positive way as a result of attending a festival. A lack of opportunities to participate in these activities can have a negative impact upon the family's happiness and QOL. Similarly, issues such as family conflict caused by stress and tiredness associated with attending a festival with children, or a lack of activities that are appropriate for different age groups, can easily tear the family apart for the day; hence the desired family togetherness, socialisation, bonding, and happiness – key determinants of family QOL – might not be achieved.

## Methods

Our research employed a mixed methodological approach and consisted of several phases. Within this chapter we discuss our focus groups, which were informed by Lloyds and Auld's (2002) theoretical perspectives on life satisfaction, happiness, and morale as well as Ragheb and Tate's (1993) theory of frequency of festival engagement against levels of satisfaction. We collected personal accounts around these variables. Focus groups were deemed appropriate to explore the broad context and a range of more specific themes and topics around family QOL, as focus groups provide an opportunity for different voices to be heard and encourage people to openly discuss topics with each other (Rubin & Rubin 1995).

We employed a snowball sampling technique to identify potential participants, contacted local community groups in St Albans and Welwyn Garden City (toddler groups, cultural groups, social media sites), and visited local festivals in Hertfordshire, UK to recruit participants. Three focus groups were conducted with 3–4 family representatives each. We used the term 'family' in its broadest sense, where a family 'includes the people who think of themselves as part of the family, whether related by blood or marriage or not, and who support and care for each other on a regular basis' (Poston et al. 2003, p. 319). The focus groups were held in local church halls or community centres, and each lasted for approximately 60 minutes. The audio recordings were transcribed verbatim and later coded and analysed using NVivo software.

## Findings and discussion

Our findings presented here are based on the family QOL frame conditions published elsewhere (Stadler & Jepson 2017): time and space; money/wealth; and rest, health, and happiness. Our findings suggest that each of these frame conditions may restrict a family's ability to attend festivals and cause negative feelings and conflict. The following sections explore and discuss our qualitative data along the themes of barriers to entry due to high ticket prices, family conflict due to overstimulated children, and lack of opportunities for family bonding. All findings and responses from family members across the three focus groups have been anonymised, and names have been changed (*Focus Group 1/FG.1, respondents A–D; Focus Group 2/FG.2, respondents E–G; Focus Group 3/FG.3, respondents H–J*).

## Barriers to entry

Families in our focus groups identified a range of challenges they face when attending festivals, such as parking, lack of childcare facilities, and bad weather. However, these were not considered as barriers to entry. High ticket prices, on the other hand, as well as having to pay for each ride once inside the festival space, were discussed by a number of participants in the focus groups as something that can limit the family's ability to attend or lead to family conflict.

> FG.1/C: Yeah, high entrance fees, you know… if you're paying £40 for a family ticket into an event and then it's sort of £2.50 per child for a ride on a merry go round, you're thinking yeah, this is going to be very expensive! So that's when it sort of tallies up and, see… I like doing free things
> 
> A: I'm desperate to take Mike to […] Festival and I'm saying well, he's two-and-a-half, it's not going to be… It's expensive! I mean we can get half price tickets but it's still going to be £70 plus petrol to get round there and everything else. So really we're better off doing something local that's free.

As expressed in earlier discussion, participants felt that ticket prices are a major factor in the decision-making process as to which festival to attend. On top of the entrance fee, families have to take into account having to pay for each ride once inside the festival space, which in addition to petrol, food, in some cases parking, and other fees adds to a substantial amount of money for a day out. Many families therefore prefer to attend local festivals that are free. This echoes Foster and Robinson's (2010) point about the importance of small-scale, local, community-type events, which tend to be more family focussed in their themes as well. Participants went on to discuss that value for money and appropriate planning are key in these decisions.

> FG.1/C: But also actually value for money because we could do sort of, you know, Legoland and all these other things but they're so expensive and they're…
> 
> A: And they're too young really to get the value out of that anyway.
> 
> C: So I tend to, especially as I, you know, I'm not earning at the moment because I'm on maternity leave, I have to really think about, also how long are we going to be there? Is it going to span over lunch? Because things spiral out and actually it can cost a fortune to go out for a family day out.

## Family conflict

Conflict within the family was identified by our participants as a common problem of attending festivals with family and with smaller children in particular. In many cases, there is too much going on at the festival, an issue that can lead to overstimulated children and, in turn, to stress, fatigue, and conflict amongst the children as well as between children and parents. This then does not create family happiness on the day and does not have a positive impact upon the family's QOL in the long run.

> FG.2/F: I prefer to go to a park, because it's not just about the financial aspect of spending lots of money, it's like funfair... a funfair with my children would be my worst nightmare because it will turn into a pester power and this and this and this and the noise and the crowds and they'd be off in all different directions because you're outnumbered. ... [laughs] It's probably me though more than, I mean they'd love it, but I just find it far too stressful and then you know, if I'm stressed then you're not dealing with them in a very positive way and a bit more snappy or whatever and then, yeah it's not the kind of experience you were hoping for.

This participant noted that the children would love to go to a funfair and would enjoy such a day out, but this would not necessarily enhance the family's overall happiness and QOL. This contradicts Robinson's (2008) findings who highlighted that the overall happiness of the family unit is almost solely dependent on the happiness of the children. Taking into account the earlier definition of family QOL by Poston et al. (2003, p. 139) which emphasises the family's 'aggregated' perspective, our focus group participants admitted that as parents they cannot always positively contribute to the family's overall QOL if the festival experience is stressful and exhausting for them. A similar issue was discussed in Focus Group 3, where participants agreed that children might get confused and overwhelmed if there is too much going on at an event, which can lead to conflict and disagreement:

> FG.3/J: I think sometimes if there's so much going on, you're sort of a bit like overwhelmed and the kids are sort of, oh I don't quite know, I'm a bit confused with what I'm...
> I: Yeah, I personally, I wouldn't want to see like loads of big rides, I mean that's nice as well but I (...) like anything you learn about a community. I find you're enriched about your community when you go to these things...
> J: Especially if there's a theme, and the kids understand that and it's easier for them to understand. Whereas if we go somewhere and it's all a bit higgledy-piggledy, they sort of don't quite know why they're there. It's too much for them, it's overstimulating. And then they start throwing tantrums and my husband and I will start blaming each other for... well, for nothing really... [laughs]. It's just too much!

For many families we spoke to, overstimulated children can cause conflict and disagreement within the family. They acknowledged that with regard to festival experiences, less is more, and in some cases, the family as a whole will get more out of participating in just one meaningful activity. This is in line with Agate et al.'s (2009) research, which emphasised that it is not necessarily the amount of time that families spend together engaging in leisure activities but how meaningful the activities are to individual family members and the family as a whole.

## Lack of opportunities for family bonding

Following on from the previous argument that family activities should be meaningful to all members of the family, a common theme and challenge for families discussed in our focus groups was the lack of activities at festivals that are appropriate for different age groups.

Families with 3–4 children at different ages identified this as a key challenge on a day out. In many cases, the parents need to split up in order to keep an eye on all children, which ultimately tears the family apart rather than bring them together. This lack of opportunities for family bonding can have a negative impact upon the family's socialisation, happiness, and QOL, and makes it difficult to understand the family's 'aggregated' perspective on QOL (Poston et al. 2003).

> FG.1/B: I mean sometimes we're finding on the weekends now that we're, my husband, and I, we'll split up. So he'll take Adam to one thing and I'll stay at home with the baby and that's, that works, but then you're not actually spending any family time together. And I'm also missing out so he'll take him to his football lessons and I don't really know what happens at those because I'm, you know, he doesn't tell me much so…
>
> FG.2/G: Up until quite recently we would split in half because of having two younger ones and then two slightly older ones, it was very difficult because of their different needs and so it was just too much going out as a family, it was just too stressful.
>
> FG.3/J: Keeping track of the kids is our main challenge, it's if the two toddlers get out of the buggy, we've got to be really hot on keeping track of them and keeping them entertained. …there's loads of things that I don't go to because it would just be too difficult. Immediately Lisa will run one way, Tommy will stand still or walk slowly in the other direction and we're immediately separated …we've got to really keep in contact about which one of us is on which child and it just gets, it just gets very stressful very quickly, so…

We previously (Stadler & Jepson 2017, p. 170) identified that festivals 'can act as a unique platform for families to share experiences and generate very powerful bonding memories', which, in turn, can enhance family happiness. Similarly, Foster and Robinson (2010) found that family togetherness was the most important motivating factor for families to attend events, closely followed by socialisation as the second most important factor. However, according to our focus group participants, it is difficult to achieve this if they have to cater for different age groups and different children's needs. This means that they do not always spend time together as a family, do not socialise and bond as a family, and do not create memories together as a family. One could therefore argue that their overall family QOL has not positively changed as a result of attending the festival.

## Conclusion

Festivals and events harbour a huge opportunity to create playfulness, social interaction, and long-lasting memories amongst members of a family group, and thus enhance their QOL together. However, this 'snapshot' of our research has demonstrated that there are a number of key issues being overlooked by event planners in relation to a family's wants and needs when they visit a festival or event.

We discovered that under the surface of the desire to take one's family to a festival or event there lies a complex decision-making process influenced by perceived barriers to attend (all of which can be linked to QOL domains: time and space; money/wealth; and rest, health, and happiness; Stadler & Jepson 2017). We found that while these domains can enable families to visit festivals and events, they also restrict their ability to do so.

The first key issue highlighted by our focus groups was high entrance fees and cost of rides/food and drink, and the family's perceptions of value for money (QOL domain: money/wealth).

The majority of families were very aware of the marketisation and meaning of festivals and events, with many preferring the low cost and familiarity of small-scale community festivals and events whilst suggesting that these types of events were more likely to appeal to their family.

The second key issue we identified was that of family conflict and the multifaceted reasons behind it (QOL domain: rest, health, and happiness). Most families suggested that a festival and event space can be very confusing to a family, even if they are given a map or directions. This is partly because the family has been placed in a new environment, and therefore extra care and attention is needed to look after one's family, which was identified as a cause of fatigue and tiredness. Additionally, if there is too much stimulation, such as bright colours, music, big rides, or too much going on, this can lead to difficulty in making decisions over what to do and can overstimulate children. This was identified as the primary cause of conflict within families.

Our third and final key issue was that of family bonding; essential for memory creation, and overall QOL (QOL domain: rest, health, and happiness). Many family-orientated events provided limited opportunities for families to interact together; the festival spaces tended to separate families rather than bring them together. Many of the events we visited tended to provide games, stalls, or activities for a very specific age range, and so activities that all of the family could take part in were limited. This effectively split up the family, so at least one of the children within a family unit became separated from their family. We believe this causes a detrimental impact on family socialisation as it reduces the opportunities to bond as a family.

There is a clear opportunity for festival planners, local authorities, and voluntary groups to develop festival spaces and programmes that cater to different age groups and offer a range of activities that are meaningful to all members of the family. Moreover, activities and events that have a strong local community element to them will be highly regarded by families local to the area. Families need to feel that they belong and that they have strong foundations; local festivals and events can achieve this if they are designed with this purpose in mind and have local inclusion within their planning processes.

In the case of family festivals and events, less is more; opportunities to engage as a family and play together can be far more beneficial than a complex programme of activities and/or bright lights and rides. One example we witnessed was a simple ball game to get balls through holes on a wooden board (all handmade by a local school teacher). There were two boards – one was the easy level aimed at small children, and the other was a larger board aimed at older children and adults. The games were side by side, which allowed good socialisation and bonding to take place across the family. Once created, family memories are powerful and emotive, and while these narratives will change over time, as they are told and retold, the point is that we tell the story, and we continue to tell the stories, and that bonds our families together over years and decades.

## References

Agate, J. R., Zabriskie, R. B., Agate, S. T. & Poff, R. (2009). Family leisure satisfaction and satisfaction with family life. *Journal of Leisure Research, 41*(2), 205–223.

Brajša-Žganec, A., Merkaš, M. & Šverko, I. (2011). Quality of life and leisure activities: How do leisure activities contribute to subjective well-being? *Social Indicators Research, 102*(1), 81–91.

Crompton, J. & McKay, S. L. (1997). Motives of visitors attending festival events. *Annals of Tourism Research, 24*(2), 425–439.

Cummins, R. (1996). The domains of life satisfaction: An attempt to order chaos. *Social Indicators Research, 38*(3), 303–332.

Foster, K. & Robinson, P. (2010). A critical analysis of the motivational factors that influence event attendance in family groups. *Event Management, 14*(2), 107–125.

George, L. K. (2006). Perceived quality of life. In Binstock, R. H., George, L. K., Cutler, S. J., Hendricks, J. and Schulz, J. H. (Eds.), *Handbook of Aging and the Social Sciences* (6th edition, pp. 320–336). Elsevier, London, 2006.

Gram, M. (2007). Children as co-decision makers in the family? The case of family holidays. *Young Consumers, 8*(1), 19–28.

Harbaugh, W. T., Krause, K. & Liday, S. G. (2003). Bargaining by children. University of Oregon Economics Working Paper No. 2002-40.

Jepson, A. & Stadler, R. (2017). Conceptualising the impact of festival and event attendance upon family quality of life (QOL). *Event Management, 21*(1), 47–60.

Lee, C. K., Lee, Y. K. & Wicks, B. E. (2004). Segmentation of festival motivation by nationality and satisfaction. *Tourism Management, 25*(1), 61–70.

Light, D. (1996). Characteristics of the audience for 'events' at a heritage site. *Tourism Management, 17*(3), 183–190.

Lloyd, K. M. & Auld, C. J. (2002). The role of leisure in determining quality of life: Issues of content and measurement. *Social Indicators Research, 57*(1), 43–71.

Murdock, G. P. (1949). *Social structure*. Oxford, England: Macmillan.

Nicholson, R. E. & Pearce, D. G. (2001). Why do people attend events: A comparative analysis of visitor motivations at four South Island events. *Journal of Travel Research, 39*(4), 449–460.

OECD (2011). Doing better for families. Available at: www.oecd.org/social/family/doingbetter. Accessed 18 August 2017.

Plagnol, A. C. & Scott, J. (2009). What matters for well-being: Individual perceptions of quality of life before and after important life events. *Applied Research in Quality of Life, 6*(2), 115–137.

Poston, D., Turnbull, A., Park, J., Mannan, H., Marquis, J. & Wang, M. (2003). Family quality of life: A qualitative inquiry. *Mental Retardation, 41*(5), 313–328.

Ragheb, M. & Tate, R. (1993). A behavioural model of leisure participation, based on leisure attitude, motivation and satisfaction. *Leisure Studies, 12*(1), 61–70.

Rapley, M. (2003). *Quality of Life Research – A Critical Introduction*. Los Angeles, CA: SAGE.

Robinson, P. (2008). *Holiday decision-making: The family perspective in tourism in visiting Britain*. University of Chichester, UK: Tourism Insights.

Rubin, H. J. & Rubin, I. S. (1995). *Qualitative Interviewing: The Art of Hearing Data*. Thousand Oaks, CA: Sage.

Stadler, R. & Jepson, A. (2017) Understanding and valuing festival and event experiences and their impacts upon family quality of life (QOL). In Armbrecht, J., Lundberg, E., Andersson, T. and Getz, D. (Eds.), *The Value of Events* (159–177). Abingdon, Oxford: Routledge.

Tomljenovic, R., Larson, M. & Faulkner, B. (2001). Predictors of satisfaction with festival attendance: A case of Storsjoyran Rock Music Festival. *Tourism (Zagreb), 49*(2), 123–132.

Uysal, M., Gahan, L. & Martin, B. (1993). An examination of event motivations: A case study. *Festival Management and Event Tourism, 1*(1), 5–10.

# 25
# FESTIVITY AND ATTENDEE EXPERIENCE
## A confessional tale of discovery

*Vern Biaett*

### Introduction

To best echo its ethnographic nature, the details of a socially constructed grounded theory method investigation of attendee behaviour at community festivals are presented as a confessional tale. A preliminary project suggested social capital bridging between disparate visitors at community festivals does not always occur (Biaett 2012). From primary exploration a substantive theme emerged, indicating lower levels of attendee social capital bonding and bridging corresponded to passive activity at community festivals. Supplementary inquiry saturated this theme, allowed it to evolve to a point of trustworthiness, and led to the conceptualisation of organic festivity theory. This neoteric hypothesis asserts that the combination of physical collaborative creative activities, stimulation of senses, and cyclically aroused emotions at community festivals creates a highly festive atmosphere giving rise to increased social capital bonding and bridging, peak liminal experience, communitas, and feelings of well-being for attendees.

### The tale begins

What is happening? This unpretentious research question launched a naturalistic inquiry (Lincoln & Guba 1985) into on-site attendee behaviour at community festivals in 2009 and the subsequent emergence of Organic Festivity Theory in early 2017. To best convey this journey I chose to present it as a confessional tale (Van Maanen 1988), an ethnographical reporting style allowing me to discuss the research design, methods, and findings of the project and insightfully reflect on the process. While ethnography in general, and a confessional tale writing style in particular, are unusual for event management studies, both address appeals to advance beyond post-positivistic research orientations with innovative methods to provide contextual understandings of visitor experience (Dixon, Igo & McGuire 2011; Holloway, Brown & Shipway 2010; Jaimangal-Jones 2014; Mair & Whitford 2013).

After three years of instructing college leisure courses following thirty years as an event practitioner, in 2008 I elected to pursue a doctorate. Festivals were not my intended focus as I considered myself an expert in the field. That assumption changed in a qualitative research methods course in 2009 when I became aware although that visitor experience had surfaced as the nucleus of event studies, research on participant behaviour remained almost exclusively a quantitative examination of pre-event motivations and post-event satisfactions (Getz 2007; Pettersson & Getz 2009). To complete a research project I opted to attend community festivals as an ethnographer and study on-site attendee behaviour. Field notes taken as an embedded participant observer were enlarged and expanded into a thick description. Short action statements extracted from these narratives were categorised. Employing reflective memo writing, peer consultations, literature review, data re-examinations, and category re-evaluations, the project concluded that social capital bridging between disparate visitor groups does not always occur at festivals. The assignment report included recommendation for future research, expressed within a required reflective poem:

> People at a Festival: Experiences?
> Uncovering the truth, protecting the truth
> People are warm, yet cold
> Bridging social capital?
> I wonder if it is going on, if anybody cares, if it is and I can't see
> Sponsors, community organizers, event producers
> They want to know, don't they?
> All I know is that I'm not sure
> Communitas?
> One day we will know more

As a festival practitioner I suffered from 'inattentional blindness' (Mack & Rock 2000). I conducted marketing research generating informative facts and figures but never saw what on-site attendees were doing around me or wrote poems about my findings. Findings were presented at a graduate symposium and international conference, but follow-up was delayed as other doctoral obligations took precedence.

## Primary exploration

My search for contextual understandings of on-site festival attendee behaviour resumed in 2011 with a dissertation on participant experiences at community festivals using a social constructivist epistemology, hermeneutic phenomenology, and ethnographic participant observation and grounded theory method strategies. Social constructivism envisions the generation of meaning and value arising from physical, social, and emotional interaction (Charmaz 2006). Recognised as an epistemology suitable for tourism curriculums, including event tourism (Tribe 2001), it was deemed an excellent fit to study attendee behaviour. Hermeneutic phenomenology which subjectively interprets individual experiences and contextual relationships was reasoned an appropriate foundational approach. Ethnographic participation observation meshed with ideas of an 'immediate conscious experience approach' to observe actual leisure behaviour (Mannell & Kleiber 1997, p. 83). Finally, grounded theory method addressed the dilemma that behavioural experiences in event studies remained a mystery due to virtually non-existent examination and theory building (Getz 2007).

## A priori *knowledge of literature*

Glaser and Strauss (1967) advocate literature review following grounded theory method data collection and analysis to prevent outside influences. Strauss and Corbin (1990, p. 48) recognise that 'we all bring to the inquiry a considerable background in professional and disciplinary literature.' Prior to starting my fieldwork I did not conduct a literature review, but I possessed *a priori* knowledge that informed my research.

A concise definition of festival is non-existent. Getz (1989) spoke of linked perspectives but believed a universal definition of festivals not possible. Others reached similar conclusions (Hall 1989; Jago & Shaw 1998), and when Getz (2010) revisited the topic he concluded a definition of festival remained only a spectrum of esoteric ideas. I was aware celebration existed since the earliest cultural hearths (Kraus 1971). As civilisation progressed and celebration became evermore structured by authorities, it continued to provide societal fabric. Following World War II, emphasis on public relations and revenue generation led to pseudo-events (Boorstin 1961) with ritualistic and profane festivity surpassed by marketing and mercantile activity. As festivals increased in numbers (Janiskee 1994) they also became strategies for rural redevelopment (Wilson, Fesenmaier, Fesenmaier & Van Es 2001), urban regeneration (Jackson, Houghton, Russell & Triandos 2005), and place branding (Derrett 2003; Jamieson 2004). During this same period, Putnam (2000) observed and reported decreases in social capital.

Authentic experience is a term of knowledge, occurrence, and emotion. Van Gennep (1960[1909]) categorised religious rituals and profane festivals as pre-liminal ventures away from ordinary routine, liminal participation in the unusual, and post-liminal returns to normalcy. Turner (1982) combined these liminal phases into a single concept of liminality, defined as periods of autonomy and freedom imparting feelings of pleasure and *communitas*. He also used the term *liminoid* to differentiate between profane and religious experiences. Research has associated authentic festival experience with *communitas* (Gilmore 2010; King 2010), visitor feelings of inner-self (Wang 1999), and desires for pleasure outside of everyday life (Timothy 2011).

Knowledge of what brings meaning to experience included Neulinger's (1981) paradigm of meaningful leisure with its variables of freedom of choice and intrinsic reward. Explaining leisure time, Nash (1953) created a pyramid where meaningful experience builds from a passive base, to emotional and active engagement, to a capstone of creativity. In flow theory (Csikszentmihalyi 1990) meaningful experience arises from a loss of self-consciousness, the merging of action and awareness, a sense of self-control, and an altered sense of time. Intangible places are created through authentic experience (Tuan 1977); short-term, flashpoint experiences connect people (Manzo 2008); and 'events without authenticity, local meaning, and culture provide only spectacular experiences in placelessness' (MacLeod 2006, p. 232).

## *Data collection and analysis*

In the absence of a definition of community festival, the term was delimited to include temporary events, open to the public, with a single location, and a theme of celebration or festivity. Primary data about attendee behaviour emerged from participant observation at seven purposively and conveniently selected community festivals near Phoenix, Arizona including holiday celebrations, fiestas, cowboy days, and art festivals. Handwritten notes from these festivals were enlarged within 12 hours and expanded into typewritten narratives within 72 hours of collection to ensure thick descriptions of attendee behaviour. Initial coding, a meticulous process of word-by-word, line-by-line, sentence-by-sentence analysis, extracted over 1,200 behavioural action codes (Charmaz 2006). These included short statements such as

> people surround the dancers, man on cell phone looks bored, people hold hands over ears when guns fire, kids crowd closer to the performer, family camps out near the stage, woman stops three men dressed in kilts, dad makes sure kids are safe on ride, and shoppers pay little attention to others.

Saturation was reached when no new codes arose from the seventh festival.

Leaving the field, with plans to add theoretical sampling to strengthen my study, I struggled when beginning to write about my journey of discovery. A qualitative research mentor suggested I consider a confessional tale. To practice this format I wrote an auto-ethnographic reflection (Biaett 2012) that provides additional detail on my dissertation research design and method, summarised earlier.

Additional data came from event manager interviews and a content analysis of International Festivals & Events Association online newsletters distributed from March 2010 to February 2013, conducted for theoretical sampling to strengthen emerging themes. The interviews with event managers were designed to create conversation regarding planned activity and attendee behaviour. Responses to questions on activity planning fixated on operational issues, not experience design factors. When asked to describe attendee behaviour at events, every event manager non-enthusiastically hemmed, hawed, and spoke only about demographic characteristics. An interesting comment was made by one interviewee of how experience at her festival was about waiting in lines, but this was OK because the festival was free. A total of 1,592 articles from 153 weekly newsletters were dissected to ascertain the prominence of stories concerned with programming of quality experiences for attendees. It was deduced that while 28.4% of articles were on financial and 16.0% marketing topics, only 2.2% concentrated on quality authentic experiences.

As subsequent festival narratives and interview transcripts added to my collective data mix I repeatedly reanalysed it through focussed coding, a process that eventually sorted, diagramed, and clustered data codes into 6 main categories and 18 subcategories. I turned to axial coding to move these categories toward stronger themes. This involved fracturing and rebuilding all categories by asking questions of 'when, where, why, who, how, and what consequences' (Strauss & Corbin 1990, p. 125) about the data codes they contained. They were answered by revaluating what action codes stated, how they originated and were located in narratives, and what had been written about them in reflective memos. This process put in greater context attendees' reactions to the structural conditions of a festival, what was going on around them, and the consequences of their actions.

Systematically, two broad categories were reconstructed. One posed community festivals are temporary special places where bonding and bridging social capital between attendees can be found and developed. The second construed correlation between quality attendee experiences at community festivals and the programming of physical, emotional, and collaborative activities. To determine if these themes should be developed independently or merged, and to establish a stronger framework for possible substantive theory, more information was needed.

## Literature review

To expand *a priori* knowledge of Putnam's (2000) theoretical concept that social capital bonding brings together those with similar social and cultural backgrounds, while social capital bridging jumps across this divide in real-life situations, more research was required. To specifically inform and advance my developing social capital category, literature was reviewed related to the topic of festival social capital. Many articles casually implied a connection between festivals and social capital. Remington (2003) recognised that social capital bonding increased within festival organiser and volunteer networks. This was reported by Arcodia and Whitford (2006) as well, who also acknowledged general senses of cohesion among visitors, increasing social capital for attendees within family and friend groups, and decreasing social capital if organisers fail to create positive celebration before, during, or after a festival. Both articles focussed on the general landscape of festival experience, not specifically on-site attendee behaviour. Guided by social capital theory, Wilks (2011) investigated attendees at music festivals in real time with critical discourse analysis and found bonding social capital highly present but minimal bridging social capital. A psychology study using structured interviews and mixed modelling analysis reported increased social capital for parents attending community festivals (Molitor, Rossi & Brantan 2011). It was felt that the literature confirmed that varying levels of bonding and bridging social capital exist at festivals.

Labelling my second emerging category as festive activity I also conducted literature review on festival experiences. Tschohl (2002) proclaimed excellence is built by creating incredible experience. A case study about a planner failing to meet guest expectations (Berridge 2012) highlighted the importance of event experience design knowledge. Outlining good festival experiences Morgan (2008) concluded that social interactions, personal experiences, shared value of performance, and a sense of communitas were key elements. Pettersson and Getz (2009) explored festival experiences finding positive experiences related to quality programming. They declared that while guests attend festivals for both generic fun atmospheres and specific experiences, and although festival experience cannot be completely designed, certain design principles enhance social interaction. Van Belle (2009, p. 8) suggests reimagining the word 'festival,' a noun, as the word 'festivalizing,' a verb. He believed by appreciating festivals as activity that does something, not as a group of activities that are something, festive experience is really a state of constant creation defined by the act of participant attendance. Proclaiming the arts as building blocks of festive experience, Ehrenreich (2006) asserts dance was the first physical manifestation of festivity and, with its accompanying music, crucial to festive experience. I believed literature substantiated the theme that programming festive activity was significant in the provision of quality attendee experiences.

## *Construction of substantive theory*

'Where is the theory in grounded theory?' (Charmaz 2006, p. 133). Theory comes from a systematic social construction of grounded data. In this research, community festival landscapes have been reduced to observational notes of attendee behaviour and, in turn, rebuilt into thick descriptive. Narratives were dichotomised into action statements with initial coding and reassembled into categories with focussed coding. The data in each category were re-evaluated by axial coding, resulting in two general themes. Literature review confirmed and added substance to themes, and with reflective theorising (Charmaz 2006) substantive theory emerged (Biaett 2013, p. 77):

> Social capital bonding is strongly evident and easily recognizable within friend and family groups at all community festivals, but minimal throughout an inflated group of unacquainted peers that share demographic similarities, at community festivals featuring low degrees of programmed festivity. Social capital bridging exists minimally, both heuristically in the form of direct social interaction between strangers with dissimilar demographics, as well as hermeneutically by attendees possessing only a sense of primal subconscious generic communitas, at community festivals featuring low degrees of programmed festivity. Event management possessing both the aspiration and knowledge to program quality festive experience has the ability to increase and accentuate the development of social capital bonding and bridging at community festivals.

This substantive theory implied it should not be assumed that social capital inherently exists at community festivals and there is a need to better understanding the essence of festive experience.

## Supplementary exploration

Qualitative research avalanches. The examination of visitor behaviour that began by asking 'what is happening' spiraled into a paradigm of social capital, festivity, and experience design. Believing there was more surrounding the relationship of festivity and attendee behaviour, I extended my exploration with a prolonged post-dissertation literature review. I inundated the collected data mix with rhetorical insights from a variety of fields. Continual re-evaluation, peer review of redeveloping themes, and reflective theorising flushed out substantive theory to a point of trustworthiness (Lincoln & Guba 1985). Strength between observation and interpretation developed, and findings linked to data could be easily compared and contrasted to other situations. An abridged synopsis of extended literature review, interjected with reflective theorising, provides a look at the ideas and reasoning ultimately leading to the emergence of organic festivity theory.

### *Antecedents of festivity*

People celebrate with festive activity. Because festivity has existed as part of every human experience (Fortes 1936) the 'discussion of the festivals of extinct or remote societies may throw light on those still to be found in ours' (Roy 2005, p. xii). Early humans met their needs of food, water, shelter, and belonging before they satisfied needs of self-actualisation (Maslow 1943). They embraced their mythological spirits (Armstrong 2005) with spontaneous juxtaposed celebrations of ecstasy and transcendence. They rejoiced in their accomplishments and relieved feelings of suffering from killing animals and death of kinfolk. Cave paintings with depictions of Palaeolithic hunters, females, and shamans engaged in celebration provide the first records of this festivity (Burkert 2001). For primitive man there was no separation of the spiritual and secular, and festivity was 'of the whole of the world and of life' (Pieper 1965, p. 3). Clans gathered nightly around bonfires adorned in red body paint (Lewis 1980), chanted, drummed, and danced (Ehrenreich 2006) to celebrate their world. Huzinga (1955) thought the festive activity of ancient celebration synonymous with spontaneous, meaningful unto itself, intrinsic, out of the ordinary, absorbing, communal play. Falassi (1987) described profane festivals as the essence of joyful and hospitable communal play. Additional matter on the antecedents of festivity can be found in my account about the missing ingredients of community festival (Biaett 2015).

Reflecting on this strain of literature I crafted a historical typology of festivity. It characterised mankind's original primordial, spontaneous, highly physical emotional collaborative celebratory activity as *organic*. The ritualised, spatial, temporal, and structured festivals of progressing civilisations were typified as *organised*, and today's marketing and economic oriented festivals were typified as *commercial organisms*. My dissertation's substantive theme evolved temporarily into what I called PX (participant experience) theory, simplified to positively state, 'Levels of social capital bonding and bridging increase when attendees engage in more organically festive forms of activity' (Biaett 2015). Although this premise, asserting the physical emotional collaborative activities of organic festivity were critical elements for increasing social capital at community festival, was accepted for publication, peer review following presentations at international conferences indicated more was needed.

## Infusion of senses and emotions

Re-evaluating, I realised attendees became active and engaged when their senses were stimulated and emotions aroused. People in lines were bored, on their phones, but as they neared the front, with sights, sounds, and strong smells of food concessions, toilets, and petting zoos, they became interactive with others. At venues with loud music, thumping bass, or flashing lights, people stood, clapped, and danced together. On scary rides, when visiting a dog adoption tent, or when upset by someone cutting in line, people were absorbed. In behavioural momentum theory Nevin and Shahan (2011) outline changes in behaviour as disruptors – stimulated senses that arouse emotions are disruptors of attendee behaviour at community festivals.

Traditional senses include sight, hearing, taste, smell, and touch, but there are other stimuli including temperature, vibration, and balance (Pediaopolis 2017). Addressing transformational experience at an event innovation forum, Rinehart (2015) informed the audience when senses are stimulated, synapses in the brain are affected by neurotransmitters that create emotional responses. Dasu and Chase (2013, p. 24) allege that 'emotions define the importance of an experience,' and Hosany and Gilbert (2010, p. 522) allege that one should 'engineer positive emotions to create enjoyable and memorable experiences.' Research recapped by Brown and Hutton (2013) found emotional festival experiences linked to atmospherics, loyal behaviour, motivation, and satisfaction. Amarante (2011), interviewing the Los Angeles Lakers' CEO, was told the team manufactures messages of anger prior, during, and after games to excite and engage fans, which paralleled literature emphasising emotional intensity as important to festival experience (Collins 2004). In the psycho-evolutionary theory of emotion Plutchik (2002) identifies eight biologically primitive primary emotions with four juxtaposed pairs (joy/sadness, trust/disgust, fear/anger, and surprise/anticipation) and notes that these, and derivative combinations, exist in varying levels of intensity.

It became obvious that stimulating senses and emotions equalled better experiences. Attendees with stimulated senses were seen to be social and creative, not passive spectators. Action statements attested, 'people stomped in unison to loud music, girls take selfie with Irish food, drunk lady gets upset and yells, and couple shows cowboy mannequin with red eyes to others.' With constant comparison of data and literature, it appeared organic festivity was best expressed as the combination of physical collaborative creative activity, stimulated senses, and aroused emotions.

## Well-being and happiness

Mannell and Kleiber (1997, p. 86) believe that 'good leisure experiences may better contribute to well-being' viewed in three paradigms: 1) happiness, delineated as short-term present feelings of experience; 2) morale, viewed as personal assessment of the future; and 3) satisfaction, described as appraisal of past experiences. Russell (2013) describes well-being in physical, emotional, intellectual, and social terms, similar to the physical collaborative creative activity of organic festivity. In flow theory (Csikszentmihalyi 1990) participants engaged in performance and competitive activities achieve optimal experience and a sense of well-being when the factors of skill level and challenge are matched and maximised. I envisioned that the three combined attributes of organic festivity should be considered as the factors which lead to flow, a sense of liminality, and feelings of well-being for attendees at community festivals.

## Organic festivity theory

This neoteric theory, emerging from socially constructed grounded theory method research, converges on three constructs. The first, with primordial roots, is the importance of having attendees engaged in physical, collaborative, and creative activity, for instance immersion in dance activity, as opposed to being simply entertained by passive spectator amusement and shopping. The second construct, sensually infused crowd enthusiasm, emphasises dynamically stimulating the basic senses and additional sensual modalities, for example strong smells and pounding deep bass beats. The third construct centres around arousing attendee emotions prior to, during, and after an event. With this foundation organic festivity theory asserts,

> At community festivals, the maximized interrelated factors of physical collaborative creative activity, stimulated senses, and cyclically aroused emotions, give rise to highly festive atmospheres during which social capital bonding and bridging flourishes and attendees attain peak levels of liminality with feelings of well-being.

And one day I knew a little more. I believe this is just the beginning of the story of festivity and attendee experience. My research concentrated on community festivals, but it has implications for future research into multiple aspects of event management and other fields. What activities, senses, and emotions best increase social capital, liminality, and feeling of well-being? Can ethnography find a home in festival research? Only tomorrow will tell.

## References

Amarante, L. (2011). *Ten factors to creating a world class event experience*. Arizona State University. Unpublished thesis. Tempe, Arizona.
Arcodia, C. & Whitford, M. (2006). Festival attendance and the development of social capital. *Journal of Convention and Event Tourism, 8*(2), 1–18.
Armstrong, K. (2005). *A short history of myth*. Edinburgh: Canongate Books.
Berridge, G. (2012). Event experiences: A case study of the differences between the way in which organizers plan an event experience and the way in which guests receive the experience. *Journal of Parks and Recreation Management, 30*(3), 7–23.
Biaett, V. (2012). A confessional tale: Auto-ethnography reflections on the investigation of attendee behavior at community festivals. *Tourism Today, 12*, 65–75.
Biaett, V. (2013). *Exploring the on-site behavior of attendees at community festivals: A social constructivist grounded theory approach*. Arizona State University. Unpublished thesis. Tempe, Arizona.
Biaett, V. (2015). Organic festivity: A missing ingredient of community festival. In Jepson, A. and Clarke, A. (Eds). *Exploring community festivals and events* (17–30). New York, NY: Routledge.
Boorstin, D. (1961). *The image: A guide to pseudo-events in America*. New York, NY: Harper and Row.
Brown, S. & Hutton, A. (2013). Development in the real-time evaluation of audience behavior at planned events. *International Journal of Event and Festival Management, 4*(1), 43–55.
Burkert, W. (2001). Shamans, caves, and the master of animals. In J. Narby and F. Huxley (Eds). *Shamans through time: 500 years on the path to knowledge* (223–227). London, UK: Thames & Hudson.
Charmaz, K. (2006). *Constructing grounded theory: A practical guide through qualitative analysis*. London, UK: Sage.
Collins, R. (2004). *Interaction ritual chains*. Princeton, NJ: Princeton University Press.
Csikszentmihalyi, M. (1990). *Flow: The psychology of optimal experience*. New York, NY: Harper Perennial.
Dasu, S. & Chase, R. (2013). *The customer service solution: Managing emotions, trust, and control to win your customer's business*. New York, NY: McGraw Hill Education.
Derrett, R. (2003). Making sense of how festivals demonstrate a community's sense of place. *Event Management, 8*(1), 49–58.

Dixon, H., Igo, L. & McGuire, F. (2011). Grounded theory methodology in research. In E. Sirakaya-Turk, M. Uysal, and W. Hammitt (Eds). *Research methods for leisure, recreation and tourism* (127–139). Cambridge, MA: CAB International.

Ehrenreich, B. (2006). *Dancing in the streets: A history of collective joy.* New York, NY: Henry Holt and Company.

Falassi, A. (1987). *Time out of time: Essays on the festival.* Albuquerque, NM: University of New Mexico Press.

Fortes, M. (1936). Ritual festivals and social cohesion in the Hinterland of the Gold Coast. *American Anthropologist, 38,* 590–604.

Getz, D. (1989). Special events: Defining the product. *Tourism Management* 10(2), 125–137.

Getz, D. (2007). *Event studies: Theory, research, and policy for planned events.* Oxford, UK: Elsevier Butterworth Heinemann.

Getz, D. (2010). The nature and scope of festival studies. *International Journal of Events Management Research, 5*(1), 1–47.

Gilmore, L. (2010). *Theater in a crowded fire: Ritual and spirituality at Burning Man.* Berkeley, CA: University of California Press.

Glaser, B. & Strauss, A. (1967). *Discovery of grounded theory: Strategies for qualitative research.* Chicago, IL: Aldine.

Hall, C. M. (1989). The definition and analysis of hallmark tourism events. *GeoJournal, 19*(3), 263–268.

Holloway, I., Brown, L. & Shipway, R. (2010). Meaning not measurement: Using ethnography to bring a deeper understanding to the participant experience of festivals and events. *International Journal of Event and Festival Management, 1*(1), 74–85.

Hosany, S. & Gilbert, D. (2010). Measuring tourist's emotional experiences toward hedonic holiday destinations. *Journal of Travel Research, 49*(4), 513–526.

Huzinga, J. (1955). *Homo ludens: A study in the play element in culture.* Boston, MA: Beacon Press.

Jackson, J., Houghton, M., Russell, R. & Triandos, P. (2005). Innovations in measuring economic impacts of regional festivals: A do-it-yourself kit. *Journal of Travel Research, 43*(4), 360–367.

Jago, L. K. & Shaw, R. N. (1998). Special events: A conceptual and definitional framework. *Festival Management and Event Tourism, 5*(1–2), 21–32.

Jaimangal-Jones, D. (2014). Utilising ethnography and participant observation in festival and event research. *International Journal of Event and Festival Management, 5*(1), 39–55.

Jamieson, K. (2004). The festival gaze and its boundaries. *Space and Culture, 7*(1), 64–75.

Janiskee, R. (1994). Some macroscale growth trends in America's community festival industry. *Festival Management & Event Tourism, 2*(1), 10–14.

King, S. A. (2010). Blues tourism in the Mississippi Delta: The functions of blues festivals. *Popular Music and Society, 26*(4), 455–475.

Kraus, R. (1971). *Recreation and leisure in modern society.* New York, NY: Appleton-Century-Crofts.

Lewis, G. (1980). *Day of shining red: An essay on understanding ritual.* Cambridge, UK: Cambridge University Press.

Lincoln, Y. S. & Guba, E. G. (1985). *Naturalistic inquiry.* Newbury Park, CA: Sage.

Mack, A. & Rock, I. (2000). *Inattentional blindness.* Boston, MA: M.I.T. Press.

MacLeod, N. (2006). The placeless festival: Identity and place in the post-modern festival. In Picard, D. & Robinson, M. (Eds). *Festivals, tourism, and social change: Remaking worlds,* 222–237, Cleveland, OH: Channel View Publications.

Mair, J. & Whitford, J. (2013). An exploration of events research: Event topics, themes and emerging trends. *International Journal of Event and Festival Management, 4*(1), 6–30.

Mannell, R. & Kleiber, D. (1997). *A social psychology of leisure.* State College, PA: Venture Publishing.

Manzo, L. C. (2008). Understanding human relationships to place and their significance for outdoor recreation and tourism. In Kruger, L. E., Hall, T. E. & Stiefel, M. C. (Eds). *Understanding concepts of place in recreation research management,* 135–174, U.S. Department of Agriculture, Forest Service, Pacific Northwest Research Station, General Technical Report PNW-GTR-744, Portland, Oregon.

Maslow, A. H. (1943). A theory of human motivation. *Psychological Review, 50,* 370–396.

Molitor, F., Rossi, M. & Brantan, L. (2011). Increasing social capital and personal efficacy through small-scale community events. *Journal of Community Psychology, 39*(6) 749–754.

Morgan, M. (2008). What makes a good festival? Understanding the event experience. *Events Management, 12*(1), 81–93.

Nash, J. B. (1953). *Philosophy of recreation and leisure.* Dubuque, IA: W.M. C. Brown Company Publishers.

Neulinger, J. (1981). *To leisure: An introduction.* Boston, MA: Allyn & Bacon.

Nevin, J. & Shahan, T. (2011). Behavioral momentum theory: Equations and applications. *Journal of Applied Behavioral Analysis, 44*(4), 877–895.

Pediaopolis, W. (2017). *The five senses,* Retrieved from http://udel.edu/~bcarey/ART307/project1_4b/. Accessed 10/01/2018.

Pettersson, R. & Getz, D. (2009). Event experiences in time and space: A study of visitors to the 2007 World Alpine Ski Championships in Are, Sweden. *Scandinavian Journal of Hospitality and Tourism, 9*(2–3), 308–326.

Pieper, J. (1965). *In tune with the world: A theory of festivity.* New York, NY: Harcourt, Brace & World.

Plutchik, R. (2002). *Emotions and life: Perspectives from psychology, biology, and evolution.* Washington, DC: American Psychological Association.

Putnam, R. (2000). *Bowling alone: The collapse and revival of American community.* New York, NY: Simon & Schuster.

Remington, S. (2003). The power of festivals to build social capital. *IE, 14*(2), 21–22.

Rinehart, B. (2015). *Why event pros need to design emotional experiences.* Event Innovation Forum, Orlando, Florida. Available at: www.youtube.com/watch?v=TA1EteF44uc. Accessed 09/01/2018.

Roy, C. (2005). *Traditional festivals: A multicultural encyclopedia.* Santa Barbara, CA: ABC-CLIO.

Russell, R. (2013). *Pastimes: The context of contemporary leisure.* 5th edition, Urbana, IL: Sagamore.

Strauss, A. & Corbin, J. (1990) *Basics of qualitative research: Grounded theory procedures and Techniques.* Newbury Park, CA: Sage.

Timothy, D. J. (2011). *Cultural heritage and tourism: An introduction.* Bristol, UK: Channel View Publications.

Tribe, J. (2001). Research paradigms and the tourism curriculum. *Journal of Travel Research, 38*(4), 442–448.

Tschohl, J. (2002). *Achieving excellence through customer service.* Minneapolis, MN: Best Sellers Publishing.

Tuan, Y. (1977). *Space and place: The perspective of experience.* Minneapolis, MN: University of Minnesota Press.

Turner, V. (1982). *Celebration: Studies in festivity and ritual.* Washington, DC: Smithsonian Institution Press.

Van Belle, D. (2009). Festivalizing performance: Community and aesthetics through the lens of three festival experiences. *Canadian Theater Review, 138,* 7–12.

Van Gennep, A. (1909). *The rites of passage,* 1960 translation by M. Vizedom and G. Coffee, Routledge and Kegan Paul, London.

Van Maanen, J. (1988). *Tales of the field.* Chicago, IL: University of Chicago Press.

Wang, N. (1999). Rethinking authenticity in tourism experience. *Annals of Tourism Research, 26*(2), 349–370.

Wilks, L. (2011). Bridging and bonding: Social capital at music festivals. *Journal of Policy Research in Tourism, Leisure & Events, 3*(3), 281–297.

Wilson, S., Fesenmaier, D. R., Fesenmaier, J. & Van Es, J. C. (2001). Factors for success in rural tourism development. *Journal of Travel Research, 40*(2), 132.

# 26
# INFORMATION AND COMMUNICATION TECHNOLOGY AND THE FESTIVAL EXPERIENCE

*Christine M. Van Winkle, Kelly J. MacKay and Elizabeth Halpenny*

## Introduction

Developments in information and communication technologies (ICTs) have transformed communication across the world (Poushter 2016). ICT can include hardware, software, netware (networked operating systems) and humanware (hardware or software built around the users' needs) used to facilitate communication across time and space (Buhalis 2003). Increasingly, festivals are integrating new ICTs into the attendee experience (Van Winkle & Comer 2011), and technology can mediate festival experiences or become the experience itself and transform the festivalscape (Neuhofer, Buhalis, & Ladkin 2014; Robertson, Yeoman, Smith, & McMahon-Beattie 2015).

While ICT has been the subject of user experience research in tourism and recreation contexts (Höpken, Gretzel, & Law 2009; Kim & Schliesser 2007; Law, Leung, & Buhalis 2009; MacKay & Vogt 2012), ICT use has received less attention in festival studies. Themed public celebrations (i.e. festivals) have been an important part of life throughout history, and events have become increasingly important because of the flexible programming offered in a time when people feel the pressure of limited time available for leisure (Getz 2012). With increased competition for attendees, festivals often try to reinvent themselves by diversifying their programming. While ICT has been commonly used at festivals for utilitarian purposes like on-line ticket sales, recently some festivals have begun to provide patrons with opportunities to interact with the event and other patrons through ICT. For example, beginning in 2016, Coachella live-streamed festival events in 360 degrees. A wide range of ICTs can be included in the festival experience. The majority of people across the globe now own a mobile device (MD) (Mobile Fact Sheet 2017), and because of the increasing popularity of mobile technologies, many festivals are finding ways to include digital mobile elements at the festival.

This chapter will examine the current state and future implications of ICT integration into festival experiences and will focus on ICTs used by attendees in festival settings; specifically, the Internet, MDs and social media use will be explored.

## Background

The evolution of ICT, including the computer, Internet and World Wide Web (WWW), has transformed society over the course of the 20th and 21st centuries (Leiner, Cerf, Clark, Kahn, Kleinrock, Lynch, Postel, Roberts, & Wolff 2009). The computer revolution began in the 1960s and continued throughout the next three decades with the development of minicomputers, modems, networks, user interfaces, less-expensive personal computers and eventually mobile digital technology (Leiner et al. 2009; Lonnquist 2011; Peter 2007). In the 1990s, complex computer networks within companies were common, but personal online networks did not yet exist limiting the scope of these networks. The development and growth of the WWW in the late 1980s and early 1990s provided people with the opportunity to share, link and connect various operating systems across organizations, communities and the globe (Lonnquist 2011).

At the turn of the new millennium, the WWW transformed again and its influence on our lives grew (Tapscott 2009). This transition to the WWW 2.0 came about when the WWW became a place where people could contribute by producing user-generated content (UGC). As of 2017, half of the world's population had access to the Internet (We Are Social 2017).

Online communication with other users began in the 1960s and 1970s with the introduction of email and evolved to include listservs in the 1880s, chat rooms in the 1990s and paved the way for online social networking sites, which were first introduced in the mid-1990s (McIntyre 2014). By the 21st century, communicating online was commonplace, and so when sites like Myspace and Facebook were introduced in the mid-2000s, millions of consumers joined these platforms within the first few years of their introduction.

MDs evolved along a similar timeline and have also drastically transformed the way we communicate and access information. The first mobile wireless phone was introduced in the 1970s. Within 20 years, mobile digital technology has advanced incredibly, and mobile phones are used by over two-thirds of the population across the globe (We Are Social 2017). MDs may be 'the most rapidly diffused technological artifact in history' (Wajcman 2008, p. 68).

As consumers use the WWW, social media and MDs to communicate, (including festivals) look for opportunities to engage with customers using these tools (Neuhofer, Buhalis, & Ladkin 2015). Research indicates that value can be added to a consumer experience when ICT is integrated in such a way that individuals can 'gather information, enrich and construct experiences' (Neuhofer et al. 2015, p. 791).

## Types of MD use

The Typology of Human Capability (THC) (Korn & Pine 2011) presents experience-enhancing digital opportunities. The THC assumes that digital technology gives people the opportunity for connecting and doing individually or as a group. Classifying technology use according to these dimensions results in the following digital experiences for users: sensing, performing, linking and organizing. *Sensing* describes how peoples' sensations can be enhanced through digital technologies. ICT can also facilitate *performing* by offering tools that enable people to accomplish something. *Linking* facilitates connection and interaction with others. *Organizing* enables groups of individuals to form and function. The four constructs can work independently, as well as collectively to enhance a person-centred experience (Korn & Pine 2011).

Van Winkle, Cairns, MacKay and Halpenny (2016) examined the THC in festival contexts and after completing 163 interviews with attendees at six different festivals, found that linking was the most common digital experience had by festival attendees, but that all experiences described by the THC were seen at festivals. Based on the interviews undertaken, operational definitions of the THC constructs were developed for the festival context. At the festival, linking using ICT involved connecting with others. Connecting occurred through speech, text or visuals and was either virtual or in-person, immediate or delayed (e.g. posting social media content). Organizing involved the use of ICT to coordinate a group of individuals at, or to, a festival. This could require immediate action and initiative by one or all of the group members (e.g. using mobile to arrange meeting up with others). Sensing provided festival attendees the opportunity to experience different sensations. These sensations could be psychological, emotional or physical. Within the physical realm, MDs offered opportunities to see, hear or feel the festival differently through digital imagery, recordings or haptic (touch) technology enabling people to experience information in a new way. Performing involved independent action, such as when an individual engages with mobile technology to accomplish something that influences their experience (e.g. purchasing tickets and locating directions).

Van Winkle et al. (2016) adapted the original version of the THC to recognize the important role that context plays in how technology affects festival experiences. The addition of context acknowledges that ICT used during a festival may or may not be used in relation to the festival and that this likely affects attendees' overall experience attending the festival. What the THC conceptualization does not offer is insight into the outcomes of ICT use and how using technology to link, sense, organize and perform may detract from or enhance a festival experience. Future research should examine the outcomes of technology use during festivals. In particular, insights into the effects on attendees' experiences in terms of engagement and satisfaction will provide needed insight for festival administrators.

## Acceptance and use of ICT in festival contexts

Theories describing user acceptance of technology provide a comprehensive understanding of the factors affecting ICT adoption in festival settings relevant to both current and future technologies. By grounding the discussion in theory, the specific technologies described become less important than considering the implications of all ICT on the visitor's experience.

The Diffusion of Innovation Theory (DIT) was an early technology acceptance theory that explored how technology is adopted over time. This framework describes the stages people and organizations go through in deciding whether or not to adopt a new technology (Rogers 1995). DIT has been criticized because while it describes adoption, it does not explain how adoption occurs or factors that lead to adoption and this limits its scope of application (Straub 2009). Two widely accepted theories exist that describe IT adoption specifically – Technology Acceptance Model (TAM) and the United Theory of Acceptance and Use of Technology (UTAUT) (Straub 2009). TAM posits that perceived ease of use and perceived usefulness affect intention to adopt and use a technology and the adoption of a new technology (Davis 1989). This model has been criticized because it does not recognize differences between users. The UTAUT evolved out of the TAM and suggests that performance expectancy, effort expectancy and social influence predict behavioural intention to use IT and, in turn, predict usage. In this model, gender, age and experience are all moderating factors for intention to use technology (Venkatesh & Davis 2000), addressing issues with the TAM. Further modification has resulted in the UTAUT2 (Venkatesh, Thong, & Xu 2012), which adds habit, hedonic motivation, price value and facilitating conditions as variable affecting intention to use one's device.

Van Winkle, Bueddefeld, MacKay and Halpenny (2017) examined the UTAUT2 variables in three festival settings and demonstrated performance expectancy, habit and hedonic motivation affect intention to use MDs at festivals. Attendees use devices because they feel they add value to their experience. The range of functions offered by mobile make it a useful tool in an intense context, and users feel that MDs facilitate their ability to perform tasks they need to undertake.

Habits, measured by people's perception that they have developed a habit of using their MD, affected their intention to use their device in the festival context (Van Winkle, Cairns, Halpenny, & MacKay 2016). With the range of functions offered by devices, many have become accustomed to using MDs on an ongoing basis. Festival visitors may be using their MDs, checking the Internet, and posting on social media due to habits formed outside of the festival context. This can be both a benefit and drawback in the festival setting. Attendees with well-formed habits will find that using mobile to coordinate activities may facilitate the festival experience. When festivals introduce novel programming using ICT, attendees with a strong habit of using mobile will likely easily adopt these new offerings. Alternatively, this habit may, at times, interfere with experiencing the festival. It seems likely that when the habit of using a device triggers festival-related MD use, then the experience will be enhanced, whereas when the habit triggers non-festival-related use, the festival experience will suffer. Further research is needed in this area to understand the implications of our MD use habits on our festival experiences.

Motivations for attending festivals have been well researched and highlight the hedonic and social value people derive from festivals (Crompton & McKay 1997; Lee, Lee, & Wicks 2004). Given the pleasure-seeking aspect of festival experiences, it is no surprise that when people use mobile in festival settings, they do so because of the hedonic elements of mobile use (Van Winkle et al. 2017). When examining how festivals are engaging audiences through ICT, the vast majority of experiences are utilitarian (ticket purchasing, schedules, maps). There is great opportunity for festivals to entice audiences with ICT programming that has hedonic elements such as fun, pleasure and entertainment.

ICT nonuse is less understood than acceptance and use (Selwyn 2003). Disconnecting from technology is becoming increasingly prevalent in leisure and tourism settings, and considering nonusers is essential to understanding the role of ICT during festival experiences (Dickinson, Hibbert, & Filimonau 2016; Pearce & Gretzel 2012). Early research on ICT non-adoption focused on the digital divide and disparate access to technology, with little recognition that there are people who choose to reject technology (Selwyn 2003). Not all festival participants are enthusiastic about integrating ICT into their festival experience. Research has found that 10–15% per cent of attendees either don't own or don't have an MD at the festival (Van Winkle, Cairns, Halpenny, & MacKay 2014). Of those that do have a device, as many as 10–20% per cent don't intend to use their device during the festival (Van Winkle et al. 2014).

Reasons for nonuse vary and include disappointed nonusers who had an unusable device, indifferent nonusers who didn't bring an MD with them and enthusiastic nonusers who felt that the presence of an MD was an unwanted interference or inappropriate for the context. There are times when nonuse is freely chosen and other times when it is imposed (Van Winkle et al. 2014). In each case, there is potential for the lack of a MD to affect the festival experience, either positively or negatively.

All festivals need to consider their audiences and the role mobile technology should play in the festival experience. Some festivals may attract audience members more likely to reject technology and who are seeking an escape from being connected. By having a disconnected festival, some festivals may be able to uniquely appeal to this niche market. Alternatively, providing novel mobile experiences may attract new audiences and distinguish a festival from its competitors. When deciding how to integrate ICT into the festival experience, festival administrators should consider the mandate of the festival, resources available, and both technology users and nonusers.

## ICT and the attendee experience

The attendee experience is paramount in a festival context. Festivals hold a range of meanings for people, and creating memorable experiences for attendees is an important consideration for festival administrators (Crespi-Vallbona & Richards 2007; Getz 2012). With the growth of the event industry (Getz & Page 2016), competition for festival funding and audience members continues to increase (Dean 2016). Festival organizations look for novel ways to provide unique experiences that appeal to diverse audiences. ICT offers the opportunity for innovative interaction and co-creation experiences, and can provide new or enhanced elements to a festival (Neuhofer at al. 2015; Tussyadiah & Fesenmaier 2008).

Neuhofer et al. (2014) presented the 'Experience Typology Matrix' to classify technology-enhanced experiences along two dimensions: intensity of co-creation and intensity of technology. Co-creation occurs when the customer is part of creating the experience and the consumer and company create value together (Prahalad & Ramaswamy 2004). This typology demonstrates how organizations can enhance experiences with technology by engaging consumers in co-creation and technology use. The typology results in a hierarchy of experiences that include (1) conventional experience, (2) technology-assisted experience, (3) technology-enhanced experience and (4) technology-empowered experience. This hierarchy suggests that the ultimate experience will have intense technology integration and intense co-creation elements that result in immersive, interactive and pervasive experiences. Even technology-assisted experiences may offer visitors new opportunities, including the ability to micro-coordinate during the festival experience (Wajcman 2008), allowing participants to make plans throughout their festival experience and connect with others regardless of time or location. While this typology provides needed insight into how attendees can be engaged through technology and co-creation, it does not acknowledge negative implications of technology integration on experience.

Festivals have often been described as liminoid spaces (Sharpe 2008; Turner 1974). The concept, first introduced by Turner (1974), presents the *liminal or liminoid* as a place to escape, away from everyday life. Within the liminoid space of festivals, people may find refuge from the routine and structure of daily life and discover a more flexible social place in which to lose oneself, if only temporarily (Picard & Robinson 2006). *Communitas* describes the unstructured community formed in festival settings and depicts the common experience shared by attendees (Turner 1974). The temporary state of togetherness formed by festivals is a unique feature of this leisure/tourism experience that has been discussed across festival genres (Laing & Mair 2015). Mobile connectivity may impact the *liminality* and *communitas* experienced at the festival. The anytime/anywhere connectivity offered by mobile technology (Green 2002) may facilitate attendees' connection to the festival and other attendees but may also make it difficult to loose oneself in the novel space of a festival. While at a festival, we are able to fill dead space/time with communication (Wajcman 2008). Unfortunately, this constant connection can reduce the spontaneity that makes a festival experience unique, and ICT may become a 'leash' that keeps us tethered to our everyday lives reducing opportunities for serendipity and discovery (Luxford & Dickinson 2015; Prasopoulou, Pouloudi, & Panteli 2006). Ballantyne, Ballantyne and Packer (2014) described four aspects of a music festival experience: music, festival, social and separation. ICT affects our experience across all of these realms, and while mobile engagement seems capable of enhancing our connection to performance, the festival and social groups, it simultaneously prevents us from separating from our everyday lives, thereby reducing our disconnection while at the festival.

ICT plays a role in the festival experience through all stages from pre-festival anticipation and planning through the return home and reflection (Berridge 2007; Clawson & Knetsch 1966; MacKay, Barbe, Van Winkle, & Halpenny 2017). While much attention is given to technology pre- and during the festival, there are opportunities for festivals to engage attendees using ICT post-festival that should not be overlooked. The unbounded time/space offered by ICT can be used to engage audiences on an ongoing basis and build lasting connections both between the festival and attendees and amongst attendees. MacKay et al. (2017) found that festival social networking sites were predominantly active during the festival with two-thirds of tweets posted during this timeframe. A third of tweets took place the week before a festival with little to no activity post-festival. This is a lost opportunity offered by ICT to enhance the value of the festival for consumers.

Festival administrators and attendees must not become complacent about how ICT is integrated into their festival experience. Administrators should carefully consider how new ICT ventures can be used to enhance experience and add value for the festival attendee. At the same time, festival attendees should avoid letting habits formed in daily life dictate how their mobile use affects their limited time at the festival.

## Trends

The integration of emerging technologies into the festival context allows festivals to offer novel experiences and add value for attendees, when integrated appropriately. In recent years, technologies like augmented reality (AR), virtual reality (VR), haptic and wearable technology, gamification and location-based ICT have been explored at some festivals and will likely emerge at festivals globally in the coming years as they become increasingly accessible (Robertson et al. 2015).

There are many possible AR and VR applications in leisure and tourism. VR technology allows users to access a 3D virtual environment that can be explored and interacted with, engaging one or more of the users' senses (Guttentag 2010). Products like Google Cardboard, which use consumers' MDs to display the environment, have made VR accessible to the masses. High-end products like Rift provide users with high-quality virtual experiences not previously accessible to consumers. At festivals, we have recently seen VR introduced as a way to experience the festival from far away locations giving people who can't attend the opportunity to be part of the experience and allowing attendees access to backstage areas. VR allows people to experience space and time anywhere, anytime. Providing access to spaces that are off-limits, offering additional content and enticing new attendees with a sense of the festival in advance of attendance are all possible with VR technology and have implications for festival marketing, experience design, education, accessibility, preparation and evaluation. AR offers similar possibilities as VR and involves superimposing computer-generated content onto reality. For example Cinemental, a Canadian Francophone film festival, used AR to enable the public to bring the festival's promotional posters to life and shared the history of the festival (Blair 2017). These types of opportunities are known to provide immersive experiences that enhance psychological presence (Gutierrez, Vexo, & Thalmann 2008).

Haptic technology engages the sense of touch and provides users with real-time tactile feedback (Hall 2014). Most smartphones already offer some haptic elements (e.g. vibration). Features such as these integrated into festival apps could easily enhance attendees' experiences. Digital maps that use haptics to guide visitors could be used by people with visual impairments or by all attendees in a dark festival space. The Apple Watch is likely the best-known haptic wearable technology, but haptic clothing has been developed, and one can imagine a future where wearing a haptic shirt that pulses with the music enhances a festival experience (Scott 2010).

Gamification involves adding game-like elements (points, levels, competition, rules) to non-game activities. By adding these elements, it is believed that people will become more engaged in the activity as a result of the clear goals and incentives provided in a rule-bound context (Rashid 2017). The Sydney Festival evolved their mobile app to add elements of gamification to enhance the app user experience (Sydney Festival 2012). The app involved real-time challenges that helped people to personalize and share their festival experience.

Location-based experiences are becoming somewhat common with smartphone technology. Many mobile users use push notifications offered by mobile apps. Products like iBeacon take location-based experiences further by integrating time and spatial recognition to deliver messages to mobile users within a certain distance of iBeacon. The Bonnaroo Festival provided proximity-based notifications to app users. With technologies like iBeacon, festival attendees can benefit from information about up-to-date program changes, crowded locations and emergency situations (Kahn 2014).

Many of these emerging technologies will provide opportunities to develop experience-enhancing ICT at festivals, moving beyond utilitarian applications. As festivals adopt and integrate new technology into the attendee experience, we all must consider the implications. Existing theories and research provide insight into the drawbacks and benefits that, if considered, can assist festivals and attendees making choices about new technology use that will enhance experiences and will not detract from the festival.

## Conclusion

To date, the research examining ICT integration into the festival experience has contributed to the development, evolution and refinement of theories about both the role of ICT in our lives and our experiences at festivals. Better integration of theories (e.g. TAM, UTAUT), frameworks (e.g. THC, Experience Typology Matrix) and concepts (e.g. habit, *liminality*, *communitas*) currently informing our understanding will enhance the contribution research makes to practice. Moving forward, transdisciplinary approaches in this field of study would enable the research to move beyond traditional disciplinary boundaries (management, marketing, geography, leisure, tourism, psychology, sociology) and provide complex insights relevant in a range of fields of study.

In the future, researchers and practitioners should continue to explore ICT users' and nonusers' behavior as well as the costs and benefits of ICT use at festivals. Much of the existing research examines particular groups, concepts and outcomes in isolation. By considering these varying perspectives simultaneously, more meaningful insights will be possible.

## References

Ballantyne, J., Ballantyne, R. & Packer, J. (2014). Designing and managing music festival experiences to enhance attendees' psychological and social benefits. *Musicae Scientiae*, 18(1), 65–83.
Berridge, G. (2007). *Events design and experience*. New York, NY: Routledge.
Blair, D. (2017). *Bitspace development*. Retrieved from http://bitspacedevelopment.com/cinemental-25-augmented-reality-festivals. Accessed 09/01/2018.
Buhalis, D. (2003). *eTourism: Information technology for strategic tourism management*. New York, NY: Financial Times Prentice Hall.
Clawson, M. & Knetsch, J. L. (1966). *Economics of outdoor recreation*. Baltimore, MD: Johns Hopkins Press and London, UK: Oxford University Press.

Crespi-Vallbona, M. & Richards, G. (2007). The meaning of cultural festivals: Stakeholder perspectives in Catalunya. *International Journal of Cultural Policy*, *13*(1), 103–122.
Crompton, J. L. & McKay, S. L. (1997). Motives of visitors attending festival events. *Annals of Tourism Research*, *24*(2), 425–439.
Davis, F. D. (1989). Perceived usefulness, perceived ease of use, and user acceptance of information technology. *MIS Quarterly*, *13*(3), 319–340.
Dean, S. (2016, July 2). Do the growing number of music festivals actually make any money? *The Daily Telegraph*. Retrieved from www.telegraph.co.uk/business/2016/07/02/do-the-growing-number-of-music-festivals-actually-make-any-money/. Accessed 09/01/2018.
Dickinson, J. E., Hibbert, J. F. & Filimonau, V. (2016). Mobile technology and the tourist experience: (Dis)connection at the campsite. *Tourism Management*, *57*, 193–201.
Getz, D. (2012). *Event studies: Theory, research and policy for planned events*. Abingdon, Oxon: Routledge.
Getz, D. & Page, S. J. (2016). Progress and prospects for event tourism research. *Tourism Management*, *52*, 593–631.
Green, N. (2002). On the move: Technology, mobility, and the mediation of social time and space. *The Information Society*, *18*(4), 281–292.
Gutierrez, M., Vexo, F. & Thalmann, D. (2008). *Stepping into virtual reality*. London, UK: Springer.
Guttentag, D. A. (2010). Virtual reality: Applications and implications for tourism. *Tourism Management*, *31*(5), 637–651.
Hall, B. (2014, October 3). Taptic, haptics, and the body fantastic: The real Apple Watch revolution. *Macworld*. Retrieved from www.macworld.com/article/2690729/taptic-haptics-and-the-body-fantastic-the-real-apple-watch-revolution.html. Accessed 09/01/2018.
Höpken, W., Gretzel, U. & Law, R. (2009). Information and communication technologies in tourism 2009. *Proceedings of the International Conference in Amsterdam, The Netherlands, 2009*. Vienna, Austria: Springer.
Kahn, J. (2014, July 14). Bonnaroo festival used iBeacons to collect valuable data about concertgoers. *9to5Mac*. Retrieved from https://9to5mac.com/2014/07/14/bonnaroo-festival-used-ibeacons-to-collect-valuable-data-about-concertgoers/. Accessed 09/01/2018.
Kempt, S. (2017, January 24). Digital in 2017: Global overview. *We Are Social*. Retrieved from https://wearesocial.com/special-reports/digital-in-2017-global-overview. Accessed 09/01/2018.
Kim, H. & Schliesser, J. (2007). Adaptation of storytelling to mobile information service for a site-specific cultural and historical tour. *Information Technology & Tourism*, *9*(3–1), 195–210.
Korn, K. C. & Pine, B. J. (2011). The typology of human capability: A new guide to rethinking the potential for digital experience offerings. *Strategy & Leadership*, *39*(4), 35–40.
Laing, J. & Mair, J. (2015). Music festivals and social inclusion – the festival organizers' perspective. *Leisure Sciences*, *37*(3), 252–268.
Law, R., Leung, R. & Buhalis, D. (2009). Information technology applications in hospitality and tourism: A review of publications from 2005 to 2007. *Journal of Travel & Tourism Marketing*, *26*(5–6), 599–623.
Lee, C. K., Lee, Y. K. & Wicks, B. E. (2004). Segmentation of festival motivation by nationality and satisfaction. *Tourism Management*, *25*(1), 61–70.
Leiner, B. M., Cerf, V. G., Clark, D. D., Kahn, R. E., Kleinrock, L., Lynch, D. C., Postel, J., Roberts, L. G. & Wolff, S. (2009). A brief history of the Internet. *ACM SIGCOMM Computer Communication Review*, *39*(5), 22–31.
Lonnquist, J. (2011, August 28). Birth of the web. *The Computer History Museum: California*. Retrieved from www.computerhistory.org/highlights/publicweb20th/. Accessed 09/01/2018.
Luxford, A. & Dickinson, J. E. (2015). The role of mobile applications in the consumer experience at music festivals. *Event Management*, *19*(1), 33–46.
MacKay, K. & Vogt, C. (2012). Information technology in everyday and vacation contexts. *Annals of Tourism Research*, *39*(3), 1380–1401.
MacKay, K., Barbe, D., Van Winkle, C. M. & Halpenny, E. (2017). Social media activity in a festival context: Temporal and content analysis. *International Journal of Contemporary Hospitality Management*, *29*(2), 669–689.
McIntyre, K. E. (2014). The evolution of social media from 1969 to 2013: A change in competition and a trend toward complementary, niche sites. *The Journal of Social Media in Society*, *3*(2), 5–25.
Neuhofer, B., Buhalis, D. & Ladkin, A. (2014). A typology of technology-enhanced tourism experiences. *International Journal of Tourism Research*, *16*(4), 340–350.
Neuhofer, B., Buhalis, D. & Ladkin, A. (2015). Technology as a catalyst of change: Enablers and barriers of the tourist experience and their consequences. In Tussyadiah, I. & Inversini, A. (Eds.). *Information and communication technologies in tourism*. Lugano, Switzerland: Springer International.

Pearce, P. L. & Gretzel, U. (2012). Tourism in technology dead zones: Documenting experiential dimensions. *International Journal of Tourism Sciences*, *12*(2), 1–20.
Peter, I. (2007). *Net History*. Retrieved from www.nethistory.info/index.html. Accessed 09/01/2018.
Pew Research Centre. (2017, January 12). *Mobile Fact Sheet*. Retrieved from www.pewinternet.org/fact-sheet/mobile/. Accessed 09/01/2018.
Picard, D. & Robinson, M. (2006). *Festivals, tourism and social change: Remaking worlds*. Frankfort Lodge, UK: Channel View Publications.
Poushter, J. (2016 February 22). Smartphone ownership and internet usage continues to climb in emerging economies. *Pew Research Center*. Retrieved from www.pewglobal.org/2016/02/22/smartphone-ownership-and-internet-usage-continues-to-climb-in-emerging-economies/. Accessed 09/01/2018.
Prahalad, C. K. & Ramaswamy, V. (2004). Co-creation experiences: The next practice in value creation. *Journal of Interactive Marketing*, *18*(3), 5–14.
Prasopoulou, E., Pouloudi, A. & Panteli, N. (2006). Enacting new temporal boundaries: The role of mobile phones. *European Journal of Information Systems*, *15*(3), 277–284.
Rashid, B. (2017 May 20). Hacking children's learning: Why gamification technology has the answers. *Forbes*. Retrieved from www.forbes.com/sites/brianrashid/2017/05/20/hacking-childrens-learning-why-gamification-technology-has-the-answer/#18660c982900. Accessed 09/01/2018.
Robertson, M., Yeoman, I., Smith, K. A. & McMahon-Beattie, U. (2015). Technology, society, and visioning the future of music festivals. *Event Management*, *19*(4), 567–587.
Rogers, E. M. (1995). *Diffusion of innovations*. New York, NY: The Free Press.
Scott, L. (2010, June 24). Glastonbury festival in the future. *Metro News*. Retrieved from http://metro.co.uk/2010/06/24/glastonbury-festival-in-the-future-415420/. Accessed 09/01/2018.
Selwyn, N. (2003). Apart from technology: Understanding people's non-use of information and communication technologies in everyday life. *Technology in Society*, *25*(1), 99–116.
Sharpe, E. K. (2008). Festivals and social change: Intersections of pleasure and politics at a community music festival. *Leisure Sciences*, *30*(3), 217–234.
Straub, E. T. (2009). Understanding technology adoption: Theory and future directions for informal learning. *Review of Educational Research*, *79*(2), 625–649.
SydneyFestival. (2012, January 17). It's play time at the Sydney Festival! Retrieved from www.gamification.co/2012/01/27/its-play-time-at-sydney-festival/. Accessed 09/01/2018.
Tapscott, D. (2008). *Grown up digital: How the net generation is changing your world HC*. New York, NY: McGraw-Hill.
Turner, V. (1974). Liminal to liminoid, in play, flow, and ritual: An essay in comparative symbology. *Rice Institute Pamphlet-Rice University Studies*, *60*(3), 53-92.
Tussyadiah, I. P. & Fesenmaier, D. R. (2008). Marketing places through firstperson stories: An analysis of Pennsylvania roadtripper blog. *Journal of Travel & Tourism Marketing*, *25*(3–4), 299–311.
Van Winkle, C. M. & Comer, A. (2011). Festivals and information technology: Stages of diffusion of innovation. *Proceedings of the 13th Canadian Congress on Leisure Research, Brock University, St Catherines, ON, Canada*.
Van Winkle, C. M., Cairns, A., Halpenny, E. & MacKay, K. J. (2014). Living on the edge: Attending a festival without my MD. *Travel and Tourism Research Association Canada Annual*, September 24–26, Yellowknife, NWT.
Van Winkle, C. M., Cairns, A., Halpenny, E. & MacKay, K. J. (2016). MD use and festivals: The role of habit. *e-Review of Tourism Research*, Enter2016: Bilbao, Spain.
Van Winkle, C. M., Cairns, A., MacKay, K. J. & Halpenny, E. (2016). MD use at festivals: Opportunities for value creation. *International Journal of Event and Festival Management*, *7*(3), 201–218.
Van Winkle, C. M., Bueddefeld, J., MacKay, K. J. & Halpenny, E. (2017). Factors affecting mobile device use at festivals. *Travel and Tourism Research Association: Advancing Tourism Research Globally*, 16.
Venkatesh, V. & Davis, F. D. (2000). A theoretical extension of the technology acceptance model: Four longitudinal field studies. *Management Science*, *46*(2), 186–204.
Venkatesh, V., Thong, J. Y. & Xu, X. (2012). Consumer acceptance and use of information technology: Extending the unified theory of acceptance and use of technology. *Management Information Systems Quarterly*, *36*(1), 157–178.
Wajcman, J. (2008). Life in the fast lane? Towards a sociology of technology and time. *The British Journal of Sociology*, *59*(1), 59–77.

# 27

# HOW DO RESIDENTS EXPERIENCE THEIR OWN FESTIVALS?

## A qualitative approach to meanings and experiences

*Nídia Brás, Júlio Mendes, Manuela Guerreiro and Bernardete Dias Sequeira*

### Introduction

Rural communities have recently been using events as tools for local development, especially if they are part of their community development policies (Richards & Palmer 2010; Ziakas & Costa 2010; Ziakas 2016). Economic benefits, feelings of belonging to the community, urban regeneration, quality of life, and cultural and social benefits are usually recognised as the main impacts of events (Fredline, Jago, & Deery 2003; Chalip 2006; Richards & Palmer 2010; Schulenkorf & Edwards 2012; Ziakas 2016). Ziakas (2016) suggests that more research into the impacts of cultural or festival events is needed (Ziakas 2016). Moreover, de Geus, Richards and Toepoel (2016, p. 276) argue that literature 'on event experiences is very scarce and fragmented'. There is little understanding of what kind of meanings and experiences residents attach to a festival that occurs in the place where they live. Therefore, this study aims to examine the meanings and experiences residents ascribe to a festival in a local community in a small inland region in Portugal – Mértola.

Mértola is a small town with 7,274 inhabitants (Instituto Nacional de Estatística [Statistics Portugal] 2011), located in the interior of Portugal. The abundant archaeological remains from the Muslim occupation in the 11th and 12th centuries have given rise to several little museums within the town, which are one of the main tourist attractions and a source of pride for the inhabitants. Known as 'Museum Town', Mértola has been the stage of the Mértola Islamic Festival since 2001. The event takes place every two years and 'seeks to evoke and preserve the heritage of the Muslim period in the south of the Iberian Peninsula' (Câmara Municipal de Mértola 2015, p. 8).

The methodology included semi-structured interviews with residents from different areas of the town and had three main objectives: (i) to understand the experiences of residents in the Islamic Festival, (ii) to understand the meanings that residents attach to the Islamic Festival and (iii) to characterise the most relevant memories of their participation in this festival. Findings of this study are likely to make significant contributions to theory and practice by furthering our understanding of how residents feel and experience the events that take place in their own cities. Also, the study highlights the often undervalued role of residents as meaning makers and as consumers of the event.

## Literature review

### *Festivals as special events in local communities*

Events have been considered as temporary and special happenings, and 'each one has a unique ambience created by the combination of its length, setting, management (i.e., its program, staffing, and design), and those in attendance' (Getz 1997, p. 4)'. The word *event* can include a wide range of typologies such as mega events like Olympics or World Fairs, hallmark events like European Capital of Culture or Rock in Rio as well as 'community festivals and local events' (de Geus et al. 2016, p. 275). When the event is specially attached to the community, and it is considered sustainable and beneficial to the place itself, it is usually recognised as a hallmark event or festival (Hall 1989; Getz 2008; Todd, Leask, & Ensor 2017). Its uniqueness and its special attachment to the community also characterise a festival as an 'event, a social phenomenon, encountered in virtually all human cultures' that 'begins with a valorisation (or sacralisation)' of the setting, a 'ritual which modifies the usual and daily function of time and space' (Falassi 1987, p. 1). Festivals are the 'products of a cultural frame conveying symbolic representations' (Ziakas 2016, p. 1148). In addition to the importance of their physical setting, they also generate affection and meaning, feelings and emotions among visitors and residents (Johnstone 2012; de Geus et al. 2016).

### *Festival performances, a source of personal experiences and meanings*

For Pine and Gilmore (1999, p. 12), from the marketing perspective, experiences are the 'set of activities in which individuals engage in personal terms'. Each event is experienced subjectively by those involved in physical, emotional, spiritual and intellectual ways (Tung & Ritchie 2011, p. 1371). An experience is a multidimensional concept of an affective, cognitive and behavioural nature (Pine & Gilmore 1999).

Each experience derives from the interaction between the staged event, the actors (like a theatrical play) and the individual's state of mind (Pine & Gilmore 1999). This is similar to Ziakas and Costa's (2012) approach when they used the event dramaturgy metaphor. In the field of events, little attention has been dedicated to the topic. De Geus et al. (2016) conceptualised and developed a scale to measure event and festival experiences. In their study, de Geus et al. (2016, p. 277) conceptualised an event experience as

> 'an interaction between an individual and the event environment (both physical and social), modified by the level of engagement or involvement, including multiple experiential elements and outputs (such as satisfaction, emotions, behaviours, cognition, memories and learning), that can happen at any point in the event journey'.

The theme of the event (in this study, a festival) represents a unified storyline, and it must drive all the design elements of the event to capture the customer emotionally (Pine & Gilmore 1999). Chalip (2006) argues that the theme, through metaphors and symbols, promotes and reinforces the meaning among those who attend the event as well as the sense of celebration and the festive atmosphere (Richards & Palme 2010) that will offer the stage for visitors to live their unforgettable experiences.

Residents' narratives and event meanings allow the development of festivals that really matter to the host population. The host community members are simultaneously performing the narrative and consumers of the experience (Pine & Gilmore 1999; Binkhorst & Den Dekker 2009). The city is prepared as a stage where residents and tourists can have memorable experiences. The preparation of the stage aims to 'engage individual customers in a way that creates a memorable event' (Pine II & Gilmore 1998, p. 98). Experiences are, thus, personal outcomes that result from the interaction between the individual, his own state of mind and the stage, like in a theatrical play. The local community, those who are performing the narrative in the stage, will be engaged in a co-creative process (Binkhorst & Den Dekker 2009; de Geus et al. 2016). In summary, events provide the attendees with a 'leisure and social opportunity beyond everyday experience' (Jago & Shaw 1998, p. 29), which can be classified as 'meaningful experiences' (Stokowski 1992, p. 12) that can influence attendees' mood, emotional state, feelings and fantasies (Hull 1990; de Geus et al. 2016).

The five human senses (sight, hearing, touch, smell and taste) 'are of crucial importance to the individuals' experience' as they can act as filters through which individuals acquire and interpret the information from the environment (Agapito, Mendes, & Valle 2013, p. 64). Therefore, experience is a perceptual phenomenon that affects the formation of meanings and belief sets (Tafesse 2016). In the case of festivals, meaning refers to 'all experiences, feelings and thoughts as well as the subsequent sense of salience that people obtain from their participation in, or attendance of, event-based activities' (Ziakas & Boukas 2013, p. 95). Festivals, as cultural performances, should be grounded in the local identity of places as they are, at the same time, a source of group and place identity itself (Green & Chalip 1998; De Bres & Davis 2001; Derrett 2003). In this sense, the meanings that residents attach to events and festivals give clear insights about local values that will be then appreciated by tourists and visitors. Thus, an understanding of festival meanings may shed light on the grounding cultural forces that determine festivals experiences.

Experiences and meanings attached to events and festivals are subjective constructions (Ziakas 2016), therefore, a case-study analysis is an appropriate method to use in order to better develop a framework that will provide policymakers and tourism and event managers with clear insights that will contribute to design the best festival settings and programme. Some research has been done to understand the event experience from the perspective of residents (Ziakas & Boukas 2013). However, it remains a subject that has not yet been fully studied.

## Methodology

### *Sampling and data collection procedures*

Since the literature is relatively scarce on the meanings residents attach to a festival performed in the place where they live, we decided to employ grounded theory (Glaser & Strauss 1967; Glaser 1978) as our main approach to data analysis. This method was chosen because the present study aims to explain and deepen the understanding of a complex social phenomenon (personal experiences and meanings residents attach to a festival).

The aim of this chapter is to improve knowledge about how policymakers can design events in order to improve attendees' experiences. In order to assess the perception of residents on the festival we conducted in-depth interviews (Miles & Huberman 1994) and semi-structured interviews (Bryman 2008). The interview script was developed based on the objectives arising from the research problem. Resident respondents were selected by purposive sampling (Bryman 2008), i.e. based on their sector of activity, experience and knowledge about the festival, in order to obtain a diversified sample. The determination of the sample size followed the criterion of data saturation (Ghiglione & Matalon 1997). After 13 interviews, the collected information content become repetitive and no new themes were emerging, so we considered that saturation point was reached and we stopped interviewing.

The interviews took place in the first week of June 2015 during the eighth Mértola Islamic Festival. Respondents were invited to participate in the study, and following their consent, the time and place of their interview was arranged. Each interview was assigned a numerical code (R1; R2; ... R13) to ensure the anonymity and confidentiality of the data.

## Data analysis

First, the data was organised and then analysed and interpreted using the coding system of grounded theory based on three coding levels: open coding, axial coding and selective coding (Strauss & Corbin 1990). *Open coding* aims to identify, name, categorise and describe phenomena presented in the text (Glaser 1992). *Axial coding* is the process in which relationships between categories and subcategories are clarified and established through a constant movement between the inductive (elaboration of concepts, categories and relations from the text) and deductive reasoning (test of concepts, categories and relations in contrast to the text) (Flick 2005, p. 184). In this stage, causal relationships between the concepts are emphasised in order to construct a matrix of analysis in which the generic relations are visible (Strauss & Corbin 1990). Finally, *Selective coding* corresponds to the process of identifying core categories around which other categories or concepts are integrated. It is thus possible to draw the data analysis storyline.

In this research, data collected through the interviews were registered, organised and then analysed through qualitative data analysis software (NVivo 9, QSR International).

## Results

### Sample characterisation

The age of the respondents ranged between 17 and 65, and the average age was 46 years. Nine respondents had a college education, nine are women and four are men. As for occupation, it should be mentioned that four respondents were directly linked to tourism and four to teaching. The municipality, the organising authority of the festival, is represented through the respondents' occupations, R2, R3, R4 and R7.

### Experiences and meanings: Mértola Islamic Festival

The analysis of the empirical data collected through interviews with residents of Mértola allowed us to identify four main central categories: (i) the experiences of the festival, (ii) the meaning of the experiences, (iii) the feelings and emotions aroused by the festival and (iv) the memories of the festival. From this, other subcategories were integrated, establishing relationships between categories and subcategories, through a constant movement between inductive and deductive reasoning (Table 27.2).

Table 27.1 Profile of respondents

|  | Gender | Affiliation | Education level | Age |
|---|---|---|---|---|
| R1 | M | Civil society: President of the Student Association | Secondary school | 17 |
| R2 | M | Sports: President of the Nautical Club | Higher education | 55 |
| R3 | F | Volunteering | Secondary school | 65 |
| R4 | F | Culture: Librarian | Higher education | 52 |
| R5 | F | Civil society: Blogger | Higher education | 52 |
| R6 | F | Education: School Director | Higher education | 47 |
| R7 | M | Municipality: President | Higher education | 43 |
| R8 | M | Education: Kindergarten teacher | Higher education | 54 |
| R9 | F | Tourism: Rural tourism owner | Higher education | 39 |
| R10 | F | Commerce: Local business entrepreneur | Secondary school | 31 |
| R11 | F | Tourism: Director of Merturis (municipal company) | Higher education | 41 |
| R12 | F | Commerce: Local business entrepreneur | Secondary school | 35 |
| R13 | F | Civil society: Retired | Primary school | 65 |

## Festival experiences

In terms of the experiences of the festival under study, the responses of the respondents led us to three subcategories: namely sensory experience, cultural experience and the stage design.

The Islamic Festival was perceived as a sensory experience insofar as the various activities in which visitors can engage were a constant stimulation of the senses. As one respondent noted,

> Sometimes we anticipate with an interactive exhibition ... in the Casa das Artes (House of Arts) ... It is an exhibition that appeals to the five senses. We set a table with tagine with mint, oranges, dates and raisins for people to savour ....
>
> (R8)

The respondents mentioned this type of stimuli several times. For example, the music filling the space continually stimulated hearing: 'A very different experience is the concerts which, despite the nature of the themes and music being from the Arab world and the unusual sounds, are very interesting experiences' (R2). Other respondents highlighted the earthy colours of the landscape sprinkled with white houses, the clothes of the vendors, some of whom come from Morocco, enchanted the eyes. The scents of the incense scattered in the air delighted the nose: 'I always mention two aspects that strike me most, the scents, and the colours! The sight, the smell, are the two senses that at this point I feel more agitated' (R5). Finally, the texture of the fluttering fabrics, carpets and artefacts sold by artisans was a source of unique tactile sensations.

The residents interviewed also considered the festival as a cultural experience wherein the past, the spaces and the experiences typical of the Arab culture are revived and where residents enjoyed an environment of multiculturalism and peaceful coexistence between different cultures. As mentioned by one respondent,

> [the Festival] focuses on a certain period of history that was important for Mértola and that over time has always maintained its historical and cultural influence in various aspects of life that we know today, whether in architecture, language or music, or gastronomy.
>
> (R11)

*Table 27.2* Categories emerging from data grouping

| Data | Open coding | Axial coding | Selective coding | |
|---|---|---|---|---|
| Interview transcripts | Sounds and music | Sensory experience | Festival experience | |
| | Gastronomy and flavours | | | |
| | Colours | | | |
| | Smells | | | |
| | Touch/sensations | | | |
| | Arab culture | Cultural experience | | |
| | Souk | | | |
| | Multiculturalism | | | |
| | Intercultural living | | | |
| | One notices how it was a few years ago | | | |
| | Discovery of the past | | | |
| | Stress | Stage design | | |
| | Tiredness | | | |
| | Needs more facilities | | | |
| | Duty accomplished | | | |
| | Desire to start over | | | |
| | Interaction among participants | Sociability | Festival meanings | Event experiences and meanings |
| | Communication | | | |
| | Call to prayer | Spirituality | | |
| | Pray time | | | |
| | Feeling of belonging | Sense of community | | |
| | Local roots | | | |
| | Sharing identities | | | |
| | Relationship with Muslim culture | Fear | Festival feelings and emotions | |
| | Positive spirit | Emotions | | |
| | Peaceful | | | |
| | Happiness | | | |
| | Joyful | | | |
| | Magic | | | |
| | Mystery | | | |
| | People | Memories | Festival memories | |
| | Sense of achievement | | | |
| | Sharing | | | |
| | Authenticity | | | |
| | Cultural mix | | | |
| | Experiences of the past | | | |
| | Very laborious | | | |
| | Last day | | | |

The souk was one of the most relevant spaces of this festival: 'What I like most is undoubtedly the visits to the souk, because I know real Arab souks in Morocco, (…). This experience here in Mértola is extremely well done and very like the real souks' (R2). Another respondent pointed out that the festival arouses the attendees' imagination: 'everything reminds me of the medinas of the Arab countries … it's like you're in a different country' (R8). Also, the harmony between different cultures was highlighted: 'The Festival celebrates a healthy coexistence between cultures (...). The Festival is also a way of demonstrating that coexistence between cultures is perfectly possible without this dark cloud of fundamentalism that in fact accompanies the word' (R11).

The organisation of the festival caused great pressure and fatigue on the residents involved in their organisation, an aspect highlighted by Respondent 7: 'There is enormous pressure on the whole organization to ensure that things go well, without accidents, thefts, problems with security forces or with visitors, or that there are enough parking spaces, etc., etc., therefore it's a general concern' (R7).

In making an overall assessment of the festival, some of the interviewees said that they wanted the festival to 'happen again': 'There is a desire to have the Festival again ...' (R2). They also referred to the need for more facilities so that future festivals can be improved, as well as a greater participation of civil society and the improvement of infrastructures, namely parking and access. Two respondents expressed such an understanding of how the festival should be 'redesigned, in a different register, more participation from civil society... I think the Festival will have to reinvent itself quickly ... it must be reconsidered and involve civil society' (R2). '... But there are details here that are not well organized ... we do not have parking lots, access, we are not prepared for so many people, and the village does not seem to have the size for that' (R10).

In the end, the assessment was positive because the sense of mission accomplished and desire to start over prevailed: 'Society is happier, people are waiting for the Islamic Festival, we already feel that desire, that the souk arrives and takes us back to other times. And there is always a wish that it happens again' (R5).

## Festival meanings

Through the content of the interviews it was possible to identify the three main meanings respondents assigned to the Islamic Festival: namely sociability, spirituality and sense of community.

Six of the respondents referred to the festival as a social experience that provided participants with opportunities to socialise and communicate with different people. It is a context of interaction and healthy coexistence between visitors and residents, where social relationships are established. One respondent was particularly clear when expressing this understanding: 'For me, it's the people, I really like to see a lot of people, completely different people, the participants, and all the conviviality there (...) this is a very interesting experience' (R11).

Some of the respondents gave the festival a spiritual significance to the extent that there are religious demonstrations related to Islam, albeit without fundamentalisms: 'hour of prayer, when they go through the streets singing and with instruments, they all follow in line, with songs so different, that seem like prayers' (R10). 'I hear the call to prayer, I hear different languages in the streets' (R8).

Seven of the respondents considered the Islamic Festival as a way of expressing the values, the identity, the history and the physical environment of Mértola related to its Arab roots; thus the festival was seen as a manifestation of identity, evoking a sense of community. According to a respondent, the festival 'is mainly culture, tradition, the common aspects with us, with our community and their identity that are similar to ours and our historic village and that is what we seek to explore' (R7). Another participant emphasised the historical aspect: 'The very historical area of the village, easily brings us back to the Arab times, to our very roots' (R3).

## Festival feelings and emotions

According to some of the respondents, the festive atmosphere of the festival provided a feeling of celebration where they felt very good, highlighting the experience of some emotions, such as a positive spirit, a sense of peace, happiness, joy, magic and mystery. A feeling of well-being was mentioned by one respondent: 'I feel good, of course always with the concern that everything goes well, but the people are very nice and above all we see happy people these days' (R4). Respondents found a good atmosphere among residents and visitors as well as among the Moroccan craft vendors: 'there are many high-spirited people, not only the visitors... the Moroccans themselves are friendly' (R10). The magic atmosphere, the surprise and the peaceful coexistence were also mentioned in the interviews: 'Concert nights that are magical, the ambience and the surroundings always surprise me positively... it is always a peaceful environment' (R3). The feelings aroused by the festival were highlighted by a respondent: 'I feel very Moroccan, very Islamic in all that charm' (R9).

Given that the festival is based on a concept associated with Islam, the staging of the event raised some fear in the local community. This feeling was highlighted by Respondent 6: 'But this year we were in some sort of fear - not that it was a confessed fear - but with some fear that one might think that our relationship with Muslims was not the right relationship to have' (R6).

## Memories of the festival

The statements of respondents showed that the strongest memories of the festival were mainly those related to people, the sharing, authenticity, cultural mix based on the acceptance of the difference and experiences from the past. Respondents also mentioned a sense of achievement, the memory of hard work and a nostalgic memory of the last day of the festival: 'When it ends, there are good memories of what we can enjoy, with our friends, the time we spend with them ... and there is the remembrance of the village with lots of people' (R1). One respondent stressed the authenticity: 'There are many festivals that are very "Tiriló", are very artificial, this one is very authentic' (R6). The local culture was also said to be as one of the elements that contributed to the success of the festival: 'the people from Alentejo always have the table set... only for a greater number of visits and that is what happens pretty much in every house of Mértola these days' (R3). Once again, the intercultural exchange of experiences is mentioned as one of the most relevant outcomes of this kind of festival: 'But what remains is also the children realizing that we respect and accept what is different. This aspect of our action in the festival is, in the first place, a sign of its interculturality' (R8).

## Conclusions

The Mértola Islamic Festival was the setting for a study that aimed to understand the meanings and experiences residents attach to a festival in a local community. Interviews were conducted with residents who, despite having diverse profiles and occupations, were involved in various ways, both in the organisation and in the experience of the Festival, as audience, exhibitors or part of the organisation.

From the residents' responses when interviewed in the town of Mértola, where the Islamic Festival takes place every two years, four main themes emerged: (i) the experiences lived throughout the preparation and during the festival, (ii) meanings associated with these experiences, (iii) the feelings and emotions aroused by the festival and (iv) the memories of the festival.

At the same time, other striking characteristics included a fondness for the past, facing the future very much aware of their roots and, in this encounter of cultures, the residents welcomed the traditions and senses of other peoples of North Africa with open arms. The festival is, above all, a paradigmatic case of openness to other cultures and the strengthening of a deep relationship between the Alentejo region and Morocco.

The experiences of this festival appear to be fundamentally lived on three levels: a sensory experience, a cultural experience motivated by permanent associations to the historical past of the village, and the preparation of the stage in which residents and visitors interact during the festival.

The meanings that the residents attach to the festival are guided by three main domains. First, the opportunities for social interaction between elements of the local community, exhibitors (many of whom are outside the community) and visitors. Second, the atmosphere of the event is guided by the moments associated with religion and spiritual life. Finally, from the perspective of the interviewed residents, the Mértola Islamic Festival seems to strengthen the sense of community by promoting a sense of belonging, valuing local roots and sharing the community's identity with visitors.

Insights from event experiences and meanings from the perspective of residents can help managers to design a festival that will contribute to the local development and, at the same time, will better meet their audience's desires and expectations. It will also contribute to develop an efficient communication strategy to the target market as well as to design and leverage meaningful event tourist experiences.

We acknowledge the need for further research before, during and after the festival, not only among residents and organisation entities but also, and especially, among the festival attendees. Knowing their opinions, satisfaction and loyalty are an essential reference for the sustainability of the Mértola Islamic Festival.

## Acknowledgements

This research was funded by national funds through the FCT – Foundation for Science and Technology under the project UID/SOC/04020/2013.

## References

Agapito, D., Mendes, J. & Valle, P. (2013). Exploring the conceptualization of the sensory dimension of tourist experiences. *Journal of Destination Marketing and Management*, 2(2), 62–73.

Binkhorst, E. & Den Dekker, T. (2009). Agenda for co-creation tourism experience research. *Journal of Hospitality Marketing and Management*, 18(2), 311–327.

Bryman, A. (2008). *Social research methods* (3rd ed.). New York: Oxford University Press.

Câmara Municipal de Mértola. (2015). *Festival Islâmico de Mértola – Plano Estratégico de Ação*. Available at www.cm-mertola.pt/municipio/projetos-co-financiados/festival-islamico-de-mertola-plano-estrategico-de-acao. Accessed on December 2015, p. 8.

Chalip, L. (2006). Towards social leverage of sport events. *Journal of Sport & Tourism*, 11(2), 109–127.

De Bres, K. & Davis, J. (2001). Celebrating group and place identity: a case study of a new regional festival. *Tourism Geographies – an International Journal of Tourism Space, Place and Environment*, 3(3), 326–337.

De Geus, S., Richards, G. & Toepoel, V. (2016). Conceptualisation and operationalisation of event and festival experiences: creation of an event experience scale. *Scandinavian Journal of Hospitality and Tourism*, 16(3), 274–296.

Derrett, R. (2003). Making sense of how festivals demonstrate a community's sense of place. *Event Management*, 8(1), 49–58.

Falassi, A. (1987). *Time out of time: essays on the festival*. Albuquerque: University of New Mexico Press.

Flick, U. (2005). *Métodos qualitativos na investigação científica*. Lisboa: Monitor – projectos e edições, Lda.

Fredline, E., Jago, L. & Deery, M. (2003). The development of a generic scale to measure the social impacts of events. *Event Management*, 8(1), 23–37.

Getz, D. (1997). *Event management and event tourism*. New York: Cognizant Communications Corporation.

Getz, D. (2008). Event tourism: definition, evolution, and research. *Tourism Management*, 29(3), 403–428.

Ghiglione, R. & Matalon, B. (1997). *O Inquérito: Teoria e Prática* (3a ed.). Oeiras: Celta Editora.

Glaser, B. G. (1978). *Theoretical sensitivity: advances in methodology of grounded theory*. San Francisco: University of California Press.

Glaser, B. G. (1992). *Basics of grounded theory analysis*. Mill Valley, CA: Sociology Press.

Glaser, B., & Strauss, A. (1967). *The discovery of grounded theory: strategies for qualitative research*. Chicago, IL: Aldine.

Green, B. C. & Chalip, L. (1998). Sport tourism as the celebration of subculture. *Annals of Tourism Research*, 25(2), 275–291.

Hall, C. M. (1989). The definition and analysis of hallmark tourist events. *GeoJournal*, 19(3), 263–268.

Hull, R. B. (1990). Mood as a product of leisure: causes and consequences. *Journal of Leisure Research*, 22(2), 99–111.

Instituto Nacional de Estatística [Statistics Portugal]. (2011). Available at www.ine.pt/xportal/xmain?xpgid=ine_main&xpid=INE. Accessed on November 2015.

Jago, L. & Shaw, R. (1998). Special events: a conceptual and differential framework. *Festival Management and Event Tourism*, 5(2), 21–31.

Johnstone, M. (2012). The servicescape: the social dimensions of place. *Journal of Marketing Management*, 28(11–12), 1399–1418.

Miles, M. B., & Huberman, A. M. (1994). *Qualitative data analysis: an expanded sourcebook* (2nd ed.). London: Sage Publications.

Pine II, B. J. & Gilmore, J. H. (1998). Welcome to the experience economy. *Harvard Business Review*, July–August, 97–105.

Pine, B. J. & Gilmore, J. H. (1999). *The experience economy: work is theatre & every business a stage*. Boston, MA: Harvard Business School Press.

Richards, G. & Palmer, R. (2010). *Eventful cities: cultural management and urban revitalization*. Amsterdam: Butterworth-Heinemann.

Schulenkorf, N. & Edwards, D. (2012). Maximizing positive social impacts: strategies for sustaining and leveraging the benefits of inter-community sport events in divided societies. *Journal of Sport Management*, 26(5), 379–390.

Stokowski, P. A. (1992). Social networks and tourist behaviour. *The American Behavioral Scientist*, 36(2), 212–221.

Strauss, A. & Corbin, J. (1990). *Basics of qualitative research*. Newbury Park, CA: Sage.

Tafesse, W. (2016). Conceptualization of brand experience in an event marketing context. *Journal of Promotion Management*, 22(1), 34–48.

Todd, L., Leask, A. & Ensor, J. (2017). Understanding primary stakeholders' multiple roles in hallmark event tourism management. *Tourism Management*, 59(April), 494–509.

Tung, V. W. S. & Ritchie, J. R. B. (2011). Exploring the essence of memorable tourism experiences. *Annals of Tourism Research*, 38(4), 1367–1386.

Ziakas, V. (2016). Fostering the social utility of events: an integrative framework for the strategic use of events in community development. *Current Issues in Tourism*, 19(11), 1136–1157.

Ziakas, V. & Boukas, N. (2013). Extracting meanings of event tourist experiences: a phenomenological exploration of Limassol Carnival. *Journal of Destination Marketing & Management*, 2(2), 94–107.

Ziakas, V. & Costa, C. A. (2010). Between theatre and sport in a rural event: evolving unity and community development from the inside-out. *Journal of Sport & Tourism*, 15(1), 7–26.

Ziakas, V. & Costa, C. A. (2012). 'The show must go on': event dramaturgy as consolidation of community. *Journal of Policy Research in Tourism, Leisure and Events*, 4(1), 28–47.

# 28
# FEMINIST POLITICS IN THE FESTIVAL SPACE

*Tasmin Coyle and Louise Platt*

## Introduction

Feminism in the context of festivals from a Western perspective has been examined across disciplines but rarely synthesised within the festival studies literature. Within the leisure studies literature, there has been a more substantive examination, and the distancing of 'event management' (within which festival studies often sits) as an area of study from leisure studies, we suggest, has led to a lack of engagement with this literature. For example, Aitchison's (1999, 2000) work is rarely drawn on in events (exceptions of work which cite these works include: Browne 2009; Finkel & Matheson 2015), and the work of Watson and Scraton (2011) on thinking intersectionally in leisure studies has only been cited in relation to sport rather than 'events management' explicitly. We contend that lack of engagement with these concepts is a missed opportunity in thinking critically about festivals in relation to intersectional feminism.

There is evidence of literature which examines gender performance within the festival space (for example Goulding & Saren 2009; Pielichaty 2015) and experiences of women at greenfield festivals (Browne 2009); however, this chapter addresses the role of feminist politics specifically in the production of festivals within the arts sector. This has been placed within the context of the 'wave narrative', the evolution of feminist politics and the influence that this has had on growing numbers of Do-It-Yourself (DIY) arts festivals in urban locations. It offers critical case studies from an organiser perspective of festivals that put feminist politics to the fore.

## The wave narrative: the evolution of feminist politics

Whilst problematic, the wave narrative is used to define specific time periods of feminist activism and social change took place. Whilst scholars are dependent on the wave narrative to articulate the evolution of feminist thought, they are consciously critical of its usage, citing that the waves are generationally divisive. This section will briefly offer an overview of the wave narrative in order to place subsequent discussions in context. It is beyond the scope of this chapter to offer a comprehensive social and political history of feminist movements, but it is important to understand their contemporary relevance in order to analyse feminist festivals.

In summary, 'first-wave' feminism refers to the period of the Woman Movement (Suffrage Movement) in the late 19th to the early 20th centuries and campaigns for votes for women. 'Second-wave' feminism (Women's Liberation Movement) is characterised as beginning in the 1960s influenced by the publication of the translation of Simone de Beauvoir's *The Second Sex* in 1953 and subsequent publication of *The Feminine Mystique* by Betty Friedman in 1963. This took place alongside events in the UK, such as the introduction of the contraceptive pill in 1961, the strike of the machinists at the Ford factory in Dagenham in 1968, and the passing of the Sex Discrimination Act in 1975. Agreement over what *equality* was within this period are debated within the movement, and this period has come under criticism for treating women as a homogeneous group; indeed, a group which was white and relatively privileged. Therefore, a key aspect that distinguishes 'third-wave' feminism is that of intersectionality (Evans 2015). Bell hook's seminal work *Ain't I am Woman* (1981) brought attention to the devaluation of black femininity within the movement. Further, queer theory defines this era with feminists working to break down gender binaries, such as Teresa de Lauretis (1991) who coined the term 'queer theory' and Judith Butler's *Gender Trouble* (first published in 1990). The 'third-wave' has been criticised for a focus on individual emancipation and micropolitics that is by no means resolved within 'fourth-wave' feminism; yet the attention to intersectionality maintains a strong focus (Brown, Ray, Summers, & Fraistat 2017; Zimmerman 2017).

Social media and online activism is often cited as the primary differential of the 'fourth-wave' (Chamberlain 2017), although there is contention over this, particularly in the UK context. In their work, Aune and Holyoak (2017) suggest that the third-wave in the UK started much later than in the US, and the cultural and political particularities of the context within which feminist politics is being enacted need to be examined. They further suggest that the affordances new technologies offer (i.e. online activism) do not alone signal a new wave.

In the UK, there has been a renewal of interest in feminism amongst young people in the early 2000s. This media-driven image is said to be undoing feminism. This neo-liberal, post-feminist sensibility is subsumed into popular culture, 'as an *identity* that any young woman might like to have – it is stylish, defiant, funny, beautiful, confident, and it "champions" women' (Gill 2016, p. 625). However, there is a danger that this critique of younger feminists renders their political activism invisible (Aune & Holyoak 2017).

Nonetheless, social media allows women to organise activism; for example, the swift organisation of 2011 'SlutWalk', a reaction to a police officer in Ontario, Canada, suggesting women should 'stop dressing like sluts' in order to avoid sexual harassment (for example Borah & Nandi 2012; Dow & Wood 2014; McCormack & Prostran 2012). Other campaigns include *No More Page 3*, calling for an end to use of topless models in British tabloid newspapers (Glozer, McCarthy, & Whelan 2015), and the Twitter account (and subsequent book) *Everyday Sexism*, which encourages women to call out sexism in everyday rhetoric (Bates 2016). More recently, debates around 'safe spaces', 'trigger warnings', and 'no-platforming' (Byron 2017; Dunt 2015; Lewis, Sharp, Remnant, & Redpath 2015) have all played out on social media as well as issues of trans identities (Jackson, Bailey, & Foucault Welles 2017; Johnson 2013).

What has also developed from this engagement in the online sphere is a 'call-out culture' (Cochrane 2013), and the phrase 'privilege checking' has emerged. This encourages women to reflect on where their viewpoint stems from and to remember that all forms of feminisms are valid (see Freeman 2013 for a summary of the emergence of the term). Further, the online environment can be viewed as facilitating intersectionality, as it allows women from different communities, ethnicities, and backgrounds to engage in conversation with each other (Chamberlain 2017; Cochrane 2013; Dobson 2016). Yet the anonymous nature and relative freedom of the internet now opens women to backlash, often in the form of threats of physical violence and sexual abuse (Baer 2016; Eckert 2017; Jane 2014).

Therefore, in summary, the wave narrative is helpful in understanding the evolution of contemporary feminist politics. Whilst contentious and often culturally specific, there is, however, a call to reframe the narrative to be more nuanced in order to avoid a privileging of one particular cultural perspective.

## Festivalising feminism

It is generally accepted that one of the roles of festivals is to provide an opportunity for catharsis (Bennett, Taylor, & Woodward 2016). Using festivity to champion a particular political viewpoint or as an act of collective activism is nothing new. Most notable examples are Pride parades, which are not only a celebration of Lesbian, Gay, Bisexual, Transgender and Queer (LGBTQ) identities but also emerged in the 1970s in the US as a 'liberation march' in commemoration of the Stonewall Riots (Browne 2007; Johnston 2007; Johnston & Waitt 2015). Further to this, there is a strong historical link between music festivals and political activism from the 1960s onwards (Martin 2016; McKay 2004, 2015; Partridge 2006). In July 2017, the leader of the UK Labour Party, Jeremy Corbyn, spoke at Glastonbury Festival. These are examples of 'civil leisure' (Mair 2002), and using festivity to engender social change is emerging as a field of interest for event scholars (de Jong 2017; Lamond & Spracklen 2014; Sharpe 2008).

Whilst festivals have always had elements of pleasure, the emphasis on political activism perhaps has diminished, and festivals are increasingly becoming commercialised and sanitised for the purpose of enhancing the visitor experience (Anderton 2008) or utilised in destination marketing (Quinn 2010). It can be argued that we are seeing a festivalisation of feminism, which could potentially be critiqued as an example of the post-feminist sensibility where activism has been subsumed into the entertainment industry. However, it is important to view feminist festivals with critical lens, one that can leave space for a critique of neoliberal post-feminism without making collective feminist activism invisible or reduced to a mere fashion trend.

### Festivals as spaces for women

Festivals have the potential to provide spaces for women to gather as a collective. Feminist geographers have reminded us that when we think about spaces, they cannot be thought of as neutral (Massey 2013; Rose 1993). Leisure spaces have been examined in relation to gender and sexuality (Aitchison 1999; Scraton & Watson 1998) with fear and apprehension of risk as a common mechanism of women's self-exclusion from public spaces.

In relation to specific festivals related to feminism and women, there is an uneasy relationship with public spaces; however, solutions are often problematic. An example widely examined in academic literature is *Michigan Womyn's Festival* (or *Michfest*) which grew out of the lesbian feminist movement in the 1970s US. The festival had a strict 'womyn born womyn's space' policy, which was challenged by those who claimed the policy was discriminatory. Whilst the inclusion/exclusion of transgender women in this festival was complex (see Gamson 1997; McConnell, Todd, Odahl-Ruan, & Shattell 2016 for an in-depth discussion), it was identified by Browne (2011) that even long-standing, dedicated festivalgoers also criticised cisgender attendees as 'weekend converts,' casting doubts on their lesbian feminist politics. As previously discussed with the wave narrative, generational divisions emerge.

The boundaries of 'woman', 'feminist', and 'lesbian' are negotiated in this space, and intersectional diversity comes under the microscope. As McConnell et al. (2016) argue, there is a danger that a dominant intersectional identity (in the case of *Michfest* – cisgender, white, lesbian, feminist) can lead to further separatist spaces and reflect oppressive systems the festival is seeking to counteract. Also, whilst the temporal festival space can be problematic in issues of inclusion/exclusion, it is also possible, as indicated earlier, that this temporal space could also mean only temporal engagement. The eventual demise of *Michfest* also exemplifies the evolution of feminist politics and its role within the rise and fall of festival trends.

Festival spaces can be spaces of risk for women; for example, there is an increasing number of sexual assaults at British greenfield festivals. Following the rape of a festivalgoer at Latitude festival in 2010, Melvyn Benn, the chief executive of Festival Republic (Topping 2010), released a statement:

> [...] When you go to a festival with your friends and you drop your guard, but you are living in what is essentially a small town, and in a town you wouldn't leave your door open without expecting some crime.

This is the familiar territory of 'victim blaming' – a key issue that has been raised on social media by contemporary feminists and echoes the 'SlutWalk' movement discussed earlier.

Festivals have experimented with so-called 'safe spaces', a notion that is tied up with contemporary feminism despite origins in 1970s US. The production of *The Sisterhood*, Glastonbury's women-only space in the area of *Shangri-La*, is described on Twitter as 'Glastonbury's first ever women only venue! Intersectional, Queer, Trans & Disability inclusive'. Whilst more inclusive than *Michfest*, it saw a backlash from women in the UK conservative press who believed it to be a patronising gesture (Whelan 2016). Indeed, just because a space is designated as a women-only space does not guarantee safety (Lewis et al. 2015). Yet, as an article in Vice Magazine's online music site *Noisey* pointed out,

> It's not as if all the women at Glastonbury are getting together to hurl all the men on a bonfire in the stone circle at dawn in a mass sacrifice, with Emily Eavis at the front chanting 'Safe space! Safe space! Safe Space!' It is just a tent for women to hang out, dance and get drunk in. It's that simple – and that's why it works.
>
> (Jones 2016)

The 'outcry' in relation to this space is an example of the prominence of highly mediated debates related to the role of online interactions in feminist politics today.

The festival space also can provide a platform for women as artists. Although women make up most of the creative workforce, they are under-represented at the top levels and on boards. This has led to women creating their own DIY spaces. For example, the Riot Grrrl movement encouraged female punk bands, self-publishing zines, and knowledge sharing amongst women. This ethos was born out of necessity and a reaction to industries that ignored women and will be evidenced in the following discussions of the festival case studies.

## Critical case studies

The chapter will now proceed to present illustrative critical case studies of UK festivals which place feminist politics to the fore. These festivals are arts-led festivals that take place in the urban environment (as opposed to greenfield festivals). The festivals (and the participants) have been anonymised for confidentiality. All four case studies festivals are small scale and voluntarily run by creative women emerging from a DIY ethos. The following discussion draws on semi-structured interviews with four festival organisers and illustrates the role that feminist festivals are playing in activism, and the challenges that they face as part of negotiating the evolution of feminist politics.

## Festivals as platforms for feminist politics

Participants all suggested that their festivals were a platform for feminist politics, but they expressed concern over the usage of the wave narrative. One interviewee stated, 'I think the Wave metaphor isn't really helpful because it kind of presupposes there's this distinction across the generations and actually that's not really true'. Further, it was agreed that the wave metaphor is problematic in moving feminism forward due to the lack of communication across generations of feminism: 'there is an issue here around, around inter-generational communication between different levels, or different generations of feminists' (Festival A). This reinforces the arguments made earlier that a more nuanced approached to the wave narrative needs to be taken.

When asked if the different forms within feminist ideology have ever posed a challenge in the organisation of the festivals, one participant responded,

> In the early stages, we found there was two different ideas of what feminism is about and what [festival] could do. So one natural division kind of happened between one kind of perspective of feminism which was a little bit more exclusionary than we were wanting to go with.
>
> (Festival B)

Another participant shared that their organisation remains open to displaying different ideas about feminism without 'eating itself up' (Festival A) and stated that the divisions within feminism are hindering the feminist movement. These participants clearly expressed a more inclusive and intersectional view of feminist politics within their organisation, which is typical of the third- and fourth-wave movements. Whilst the four festivals had different ideologies across their organisations and found the wave narrative problematic, it was found that having a clear vision of what feminism meant to *them* was integral to the success of the festival.

Further, all participants viewed their festivals as a potential catalyst for their audiences to become more engaged in feminist politics:

> Our thinking is that you don't go from your sofa to the picket line in one fell swoop, you have to have those interactions along the way and that's what we're trying to do, is be something which doesn't feel really overwhelming and academic or like elitist or exclusive.
>
> (Festival A)

Helping women become more confident in engaging in both feminist politics and politics in general is something all participants agreed on. These festivals could potentially provide women with an accessible introduction to politics. There is the danger, however, like *Michfest*, that 'versions' of feminist politics can become outmoded and fall out of favour, challenging the sustainability of such festivals.

There was an acknowledgement of the increased popularity of feminism, and it was felt that a post-feminist sensibility was an opening to develop meaningful discussions about activism in the festival space:

> Suddenly every pop star was like, I'm a feminist. And it did maybe feel a little motivated by something that wasn't quite feminist, but at the same time like that is exposing loads of young girls who've never heard that word to the word feminist, that'll hopefully go and Google it and find out like what it actually is.
>
> *(Festival A)*

However, there was a more critical view which could present a challenge in maintaining political relevance of the festivals, especially in light of individualistic narratives of feminism:

> I sometimes go to things and I talk to younger generations of feminists, you know it seems to be they're only engaged with a very tiny aspect of what affects them personally. There's a lack of global awareness, there's a lack of international perspective.
>
> *(Festival C)*

There was evidently a challenge in engaging new audiences. Social media provided a platform, but it had to then translate into physical spaces:

> I think we've managed to build this community which very much does exist online but also translates to the real world and kind of like the vibe that we're giving off online… I think that's something that we're really conscious of … we don't just want to be another social platform sharing inspirational memes.
>
> *(Festival A)*

Taking the example of the SlutWalk mentioned previously, this campaign may have mobilised online; however, it was only able to deliver an impact once it manifested in a physical space. Therefore, festivals offer the opportunity to blur the online/offline activism spaces and further challenge the distinction of 'fourth-wave' being defined by online activism or indeed the existence of this wave at all.

## *Feminist festivals as space of empowerment*

When asked if feminist festivals could provide a solution for women to safely engage in the festival scene, participants were keen to stress that what they can offer is an 'add on', not a solution due to the temporality of the festival format.

> Feminist festivals are not a substitute for, they're an addition to. And it's really important to make sure that is your aim, it's like this is just one aspect where you can talk about issues where you can kind of maybe come up with a plan.
>
> *(Festival B)*

It is also possible that feminist festivals can offer women support in their creative practice. One festival organiser commented that

> Learning how to design your own flyers and to do decent social media marketing and to write a good press release and empower yourself to be able to know how to run your

own tech, all those skills are really important to then be able to produce and run your own shows and therefore be a more successful artist. And they're the kind of things that we try and offer within the Festival, but we are limited at capacity.

*(Festival D)*

This supportive and DIY ethos was something that all participants interviewed commented on and stated was deeply ingrained in their festivals ethos. This DIY style is reminiscent of the third-wave feminist movements, empowering each other to take control in a male-dominated industry. Since there is still a serious inequality issue in the creative industries, this DIY ethos is still driving feminist creative as a collective.

I think feminist festivals have had to fight really hard because those positions, [...] we've had to prove that we can do it and then also we end up doing it 20 times better because we're working harder.

*(Festival B)*

Yet, whilst these festivals offer a supportive environment, nonetheless, they were mindful of their capacity to pay.

There's always a debate, an issue around payments of performers and payment of participants, and that is a feminist issue as far as I'm concerned because there's so much expected as goodwill from participants, particularly women and women are always underpaid, or not paid.

*(Festival C)*

Whilst these festivals can form a supportive community for women artists, due to their lack of funding, there is an issue with the fair payment of artists. Again, this tension emerges around a DIY ethos, but it creates limitations around being financially sustainable.

## *Festivalisation of feminism*

Wider institutions potentially take advantage of feminist festivals for their own marketing gains, and there is perhaps a festivalisation of feminist politics to serve a particular agenda. At least two of the festivals noted that established institutions were starting to approach them with collaboration opportunities. However, they were both cautious when choosing who to work with in order to maintain their DIY ethos.

I think we're going to have to be quite careful about how we negotiate that... but often what venues want to do is basically tap into your audience and be like, oh you've got loads of like women under 30.

*(Festival A)*

Some expressed frustration related to *International Women's Day*: 'everybody is like Rent a Feminist for the month because it's International Women's Day in March' (Festival A). The trend for feminist politics, as examined earlier, can make activism less visible, and it is important that these festivals maintain a balance between establishing a profile for what they do, which might mean collaborating on national events or with wider institutions, but ensure that the politics remain meaningful.

In order to achieve this, there was an awareness that organisers had to engage with audiences outside of themselves and existing feminist activists. If the festivals are unable to engage with wider audiences, it becomes difficult to establish to what extent they are achieving bringing communities together and translating the temporal space of the festivals into activism and social change. 'It was showcasing some sort of feminist work that's taking place but it didn't really connect with audiences outside of itself' (Festival C).

## Conclusions

The four festivals examined in this chapter are helping women become more confident in engaging in both feminist politics and general politics by providing them with an accessible introduction to politics. There is also a deliberate effort to engage with popular culture but not to allow the collective aspect of feminist activism to be diminished. Indeed, the power that the online sphere offered was recognised, but the interaction of festivalgoers in physical spaces is still salient. This is all the more true in relation to festivals that intend to inspire social change and collective action. However, there needs to be further consideration around how to make the physical spaces of such festivals as accessible as online spaces in terms of collective activism (whilst acknowledging debates around online access).

Aligned with the contentious nature of the wave narrative, feminists who are organising these festivals are conscious of what feminism means to different audiences and how they can present bring younger women into activism. A continued engagement with the wave narrative as affective rather than hierarchical is essential in order to create inclusive spaces that are relevant and sustainable, and able to respond to the changing and evolving nature of politics today without forgetting the activism of those that came before or diminishing the lived experiences of diverse groups of women.

There is rich potential for further study in this area, not least as the work presented here is solely offered from an organiser perspective. Further research could focus on how feminist festivals are spaces where multiple identities are negotiated. This would build on previous leisure studies work on intersectionality and further related critical festival studies under a critical feminist lens.

## References

Aitchison, C. (1999). New cultural geographies: the spatiality of leisure, gender and sexuality. *Leisure Studies*, 18(1), 19–39.
Aitchison, C. (2000). Poststructural feminist theories of representing others: a response to the 'crisis' in leisure studies' discourse. *Leisure Studies*, 19(3), 127–144.
Anderton, C. (2008). Commercializing the carnivalesque: the V Festival and image/risk management. *Event Management*, 12(1), 39–51.
Aune, K. & Holyoak, R. (2017). Navigating the third wave: contemporary UK feminist activists and 'third-wave feminism'. *Feminist Theory*. doi:10.1177/1464700117723593.
Baer, H. (2016). Redoing feminism: digital activism, body politics, and neoliberalism. *Feminist Media Studies*, 16(1), 17–34.
Bates, L. (2016). *Everyday Sexism: The Project that Inspired a Worldwide Movement*. London: Simon & Schuster.
Bennett, A., Taylor, J. & Woodward, I. (eds.). (2016). *The Festivalization of Culture*. Oxon & New York: Routledge.
Borah, R. & Nandi, S. (2012). Reclaiming the feminist politics of 'SlutWalk'. *International Feminist Journal of Politics*, 14(3), 415–421.
Brown, M., Ray, R., Summers, E. & Fraistat, N. (2017). # SayHerName: a case study of intersectional social media activism. *Ethnic and Racial Studies*, 40(11), 1–15.

Browne, K. (2007). A party with politics? (Re)making LGBTQ Pride spaces in Dublin and Brighton. *Social & Cultural Geography*, 8(1), 63–87.

Browne, K. (2009). Naked and dirty: rethinking (not) attending festivals. *Journal of Tourism and Cultural Change*, 7(2), 115–132.

Browne, K. (2011). Beyond rural idylls: imperfect lesbian utopias at Michigan Womyn's music festival. *Journal of Rural Studies*, 27(1), 13–23.

Butler, J. (1990). *Gender Trouble*. New York: Routledge.

Byron, K. (2017). From infantilizing to world making: safe spaces and trigger warnings on campus. *Family Relations*, 66(1), 116–125.

Chamberlain, P. (2017). *The Feminist Fourth Wave: Affective Temporality*. New York: Springer.

Cochrane, K. (2013). *All the Rebel Women: The Rise of the Fourth Wave of Feminism*. London: Guardian Books.

de Jong, A. (2017). Rethinking activism: tourism, mobilities and emotion. *Social & Cultural Geography*, 18(6), 851–868.

De Lauretis, T. (1991). *Queer Theory: Lesbian and Gay Sexualities*. Bloomington: Indiana University Press.

Dobson, A. S. (2016). *Postfeminist Digital Cultures: Femininity, Social Media, and Self-Representation*. New York: Springer.

Dow, B. J. & Wood, J. T. (2014). Repeating history and learning from it: what can SlutWalks teach us about feminism? *Women's Studies in Communication*, 37(1), 22–43.

Dunt, I. (2015). Safe space or free speech? The crisis around debate at UK universities. *The Guardian*, 6 February. Available from: www.theguardian.com/education/2015/feb/06/safe-space-or-free-speech-crisis-debate-uk-universities. Accessed 18 August 2017.

Eckert, S. (2017). Fighting for recognition: online abuse of women bloggers in Germany, Switzerland, the United Kingdom, and the United States. *New Media & Society*. doi:10.1177/1461444816688457.

Evans, E. (2015). *The Politics of Third Wave Feminisms: Neoliberalism, Intersectionality, and the State in Britain and the US*. New York: Springer.

Finkel, R. & Matheson, C. M. (2015). Landscape of commercial sex before the 2010 Vancouver Winter Games. *Journal of Policy Research in Tourism, Leisure and Events*, 7(3), 251–265.

Freeman, H. (2013). Check your privilege! Whatever that means. *The Guardian*, 5 June. Available from: www.theguardian.com/society/2013/jun/05/check-your-privilege-means. Accessed 17 August 2017.

Gamson, J. (1997). Messages of exclusion: gender, movements, and symbolic boundaries. *Gender & Society*, 11(2), 178-199.

Gill, R. (2016). Post-postfeminism? New feminist visibilities in postfeminist times. *Feminist Media Studies*, 16(4), 610–630.

Glozer, S., McCarthy, L. & Whelan, G. (2015). # NoMorePage3: feminism and institutional work in corporate constructed arenas of citizenship. *Academy of Management Proceedings*, 2015(1), 16085.

Goulding, C. & Saren, M. (2009). Performing identity: an analysis of gender expressions at the Whitby goth festival. *Consumption Markets & Culture*, 12(1), 27–46.

hooks, b. (1981). *Ain't I a Woman Black Women and Feminism*. Boston, MA: South End Press.

Jackson, S. J., Bailey, M. & Foucault Welles, B. (2017). #GirlsLikeUs: trans advocacy and community building online. *New Media & Society*. doi:10.1177/1461444817709276.

Jane, E. A. (2014). 'Back to the kitchen, cunt': speaking the unspeakable about online misogyny. *Continuum*, 28(4), 558–570.

Johnson, J. R. (2013). Cisgender privilege, intersectionality, and the criminalization of CeCe McDonald: why intercultural communication needs transgender studies. *Journal of International and Intercultural Communication*, 6(2), 135–144.

Johnston, L. (2007). Mobilizing pride/shame: lesbians, tourism and parades. *Social & Cultural Geography*, 8(1), 29–45.

Johnston, L. & Waitt, G. (2015). The spatial politics of gay pride parades and festivals: emotional activism. In: Patternotte, D. & Tremblay, M. (eds.), *The Ashgate Research Companion to Lesbian and Gay Activism* (pp. 105–120). Surrey and Burlington: Ashgate.

Jones, D. (2016). Do we need a women's only venue at Glastonbury? *Noisey*. Available from: https://noisey.vice.com/en_uk/article/6e4e3k/do-we-need-a-womens-only-venue-at-glastonbury. Accessed 18 January 2017.

Lamond, I. R. & Spracklen, K. (2014). *Protests as Events: Politics, Activism and Leisure*. London: Pickering & Chatto Publishers.

Lewis, R., Sharp, E., Remnant, J. & Redpath, R. (2015). 'Safe spaces': experiences of feminist women-only space. *Sociological Research Online*, 20(4), 9–17.

Mair, H. (2002). Civil leisure? Exploring the relationship between leisure, activism and social change. *Leisure/Loisir*, 27(3–4), 213–237.

Martin, G. (2016). The politics, pleasure and performance of new age travellers, ravers and anti-road protestors: connecting festivals, carnival and new social movements. In: Bennett, A., Taylor, J., and Woodward, I. (eds.), *The Festivalization of Culture* (pp. 87–106). Oxon and New York: Routledge.

Massey, D. (2013). *Space, Place and Gender*. Oxford: John Wiley & Sons.

McConnell, E. A., Todd, N. R., Odahl-Ruan, C. & Shattell, M. (2016). Complicating counterspaces: intersectionality and the Michigan Womyn's Music Festival. *American Journal of Community Psychology*, 57(3–4), 473–488.

McCormack, C. & Prostran, N. (2012). Asking for it. *International Feminist Journal of Politics*, 14(3), 410–414.

McKay, G. (2004). 'Unsafe things like youth and jazz': Beaulieu jazz festivals (1956–61), and the origins of pop festival culture in Britain. In Bennett, A. (ed.), *Remembering Woodstock* (pp. 90–110). Aldershot: Ashgate Publishing.

McKay, G. (2015). *The Pop Festival: History, Music, Media, Culture*. New York: Bloomsbury Publishing USA.

Partridge, C. (2006). The spiritual and the revolutionary: alternative spirituality, British free festivals, and the emergence of rave culture. *Culture and Religion*, 7(1), 41–60.

Pielichaty, H. (2015). Festival space: gender, liminality and the carnivalesque. *International Journal of Event and Festival Management*, 6(3), 235–250.

Quinn, B. (2010). Arts festivals, urban tourism and cultural policy. *Journal of Policy Research in Tourism, Leisure and Events*, 2(3), 264–279.

Rose, G. (1993). *Feminism and geography: the limits of geographical knowledge*. Minneapolis: University of Minnesota Press.

Scraton, S. & Watson, B. (1998). Gendered cities: women and public leisure space in the 'postmodern city'. *Leisure Studies*, 17(2), 123–137.

Sharpe, E. K. (2008). Festivals and social change: intersections of pleasure and politics at a community music festival. *Leisure Sciences*, 30(3), 217–234.

Topping, A. (2010). Rapes at Latitude prompt launch of safety awareness campaigns. *The Guardian*. Available from: www.theguardian.com/culture/2010/jul/19/latitude-festival-safety-campaign. Accessed 24 June 2017.

Watson, B. & Scraton, S. J. (2013). Leisure studies and intersectionality. *Leisure Studies*, 32(1), 35–47.

Whelan, E. (2016). Glastonbury's 'women-only' venue deserves to sink into the mud. *The Spectator*, 6 June. Available from: https://blogs.spectator.co.uk/2016/06/glastonburys-women-venue-deserves-sink-mud/. Accessed 18 August 2017.

Zimmerman, T. (2017). #Intersectionality: the fourth wave feminist Twitter community. *Atlantis: Critical Studies in Gender, Culture & Social Justice*, 38(1), 54–70.

# PART VII

# Types of festivals

# 29
# FOOD AND WINE FESTIVALS AS RURAL HALLMARK EVENTS

*Jennifer Laing, Warwick Frost and Melissa Kennedy*

### Introduction

The small town of Bluff is located at the southern tip of New Zealand's South Island. Like many rural towns, Bluff decided to theme their annual festival around a distinctive local product. In 1996, they started staging the Bluff Oyster Festival, a hallmark event that involved the local community, attracted tourists and reinforced a strong sense of place. In 2007, the festival organisers Venture Southland – a joint initiative of three local councils – planned to increase its patronage by moving it nearly 30 kilometres north to the regional city of Invercargill. The local people of Bluff were outraged by this attempt to take over what they saw as *their* festival. A public meeting voted to take the festival away from Venture Southland and its council backers and to organise the 2008 festival at Bluff (NZPA 2007). John Edminstin, the new chairman of the organising committee, proclaimed that they would 'set about taking the festival 'back to basics' and putting the focus on people'. As a result, they found that when 'the committee scrapped the 'corporate feel' introduced by Venture [they] immediately saw an increase of more than 1,000 people through the gates' (quoted in Foden 2015).

While the expanding literature on hallmark events is primarily focussed on large cities, many rural towns are increasingly looking to develop and foster festivals that can be categorised in this fashion. They are so intertwined with the destination and what is located there that they reinforce its spirit or sense of place (Getz 2008; Kennedy 2018; Robertson & Wardrop 2004). Often the name of the festival includes the name of the town, which again reinforces local links. An exemplar is the Gilroy Garlic Festival which has run annually in the Californian town of that name since 1979.

In a crowded tourism marketplace, this strong emphasis on distinctive local features may form the basis of a strategic competitive advantage, depending on how difficult it is for competitors to replicate these themes. Staging these events can help to regenerate and reinvigorate rural communities that have struggled to deal with a decline in traditional industries and changes in demographics. Rural hallmark events – as distinct from those in major cities – are therefore worthy of attention, both from a theoretical and from a practical perspective.

## Rural food and wine festivals

Many rural hallmark events take the form of food and wine festivals, where the bounty of what is available and grown locally is a source of community pride and identity and can be argued in some cases to be distinctive to a region (Richards 2015). The Bluff Oyster Festival is an instructive example, focussing on an attractive local food product, and restaurants in New Zealand often proudly refer to the Bluff Oyster on their menus. In the case of wine festivals, there are links to notions of *terroir*, based on local climate and soil, manifesting itself in certain locations being known for distinctive grape varieties and styles. Such a concept can also be extended to other forms of rural production, as certain foods are often endemic to particular places, sometimes because of geographical or climatic conditions, but also because of the existence of a creative food economy that supports and promotes the local harvest (Richards 2015). In some cases, the choice of a food or wine theme is quite strategic, with the aim of filling a gap in the market in order to attract visitors (Lee & Arcodia 2011; Lewis 1997).

Whilst much of the focus on rural hallmark events has been on their role in gaining economic benefits through increased tourism, there are other dimensions that require study, particularly in the context of food and wine festivals. Producers often participate in these festivals to earn revenue, seeing them as a medium for direct sales and building their product image and market base (Beverland, Hoffman, & Rasmussen 2001; Frost & Laing 2018). In rural areas, involvement in food and wine festivals is critical for the development of small-scale entrepreneurs, particularly those involved in organic and alternative production (Bosworth & Farrell 2011; Dana, Gurau, & Lasch 2014; Herslund 2012; Moscardo 2014; Mottiar 2016; Nel & Stevenson 2014). Often these entrepreneurs are amenity migrants, attracted to areas through earlier tourist visits or the search for a change in lifestyle (Akgün, Baycan-Levent, Nijkamp, & Poot 2011; Argent, Tonts, Jones, & Holmes 2013; Perkins, Mackay, & Espiner 2015). There may be a juxtaposition of old and new industries, which may be either an opportunity or a problem for the region (Perkins et al. 2015).

In terms of social impacts, rural food and wine festivals that have become hallmark events may build resilience in their local communities through encouraging community spirit and celebrating local identity. In some areas, food and wine festivals are themed around minority ethnic groups – who may be diasporas – and their distinctive foodways and products (Laing & Frost 2013; Timothy & Pena 2016). Rural festivals are a source of pride, often seen as highly authentic, creating well-being, social inclusion and leadership amongst locals and leaving behind community legacies. However, much of the research to date has either been in terms of food and wine producers and their interactions (Alonso & Bressan 2013; Bosworth & Farrell 2011; Dana et al. 2014; Moscardo 2014), or on rural festivals in general rather than on those themed on food and wine specifically (Black & Black 2016; Davies 2015; Gibson & Connell 2015).

Despite all these potential positive outcomes, rural festivals face many challenges, including lack of resources and expertise to keep the festivals viable in the long term and attracting tourists to places that are geographically isolated (Frost & Laing 2011, 2015). California's Stockton Asparagus Festival, for example, was initially hailed as a success for the strategic branding adopted by its organisers (Lewis 1997). However, in 2014 it closed due to declining attendances and the local council's insistence that the festival pay a higher proportion of government costs (Parrish 2014).

Given these concerns, rural hallmark events such as food and wine festivals provide important opportunities to understand how the leveraging of 'place' can contribute to economic and social sustainability. Our aim in this chapter is to go beyond seeing hallmark events simply in tourism terms. Focussing on food and wine festivals, we examine their economic importance more broadly, as well as considering the role of collaboration, and their impact on identity.

## Methods

The chapter is based on a qualitative phenomenological study involving long interviews with seven key stakeholders of festivals in rural south-east Australia (Victoria, southern New South Wales and South Australia). These included managers of festivals, destination marketing organisers and agricultural producers. Interviews were recorded and transcribed, then analysed thematically. Transcripts were sent to the interviewees for reflection, which increases the trustworthiness of the study (Tracy 2010). Each interviewee was given a number (P1, P2, etc.) to maintain their anonymity and thus confidentiality in what they said during their interviews. A fuller and more detailed explanation of the methodology used in this study, notably the data collection and data analysis process, may be found in Laing and Frost (2015).

## Findings

### *The changing landscape of rural Australia*

The backdrop to the development of rural hallmark events is the changing nature of the economy, with rural restructuring resulting in employment shifting away from traditional agriculture towards tourism, recreation and services (Ooi, Laing & Mair 2015). There are also changes in migration patterns, with younger people leaving small towns for perceived greater opportunities in larger urban centres. P6 noted that rural Australia has traditionally focussed on

> Agricultural production and we all know that that's under pressure in terms of being a major economic driver ... if you go back to the '70s and '80s on any given little country road there were seven farms and seven families and all the economic activity that brings with it in terms of kids at the school and all those things in that village. Now there's two farms that are three times bigger than they used to be for them to be viable so that means there's only two families and those kids have now grown up.

In addition, there has been a move towards artisanal and niche production. As P7 observed, 'traditional agriculture has certainly shifted, but we're seeing more of that more intensive smaller property activity coming to the fore. We see agri-tourism as probably our next significant tourism product for the region'. P7 went on to refer to this transition in more depth:

> All of the towns around here have all had some degree of change. [One town] had a $100 million tobacco industry close down overnight ...The transition to something else has been, probably in the eyes of those that are right in the middle of it, quite slow, but those looking from the outside can really see that the town is shifting and really embracing that tourism message. There's a lot of food venues that are now popping up.

This aligns with changes in the demographic make-up of rural communities, where there may be an influx of older people, often retired, known as *tree-changers*. Typically, these newcomers are looking for cheaper housing to free up their capital, a more unhurried lifestyle and amenities such as shops and cafes (Wheeler & Laing 2008). Many of these people are interested in food and where it comes from. According to P6, 'Every person out there is now a gourmet chef ... they're googling Jamie [Oliver] and making all this stuff ... the consumers are more educated about organic, they're more educated about the issue with the duopoly of the supermarkets'. The latter comment refers to the fact that there are essentially only two major supermarket chains in Australia, with a commensurate purchasing power which has led to some farmers having to sell their products unduly cheaply to remain on supermarket shelves. This concern about the food that they eat and the moral choices that this represents provides an opportunity for a festival to promote local produce and food products to the community and to develop a sense of pride in how it is grown or made.

Not all rural festivals are successful, and some of this is traced to these changes in the community, as newcomers arrive and take time to assimilate or have different needs which need to be accommodated over time. According to P7,

> We've seen a drop off in events ... in the last two years, and the best guess we've got is simply the community, the structure of the community, has changed. The events that the community traditionally got behind don't align with the new residents to town. But what we're seeing is those new residents are coming up with other ideas and it's going to take some time for those ideas to be fully formed, but I think we'll see a change and a re-emergence of events and festivals as they understand a little bit more about where their passion is and how it could work.

### *Economic importance of rural hallmark festivals*

Rural hallmark festivals themed around food and wine were perceived by the interviewees as having a number of economic benefits. They raise awareness of the town and thus visitation. P1 explained, 'We're open seven days a week now – I'm pretty sure if it wasn't for the festivals that we do, we probably wouldn't be opening as much as we do, because it's just given the area the exposure'. Similarly, P2 observed, 'Events have historically been absolutely critical in the driving of visitation to the region', and explained how this occurs:

> [The festivals play] a big promotional role, very big. People will come to these events and go 'we had a good time'. Then they will come outside of those events. That's what we hope for, not just to attract them to the event. It's about getting people in the door, so they get to know us and then they want to come back.

By working collaboratively, the numbers of visitors are far greater than they would be to an individual attraction such as a winery. However, in some cases, there is a limit to the number of attractions that should optimally take part to avoid splitting the audience too finely:

> We find as a region when we do events, if we all do an event on the same day, there's not enough people ... but if four or five wineries have events over the course of a weekend that works quite well.

*(P5)*

From a marketing perspective, the festivals expand the tourism product for visitors. Thus for P3, a winery representative, 'Attracting the visitor is a little broader than just cellar doors ... [it's] how the area is pitching events, which are the main drivers to get people up here'. They may also increase the potential market segments for their products, particularly in terms of attracting younger people. P4 talked about the rural hallmark festival they took part in, which is

> geared towards the younger generation for sure. That's bands, it's fun, it's the fun wines – the [sweet] moscatos ... so that's targeted fairly and squarely at the younger generation ... so you're trying to engage people on a more equal footing ... people aren't coming to us for pure unadulterated wine education. There's a sort of lifestyle element that has really taken over wine appreciation over the last couple of decades, so you need to introduce regional food produce.

Staging a rural hallmark festival can overcome the problems of seasonality, particularly in the colder months. P5, for example, had success in focussing events on a quiet month, promoting red wine in winter: 'So now July is one of our stronger months. You'll find through that month that probably a dozen or more wineries will have events scattered through that month. So that helps visitation. It helps the accommodation in town'. They also offer individual businesses the benefits of leveraging off the resources of other businesses in the region. P1 provided the example of a lack of tourist infrastructure at their winery: 'Individual cellar doors causes a bit of grief for people sometimes. Especially if you are not set up for food. Like we're not set up, we don't have a commercial kitchen'. Involvement in a rural hallmark festival allows these businesses to attract tourists, even if the winery can't offer meals or snacks to their visitors. For producers, these festivals allow the consumer to come directly to them, rather than the producer being required to seek out sales. These festivals were therefore convenient and efficient in terms of reaching the market. P5, for example, was clear about the role that festivals play in the marketing strategy of their winery: 'In terms of how we spend time and money on promotion, we look at local events first ... where people come to us versus where we go to people'.

## Collaboration and networking

The social benefits of staging rural hallmark festivals were also discussed. Many outcomes related to the facilitation of collaboration and networking, through working with other members of their local community on the festival organisation. Without this impetus, the community may lose their sense of togetherness, perhaps a reference to social capital (Alonso & Bressan 2013). Thus, P1 observed,

> We did go through a little stage when we didn't have any festivals. Probably nine or ten years ago ... I think everyone did lose out, they got a bit involved in their own area, but now we are working as a group ... we can provide support to each other.

It encourages *coopetition* rather than competition: 'We're all willing to help each other ... we don't view each other as competitors, we need to work together as a region to be successful. That's what a lot of the bigger regions have done' (P1).

While this strategy can be costly, in time or resources, it is seen by some as having clear benefits in terms of building a strong and healthy community, reflecting Richards's (2015) findings in relation to food networks. It can be the outcome of joining a destination marketing organisation, where festivals are organised on a regional basis. According to P3,

> Joining a regional marketing organisation, that's been a huge marketing cost to us. That's been the main financial commitment in one place that we've ever had ... one of

the reasons why I joined was to gain some community inclusion, because I think the country doesn't work like the city.

However, this made participating in these festivals mandatory for the members rather than an individual decision.

The other issue that was often raised by participants was the grass-roots nature of many of these festivals, which started within the community, rather than being imposed on a community: 'Most of the festivals that are still going after 25 years all started in the backyard of a pub, or over a beer while someone was having a chat, or in a pop-up gallery' (P6).

## *Identity*

It was emphasised by the interviewees that their festivals were well patronised by locals, who saw them as *their* festival: 'The food and wine thing 10 years ago was a visitor thing, but if you go to our wine festival in a couple of weeks' time ... there'll be 5,000 people and 2,500 of them will be local people' (P6). The nature of food lends itself to creating a sense of identity, through stimulating the economy but also encouraging conviviality. P7 explained what that might mean for a small rural town:

> Food is the precursor to further development; it seems to stimulate a confidence within the local community to see their neighbour out [eating]; they're spending money, they're conversing, they're celebrating their town, which then supports them getting excited about it and investing themselves. Tourism operators may be coming in from outside that also get involved in that.

However, there may be a disconnection between how tourists see a place and how locals see it, which has implications for festival development. While locals might think their town is distinctive, visitors might see it as similar to others they have visited. The same may be said about local festivals. P6 unpacked this dilemma:

> Our challenge to the villages is give me [tourists] a reason to come to your village which doesn't include historic buildings, quaint main street and boutique shopping because that just describes every village in the state ... [otherwise] if I've seen this one, I've seen them all.

## *Challenges of staging rural hallmark festivals*

While there were perceived benefits in staging festivals themed around food and wine, there were also challenges to overcome. One of the most important was the need to avoid the festivals becoming so big that it was difficult to deal with the number of visitors and the logistics involved in staging them. For P1, the increase in exposure and awareness had to be balanced by the impact on the region itself: 'The main reason is to promote the area and give us a bigger name ... it is a bit of a balancing act. We want to be careful about not being perceived as too big'. A few interviewees mentioned the need for de-marketing. For example, P2 stated,

> We don't want [our numbers of attendees] to get more than 4000, that would be way too many. If it got to 4000, we would stop trying to promote it. We'd start to pull back, because it's more about getting the quality visitor.

According to P1, 'We've learnt a lot off ... [another festival]. They had all sorts of disasters from that. From getting too big. So I think we need to be clever about marketing and clever about who we're marketing it to'.

Sometimes, resources, particularly staff, are too thin on the ground to cope with the influx of visitors. P2 explained how a coordinated wine festival across their region ended up being fractured into smaller events to make it easier for individual wineries to cope with:

> There was a time that everyone went to the one spot [a central venue] and did tastings and food. Then as that grew, it got a little bit out of control. So it went back to the wineries ... and each winery held their own event.

These festivals might also highlight a lack of accommodation when so many people visit at the same time: 'A small problem with accommodation in that there is not enough of it. The festival weekends book out years in advance so it can be a bit difficult, especially for new visitors' (P1).

Keeping the festival small was perceived by some interviewees as providing a point of difference:

> They all claim to be different, but they're really not ... a lot of them are just – we have entertainment, we have food, we have wine, come along, skip from place to place. Essentially, that's what ours is. But we just have [something different in] that we're smaller.
>
> *(P2)*

Keeping it small ensured a warm and intimate ambience:

> So our atmosphere is different ... I don't really like big events, because if you're really wanting to know about this particular winery, you just really can't get a sense of it ... that's one of the reasons we don't want to grow too big, because we want to keep that experience happening.
>
> *(P2)*

This trend towards intimacy of gastronomic experiences has been highlighted by Richards (2015) in his analysis of the changing nature of gastronomy in the modern economy.

A number of interviewees mentioned concerns about crowd behaviour when festivals became too large, notably around drunkenness. According to P1,

> It's just trying to combat things getting out of control and trying to avoid the real drunken antics because it's marketed as a family friendly event ... [if] you turn into a bar, you lose that aspect of a wine tasting and a wine and food event.

Paradoxically, dealing with the risk of drunk driving by providing transport might also lead to the festival becoming too large, as it becomes more attractive to those who might otherwise be forced to abstain from drinking during the festival. P1 observed,

> We were talking last year about running a bus [from the nearby large town] ... we initially thought of doing it to try and combat drink driving ... but our board actually said no to it ... they said it'll make it too big.

Another issue involved attracting the right kind of visitor to the festival. P2 noted, 'We don't want it to be a drinkfest. It's a relaxed atmosphere. It's not a drunken atmosphere'. One long-running wine festival made changes in order to target people who were looking to learn about the product, rather than taking part in a party weekend: 'It was more around the audience and creating a better experience for people who are genuinely interested in the product ... [and] removing part of that party element from it, which [potentially] decreases numbers, but that hasn't played out' (P7). They were prepared to see numbers of visitors fall rather than risk a decline in the experience.

## Conclusion

This chapter provides a number of insights into the role of hallmark food and wine festivals in strengthening the economic and social sustainability of rural towns or regions. First, many of these festivals boost tourist visitation, the conventional view of the impact of hallmark events. This is vital in rural places where traditional industries have declined, although our findings suggest that there are potential economic benefits that go beyond tourism. This has been underplayed or overlooked in the literature to date. Second, these festivals can act as a strategic device in building a creative food economy or *cluster* – mobilising diverse stakeholders to work together and brand local food/wine and the region (as noted by P1). Third, they provide a marketplace to connect producers to educated or conscious consumers, or 'quality visitors', as P7 noted, forming relationships and creating new market segments, e.g. the younger market targeted by P4. The changing make-up of these regions was noted, which may have implications for the continuity of festival organisations, but can also provide new sources of support for the festivals, ensuring their survival.

Fourth, hallmark rural food and wine festivals link to Richards's (2015) idea of *co-creating communities* through gastronomic networks. This means moving beyond studies focussed on individual gastronomic tourists and events. As shown here, these networks are based on strong relations between local producers, local residents, tourists and tourism operators, as P7, in particular, acknowledged. This bonding process may strengthen social capital (Alonso & Bressan 2013). Bridging social capital may also result from newcomers to the community connecting to others and thus feeling accepted through their involvement in these festivals.

Fifth and finally, the *barriers* to growth of hallmark rural food and wine festivals and the need for de-marketing highlighted in the findings can actually be opportunities for these places to distinguish themselves from the *sameness* problem of other towns through providing small-scale and personal creative tourism experiences and relational encounters with locals (Richards 2015). In the case of food and/or wine, the links with producer and region can be emphasised, providing a distinctive local story that sets the town and its festival apart and makes the experience more authentic. This might, in turn, build feelings of community identity and pride about local achievements, making rural regions and towns potentially attractive places to live in as well as to visit.

## References

Akgün, A.Y.A., Baycan-Levent, T.N., Nijkamp, P. & Poot, J. (2011). Roles of local and newcomer entrepreneurs in rural development: A comparative meta-analytic study. *Regional Studies, 45*(9), 1207–1223.

Alonso, A. & Bressan, A. (2013). Small rural family wineries as contributors to social capital and socioeconomic development. *Community Development, 44*(4), 503–519.

Argent, N., Tonts, M., Jones, R. & Holmes, J. (2013). A creativity-led rural renaissance? Amenity-led migration, the creative turn and the uneven development of rural Australia. *Applied Geography*, *44*(October), 88–98.

Beverland, M., Hoffman, D. & Rasmussen, M. (2001). The evolution of events in the Australasian wine sector. *Tourism Recreation Research*, *26*(2), 35–44.

Black, N. & Black, N. (2016). Festival connections: How consistent and innovative connections enable small-scale rural festivals to contribute to socially sustainable communities. *International Journal of Event and Festival Management*, *7*(3), 172–187.

Bosworth, G. & Farrell, H. (2011). Tourism entrepreneurs in Northumberland. *Annals of Tourism Research*, *38*(4), 1474–1494.

Dana, L.P., Gurau, C. & Lasch, F. (2014). Entrepreneurship, tourism and regional development: A tale of two villages. *Entrepreneurship & Regional Development*, *26*(3–4), 357–374.

Davies, A. (2015). Life after a festival: Local leadership and the lasting legacy of festivals. *Event Management*, *19*(4), 433–444.

Foden, B. (2015). Bluff Oyster Festival: How $10 helped make the world Bluff's oyster. *Stuff.co.nz*, May 23. www.stuff.co.nz/life-style/food-wine/68759987/Bluff-Oyster-Festival-How-10-helped-make-the-world-Bluffs-oyster, accessed 13 September 2015.

Frost, W. & Laing, J. (2011). *Strategic Management of Festivals and Events*. Melbourne: Cengage.

Frost, W. & Laing, J. (2015). Avoiding burnout: The succession planning, governance and resourcing of rural tourism festivals. *Journal of Sustainable Tourism*, *23*(8/9), 1298–1317.

Frost, W. & Laing, J. (2018). Understanding international exhibitions, trade fairs and industrial events: Concepts, trends and issues. In Frost, W. & Laing, J. (Eds.) *Exhibitions, Trade Fairs and Industrial Events* (pp. 1–20). Abingdon and New York: Routledge.

Getz, D. (2008). Event tourism: Definition, evolution and research. *Tourism Management*, *29*(3), 403–428.

Gibson, C. & Connell, J. (2015). The role of festivals in drought-affected Australian communities. *Event Management*, *19*(4), 445–459.

Herslund, L. (2012). The rural creative class: Counterurbanisation and entrepreneurship in the Danish countryside. *Sociologia Ruralis*, *52*(2), 235–255.

Kennedy, M. (2018). Beyond branding: The role of booktowns in building a relational marketplace. In Frost, W. & Laing, J. (Eds.) *Exhibitions, Trade Fairs and Industrial Events* (pp. 183–196). Abingdon and New York: Routledge.

Laing, J. & Frost, W. (2013). Food, wine… heritage, identity? Two case studies of Italian diaspora festivals in regional Victoria. *Tourism Analysis*, *18*(3), 323–334.

Lee, I. & Arcodia, C. (2011). The role of regional food festivals in destination branding. *International Journal of Tourism Research*, *13*(4), 355–367.

Lewis, G. H. (1997). Celebrating asparagus: Community and the rationally constructed food festival. *The Journal of American Culture*, *20*(4), 73–78.

Moscardo, G. (2014). Tourism and community leadership in rural regions: Linking mobility, entrepreneurship, tourism development and community well-being. *Tourism Planning & Development*, *11*(3), 354–370.

Mottiar, Z. (2016). The importance of local area as a motivation for cooperation among rural tourism entrepreneurs. *Tourism Planning & Development*, *13*(2), 203–218.

Nel, E. & Stevenson, T. (2014). The catalysts of small town economic development in a free market economy: A case study of New Zealand. *Local Economy*, *29*(4–5), 486–502.

NZPA. (2007). Bluff keeps oyster festival after community rallies. *NZ Herald*, 13 December. www.nzherald.co.nz/lifestyle/news/article.cfm?c_id=6&objectid=10482182, accessed 8 September 2015.

Ooi, N., Laing, J. & Mair, J. (2015). Socio-cultural change facing ranchers in the Rocky Mountain West as a result of mountain resort tourism and amenity migration. *Journal of Rural Studies*, *41*(October), 59–71.

Parrish, K. (2014). After 29 delicious years, Stockton's Asparagus Festival is no more. *Recordnet.com*, 11 June, www.recordnet.com/article/20140611/A_NEWS/406110328, accessed 28 October 2017.

Perkins, H.C., Mackay, M. & Espiner, S. (2015). Putting pinot alongside merino in Cromwell District, Central Otago, New Zealand: Rural amenity and the making of the global countryside. *Journal of Rural Studies*, *39*(June), 85–98.

Richards, G. (2015). Evolving gastronomic experiences: From food to foodies to foodscapes. *Journal of Gastronomy and Tourism*, *1*(1), 5–17.

Robertson, M. & Wardrop, K.M. (2012). Events and the destination dynamic: Edinburgh festivals, entrepreneurship and strategic marketing. In Yeoman, I., Robertson, M., Ali-Knight, J., Drummond, S. & McMahon-Beattie, U. (Eds.) *Festival and Events Management: An International Arts and Culture Perspective* (pp. 115–129). Oxford: Elsevier.

Timothy, D. & Pena, M. (2016). Food festivals and heritage awareness. In Timothy, D. (Ed.) *Heritage Cuisines: Traditions, Identities and Tourism* (pp. 148–165). London and New York: Routledge.

Tracy, S.J. (2010). Qualitative quality: Eight 'big-tent' criteria for excellent qualitative research. *Qualitative Inquiry*, *16*(10), 837–851.

Wheeler, F. & Laing, J. (2008). Tourism as a vehicle for liveable communities: Case studies from regional Victoria, Australia. *Annals of Leisure Research*, *11*(1 & 2), 242–263.

# 30
# POSITIONING IN MONTSERRAT'S FESTIVALS

## Music, media, and film

*Joseph Lema, Gracelyn Cassell, and Jerome Agrusa*

### Introduction

Cultural aspects of a society are of growing interest in the relationship that exists between community development, the arts, and tourism activities. This interest and involvement extends beyond economics and has given rise to a number of critical questions concerning the value and potential opportunities as well as the challenges that exist for a tourism destination. The prospects and potential for developing unique cultural offerings or products, including music-related events, provide numerous benefits. When managed effectively, this can diversify tourism activities and help sustain tourism during challenging times of economic downturn, social or environmental crises, along with providing resourceful connections between visitors and the host community.

Festivals and events, for instance, are increasingly used to market tourism destinations while also being closely associated with other tourism marketing and branding initiatives (Baez & Devesa 2014; Getz 1991; Hall 1992; Quinn 2006; Tikkanen 2008; Yu & Turco 2000). However, festivals and events have often been singularly dominated by measures of value in terms of economic significance of the festival or event itself with less investigation into the overall impact of the event that are not as easily identifiable or objectively measurable (Getz & Frisby 1988; O'Sullivan & Jackson 2002; Quinn 2006). As part of cultural tourism, interest in the history of a location and those that have lived in the local community offers a wealth of contribution to the tourism product for a location. This information for the tourist may assist a mindful traveler who may leave a destination with a heightened awareness and increased appreciation of the many unique historical and cultural components of the area (Moscardo 1999). In this regard, music and destinations that have influenced music may also help to enhance images and memories that leave a lasting impression far beyond the activities of the trip itself. Music, for example, which often captures the celebrations of the past, trials, and tribulations or even possible events of the future, may help enhance the tourism experience along with affinity to the destination or event associated with a region (Getz 2008). For example, Calypso and Soca musician Alphonsus "Arrow" Cassell's legendary global hit track, "Hot Hot Hot", easily connects to the ongoing and active volcanic eruptions that exist on the island of Montserrat, which also captures the challenges and opportunities that this island faces with the continuous natural disaster and threats of pyroclastic volcanic eruptions.

With a population of approximately 5,100 residents, music is a hallmark of this tiny British Overseas Territory with even a *Montserrat Idol* talent competition among up and coming resident artists (Discover Montserrat 2017).

A number of famous artists have recorded sessions at *AIR Montserrat*, including Sir Paul McCartney, Sir Elton John, Black Sabbath, Dire Straits, Duran, Eric Clapton, Lou Reed, Michael Jackson, Stevie Wonder, Sting, The Rolling Stones, The Police, and Ultravox (Air Studios 2013). Sharing with the world where Alphonsus "Arrow" Cassell emerged, and how the beauty of the island of Montserrat has inspired his music, will provide another marketing attribute to the current tourism marketing product. Tourists may similarly also attach themselves to the destination as well as the artist on a deeper level than merely for arousal or limited entertainment enjoyment. Lashua, Spracklen, and Long (2014) proposed that music tourism is a historical phenomenon of modernity with the cultural aspect of live music connecting travelling musicians with locals and tourists at festivals, concerts, orchestras, music halls, and impromptu street performances. The encounters tourists have with music can also have a representative sense of place with a tourism destination with distinct memories and narratives among people, music, and place (Connell & Gibson 2003). The emergence of celebrity endorsement in a wide array of fields is becoming very common in the vast global area of advertisement, marketing, and brand recognition (Kim, Long, & Robinson 2009). In an era where celebrity personality or identity provides a symbolic meaning and value to the associated environment, the marketing potential can be recognized through a number of channels and forms (Stern 1994; Wee & Ming 2003).

## Literature review

### *Celebrities, music, and tourism*

While many studies have investigated celebrity endorsement, the influence of celebrities, and persuasion in a number of diverse areas, this topic has not been closely linked to tourism (Johns, Weir, & Weir 2015; Kim, Agrusa, Lee, & Chon 2007; Kim, Lee, & Prideaux 2014; McCartney & Pinto 2014). Celebrity- or film-induced tourism, however, has seen accelerated attention for ongoing business development and the creation of new tourism markets in addition to associated licensing and merchandising (Beeton 2008). Furthermore, research suggests that the intangible benefits of hosting a film or television and audio music broadcast, as well as having a celebrity from an area, can enhance the image and increase awareness of the image of a destination (Han & Lee 2008; Kim et al. 2007) just as a film-induced festival can help to enhance the image of a destination (Frost 2017). Graceland in Memphis, Tennessee, for instance, has hosted an average of 500,000 annual visitors to the exhibit area and mansion since opening June 7, 1982 with over $32 million annual revenues in worldwide merchandising and licensing for the brand of Elvis or the "King of Rock & Roll" (Sanz 2012). The *Sound of Music* is another illustration – released in 1965 and having received five Academy Awards, more than 40 years later, it is still the most popular organized tour of all time in Salzburg, Austria (Im & Chon 2008). The movie *King Kong* set in the backdrop of Trang An Landscape Complex located in Ninh Binh Province of North Vietnam has experienced accelerating visitor interest (Tong 2017) coupled with recently being designated a World Heritage Site by the United Nations Educational, Scientific and Cultural Organization (UNESCO). In the Caribbean, Trench Town, Jamaica, home of legendary artist Bob Marley, is a world famously designated the home of reggae and has developed as an alternative tourism attraction (Boxill 2004; Rhiney & Cruse 2012).

Similarly, by way of example, interest in Korean pop artists and TV dramas has been attributed to the release of widely exposed TV and audio programming in a wide number of countries, particularly, although not exclusively, in Asia (Kim et al. 2009). Africa, North America, and Europe have also experienced increased growth in popularity along with an increased interest in the associated Korean cultural activities such as music, food, fashion, and cosmetics to name a few. In addition to the direct economic impact of the production itself, substantial benefits have emerged and increasingly realized through tourism (Kim et al. 2007).

Music, film, or a TV program can provide a medium to spread philosophical, cultural, or even political messages and meanings of a region (Mercille 2005). Furthermore, symbolic themes of featured events, historical cultural traits, and physical characteristics can be linked from the ordinary everyday life to the world of mass media (Iwashita 2008). While mass media has emerged from a number of forces, the idolization of celebrities, including musicians and actors, may represent a contemporary cultural trend that is evident in many parts of society today (Koernig & Boyd 2009; Lord & Putrevu 2009).

A number of risks associated with film-induced and music tourism may include the potential negative impacts on the host community including increased congestion, loss of privacy, dilution of cultural authenticity through commercialization, and the demonstration effect which has been acknowledged through a number of related studies in various tourism destinations (Beeton 2008; Fisher 2004). In the case of film-induced tourism, for example, Jewell and McKinnon (2008) argued that misinterpretations and misconceptions result when the image of the destination that is portrayed on screen differs from the authentic history and culture of that destination. When a destination duplicates the consumptive patterns of the portrayed culture through the media, a demonstration effect occurs through this borrowed commercialization process (Fisher 2004). Furthermore, a number of studies indicate that invented stories or characters at filming destinations draw attention to issues of authenticity of the tourism product and gaps in the associated images that really exist along with unrealistic expectations of the destination itself (see, for example, Jewell & McKinnon 2008).

Characteristics of celebrity icons may also lead to differentiated risks throughout various cultures that have widely varying interpreted cultural meanings (Gakhal & Senior 2008; Parulekar & Raheja 2006; Wang, Hsieh, & Chen 2002). The symbolic communications model proposed by Spears, Mowen, and Chakraborty (1996) attempts to demonstrate the culturally connected world through linkages on a continuum relative to culture and nature. Product meaning is then created through associations with a bundle of symbols that can transfer the meaning between the symbol and product and advertised to the consumer through different systems of communication (Spears et al. 1996).

Challenges exist, however, that can lead to misinterpretations or misconceptions if not carefully positioned. Destination Product Placement (DPP) in films is a concept that refers to the deliberate and explicit use of a destination in a film that offers significant growth opportunities to promote a destination or even a fictitious destination as demonstrated in the latest two Disney movies including *Frozen* staged with the backdrop of Norway and *Moana* staged in Hawaii. With significant worldwide media exposure through the two films, controversy (among natives, residents, and tourists) continues to surround the cultural depiction of the characters and representation of the area. Nonetheless, it is likely that as technology such as mobile, cloud, and cognitive technologies, including digital storytelling, evolve, there will be more strategic placement of music, film, and media sources to complement the attributes of a festival, event, and tourism destination.

Tourism destinations can host spotlight events for small destinations that focus on a unique aspect of the place in order to reposition an image that may overcome negative media coverage of a disaster or unsafe location by using celebrities or opinion leaders who can assure traveler safety from their own opinion and experiences (Avraham 2014). The celebrity or opinion leader endorsement can also reinforce a unique cultural attribute such as a music festival, for instance, that may benefit a tourist want or need. The relationship between a festival or special event and tourism is a way for associated images that can be transferred to changing the destination brand as well as strengthening and enhancing the benefits of the brand through the physical, natural, and cultural aspects of the destination (Jago, Chalip, Brown, Mules, & Ali 2003). Destinations engaged in supply-side marketing and development promote messages that focus on trends, unique attributes, authenticity, and high quality to enhance a sense of place. A holistic approach proposed by Richards (2017) aims at broader placemaking activities through the use of special events to involve local stakeholder groups for increased social cohesion and investment opportunities. In the case of a natural disaster, bringing together community residents and local businesses with tourists can help to increase consumer confidence as well as investor relations in having an operating environment that offers synergies to stimulate visitation and spending in addition to increasing the profile of a destination.

## Case study of Montserrat

Montserrat is an island of less than 103 square kilometers and is part of the Leeward group (Lesser Antilles) located in the Eastern Caribbean between Antiqua and Guadeloupe. From a previous high of 12,000, there are now only 5,000 residents that remain in a safe zone on the island following the volcanic eruption of the Soufriere Hills volcano in 1995 which left two-thirds of the island uninhabitable including the capital of Plymouth (UN data 2015). Active volcanos remain a part of Montserrat with ongoing threats of pyroclastic volcanic eruptions as well as hurricanes passing through the warm Caribbean waters. An overseas territory of the United Kingdom, Montserrat is governed by a chief minister, executive council, and a legislature consisting of eleven members, of which nine are elected (Riches & Stalker 2016). Construction of port facilities, including a ferry service from Antigua and the opening of Gerald's Airport in the newly developing capital of Little Bay, has improved communication and access to the island. For volcano monitoring, the Montserrat Volcanic Observatory serves the island for both scientists and officials in addition to hosting educational tours for locals and tourists.

### *Event bundling in Montserrat*

In 2010, a unique literary festival entitled "The Alliouagana Festival of the Word" took place at the Cultural Centre in Little Bay on the island of Montserrat as a world-class literary festival, with presentations by internationally recognized authors providing storytelling, book-signings, readings, music, dramatic presentations, and workshops. Alliouagana is a name derived from the Amerindians referring to Montserrat as the land of the prickly bush (Fergus 1975). Preceding the event was the first symposium in the Alphonsus "Arrow" Cassell memorial lecture series that has continued annually to date. This engaging event attracts visitors to Montserrat from a number of markets including the creative and cultural industries which is naturally of significance to developing economies. The local community as well as external supporters make it possible to host the annual literary festival in

Montserrat with volunteers providing specialized services throughout the event. Involving the community in this approach also provides a wealth of reciprocal learning opportunities among the different generations in the community, and this, in turn, has helped to facilitate and promote positive dialogue and change in the tourism management system. Furthermore, other celebratory events such as St. Patrick's week that recognizes the African and Irish heritage, the Montserrat Christmas Festival featuring the Masquerades, and Calabash Festival also help to convey many of the traditions and customs of Montserrat in a festive spirit (Fergus 2006).

While Montserrat has been the location set for a number of films, the history of Calypso music along with the famed music success of "Arrow" predominates in media recognition and celebrations. Ironically, an advantage for Montserrat in attracting a niche tourism market, as well as literary and music inspired artists, is the appeal of the active volcano which also fascinated Henry Nelson Coleridge when he visited Montserrat in 1825. The spectacle of volcano can be linked to some of the disaster literature that has emerged from Montserrat in an attempt to show how life engenders the creative arts. Therefore, the significance of the literary festival and symposium enriches the depth of understanding and cultural inquiry into the richer aspects of Montserrat that exists beyond the celebratory effect of hosting the festival that has typically taken place on the island on an annual basis. Bundling the symposium with the festival allows synergies to sustain both the events. Being relatively low-scale events with less than 300 participants, economies of scale are a challenge, as well as attracting ongoing vendor support. Sponsorships, associated vendor participation, along with event participation among locals are necessary for the continuation of the complementary events.

A bundled package which includes Montserrat's attractions (diving, hiking, bird watching, snorkeling, volcano viewing and education) combined with special rates for accommodation and on island transportation was proposed as part of advertising the Festival in an effort to fill as many of the 150 beds available for visitors. November being a shoulder season for tourism on the island, hoteliers were encouraged to provide attractive rates to extend hotel occupancies. Groups of writers around the world were one of the target market segments, with special attention paid to the regional potential market in Guadeloupe, which has historically had a high interest but underutilized inbound market to Montserrat (Government of Montserrat 2017). Attracting the Montserrat diaspora back to the island for the festival and encouraging them to remember the island the way it was before the volcanic eruptions is another significant niche market. Having the Festival during the second weekend in November positions it well for the availability of scheduled flights and lower travel costs, and as the cold sets in up north, this makes the Caribbean a more attractive destination. The art and craft sector was involved in developing a range of attractive handmade and souvenir items displayed for sale at the venue, with locally produced items carrying the event's logo, such as bags, visors, and hats, along with other representative commodities and memorabilia.

Collaboration with such agencies as the Montserrat Tourist Board, the Hospitality Association, the Montserrat Arts and Crafts Association, ground transportation, and tour Guides Association was essential for the success of events along with forging alliances with other festivals that are held throughout the region. As a corollary to the weekend activities, a book stall with selected titles for sale, music offerings, a food court offering local and regional cuisine, a craft market and pampering sessions with massage therapists and reflexologists was also of high interest to the event participants. Dramatic performances are much loved by Montserratians at home and abroad with music shows that have tended to draw sizable crowd including high participation from local residents. Presentations were recorded and guest presenters interviewed by the media to provide advertising content for future festivals. The potential is there for income generation through the sale of recordings of performances of each year's festival, but this has implications for various rights including those of the authors and so require skillful negotiation.

The future of the festival and symposium events is strongly linked to the new developments in the country as well as evolving creative, entertaining, and life enrichment themes. Having the festival in close proximity to accommodation units reduces the administrative costs of the events along with making use of the existing resources, available infrastructure, along with active local participation and creative human potential that exists on the island.

## Conclusion

The uniqueness of cultures through creative works such as music that can portray a "way of life" may be as appealing to tourists as an unspoiled beach or breathtaking landscape (Agrusa 2006). More than ever, tourists are seeking experiences which expose them to unique offerings at a travel destination, including distinct cultural resources. Music is one form of cultural expression that may help to provide another opportunity for tourists who may want to learn the different ways of life and experience those new cultures, first hand.

With tourists increasingly seeking to experience unique cultures and traditions on a more personal level to enrich their own lives, contact with the local population can promote mutual understanding that benefits both tourists and the local residents (Fredline & Faulkner 2000; McDonnell, Allen, & O'Toole 1999). Significant opportunities to diversify the economic base through increased employment opportunities and investment in conservation of the environment, along with projects to help preserve the local culture and traditions of the past, can evolve through responsible tourism development (Dwyer, Mellor, Mistilis, & Mules 2000).

Such an approach to responsible cultural tourism encourages tourists to "get off the road" in order to encounter the authentic traditions of a culture while providing an enriching experience for both residents and tourists (Agrusa 2006). In the process, cultural tourism also encourages local residents to be more engaged with tourists because they are more closely involved in participating in how their culture will be represented to others. Travel marketers are becoming more aware that the increasing demand for cultural tourism is a lucrative economic and social benefit to a region. Increasing recognition in terms of providing a richer tourism experience that builds on cultural opportunities, community involvement, and environmental quality is becoming more apparent to tourism planners along with local and regional development authorities (Madrigal 1995). Integrating the local cultural and artistic aspects can provide tourists the opportunity to engage in an array of activities; therefore, strategic bundling may also allow Montserrat to differentiate itself from competing destinations that may be able to offer similar commodities. Therefore, bundling to sustain the niche events should include products and service that embrace an authentic flair of local culture and highlight the talented artists who have contributed to the uniqueness of Montserrat while also engaging those residents who aspire to share their artistic and creative talents with tourists in the future.

Music and literary festivals can support a sense of place for Montserrat and help to communicate the challenges the island has yet highlight the unique cultural underpinnings of the culture. Music and literature can support the old with the new, and in the case of Montserrat, with a troubled history, from the devastating Hurricane Hugo in 1989 to the ongoing pyroclastic volcanic eruptions and environmental threats that still exist, the constructed historical structures and landscape may be covered with ash, but the reconstruction and expressions through music and literature are thriving. Celebrating the past through music and literary festivals can bridge the memory of past events with the present as well as provide a hope for the future. The positioning of festivals to connect tourists and locals among a wide range of demographic segments and characteristics is fluid. Staiff and Bushell (2017) propose that co-determination of events provides placemaking while the place provides the underpinning for events. The reciprocity of this dynamic relationship can be realized and communicated through the music and literary event that enhance the cultural capital of a tourism destination.

With the increased presence of social media, even some of the smallest, most remote destinations and small-scale festival events can have a worldwide presence to share their story. Prentice and Andersen (2003) argued that festivals can help to reposition the image of a destination as well as a region, while social media, according to Garay and Soledad Morales Pérez (2016), can widely enhance the image of a festival through greater channels of communication and integration of collaborating marketing intelligence. The potential exists for increased exposure, targeted and personalized marketing, along with sponsorship opportunities to support the sustainability of an event. Music and literary festivals in particular are akin to storytelling, and in the era of digital technology, with mobile, cloud, and cognitive computing applications, a new channel of opportunity exists to promote sense of place among increasingly integrated platforms. For small-scale festivals taking place in Montserrat, crowdsourcing and cloud-based applications for new knowledge and sources of cultural capital can provide new sources of continuity to not only communicate and engage festival participants, tourists, and locals but sustain the memories and voices of calypsonians.

## References

Agrusa, J. (2006). The role of festivals and events in community tourism destination management. In W. Jamieson (Ed.), *Community destination management in developing economies* (pp. 181–192). New York: Haworth Hospitality Press.

Air Studios. (2013). Retrieved from www.airstudios.com/about-us/history/air-montserrat/. Accessed 30/11/2017.

Avraham, E. (2014). Hosting event as a tool for restoring destination image. *International Journal of Event Management Research, 8*(1), 61–75.

Beeton, S. (2008). Location, location, location: Film corporations' social responsibilities. *Journal of Travel & Tourism Marketing, 24*(2/3), 107–114.

Baez, A. & Devesa, M. (2014). Segmenting and profiling attendees of a film festival. *International Journal of Event and Festival Management, 5*(2), 96–115.

Boxill, I. (2004). Towards an alternative tourism for Jamaica. *International Journal of Contemporary Hospitality Management, 16*(4/5), 269–272.

Connell, J. & Gibson, C. (2003). *Sound tracks: Popular music, identity and place*. London: Routledge.

Discover Montserrat. (2017). Montserrat idol. Retrieved from https://discovermni.com/tag/montserrat-idol/. Accessed 30/11/2017.

Dwyer, L., Mellor, R., Mistilis, N. & Mules, T. (2000). A framework for assessing 'tangible' and 'intangible' impacts of events and conventions. *Event Management, 6*(3), 175–189.

Fergus, H.A. (1975). *History of Alliouagana: A short history of Montserrat*. [Plymouth] Montserrat: University Centre.

Fergus, H.A. (2006). *Montserrat: Defining moments*. Toronto: Kimagic Publishing.

Fisher, D. (2004). The demonstration effect revisited. *Annals of Tourism Research, 31*(2), 428–446.

Fredline, E. & Faulkner, B. (2000). Community perceptions of the impacts of events. In J. Allen, R. Harris, L. Jago, & J. Veal (Eds.), *Events beyond 2000: Setting the agenda. Proceedings of conference on event evaluation, research and education*, Sydney.

Frost, W. (2008). Projecting an image: Film-induced festivals in the American west. *Event Management, 12*(2), 95–103.

Gakhal, B. & Senior, C. (2008). Examining the influence of fame in the presence of beauty: An electrodermal neuromarketing study. *Journal of Consumer Behavior*, 7(4–5), 331–341.

Garay, L. & Pérez, S. M. (2017). Understanding the creation of destination images through a festival's Twitter conversation. *International Journal of Event and Festival Management*, 8(1), 39–54.

Getz, D. (1991). *Festivals, special events and tourism*. New York: Van Nostrand Reinhold.

Getz, D. (2008). Event tourism: Definition, evolution, and research. *Tourism Management*, 29(3), 403–428.

Getz, D. & Frisby, W. (1988). Evaluating management effectiveness in community-run festivals. *Journal of Travel Research*, 27(1), 22–27.

Government of Montserrat. (2017). Statistics department. Retrieved from www.gov.ms/pubs/statistics-department/. Accessed 30/11/2017.

Hall, C.M. (1992). *Hallmark tourist events: Impacts, management and planning*. London: Belhaven.

Han, H. & Lee, J. (2008). A study on the KBS TV drama Winter Sonata and its impact on Korea's Hallyu tourism development. *Journal of Travel & Tourism Marketing*, 24(2/3), 115–126.

Im, H.H. & Chon, K. (2008). An exploratory study of movie-induced tourism: A case of the movie The Sound of Music and its locations in Salzburg, Austria. *Journal of Travel & Tourism Marketing*, 24(2/3), 229–238.

Iwashita, C. (2008). Roles of films and television dramas in international tourism: The case of Japanese tourists to the UK. *Journal of Travel & Tourism Marketing*, 24(2/3), 139–151.

Jago, L., Chalip, L., Brown, G., Mules, T. & Ali, S. (2003). Building events into destination branding: Insights from experts. *Event Management*, 8(1), 3–14.

Jewell, B., & McKinnon, S. (2008). Movie tourism—a new form of cultural landscape?. *Journal of Travel & Tourism Marketing*, 24(2–3), 153–162.

Johns, R., Weir, B. & Weir, R. (2015). The power of celebrity: Exploring the basis for Oprah's successful endorsement of Australia as a vacation destination. *Journal of Vacation Marketing*, 21(2), 17–130.

Kim, S.S, Agrusa, J., Lee, H. & Chon, K. (2007). Effects of Korean television dramas on the flow of Japanese tourists. *Tourism Management*, 28(6), 1340–1353.

Kim, S.S., Lee, J., Prideaux, B. (2014). Effect of celebrity endorsement on tourists' perception of corporate image, corporate credibility and corporate loyalty. *International Journal of Hospitality Management*, 37(0), 131–145.

Kim, S.S., Long, P., & Robinson, M. (2009). Small screen, big tourism: The role of popular Korean television dramas in South Korean tourism. *Tourism Geographies*, 11(3), 308–333.

Koernig, S. & Boyd, T. (2009). To catch a tiger or let him go: The match-up effect and athlete endorsers for sport and non-sport brands. *Sport Marketing Quarterly*, 18(1), 25–37.

Lashua, B., Spracklen, K. & Long, P. (2014). Introduction to the special issue: Music and Tourism. *Tourist Studies*, 14(1), 3–9.

Lord, K. & Putrevu, S. (2009). Informational and transformational responses to celebrity endorsement. *Journal of Current Issues and Research in Advertising*, 31(1), 1–13.

Madrigal, R. (1995). Residents perceptions and the role of government. *Annals of Tourism Research*, 22(1), 86–102.

McCartney, G. & Pinto, J.F. (2014). Influencing Chinese travel decisions: The impact of celebrity endorsement advertising on the Chinese traveler to Macao. *Journal of Vacation Marketing*, 20(3), 253–266.

McDonnell, I., Allen, J. & O'Toole, W. (1999). *Festival and special event management*. Brisbane: John Wiley and Sons.

Mercille, J. (2005). Media effects on image: The case of Tibet. *Annals of Tourism Research*, 32(4), 1039–1055.

Moscardo, G. (1999). *Making visitors mindful: Principles for creating sustainable visitor experiences through effective communication*. Champaign, IL: Sagamore Publishing.

O'Sullivan, D. & Jackson, M.J. (2002). Festival tourism: A contributor to sustainable local economic development? *Journal of Sustainable Tourism*, 10(4), 325–342.

Parulekar, A.A. & Raheja, P. (2006). Managing celebrities as brand: Impact of endorsements on celebrity image. In L.R. Kahle and C.-H. Kim (Eds.), *Creating images and the psychology of marketing communication* (pp. 161–169). Erbaum: St. Louis.

Prentice, R. & Andersen, V. (2003). Festival as creative destination. *Annals of Tourism Research*, 30(1), 7–30.

Quinn, B. (2006). Problematising 'Festival Tourism': Arts festivals and sustainable development in Ireland. *Journal of Sustainable Tourism*, 14(3), 288–306.

Rhiney, K. & Cruse, R. (2012). Trench Town Rock: Reggae music, landscape inscription, and the making of place in Kingston, Jamaica. *Urban Studies Research*, 1–12. Retrieved from www.hindawi.com/journals/usr/2012/585160/cta/. Accessed 30/11/2017.

Riches, C. & Stalker, P. (2016). *A guide to countries of the world*. Oxford University Press. Retrieved from www.oxfordreference.com. Accessed 30/11/2017.

Richards, G. (2017). From place branding to placemaking: The role of events. *International Journal of Event and Festival Management*, 8(1), 8–23.

Sanz, A. (2012, June 17). Graceland celebrates 30 years of Elvis pilgrimages. USA Today. Retrieved from http://travel.usatoday.com/destinations/story/2012-06-17/Graceland-celebrates-30-years-of-Elvis-pilgrimages/55644436/1. Accessed 30/11/2017.

Spears, N., Mowen, J. & Chakraborty, G. (1996). Symbolic role of animals in print advertising: Content analysis and conceptual development. *Journal of Business Research*, 37(2), 87–95.

Staiff, R. & Bushell, R. (2017). The "old" and the "new": Events and placemaking in Luang Prabang, Laos. *International Journal of Event and Festival Management*, 8(1), 55–65.

Stern, B. (1994). Authenticity and the textual persona: Postmodern paradoxes in adverting narrative. *International Journal of Research in Marketing*, 11(4), 387–400.

Tikkanen, I., (2008). Internationalization process of a music festival: Case Kuhmo Chamber Music Festival. *Journal of Euromarketing*, 17(2), 127–139.

Tong, K.D. (2017, March 23). Vietnam tries to cash in on King Kong. Nikkei Asian Review. Retrieved from https://asia.nikkei.com/magazine/20170323/Business/Vietnam-tries-to-cash-in-on-King-Kong. Accessed 30/11/2017.

UN data. (2015). *World statistics pocketbook: United Nations statistics division*. Retrieved from http://data.un.org/CountryProfile.aspx?crName=Montserrat. Accessed 30/11/2017.

Wang, K.-C., Hsieh, A.-T. & Chen, W.-Y. (2002). Is the tour leader an effective endorser for group package tour brochures? *Tourism Management*, 23(5), 489–498.

Wee, T. & Ming, M. (2003). Leveraging on symbolic values and meanings in branding. *Brand Management*, 10(3), 208–221.

Yu, Y. & Turco, D. (2000). Issues in tourism event economic impact studies: The case of the Albuquerque international balloon fiesta. *Current Issues in Tourism*, 3(2), 138–149.

# 31
# MUSIC EVENTS AND FESTIVALS
## Identity and experience

*Michelle Duffy*

## Introduction

Music has long been a significant component of rituals, festivals and other community events. Historians point out that music and dance were integral to religious ceremonies and political meetings in ancient Egypt, while the Pythian Games held in Delphi – a 6th-century precursor to the Olympic Games – included music performance as well as music and poetry competitions (Hudson, Roth, Madden, & Hudson 2015). What we might recognise as a music festival today is evident in the festivities associated with the troubadour guilds of 11th-century southern Europe (Frey 1994). The music festival as a format is particularly long lived; for example, for a little over 300 years, the Three Choirs Festival has rotated between the English cathedral cities of Gloucester, Hereford and Worcester, making it one of the oldest continuing music festivals in Europe (Boden & Hedley 2017). Many contemporary music festival practices and programmes continue to maintain a focus on specific music genres, which some scholars argue was in response to the lack of live performance opportunities in society following the Second World War (Robertson, Yeoman, Smith, & McMahon-Beattie 2015). Even so, the music festival format remains an important live music strategy in the face of issues such as policy regulations in regard to noise, urban and regional development strategies, and the rapid increase in the development and democratisation of participation in the online world. Indeed, as numerous studies have demonstrated, the number of music festivals has grown exponentially (Getz & Page 2016), and with this the range, goals and formats of music festivals have increased (Gibson 2013). The prevalence and scope of music festivals means that the study of music festivals is more than an examination of musical genre and style. Scholars have sought to better understand the role these festivals play in such things as the formation of identity and community; inclusive and exclusionary practices of social formation; the maintenance of tradition, urban and rural regeneration and development; health and well-being; tourism; and the experiential economy (Ballantyne, Ballantyne, & Packer 2014; Gibson 2013; Laing & Mair 2015).

## Music genres and identity

Most music festival research has focused on music genres as forms of representation that are linked to specific groups or communities (Connell & Gibson 2003; Quinn 2003). The music genres performed – the song lyrics, instrumentation, melodic structures or performance styles – are understood as constructions of identity that are associated with specific cultural groups or lifestyles (Curtis 2010; Gibson & Connell 2005; Goulding & Saren 2009). This approach aligns with studies of music that have, until recently, conceptualised music in terms of highly patterned and stable sound profiles that served to identify the social group from which the music originated (Lomax 1976). Critiques of this approach have pointed out that there is no simple relationship between music and meaning (DeNora 2000; Frith 1996). Rather, the interactions between musician, listener and the cultural context in which music is performed result in complex and varied sets of meanings that are not static, but shift in response to different situations. In this way, ideas about identity and belonging emerge through performance. The ways in which musical practices are perceived by performers and audience lead to the formation of particular alliances and the creation of a sense of group identity. The identity or identities of individuals and groups are actively constructed through the production and consumption of various musical practices and genres. The relationship, then, between music and identity is always ambiguous and contextualised, and therefore the arrangement of sounds into music does not result in a transparent and stable set of meanings (Martin 1995).

Many studies in sociology, anthropology and human geography have explored ways in which music festivals help to create and express ideas about the identity of a community through distinctive cultural artefacts and activities, in which music is presented in conjunction with dance, costume and food (Derrett 2003; Gibson & Connell 2005; Quinn 2003). Often such music festivals are a means to preserve traditions and group identity, particularly in spaces of contestation and transition (Brennan-Horley, Connell, & Gibson 2007; Costa 2002; Fortier 1999; Mair & Duffy 2015; Matheson 2005). The community festival provides a popular framework for such goals and is closely associated with the multicultural festival as this format can help contribute to processes that facilitate new forms of belonging, especially for migrant, diasporic and transnational groups (Duffy 2003; Keller 2007; Permezel & Duffy 2007; White 2015). Multicultural festivals are often promoted as sites for ongoing dialogues and negotiations within diverse communities, and music's role is often that of a medium for such dialogue as well as providing an atmosphere in which social harmony and integration may be fostered (Duffy 2005; Lee, Arcodia & Lee 2012; Osterlund-Potzsch 2004; Permezel & Duffy 2007). However, such notions of belonging can also be problematic because of the sort of identities or social relations invoked (Cornish 2015; Jodie 2015), or because members of a community may feel excluded due to such things as ticket prices.

The significance of music in the festival format is that music can be viewed as processes or performances that act out, create and negotiate various forms of identity. Music is a conceptual and symbolic practice, and can be interpreted in idiosyncratic ways by individual listeners, but collective meaning is also attributed to musical sounds. In this way, music can be associated with places and particular images, emotions and meanings, as well as a way of shaping social action. Yet music can also be used to erect boundaries, thus serving to maintain distinctions between groups of people. As Erlmann (1996) suggests in relation to world music, there are border zone relations in which different styles and genres of music are performed that are zones of contestation and negotiation between different groups with different agendas. The official discourses of those groups controlling the festival operate to produce an official 'imagined' community (Anderson 1983), which the festival is then planned to address. Yet the transitory nature of the event – the brief encounters and exchanges occurring within the festival space – produces other ways of being, resulting in a performative set of identities that are constituted at the time of the festival and in that place. Such processes produce different and often conflicting configurations of identity, place and music. Music festivals are therefore complex sites of identity formation and community building. Nonetheless community music festivals can facilitate a space for ongoing dialogue between differing groups and communities, each trying to negotiate some form of local identity that then has input into a framework of belonging (Permezel & Duffy 2007).

The focus on the relationship between music, performance and identity has also raised ideas about authenticity and authentic practices, in which music practice and performance are often linked to geographically distinct locations and communities (Carney 1997; Duffy 2005). Authenticity is a highly problematic concept because it often reproduces oversimplified categories about the relationships between music and community, and hides the ideological framings of tradition that condemns 'change' (Waitt & Duffy 2010). Nonetheless, there is some correlation between sound structures and social structures, because, as with language acquisition, we learn to recognise certain musical patterns or conventions as 'correct' (Attali 1992; Feld 1984). Even so, scholars continue to question what is meant by authenticity and the impact this may have on music festival participation (Kim & Jamal 2007; Szmigin, Bengry-Howell, Morey, Griffin & Riley 2017). However, it is not musical practices alone that raise issues of authenticity. In the tourism literature there is a differentiation between an authenticity attributed to objects or events deemed 'genuine' (MacCannell 1976) such as attending particular performances or prototypical events such as Glastonbury, and events that *feel* more authentic to the individual because s/he perceives his or her participation as a means of (re)connecting to a sense of a 'true' self (Steiner & Reisinger 2006). This framing of the music festival has strong links to a conceptualisation of the festival as something outside of daily life and extraordinary, and where festival activities serve to help bind people together as a community (Durkheim 1912/1976).

Yet what constitutes authentic music festival practice does have some relationship to spatial scale. The emotional impact aroused while participating in these music festival events has become significant for those tourists seeking to experience some notion of an authentic 'other'. In a highly competitive market, some festival destinations have sought to provide a unique experience through the use of music festivals, a particular feature of regional and non-metropolitan development strategies (Croes, Semrad, & Rivera 2016; Gibson 2013). In these festival settings, music can be deployed to create an 'emotive narrative for tourists, as an expression of culture, a form of heritage, a signifier of place and a marker of moments' (Lashua, Spracklen, & Long 2014, p. 4). Small music festivals may foster a sense of uniqueness and intimacy, yet major outdoor music festivals are nevertheless perceived as authentic sites of freedom, perhaps because of a nostalgia associated with the counterculture music festivals of the 1960s. Major music festivals also have links to Bakhtin's (1984) notion of the carnivalesque, offering 'temporary bounded spheres of 'licensed transgression' (Griffin, Bengry-Howell, Riley, Morey, & Szmigin 2016, p. 1) in which the usual constraints of the everyday can be abandoned, thus resonating with Turner's (1984) notions of *communitas*.

## Music festival experiences

### *Liminality and communitas*

Music festivals offer important forms of participation that facilitate belonging and identification through representational and experiential processes. Engagement with music and its contribution to feelings of connectedness (as well as at times a sense of disconnection) during the festival event has been explored through the concepts of liminality and *communitas*.

Liminal events are most often understood as offering some contact with the sacred or divine, and hence facilitate the individual's transformation into a full participant of the community or group, exemplified in anthropological literature by ceremonies of initiation (Lewis & Dowsey-Magog 1993; Turner 1984). In the anthropological literature, this liminal period is conceived as a time of possibility and transformation (Turner 1974). An important part of this process of sociality is the generation of strong, often spontaneous feelings of connectedness that arise out of involvement in the community event, producing what Turner (1984) calls *communitas*. While some argue that truly liminal events can only occur within small-scale, integrated or indigenous societies, there is empirical evidence arising in cognitive neuroscience of a 'communicative musicality' (Malloch & Trevarthen 2009; Trevarthen 2002) that helps facilitate new forms of social being (Benzon 2001). Examples of such new forms of social being can be found in contemporary performative events such as electronic dance music festivals, which are understood as deliberate responses to contemporary feelings of alienation and instability. Nor are they limited to small-scale participation. Indeed, many electronic dance music festivals have become platforms for associated art and lifestyle industries with audiences at some events attracting large-scale audiences in the thousands (St John 2015). As this body of research on music festivals suggests, even while transient, the generation of feelings of attachment is important to consolidating feelings of belonging to a specific community that continues beyond the event period.

The reference to liminality and *communitas* in the conceptualisation of the music festival as an event apart from the everyday is a common grounding for many studies on festivals. The festival is conceived as a liminal and temporary spatialised process in which participation can lead to an 'enacting [of] lifestyles' and experiments with identities that are often created through playing with notions of the authentic and the tribal/primitive other (Lavenda 1992; Melucci 1989; St John 1997). Moreover, many alternative music festivals become sites for a 'pilgrimage to a location outside the parameters of the everyday where inspired travellers seek affirmation and wholeness, orchestrat[ing] the (re)production, the becoming, of self, identity, attitude, lifestyle' (St John 1997, p. 173). Such music festivals are explicitly framed in terms of facilitating access to something sacred or fundamental within a community or group, and participation enables the creation of a sense of connectivity and belonging. Yet the affect and impact reaches beyond that of the immediate time and space of the event. In this framework, a sense of community comes into being within the festival event and then disperses, to be reformed and reactivated at the next festival. The generation of intense feelings of belonging can operate across different social structures, including class, ethnicity or gender, and serve to reaffirm group identity and belonging, and this sense of deep connection is significant to the maintenance of social structures (Costa 2002; Falassi 1987; Prorok 1998; St John 1997).

## *Emotion, affect and the senses*

Research in a range of disciplines has started to think about the relationship between place and music more specifically in terms of music's unique qualities. A focus on music can help us explore the emotional and intuitive aspects of our social life, qualities missing from the visual and rational modes of study (DeNora 2000; Duffy, Waitt, & Gibson 2007; Smith 1994; Wood & Smith 2004; Wood, Duffy, & Smith 2007). This approach to music and its emotional affects is significant to understandings of how the world works. Our emotional responses locate us within specific networks of human and non-human relations (Wood & Smith 2004). Music is significant to the ways in which individuals experience themselves and others, in part helping people to feel their subjectivity in certain contexts: for example, in terms of ethnicity, class or subcultural group. Music operates by tapping into our emotional and intuitive selves, and this provides a means through which to examine how the emotions influence social interactions (DeNora 2000; Juslin & Sloboda 2001). Simultaneously, space becomes shaped by how people respond to the embodied, emotional and fleshy experience of music (Waitt & Duffy 2010). The significance of music performance within the festival is because it arouses feeling:

> [m]usic's evocative qualities are used to add credence to the visual images, to convey excitement, tradition, continuity with the past, elegance or escape. Why music is powerful in this regard is in part simply because of its ability to elicit emotional responses from audiences – excitement, energy or melancholy.
>
> *(Gibson & Connell 2005, p. 72)*

Emotional and bodily responses to sound, music and the presence of others can set up an ambiance in which music festival attendees are caught up by the thrill of an event in ways that bring individuals 'into the groove together' (Keil & Feld 1994, p. 167). Work in the social sciences in the past few decades has emphasised the significance of the senses and the body in instituting forms of sociality because of the ways in which sensory experience contributes to concepts of the self and culture and their interrelationship (Lowe 2012). The generation of strong, often spontaneous feelings of connectedness arising out of participants' responses to the sensual (visual, oral, olfactory and haptic) elements of an event is a significant part of the process of sociality and producing *communitas* (Turner 1984).

However, musical engagement is not a benign process. Listening to and engaging with music can create an affective ambience that encourages an openness to others and belonging together (Fiumara 2006), or, conversely, individuals and groups may feel alienated and excluded. Music is significant to reinforcing hegemonic sociocultural views. It also has an important role in disrupting as well as creating forms of social cohesion (Duffy 2005). Thus, the sonic and visceral experiences of a music festival structure the social, spatial, cultural, economic as well as political relationships of everyday life (Attali 1992; DeNora 2000).

Rodaway (1994, p. 4) argues that we need to critically examine the role of the senses because such an approach contributes to 'the fullness of a living world or everyday life as a multisensual and multidimensional situatedness in space an in relationship to places'. Visual and textual frameworks and methodologies have provided important insight into the representational processes and practices of music festivals, yet these approaches are less appropriate for capturing the aural characteristics of sound and music and their associations with the emotional, affective, sensual and visceral ways we engage at a music festival (Duffy, Waitt, Gorman-Murray, & Gibson 2011; Saldanha 2007; Waitt & Duffy 2010; Wood et al. 2007). Recent work in this area has utilised a variety of methods, including a focus on listening (Duffy & Waitt 2011; Waitt & Duffy 2010), the senses (Duffy & Mair forthcoming) and ethnography (Duffy 2005; Morton 2005). All of these have 'the potential to reconfigure listeners' relationships to place, to open up new modes of attention and movement, and in so doing to rework places' (Gallagher 2015, p. 468).

## Music festivals, economic development strategies and tourism

Florida's (2002) creative industries framework can help conceptualise the role of music festivals – and festivals more broadly – in local economic development (Cudny 2014). Music festivals are understood as part of a range of cultural activities that attract the so-called creative classes into economically depressed urban areas that then help initiate urban regeneration through a cultural economy (Gibson 2013). In addition, cultural industries have also given rise to what has been termed 'experience societies' (Schulze 1993) and the 'experience economy' (Freire-Gibb 2011), where, particularly in developed countries, surplus time and money allow for increased participation in leisure activities and heightened emotional experiences (Aikaterini, Seonjeong, Liang, & Lanlung 2014; Cudny 2014). Music festivals readily fit within this experiential framework (Aikaterini et al. 2014; Ballantyne et al. 2014; Lee et al. 2012; Morgan 2008). An enjoyable festival experience is not only desirable but a source of competitive advantage. According to Ballantyne et al. (2014) the music festival experience can provide a range of psychological benefits such as attendees developing or reflecting on their understanding of themselves and the cultivation of new expressions of self-identity. There are also social benefits, such as connecting with others who share similar or different beliefs, creating a sense of community, participating in social activities and engaging in intense and concentrated interaction (Ballantyne et al. 2014). While the location of music festivals has been an important component of development strategies in specific locations, the tourism industry has also started to consider the benefits arising from a focus on experience. For example, music festivals on cruise ships are increasingly significant in the calendar of cultural tourism experience (Cashman 2017). Typically devoted to a specific genre of music, modern cruise music festivals combine the luxury of a cruise with the 'hedonistic, neo-tribal experience of a music festival' (Cashman 2017, p. 249).

## Conclusion

The boundaries between the music festival and its geographical and social context have also become increasingly the focus for understanding the influences and effects of a festival. A festival may spill beyond its temporal and spatial boundaries, a process called festivalisation (Cremorna 2007; Roche 2011). As Roche (2011) argues, festivalisation processes draw on collective understandings and practices of space, time and agency that are then deployed so as to shape communal notions of identity and belonging. Moreover, these events are interpellated into a community's calendar of 'memorable and narratable pasts, with the sociocultural rhythm of life in the present, and with anticipated futures' (Roche 2011, pp. 127–128; see also Duffy et al. 2011). Festivals, rather than transcending the everyday, are now also examined for the ways they are intimately embedded within the public sphere as normative and at times transformative processes (Giorgi & Sassatelli 2011). Thus, music festivals are becoming increasingly important in developing economic and social development strategies.

## References

Aikaterini, M., Seonjeong, L., Liang, T. & Lanlung, C. (2014). The experience economy approach to festival marketing: vivid memory and attendee loyalty. *Journal of Services Marketing, 28*(1), 22–35.
Anderson, B. (1983). *Imagined Communities*. London: Verso.
Attali, J. (1992). *Noise: The Political Economy of Music*. Minneapolis: University of Minneapolis Press.
Bakhtin, M. (1984). *Rabelais and His World*. Trans. by H. Iswolsky. Bloomington: Indiana University Press.
Ballantyne, J., Ballantyne, R. & Packer, J. (2014). Designing and managing music festival experiences to enhance attendees' psychological and social benefits. *Musicae Scientiae, 18*(1), 65–83.
Benzon, W. (2001). *Beethoven's Anvil: Music in Mind and Culture*. New York: Basic Books.
Boden, A. & Hedley, P. (2017). *The Three Choirs Festival: A History (New and Revised Edition)*. Melton: Boydell & Brewer.

Brennan-Horley, C., Connell, J. & Gibson, C. (2007). The Parkes Elvis Revival Festival: economic development and contested place identities in rural Australia. *Geographical Research*, 45(1), 71–84.

Carney, G. (1997). *The Sounds of People and Places: Readings in Geography of American Folk and Popular Music*. Lanham, MD, University Press of America.

Cashman, D. (2017). 'The most atypical experience of my life': the experience of popular music festivals on cruise ships. *Tourist Studies*, 17(3), 245–262.

Connell, J. & Gibson, C. (2003). *Sound Tracks: Popular Music, Identity, and Place*. London: Routledge.

Cornish, H. (2015). Not all singing and dancing: Padstow, folk festivals and belonging. *Ethnos: Journal of Anthropology*, 81(4), 631–347.

Costa, X. (2002). Festive identity: personal and collective identity in the Fire Carnival of the 'Fallas' (València, Spain). *Social Identities*, 8(2), 321–345.

Cremorna, V.A. (2007). Introduction: the festivalising process. In Hauptfleisch, T., Lev-Aladgem, S., Martin, J., Sauter, W. & Schoenmakers, H. (Eds.), *Festivalising! Theatrical Events, Politics and Culture* (pp. 5–13). Amsterdam: Rodopi.

Croes, R., Semrad, K. & Rivera, M. (2016). The relevance and value of music festivals as relational goods in SIDS. *Tourism Travel and Research Association: Advancing Tourism Research Globally*, 24. Available at http://scholarworks.umass.edu/ttra/2012/Oral/24.

Cudny, W. (2014). Festivals as a subject for geographical research. *Geografisk Tidsskrift-Danish Journal of Geography*, 114(2), 132–142.

Curtis, R.A. (2010). Australia's capital of jazz? The (re) creation of place, music and community at the Wangaratta Jazz Festival. *Australian Geographer*, 41(1), 101–116.

DeNora, T. (2000). *Music in Everyday Life*. Cambridge: Cambridge University Press.

Derrett, R. (2003). Making sense of how festivals demonstrate a community's sense of place. *Event Management*, 8(1), 49–58.

Duffy, M. (2003). 'We find ourselves again': (re)creating identity through performance in the community music festival. *Australasian Music Research*, 7, 103–112.

Duffy, M. (2005). Performing identity within a multicultural framework. *Social and Cultural Geography*, 6(5), 677–692. Duffy, M. & Mair, J. (forthcoming). Engaging the senses to explore community events. *Event Management*.

Duffy, M. & Waitt, G. (2011). Sound diaries: a method for listening to place. *Aether: The Journal of Media Geography*, 7, 119–136.

Duffy, M., Waitt, G. & Gibson, C. (2007). Get into the groove: the role of sound in generating a sense of belonging through street parades. *Altitude*. Available at www.thealtitudejournal.com/.

Duffy, M., Waitt, G., Gorman-Murray, A. & Gibson, C. (2011). Bodily rhythms: corporeal capacities to engage with festival spaces. *Emotion, Space and Society*, 4(1), 17–24.

Durkheim, E. (1912/1976). *The Elementary Forms of the Religious Life*. Trans. J. Swain. London: Allen and Unwin.

Erlmann, V. (1996). The aesthetics of the global imagination: reflections on world music in the 1990s. *Public Culture*, 8, 467–487.

Falassi, A. (Ed.). (1987). *Time Out of Time: Essays on the Festival*. Albuquerque: University of New Mexico Press.

Feld, S. (1984). Sound structure as social structure. *Ethnomusicology*, 28(3), 383–409.

Fiumara, G.C. (2006). *The Other Side of Language: A Philosophy of Listening*. London and New York: Routledge.

Florida, R. (2002). *The Rise of the Creative Class*. New York: Basic Books.

Fortier, A.-M. (1999). Re-membering places and the performance of belonging(s). *Theory, Culture & Society*, 16(2), 41–64.

Frey, B. (1994). The economics of music festivals. *Journal of Cultural Economics*, 18(1), 29–39.

Freire-Gibb, L.C. (2011). The rise and fall of the concept of the experience economy in the local economic development of Denmark. *European Planning Studies*, 19(10), 1839–1853.

Frith, S. (1996). *Performing Rites: Evaluating Popular Music*. Oxford: Oxford University Press.

Gallagher, M. (2015). Sounding ruins: reflections on the production of an 'audio drift'. *Cultural Geographies*, 22(3), 467–485.

Getz, D. & Page, S.J. (2016). Progress and prospects for event tourism research. *Tourism Management*, 52(February), 593–631.

Gibson, C. (2013). Music festivals and regional development policy: towards a festival ecology. *Perfect Beat*, 14(2), 40–157.

Gibson, C. & Connell, J. (2005). *Music and Tourism: On the Road Again*. Clevedon: Channel View.
Giorgi, L. & Sassatelli, M. (2011). Introduction. In Delanty, G. (Ed.), *Festivals and the Cultural Public Sphere* (pp. 1–11). London and New York: Routledge.
Goulding, C. & Saren, M. (2009). Performing identity: an analysis of gender expressions at the Whitby goth festival. *Consumption, Markets and Culture*, 12(1), 27–46.
Griffin, C., Bengry-Howell, A., Riley, S., Morey, Y. & Szmigin, I. (2016). 'We achieve the impossible': discourses of freedom and escape at music festivals and free parties. *Journal of Consumer Culture*. doi:10.1177/1469540516684187.
Hudson, S., Roth, M., Madden, T. & Hudson, R. (2015). The effects of social media on emotions, brand relationship quality, and word of mouth: an empirical study of music festival attendees. *Tourism Management*, 47(April), 68–76.
Jodie, G. (2015). Examining the cultural value of festivals. *International Journal of Event and Festival Management*, 6(2), 122–134.
Juslin, P.N. & Sloboda, J.A. (2001). *Music and Emotion: Theory and Research*. Oxford: Oxford University Press.
Keil, C. & Feld, S. (1994). *Music Grooves*. Chicago, IL: University of Chicago Press.
Keller, M.S. (2007) Transplanting multiculturalism: Swiss musical traditions reconfigured in multicultural Victoria. *Victorian Historical Journal*, 78(2), 187–205.
Kim, H. & Jamal, T. (2007). Touristic quest for existential authenticity. *Annals of Tourism Research*, 34(1), 181–201.
Laing, J. & Mair, J. (2015). Music festivals and social inclusion: the festival organisers' perspective. *Leisure Sciences*, 37(3), 252–268.
Lashua, B., Spracklen, K. & Long, P. (2014). Introduction to the special issue: music and Tourism. *Tourist Studies*, 14(1), 3–9.
Lavenda, R. (1992). Festivals and the creation of public culture: whose voice(s)? In Karp, I., Mullen Kreamer, C. & Lavine, S. (Eds.), *Museums and Communities: The Politics of Public Space* (pp. 76–104). Washington, DC: Smithsonian Institute Press.
Lee, I., Arcodia, C. & Lee, T.J. (2012). Benefits of visiting a multicultural festival: the case of South Korea. *Tourism Management*, 33(2), 334–340.
Lewis, L. & Dowsey-Magog, P. (1993). The Maleny 'fire event': rehearsals toward neo-liminality. *The Australian Journal of Anthropology*, 4(3), 198–219.
Lomax, A. (1976). *Cantometrics: An Approach to the Anthropology of Music*. Berkeley: University of California Press.
Lowe, K. (2012). The social life of the senses: charting directions. *Sociology Compass*, 6(3), 271–282.
MacCannell, D. (1976). *The Tourist: A New Theory of the Leisure Class*. Berkeley and London: University of California Press.
Mair, J. & Duffy, M. (2015). Community events and social justice in urban growth areas. *Journal of Policy Research in Tourism, Leisure and Events*, 7(3), 282–298.
Malloch, S. & Trevarthen, C. (2009). Musicality: communicating the vitality and interests of life. In Malloch, S. & Trevarthen, C. (Eds.), *Communicative Musicality: Exploring the Basis of Human Companionship*. Oxford: Oxford University Press.
Martin, P. (1995). *Sounds and Society: Themes in the Sociology of Music*. Manchester and New York: Manchester University Press.
Matheson, C. (2005). Festivity and sociability: a study of Celtic music festival. *Tourism Culture & Communication*, 5(3), 149–163.
Melucci, A. (1989). *Nomads of the Present: Social Movements and Individual Needs in Contemporary Society*. London: Hutchinson Radius.
Morgan, M. (2008). What makes a good festival? Understanding the event experience. *Event Management*, 12(2), 81–93.
Morton, F. (2005). Performing ethnography: Irish traditional music sessions and new musical spaces. *Social & Cultural Geography*, 6(5), 661–676.
Osterlund-Potzsch, S. (2004). Communicating ethnic heritage: Swedish-speaking Finn descendants in North America. In Kockel, U. & Craith, M.N. (Eds.), *Communicating Cultures* (pp. 14–41). Munster: LIT.
Permezel, M. & Duffy, M. (2007). Negotiating cultural difference in local communities: the role of the body, dialogues and performative practices in local communities. *Geographical Research*, 45(4), 358–375.

Prorok, C. (1998). Dancing in the fire: ritually constructing Hindu identity in a Malaysian landscape. *Journal of Cultural Geography*, *17*(2), 89–114.

Quinn, B. (2003). Symbols, practices and myth-making: cultural perspectives on the Wexford Festival Opera. *Tourism Geographies*, *5*(3), 329–349.

Robertson, M., Yeoman, I., Smith, K. & McMahon-Beattie, U. (2015). Technology, society, and visioning the future of music festivals. *Event Management*, *19*(4), 567–587.

Roche, M. (2011). Festivalisation, cosmopolitanism and European culture: on the sociocultural significance of mage-events. In Giorgi, L. Sassatelli, M. & Delanty, G. (Eds.), *Festivals and the Cultural Public Sphere* (pp. 124–141). London and New York: Routledge.

Rodaway, P. (1994). *Sensuous Geographies: Body, Sense and Place*. New York: Routledge.

Saldanha, A. (2007). *Psychedelic White: Goa Trance and the Viscosity of Race*. Minneapolis: University of Minnesota Press.

Schulze, G. (1993). *Die Erlebnisgesellschaft: Kultursoziologie der Gegenwart* [*The experience society: Cultural Sociology of the Present*]. Frankfurt: Campus Verlag.

Smith, S. (1994). Soundscape. *Area*, *26*(3), 232–240.

Steiner, C. & Reisinger, Y. (2006). Understanding existential authenticity. *Annals of Tourism Research*, *33*(2), 299–318.

St John, G. (1997). Going feral: authentica on the edge of Australian culture. *The Australian Journal of Anthropology*, *8*(2), 167–189.

St John, G. (2015). Introduction to weekend societies: EDM festivals and event-cultures. *Dancecult: Journal of Electronic Dance Music Culture*, *7*(1), 1–14.Szmigin, I., Bengry-Howell, A., Morey, Y., Griffin, C. & Riley, S. (2017). Socio-spatial authenticity at co-created music festivals. *Annals of Tourism Research*, *63*, 1–11. doi:10.1016/j.annals.2016.12.007.

Trevarthen, C. (2002). Origins of musical identity: evidence from infancy for musical social awareness. In Macdonald, R. Hargreaves, D. & Miell, D. (Eds.), *Musical Identities* (pp. 21–38). Oxford: Oxford University Press.

Turner, V. (1974). *Dramas, Fields, and Metaphors: Symbolic Action in Human Society*. Ithaca, NY: Cornell University Press.

Turner, V. (1984). Liminality and performance genres. In MacAloon, J. (Ed.), *Rite, Drama, Festival, Spectacle: Rehearsals toward a Theory of Cultural Performance* (pp. 19–41). Philadelphia, PA: Institute for the Study of Human Issues.Waitt, G. & Duffy, M. (2010). Listening and tourism studies. *Annals of Tourism Research*, *37*(2), 457–477.

White, L. (2015). Swiss and Italian identities: exploring heritage, culture and community in regional Australia. In Jepson, A. and Clarke, A. (Eds.), *Routledge Advances in Events Research Book Series: Exploring Community Festivals and Events* (pp. 197–211). Oxon and New York: Routledge.

Wood, N. & Smith, S.J. (2004). Instrumental routes to emotional geographies. *Social & Cultural Geography*, *5*(4), 533–548.

Wood, N., Duffy, M. & Smith, S.J. (2007). The art of doing (geographies of) music. *Environment and Planning D: Society and Space*, *25*(5), 867–889.

# 32
# RELIGIOUS AND SPIRITUAL FESTIVALS AND EVENTS

*Ruth Dowson*

## Introduction

This chapter attempts a critical review and appraisal of the current state of research into religious and spiritual festivals and associated events. The literature emerges from a wide range of multidisciplinary sources, which have historically been situated in separate, traditional disciplinary silos. The chapter also investigates research into the religious origins of contemporary festivals, and questions whether and how meanings can be separately, or both, spiritual and religious. It notes the de-spiritualisation of religious festivals. Finally, the chapter assesses the future development of conceptual and theoretical approaches to religious and spiritual festivals, from empirical positioning to qualitative ethnographic perspectives (Sparkes & Smith 2013) and critical events research (Lamond & Platt 2016).

## Research on religious and spiritual festivals

Whilst the study of festivals from an events management perspective is fairly new (for only the past 20 years at most: Bowdin, Allen, O'Toole, Harris, & McDonnell 2011; Getz 2012), historically, academic writers have previously addressed the theme of festivals through the lenses of religion and spirituality, celebration and ritual. For example, the French sociologist and philosopher Emile Durkheim, whose 1912 publication 'The Elementary Forms of Religious Life' contemplated a theory of religion, identified the concept of 'collective effervescence' (Durkheim 2008 [1912]), inspired by and imbued within religious celebrations and festivals. During the Second World War, the Russian philosopher Mikhail Bakhtin explored the carnivalesque (Hirschkop & Shepherd 2001), a concept emanating from religious festival origins. The British anthropologist Victor Turner authored compelling studies of religious rituals, rites of passage, celebration and festivity (Turner 1982), and the Italian anthropologist and folklorist Alessandro Falassi (1987) focussed his research on festivals and ritual, identifying an influential typology of ritual characteristics found within religious festivals. These four researchers in particular have contributed to the formation of academic thinking on the topic of religious and spiritual festivals, although it seems unlikely that any would have considered this area outside of their own disciplinary contexts.

An examination of more recent literature continues to demonstrate the multidisciplinary nature of the study of festivals in general – and even explicitly religious and spiritual festivals – but such research is generally undertaken within and from separate disciplinary silos. The range of disciplines is surprisingly broad, and an investigation of journal titles in which such articles are published, as well as article and monograph titles themselves, finds examples in a range of subject areas (see Table 32.1).

However, historical silos are beginning to blend across disciplines, with the emergence of interdisciplinary fields of study. These include the sociology of religion (Brown 2006; Davie, Heelas, & Woodhead 2003; Flanagan & Jupp 2010; Lundskow 2008; Woodhead & Catto 2012); the more recent appearance of religious tourism, events and pilgrimage as an area of research (Laing & Frost 2016; Leppakari & Griffin 2017; Norman 2011; Pinho & Garofalo 2016; Raj & Morpeth 2015; Timothy & Olsen 2006); and the new development of the critical event studies turn (Hall & Page 2015; Jepson & Clarke 2016; Lamond & Platt 2016; Lamond & Spracklen 2014; Merkel 2015; Robinson 2016; Rojek 2013; Spracklen & Lamond 2016; Stanton 2015). This indicates the coming of age of the study of events and festivals from their management and logistics subject origins (Bowdin, Allen, O'Toole, Harris, & McDonnell 2011; Getz 2012). Figure 32.1 suggests a framework that maps the

*Table 32.1* Range of disciplines with research related to religious and spiritual festivals

| Discipline | Authors |
|---|---|
| Anthropology | Bilby (2010), Karin (2014), Kuligowski (2016), Miles (2011) and Smith (1989) |
| Cultural history | Rao and Dutta (2012) |
| Cultural theory | Hirschkop and Shepherd (2001) |
| Drama | Chen (2011) |
| Economics | Akay, Karabulut, and Martinsson (2015) |
| Environmental psychology | Ruback, Pandey, and Kohli (2008) |
| Environment and water | Viji and Shrinithivihahshini (2017) |
| Ethnology | Håland (2014) and de Maaker (2013) |
| Geography | Alvarado-Sizzo, Frejomil, and Crispín (2017), Egresi and Kara (2014) and Justin (2017) |
| Linguistics | Pena Nunez (2016) |
| Marketing | Pfadenhauer (2010) and Quezado, Alcântara, Costa, Arruda, and Mota (2016) |
| Mental health | Bottorff (2015) and Mellor, Hapidzal, Teh, Ganesan, Yeow, Latif, and Cummins (2012) |
| Religion | Liu (2015), Ross (2013), Sadovina (2017) and Yazbak (2011) |
| Risk | Illiyas, Mani, Pradeepkumar, and Mohan (2013) |
| Spirituality | Cheer, Belhassen, and Kujawa (2017) |
| Theology | Chryssides (1999), Cobb (2005), Evans (2006), Mart (2015), Plantinga and Rozeboom (2003), Ross and Baker (2015), Ross (2013), Spinks (2010), Ward (2005), White (2000) and Wroe (1988) |
| Tourism | Aragão (2014), Borges, Moreira, and Perinotto (2015), Cheer, Belhassen, and Kujawa (2017), Cohen (2012), Collins-Kreiner (2010), Kalman (2014), Lee and Huang (2015), Lee, Fu, and Chang (2015), Matheson, Rimmer, and Tinsley (2014), Shinde (2011) and Suntikul and Dorji (2016) |

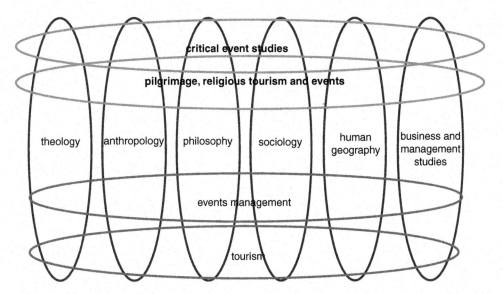

*Figure 32.1* The development of interdisciplinary research into religious and spiritual festivals

development of the study of religious and spiritual festivals from the perspectives of separated silos, into the more recent emergence of critical event studies, linking with the study of pilgrimage, religious tourism and events.

While spirituality and religious aspects may only appear tangentially in some of the relevant research published in these silos, nevertheless such studies can still inform the body of knowledge. For example, recent research on contemporary music festivals by Robinson alludes to the spiritual or mystical elements of the festival experience, especially in those festivals that embrace collaborative forms of participation (Robinson 2015; McKay 2015). Robinson connects these participative or 'No Spectators' festivals with Bakhtinian carnivalesque, in opposition to the 'perverted... spectator-inducing aspects of concert-model festivals' (Robinson 2015, pp. 144–145), which have arguably been overwhelmingly corrupted by commercialisation and sponsorship. Related research into raves and freeparties by Dowson, Lomax and Theodore-Saltibus (2015) observed participants' explicitly spiritual experiences within the sacred space of such illicit festive events. Indeed, some sound collectives have evolved through the rave and freeparty scene into producing independent rave-themed festivals of their own, followed by the introduction of specific rave-stages at larger (and more commercial) music festivals. Such occurrences might be a reflection of the commercialisation of festivals generally, but there is a gap in current research concerning the spiritual experiential aspects of mainstream music festivals that might be explored through the critical event studies route.

Equally, studies of religion and spirituality may either make tangential reference to, or ignore, the elements of festival. For example, Brown (2006) examines developments within the religious context of British society but makes no explicit mention of religious or spiritual festivals, despite a short discussion of Catholic pilgrimages. Instead, Brown focusses elsewhere on the charismatic renewal of the 1980s which has influenced the evolution of Christian festival-like events in the 21st century. Descriptions of charismatic church gatherings in which 'ecstatic people sway in unison' (Brown 2006, p. 299) more resemble the drug-fuelled bliss of the rave than a traditional church service, yet the comparison remains unmade. Ward's 2005 monograph provides a deep theological analysis of the impact of cultural change and transformation on religious practice but makes no mention of religious or spiritual festivals, or their consequences for churches. Even the 'holy trinity' of leading sociology of religion academics, Davie, Heelas and Woodhead, also omit to consider explicitly the impact of religious festivals in their work on the future of religion. This is despite their recognition of the influence of the experiential in teaching religious studies in schools (2003, p. 2) and their recognition that both the Church of England and Roman Catholic churches in the UK provide a focus of celebration during major Christian festivals (Christmas, Easter), along with rites of passage (baptisms, weddings and funerals) (2003, p. 93). Perhaps this omission should not come as a surprise, as these authors' perspectives (or their hermeneutical lens, to borrow a theological term) originate from within the scope of mainstream theology and sociology of religion, so why should they therefore be expected to consider festivals within their studies? And yet across the globe, beyond the windows of the ivory towers of traditional theological academia, lie lands where festivals flourish, whether religious, spiritual or secular in nature, attended by millions of people, affecting not only their beliefs but also their everyday lives and even providing employment. Or might such considerations resemble the 'distortion and manipulation' (Turner 1982, p. 297) of Boorstin's 'pseudo-events' (1962), and therefore be deemed as unacceptable for study by academics from disciplines such as theology or sociology of religion? Sadly, the responses of events management academics (and perhaps more so for practitioner-academics, like myself), and especially for those with an inclination towards critical event studies, to what perhaps appears to be not only ignorance of the nuances of our subject but sometimes even a lack of awareness of its very existence, result in an achingly frustrating view of those who either ignore or write about 'our' subject yet come from a non-events background. Such resentment might be addressed by the collaborative efforts of truly interdisciplinary approaches to research.

However, the recent corpus of research into new developments in Christian worship provide evidence of a more insightful approach, acknowledging the positive impact of the advance of new Christian festivals that resemble the secular music festival, often with a greater emphasis on the ecstatic experience of a freeparty (Evans 2006; Mart 2015; Plantinga & Rozeboom 2003; Ross 2013; Ross & Baker 2015; Spinks 2010; Ward 2005; White 2000; Wroe 1988).

## Festivals: religious and spiritual?

Classic studies of festival have often selected autochthonous (indigenous, aboriginal) tribes and groupings for comparison with contemporaneous practices. Durkheim (2008 [1912]), for example, studied aboriginal tribes, and whilst his work was met by strong methodological challenges, the assumptions he made have influenced deeply the subsequent development of theory, such as the social nature of religion, and the foundations of community cohesion through the celebration of sacred times, places and occurrences. Jepson and Clarke's (2016) study of contemporary festivals, situated within the emerging turn to critical event studies, recognises the depth of connectivity with the religious origins of 'festival', particularly in producing the experience of togetherness and transcendence, or what Turner labelled '*communitas*' (Turner & Turner 1978).

So, how do the religious origins of festivals influence religious and spiritual festivals, or even the non-religious and non-spiritual festivals, of today?

The celebrations of the three Abrahamic religions (Judaism, Christianity and Islam) are structured around the concepts of times and seasons. For example, the way we use our time, the amount of time we allocate to different activities, the way those activities are structured, and what activities take precedence, indicate the value we place on those activities. Observant Muslims will stop all other activities to pray five times during a 24-hour period, often traveling to the nearest mosque or masjid. The Muslim calendar is lunar and shorter than the solar year, so Ramadan, a month-long period of fasting, moves forward each year by approximately ten days, migrating slowly through the seasons.

Similarly, Christian practices and festivals reflect the priorities of the early church. Sunday is the day of rest, and so the flow of the week is important to Christian ritual and worship. Within each day itself, the church adopted the Jewish practice of the day beginning as night fell. As a result, there are celebrations of the Eve of a festival, such as All Hallows' Eve (celebrated as Halloween by the secular world), and Christmas Eve; whilst morning, mid-day, evening and night prayer form a daily structure of worship and prayer, in addition to Sunday services (White 2000).

Christian rites, rituals and festival celebrations are ordered around the three seasons of Christmas, Easter and Pentecost (White 2000, p. 57), with special time prior to Christmas (Advent) and Easter (Lent), whilst in between comes 'Ordinary Time' (White 2000, p. 66). Some dates are fixed (sanctoral cycle), whilst others move (temporal cycle) (White 2000, p. 63). Some additions were made after the 4th century, including All Saints' Day, the Assumption of the Blessed Virgin Mary and Corpus Christi. The Roman Catholic and Orthodox churches also honour saints' days and festivals commemorating holy people, acts and places, celebrated in different ways in different places, initiating pilgrimages, processions and feasting. Thus, religious practice has influenced the concepts of sacred and profane time, and liminal space. The sacred time of religious festivals provides a 'time out of time' (Falassi 1987), as well as a time before and after sacred time, which is not sacred. These precepts have influenced the development of the festivals we know today.

Having identified the origins of religious festivals, it may also be helpful, in today's context, to attempt to define terms – what do we mean by 'religious' and 'spiritual' festivals? Unfortunately, the answer is complex and longer than the space available here. However, Flanagan and Jupp offer a comprehensive discussion of the meaning of spirituality from a sociological perspective, concluding that 'spirituality partly overlaps with theology, but also belongs to religion' (2010, p. 2). This understanding is evidenced by the traditions of the major faiths that contain elements of organised religious practice, as well as individual spirituality.

## Festivalisation and eventisation of faith

Religious festivals, feasts, fasts and mystery plays of past millennia have developed into the festivals and events that monopolise the postmodern cultural landscape of the 21st century in what might be recognised as the 'eventization of life' today (Dowson 2015). Whilst the Internet age impacts on social aspects of daily life, bringing with it private individualisation, the 21st century has witnessed an explosion in experiential marketing as organisations review their strategic direction in an effort to better to attract, involve and animate their customers and clients within relationships. Religious organisations of all faiths are no different, engaging with communities and building new relationships through celebratory festivals and other events (Dowson 2015). The 'eventization of faith' was introduced by Pfadenhauer, who applied the concept of experiential marketing to a study of an international Roman Catholic youth festival held in Germany in 2005 (Pfadenhauer 2010).

A question arises regarding the meanings of religious and spiritual festivals: can they be both spiritual and religious? A thorough literature search identifies tens of thousands of possible sources, more for 'religious festivals' than for 'spiritual festivals', with some overlaps. From an analysis of this literature, there appear to be identifiable thematic groupings of research, outlined later.

The first theme discusses and analyses specific religious and spiritual festivals. Some publications discuss specific Hindu festivals, including Kumbh Mela, Holi (Rao & Dutta 2012), Thaipusam (Mellor et al. 2012) and Mela (Carnegie & Smith 2006) as well as specific Hindu saints (Pechilis 2009). Others consider Muslim festivals, including Hajj (Al-Muhrzi & Alsawafi 2017; Raj & Morpeth 2015), Muharram (Rao & Dutta 2012) and Nabi Rubin (Yazbak 2011). Roman Catholic and Orthodox Christian festivals are widely investigated, whether directly associated with a holy person (e.g. a saint), or a holy place, or time (Alvarado-Sizzo et al. 2017; Pena Nunez 2016; Pinho & Garofalo 2016; Viji & Shrinithivihahshini 2017). Some studies focus on specific age groups (Pfadenhauer 2010; Quezado et al. 2016), whilst others examine New Age, spiritual and syncretic festivals (Sadovina 2017; Chen 2011), along with pagan aspects (Håland 2014), animism and folk religion (Liu 2015).

A second theme assesses the 'spiritual' aspects of festivals, from motivations and attitudes (Raj & Morpeth 2015), to multicultural festivals which may have religious origins (Lee & Huang 2015), and festivals with or without explicit connections to religion and spirituality (Bottorff 2015; Ross 2013). A third theme finds explicit or implicit inclusion of festival within studies of aspects of spirituality or religion: those publications that make explicit mention of religious and spiritual aspects of festivals tend to be found in specific journals, such as the *International Journal of Religious Tourism and Pilgrimage*, which provides many examples and encourages such academic discussion. Additional minor themes include the study of festivals within a wider context and the de-spiritualisation of religious festivals, which would traditionally be addressed through the lens of sociology or anthropology, but which is found more recently within critical tourism (Yazbak 2011).

However, there appears to be a gap in academic discussion of religious festivals' meanings being overtaken by cultural appropriation, such as the Hindu Holi festival, whereby a religious festival morphs into a non-spiritual, secular 'colour run', appropriating parts of the religious festival's culture, actions and structure, but not its meaning.

The Hajj is the most-discussed mass participation event in academic literature, along with many Roman Catholic pilgrimages, yet events and festivals attended by the Pope attract large crowds but little research, including the largest event in papal history, which took place in Manila, Philippines in 2015, with an estimated attendance of up to seven million people (ABS-CBN News 2015).

## Future development of theory and research

There are several areas which could usefully be researched in future. The concept of 'eventization of faith' proposed by Pfadenhauer (2010) could be advanced, following the process of the conceptual maturity of festivalisation. Future research might explore the spiritual experiential aspects of mainstream music festivals, through the critical event studies route. Additionally, emerging themes identified through this research that could be addressed in future research include identity, community, growth/learning/development/self-awareness, protest/hegemony and spectacle.

Whilst there has been a preponderance of quantitative analysis in recent research, the development of qualitative ethnographic approaches (Sparkes & Smith 2013) is increasing and would complement critical events research. Finally, encouraging dialogue across disciplinary boundaries through international research, with researchers from different perspectives would aid a move away from silos towards critical integrated perspectives. Engagement between new and existing academic associations could support such measures.

## References

ABS-CBN News. (2015). *Luneta Mass is largest event in papal history.* Retrieved from http://news.abs-cbn.com/nation/01/18/15/luneta-mass-largest-papal-event-history.

Akay, A., Karabulut, G. & Martinsson, P. (2015). Cooperation and punishment: The effect of religiosity and religious festival. *Economics Letters, 130*(1), 43–46.

Alvarado-Sizzo, I., Frejomil, E. P. & Crispín, Á. S. (2017). Religious tourism in southern Mexico: Regional scopes of the festival of the Immaculate Conception. *Geoforum, 83*(1), 14–25.

Aragão, I. R. (2014). Turismo Cultural-Religioso, Festa Católica e Patrimônio em São Cristóvão - Sergipe – Brasil (Cultural Tourism: Religious, Catholic Feast and Heritage in São Cristóvão, Sergipe, Brazil). *PASOS Revista de Turismo y Patrimonio Cultural, 12*(1), 145–158.

Bilby, K. (2010). Surviving secularization: Masking the spirit of Jankunu (john canoe) festivals of the Caribbean. *New West Indian Guide, 84*(3–4), 179–223.

Boorstin, D. J. (1962). *The Image: A Guide to Pseudo-Events in America.* New York, NY: Harper & Row.

Borges, D. M., Moreira, G. L. & Perinotto, A. R. C. (2015). Turismo Religioso E. Circulacao midiatica: Festas religiosas de Sao Francisco E. Sao Sebastiao Em Parnaiba/Pi (Religious Tourism and Media Circulation: At Parnaiba's Religious Festivals "St Francisco" and "St Sebastiao"). *Turydes: Revista Turismo Desarrolio Local, 8*(18), 1–22.

Bottorff, D. L. (2015). Emerging influence of transmodernism and transpersonal psychology reflected in rising popularity of transformational festivals. *Journal of Spirituality in Mental Health, 17*(1), 50–74.

Bowdin, G., Allen, J., O'Toole, W., Harris, R. & McDonnell, I. (2011) *Events Management.* 3rd ed. London, UK: Butterworth-Heinemann.

Brown, C. G. (2006). *Religion and Society in 20th-Century Britain.* Harlow, UK: Pearson Educational.

Carnegie, E. & Smith, M. (2006). Mobility, diaspora and the hybridisation of festivity: The case of the Edinburgh Mela. In Picard, D. & Robinson, M. (Eds.), *Festivals, Tourism and Social Change* (pp. 255–268). Clevedon, UK: Channel View Publications.

Cheer, J. M., Belhassen, Y. & Kujawa J. (2017). The search for spirituality in tourism: Toward a conceptual framework for spiritual tourism. *Tourism Management Perspectives, 24*, 252–256.

Chen, C. (2011). Spectacle and vulgarity: Stripper dance at temple festivals in contemporary Taiwan. *TDR: The Drama Review, 55*(1). Retrieved from https://muse.jhu.edu/article/414682.

Chryssides, G. D. (1999). *Exploring New Religions.* London, UK: Cassell.

Cohen, E. (2012). The Vegetarian Festival and the city pillar: The appropriation of a Chinese religious custom for a cult of the Thai civic religion. *Journal of Tourism and Cultural Change Volume, 10*(1), 1–21.

Cobb, K. (2005). *The Blackwell Guide to Theology and Popular Culture.* Oxford, UK: Blackwell Publishing.

Collins-Kreiner, N. (2010). Current Jewish pilgrimage tourism: Modes and models of development. *Tourism, 58*(3), 259–270.

Davie, G., Heelas, P. & Woodhead, L. (2003). *Predicting Religion: Christian, Secular and Alternative Futures.* London, UK: Routledge.

de Maaker, E. (2013). Performing the Garo Nation? Garo Wangala dancing between faith and folklore. *Asian Ethnology, 72*(2), 221–239.

Dowson, R. (2015). Religion, community and events. In Jepson, A. & Clarke, A. (Eds.), *Exploring Community Festivals and Events.* London, UK: Routledge.

Dowson, R., Lomax, D. & Theodore-Saltibus, B. (2015). Rave culture: Freeparty or protest. In Lamond, I. R. & Spracklen, K. (Eds.), *Protests as Events: Politics, Activism and Leisure.* London, UK: Rowman & Littlefield International Ltd.

Durkheim, E. (2008). [1912] *The Elementary Forms of Religious Life.* Cladis, M. S. (Ed.), Cosman C. (Trans.). Oxford, UK: Oxford University Press.

Egresi, I. & Kara, F. (2014). Motives of tourists attending small-scale events: The case of three local festivals and events in Istanbul, Turkey. *Geojournal of Tourism & Geosites, 14*(2), 93–110.
Evans, M. (2006). *Open Up the Doors: Music in the Modern Church*. London, UK: Equinox Publishing.
Falassi, A. (1987). Festival: Definition and morphology. In Falassi, A. (Ed.), *Time Out of Time: Essays on the Festival* (pp. 1–10). Albuquerque: University of New Mexico Press.
Flanagan, K. & Jupp, P. C. (Eds.). (2010). *A Sociology of Spirituality*. Farnham, UK: Ashgate Publishing.
Getz, D. (2012). *Event Studies: Theory, Research and Policy for Planned Events*. 2nd ed. London, UK: Routledge.
Håland, E. J. (2014). The legend and popular festival of Agios (Saint) Charalampos, and its parallels in the wider Greek context. *Ancient and Modern. Folk Life, 52*(1), 13–48.
Hall, C. M. & Page, S. (2015). Geography and the study of events. In Page, S. J. & Connell, J. (Ed.), *The Routledge Handbook of Events*. London, UK: Routledge.
Hirschkop, K. & Shepherd, D. (2001). *Bakhtin and Cultural Theory*. 2nd ed. Manchester, UK: Manchester University Press.
Illiyas, F. T., Mani, S. K., Pradeepkumar, A. P. & Mohan, K. (2013). Human stampedes during religious festivals: A comparative review of mass gathering emergencies in India. *International Journal of Disaster Risk Reduction, 5*(2), 10–18.
Jepson, A. & Clarke, A. (2016). *Managing and Developing Communities, Festivals and Events*. Basingstoke, UK: Palgrave Macmillan.
Justin, A. T. (2017). The aesthetics and cultural relevance of the Ier ritual festival among the Tiv of central Nigeria. *Journal of Pan African Studies, 10*(1), 325–336.
Kalman, H. (2014). *Heritage Planning: Principles and Process*. London, UK: Routledge.
Karin, V. (2014). Unto our kin and posterity – The festival of spiritual and material creativity of Dinaric Serbs, who colonized Vojvodina, as a rite of passage. (English). *Issues in Ethnology Anthropology, 9*(1), 127–132.
Kuligowski, W. (2016). Festivalizing tradition. A fieldworker's notes from the Guča Trumpet Festival (Serbia) and the Carnival of Santa Cruz de Tenerife (Spain). *Lithuanian Ethnology: Studies in Social Anthropology & Ethnology/Lietuvos Etnologija: Socialines Antropologijos Ir Etnologijos Studijos*, (16), 35–54.
Laing, J. & Frost, W. (2016). Religious events and their impacts: A new perspective for religious tourism. *International Journal of Religious Tourism and Pilgrimage, 4*(12), i–iii.
Lamond, I. & Platt, L. (2016) *Critical Event Studies: Approaches to Research*. London, UK: Palgrave Macmillan.
Lamond, I. R. & Spracklen, K. (2015). *Protests as Events: Politics, Activism and Leisure*. London, UK: Rowman & Littlefield International Ltd.
Lee, I. S. & Huang, S. (2015). Understanding motivations and benefits of attending a multicultural festival. *Tourism Analysis, 20*(2), 201–213.
Lee, T. S., Fu, C. -J. & Chang, P. -S. (2015). The support of attendees for tourism development: Evidence from religious festivals, *Taiwan, Tourism Geographies, 17*(2), 223–243.
Leppakari, M. & Griffin, K. (Eds.). (2017). *Pilgrimage and Tourism to Holy Cities: Ideological and Management Perspectives*. Wallingford, UK: CABI.
Liu, D. (2015). The animistic aspects in the Chinese Zhong Yuan Festival. *Asian Journal of Pentecostal Studies, 18*(2), 53–70.
Lundskow, G. (2008). *The Sociology of Religion: A Substantive and Transdisciplinary Approach*. Los Angeles, CA: Pine Forge Press.
Mart, G. (2015). Unearthing spirituality: Through the arts. In Ross, C. & Baker, J. (Eds.), *Pioneering Spirituality: Resources for Reflections and Practice*. Norwich, UK: Canterbury Press.
Matheson, C. M., Rimmer, R. & Tinsley, R. (2014). Spiritual attitudes and visitor motivations at the Beltane Fire Festival, Edinburgh. *Tourism Management, 44*, 16–33.
McKay, G. (Ed.). (2015). *The Pop Festival: History, Music, Media, Culture*. London, UK: Bloomsbury Academic.
Mellor, D., Hapidzal, F. M., Teh, K., Ganesan, R., Yeow, J., Latif, R. A. & Cummins, R. (2012). Strong spiritual engagement and subjective well-being: A naturalistic investigation of the Thai Pusam Festival. *Journal of Spirituality in Mental Health, 14*(3), 209–225.
Miles, W. (2011). Among the "Jubos" during the Festival of Lights. *Transition, 105*, 30–45.
Norman, A. (2011). *Spiritual Tourism: Travel and Religious Practice in Western Society*. London, UK: Bloomsbury Academic.

Pechilis, K. (2009). Experiencing the Mango Festival as a ritual dramatization of Hagiography. *Method & Theory in the Study of Religion*, 21(1), 50–65.

Pena Nunez, C. B. (2016). El Inca abraza a la predicación: El juego de la sortija y la conquista espiritual en la fiesta barroca en honor de Santa María de Guadalupe en Potosí, 1601 (The Inca embraces preaching: The game of the ring and the spiritual conquest in the Baroque style in honour of Santa Maria de Guadalupe in Potosí, 1601). *RILCE. Revista De Filología Hispánica*, 32(3), 715–736.

Pfadenhauer, M. (2010). The eventization of faith as a marketing strategy: World Youth Day as an innovative response of the Catholic Church to pluralization. *International Journal of Nonprofit and Voluntary Sector Marketing*, 15(4), 382–394.

Pinho, T. F. & Garofalo, G. de L. (2016). The candle of Nazareth' Feast, devotion and tourism in Para (Brazil) O 'Círio de Nazaré': festa, devoção e turismo no Pará (Brasil). *International Journal of Religious Tourism and Pilgrimage*, 4(2), 1–11.

Plantinga Jr., C. & Rozeboom, S. A. (2003). *Discerning the Spirits: A Guide to Thinking about Christian Worship Today*. Grand Rapids, MI: William B. Eerdmans Publishing Company.

Quezado, I., Alcântara, A. J. F., Costa, J. S., Arruda, D. M. & Mota G. (2016). So Jesus na causa: Fe e percepsao de crowding em evento religioso (Only Jesus in the cause: Faith and perceptions of crowding in a religious event). *ReMark: Revista Brasileira de Marketing*, 15(4), 486–495.

Raj, R. & Morpeth, N. (2015). *Religious Tourism and Pilgrimage Management: An International Perspective*. 2nd ed. Wallingford, UK: CABI.

Rao, H. & Dutta, S. (2012). Free spaces as organizational weapons of the weak: Religious festivals and regimental mutinies in the 1857 Bengal Native Army. *Administrative Science Quarterly*, 57(4), 625–668.

Robinson, R. (2015). No Spectators! The art of participation, from Burning Man to boutique festivals in Britain. *The Pop Festival: History, Music, Media, Culture*, 165–82.

Robinson, R. (2016). *Music Festivals and the Politics of Participation*. Abingdon, UK: Ashgate Publishing.

Rojek, C. (2013). *Event Power: How Global Events Manage and Manipulate*. London, UK: Sage.

Ross, C. (2013). Spectacle, ecstasy, and music festivals: The spiritual longing of the lost generation, *Liturgy*, 28(3), 42–50.

Ruback, R. B., Pandey, J. & Kohli, N. (2008). Evaluations of a sacred place: Role and religious belief at the Magh Mela. *Journal of Environmental Psychology*, 28(2), 174–184.

Sadovina, I. (2017). The new age paradox: Spiritual consumerism and traditional authority at the Child of Nature festival in Russia. *Journal of Contemporary Religion*, 32(1), 83–89.

Shinde, K. A. (2011). Placing communitas: Spatiality and ritual performances in Indian religious tourism. *Tourism*, 59(3), 335–352.

Smith, V. L. (1989) *Hosts and Guests: The Anthropology of Tourism*. 2nd ed. Philadelphia: University of Pennsylvania Press.

Sparkes, A. & Smith, B. (2013). *Qualitative Research Methods in Sport, Exercise and Health: From Process to Product*. London, UK: Routledge.

Spinks, B. D. (2010). *The Worship Mall: Contemporary Responses to Contemporary Culture*. London, UK: SPCK.

Spracklen, K. & Lamond, I. R. (2016). *Critical Event Studies*. London, UK: Routledge.

Stanton, A. L. (2015). Celebrating Muhammad's birthday in the Middle East: Supporting or complicating Muslim identity projects? In Merkel, U. (Ed.), *Identity Discourses and Communities in International Events, Festivals and Spectacles*. Basingstoke, UK: Palgrave Macmillan.

Suntikul, W. & Dorji, U. (2016). Local perspectives on the impact of tourism on religious festivals in Bhutan. *Asia Pacific Journal of Tourism Research*, 21(7), 741–762.

Timothy, D. J. & Olsen, D. H. (2006). *Tourism, Religion and Spiritual Journeys*. Abingdon, UK: Routledge.

Turner, V. (1982). *Celebration: Studies in Festivity and Ritual*. Washington, DC: Smithsonian Institution.

Turner, V. & Turner, E. L. B. (1978). *Image and Pilgrimage in Christian Culture: Anthropological Perspectives*. New York, NY: Columbia University Press.

Viji, R. & Shrinithivihahshini, N. (2017). An assessment of water quality parameters and survival of indicator in pilgrimage place of Velankanni, Tamil Nadu, India. *Ocean and Coastal Management*, 146(1), 36–42.

Ward, G. (2005). *Cultural Transformation and Religious Practice*. Cambridge, UK: Cambridge University Press.

Ward, P. (2005). *Selling Worship: How What We Sing Has Changed the Church*. Milton Keynes, UK: Paternoster Press.
White, J. F. (2000). *Introduction to Christian Worship*. 3rd ed. Nashville, TN: Abingdon Press.
Woodhead, L. & Catto, R. (2012). *Religion and Change in Modern Britain*. London, UK: Routledge.
Wroe, M. (Ed.). (1988). *Dancing in the Dragon's Jaws: Rock and Roll, Its Music and Culture – A Christian Appreciation*. London, UK: Greenbelt Festivals.
Yazbak, M. (2011). The Muslim festival of Nabi Rubin in Palestine: From religious festival to summer resort. *Holy Land Studies, 10*(2), 169–198.

# 33

# AUSTRALIA CELEBRATES

## An exploration of Australia Day festivals and national identity

*Leanne White and Elspeth Frew*

### Introduction

Tourists receive messages from the various sites they visit, sent to them by the creators of those sites. These places, presented as aspects of a national heritage, help to shape a common national identity or 'imagined community' amongst a diverse population. This shared identity is often an official goal of countries comprised of many different cultures where there exists a common urge to create a national identity to overcome diversity and difference within the nation-state (Pretes 2003). If sites can help create a common identity or imagined community among a diverse population, can a series of events held on a country's national day represent aspects of the nation's culture and help to develop a common national identity?

This chapter explores how Australians celebrated Australia Day historically and in 2017 and considers these festivals and events in the context of national identity development and Australian nationalism. Australia Day, held on 26 January, is Australia's national day, commemorating the day in 1788 when European settlers first arrived in Botany Bay. Throughout the country, many federal, state, territory and local council-supported events are staged to celebrate Australia as a country and to celebrate being Australian. The Australia Day festival celebrations range from formal occasions supported by government funding such as citizenship ceremonies, to independent informal gatherings of friends and neighbours holding Australia Day barbeques and idiosyncratic and irreverent events and activities. The celebration of Australia Day on 26 January has become a topic of controversy in recent times, with some municipalities (including Melbourne's City of Yarra and City of Darebin) voting to cancel Australia Day festivities altogether from 2018. Indeed, Councillors at the City of Yarra unanimously voted to no longer refer to 26 January as Australia Day (Australian Associated Press 2017).

Such diverse celebratory events taken together can be viewed as a festival reflecting Falassi's belief that a festival can be based on 'power, class structure, and social roles' and can be staged 'by the people for the people' or 'by the establishment for the people' (Falassi 1987, p. 3). In addition, Falassi notes at festival times, people engage in activities they do not normally engage in, and they 'invert patterns of daily social life' (1987, p. 3), which reflects the many unusual and quirky events staged on Australia Day, as discussed later. From a festival typology perspective, the Australia Day festival reflects many of the rites or 'movements' that occur during the festival from the beginning to end, namely the rites of purification, passage, reversal, conspicuous display, conspicuous consumption, drama, exchange, competition and devalorisation (Falassi 1987). Getz (2010, p. 7) notes that festivals are cultural celebrations and they 'always have a theme and they have potentially very diverse programs and styles, all in pursuit of fostering a special kind of experience'. He explains that festivals are 'connected to cultures and to places, giving each identity and helping to bind people to their communities' and can 'foster and reinforce group identity' (Getz 2010, p. 8). By examining some of the themes, rites and rituals surrounding national celebrations such as Australia Day, we can perhaps rethink our understanding and awareness of national heritage and tradition 'in our everyday lives' (Waterton 2010, p. 206).

## Nationalism and national identity in Australia

An exploration of the concepts of nation and nation-state and some consideration of the arguments surrounding the debate on these terms provides a useful basis from which to examine theories of national identity and nationalism, particularly with reference to how nationalism is celebrated in Australia. There is no question that the nation has a significantly broader meaning than the geographical boundaries of a country. The term encompasses more far-reaching notions than territory alone. It is acknowledged that the nation can embrace a combination of political, social, cultural, historical, economic, linguistic and religious factors (Anderson 1983). When an individual is said to belong to a nation, it is generally understood that the person has their foundations in that country. The word nation originated from the Latin term 'natio' or community of birth. Nation is therefore associated with words such as native, nature, innate, natal and renascent.

While numerous theorists have analysed nationalism, Benedict Anderson's groundbreaking 1983 work (revised a few times since) *Imagined Communities: Reflections on the Origin and Spread of Nationalism* has reconceptualised the way scholars have come to think about nationalism. Anderson popularly conceptualised the nation as an 'imagined political community'. Of the academic literature produced on theories of nationalism over the past 30 or so years, Anderson is among the most frequently cited (Culler & Cheah 2003, p. vii). Ozkirimli argues that Anderson's work 'constitutes one of the most original accounts of nationalism to date' (Ozkirimli 2000, p. 151), while James claims that Anderson's key text 'remains the most insightful book written in the area' (James 1996, p. ix). According to Anderson, nationalism is a taken-for-granted frame of reference (1991, p. 12). It is the daily ritual, undertaken by individuals of the nation separately, of reading about the events that have been selected as newsworthy that cement the concept of a common national identity. Billig refers to the way in which symbols of the nation are reproduced daily as 'banal nationalism' (Billig 1995, p. 6). As Billig explains, banal nationalism (everyday nationalism) is evidenced not by the flag but by the flag that might be relatively unnoticed in a public space. For the individual celebrating national festivals and events such as the highlights of Australia's Bicentennial celebrations in 1988 or the Opening Ceremony of the Sydney 2000 Olympic Games, heritage becomes somehow embodied and personified by their own experiences and those of others – along with the many photographs of the experiences that may be taken and shared. If we understand heritage as a process that constructs meaning about the past, then the construction of the related rituals and traditions is illustrative of this process. It is, essentially, a construction of national heritage based on stories, memories, reports and photographs that have been documented and passed down through the ages by family and friends.

In this chapter, we discuss three main types of nationalism – official, popular and commercial. Official nationalism is the civic, formal and ceremonial nationalism such as the Australian Government's planning of the Bicentennial celebrations in 1988 or the Centenary of Federation celebrations in 2001 (Anderson 1983). National anthem, flag and official symbols are part of official nationalism. The concept of popular nationalism was examined by Ward (1966) and can include nationalist messages and images as depicted in popular culture texts such as Australian film, television drama, popular songs and sport. Mackay argues that 'Our belief in a distinctive, homogenous set of Australian characteristics – an essential Australianness – is sustained by the rural myth' (Mackay 1999, p. 44). Such rural myths are evidenced in texts such as the 1895 poem *The Man from Snowy River* and the numerous related texts that have been produced since that time, along with associated commercial industries. Consequently, the connected texts work to perpetuate the myth amongst Australian and overseas visitors in industries such as fashion and tourism (White 2009). Commercial nationalism refers to consumer-related uses of these national symbols, images and icons. It is the nationalism represented by companies and through products such as Qantas and Vegemite. Seal (2004) acknowledges official and unofficial factors in telling a nation's story by stating in the preface of *Inventing Anzac: The Digger and National Mythology*, that his book 'demonstrates how the official and the unofficial, the formal and the folkloric, the institutionalised and the communal have colluded – and continue to collude – in the construction of a potent national mythology' (p. vii).

## Historic celebrations of Australia's national day

Australia Day was celebrated during previous major anniversaries of European settlement (1838, 1888, 1938 and 1988) with the various themes and representations of Australian history being modified over time at the 50th, 100th, 150th and 200th anniversaries. In examining the ways in which the act of European settlement had been marked in the past, it appears that specific events such as fireworks, regattas and re-enactments of the arrival of the First Fleet were part of the ritual which organisers thought it appropriate for the national birthday to be celebrated.

26 January, 1838 marked the passing of 50 years since the establishment of a penal colony at Sydney Cove at which the British flag was unfurled. The 1838 celebration was known as Anniversary Day, and loyalty was directed towards Great Britain. A public holiday was declared, and events such as a 50-gun salute, regatta, jubilee waltz and fireworks display took place. The national newspaper, *The Australian*, reflecting the attitude of the day, proudly reported that 'instead of savages and beasts of the field, human beings now populate the land' (Horne 1981, p. 16). Various reports of Aboriginal maltreatment by white settlers had reached Great Britain, and a report tabled in the House of Commons made recommendations for the protection of Australia's original inhabitants.

The Centenary celebrations of 1888 had many similarities with the Bicentennial celebrations that would be held 100 years later. The Centennial festivities were mainly centred in and around Sydney, and the harbour regatta of 1888 was a forerunner to the Tall Ships and First Fleet parades of sail that were held in 1988. In 1888, an area known as the Lachlan Swamps was renamed Centennial Park and dedicated to the people of Sydney, while a site of 100 hectares in the geographical centre of metropolitan Sydney was named Bicentennial Park 100 years later. During the Centenary celebrations, a foundation stone for the New South Wales (NSW) Parliament building was uncovered, while in 1988, Australia's first permanent Parliament House in Canberra was declared officially opened. Finally, the

Centennial International Exhibition held at Melbourne's Exhibition Buildings was essentially the 19th-century equivalent of the World Expo held on the banks of the Brisbane River for the Bicentenary. However, the Centenary celebrations were not without their detractors. The widely read national journal, *The Bulletin,* described the celebrations as 'childish, frothy and boastful' – similar sentiments to those that were also to emerge 100 years later for the Bicentenary.

Australia's Sesquicentenary celebrations in 1938 had two main features in common with the Bicentenary: organisers focussed on the nation, and the Aboriginal community expressed their opposition. Australia had changed significantly in the past 50 years, and two key dates which contributed to this change were the 1st of January 1901 and the 25th of April 1915. On the first day of the 20th century, the Commonwealth of Australia came into being and the proclamation of the Federal Constitution was celebrated at Sydney's Centennial Park. In May of that year, Australia's first Federal Parliament was formed, and four months later the flag, a crucial symbol for a new nation, was launched. Ironically Australia's official birth as a nation took place in the same year that Queen Victoria died, having reigned for 63 years. While the political genesis of Australia can be traced to the events of 1901, some historians have argued that it was the Australian and New Zealand Army Corps (ANZAC) landing at Gallipoli in 1915 that marked the emergence of Australia as a nation. The Aboriginal community declared 26 January, 1938 a 'Day of Mourning and Protest' and held a conference which attracted more than 100 supporters. However, unlike the Bicentenary when Aboriginal issues were given a reasonable amount of media coverage, this event was almost entirely ignored by the media. The national day only became known as 'Australia Day' in 1946 and was generally celebrated as a long weekend as the nearest Monday was taken as a public holiday.

Having provided an overview of some of the theories of nationalism and national identity, the way Australia Day has been celebrated historically was explored. The following provides an examination of the various ways in which the nation was celebrated on Australia Day in 2017. The meanings conveyed in the presentation of signifiers of nation and nationalism are investigated.

## Australia Day 2017

On 26 January 2017, each state and territory is involved in the Australia Day festival by hosting a variety of events to celebrate Australia Day. Most of these events were staged outdoors, reflecting the summer weather across Australia which supports and encourages outdoor activities at that time of year. Many Australia Day festival events were held at iconic venues such as on and around Sydney Harbour, on rivers, and at local parks and beaches. An example of a traditional Australia Day event held in 2017 at an iconic venue was the 181st Australia Day Regatta, held on Sydney Harbour, with the Australia Day website stating,

> Enjoy the world's oldest continuously conducted annual sailing event, now in its 181st edition, which will see scores of vessels – including vintage yachts and 18-foot skiffs – compete in events for all classes in the Eastern area of Sydney Harbour.
> *(Australia Day Council of NSW 2017)*

As in previous iterations of Australia Day, the events held on Australia Day 2017 can be divided into Official events, Commercial Events and Popular Events. The Australia Day 2017 Official events involved activities such as flag raising, citizenship events and open houses of government buildings. Some states or territory governments hosted events to announce the Australian of the Year and stage award ceremonies. There was also a Welcome to Country and Indigenous dancing session. For example, in the town of Singleton in NSW, an Australia Day Ceremony was held in the Civic Centre and featured a citizenship ceremony, the announcement of the local Citizen of the Year and the town's Young Achiever of the Year, with the Australia Day address delivered by a special guest appearance of a TV personality. In Toowoomba, Queensland, an official flag-raising ceremony held at 8.30 am was followed by some Australian damper, lamingtons and cups of tea. Damper is a traditional Australian bread, eaten by swagmen, drovers and stockmen in the 1800s, while lamingtons are chocolate and coconut cubes of sponge cake that are reported to have been named after Baron Lamington, the first governor of Queensland from 1895 to 1901 (Symons 2007).

In Newcastle, the day started at 9 am with a traditional Australia Day citizenship ceremony, where 100 people became new citizens, and there were also awards for the City of Newcastle Citizen, Young Citizen and Community Group of the Year. The Northern Territory staged their 2017 Australian of the Year Awards during an Australia Day Black Tie Ball and was the only Official Event in the sample held in the evening, possibly reflecting that January in Darwin is during the Northern Territory's wet season and so an inside event is more suitable. An example of a Popular Event was 'Australia Day 2017 – Live at the Sydney Opera House' which was a concert staged at the Sydney Opera House featuring many of Australia's best musicians performing in front of a capacity crowd. The concert was also broadcast live on television and was organised by the NSW Government through its tourism and major events agency Destination NSW. These ceremonial events staged as part of the Australia Day festival reflect Falassi's rites of conspicuous display whereby the 'ruling groups typically display themselves as guardians and keepers, and as depositories of religious or secular power, authority, and military might' (Falassi 1987, p. 4).

## *Family activities*

The attendees at the 2017 Australia Day festival were either passive or active participants, with the passive audience members simply watching the events as they unfolded in front of them and the active participants being physically involved in some capacity during the event. There were many examples of events staged for fun and engagement by families which encouraged active participation. Many of these events encouraged families to visit a variety of outdoor settings such as local parks to take part in a range of activities for the children. The most frequently organised children's activities included activities such as jumping castles, face painting, petting zoos, balloon twisting, family trivia quizzes, pony rides, colouring competitions, roving entertainment and give-aways. These activities were held throughout the day, from early in the morning until late at night, often culminating in fireworks displays. These were described as fun and interactive, designed to entertain the whole family.

There were also some Australian-themed activities which strongly reflected aspects of Australia's history, geography, economy and culture. In rural and regional areas there was a reflection of the country in activities such as blacksmithing, cow milking, whip cracking, sheep shearing and sheep dog demonstrations reflecting Australia's strong agricultural background. There were also ute musters and motorbike displays. Utility vehicles or pickups (referred to as the ute) are seen across the length and breadth of Australia as they are a key tool for rural farmers and urban tradesmen. The first ute was launched in 1951 and remains a symbol of Australia's supposed egalitarianism to this day. The ute is celebrated in regional parts of Australia with 'ute musters' whereby owners converge to celebrate the different styles and forms of ute. At Bella Vista Farm, an hour's drive inland from Sydney, the Australia Day web page noted that 'convict floggings are set to run throughout the day' (National Australia Day Council 2017a). There were several examples of thong (flip-flop) throwing competitions reflecting the ubiquitous Australian practice and tradition of wearing thongs in informal settings whereby the thong is an Aussie icon and is considered the essential footwear item of summer. The humble thong has been an essential part of beach culture in Australia since the 1950s. There were examples of native animal and reptile displays reflecting Australia's unique fauna. For example, the Maitland City Council organised the following Australian-themed activities: a backyard sprinkler playground, a cubby house corner, backyard cricket and yard games and a lawn mower obstacle course for children. The lawn mower is a particularly iconic item which was also featured at the Sydney 2000 Olympic Games. The town of Mindarie in Western Australia had Australian-themed events staged all day:

> Keep the kids entertained from 11 am – 4 pm at the giant sandpit with free activities including a jumping castle, surf simulator, temporary tattoos, the big dig, Vegemite finger painting and a bubble zone… Then finish the evening with a choc-top and popcorn while watching the classic Aussie movie *Crocodile Dundee* on the silver screen.
> (National Australia Day Council 2017b)

Such events reflect the mostly informal events staged as part of Australia with only a couple of examples of formal events such as the Northern Territory government hosting a black tie dinner. The variety of events reflects Falassi's rites of exchange and reinforces the idea that attendees at festivals engage in activities they would not normally engage in and they invert patterns of daily social life.

## *Music and food*

The use of music was evidenced throughout Australia as part of Australia Day festival events in 2017 and involved local bands performing in local parks. Some local councils had organised for cover bands to play who specialised in imitating traditional Australian bands such as The Australian INXS show and the Australian Divinyls show. Some events engaged DJs to play 'Aussie Anthems all day' or 'spinning the decks with all your top Aussie hits from the 1970s' (Central Coast Tourism 2017). Some destinations also allowed coverage of youth Radio Station Triple J to broadcast the Hottest 100 Countdown, which has been running since the late 1980s. Since music is a great unifier and can encourage nostalgia (Barrett et al. 2010), these activities appeared to reinforce Australian nationalism.

On Australia Day 2017 there were many examples of the use of food, and Australian culture was reflected in the provision of various types of food which highlighted aspects of Australian food culture and often showcased the region. Some commercial operators promoted their Australia Day lunches or dinners, where people could choose from Australian-themed food, which included 'Aussie-inspired tucker' such as barbecued chicken, lamb and prawns, with desserts including pavlova with fresh fruit and cream and fairy floss. Local councils staged barbecues in local parks and offered 'sausage sangas, shrimps on the BBQ' and a variety of food stalls. In addition, there were more informal and humorous uses of food on Australia Day, including such activities as lamington-making, watermelon-eating and pie-eating competitions. Falassi (1987, p. 4) notes that rites of conspicuous consumption 'usually involve food and drink' and that rites of competition include 'various forms of contest and prize giving'. During the Australia Day festival, there are many examples of Australians consuming food and drink that are representative of Australian culture. Some of the eating competitions reflect Falassi's suggestion that the rite of conspicuous consumption is often abundant, excessive or wasteful.

On the official Australia Day website there was encouragement for Australians to choose whatever an individual wanted to do to celebrate Australia Day, with the suggestion that whatever activity anyone chose to celebrate the day was acceptable. This may reflect the diverse nature of the population of Australia from multiple countries and across diverse cultures. The slogan 'Celebrate #AustraliaDay Your Way' reinforced the individual and varied nature of celebrating Australia Day. A series of associated videos were provided featuring well-known Australians discussing what Australia Day meant to them and how they have celebrated it.

## Discussion

The Australia Day 2017 events ranged from the serious to the frivolous and the formal to the informal. The event organisers ranged from local councils and tourism boards, to voluntary non-profit organisations and private-sector companies. They ranged from barbeques and games to sporting activities, and there were federally sponsored events, state-sponsored events and locally supported events. The variety and type of events taking place on Australia Day may reflect Spillman's (1997) suggestion that, in a diverse country, diversity itself becomes an aspect of national identity. Some events were organised by commercial operators aiming to make money. However, most events were free, sponsored by the state or territory government or local council.

Some Australia Day events were held at locations that had no obvious link to the event being held, so, in effect, the event could be held on any site, as the location is incidental to the core activity of the event. Robinson, Picard and Long (2004, p. 187) suggest that 'generic and socially decontextualised – placeless – festival forms are increasingly being invented and scheduled with a main purpose of attracting tourist audiences as well as catering for various types of communities'. The Australia Day festival events were not designed to attract tourists, but rather citizens; nonetheless, the events have a strong association with the location, reflecting the culture and identity of the area. For example, the Best Pioneer Costume competition held in Gympie, Queensland reflects the pioneering element of the early white settlers to the region. Physical participation in the event through competition is offered at Australia Day festival events, with the opportunity provided for the attendee to experience and participate in the core activity of the event. The participants in the Australia Day events did not require a range of specialist skills, knowledge or expertise to fully engage in the core activity of the event. Effectively, the events were open to all types of people, perhaps reflecting Australian egalitarianism.

Many Australia Day events are not serious but simply provide an opportunity for participants and spectators to have fun and enjoyment. Weed (2006, p. 306) notes that sport, 'while still pursued by some for traditional motives of fitness, health, competition and achievement, is now increasingly participated in simply for fun and pleasure'. Similarly, Frew (2006) notes that when tourists experience fun at humorous events and festivals it helps ensure the experience is a positive one for all involved namely, the tourist, the tourism employees and the locals. She suggests that the generation of pleasant emotions when attending a humorous event may result in high satisfaction levels and positive word-of-mouth recommendation about the experience and/or destination. Therefore, the provision of fun and light-hearted activities such as Australia Day events may have numerous tourism-related benefits and may reflect the Australian satirical sense of humour.

## Conclusion

This chapter has considered the variety of events organised when Australians celebrate their national day and discusses what this tells us about who Australians are and how they view themselves as a nation. Horne noted that national identity entails more than simply 'flapping flags, singing folk songs or telling heroic anecdotes' (1981, p. 62). Indeed, this chapter has noted that the Australia Day festival includes many ways to celebrate nationalism, from mainstream events funded by the government to self-effacing, satirical and offbeat events such as backyard cricket, lamington-making, whip-cracking displays and pie-eating competitions.

The Australia Day festival celebrations in 2017 were similar in many ways to the Australian Centenary of Federation celebrations in 2001 when it was reported that 'Australia yesterday managed to pull off a medley of the sentimental, the commemorative and the down-right bizarre' (Hurrell 2001, p. 4). The staging of such 'down-right bizarre' events on Australia Day is appropriate in a country that prides itself on not taking itself too seriously, where the off-beat events highlight and reinforce the non-conformist and irreverent mocking nature, with a clear preference for the irreverent, the unauthorised, and the sometimes uncouth. While Australia Day committees across the country can work to encourage patriotic flag-raising and citizenship ceremonies, the many events staged on a limited budget provide an attractive lure for Australians.

This chapter has demonstrated the ways in which Australia Day remains an important part of the Australian national consciousness. Official, popular and commercial celebrations of Australia Day tell us much about who we are as a nation. The commemoration of this important national day at the local, state and national levels and adopting official, popular and commercial styles of nationalism appears to be gaining in momentum and shows little signs of slowing down. The chapter also used Falassi's theory of rites or 'movements' at festivals to demonstrate that Australia Day events reflect many of these aspects.

As Australians, we learn much about our contemporary social and cultural environment when we take the time to explore the diverse ways in which Australia Day is celebrated. Examining a variety of manifestations of the Australia Day festival celebrations in 2017 can assist us in moving closer to answering some of the deeper questions about the ubiquitous and endearing characteristic that we know as the Australian national identity. The highly ironic and irreverent events staged reflect that Australians do not have a problem with mocking themselves or the quirky items that form a unique part of their culture and the diversity of the events reflect the diversity of the culture of Australians from many parts of the world.

Further research might attempt to explore why some celebrations and legacies of Australia Day continue to generate such distinct and unique meanings. Some official, popular and commercial Australia Day festival celebrations and imagery swim to the top, while others sink to the bottom and do not develop currency. An area worthy of further examination would be to determine the nature and intensity of the more persistent and regular types of Australia Day events. The movement of local councils banning Australia Day celebrations from their local area in recognition of the negative connotations of day for Indigenous Australians makes this an issue to follow with interest in the future.

## References

Anderson, B. (1983) *Imagined Communities: Reflections on the Origins and Spread of Nationalism*, London: Verso.

Anderson, B. (1991) *Imagined Communities: Reflections on the Origins and Spread of Nationalism (Revised Edition)*, London: Verso.

Australian Associated Press (2017) Melbourne's Yarra Council votes unanimously to move Australia Day citizenship ceremonies. Online: www.theguardian.com/australia-news/2017/aug/16/melbournes-yarra-council-votes-unanimously-to-move-australia-day-citizenship-ceremonies (accessed 16 August, 2017).
Australia Day Council of New South Wales (2017) Australia Day. Online: www.australiaday.com.au (accessed 1 August, 2017).
Barrett, F. S., Grimm, K. J., Robins, R. W., Wildschut, T., Sedikides, C. and Janata, P. (2010) Music-evoked nostalgia: Affect, memory, and personality, *Emotion*, *10*(3), 390–403.
Billig, M. (1995) *Banal Nationalism*, London: Sage.
Central Coast Tourism (2017) Australia Day on the Central Coast. Online: www.visitcentralcoast.com.au/events/t/australia-day-on-the-central-coast (accessed 1 August, 2017).
Culler, J. and Cheah, P. (eds.) (2003) *Grounds of Comparison: Around the Work of Benedict Anderson*, New York: Routledge.
Falassi, A. (1987) Festival: Definition and morphology. In Falassi A. (ed.) *Time Out of Time: Essays on the Festival*, Albuquerque: University of New Mexico Press, pp. 1–10.
Frew, E. A. (2006) The humour tourist: A conceptualisation, *Journal of Business Research*, *59*(5), 643–646.
Getz, D. (2010) The nature and scope of festival studies, *International Journal of Event Management Research*, *5*(1), 1–47.
Horne, D. (1981) *Nationalism and Class in Australia: 1920–1980*, Brisbane: Australian Studies Centre, University of Queensland.
Hurrell, B. (2001) Stand up and enjoy being silly, *Herald Sun*, January 2, p. 4.
James, P. (1996) *Nation Formation: Towards a Theory of Abstract Community*, London: Sage.
Mackay, H. (1999) *Turning Point: Australians Choosing Their Future*, Sydney: Macmillan.
National Australia Day Council (2017a) Australia Day. Online: www.australiaday.org.au (accessed 22/6/2018).
National Australia Day Council (2017b) The Marina Mindarie Australia Day. Online: www.australiaday.org.au/events/view/2365/the-marina-mindarie-australia-day (accessed 1 August, 2017).
Ozkirimli, U. (2000) *Theories of Nationalism: A Critical Introduction*, Houndmills: Macmillan.
Pretes, M. (2003) Tourism and Nationalism, *Annals of Tourism Research*, *30*(1), 125–142.
Robinson, M., Picard, D. and Long, P. (2004) Introduction: Festival tourism: Producing, translating, and consuming expressions of culture(s), *Event Management*, *8*(4), 187–189.
Seal, G. (2004) *Inventing Anzac: The Digger and National Mythology*, St Lucia: University of Queensland Press.
Spillman, L. (1997) *Nation and Commemoration: Creating National Identities in the United States and Australia*, New York: Cambridge University Press.
Symons, M. (2007) *One Continuous Picnic: A Gastronomic History of Australia*, Carlton: Melbourne University Press.
Ward, R. (1966) *The Australian Legend*, Melbourne: Oxford University Press.
Waterton, E. (2010) *Politics, Policy and the Discourses of Heritage in Britain*, Hampshire: Palgrave Macmillan.
Weed, M. (2006) Sports tourism. In Beech, J. and Chadwick, S., *The Business of Tourism Management* (157–189), Essex: Pearson Education.
White, L. (2009) The man from Snowy River: Australia's bush legend and commercial nationalism, *Tourism Review International*, *13*(2), 139–146.

# PART VIII
# Cultural perspectives on festivals

# 34
# HERDING LIVESTOCK AND MANAGING PEOPLE
The cultural sustainability of a harvest festival

*Guðrún Helgadóttir*

## Introduction

Harvest has been a cause for celebration for humans from time immemorial, and with the growth of tourism, these festivals attract visitors from outside the celebrating communities. As with other forms of cultural tourism, there is a certain balance between maintaining the original focus of the festival, its authenticity if you will, and catering to the growing number of visitors not directly involved in the core activity. This balance is the theme in this study. It expands on previous studies of horse round-ups or horse gathering in Northern Iceland conducted by participant observations and visitor surveys (Helgadóttir 2006, 2015; Helgadóttir & Sturlaugsdóttir 2009). Here the focus is on the subjective experience of the horse farmers as expressed in semi-structured interviews.

Harvest festivals are not only celebrations of ripe fruit and grains, a loaded Thanksgiving dinner table, pressing grapes or the excess of tomatoes flowing through the streets at La Tomatina. In the arctic and sub-arctic north, human sustenance traditionally consisted largely of animal protein. Hence, what counts for a harvest festival in Iceland is *réttir*, the gathering of livestock from summer pasture.

The research question addressed here is how residents perceive the changes in the harvest festival, Laufskálarétt, over the timespan they have participated in the festival.

## Literature review

It has long been acknowledged that harvest festivals attract tourists or as Janiskee (1980) dubbed them 'Rural delights for day tripping urbanites' (p. 96), with a concern for the cultural sustainability of the harvest festivals suffering from commodification or 'gimmickry'. These concerns have by no means subsided in the period of festivalisation of culture (Richards 2007) and are exacerbated today by renewed concerns over mass tourism that have led residents in heavily visited city destinations to protest (Golomb & Novy 2017). A common theme in these concerns is the negative effect of commodification, the devaluation of cultural assets in the tourism marketplace.

Tourism in cultural attractions is a complex phenomenon, and conventional marketing that relies on simple, easy to grasp messages can hardly do justice to these cultural assets.

The tourist has a transient relationship with the destination, while the resident has a long-term, even lifelong and transgenerational investment in the destination culture. The understanding of the tourist informed by marketing can therefore be explained by Baudrillard's (2000) concept of simulacra, where the marketing message is but a shadow of the deeper truth on which the attraction rests. Destination marketing is in many respects a case in point of this theory as destination marketing, nation branding, nation building and contemporary cultural movements shape the cultural experience.

Acceptance and positive attitudes to tourism are closely linked to perceived positive economic impact for residents and community (Kim, Uysal & Sirgy 2013). The conclusion of research on the social impacts of tourism is that in the organisation and development of tourism, the residents' quality of life is an important sustainability factor. Residents experience the impacts of visitation differently, which is important to take into account in the internal marketing and planning of tourism-related activities. Residents who value peacefulness and quiet are, for example, less likely to accept the impact of people congregating in their neighbourhood than residents who value access to cultural events (Andereck & Nyaupane 2011; Canavan 2014; Ridderstraat, Croes & Nijkamp 2016).

The cultural clash between tourists and residents has mainly been explored in developing countries and in destinations for indigenous tourism (Smith 2009). However, residents in developed countries also have negative experiences of tourists not respecting the norms and values of the destination community hence the concern with overtourism. In the case of Barcelona, tourist nudity in public sparked an outcry, and this became an outlet for a long-brewing frustration with the pressures of increasing visitor numbers and the increasing presence of the tourism industry (Golomb & Novy 2017).

The presence at festivals of guests that show disrespect for the occasion, the community and the values celebrated is a threat to the cultural sustainability of the festival. Furthermore, the outsider at the festival may not intend to be disrespectful; he or she may simply be ignorant, not getting it. This raises the question of how wide destination marketers can, or should, cast the net to promote festivals (Helgadóttir & Dashper 2016).

## Background

Sheep and horse farming in North-West Iceland relies partially on the use of common lands, that is, mountain pastures, for summer grazing. Farmers drive or herd their sheep to the pastures after lambing season, and their horses later in the summer when the pastures can carry their grazing and trampling. In autumn, the sheep and horses are gathered and herded back to the lowlands and sorted at communal corrals, before herding or driving them back to their respective farms (Aldred 2012; Helgadóttir 2015).

The sorting at the corral is a community gathering, the core of the festival that has developed to celebrate the success of bringing back the animals that grazed freely in the summer. Around this core, the festival has grown, spawning satellite events, products and services for visitors. The growth is mainly due to marketing efforts by Destination Management Organisations (DMOs) and the tourism sector in those rural areas. The timing is late September, which extends the shoulder season of tourism in the areas by a month. Tourism is, therefore, a stakeholder in these harvest festivals in addition to the main stakeholders, the farmers (Helgadóttir 2015).

The farmers are responsible for the management of the livestock and the pastures, for the corral, fences and for the organisation of the gathering and sorting, the core attraction in the event. The municipality nominates members to the committee responsible for managing the commons, the fences and corral as well as organising the gathering and sorting of livestock (*Fjallskilareglugerð*). Although this is strictly speaking not the role of the committee, it organises a dance on the evening of the gathering. Tourism is not their business, but tourism is there to stay at the harvest festival as it attracts crowds of spectators who are not directly involved in the core activity. This is a mixed blessing as the corrals are for animals, rather than people. They are in use 1–2 days per year, and the farmers who are responsible for them have no direct gain from the visitors. Tourist operators, on the other hand, have gain from the visitors but do not manage the core event and have no jurisdiction on the corral site.

Laufskálarétt is perhaps the most visited of the horse gatherings in Iceland. In 2017, there were 380 adult horses from 23 farms grazing on the commons in Kolbeinsdalur. The maximum number of horses allowed grazing there in the summer of 2017 was 400. According to information from the commons committee (*fjallskilastjórn*) about 50 per cent of the horses belong to five of the farms. On the day of the gathering about 300 riders participate, and an estimated number of visitors at the corral is 2,000–2,500 (Helgadóttir 2015).

In the case of the harvest festival of horse gathering, the actual work of gathering and sorting the horses is the harvesting, that is the core activity in the event. While a tourist presence is expected (Helgadóttir & Sturlaugsdóttir 2009), their participation can be problematic as they can get in the way of the people carrying out the work, which of course leads to resident dissatisfaction with the touristification of the festival. The harvesting takes place in public, but the festivities take place not only in public venues such as bars and restaurants but also in most homes in the region. Traditionally the homes were open to visitors, as most of them were in some way connected to the region, but as the numbers grow, the chances of a total stranger making an appearance at your party increase.

While everyone loves a good party and the tradition is to have a house full of guests, and good cheer, an inherent stakeholder conflict must constantly be resolved. This resolving process is key to the cultural sustainability (Soini & Birkeland 2014) of the event. In one of the few studies conducted on Laufskálarétt, Gísladóttir (2012) took an ethnographic look at the festival. She concluded that the locals are actors on a heritage stage where guests can feel a belonging to space and place through the heritagised image of country culture, 'be an Icelandic farmer for a moment' (p. 63). The tension described earlier, between attending to the core activity of horse husbandry and the increasingly demanding role of host, forms the research problem addressed in this chapter.

## Method

This chapter is part of a longitudinal study of the horse gathering in North-West Iceland and is hence a case study. The author has been conducting research at this annual festival since 2002, some years with assistance from students in the event management programme at Hólar University College. Various methods have been used for data collection: visitor surveys on-site, participant observation and semi-structured interviews. This chapter focusses on the festival from the resident rather than visitor perspective and is based on short semi-structured interviews with residents in the immediate vicinity of the most visited round-up, Laufskálarétt. It should be noted that the author is a resident and has participated in the horse gathering since 1996.

A convenience sample of residents was approached, and the sample snowballed as the initial interviewees suggested others and in total six people of varying age and attachment to the festival were interviewed. They were first asked when they first attended Laufskálarétt and what changes they have seen over the period in which they have been participating. This main question was followed up with questions about the festivalisation of the horse gathering, when and to what extent it became a celebration, who participates and how they experience this development. Apart from the initial question, the interviews were unstructured, meaning that the residents told their story and questions were used only to follow up on the initial question. For reasons of anonymity in a very small community, the interviewees are given numbers and their gender and age not reported.

## The horse gathering

Horse round-up or horse gathering is used to describe the act of searching the commons for livestock and herding them to the corral. The 'commons' refers here to that part of the Kolbeinsdalur valley that is used for summer grazing by a number of farms that have in common the right to use the area. The herding on the commons takes place on the same day as the sorting at the corral. The riders set out early morning, and the *fjallkóngur* is in charge of the herding, directing people to where they should be and who should do what and when. The herd is on the east side of a river, and those who herd and those that want to ride with the herd cross the river. Visitors on organised tours stay on the west bank with their guides to watch the herding and then follow the herd when it has crossed the river and moves west toward the corral.

Usually the horses arrive at the corral around noon; the riders and herd appear at the top of a hill and flow down in a long line toward the corral. The sorting starts when all the horses have been herded to a pasture adjacent to the corral, the sorting takes a few hours and the farmers and assistants ride home with their horses in the late afternoon.

The corral is made of concrete walls and serves the purpose of enclosing the horses to sort them according to farms. The centre of the corral is the *almenningur* and radiating from there like pieces of a pie are the *dilkur* or the enclosures belonging to each farm. There is a wide entryway to the *almenningur*, where the horses are driven in larger groups to sort. When sorted, each horse has to pass through narrower doors to the *dilkur* of the farm. The older horses know the routine, but younger horses can have trouble understanding where they are supposed to go and hence become stressed.

The corral stands on a low hill by a river. To the north of it is a parking lot, to the south a field where the horses wait to be driven into the *almenningur*. When the horses and riders stream down the hillside from Kolbeinsdalur down to the corral, many visitors line up along the fence of this field to take pictures of the herd. While the farmers and their assistants are working in the *almenningur* and *dilkur* to sort their horses, the visitors mainly stay on the outside of the corral, walking around it, looking at horses and meeting people. However, there is a tendency among visitors to enter the corral, sitting on the walls and even walking among the horses.

Based on 20 years of participant observation this author contends that the people at the corral roughly fall into three categories: (1) the core group, those working at the corral sorting horses and bringing them home; (2) the experienced guests, those who are repeat visitors and local people who are not involved in the sorting but may be riding with the herd; and (3) the novices, that is, people who are there for the first time or are so loosely connected to the community at the festival that they have not 'learned the ropes' of participation.

The first group is mainly the farmers and horse owners who are busy with sorting their horses and do not really take part in the festivities outside the corral. The second group of experienced guests adds a distinctive ethos to the occasion, as among them are people, mostly men, who stand around often with a beer or flask in hand and sing, thereby displaying the tradition of singing and cheer. This group is often dressed in the traditional Icelandic sweater, the occasional one even sporting a cowboy hat. The majority of this group is, however, there to meet people and enjoy the sight of the horses, speculating which of the foals have potential and greeting friends and relatives. The novices, or the third group, is a large group and potentially disruptive as they may not realise that by entering the corral they can interfere with the work and expose themselves to danger from running horses. On the outside of the corral they might try to participate in the singing without realising that, for this too, there are rules of the game; men stand shoulder to shoulder in a circle, singing songs they know all the words to in harmony. An out-of-key voice from an out-of-place body is tolerated but not particularly welcomed.

The sorting of horses takes about 3 hours, and when it is done the *réttarstjóri*, who directs the work at the corral, will allow the farms to leave with their horses one by one. It is important to give each group enough time and space so that they will not mix again on the way home.

It should be noted that farmer refers here both to male and female horse farmers and that many of the female farmers are actively herding and sorting their horses. However, the traditional division of tasks in the household means that the women are to the larger extent responsible for providing food for their family and guests. It is also worth noting that despite the fact that farmers are both male and female, all the formal roles within the event are played by males. The *fjallkóngur* and the *réttarstjóri* are men, although in other communities such roles have occasionally been held by women.

## Findings

Three themes from the interviews are reported here: the festivalisation of the horse gathering (that is the change from a working to leisure event), the perceived sociocultural aspects of this festivalisation on the community, and the lived experience of the interviewees of the festival as it is today.

### *Festivalisation of the horse gathering*

The informants agree that in their lifetime the horse gathering has changed from being simply one of the tasks of horse farming to becoming a festival. Before, they recall mostly the people directly involved with the gathering at the corral:

> Around 1970 this was no festival or event, it was just people gathering their horses, just those working at the corral. Then there was a change when people moved here that started to invite acquaintances from the [national] horse sector. And then they started the round-up dance.
>
> *(Informant A)*

Informant C remembers that in his childhood 30–40 years ago,

> You did not enter the *almenningur* if you wanted to survive, it was no place for the children or the elderly! It was more just work then, to get the horses and maybe we were 3–4 driving them home and no partying. Now we have maybe 30–40 people riding home with us; relatives, friends and friends of friends.

There are several key changes that the interviewees felt began to make the event into a festival over the last 40 years. First, the instigation of satellite events. The first of those was a dance with live music on the evening of the gathering, which has attracted people for several decades now and a source of income for the local commons committee. In later years all the pubs and bars in the municipality offered live music on the Saturday and even the Friday evening. In the 1990s, a horse show in the then newly erected riding hall in the community was first held on the Friday evening, and this has become a tradition. The third satellite event is open house at horse farms on the Sunday, and last but not least, many homes in the vicinity of the corral now have private parties on the eve of the gathering.

Second, around 1980, interest arose in the event as a tourism magnet, and in the 1990s, the date of the gathering was set for perpetuity on the last Saturday in September. Before that, the date was set annually depending on the local farming and grazing conditions. From then on, the gathering has been marketed by the municipality of Skagafjörður and visitor numbers have risen. The municipality has also provided resources for improvements of the parking lot and the temporary toilet facilities. This happened in tandem with municipal tourism policy.

Third, developments in horse husbandry in the region have resulted in changes in how horses and people behave at the gathering, thus changing the ethos of the event. Previously, farmers kept large herds of horses where the mares were largely without contact with humans year round. 'Before, these old brood mares, they were so wild and shy of humans' (Informant A). It was therefore not without conflict to get them into their *dilkur*. It became for a while somewhat of a sport to wrestle with the horses at the corral, but in the 1990s an effort was made to stop this. This, combined with the changes in the horse husbandry, means that 'today, horses are fewer and they are trained and fed, so they are used to the human touch' (Informant C), which has led to a calmer atmosphere at the corral. 'The old mares know their *dilkur* and if you are quick enough to open before they need to move with the whirl, they just walk in' (Informant B).

## *Sociocultural aspects of the festivalisation*

There is a long-standing tradition of hospitality and festivities in the municipality, and a common saying in Iceland is that the locals in Skagafjörður cheer and sing. When the author moved to Skagafjörður in the late 1990s a friend explained that this was a place where you could have a party in the middle of harvesting. This suggested that compared to other communities, there was more interest in having fun than profiting. This image has been used in the marketing of Skagafjörður as a destination for tourism and of Laufskálarétt as a festival. The interviewees were not quite sure how it came about that this horse gathering in particular became so popular and developed into a festival weekend but speculate that it may have to do with this old image of their community as prone to festivities.

Laufskálarétt is now firmly established as a festival in the community. The date is fixed, visitor numbers have been growing for over a decade and the festival has become a tourism attraction. Local homes receive a high number of visiting friends and relatives, both for accommodation and for food and drink. While this is in line with the hospitality tradition of the community, there are some concerns, which are manifested in discontentment with two things: lack of revenue from the commercial tourism presence and inappropriate behaviour by guests.

'It is a pity that little else than effort remains on the farms', says Informant C, commenting on the rising number of visitors and the fact that commercial tourism enterprises use attendance at the festival as an attraction. 'It is one thing to have guests, but it is another matter when businesses bring people in and the farmers get nothing but extra work from it'

(Informant C). The informants also agree that today the sale of horses at the corral is negligible, thus losing another traditional aspect of the event:

> But there is no sale to speak of nowadays at the corral, before people sold maybe 2–3 foals but now people only buy trained horses. Before people would come to the farms to buy foals and colts, but now it is all online.
>
> *(Informant B)*

Informant A recalls that the festivities grew from just family and friends enjoying the evening to 'a hundred people passing through the home, many of whom we didn't know, they were just drinking and partying', which the family experienced as way out of hand. This overstepping of the boundaries that locals have also happens at the corral: 'It is frustrating that people do not seem to realize that the *dilkur* belongs to a farm and is for horses, one is almost fighting with people to be able to sort the horses' (Informant B). Not only does this interfere with the work, but it can also be dangerous for the visitors to be in the way when gates open, and horses charge through. During the herding, tourism operators keep order among their guests. 'The foreigners, they are easy – there is no problem with them getting in the way' (Informant C).

It is more likely that visitors who are on their own or with experienced guests may step out of line. The author recalls an incident where an Icelandic man opened the gate for the herd without the *fjallkóngur's* permission, much sooner than planned, and turned to his companions, saying, 'There, didn't I do a great job!' Which wasn't the case at all – not to mention the disrespect to the organisers of the herding that this action by an outsider shows.

Much of the undesired behaviour is associated with inebriation. Informant A recalls an incident where an Icelandic visitor was quite drunk at the corral but really wanted to ride home with his friends. So, he went around asking for a horse and was constantly turned down. But an opportunity availed itself when he saw an older gentleman who was loosely holding the rein of his saddled horse while chatting with another man. The drunk man clambered on the horse, took the reins and galloped away before the owner realised what was happening! While inebriation can be a problem and the locals try to manage it, they are not averse to drinking in moderation at the festival. The flask and bottle are a common sight, especially among the domestic visitors, many of whom are repeat visitors.

This is not to say that all informants had stories of troublesome domestic visitors; Informant E described what he believes is the attraction for the experienced guest:'

> I know of people who come to Laufskálarétt and tell me, I'm just there to see the herd come down [to the corral], this is something that moves me, I enjoy it and not because horses are my special interest, I like horses and like to be at the corral on the outside and meet friends and acquaintances for a chat while you guys are working your butt off herding and managing the herd I'm just here on the outside and the place is full of old and new friends'.

So, in this case, there is keen awareness of the distinction between participating as work and participating as leisure.

## Lived experience of the festival

Despite the negative experiences, the informants near unanimously agree that Laufskálarétt is a festival that they enjoy and that it has a positive impact on the image of their community.

Most of them always go unless they are incapacitated by illness, childbirth or other major eventualities. Informant D explained it this way:

> It is a festival of a kind of course for the locals who have horses on the commons to see them after the summer, it is always fun and exciting in my experience. This is not a boring task, it is a lot of fun to herd the horses and sort them.

An informant from the next municipality added, 'When I'm at Laufskálarétt I feel as if I'm at an outdoor festival!' (Informant E), and a horse tourism operator in the region feels the same way: 'I feel Laufskálarétt is like, it is a people's festival, a huge crowd'.

## Implications

Laufskálarétt has in the lifetime of one generation changed from being a working event on the calendar for horse farmers in a small community in Northern Iceland to being a festival for the whole community attracting domestic and international visitors. What their experience shows is that much of this change was not anticipated by the locals, and that the dialogue between the farmers and the marketers and managers of tourism has been limited so that the community is vague on to what extent the development was planned and by whom.

The municipality, having a vested interest in the sustainability of both farming and tourism, comes in as a liaison in dialogue with both parties. The municipality contributes both to increasing the capacity of the site with improved parking and temporary toilet facilities, and to the marketing that makes this necessary. While these are expenses from the municipal budget, there is no direct revenue to cover those. The indirect benefits are identified in the tourism policy as profiling the municipality as a place where festivities are a strong feature.

How and to what extent the development of Laufskálarétt as a festival improves the quality of life for residents is still a question that needs to be asked now and should perhaps have been posed in the community decades ago. The answers might have reduced the risk of friction between the working event and the revelry, in terms of crowd management and transparency regarding the revenue and resource allocation. As the festival has become important to the community it is vital to address these questions to ensure the cultural, social and economic sustainability of the festival.

Whether and how it will be for the next generation needs to be discussed in relation to foreseeable changes in horse husbandry as the core attraction is the herding and sorting of horses. What would there be left to celebrate if there was no herd to gather for the harvest festival? Would it still be a celebration if the crowd of people disappears? Given the propensity for festivities in the community, as well as the centrality of horses in the destination, these are almost unthinkable questions. However, they need to be asked to find the way to the most feasible future scenario.

## References

Aldred, O. (2012). Mobile communities: The gathering and sorting of sheep in Skútustaðarhreppur, Northeast Iceland. *International Journal of Historical Archaeology, 16*(3), 488–508.

Andereck, K.L. & Nyaupane, G.P. (2011). Exploring the nature of tourism and quality of life perception among residents. *Journal of Travel Research, 50*(3), 248–260.

Baudrillard, J. (2000) Framras likneskjanna. In Svansson, G. (Ed.), *Fra eftirlikingu til eydimerkur*. Translated from French by G. Svansson (pp. 42–60). Reykjavik: Bjartur & Reykjavikurakademian.

Canavan, B. (2014). Sustainable tourism: Development, decline and de-growth. Management issues from the Isle of Man. *Journal of Sustainable Tourism, 22*(1), 127–147.

Gísladóttir, S.F. (2012). *'Skála og syngja Skagfirðingar' Rannsókn á ímynd Skagfirðinga og aðkomufólks í tengslum við Laufskálarétt.* Unpublished thesis, University of Iceland.

Golomb, C. & Novy, J. (eds.). (2017). *Protest and Resistance in the Tourist City.* New York: Routledge.

Helgadóttir, G. (2006). The culture of horsemanship and horse based tourism in Iceland. *Current Issues in Tourism, 9*(6), 535–548.

Helgadóttir, G. (2015). Horse round-ups: Harvest festival and/or tourism magnet. Cheval, tourisme et Mondialisation, *Editions Spéciale Monde du tourisme*, Paris: Parution.

Helgadóttir, G. & Dashper, K. (2016). 'Dear International Guests and Friends of the Icelandic Horse': Experience, meaning and belonging at a niche sporting event. *Scandinavian Journal of Hospitality and Tourism, 16*(2), 422–441.

Helgadóttir, G. & Sturlaugsdóttir, R. (2009). Stóðréttir: Ávinningur af komu ferðafólks. [Horse roundups: Economic impact of tourism] *Ráðstefna um íslenska þjóðfélagsfræði*, Háskólinn á Akureyri, 8–9 May.

Janiskee, B. (1980). South Carolina's harvest festivals: Rural delights for day tripping urbanites. *Journal of Cultural Geography, 1*(1), 96–104.

Kim, K., Uysal, M., & Sirgy, M. J. (2013). How does tourism in a community impact the quality of life of community residents?. *Tourism Management, 36*, 527–540.

Richards, G. (2007). The festivalization of society or the socialization of festivals? The case of Catalunya. In Richards, G. (Ed.), *Cultural Tourism: Global and Local Perspectives* (pp. 257–280). New York: Haworth Hospitality Press.

Ridderstraat, J., Croes, R. & Nijkamp, P. (2016). The tourism development-Quality of life nexus in a small island destination. *Journal of Travel Research, 55*(1), 79–94.

Smith, M. (2009). *Issues in Cultural Tourism Studies*, 2nd edition. London: Routledge.

Soini, K. & Birkeland, I. (2014). Exploring the scientific discourse on cultural sustainability. *Geoforum, 51*(January), 213–223.

# 35
# FESTIVALS AS PRODUCTS
## A framework for analysing traditional festivals in Ghana

*Oheneba Akwesi Akyeampong*

### Introduction

In Ghana, traditional festivals (TFs) account for the largest flow of domestic tourists (Akyeampong 2007; Amenumey & Amuquandoh 2008; Ministry of Tourism/Ghana Tourist Board 1996). Some slave forts and castles in the country, including three UNESCO World Heritage Sites, and a couple of national parks are highly popular on the international tourism circuit (Akyeampong 2011). However, largely because they are celebrated all over the country, TFs constitute the leading tourist attractions in the country.

Contemporary events, e.g. Farmers Day and Teachers Day, are the second major category of the country's events tourism market. However, these are organised by the state, with the location being rotated among the ten administrative regions, annually. Beauty pageants, e.g. Miss Ghana, Miss Malaika, also belong to this category except that they are organised by private event management companies; they are typically urban-based and patronised mostly by the middle class. The Pan-African Festival of Arts and Culture (PANAFEST), which seeks to celebrate African history and cultural achievements as well as the ideals of Pan-Africanism, is a nontraditional festival instituted in 1992, initially as a biennial event but now held quadrennially (Amenumey & Amuquandoh 2008; GoG/UNDP 2010; Mensah & Dei-Mensah 2013; MoT/GTB 1996). PANAFEST used to attract both continental as well as diasporan Africans.

Largely on account of their wide geographical spread, diversity and the opportunity they create for family gathering, TFs generate the largest volumes of domestic tourists, with a wide array of consequences for their respective communities. Thus, as major domestic tourism resources, TFs, among others, contribute immensely to the preservation and/or revival of ancient traditions (Mathieson & Wall 1982) and to redistribution of incomes (Archer 1978; Sharpley & Telfer 2002). The increasing significance of TFs as tourism resources in Ghana is manifested in a number of areas. First is the revival of dormant festivals and establishment of new ones. Examples of TFs instituted since the mid-1980s – when tourism was declared a 'priority sector' in the country by PNDC Law 116 (1986) – are *Akwantu-kese* (literally, the 'great trek') celebrated by the people of New Juabeng; Koforidua in the Eastern Region (Figure 35.1); *Akwantu-tenten* (i.e. the 'long trek'), celebrated by the people of Akan-Buem; Nkwanta in the northern part of Volta Region; and *Kente festival* (*kente* is a uniquely

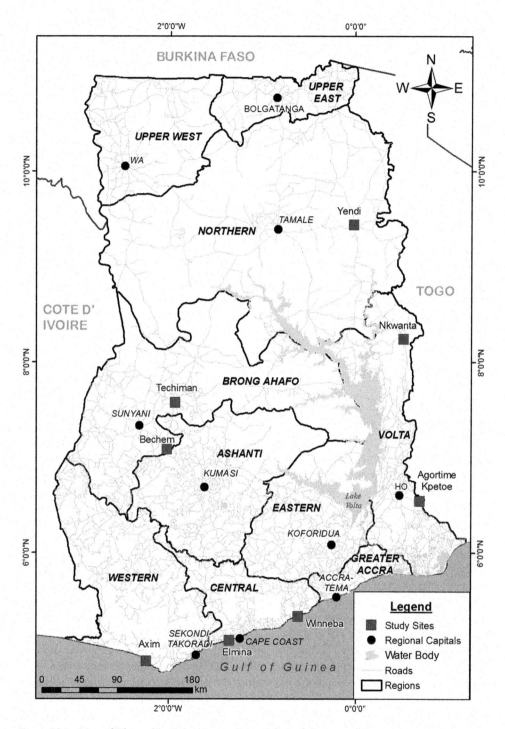

*Figure 35.1* Map of Ghana showing major traditional festival towns

Ghanaian hand-woven fabric), celebrated by the people of Agortime-Kpetoe, Volta Region as the home of the expensive fabric which in times past was an exclusively royal garb.

Next is the event management industry, spawned by the expanding number of festivals. In recent times, the country has witnessed a boom in event management companies as well as tertiary-level academic programmes in events management. On its part, the Ghana Tourism Authority (GTA, until 2011 it was Ghana Tourist Board), the national tourism organisation, has thrown in its weight by highlighting TFs in its promotional activities. As at 2012, the GTA published a calendar of some 85 TFs in its brochures (Mensah & Dei-Mensah 2013).

Finally, a major off-shoot of the growing interest in TFs has been the large volume of scholarly works into festivals in Ghana. These include Akyeampong and Yankholmes (2016), Amenumey and Amuquandoh (2008), Ewusi (2005), Amenumey (2003), Odotei (2002), Clarke-Ekong (1995, 1997), and Wyllie (1994). It is this interest by academia that prompted this chapter.

From a tourism development perspective, the foregoing works lack a theme or collection of themes that allows for a comparative analysis of two or more TFs. Besides their historical origins, there is hardly any other common sub-theme(s) that facilitate comparative studies. The conceptual basis and formats are as diverse as the origins and types of the TFs studied.

The eclectic approaches to research into TFs can be attributed to the significant differences in key parameters such as scale, location, cultural practices, level of popularity and impact in addition to historical origins. These conceptual and empirical issues are compounded by unspoken motives underlying the celebration of modern-day TFs in Ghana. A festival may be celebrated ostensibly to commemorate a historic landmark or thank the gods and ancestors for protection, guidance or good harvest. But at the end of it all, organisers hope to raise enough funds at least to cover expenses incurred, hence the inclusion of such aspects as launching, promotional activities and proposal for sponsorship in the modern-day TF.

In this chapter, it is argued that a common theme in which all stakeholders, from host communities and organisers to service providers, attendees and sponsors, can find a niche is the product approach. By definition, a product yields satisfaction to customers while generating incomes to designers, manufacturers and sellers. Hence, all stakeholders should easily relate to 'the festival-as-product' framework in ways that can be systematically appraised.

## Conceptual issues, definitions and proposed framework

According to Middleton (1989, p. 373), 'the concept of the "tourist product" is central to understanding the meaning and practice of management in all sectors of the travel and tourism industry'. Middleton then goes on to cite Kotler's (1984) definition of a 'product', which is reproduced verbatim here because it is considered an appropriate starting point as well as a useful conceptual basis for this chapter. A product, in the view of Kotler (1984, p. 463), is 'anything that can be offered to the market for attention, acquisition, use or consumption that might satisfy want or need. It includes physical objects, services, persons, places, organisations and ideas'.

Therefore, a TF is a 'product'; it attracts people's attention; people travel from far and near to witness, participate or simply 'consume' a TF. A TF satisfies the psychological and social needs of residents and attendees. For host communities, organisers, crew and performers, the economic benefits derived cannot be overemphasised. Corporate organisations are not charities; they consider the gains to be made before sponsoring a TF. To all intents and purposes, therefore, TFs are products in their own right and constitute a vital component of the 'total tourist product' in which people undertake package or inclusive tours.

A festival is a special event which after years of continuous celebration has become identified with a given locality or people (Allen, O'Toole, McDonnell & Harris 2011, p. 28). For the South Australian Tourism Commission (1997), a festival is a celebration of something the local community wishes to share and which involves the public as participants in the experience. For our purposes, a TF combines elements in the two definitions and goes further to stress the role of traditional leadership as the initiators and chief celebrants. A TF in Ghana is often identified with a traditional area (TA), which can be described as a group of communities with a common traditional leadership through whom all other traditional officers obtain authority, having a common ancestry, cultural practices and dialect. For our purposes, an arbitrary distinction is made between 'ancient' and 'modern' TFs; the former is one celebrated from time immemorial, e.g. *Apuor*, while the latter is one instituted since the mid-1980s, e.g. *Adekyem*. Finally, TFs have their exoteric components, marked by rituals often not for public consumption, but TFs also have their public segment. It is the latter that makes the festival a tourism resource. The ancient celebrations take centre stage, but increasingly, secondary activities such as fun-games, health walks and beauty pageants are added in a bid to extend the festival period. Leading TFs in the country include *Aboakyer* (of the *Effutus* of Winneba) (Figure 35.1), *Bakatue* (of *Edina* or Elmina), *Fetu Afahye* (Oguaa people, Cape Coast), *Bugum* (Fire Festival of *Dagbon*, Yendi, and Tamale), *Kundum* (*Ahanta*, Axim) and *Homowo* (of the *Gas*, Accra).

In project management terminology, a special event is described as a 'deliverable' (Bowdin, Allen, O'Toole, Harris & McDonnell 2006). However, their peculiarities are such that TFs do not fit the 'deliverable' designation. A TF is organised and celebrated by the community led by their traditional leaders who initiate the festival and preside over it as the chief celebrants. A deliverable connotes the handiwork of an outsider, typically a consultant, tasked to 'deliver' a 'project' within a given timeframe. However, for TFs, traditional leaders and *Asafo* (traditional militia) groups are not 'outsiders' or consultants who plan, organise and 'deliver' a TF as implied in project management because they are the key participants in any TF.

The product approach greatly enhances the discourse on TFs within the larger context of tourism development and facilitates the generation of theories. The product approach utilises the main attributes/facets of a festival, such as historical origins, life cycle stage, pre-festival activities, event product, promotion, sponsorship and impact (Figure 35.2) as the building blocks for research and write-up on TFs. Since these are common to all TFs, the framework constitutes a basis for scientific enquiry into all TFs.

In their oft-cited work, i.e. *Tourism: economic, physical and social impacts*, Mathieson and Wall (1982) identify three key elements that underpin the tourism phenomenon, namely the dynamic, static and consequential elements. The dynamic element refers to the movement or travel to and from the destination; specific areas for enquiry here include search for information about the potential destination, travel party size, mode of travel, etc. The static element is about the stay, and sub-areas worth investigating include attractions visited, other activities undertaken, expenditure patterns, visitor satisfaction, attendee profiling, etc. The consequential element, or simply stated, impacts, are the economic, sociocultural and environmental fallouts of the visit. In short, the discourse on TFs as tourism resources should highlight their appeal and ability to induce discretionary travel; specifically, get people to voluntarily relocate to the festival venue.

Unlike the Mathieson and Wall model that focusses more on the demand side of the equation, the product approach encapsulates both the demand and supply elements of events.

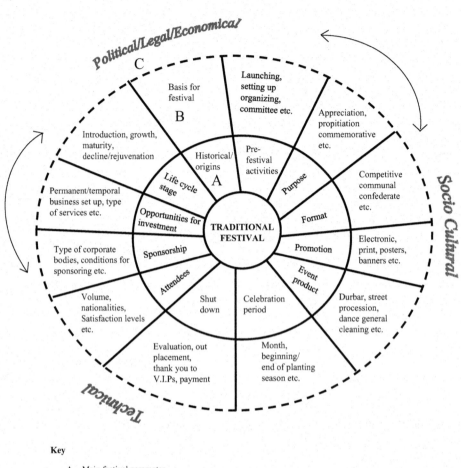

*Figure 35.2* Festival-as-a-product framework

## Research design and data collection

The two festivals selected for study are celebrated in the Techiman and Bechem TAs, both in the Brong-Ahafo Region (BAR), one of Ghana's ten administrative regions. BAR is located outside what used to be described as the country's 'Golden Triangle' with Accra, Kumasi and Sekondi-Takoradi as the vertices (Figure 35.1). The area earned that accolade on account of its resource endowment at the peak of the colonial mercantile system. Today, largely on account of the location of her leading attractions, the country's tourism hub is, somehow, coterminous with the Golden Triangle. It can thus be deduced that the 'tourist characteristics' as well as 'destination characteristics' (Mathieson & Wall 1982, pp. 22–23) are likely to be similar and comparable, despite the significant differences between the festivals. *Apuor* is one of Ghana's oldest TFs, at least 200 years old, whereas *Adekyem* is barely a decade old (Anane Agyei 2012). Coincidentally, Bechem and Techiman hosted the national Farmers Day awards in 1997 and 2008, respectively, a fact which hotelier interviewees alluded to frequently in responses regarding the economic gains made from festivals (and events).

A descriptive case-study design was adopted, while qualitative techniques, specifically in-depth interviews and focus group discussions (FGDs), were used for data collection. The case-study approach was preferred over a cross-sectional method because of the uniqueness of the phenomenon being studied (Sarantakos 1998). Primary data were obtained from key informants, namely traditional authorities and hoteliers, as well as FGD participants. Traditional authorities were recommended by the palaces of the traditional overlords of the two study areas. Participants in the two FGDs were selected accidentally from various segments of the communities, while two hoteliers were conveniently sampled, one each from budget and star-rated facilities.

Interviews and discussions covered wide spectrum of the two TFs. However, in the narrations reported later, a premium was placed on the views of traditional authorities on the origins, benefits and challenges facing each festival, while the views of hoteliers on the economic gains of festivals were elicited. Extracts from FGDs are reported here as substantive matters on their own or as corroborators of other views.

All interviews were conducted in the homes and hotels of the respective interviewees. At Techiman, the FGD with 11 participants took place under a tree near the main (open-air) marketplace, while that of Bechem (involving nine participants) was at a corner of the town's lorry station. All interviews and FGDs were recorded and later transcribed verbatim. The transcripts were then content-analysed. This allowed the data to speak for itself. The transcripts were then returned to the interviewees to check and verify that the notes represented an accurate record of the interviews (Strauss & Corbin 1998). In a couple of instances, some changes had to be made at the request of the interviewees in order to capture what they insisted were an accurate reflection of their sentiments.

Quotes by informants are presented with their anonymous number as well as status and town. In all, 26 people, aged between 38 and 62, participated in the study. Data collection took place between the 17th and 28th of October 2015.The following have been used to identify the interviewees and FGD participants whose quotations were used:

TECH – Techiman; BECH – Bechem; TRA – traditional authority; HOT – hotel proprietor or manager; FGD – FGD participant; M – male; and F – female. Each identifier begins with the anonymous number assigned to interviewees and participants.

## Results and discussion

In the following analysis, the variables selected for comparison cover both those common as well as those not so familiar in the literature.

### Case #1: *Apuor* Festival of Techiman; celebrated April/May

#### *Historical origins*

Oral tradition has it that about two centuries ago, an epidemic broke out in the Bono Kingdom that claimed several lives in the communities, including Techiman, the capital. Consultations with the gods revealed that the abominations of the people had reached the high heavens, hence the grim mortality rates. The oracle directed that only a 'rejection' of such iniquities would turn away the wrath of the

*Table 35.1* An overview of the main attributes/facets of *Apuor* festival

| Type/format | Commemorative/communal |
|---|---|
| Event product(s) | The core product is a durbar of chiefs and people as well as mock battle in remembrance of the past wars fought by their ancestors. |
| Additional product(s) | Ban on noise making four weeks to real celebration. |
| Key ritualistic component(s) | Cleansing of shrines of the local deities as a symbol of rededication of the community to the cherished traditions of their forebears. Visit to the royal mausoleum by chiefs and elders to pacify the ancestors. |

gods. *Apuor* is an Akan word meaning 'rejection', a 'denunciation' or an end to the evil deeds of the past. Rejection of sinister deeds was symbolised by the subjection of community leaders to public ridicule. Thus, for one week every year, the citizens are at liberty to criticise their leaders without let or hindrance. The objective was that community leaders would then be scrupulous in the discharge of their official duties, while the citizenry were expected to abstain from moral decadence. *Apuor* is, therefore, a celebration of decency, moral uprightness in society. *Apuor* is essentially a commemorative festival that has increasingly been overtaken by cleansing or purification rituals as the public ridicule component has waned over the years.

## Cultural practices (event product)

Because of its genesis, it is difficult to discuss its economic or other consequences without placing the modern-day *Apuor* in its right context. As one traditional elder put it,

> Ours is a centuries-old tradition; a week is set aside every year for the citizens to castigate traditional elders for their misdeeds and other infractions in the course of the year. But I must confess, however, that the practice is now dying out. Citizens seldom chide the elders these days. In fact, I have never witnessed people pouring scorn on the *Omanhene*, (overlord of the traditional area) or other elders since my adolescent days, even though the practice has not been officially proscribed. Participation in the festival keeps growing, nevertheless.
> 
> (#1/M/TECH/TRA)

These sentiments were corroborated by a female FGD participant who maintained that

> These days; most citizens are more interested in the merry-making components of the festival. The real purpose of the festival is lost on the attendees. The public ridicule seems to have been popular in those days when a sort of class system prevailed; an upper class and a lower class made up of ordinary citizens.

> This is no longer the case even though the family reunions still take place. Young attendees are engaged in merry-making while the elders attend to the purification rites.
>
> (#7/F/TECH/FGD)

Despite the differences in their ages and social status, the two agree on the cultural practices of today. Culture is dynamic; hence, in spite of its inherent virtues, the tradition of public ridicule was bound to give way as happened in Ancient Rome around the Renaissance era (Fridgen 1991). Nevertheless, it would be interesting to undertake an enquiry into the touristic – and sociological – implications of celebrating *Apuor* as originally intended. For instance, would residents and visiting indigenes participate at the same level? Would non-indigenes be attracted to such a festival?

## Economic benefits (impact)

On the economic benefits of *Apuor*, the two hoteliers provided very useful insights. According to the proprietor of a one-star hotel,

> There is generally a significant increase in patronage (of hotel rooms) during *Apuor* festival. However, these annual hikes cannot be compared to the level we witnessed when Techiman hosted the 2008 National Farmers day Awards. Usually, the demand for food and beverages (F & B) does not match demand for rooms, apparently because most guests tend to consume these from family homes during *Apuor*. The situation was significantly different from the 2008 Farmers Day event when demand for F & B was almost as high as that for rooms.
>
> (#3/M/TECH/HOT)

On her part, the owner-manager of a budget facility added that

> The volume of business expands considerably during the celebration of *Apuor* so we eagerly look forward to that occasion. We were, therefore, highly disappointed a couple of years back when it was called off.
>
> (#2/F/TECH/HOT)

Thus, to a very large extent, the owner of the budget facility acquiesced in the views of her counterpart that *Apuor* brings about a hike in the hotel business. She, however, made no comparison between demand during *Apuor* and that of Farmers Day. She also made no reference to demand for F & B. This may be so because in Ghana, it is not obligatory for budget hotels to serve F & B on their premises (Ghana Tourist Board 2005). It is also possible that budget facilities may be shunned by attendees to contemporary events who tend to be high-ranking government officials. Generally, in Ghana, the F & B departments of hotels face competition from low-priced eateries known locally as *chop-bars* (Akyeampong 2007; Briggs 1999). Finally, given that many attendees would be returning home for the event, they may be eating with family and friends rather than commercial establishments.

## Case #2: *Adekyem* of Bechem; celebrated in April–May

### Historical origins

*Adekyem* is a very recent creation that is not even a decade old. But the events it seeks to commemorate are quite old, between two hundred and three hundred years old. *Adekyem* means 'sharing', a direct linkage to Bekyem – the vernacular for Bechem (or the place for sharing). According to history, Ashanti warriors returning from expeditions to the lands in north-western parts of modern Ghana and beyond stopped at a particular place to share their booty. With time, as the Asante empire declined and wave after wave of retreating warriors decided to settle, the place became known after its originating activity – war booty sharing – or 'Bekyem' in the vernacular. This was preferred to 'Behyiase', an earlier name which literally meant 'meeting place'. The people of Bechem are full-blooded Ashantis and for over two centuries celebrated no TF except *Akwasidae*, celebrated in the palace every seventh Sunday to pacify the gods, just as their kith and kin in Ashanti Region proper. However, in 2011, the Omanhene (overlord) of Bechem TA, Nana Fosu Gyeabour Akoto II, instituted *Adekyem* to commemorate the origins of the TA. The 2011 maiden edition of *Adekyem* was graced by Otumfuo Osei Tutu II, the *Asantehene* or grand overlord of the Asante kingdom. The gesture was meant to underscore their Ashanti origins. An educational endowment fund was launched at the maiden edition (Anane-Agyei 2012).

### Cultural practices (event product)

A traditional elder quizzed on the topic revealed that

> On the eve of the durbar, the *Omanhene* (traditional over-lord) and a small group of royals enter the stool room at night to perform rituals. Despite my position, I am not privy to what goes on there. I, however, join in the procession on Saturday mid-morning to the durbar grounds.
>
> *(#15/M/BECH/TRA)*

*Table 35.2* An overview of the main attributes/facets of *Adekyem* festival

| Type/format | Commemorative/communal |
| --- | --- |
| Event product(s) | Besides the grand durbar of chiefs and people, *Adekyem* lacks a core product, obviously as a result of its recent origins. It may take a while for one product to crystallise as the core. |
| Additional product(s) | There is a miscellany of event activities that should pass for secondary products common with other festivals. For *Adekyem*, the most outstanding ones are the exchange of gifts and the display of voluntarism. Besides being innovative, they also capture the essence and spirit of the festival. |
| Key ritualistic component(s) | None – nontraditional festival. |

This revelation confirms what is in the literature (e.g. Anane-Agyei 2012) that the climax or main event product is the durbar of chiefs and people. As stated from the outset, exoteric rituals undertaken out of public view cannot pass as touristic events. One can, thus, posit that after the inception of a festival, a couple of add-ons eventually crystallise as core event products. It may, therefore, take a while for some activity(ies) to emerge as cultural practices or event product associated with *Adekyem*.

Notwithstanding its recent origins, *Adekyem* was bound to have one or the other impact. On economic gains, one traditional leader had this to say:

> Since the institution of *Adekyem* in 2011, we have enjoyed an appreciable increase in trading activities during celebrations. I am not in the hospitality industry which is of interest to you but the increased sales in basic goods and services is very evident during celebrations. For me, however, the occasion is as culturally significant as its economic fall-out.
>
> (#15/M/BECH/TRA)

This view was corroborated by a FGD participant who remarked that

> Well, I feel satisfied with the rise of commercial activities. As a trader myself, I have over the past two years made extra sales during the festival. Remember that the essence of the festival is the exchange of gifts and I believe that most visitors (i.e. indigenes living outside Bechem) might purchase their gifts from elsewhere, so only a small percentage of gifts are bought locally. Nevertheless, I'm okay with business during the celebration.
>
> (#21/F/BECH/FGD)

The foregoing quotes indicate a consensus about the potential economic gains to be made from *Adekyem*, especially because of the gift-exchange involved. Meanwhile, hotel proprietors had these sentiments to share:

> I have observed an increase in business during the celebration of *Adekyem*, though I will not say the hotel is over-booked. Most of the guests are natives living in Sunyani, Kumasi, Accra and Techiman. Demand reaches its peak from Friday to Sunday.
>
> (#16/M/BECH/HOT)

While confirming this scenario, the second proprietor added that

> *Adekyem* festival has really resulted in increase in demand for our products. It's our third year and there has been visible expansion in sales during celebrations. Of course, the demand for rooms far exceeds that for food and beverages but that is not peculiar to us. Other occasions when we do such brisk business are the funerals of dignitaries but *Adekyem* is exceptional because it is a community-wide event.
>
> (#17/BECH/HOT)

It is clear that the two hoteliers enjoy a boom in business during the festival, a feature that is common in all major TF towns around the country. However, one can infer from the narratives that the 'pulling power' of *Adekyem* is not as high as with older festivals. Similarly, the resulting increase in general commercial activities is moderate.

## Challenges

Though a fairly recent festival, one cannot rule out challenges associated with *Adekyem*. According to the traditional authority,

> Ours is a relatively 'young' festival; it may not be as old and popular as *Munufie* or *Apuor*. I want to believe that the economic gains from these older festivals in the region might have influenced the *Omanhene* into instituting *Adekyem*. It is currently in its formative stages and so we cannot point to any definitive challenge(s). Perhaps, as an evolving TF, we can rather talk of missing activities (event products) that could be added to place *Adekyem* on the same pedestal as the established ones in the region and beyond.
>
> *(#15/M/BECH/TRA)*

However, other interviewees expressed different views, one of which is cited here. An FGD participant maintained that

> The composition of the organising committee should change drastically. It should include more of the young people, possibly event management professionals and less of the traditional elders. Such people serving on the committee should be able to inject more innovative ideas that will increase the volume of attendees, especially non-indigenes.
>
> *(#22/F/BECH/FGD)*

The last quote touches on a very sensitive topic. By definition, the organisation of a TF is the preserve of traditional authorities; elected or appointed local and central government officials only lend a helping hand. Though an organising committee comprises a cross section of the community, e.g. farmers, traders, the youth and major migrant groups, it is, invariably, dominated by traditional leaders. In the Ghanaian setting, it is not common to have an 'ordinary' citizen chairing a committee when there is a chief around. In traditional matters such as a TF, it is indeed rare; yet, young and educated members of a community might have more progressive ideas. The counterargument is that a TF risks being unduly modernised or even commercialised if the role of traditional authorities is played down. The problem is, therefore, not likely to be peculiar to *Adekyem*.

## Conclusion

TFs have in recent times attracted increased attention as the leading triggers of domestic tourist flow in Ghana. From a tourism perspective, however, the conceptual bases of most scholarly works are as convoluted as the festival types. This chapter sought to demonstrate that the product approach enriches the discourse on TFs within the larger context of tourism development by bringing convergence to an otherwise disparate field. The product attributes are common to all TFs, irrespective of type, scale, age or level of popularity. Thus, despite the obvious differences between them, the framework could be systematically applied to a comparative study of *Apuor* and *Adekyem* festivals. In fact it could have been applied to a comprehensive case study of each of them – and be meaningfully replicated anywhere else.

Just as a product has value, price, sellers, etc. and is found in every household, so one can identify attributes, facets or phases in every TF to facilitate thorough appraisal. Each attribute can be subjected to in-depth analysis either in a case or comparative study. Another advantage is that it can be easily adapted to suit the research objectives and design. For practice, all stakeholders, from host communities and sponsors to attendees and municipal authorities, should easily relate to a 'product', as either producers, intermediaries, patrons or regulators.

# References

Akyeampong, O. (2007). *Tourism in Ghana: The Accommodation Sector.* Accra: Janel Publications.
Akyeampong, O. (2011). Pro-poor tourism: Residents' expectations, experiences and perceptions in the Kakum National Park Area of Ghana. *Journal of Sustainable Tourism, 19*(2), 197–214.
Akyeampong, O. A. & Yankholmes, K. B. (2016). Profiling Masquerade Festival attendees in Ghana, *Event Management, 20*(2), 285–296.
Allen, J., O'Toole, W., McDonnell, I. & Harris, R. (2011). *Festival and Special Event Management*, 2nd edn. Milton: John Wiley and Sons.
Amenumey, E. (2003). PANAFEST 97': Perceptions from foreign participants. *Oguaa Journal of Social Science, 4*, 16–38.
Amenumey, E. & Amuquandoh, F. E. (2008). Event tourism in Ghana. In Akyeampong, O. & Asiedu, A. B. (Eds.), *Tourism in Ghana: A Modern Synthesis* (pp. 24–40). Accra: Assemblies of God Literature Centre.
Anane-Agyei, N. A. K. (2012). *Ghana's Brong-Ahafo Region: The Story of an African Society in the Heart of the World.* Accra: Abibrem Books.
Archer, B. (1978). Domestic tourism as a development factor. *Annals of Tourism Research, 5*(1), 120–141.
Bowdin, G., Allen, J., O'Toole, W., Harris, R. & McDonnell, I. (2006). *Event Management.* London: Elsevier Ltd.
Briggs, P. (1999). *Guide to Ghana.* Guildford: Brandt Publications.Clarke-Ekong, S. F. (1995). Ghana's festivals: Celebrations of life and loyalty. *Ufahamu, 23*(3), 16–33.
Clarke-Ekong, S. F. (1997). Traditional festivals in the political economy: The case of contemporary Ghana. *Journal of Social Development in Africa, 12*(2), 49–60.
Ewusi, B. K. (2005). *Social Conflict in Contemporary Effutu Festivals.* Unpublished Master's thesis, Bowling Green State University, Ohio, United States.
Fridgen, J. D. (1991). *Dimension of Tourism.* East Lansing, MI: Educational Institute of the American Hotel and Motel Association.
Ghana Tourist Board. (2005). *New Harmonized Standards for Accommodation and Catering Establishments in Ghana.* Accra: GTB.
Government of Ghana and UN Development Programme. (2010). *Ghana Millennium Development Goals Report.* Accra: Ghana: UNDP Ghana and National Development Planning Commission/Government of Ghana.
Kotler, P. (1984). *Marketing Management-Analysis, Planning and Control*, 5th edn. New York: Prentice Hall.
Mathieson, A. & Wall, G. (1982). *Tourism: Economic, Physical and Social Impacts.* Essex: Longman.
Mensah, I. & Dei-Mensah, R. (2013). *Management of Tourism and Hospitality Services.* Cape Coast: Edsam Press.
Middleton, V. (1989). Tourist product. In Moutinho, L. & Witt, S. (Eds.), *Tourism Marketing and Management Handbook* (pp. 573–576). New York: Prentice Hall.
Ministry of Tourism/Ghana Tourist Board. (1996). *15-Year Tourism Development Plan (1996–2010).* Accra: MoT/GTB.

Odotei, I. (2002). Festivals in Ghana: Continuity, transformation and politicisation of tradition. *Transactions of the Historical Society of Ghana*, New Series, *6*, 17–34.

Sarantakos, S. (1998). *Social Research*, 2nd edn. London: Macmillan.

Sharpley, R. & Telfer, D. J. (2002). *Tourism and Development: Concepts and Issues*. Clevedon: Channel View Publications.

South Australian Tourism Commission. (1997). *Planning Special Events and Festivals*. Adelaide, SA: The South Australian Tourism Commission.

Strauss, A. & Corbin, J. (1998). *Basics of Qualitative Research: Techniques and Procedures for Developing Grounded Theory*. London: Sage Publications, Inc.

Wyllie, R. W. (1994). Gods, locals, and strangers: The Effutu *Aboakyer* as visitor attraction. *Current Anthropology*, *35*(1)78–81.

# 36
# TOURISM PRESSURE AS A CULTURAL CHANGE FACTOR
The case of the Guelaguetza festival, Oaxaca, Mexico

*Marco Hernández-Escampa and Daniel Barrera-Fernández*

## Introduction

Cultural experiences nowadays constitute the basis of leisure and function as a repository of the values of modern society (MacCannell 1976; Rifkin 2001). As a result, such cultural experiences, especially events and attractions, now play a key role in global society, due to their function as 'factories of meanings' (Rooijakkers 1999) for the visitors' consumption. This means that traditional festivals might become in high demand for those seeking the appeal of authenticity. This is the case of the Guelaguetza, an indigenous festival in Mexico, which yearly attracts thousands of visitors nationwide and from abroad, all interested in experiencing ancient values and cultural expressions.

### *Tourist pressure at traditional festivals*

Tourists make an intense and short-time use of a very limited number of heritage assets and cultural attractions. The reason is to be found in the fact that tourist experience in cities is measured in days and hours, even in minutes in the case of cultural attractions or seconds in particular sites. In addition, cultural tourists do not often repeat their visits to the same place, and they are continuously looking for new attractions (Ben-Dalia, Collins-Kreiner & Churchman 2013). As a result of this, a process of selection of cultural assets takes place since only a few buildings and social representations are able to be adapted to the tourist visit. Furthermore, the cultural attractions they choose must be easy to comprehend, in order to meet their expectations and take into account the visitors' limited knowledge of local history and culture (Meethan 2003; Ashworth 2009). The main difference between the selection of cultural assets made by locals and the one made by tourists is that, for the latter, only a limited choice is made, usually among the largest, most spectacular and unique resources.

The tourist's approach to a local culture or 'tourist gaze' (Urry 1990) is built on socially constructed images, implying that sometimes they are flexible. These preconceptions mean that one of the main objectives of a journey is to see what must be seen (Delgado 2002), i.e. what is presented by tourist guides, leaflets, advertisements, movies, TV shows, web pages and social media. In the creation of the 'tourist gaze', markers are also crucial since they help identify places that 'deserve' a visit. As a result, signage, sculptures and urban landscape all help to reinforce a tourist's selection of attractions. The power of markers has been widely studied in places such as Stratford-upon-Avon, where the Shakespeare Birthplace Trust has achieved a key role in defining which places are considered as authentically related to Shakespeare and which are not (Urry 1990).

Such decisions as to the 'must see' status of various cultural assets imply a change of values conferred on heritage in particular, taking into account that heritage is a political resource used to give legitimacy to a social reality, dividing between 'them' and 'us'. As a result, tourists need to feel that the heritage assets that they have selected are especially relevant for them. At this point, Poria and Ashworth (2009) distinguish between conservation and 'heritagisation'. Conservation seeks to protect the past as exactly as possible, while 'heritagisation' refers to the use and abuse of an idealised or even invented past for the occasion. Such a dual dynamic is especially powerful when deeply rooted representations of culture strive to adapt to modern tourist demands.

As Gunay (2008) points out, the tourist use of local culture and heritage can serve to reinforce identity thanks to its outward projection. However, when interest is exclusively economic, the value of displaying the culture and legacy of a social group is lost and only those representations of culture seen as relevant for tourists are promoted, always with the aim of achieving the maximum economic profit. As a result, when the selection of heritage assets and cultural representations made by and for tourists and locals differs significantly, conflict may arise, not only in the choice of resources but also in their interpretation and use. This situation is especially likely when locals and visitors are from very different cultural backgrounds or when relatively recent cultural representations are considered.

In addition, the kind of heritage selection that gives priority to commercial value has the disadvantage of short duration, since it is viable only while economic benefit is considered adequate. This is because cultural tourism is closely linked to changes in fashion and lifestyles, and thus is clearly a volatile market. In fact, it has been estimated that investments in cultural tourism last for only ten years in average (Ashworth & Larkham 1994). Consequently, tourist products are quickly perishable in essence, and new products need to be offered once again.

This work focusses on the Guelaguetza festival, held yearly in Oaxaca, Mexico, and whose origins can be traced back more than 500 years. This case is of particular interest not only because of its importance as an indigenous celebration but also due to the tensions between tradition and cultural change. The main aim of this research was to clarify the role of tourist pressure in cultural change. On the one hand, adaptations to modern visitors' requirements imply the production of new cultural displays, but at the same time, the process arguably reinforces identity and traditions. Sometimes, the new adaptations might lead to new heritage creation, as it is the case of architecture, accessories, designs and even gastronomy in terms of installations. In order to achieve this aim, direct participant observations were performed during the 2017 edition of this festival, questionnaires were administered to visitors and also local authorities were interviewed regarding the organisation of the event. Initially, the history and meaning of the festival will be summarised in order to create a background for the reader, due to the complexity of meanings implied in such a long historic process as is the case for the Guelaguetza. Thereafter, the remainder of the results of the research will be presented.

## Oaxaca: diversity as background

Located in the southern portion of North America, Mexico represents the interface between two major biogeographical zones, and due to its great number of species, it is considered to be a megadiverse country (Cantu, Wright, Scott & Strand 2004). Cultural diversity is also relevant since the country was home to most of the Mesoamerican civilisations, and contact with the cultures from other parts of the world has only added to its sociocultural complexity (Fuentes & Reyes 2000). The state of Oaxaca is located to the south, and it is the most diverse Mexican area, both naturally and culturally (Poole 2007; Robson 2007).

Oaxaca conjures up images of time, continuity and change. The Central Valleys, where the capital city is located, constitutes one of the most recognised archaeological regions in the world. Universally relevant social processes such as the origin of agriculture, invention of writing and the rise of complex societies occurred in the area, producing astonishing examples of material culture exemplified in archaeological sites like Monte Albán, Mitla, San José Mogote, Yagul, Dainzú, Zaachila and many others (Marcus 1990; Brumfiel & Fox 2003; Flannery & Marcus 2005). It is worth mentioning that the historic city of Oaxaca, together with Monte Albán archaeological site, is listed on the United Nations Educational Scientific and Cultural Organisation (UNESCO) World Heritage List (Niglio, Cruz & Alfonso 2013). The introduction of Christianity and Western culture during colonial times indeed eroded the ancient social structures; however, syncretism and resistance eventually yielded new results. Just to give an idea of cultural richness in Mexico, besides Spanish and other introduced languages, 11 linguistic families are still spoken in the country, 6 of them in Oaxaca (Martin et al. 2011).

## Guelaguetza, the great *Fiesta* of Oaxaca

Guelaguetza is a Zapotec word which can be translated as 'to share' or 'to cooperate'. The origins of the contemporary festival can be traced deep into history. During Pre-Hispanic times, the Central Valleys of Oaxaca had been inhabited by a number of ethnolinguistic groups, including the Zapotecs and later the Mixtecs. These societies created complex systems until the Mexicas, also known as Aztecs, conquered the region in the 15th century. Following this, a city was founded whose name was Huayxácac, which can be translated as 'in the nose of the *huaje* tree' (*huaje* is a particular kind of tree). This city was multicultural from the beginning as a range of groups thrived there until the next century when the Spanish conquerors arrived. It has been documented that these indigenous people used to perform rites which included offerings to a dual or bisexual God/Goddess of the maize called Centéotl. These ceremonies presumably used to take place in a nearby hill nowadays known as '*Cerro del Fortín*' (Hill of the Small Fortress) which has been since those times the site of the Guelaguetza or its preceding versions (Lizama Quijano 2006; Flores-Marcial 2015).

Once the Spanish domain was established in the Central Valleys, Huayxácac was refounded as Antequera, in honour of the Andalusian city of the same name (Niglio et al. 2013). Still other names have been used for the site, such as the original Luá (Zapotec) or different versions of the Náhuatl name Huayxácac which ended as Oaxaca and was eventually formally selected. As happened in other places in Mexico, the ancient rites were deeply rooted in the indigenous culture. A strategy of the evangelising friars was the adaptation of traditional ceremonies in order to make them look Catholic, with the aim of completing the shift away from the indigenous cultures; however, this was never totally accomplished. In fact, this process has been studied in one of the Guelaguetza dances called 'Danza de la Pluma' (Oleszkiewicz 1997). As part of this process, a Catholic temple devoted to the Carmen Virgin was built near *Cerro del Fortín*. By this stage, Centéotl had acquired a level of acceptability to the conquerors. Since this virgin is venerated on July 16th according to the Catholic ritual calendar, it was established that the nearest two Mondays to that date would be festive. This is why nowadays, the Guelaguetza is celebrated in two Mondays of July, known as Lunes del Cerro (Mondays of the Hill). Exact dates can fluctuate, especially if they overlap other festivities. Another important fact during colonial times was that tribute to the Spaniards was imposed over the natives, sometimes associated to this festivity (Oaxaca State Government 2015).

The Independence War in Mexico, initiated in 1810, provoked a tumultuous historic period not surpassed until the Mexican Revolution ended in the early 20th century. Governments in the post-revolutionary period had to guarantee peace and also encourage a sense of nation in order to legitimate their rising powers. Both Marxism and Indigenism were rooted in the country, which led to the indigenous past being emphasised in the nationalistic official discourse. Most foreign elements were regarded as imperialist and therefore potentially harmful to the new regime. Art and imagery in general took inspiration from the Pre-Hispanic past and also from the rich Mexican folklore. For example, painter Frida Kahlo dressed herself as *tehuana* (woman from the Isthmus of Tehuantepec region) to create her appealing personal image (Helland 1990). In the specific case of dance, this art contributed in many ways to reinforce the nationalistic imaginary (Pérez Montfort 1994). In Oaxaca, a vast array of traditional dances and dresses had survived during the colonial period, sometimes with Pre-Hispanic content. The modern Guelaguetza contributes to this regional and national identity.

In 1932 the 400th anniversary of the designation of Oaxaca as a city took place. To celebrate it an 'ethnic tribute' was organised, where all the regions of the state performed their traditional dances and music, and gave offerings of local products such as food and handicrafts to Miss Oaxaca and the public (Lizama Quijano 2006). Until 1973, this modern Guelaguetza took place in a natural slope of the Cerro del Fortín, where every year wooden structures were built for the occasion (Oaxaca State Government 2015).

The main part of the Guelaguetza is framed by the two consecutive festive Mondays. The scene for this event is the auditorium at Cerro del Fortín. On both of these days, a woman, representing Centéotl, the ancient deity, opens the festival. After that, the dances from the regions start (Figure 36.1). After each performance, the dancers throw gifts to the

*Figure 36.1* *Tehuanas* during the Guelaguetza
Source: G. Feria Alonso.

audience to share, but also as reminiscence of the colonial tributes. Prior to these Mondays, the delegations march on Saturdays in a parade through the main streets of the historic city as open invitation for the main events. The auditorium is also used for other complementary spectacles such as concerts or performance arts. Many other squares and buildings in Oaxaca City also stage cultural events through the Guelaguetza season. Gastronomy and handicrafts are also offered to the visitors in special events. One of the most visited venues established during Guelaguetza is the Feria del Mezcal, where visitors can taste and buy this alcoholic beverage obtained from different species of agave plants. The liquor is similar to tequila.

## Tourism pressure and cultural displays during the Guelaguetza

Oaxaca and surrounding sites have a concentrated set of tourist resources which include the city itself and its colonial monuments such as baroque churches, palaces and the cathedral. A number of museums exist in Oaxaca, including one located in Santo Domingo Monastery which is home to the famous archaeological treasures found in Monte Albán. The typical market of the city is another key attraction where diverse merchandise can be bought, including local food. One-day tours to surrounding sites, such as archaeological sites, mezcal factories and the Hierve el Agua petrified cascades, are offered. Nearby towns like Teotitlán del Valle, Tlacolula and Zaachila can also be visited. Another important attraction is the Tule tree located in Santa María del Tule village. This tree is more than 2,000 years old, and it is considered the largest living organism in the world. Ecotourism is also developing in the nearby northern mountain range.

Oaxaca is visited by national and foreign tourists year round. Even so, a major peak is caused by the Guelaguetza. In 2006, social disturbances in the historic city affected the festival, causing a decrease in the number of visitors, which lasted a few years. However, more recently, the festival has become increasingly popular, and it has been announced by the Tourism Department that the 2017 edition of this event finally surpassed the 2005 statistics with nearly 100 per cent of hotel occupation (Rodríguez 2017). In fact, the tourist sector wants to extend the Guelaguetza to a third week in recognition of this success, which seen from another viewpoint, would be inconsistent with the traditional setup of the event.

At this point, it is becoming clear that the Guelaguetza traditional indigenous event is under heavy pressure from tourism. In order to produce economic profit and tourist satisfaction, several adaptations have occurred. For example, there have been urban and architectural modifications in the city. Street modifications for pedestrian use are currently a global trend; however, in the specific case of Oaxaca, such a decision has followed tourist demand and not local preference. In fact, the historic city of Oaxaca has been subject to heavy gentrification, especially northwards from the main square. Currently, Macedonio Alcalá, a pedestrian street, joins the main square with the Santo Domingo Monastery, and it accommodates most of the tourist stores and restaurants. Since the market is located just south to the main square and has kept its original commerce function, the southern portion of the historic city is more frequented by locals. As a result, the tourist activity concentrates around Santo Domingo, although tourists also are present around the main square.

Architectural additions to the city are also clearly related to tourism activity and specifically to the Guelaguetza festival. It could be expected that a pedestrian path would link the historic city and Cerro del Fortín. Instead, and paradoxically in respect to the pedestrian adaptations in the city centre, a massive car park was built in the slope of the hill causing a number of urban difficulties such as traffic congestion during the celebrations. In fact, the site of the celebration had been previously been segregated from the city because of the construction of a highway. In practice, it is becoming difficult to get there for tourists unless taxi or car is used. Further, originally, the location for the Guelaguetza was an open-air auditorium. However, a structure has been built to partially cover the site. The structure is clearly visible from many points in the central valleys, and beyond aesthetic appreciations it has become part of the landscape. Shocking as it was to some people, the new auditorium now is another urban icon.

In relation to social organisation, a relevant feature in Oaxaca is that many stores in the city are run by communities. People from surrounding towns have created cooperatives to produce and sell handicrafts by themselves. These cooperatives rent or own a number of premises in the city centre. Local producers sell their handicrafts to the tourists and later divide the profits according to their internal social organisation. Some cooperatives are actively run by women. In the state of Oaxaca, many different traditional dress designs are currently used in the daily life, especially by women. In most cases, men have abandoned their traditional clothes to adapt themselves to modern urban styles trying to get better jobs. Still, it can be seen that some handicraft sellers are dressed in traditional ways. This represents at the same time authenticity and social performance directed to tourists. In part, tourist pressure is helping to preserve this kind of heritage. In contrast, most clothes sold to tourists in the streets contain indigenous designs, but are adapted to modern trends. As example, modern shoes or purses can be bought which are modern in shape and use, but created with textile indigenous designs. This implies a commercial strategy but also ethnic differentiation. Only true indigenous people may use authentic traditional clothes, and these can be appreciated in the streets or in major splendour during Guelaguetza dances.

Traditional cultural attractions include tangible heritage and activities where the visitor is a simple consumer, while creative tourism implies participation and experience (Richards & Wilson 2007). In this sense, social performances and intangible heritage increasingly play a leading role as tourist attractions by themselves. Creative tourism conceives culture as a process (Landry 2008), where the work of the artists, actors, dancers and cooks is more important than the final product. Creative tourism can be observed in Oaxaca in different ways. Traditional activities have been given renewed attention by tourists searching for the authentic or indigenous, of which Oaxaca is one of the most important representatives in Mexico. That is the case of the traditional food market in the city centre, where all kinds of local products are perceived as 'exotic' especially by foreign visitors. Apart from going into the market to take pictures and try some local specialties, nowadays a wide range of activities related to local gastronomy are offered, including city tours to taste mezcal or chocolate and Oaxacan cooking classes. The increasing demand from creative tourists has resulted in the creation of new facilities such as the Gourmet Market. It complements the traditional market with more avant-garde products. This case exemplifies how creative tourism not only helps by revitalising traditional activities but also adds to the intangible cultural offer of a destination.

## Perception of experiences during the Guelaguetza

The State's Secretary of Tourism is the main organiser of the festival, showing the high relevance that this event has for the state's administration. There is an Organising Committee assisted by three departments with strategic functions: Legal-Administrative, Logistical-Operative and Promotion-Marketing. Every department is divided in a number of subcommittees, 17 in total, including ticketing, security, staging and tourist information (Oaxaca State Government 2015). However, so far no measurement of experiences has been performed for this event.

In order to analyse the perception of visitors during the 2017 edition of the Guelaguetza, 200 questionnaires were applied in total in both the auditorium and the Feria del Mezcal. Initial data analysis shows that foreign visitors are well represented, especially from USA, Canada, Brazil, Argentina, Germany, Italy, China and Japan. Mexican visitors come from basically every part of the country. Most of respondents had visited the festival before, and they plan coming again. In addition, most of people answered that the festival was the main reason to come to Oaxaca. These two statements show high levels of loyalty to this festival, something uncommon in cultural tourism (Ben-Dalia, Collins-Kreiner & Churchman 2013). Emotional experience during the festival was highly rated and clearly surpassed any difficulties. The most common complaint related to urban mobility and difficulty in accessing and leaving the auditorium. In fact, a section of the auditorium has free entrance, and a more than 2 km long queue was recorded, formed by people waiting hours and hours to get a place.

In contrast to the visitors' enthusiasm, the Guelaguetza has been criticised by the academy. Despite the contemporary sense of the event, devoted to highlighting local traditions and thus creating a sense of identity, it also promotes division and may even encourage racism (Montes García 2005). This may be a consequence of the colonial system, where social strata were related to the concept of race and were used to imply a pyramidal structure in society that is being reinforced in the festival. Another possible criticism derives from direct observation relates to gender roles. Indigenous traditions tend to promote hetero-patriarchal behaviour in an already rigid society. This can be observed in some dances related to courtship, where women are depicted as male possessions or they play submissive roles. In this sense it is interesting to note that in the Isthmus region, some traditional cultures conceive a third gender called *muxhe* consisting of biological male individuals who play feminine roles (Martos 2010). However, they are not depicted in any way in the festival. A final observation relates to animal welfare since in a specific dance a living turkey is put on public show with the consequent stress for the animal. All these topics represent future challenges for this ancient festival within a postmodern context.

## Conclusions

Despite its multiple contradictions, the Guelaguetza constitutes one of the major cultural events in the American Continent. Its origins can be traced back, in the form of precedents, to more than 500 years ago. Some of its primordial elements are clearly still identifiable, such as the figure of the ancient deity called Centéotl. Another long-term component is the location itself because its site at Cerro del Fortín has also been preserved, even though modern accommodations have been built to satisfy contemporary visitors' requirements. As a display of culture, its inherent essence has been expanded throughout the years, an example being the symbolised colonial tribute now performed as offering gifts to the audience.

As in any major festival, there are some challenges for improvement. Transport in general and accessibility to the auditorium have been identified as two of the major issues to be resolved. It is also very important to underline the fact that a considerable degree of authenticity is still one of the main values of this indigenous event. Indeed, modern tourist pressure may have modified the nature of some elements but has also created new heritage manifestations. Examples of material cultural such as handicrafts have evolved to satisfy postmodern tourist demands. On the other hand, gastronomy and other intangible kinds of heritage remain reasonably unchanged. Paradoxically, cultural change can become a means of survival, and the Guelaguetza represents a compromise between tradition and modernity, with efforts placed on preserving what is considered genuine.

This event contributes effectively to the locals' identity, pride and economy even if some of its traditional traits such as ethnicity, social domain or gender roles have been criticised as not representing what is considered to be progress. In the case of visitors, in many cases, cultural distance between the visitors and the full cultural meaning implied in the social representations might become an interpretive obstacle. Still, any person visiting Oaxaca during this grand event is likely to become satisfied intellectually, aesthetically as well as emotionally, and evidence for this is provided in the results of this study. So far, history suggests that this sacred hill of Oaxaca will receive worship from locals and foreigners, and the dance and music will go on.

## Acknowledgement

The authors thank Gustavo Roldán Feria Alonso for providing photographic material for this research.

## References

Ashworth, G. J. (2009). Do tourists destroy the heritage they have come to experience? *Tourism Recreation Research, 34*(1), 79–83.

Ashworth, G. J. & Larkham, P. J. (1994). *Building a new heritage: Tourism, culture and identity in the new Europe.* London, UK: Routledge.

Ben-Dalia, S., Collins-Kreiner, N. & Churchman, A. (2013). Evaluation of an urban tourism destination. *Tourism Geographies: An International Journal of Tourism Space, Place and Environment, 15*(2), 233–249.

Brumfiel, E. M. & Fox J. W. (2003). *Factional competition and political development in the new world.* Cambridge, UK: Cambridge University Press.

Cantu, C., Wright, R. G., Scott, J. M. & Strand, E. (2004). Assessment of current and proposed nature reserves of Mexico based on their capacity to protect geophysical features and biodiversity. *Biological Conservation, 115*(3), 411–417.

Delgado, M. (2002). Los efectos sociales y culturales del turismo en las ciudades históricas. *Congreso Internacional sobre el desarrollo turístico integral de ciudades monumentales*, Granada, Spain, 19–22 February 2002. Granada: Turismo de Granada.

Flannery, K. V. & Marcus, J. (2005). *Excavations at San José Mogote 1: The household archaeology*, 1. Ann Arbor: University of Michigan Museum.

Flores-Marcial, X. M. (2015). *A History of Guelaguetza in Zapotec communities of the central valleys of Oaxaca, 16th Century to the Present*' PhD thesis, University of California, Los Angeles.

Fuentes, J. M. L. & Reyes, A. L. (2000). *Historia general de México.* Mexico City, Mexico: Grupo Editorial Patria.

Gunay, Z. (2008). Neoliberal urbanism and sustainability of cultural heritage. *44th ISOCARP Congress*, Dalian, China. 19–23 September 2008.

Helland, J. (1990). Aztec imagery in Frida Kahlo's paintings: Indigeneity and political commitment. *Woman's Art Journal, 11*(2), 8–13.

Landry, P. F. (2008). *Decentralized authoritarianism in China.* New York, NY: Cambridge University Press.

Lizama Quijano, J. (2006). *La Guelaguetza en Oaxaca: Fiesta, relaciones interétnicas y procesos de construcción simbólica en el contexto urbano.* Mexico City, Mexico: CIESAS.

MacCannell, D. (1976). *The tourist: A new theory of the leisure class.* London, UK: Macmillan.

Marcus, J. (1990). *Debating Oaxaca archaeology*, 84. Ann Arbor: University of Michigan Museum.

Martin, G. J., Camacho Benavides, C. I., Del Campo García, C. A., Anta Fonseca, S., Chapela Mendoza, F. & González Ortíz, M. A. (2011). Indigenous and community conserved areas in Oaxaca, Mexico. *Management of Environmental Quality: An International Journal, 22*(2), 250–266.

Martos, J. A. F. (2010). Travestidos de etnicidad Zapoteca: Una etnografía de los Muxes de Juchitán como cuerpos poderosos. *Anuario de hojas de Warmi, 15.*

Montes García, O. (2005). La fiesta de la Guelaguetza: Reconstrucción sociocultural del racismo en Oaxaca. *Revista de Ciencias Sociales, 11*(1), 9–28.

Meethan, K. (2003). Mobile cultures? Hybridity, tourism and cultural change. *Journal of Tourism and Cultural Change, 1*(1), 11–28.

Niglio, O., Cruz, S. & Alfonso, P. (2013). Oaxaca, patrimonio de la humanidad. *Acontragolpe Letras, 77,* 19–20.

Oaxaca State Government. (2015). *Manual de Organización. Guelaguetza.* Oaxaca, Mexico: Oaxaca State Government.

Oleszkiewicz, M. (1997). La danza de la pluma y el sincretismo cultural en México. *Revista de crítica literaria latinoamericana, 23*(46), 105–114.

Pérez Montfort, R. (1994). *Estampas de nacionalismo popular Mexicano: Ensayo sobre cultura popular y nacionalismo.* Mexico City, Mexico: CIESAS.

Poole, D. (2007). Political autonomy and cultural diversity in the Oaxaca rebellion. *Anthropology News, 48*(3), 10–11.

Poria, Y. & Ashworth, G. J. (2009). Heritage tourism – current resource for conflict. *Annals of Tourism Research, 36*(3), 522–525.

Richards, G. & Wilson, J. (2007). Creativities in tourism development. In Richards, G. & Wilson, J. (Ed.), *Tourism, creativity and development* (255–289). London, UK: Routledge.

Rifkin, J. (2001). *Los bienes culturales en la era del acceso.* Madrid, ES: Fundación Autor.

Robson, J. P. (2007). Local approaches to biodiversity conservation: Lessons from Oaxaca, southern Mexico. *International Journal of Sustainable Development, 10*(3), 267–286.

Rodríguez, O. (2017). Oaxaca recupera turismo perdido en una década con la Guelaguetza, Retrieved from www.milenio.com/estados/oaxaca_recupera_turismo_perdido_en_una_decada_con_la_gulaguetza_0_999500515.html. Accessed 08/01/2018.

Rooijakkers, G. (1999). Identity factory South-East towards a flexible cultural leisure infrastructure. In Dodd, D. & Van Hemel, A. M. (Eds.), *Planning European cultural tourism* (78-99). Amsterdam, NL: Boekman Foundation.

Urry, J. (1990). *The tourist gaze: Leisure and travel in contemporary societies.* London, UK: Sage.

# 37
# FESTIVALS FOR SUSTAINABLE TOURISM DEVELOPMENT
## A case study of Hadoti region, Rajasthan

*Anukrati Sharma*

## Introduction

Festivals work as blood for our culture and heritage. Janiskee (1980, pp. 96–104) clarified that festivals and events can be comprehended as 'formal periods or projects of pleasurable movements, stimulation or festivals having a festive character and openly commending some idea, event or truth'. However, in the era of digitalization and modernization, the new generation appears to have limited or no interest in engaging in the traditional, local and small festivals, either as participants or audience. This is despite the fact that in a country like India, festivals have their own importance to educate people about our culture, traditions, values and beliefs. Certainly, the festivals of different states have diverse importance. This chapter aims to focus on the festivals and fairs of the Hadoti region of Rajasthan state. The state of Rajasthan is located in the northwestern part of the subcontinent. The state has an area of 132,140 square miles. The Great Indian Desert, also known as Thar Desert, is located in the west of Rajasthan. Hadoti region is located in the southeast of the state. The best season to visit Rajasthan and Hadoti region is from July to December. The Hadoti region is quite rich in culture and heritage tourism. Being on a research project searching for opportunities for tourism in the last two years, I have carried out fieldwork in some of the festivals and fairs with the objective of gathering information and records, such as photographic resources and other information related to the organisation and management of these festivals and fairs. Hence, my fieldwork gave me an opportunity to directly observe these festivals. Through the fieldwork observations, I found that the essence of tourism success and suitability lies in the festivals, fairs and events of this region. The music, songs, dance forms, costumes, jewellery, food and language are unequalled by any other place in the state. The festivals are so overpowering that no matter from where the tourists come, what are their language preferences, etc., the rhythm, sounds and environment will never fail to impress them. However, in spite of immense potential of festival tourism, the region is not benefiting from the potential advantages of and support for showcasing the hidden and unexplored festivals to the community at large. The aim of this research is to investigate in more depth issues related to festivals and tourism in Hadoti region of Rajasthan.

The specific objectives of this study focused upon:

- Whether inevitable festival growth and promotion contribute to community empowerment in the region.
- How to identify challenges faced by local people and festival organizers.

The chapter also aimed to examine the festivals as an important tourism product for economic development.

## Literature review

Waitt (2003) states that arranging/managing tourism in a way that is suitable to personal satisfaction and values results in socioculturally sustainable tourism. Sustainability in tourism expects hosts to be strongly positive towards improvements, to upgrade the visitors' involvement and add to the place attraction quality. Schuster (2001) has contended that festivals yield financial advantages by raising the profile of places, their items and establishments and pulling in streams of visitors, capital and internal speculation. For some western urban communities, a key inspiration in creating festivals has been to recover from long-term monetary decay. Festivals and occasions have been only one piece of a more extensive range of new 'social procedures' (Fox Gotham 2005a) used to revitalise traditional economies (Zukin 1995) where relaxation, diversion and tourism support an 'encounter economy' (Pine & Gilmore 1999).

In terms of financial effects, as Formica (1998) confirms, festival profiles, sponsorship, management and estimating economic drift portrayal are the fundamental subjects. Moscardo (2007) attests that the current tourism research on festivals and occasions is centered on four fundamental themes including financial effects, assessing and improving advertising and administration quality, the administration of festivals with a specific focus on showcasing their potential benefits and evaluating the more extensive festival impacts as experienced by local residents and communities. Concerns about the huge dominating effect of monetary issues have led to a concentration of research on mega-scale festivals (Gibson, Willming & Holdnak 2003). However, local and more parochial festivals can likewise produce positive financial effects. Experimental investigations of assorted local and parochial festivals, for example, the Creoli Christmas Festival, New Orleans (Chacko & Schaffer 1993); the Carbondale Mountain Fair, Arizona (Long & Perdue 1990); the Umbria Jazz celebration, Italy (Formica & Uysal 1996); and the stone music celebration in Loch Lomond, Scotland (Senior & Danson 1998), demonstrate the potential positive impacts.

However, it is good to know that local festivals and events are now being recognized as a tool and source for enhancing and promoting regional identity and development. One of the major reasons behind this acceptance of the local festivals and events is the inadequate income sources in the rural areas in comparison to metro cities (Felsenstein & Fleischer 2003; Jackson, Houghton, Russell & Triandos 2005). In context of the present research, the local festivals can work as a backbone not only for income but also for the development and reimaging of a region. Events can make a positive representation for the local community and give a healthy marketing benefit in the context of alike communities (Allen, O'Toole, McDonnell & Harris 2002). The important part here is to consider that we need ample resources and investments for promoting local festivals. Making huge investments and developing extra facilities are not always necessary to market an event (Bailey 1998 cited in Smith &

Forest 2006; Law 1993 cited in Smith & Forest 2006). The community involvement, belief in their culture and values itself are sufficient to promote the local festivals and events. The merger of festivals and events with tourism can certainly bring many benefits to the society at large. Numerous regions consider festivals to be extremely significant components of the tourism product (Jackson et al. 2005; McMorland & Mactaggart 2007), and festivals are one of the best tourism products which a region can offer to differentiate it from its competitors.

## Research methodology

For the present study, both cross-sectional and longitudinal data, and primary and secondary data have been collected. The reason to adopt longitudinal data in this research is to enhance the authenticity of the study as many researchers are of the opinion that longitudinal data are superior to cross-sectional data for calculating growth (Singer & Willett 2003). The study used mixed methods. The primary data were collected through a questionnaire, key informant interviews and focus groups, and the secondary data were collected through relevant published studies in libraries and search engines.

The questionnaire was designed to include both closed and open-ended questions, and covered topics such as demographics, socioeconomic information, the benefit flow from festivals, challenges faced by local festival organizers and suggestion for improvements. In all, 50 respondents completed the questionnaire. Focus group discussions were held with groups comprising 5–10 respondents. The focus groups were used to collect in-depth information from festival artists, festival organizers and local people. Issues which were discussed included benefits realized from festivals in the area, barriers to accessing benefits from festivals and suggestions to increase benefits from festivals. Interviews were conducted with various festival stakeholders such as festival organizers, festival artists, tourism entrepreneurs and local communities. These stakeholders were considered to be important due to their extensive local knowledge, experience, expertise and their involvement with the festivals in the study area in question. A total of five interviews were carried out. Finally, visits to some festival-related places in the study area were conducted with the intention of observing and interacting with the stakeholders. The visits also enabled the researchers to personally view various socioeconomic activities and also provided better understanding of what happens on the ground in relation to festivals investment and benefits flow.

## Background

### Festivals of Hadoti

There are many festivals in the Hadoti region, but no complete synopsis of all offered festivals exists, especially of the small local festivals. The region comprises four districts, namely Kota, Bundi, Baran and Jhalawar. The interesting thing about this region is that all the districts have different festivals. The region offers an amalgamation of big and small festivals. Guided and planned tours, exhibitions and shows are also organized during these festivals. These festivals also perform the role of educating and spreading knowledge about the cultural, heritage and religious beliefs in the area.

The best-known festival in Kota, in the Hadoti region, is the *Dusshera* Festival, which is also known as *National Dusshera* Festival. The other important and famous festivals and fairs of the region are *Kajali Teej* of Bundi, also known as the *BundiUtsavKarthik* Fair, and the *Chandrabhaga* Fair. Festivals like the *Dol* Fair of Baran, *Nahan* Fair of Sangod (near Kota) and the Tribal Fair of Sitabariand *Ramleela* of Patunda (Baran) are of great importance in terms of local community engagement, but they are quite neglected by the tourists as well as by the Government. Results from this study suggest that the local artists who are actually presenting the culture and maintaining the intangible heritage through organizing these festivals and fairs are facing many problems. As a representative of the aforesaid neglected festivals, the *Ramleela* festival of Patunda village will be used as an example in the chapter.

## *Uniqueness of* Ramleela *at Patunda village*

Dramatic presentations of the epic Ramyanaare are known as *Ramleela*. In India, this type of *Ramleela*, as of Patunda village in Rajasthan, is rare to find (Goel 2017). There are a few other examples of this type of festival in Uttarakhand and Rohtak, Haryana. Patunda is a small village with a population of 2,566 people located on the banks of Kali Sindh River. This village is setting a different way to protect our culture and to pay respect to our epics through the medium of *Ramleela*. The artists who perform the *Ramleela* are from every age group, from 10 to 82 years old. The artists of *Ramleela* are teachers, students and farmers. In total, 30 artists perform the entire drama. The festival treasurer noted, 'They are not facing major problem related to funds but still they need support for their survival'. The costumes for the artists cost approximately 30,000–40,000 INR (US$463–617). Other than this, they need to expand money in buying the curtains, etc. for creating the scenes for the drama. However, through discussions with the organizer and other artists, it has been demonstrated that small and local festivals are facing a major problem in relation to lack of interest among the public in coming and watching the activities of the occasions/festivals and dramas. One of the respondents even said, 'Television serials and movies are replacing the charm of local festivals and dramas'.

The *Ramleela* at this village has been running for the last 150 years. Many unique factors make this festival different from other *Ramleela* events in the state and outside the state. While all the other *Ramleela* festivals are celebrated when Lord Ram won over Ravan, this dramatic presentation at Patunda celebrates the birthday of Lord Ram, i.e. *Ramnavmi*. The artists who perform in the play are the local people – they are not the trained professional actors and singers. In fact, most of them are farmers. Male artists also play the characters of females. This is because females in the village areas are still not free to dance and sing in public places.

The features and origin of this *Ramleela* are distinct, but the place where it is organized is also unusual. It is not performed on a stage, but rather in an 11th-century old temple of Lord Laxmi Narayan. To make it even more interesting, and according to the epic, three processions are performed. The first is on the opening day of the *Ramleela*, the second celebrates the marriage procession of Lord Ram and the final one focuses on the death of the evil character Ravan.

## Discussion

While surveying the impact of the festival as a tourism or pecuniary advancement tool, the standard approach is to create some type of impact assessment. On many occasions, this includes assessing a total measure of earnings and business change owing to the festival. Constantly, the outcomes are often great and are then used to reinforce requests for financial help for the festival. However, by and large, such assessments rely on local multiplier estimates without explaining how this converts into local financial benefits (Gazel & Schwer 1997;

Kim, Scott, Thigpen & Kim 1998; Long & Perdue 1990). Festivals have an enormous impact on tourism. According to Deco and Balogu (2002), tourism can protect the surroundings and local heritage in a way that would not be possible if mega occasions were not organized. Festivals represent a key that is able to open access; thus, they represent solutions to resolve a variety of broader social issues and support in achieving many hidden benefits. Furthermore, festivals offer an opportunity to empower women – as noted previously, women are relatively limited in terms of what they are allowed to do and how they are allowed to behave in public. Festivals can provide an occasion where social issues can be brought to light and where existing barriers to women's participation in society can be broken down. It is essential to empower women through festivals in order to unravel these social issues, or in other words, to remove these barriers.

## *Festivals and economic development*

Festivals are becoming a popular destination marketing tool for certain destinations. The reason behind this is probably because the festivals not only create an image of the tourist destination but also develop new avenues of income. According to Getz (1997), the utilization of local festivals has achieved increased impetus in recent decades as a source for tourism development. It could be traditional, cultural or religious festivals, or it could be a new 'made-up' festival. Boo and Busser (2006) investigated the contribution of festivals in changing destination image and call for longitudinal research on this inquiry. The purpose behind organizing these festivals is to attract visitors to the destination. Festivals can be easily accepted as a promotional tool as festivals enhance demand for domestic tourism. Festivals that have been well organized are helpful in the reimaging of a place. For a region like Hadoti, where tourism is in the developing stage, a key question is whether potential exists for economic growth, destination marketing and reimaging through festivals? As Pugh and Wood (2004) stress, there is a need to embrace a better way to deal with festivals in order to take full advantage of what is possible for the host economy/group.

Festivals often catch the attention of social organizations, politicians, businesses and tourism stakeholders. The recognition that the festival contributes economically to the destination makes it easier for the organizers to get financial support from the public to conduct activities during the festival. Prevalent celebrations held, for example, in Edinburgh, Salzburg and Glyndebourne are considerably more than just social occasions. Changes in both the delivery and marketing activity for festivals have brought about monetary impacts that frequently overshadow the festivals' social messages (Frey 1994).

An immensely effective growth indictor of festivals has been their successful outcomes in relation to delivering satisfaction to visitors, economic gains, increased number of tourists and reimagining of place as festival tourist destinations.

## *Marketing and information technology strategies for promoting festivals*

In essence, seeking ways to strengthen discourse and exchange between the local community, place, society, culture and tourist/visitor are core concerns in relation to developing a marketing strategy and using information technology to promote festivals. Falassi (1987) characterizes festivals as an occasion, a social wonder, experienced in practically all human societies. The bright assortment and sensational intensity of their dynamic choreography and stylish perspectives, the indications of profound meaning underlying them, their authentic roots and the contribution of the locals have attracted the attention of casual visitors and have drawn in explorers and men of letters alike. Government, and the private players who are engaged in organizing festivals, need to develop a strategy to enhance a mutually beneficial plan for local community development and tourist recreation. It is, therefore, important to focus upon 'how can we plan and promote festivals so they efficiently able to attract more visitors/tourist?'

Waitt (2003) notes that good planning and administration as well as personal satisfaction for attendees and equitable results are all fundamental for sustainable tourism. Waitt (2003) identifies a range of ways in which festivals can best promote themselves and contribute to sustainable tourism. These include creating official web pages for all festivals; using content marketing for promotion; maximizing promotion through social networks and sites, including Twitter, Facebook, etc.; providing platforms for local people to discuss and present their ideas for organizing festivals; creating opportunities to solicit feedback and suggestions from visitors at festivals; and developing courses on events and event management in universities and other educational institutions.

During these festivals and fairs, a series of activities are organized, such as guided tours, exhibitions, conferences, shows, theater and workshops. One of the aims of educational and leisure activities is to spread knowledge about the history and cultural heritage of towns and cities. Therefore, there is a willingness to reach a varied audience, spreading knowledge through educational, fun and festive activities. A key element is the set of reenactment activities that provide visitors with the opportunity to relive history. These representations are presented by theater groups and historical reenactment groups. The former stage theatrical representations, while the latter are more educational and base their representations on historical and archaeological research. These strategies needed to be highlighted in the promotion of festivals in the Hadoti region. Many of the existing festivals and fairs, in spite of having immense potential, are not well recognized by the tourism and events industry. The stakeholders of the tourism, events and education industries need to understand the importance of festivals. Merely assuming that festivals are a source of entertainment will not work. Festivals are the milestones that showcase the real heritage and culture of a place. Moreover, educational institutions and universities can promote these festivals by encouraging the students to participate and perform in the festivals at state, national and international levels.

## Conclusion

The local festivals of Hadoti region are naturally instrumental in enhancing local tourism and in making a major contribution to the economy. Festivals are a key strategy in promoting those places that have suffered from underinvestment and have been essentially abandoned. Tourism, event and hospitality industry stakeholders and local officials need to view local festivals as crucial activities for providing income and business opportunities, especially for the local people who are suffering from economic scarcity. Festivals are not merely a medium of entertainment in the Hadoti region; they have an important social function and provide economic development resources. This chapter suggests that the local festivals of Hadoti have both social and economic impacts. However, there are some important lessons to be learned. Focused training on marketing and promotion strategies is needed. Additionally, government support is needed in order to allow local festival organisers to conduct well-planned and well-operated festivals. Finally, amenities should be provided to the attendees, visitors and tourists at the place of festival.

Respondents in this study believe strongly that the *Ramleela* that they perform in their village can play a vital role in enhancing the number of tourists in the region. The event offers an opportunity to showcase the talents of local people, plus the event itself can become an important tourist attraction as long as they received large-scale support. The respondents felt that as well as creating the identity of their place and strengthening their efforts to bring their culture back, their version of the *Ramleela* is unique and different. It was felt that not only Patunda village or the Hadoti region could benefit but that the whole state could benefit.

It is important to have a positive outlook towards these types of festivities organized by local people. Government, private companies and other stakeholders should recognize that by supporting these hidden talents, the events like the *Ramleela* of Patunda can sustain in long run. Respondents felt that if Government can support their efforts, then more tourists would come to see the festival, thus contributing more in the long term. However, youngsters also have to take a step forward to support such events. For that to happen, creating awareness is very much needed. In order to be successful, other stakeholders also have to get involved. For example, other stakeholders in the tourism and hospitality industry could arrange food stalls with the local recipes to promote food tourism. Information technology, which can spread information about the unique features of these festivals, could also be harnessed to improve marketing efforts. In particular, to promote local festivals, stakeholders may use social media marketing and virtual tours of the festivals. Festivals, especially local festivals in India, are starting to be recognized as significant resources for regional growth. Festivals are important elements of tourism product at the regional level. Surely, the way we develop these festivals will lead to future growth of tourism not only at the regional level but also at the national and international levels. Indeed, study and evaluation of the social, cultural, emotional and economic impacts of these festivals is badly needed. Local festivals in this region have much to offer both locals and visitors, but further work is required to ensure both a satisfactory visitor experience and a positive outcome for host communities.

## References

Allen, J., O'Toole, W., McDonnel, I. & Harris, R. (2002). *Festival and Special Event Management*. Milton: Wiley.

Bailey, H. (1998). Local heroes. *The Leisure Manager*, 16(10), 24–27.

Boo, S. & Busser, J. A. (2006). Impact analysis of a tourism festival on tourist destination image. *Event Management*, 9(4), 223–237.

Chacko, H. E. & Schaffer, J. D. (1993). The evolution of a festival: Creole Christmas in New Orleans. *Tourism Management*, 14(6), 475–482.

Deco, E. & Balogu, A. (2002). *The Need to Harness Nigeria Publishers*. Abuja: Federal Ministry of Tourism and Trade.

Falassi, A. (1987). *Time Out of Time: Essays on the Festival*. Albuquerque, NM: University of New Mexico Press, 91–100.

Felsenstein, D., & Fleischer, A. (2003). Local festivals and tourism promotion: The role of public assistance and visitor expenditure. *Journal of Travel Research*, 41(4), 385–392.

Formica, S. (1998). The development of festivals and special events studies. *Festival Management and Event Tourism*, 5(3), 131–137.

Formica, S. & Uysal, M. (1996). A market segmentation of festival visitors: Umbria Jazz festival in Italy, *Festival Management and Event Tourism*, 3(4), 175–182.

Fox Gotham, K. (2005a). Theorizing urban spectacles: Festivals, tourism and the transformation of urban space. *City*, 9(2), 225–245.

Frey B. S. (1994). The economics of music festivals, *Journal of Cultural Economics*, 18(1), 29–39.

Gazel, R. C. & Schwer, R. K. (1997). Beyond rock and roll: The economic impact of the Grateful Dead on a local economy, *Journal of Cultural Economics*, 21(1), 41–55.

Getz, D. (1997) *Festival Management and Event Tourism*. Elmsford, NY: Cognizant Communications.

Gibson, H., Willming, C. & Holdnak, B. (2003). Small-scale event sport tourism: Fans as tourists. *Tourism Management*, 24(2), 181–190.

Goel, A. (31 March 2017). The Harmonious Ramleela of Patoonda. *The Hindu Newspaper*.
Jackson, J., Houghton, M., Russel, R. & Triandos, P. (2005). Innovations in measuring economic impacts of regional festivals: A do-it-yourself kit. *Journal of Travel Research*, *43*(4), 360–367.
Janiskee, R. (1980). South Carolina's harvest festivals: Rural delights for day tripping urbanites. *Journal of Cultural Geography*, *1*(Fall/Winter), 96–104.
Kim, C., Scott, D., Thigpen, J. F. & Kim, S. (1998). Economic impact of a birding festival. *Festival Management and Event Tourism*, *5*(1–2), 51–58.
Law, C. (1993). *Urban Tourism: Attracting Visitors to Large Cities*. London: Mansel.
Long, P. T. & Perdue, R. (1990). The economic impact of rural festivals and special events: Assessing the spatial distribution of expenditures. *Journal of Travel Research*, *28*(4), 10–14.
McMorland, L.-A. & Mactaggart, D. (2007). Traditional Scottish music events: Native Scots attendance motivations. *Event Management*, *11*(1–2), 57–69.
Moscardo, G. (2007). Analysing the role of festivals and events in regional development. *Event Management*, *11*(1–2), 23–32.
Pine, B. J. & Gilmore, J. H. (1999). *The Experience Economy*. Boston, MA: Harvard University Press.
Pugh, C. & Wood, E. H. (2004). The strategic use of events within local government: A study of London borough councils. *Event Management*, *9*(1/2), 61–71.
Schuster, J. M. (2001). Ephemera, temporary urbanism and imaging. In Vale, L. J. & Warner, S. B. (Eds.), *Imaging the City: Continuing Struggles and New Directions* (pp. 361–196). New Brunswick: CUPR Books.
Senior, G. & Danson, M. (1998). Liam and Noel in Balloch: An economic impact assessment. *Tourism Economics*, *4*(3), 265–278.
Singer, J. D. & Willett, J. B. (2003). *Applied Longitudinal Data Analysis: Modeling Change and Event Occurrence*. London: Oxford University Press.
Smith, M. & Forest, K. (2006). Enhancing vitality or compromising integrity? Festivals, tourism and the complexities of performing culture. In Picard, D. & Robinson, M. (Eds.), *Festivals, Tourism and Social Change: Remaking Worlds* (pp. 133–151). Clevedon: Channel View Publications.
Waitt, G. (2003). Social impact of the Sydney Olympics. *Annals of Tourism Research*, *30*(1), 194–215.
Zukin, S. (1995). *The Cultures of Cities*. Cambridge, MA: Blackwell Publishers.

# 38
# PLACEMAKING BETWIXT AND BETWEEN FESTIVALS AND DAILY LIFE

*Burcu Kaya Sayari and Tuba Gün*

## Introduction

Festivals are highly influential elements in public life. This stems from their power to operate outside the limits and borders of daily life while still being situated in a socially constructed realm. This attribute of being 'betwixt and between' daily life and performances nourishes both the festivals and daily routines by providing a chance for a connection among local people, between generations, and between traditional and popular culture. Even though there is not a consensus in the literature about which is more powerful in this interaction, it is certain that festivals and daily life are intertwined. As elements of the festival become extended into daily life, we are also witnessing the infiltration of the roles and rules of the festivals into our daily life as well.

One way to investigate events is by considering their form and content (Bowdin, O'Toole, Allen, Harris & McDonnell 2006, p. 22). While content refers to elements of collective cultural memory such as myths and customs, form points to performances such as songs and dances, and together they shed light on the festival structure (Brandt 2012, p. 141). The formation and combination of these elements determine the flow and the borders of the festival. These, in turn, actively shape the placemaking attributes of festivals. The form and content of the festivals change not only the way place operates but also the rules of this operation. In the flux of festivals, places may be transformed consecutively many times, owing to the practices festivals involve. The same place may have various formations as the festival exerts its power over it by reshaping its borders and rules. During festivals, symbols, meanings and practices create distinct atmospheres and identities of places.

Cultural anthropology has a significant ability to uncover the symbols, meanings and processes woven into the festival atmosphere. Yet it is only recently that anthropology is gaining prominence in the contemporary debate around festivals with its insightful ethnographic methods and theoretical frameworks (Frost 2016). It is vital that we allow cultural anthropology and its valuable tools to contribute to festival studies (Frost 2016, p. 578). This chapter examines the flow between the festival and daily life through an ethnographic analysis of liminalities that occur as part of the placemaking of Water Festival, in the small Turkish county of Kızılcahamam. The thermal springs of Kızılcahamam have historical roots which go back to the Roman Empire.

The springs have long been appreciated not only for their curative powers and their appeal to tourists and travellers but also for creating an excellent opportunity for the promotional efforts of the county. The festival lasts 3–5 days and has been taking place since the 1930s. As such, it enjoys a significant place in the community. In addition to the contemporary entertainment activities and concerts, it embraces traditional and religious rituals such as oil wrestling and whirling dervishes ceremonies as a juxtaposition between the past and the present. Given this festival is at once a varied assemblage of heritage and popular culture, it is a significant tourist attraction. Moreover, it simultaneously reflects symbolic, social and doxastic elements of the county.

## History of the festival

According to the official records of the Ottoman Empire, the history of the town dates back to the 1820s. These records show that there was a small village of Yabanâbâd, which was the predecessor of Kızılcahamam (Ünal 2016, pp. 148–149). The population of the county is currently 25,000. The first occurrence of the festival in the 1930s was in the form of a street fair that later evolved into the present form. The festival has moved locations over time, but each of the selected locations has been the common point at which inhabitants usually gather in their daily lives. In the beginning, the fairs took place in the valley, which was part of the town's common land. As time passed, the street fair turned into a festival, and the festival moved to the area in front of the thermal springs, then to the main street, and then to the entrance of the national park, respectively.

The changes are not limited to the festival site. The original name of the festival was 'Festival of Soguksu', but it was changed into 'Kızılcahamam Culture, Art and Water Festival' in 1994. The name change was the result of the primary aim of the municipality, which was to foster and promote three different water sources of Kızılcahamam, which are thermal, mineral and spring water. Moreover, in parallel with the different practices of changing municipalities in charge, the performances and rituals that take place in the festival have been changing. While the oil wrestling activities and concerts remain the same, activities such as the staging of traditional marriage ceremonies, the amateur dramatics reviving historical events, Qur'an chanting and whirling dervishes have been added over time. In addition to these performances, the festival has included *jereed* (Turkish: *Cirit*): a traditional Turkish equestrian sport in which the object of the game is to throw the javelin accurately enough to hit the opponent (Sheehan 2004, p. 113), *sinsin* (a traditional fire play acted by men), reciprocal satires, folk dances and concerts. Nowadays, there is a marked shift from traditional performances to the combination of religious and modern activities. However, the oil wrestling activities continue to take place.

Naturally, opportunities for entertainment activities as part of daily life were limited in the past. It was not until the 1970s that TV arrived in the town. However, the social life of the town people was colourful. There were five cinemas in the town, and it was common for the townspeople to spend their leisure time in groups. As the festival was significant for the locals, it also represented a chance to dress up:

> I even remember people who dressed up as if they were attending a wedding. They were wearing evening dresses while they were going to the picnic of the festival. Wearing ordinary clothes to the concert of popular singers was considered to be disgraceful.
> *(Man, 48)*

## Festivals in the nexus of heterotopia and cultural capital

Festivals vary depending on different aspects such as their venues, season, scale, repeatability, theme and attitude to religion (Cudny 2016, pp. 32–33). The scope and components of each festival render it open to interpretation through different conceptual frameworks. Since 'festivals provide unusual activities and evoke feelings and emotions that are very different to the regular and material routines of the workday' (Davies 2015, p. 535), this fact makes the places of festival compatible with the notion of 'heterotopia' (Foucault 1986). Foucault (1986, p. 24) defines heterotopias by saying that

> There are also, probably in every culture, in every civilization, real places—places that do exist and that are formed in the very founding of society—which are something like counter-sites, a kind of effectively enacted utopia in which the real sites, all the other real sites that can be found within the culture, are simultaneously represented, contested, and inverted. Places of this kind are outside of all places, even though it may be possible to indicate their location in reality. Because these places are absolutely different from all the sites that they reflect and speak about, I shall call them, by way of contrast to utopias, heterotopias.

We also consider the festival to be a habitus, which covers different activities and places at once. Bourdieu describes the habitus as

> Both a system of schemes of production of practices and a system of perception and appreciation of practices. And, in both of these dimensions, its operation expresses the social position in which it was elaborated. Consequently, habitus produces practices and representations which are available for classification, which are objectively differentiated; however. They are immediately perceived as such only by those agents who possess the code, the classificatory schemes necessary to understand their social meaning.
> *(Bourdieu 1989, p. 19)*

The festival as a whole carries the attributes of an established order since it has its own internal rules. Therefore, drawing upon Bourdieu, we also question the degree to which this festival establishes itself as doxa, an 'established order that tends to produce the naturalisation of its own arbitrariness' (Bourdieu 1977, p. 164). Bourdieu draws our attention to the 'quasi-perfect correspondence between the objective order and the subjective principles of organisation (as in ancient societies) the natural and social world appears as self-evident' (Bourdieu 1977, p. 164). Even though the agents' apprehension of the world is 'the product of double structuring', with its objective (social structures) and subjective (schemes of perception and appreciation) sides (Bourdieu 1989, p. 20), subjective construction of the agent's vision emerges within the limits of structural constraints (Bourdieu 1989, p. 18).

This portrayal is very similar to the festival places. Wilks and Quinn (2016, p. 25) consider festivals as a heterotopia that not only 'require certain acts, performances or rituals to gain entry to them' but also juxtapose several incompatible spaces within a single space. In this juxtaposition, festivals can be evaluated 'as a mode of meaning and a process of communication' (Piette 2014, p. 231). From this point of view, festivals not only offer a reality that is distinct from the mundane, but they also present 'an ambivalent world which leaves room for fluid realities with contrary or contradictory aspects' as Piette (2014, p. 231) reveals.

In the same vein as Wilks and Quinn (2016, p. 25), Karaosmanoğlu (2010) builds on Foucault and Bourdieu and characterises Ramadan as one of the celebrations in Islam which creates a temporal heterotopia once a year by rearranging routine activities through 'a new discourse of time' (Karaosmanoğlu 2010, p. 293). Moreover, this month 'produces a multi-cultural and a multi-religious space' through universal values such as tolerance, peace and love (Karaosmanoğlu 2010, p. 294). However, not every event can create such heterotopias. Thus, these incidences are crucial. Moreover, Howell (2013, p. 57) argues that a festival with heterotopic characteristics can create a significant awareness in the participants' sense of place while admitting that 'not all (festivals) offer universals of place that can jolt, transport, or confront our sense of reality'.

In order to go beyond the existing festival literature, the chapter will elaborate on Bourdieu's (1977) notion of doxa, since we believe it has more explanatory power of the festival's placemaking process. While doxa and heterotopia enable us to scrutinise a festival's placemaking attributes, the liminality approach of Van Gennep (2010 [1960]) and Turner (1967) will allow us to dismantle the flow of a festival as a social practice. Van Gennep (2010 [1960]) focusses on 'the ceremonial patterns which accompany a passage from one situation to another or from one cosmic or social world to another' (p. 10), which, in turn, points to *rites of passage*. He scrutinises these ceremonies in three phases: separation, transition and incorporation. He describes the process that participants go through as a complete scheme which consists of 'preliminary rites (rites of separation), liminal rites (rites of transition) and post-liminal rites (rites of incorporation)' (Van Gennep 2010 [1960], p. 11). Turner builds on Van Gennep's concept of liminality. He deems liminality to be in between on a scale where at one end is the structured society and at the other unstructured positions (Turner 1966, p. 96). The use of such a scale highlights ambiguous positions that are 'neither here nor there; they are *betwixt and between* the positions assigned and arrayed by law, custom, convention, and ceremonial' (Turner 1966, p. 97; our italics). He focusses on the liminal stages in rites of passage since processes of mid-transition 'expose the basic building blocks of culture just when we pass out of and before we re-enter the structural realm' (Turner 1967, p. 110).

Turner (1974) distinguishes between liminal and liminoid phenomena. While liminoid experiences/spaces tend to appear in societies characterised by organic solidarity, in Durkheim's term, and fragmentary formation, liminal experiences/spaces tend to occur in societies characterised by mechanical solidarity (Turner 1974, pp. 84–85). Liminal experiences/spaces tend to unfold 'in the flow of natural and social processes' and may have a calendrical and rhythmic structure (Turner 1974, p. 85). Last but not least, by having a composite character, 'they reflect ... the history of the group' (Turner 1974, p. 85). We will use the term of liminality since it is more compatible with our case study.

Liminality also has spatial links. During the threshold phase, 'the passage from one social status to another is often accompanied by a parallel passage in space, a geographical movement from one place to another' which is accompanied by 'the literal crossing of a threshold which separates two distinct areas' (Turner 1974, p. 58). Thus, liminality assembles 'ritual and spatial relations'. These spatial elements not only determine the borders of the ritual process but also 'become charged themselves because their relations with other ritual symbols are activated during the rites' (Lawrence 1992, p. 213). Moreover, these symbols may not be at the forefront of the ritual, and their symbolic meaning may perish as the ritual is replaced by daily life (Lawrence 1992, p. 214).

The chapter interrogates the placemaking process together with the experiences and backgrounds of the agents participating in the festival and adopts a constructivist approach. Drawing from the work of Turner (1967) and Van Gennep (1960), the flow of the festival will be scrutinised as comprising three phases: preparation, festival duration and post-festival periods. The festival and its components are evaluated in each part through a 'time' element. This framework is compatible with Van Gennep's and Turner's points of view, which scrutinise activities on three levels.

The basis of this study was a number of sources of data. First, the authors collected information about the festival from historical collections, texts, photos and local newspapers. Then, in order to represent all groups involved in the festival, interviews were conducted with 13 residents of Kızılcahamam county centre and two villages in the county, who were festival organisers (1), prior and current local authorities (2), performers (3), audience members (5) and amateur researcher-writers (2). Semi-structured interviews were reinforced by participant observations over a one-week period in the summer of 2017. All data were kept confidential. Interviews ranged in duration from 30 to 120 minutes and were tape-recorded. Locals were interviewed in their homes, offices and cafes. In the analysis of these sources, the authors drew upon Turner (1967), Foucault (1986) and Bourdieu (1977).

## *Preparation period of Water Festival*

The preparation period comprises different elements for different stakeholders of the festival such as inhabitants, the local authorities and visitors from outside of the county. First, the festival is announced, and invitations are sent to ensure a high level of participation involving all groups. In terms of the festival landscape, there are various preparations. Environmental preparations take place so that the traffic flow is arranged in a way that does not affect daily life. Moreover, food and harvest stands are erected for the sellers who come from the city centre, other towns and surrounding villages. The festival area is designated by the hanging of local and national flags.

The festival is a source of excitement for the local people who look forward to this time of the year. In previous years (although it is not a current practice), local people used to leave cushions at the festival site one day prior in order to hold a place:

> We were going the night before and arranging our place. Let me put in this way: we used to go at night time and leave a blanket. I mean it was fascinating to us. Also it used to influence our lives.
>
> *(Man, 61)*

Further, the women prepare provisions the night before, since the family will be at the festival area throughout the day. As a part of their community spirit, it was, in the past, very typical for the women in the same neighbourhood to gather and prepare food for every family on special occasions such as *Bayram* (*fest*) and festivals. On such occasions, traditional foods were being prepared meticulously:

> Preparations were beginning at least a week beforehand. My mother used to do Turkish crepes; Aunty Hacer was cooking flatbread. Aunty Zeliha used to ferment yoghurt. The others were preparing stuffed vine leaves. Others were stuffing dried eggplants.
>
> *(Man, 53)*

It is not only the audience who gets prepared beforehand but also the team who will perform the folk dances. Their rehearsals take place for approximately two months before the festival.

Moreover, the *mise en scènes* based on historical realities are also put in place. These activities are seen as a valuable part of the festival and the pride of the county.

The festival was a source of excitement in the county's life. It used to imply a break in the mundane flow of daily life:

> I will tell how it was before. We used to be very curious about it and getting very excited. We knew that we would have a good time. I mean our participation was heartfelt and enthusiastic. Tradespeople were making preparations and see it as an opportunity. They used to feel that it was going to be good for them.
>
> *(Woman, 61)*

As life in the county changes in parallel with the technological improvements, such as television and the internet, the festival is losing its power to break the ordinary flow of daily life. In the past, it was the only way to listen to good music or to see famous singers. Moreover, neighbourhood relations were closer in the past, and it was more common to spend time in groups for all age groups. Today, the festival still has an important place in the county. However, the experiences of attendees and the community are different. It is the passage of time that has changed these experiences and the way of life in the county. Therefore, time is an illuminating element for each level of the festival.

## Festival duration and liminalities of the Water Festival

The festival site has different facets that make it a distinct place that is apart from daily life. First, even though this is not the case anymore, entrance to the festival originally required payment at the door. This was a strict demarcation line that draws attention to the fact that one has arrived in a place that is separated from daily routine. Since one of the traits of heterotopia is that it is not accessible to just anyone who wishes to enter, the festival site was, in a way, quite similar to heterotopias. As Foucault points out,

> In general, the heterotopic site is not freely accessible like a public place. Either the entry is compulsory, as in the case of entering a barracks or a prison, or else the individual has to submit to rites and purifications. To get in one must have a certain permission and make certain gestures.
>
> *(Foucault 1986, p. 26)*

The festival also captures divergent points in time. Wedding ceremonies and oil wrestling, which belong to the past, and concerts, which are elements of modern times, come together in the same festival. All these activities and performances belong to different time 'slices' as Foucault calls it which also contributes to making them a heterotopic site: 'We are in the epoch simultaneity: we are in the epoch of juxtaposition, the epoch of the near-far, of the side-by-side, of the dispersed' (Foucault 1986, p. 22). Another example, which vividly demonstrates this case, is the re-enactment of Atatürk's (the founder of the Republic of Turkey) visit to the town that happened in 1934. Until recently, the celebrations had been staging the events of this visit using cars and clothes authentic to the period.

The festival, as a regional custodian of cultural memory, encapsulates those historical occasions, which have a particular significance for the locals as well as traditional rituals. Therefore, it narrates a past event that flows into the present. As two different time slices – past and present – are intertwined, this event also creates another heterotopia.

In the same vein, almost every performance in the festival has its own rules that the locals are conversant with. Thus, there is a limit to how much performers can change their performances. When their practices are not compatible with the traditional, recognised and expected practices, there is a risk of them not being able to continue. One of these practices in danger of vanishing is *sinsin* (*fire dance*). In criticising the young *sinsin* performers, one of the locals underscores the importance of the correct moves.

> Young men performed it improperly. This game is not like that. *Sinsin* has a distinct music, atmosphere and figures. Those figures require a special talent. I mean they require much experience. Later, the villagers performed it. They were at a certain age, over 60–70s. They perform it properly. Each move has a special meaning. One performs these moves while there is a fire in the middle. Then, the rival appears and he chases him. If the rival catches him, he beats him, but only slightly.
>
> (Man, 66)

The festival makes use of a range of places, moving from one to the next. Each activity is associated with specific places. Moreover, the activities that take place in the form of corteges produce a different kind of place, which is a temporary one. As the cortege moves, it incorporates the places it is passing by into the festival space. As soon as the cortege leaves one place, daily life regains its superiority. Thus the borders of the places that the festival constructs are porous. In addition, some activities and performances use the whole town centre as a performative stage and create their flow instead of being stabilised in a particular place. There are two incidences of this case. One of them is the mise en scène of 'bride receiving', which includes taking the bride from her house to the performance of a wedding ceremony. The bride rides up to the festival location on horseback with the accompanying crowd.

> They took me on horseback. There was a retinue whose heads were all covered in white. The horses came from the villages. I wore a red veil that has a tiny slit in the front, but in a way so as not to show my face. They used to call it a *veil*. We went to the festival, but before, wandered in the town: 'there is a festival'. We wandered in the town. Everybody looked at us. It was not possible to find such a leisure activity easily in the past. I mean these events… they were something we had never seen before.
>
> (Woman, 82)

The second example is the revival of Atatürk's arrival to the town, which includes a long cortege. As the cortege moves through the main street of the town, one can be just passing by the same street. S/he will step into the festival habitus as the habitus is written into the place and equates its borders with the place. S/he may just continue to walk and return to daily life again in just a couple of moments. Therefore, there are multiple passages (in/out/in…) rather than only two (in/out). However, the borders – or thresholds – are still flexible as Bourdieu depicts within the habitus. Since the festival is surrounded by thresholds, they are implied by the divides of the place itself. From the traffic flow that is arranged by taking into consideration the festival to the flags that demarcate the festival area, there are lots of liminal zones that embody the boundaries between daily reality and the festival. Thus, there are different doxas in different liminal zones since every performance and daily life itself carry their common rules with them. These physical but invisible borders are not only porous but also define the rules that should be followed if one steps inside. The boundaries within which wearing performance costume is normal

*Figure 38.1* The retinue of bride receiving
*Source:* Ertuğrul İpek.

will be equated within the physical borders of performance zone. When the performer leaves these borders, since the costume is not compatible with common expectations, it will be seen as unusual.

## *Residual effects of the festival*

Some effects of the festivals do not quickly fade away and may penetrate into daily life. One of these effects is the privileged status of performers. Even though performers act their roles as a requirement of the festival doxa and leave them as a requirement of the daily life doxa, some extensions of the role still stay alive. Owing to the liquid form of the borders between the festival and real life, performers carry the status associated with their roles into their daily lives.

> When we win, we like it to be ranked first. Of course, we pride ourselves on victory. Wrestlers are well-known in the county. Especially, if he is a successful one, he becomes popular. People follow him.
>
> *(Man, 69)*

> They still respect me in the villages. When I go to the outskirts of the village, they call out to me '*Pehlivan! Pehlivan!*' (Wrestler! Wrestler!)
>
> *(Man, 82)*

On the other hand, it is sometimes the social capital or status accrued in daily life that defines the status that will be gained during the festival. For example, when asked the reason she did not perform as a bride in the festival, one of the interviewers answered,

> She was the wife of a teacher. I am just a daughter of a peasant and a wife of a peasant. Who would accept me?
>
> *(Woman, 66)*

Alternatively, social capital which infiltrates into the festival space is reflected back to the realm of daily life again as symbolic capital. Most of the people believed that the performance was real:

> For example, when my husband was passing through the villagers, they said, 'Look at that man, he must be a wealthy man, look at that wedding!' That is what they said to me: 'Here comes the bride who rode the horse!'
>
> *(Woman, 82)*

Another flow that occurs between the festival and daily life is the revival of some historical traditions that had been forgotten. One of the examples of this is the traditional wedding ceremony that had died out in the past and was revived after being placed in the context of the festival:

> Regarding their own weddings, young people were saying 'we want them (*traditional ceremonies*) too.', 'I want bridal procession.' It is like a chicken-egg relationship. A tradition, which is already rooted in the community before, goes on being performed by virtue of the festival.
>
> *(Woman, 56)*

## Conclusion

We discussed in this chapter the Kızılcahamam Water Festival's processes by drawing upon the theories of Turner (1967), Foucault (1986) and Bourdieu (1977). The temporal framework of Turner enabled us to scrutinise the festival in three phases, alongside the liminality inscribed into the place of the festival as it transforms the place and the flow occurs between the place of daily life and festival. We pointed out these liminal zones. We used doxa and heterotopia frameworks to scrutinise the festival's placemaking attributes. The liminal zones, doxa of the festival and daily life revealed that festival has porous borders. Thus, we could not consider our festival as a heterotopia. Even though we admit that the festival requires a social and cultural capital, these forms of capital are always in transition between everyday life and the festival.

As a doxa which has its own rules and order, the festival has its own borders that are equated with the physical place as well. Liminalities are intrinsic to these borders. Therefore, there are various interactions between this doxa and the doxa that belongs to the daily life. These two doxas embrace a flow of reciprocal exchange of roles and values. These reciprocal relations nourish the festival as well. However, the substantially unalterable and non-transferable rules of both the festival and routine life materialize the idiosyncratic framework of these places.

## References

Bourdieu, P. (1977). *Outline of a Theory of Practice* (Vol. 16). Cambridge: Cambridge University Press.
Bourdieu, P. (1989). Social space and symbolic power. *Sociological Theory*, 7(1), 14–25.
Bowdin, G., O'Toole, W., Allen, J., Harris, R. & McDonnell, I. (2006). *Events Management*. New York: Routledge.
Brandt, J. R. (2012). Content and form: Some considerations on Greek festivals and archaeology. In Brandt, J. R. & Iddeng, J. W. (Eds.), *Greek and Roman Festivals. Content, Meaning, Practice* (pp. 139–198). Oxford: Oxford University Press.

Cudny, W. (2016). *Festivalisation of Urban Spaces: Factors, Processes and Effects.* Cham: Springer.
Davies, W. K. D. (2015) Festive cities: Multi-dimensional perspectives. In: Davies, W. K. D. (Ed.), *Theme Cities: Solutions for Urban Problems* (pp. 533–561). London: Springer.
Foucault, M. (1986). Of other spaces. *Diacritics, 16*(1), 22–27.
Frost, N. (2016). Anthropology and festivals: Festival ecologies, *Ethnos, 81*(4), 569–583.
Howell, F. C. (2013). Sense of place, heterotopia, and community: Performing land and folding time in the Badalisc Festival of Northern Italy. *Folklore, 124*(1), 45–63.
Karaosmanoğlu, D. (2010). Nostalgia spaces of consumption and heterotopia: Ramadan festivities in Istanbul. *Culture Unbound: Journal of Current Cultural Research, 2*(2), 283–302.
Lawrence, D. L. (1992). Transcendence of place. In Altman, I. & Low, S. M. (Eds.), *Place Attachment* (pp. 211–230). New York: Plenum Press.
Piette, A. (2014). To be or not to be in a ritual: Essay about the mitigated presence. *Studia Nauk Teologicznych, 9,* 231–245.
Sheehan, S. (2004). *Turkey (Cultures of the World).* New York: Benchmark Books.
Turner, V. (1966). *The Ritual Process: Structure and Anti-Structure.* New York: Cornell University Press.
Turner, V. W. (1967). *The Forest of Symbols: Aspects of Ndembu Ritual* (Vol. 101). New York: Cornell University Press.
Turner, V. (1974). Liminal to liminoid, in play, flow, and ritual: An essay in comparative symbology. *Rice Institute Pamphlet-Rice University Studies, 60*(3), 53–92.
Ünal, U. (2016). Arşiv Belgelerinde Kızılcahamam ve Kızılcahamam İstiklal Harbi Şehitleri. In Erşahin, S., Çınar, H. & Arıoğlu, İ. E., (Eds.), *Kızılcahamam 100 Yaşında* (pp. 143–164). Ankara: Semih Ofset Matbaacılık.
Van Gennep, A. (2010 [1960]). *The Rites of Passage.* New York: Routledge.
Wilks, L., Quinn, B. (2016). Linking social capital, cultural capital and heterotopia at the folk festival. *Journal of Comparative Research in Anthropology and Sociology, 7*(1), 23–40.

# 39

# A FESTIVAL OF SONG

## Developing social capital and safeguarding Australian Aboriginal culture through authentic performance

*Candace Kruger*

**Introduction**

The preservation of performance traditions is one of the highest priorities for Indigenous people, as it is through song, dance and associated ceremony that Indigenous people maintain lore and a sense of self within the world. Without immediate action, many Indigenous music and dance traditions are in danger of extinction.
*(Yunupingu, Langton & Marett 2002)*

An appropriate and effective vehicle for facilitating the ongoing preservation and future development of Indigenous performance traditions is the festival. Historically, festivals around the globe have been utilised as vehicles to preserve, maintain and/or showcase Indigenous performance, knowledges and culture while concomitantly facilitating the development of social capital traditions (Whitford & Dunn 2014). Similarly, authentic Indigenous song taught to children and performed at festivals (among other events) is highly charged with cultural capital (Johnson 2012), and through participation, engagement and trust in what they learn, as a collective group, Aboriginal *jarjum* (children) provide community with local cultural knowledge when they perform.

This chapter presents a case study focussing on the extent to which the *Yugambeh* Language and Song Project (YLSP), in the *Yugambeh* language region (Gold Coast, Logan and Scenic Rim local government boundaries of South-East Queensland, Australia, *Yugambeh* 2015), highlighting the *Yugambeh* Youth Choir (YYC) – an Australian Aboriginal youth choir – facilitates the development of social capital and safeguards Aboriginal culture through performances at festivals and events, including National Aborigines and Islanders Day Observance Committee (NAIDOC) week events, National Reconciliation Week events and, in particular, the *Yugambeh Mobo* (tomorrow) Festival.

**Corroboree** (a time to gather for singing, dancing and storytelling).

The *Yugambeh Mobo* Festival is an annual community festival developed and staged by the *Yugambeh* Museum, Language and Heritage Research Centre, situated in Beenleigh, Queensland, Australia. The museum was formally opened in 1995 and is one of twenty-three

Indigenous Languages and Arts Program Language Centres supported by the Australian Government (Department of Communications and the Arts, Australian Government 2017).

The *Yugambeh Mobo* Festival is the Gold Coast's largest celebration of Aboriginal culture and is hosted annually during Reconciliation Week (27 May–3 June). By nature, Indigenous cultural expression is fluid, and therefore community festival programming requires flexibility and adaption over time. The *Yugambeh Mobo* Festival, activated in 2014, is one such example, a continuation of previous *Yugambeh* Festivals and events adapted from other events, i.e. The Drumley Walk. *Yugambeh Mobo* is a free event showcasing stories, music, song, dance and art as an expression of living Aboriginal culture based on traditional language and stories. The formation of the *Yugambeh Mobo* Festival experience is aimed at encouraging all Australians to become part of the cultural and educational exchange that is vital for Indigenous legacy (Yugambeh Museum, 2016).

Historically, *Yugambeh* Elders have always maintained language, lore and story both formally and informally within community (Best & Barlow 1997). The idea of the festival, where local community celebrates a shared experience and the public participates in the experience (South Australian Tourism Commission 1997), is not new to Indigenous communities of South-East Queensland. Arcodia and Robb (2000) acknowledged that festivals have emanated from cultural traditions and as such are a vehicle to demonstrate cultural traditions to non-Indigenous communities. In this case, *Yugambeh Mobo* Festival acts as the agent for the way Aboriginal communities have always preserved and celebrated their own culture.

> *Yugambeh* people are descendants of *Yarberri*. In *Yugambeh* legend he is known as *Jabreen*. *Jabreen* created his homeland by forming the mountains, the river systems and the flora and fauna. *Jabreen* created the site known as *Jebbribillum* (*bora* ground) when he came out of the water onto the land. As he picked up his fighting *waddy* (club), the land and water formed into the shape of a rocky outcrop (little Burleigh). This was the site where the people gathered to learn and to share the resources created by *Jabreen*. The *corroboree* held at this site became known as the *Bora* (sacred ground) and symbolised the ignition of life. Through the ceremony, people learned to care for the land and their role was to preserve its integrity.
>
> *(O'Connor 1993)*

*Bora* rings are a network of significant places for Aboriginal people. They are found within the region of Maryborough, Queensland extending south to northern New South Wales (Michael 2016) and are culturally significant sites which have provided a tangible framework for the structuring of social and cultural interaction. Knowledge of important places fosters and strengthens the ties to place, knowledge, language and the formation of cultural identity (Satterthwait & Heather 1987) and empowers traditional owners to be socially and culturally connected within their own community.

European settlers to the South-East Queensland region wrote several accounts of their experiences through memoirs and press articles about Aboriginal *bora* ceremonies and *corroboree* gatherings in which music, dance and storytelling formed a fundamental part of the ceremony and effectively broke down cross-cultural obstacles because both Aboriginal communities and European settlers were invited to attend (Hanlon 1951). As such, contributing memoirs and recordings from settlers were the first phase of safeguarding South-East Queensland Aboriginal culture through the shared experience of public *corroboree*, arguably also the humble beginnings of festival and the development of social capital within the region (Pardy 1991).

The *Yugambeh Mobo* Festival, through its fundamental structure, intrinsically provides the vehicle for the sharing of local Indigenous resources and knowledge. *Yugambeh* Mobo is an event generated for local Indigenous community, where non-Indigenous community can share in local cultural experiences and where opportunity is created for a common social purpose. The YYC is one example of a conceptualised idea created by me (a local *Kombumerri* and *Ngughi* woman), from the opportunity provided by the social and cultural objectives of the *Yugambeh Mobo* Festival.

**Ngulli nabai yarrabil** (we begin to sing).

Koen's (2009) view that an outward-looking orientation results from an aspiration to do work of value, import and benefit to others underpins the principle aspirations of the YYC; teach, learn and connect. The YYC is the first Indigenous (Aboriginal and Torres Strait Islander) youth choir of its kind where urban indigenous youth aged 5–25 years can learn to *yarrabil* (sing) in *Yugambeh* Aboriginal language, whilst learning *Yugambeh* language and culture. The YYC has grown significantly, from 10 participants at their first performance at the *Yugambeh Mobo* Festival 2014 to nearly 50 regular participants at *Yugambeh Mobo* 2016.

*Yugambeh Mobo* is the choirs' *nabei* (to begin to play) and can be accredited as the place which directly increased community awareness of *jarjum* singing heritage language. The *Yugambeh Mobo* Festival, whilst providing the opportunity for *jarjum* to perform songs of the region in the traditional *Yugambeh* language and tell the *gaureima* (story) of each songline, has provided substantial networking opportunities for the YYC.

From humble beginnings, with just a desire to learn and share *Yugambeh* language songs with *Yugambeh* family, this unique Australian Aboriginal choral group has grown to regularly perform for Indigenous community, local community and the broader community of South-East Queensland and are always warmly received. Their distinct ability to transmit cultural knowledge by singing *Yugambeh* language alive for the community and at festivals is highly sought after, and therefore the group perform approximately twice per month.

These performance opportunities have also meant that *Yugambeh jarjum* have been able to meet and talk to the Governor General of Australia, Sir Peter Cosgrove; High Court and Supreme Court Justices; Federal, State and local politicians; sporting and cultural identities; university educators; and business and community leaders. Through performance and conversation with community leaders, choir participants have come to understand that *Yugambeh* culture becomes visible when they perform and that through choir performativity, choir teaches community about local Aboriginal culture.

In 2016, 38 members of the YYC, aged 5–18 years, additionally participated in the YLSP, an investigation into the effects of participation in an Aboriginal language choir for urban indigenous children. Five themes were identified as being of benefit to the participants, including youth leadership, well-being (including self-efficacy), language acquisition, identity and Aboriginality, and sociocultural capital (Kruger 2017).

The purpose of this chapter is to demonstrate that the power of the festival can be viewed as a communication vehicle for the development of social capital and as a vehicle for safeguarding culture. Thus, the chapter will discuss the final theme, developing social capital and safeguarding Australian Aboriginal culture through authentic performance at festivals and events.

## Methodology

The YLSP followed the systemic development of knowing and knowledge principles of participatory action research (PAR) as outlined by Reason and Bradbury (2008). In this research, the use of PAR involved the examination of action and reflection, and theory and practice, and through participation with others it facilitated the pursuit of practical solutions for the flourishing of individual persons and communities. For further details on this, see Kruger (2017). Additionally, in consideration of Rigney's (1999) earlier work on Indigenist methodology where Indigenous voices are privileged within research, *Yugambeh* language words were incorporated throughout the project and can be seen in this chapter as italicised words followed by the English meaning the first time the word appears.

*Migunn Yugambeh* (what it means to know *Yugambeh*), from the *jarjum* perspective was observed and recorded through the combination of qualitative and quantitative research methods. Utilising a number of methods ensured validity to the emerging themes and credibility of the information given by the participants, and allowed for greater versatility when working with children (Creswell 2009). To do this surveys, *wula bora* (to give or share in a gathering at a significant space) sessions, interviews, video observation and personal reflections were utilised to stimulate evidence from participants.

The choir is also guided by my principle purpose, to action change for my community and to build 'cultural capital' (Jeannotte 2003) within my community, where the YYC is an applied ethnomusicological endeavour to begin to action such change. To engage *jarjum* I combine learning the skill of singing and having 'fun' and 'enjoyment', with learning language through song as a methodology for preservation. Grant's (2012) theory that grassroots community choir initiatives, which safeguard language, should utilise various methodologies for preservation, supports my principle purpose and methodology. Therefore, when teaching the YYC, I follow a combination of the following two principles: rehearsals that teach culture and language which safeguards our culture, and rehearsals that prepare performance material to build cultural capital in community.

I acknowledge that younger *jarjum* do not necessarily distinguish between these methods because I teach that learning is a way to know and knowledge should be passed on. I say, 'Once you have learnt these songs you can share them with anyone', and then *jarjum* will tell me when they have passed culture on and to whom they have shared it with. However, the older *jarjum* are beginning to understand the concepts of 'cultural capital' and 'performativity' through the choir's artistic intent. Their thoughts on 'cultural capital', 'preserving language' and 'sharing culture' are evidenced in the following sections.

## Social cultural capital

The YYC is an arts activity in community. At the most rudimentary level this arts activity engages, teaches and passes on Aboriginal language and culture through song. Jeannotte (2003) reported that the arts have a positive effect on social cohesion; they promote intercultural understanding, empower communities, regenerate neighbourhoods, encourage active communities and celebrate local culture and tradition.

The members of the choir participate when they want to and when they (and their parents) are available. Not every member performs at every performance; it is always optional, but at least 20–30 members perform regularly and participants of the YLSP had performed in a minimum of five festivals and/or events by the end of the research period.

Ruhanen and Whitford (2012) found that Indigenous groups who performed at Indigenous festivals increased their sociocultural benefits as they became recognised components of their community development. Independently, during the time of this research, *jarjum* from the choir were individually invited to perform at various events within the local community, including performances at their schools. YYC *jarjum* are becoming recognised components of their community development; they are now known as Indigenous youth who celebrate local culture and promote intercultural understanding.

Importantly, Child A (17+) understands the notion of promoting intercultural understanding. In the following interview excerpt he surmised he will be happy when schools in the area learn about *Yugambeh* language and sing the songs.

> CANDACE: So we tried our first days of Christmas and it was all giggly and funny, but you've taken a song that belongs to the world and put our own spin and language on it, so what did you think of that?
> CHILD A: I think it's quite awesome… oh (he gets excited) it's like, I can't explain, it's just pretty awesome how we just like (he does some animal actions that we do with the song) and with that number counting and stuff (he refers to singing the 12 days of Christmas counting the numbers in *Yugambeh* language) that will probably be used in schools around our Mob area.
> CANDACE: Our region, yes.
> CHILD A: It's gonna be helpful for the future and showing people like, showing that there's actually a language out there, it's amazing.
>
> *(Child A, interview, 30 October 2016)*

Child B (8–10) transmits culture with others at school, she creates performances, including her S-Factor performance, and she shares that she celebrates local culture and tradition at school. Through choir, Child B has learnt how to perform and share knowledge, song, language and tradition. In the following interview, we can see how she additionally shares that her happiness in sharing is transmitted to others and consequently she is building cultural capital in community.

> I am doing a performance at school in the S-Factor (school competition). I'm doing a traditional eagle dance with my brother and sister; we are doing a story about two eagles. I move my arms to show me catching fish and flying away. Then I begin to flap my wings. I use this dance to tell stories like I would in choir. I like sharing culture. I take Mum's possum skins to school, rattle sticks, boomerangs, I chose to take them. I showed and did the 'night bird dreaming story' to my class, I don't think I did well, but my class said they have never heard something more wonderful and I think I should be happy for what I have because this song is about not being selfish. I sing songs and do dances to my friends and class. I'm making them feel happy and giving them a different culture that they didn't know.
>
> *(Child B, interview, 15 October 2016)*

Recently we gained two new choir members. These new participants are not through their parents seeking a community connection, but rather through the recommendation of choir parents and *jarjum* actively seeking others in community to join them. The *jarjum* are recruiting other Indigenous *jarjum* that they know to strengthen social cohesion. Child C (11–13) likes the idea of new people joining choir 'because the more people join the bigger the choir gets'. She tells me that she 'lets others know that she is in choir' and she happily assists the building of the community because she 'wants to meet more Aboriginal kids in my area'.

*Jarjum* particularly understand and are able to reason, that after a festival performance or event such as the Gold Coast Show and NAIDOC celebrations, how they have shared culture with others and how members of the community can then pass cultural knowledge on.

When participants were asked if they 'liked sharing Aboriginal songs with others', all participants answered 'Yes' and shared their reasons.

Some *jarjum* are just happy to share culture:

> 'Because I can share my culture with other people',
> 'I like my culture and I like sharing it and teaching to others'.

Others recognise that it is a teaching moment:

> 'I like teaching my culture to other people',
> 'I get a chance to teach others about my language and share my culture'.

And some understand that the community recognise and appreciate the culture that has been shared:

> 'Because it makes us more visible, I can show them what the land used to be',
> 'So people can know who we really are and belong to',
> 'If other people learn language, the language will survive',
> 'It helps you and others learn more about the *Yugambeh* language',
> 'Because I can share our language, because sometimes they can tell other people',
> 'Because other people aren't Aboriginal'.

Overwhelmingly *jarjum* understand that when they perform at a festival or event they become teachers of culture. For them this is through the tradition of singing traditional and contemporary song in traditional language. They will become the *yarrabilgin* (songmen) and *yarrabilgingunn* (songwomen) of their community. Child D (8–10) directly articulated this concept:

> I'm sharing the lost language with other people who don't know the language and I'm telling them stories that they wouldn't hear anywhere else.
> (Child D, interview, 16 October 2016)

Along similar lines to Johnsons's (2012) claim that projects that look at language and identity are highly charged with cultural capital, the YYC, as a collective group, have become teachers of *Yugambeh* language and culture in their region and beyond. Through participation, engagement and trust in what they do, *jarjum* concomitantly provide community with local knowledge when they perform locally and local knowledge to a wider audience when they perform outside their region at events, festivals or live on media outlets.

Child E (17+) already understands he teaches culture. He stated that he needs to 'have an interest in my culture, because we perform culture. I need to know what I am singing about; I have a responsibility to know what it is I am sharing with others'. And he demonstrates a deeper understanding that through choir performativity 'this choir teaches community about the local Aboriginal culture, to share with others'.

Child F (14–16) had a similar understanding and reflected that sometimes choir performs at ceremony which is aimed to engage people of any culture.

> During NAIDOC week, the choir performed at one of the ceremonies held at the Burleigh RSL [*bora* ground]. The theme for this year was song lines and I was asked to speak about what song lines has meant to me, particularly after joining the choir when it started in 2014. The ceremony aimed to engage people not only of Aboriginal or Torres

Strait Islander descent, but of any culture. It was a big turn out with many people of many different cultures attending, which filled me with pride to express the significance of song lines in my life and my culture.

(Child F, participant reflection, 19 July 2016)

On the basis of the evidence from *jarjum* who regularly perform traditional Indigenous language through song at festivals and events, the YYC can claim that participation in an urban Aboriginal and Torres Strait Islander children's and youth choir assists children and youth to build a community, to support each other through this community and to become invested in each other's lives. Concomitantly, the *Yugambeh* community is building a secure and safe environment for *jarjum* enriched with social and cultural capital through the communal activity of *jarjum* learning and singing heritage language. *Jarjum* provide confirmatory evidence that performativity of Indigenous cultural knowledge crosses cultural barriers and builds social capital within community.

## Safeguarding culture

The group and I have evolved continuously and concurrently through the opportunities that are presented to us. The knowledge that is gained by learning language through song leads to a deeper understanding of culture, and as the *jarjum* mature or become curious they ask more in-depth questions. An example of this curiosity and thirst for cultural knowledge was demonstrated in Child G (11–13) and Child H (8–10) *wula bora* (interview) session. They asked for some cultural explanations:

CHILD H: Can I ask you something?
CANDACE: Yes.
CHILD G: How come the *Bora* ring, we can't go in it?

(There is a section of the *wula bora* session here that has been intentionally left out of the transcript as it contains culturally sensitive material. The girls and I have a discussion about *Bora* ring ceremony and the *Bora* ring that we attend for celebration and ceremony at Burleigh Heads, QLD).

(Wula bora session, 7 September 2016)

Although not formally part of the research (Kruger 2017), just like the *jarjum*, when community hear us and see us perform at festivals and events they also want to know more. The choir members, parents and myself are often asked questions after a performance by community members, or comments are made to us such as 'I didn't know any of this information', 'I really liked hearing the children sing and learning about the region' and 'Thank you for sharing your culture with us'. Comments about YYC performances are also made on community social media or news media websites where the choir has featured. Community bystanders leave remarks such as 'beautiful', 'enjoyed it', 'well done', 'I wish we had always combined cultures', 'I loved hearing Aboriginal language', 'deadly and proud' and 'this performance makes me proud too'.

These community experiences have additionally evolved the choir into a commodity with its own identity; essentially the choir performs for community. Importantly however, the choir is not a 'product' nor should we become subject to labels such as 'cultural cringe'; the YYC is simply Aboriginal and Torres Strait Islander *jarjum* learning *Yugambeh* Aboriginal culture and sharing it authentically with community.

Grant's (2012, p. 110) view on safeguarding culture through music is 'that the odds of successfully safeguarding music might be higher than of language, perhaps because of music's greater ability to recontextualise or its greater commercial potential'. Therefore, it is with Grant's contextual view on safeguarding music and commercial potential in mind that I develop a similar claim to acknowledge how our commodity works in our community. *Jarjum* are sustaining and safeguarding their music traditions, in addition to their language, through choral performativity which communicates culture to the community.

On this topic, I was able to share my thoughts with Pat Hession, ABC Radio 630 North Queensland, on the 3rd of June 2016 in Townsville, prior to the 2016 QLD Reconciliation Award Ceremony, where the YYC was named the 2016 winner of the Queensland Reconciliation Award – Community Division. Pat and I discussed the themes of safeguarding music and tradition, commercial product and sharing culture with community:

PAT: I know when I've travelled overseas, I've seen people doing traditional performances and I've thought 'there's a bit of cultural cringe in there'. I'm worried that people are putting on a show rather than giving me an authentic interpretation of what their culture means to them.

CANDACE: 'Authentic' is an interesting word. We are working with urban children who are demonstrating living culture, so for us it is about sharing the stories. You'll see kids hop up and sing and we're actually telling the tales of our area and it may not be exactly what someone expects to see, but it is what we do. So we use our voices and we sing, and the kids have beautiful voices and I'm training them to sing well, correctly as well and to sing in harmony and we're just doing our 'thing'. And our 'thing' is to share our story in community.

*(ABC Radio 630 North Queensland interview, 3 June 2016)*

Pat Hession's question about the perception of authenticity by an audience was surprising as I had not considered that an audience would view the choir as disingenuous. Adverse thoughts about a living culture choir or the practice of learning culture do not assist the safeguarding of language or culture. The choir's experiences to this point have not demonstrated that there is negativity surrounding urban *jarjum* learning *Yugambeh* tradition; rather it has been the opposite. The YYC's body of experience has demonstrated acceptance, popularity and community pride alongside an eagerness for more. These results are based along similar lines to Arcodia and Whitford's (2006) findings where performances in community, particularly festivals, encourage participation, create and maintain cultural activities, and facilitate the development of social capital, which develops in a positive environment.

## Concluding thoughts

Knowledge of Aboriginal language and cultural practice is vital for the survival of Australian Indigenous cultural heritage. The YLSP validates the power of the festival as a communication vehicle for the development of social capital and as a vehicle for safeguarding culture. Additionally, it demonstrates the necessity for other Australian Indigenous communities to engage their children and youth in living culture practice because *jarjum* enjoy learning their culture through the method of song and active participation.

The YYC is one ongoing endeavour to *girrebbah* (wake up) Aboriginal language in the *Yugambeh* language region of South-East Queensland, Australia. The evidence gathered from the YLSP demonstrated how performances at festivals by an Aboriginal and Torres

Strait Islander children's language choir can safeguard heritage language and culture while concomitantly building social cultural capital (among other things) within an Indigenous community. It is critically important then that other Indigenous communities become empowered and begin to consider similar programmes for their *jarjum*.

Thus, further action and in particular research is required to discover and facilitate ongoing learning of Australian Indigenous song material resources for many Indigenous communities. Additionally, future research must investigate further development of Indigenous community identity and engagement through performativity at festivals such as the *Yugambeh Mobo* Festival. Finally, there is also an opportunity to explore and gain a more nuanced understanding of the extent to which Indigenous language, song and cultural practices can also act as an effective communication vehicle for the ongoing, sustainable development of sociocultural legacy for community.

## References

Arcodia, C., & Robb, A. (2000). A Future for Event Management: a taxonomy of event management terms. *Events Beyond 2000: Setting the Agenda*, University of Technology Sydney, Australia.

Arcodia, C. & Whitford, M. (2006). Festival attendance and the development of social capital. *Journal of Convention & Event Tourism*, 8(2), 1–18.

Best, Y. & Barlow, A. (1997). *Kombumerri – Saltwater People*. Melbourne, Australia: Heinemann Library.

Creswell, J. (2009). *Research Design: Qualitative, Quantitative, and Mixed Methods Approaches* (3 ed.). Thousand Oaks, CA: Sage Publications.

Department of Communications and the Arts, Australian Government. (2017, February 22). *Indigenous Languages and Arts Program Language Centres*. Available at: www.arts.gov.au/documents/indigenous-languages-and-arts-program-language-centres. Accessed 23/8/2017.

Grant, C. (2012). Rethinking safeguarding: Objections and responses to protecting and promoting endangered musical heritage. *Ethnomusicology Forum*, 21(1), 31–51.

Grant, C. F. (2012). *Strengthening the Vitality and Viability of Endangered Music Genres: The Potential of Language Maintenance to Inform Approaches to Music Sustainability*. Brisbane, Australia: Queensland Conservatorium Arts, Education and Law, Griffith University.

Hanlon, W. (1951). *Reminiscences of Mr WE Hanlon*. Unpublished manuscript. Held in the Fryer Library. University of Queensland, Brisbane, Queensland.

Jeannotte, M. S. (2003). Singing alone? The contribution of cultural capital to social cohesion and sustainable communities. *The International Journal of Cultural Policy*, 9(1), 35–49.

Johnson, H. (2012). The Group from the West: Song, endangered language and sonic activism on Guernsey. *Journal of Marine and Island Cultures*, 1, 99–112.

Koen, B. (2009). *Beyond the Roof of the World: Music, Prayer, and Healing in the Pamir Mountains*. New York: Oxford University Press.

Kruger, C. (2017). *In The Bora Ring: Yugambeh Language and Song Project – An Investigation into the Effects of Participation in the 'Yugambeh Youth Choir', An Aboriginal Language Choir for Urban Indigenous Children*. Unpublished manuscript. Master of Arts Research Thesis, Griffith University, Australia.

Michael, S. (2016). 'One Ring to Rule Them All?' Towards understanding the plethora of bora grounds in southeastern Queensland. *Queensland History Journal*, The Royal Historical Society of Queensland, 22(12), 859–877.

O'Connor, R. (Ed.). (1993). *Yugambeh in Defence of Our Country: mibun wallul mundindehla malinah dhagun*. Queensland, Australia: Kombumerri Aboriginal Corporation for Culture.

Pardy, S. (1991). *A Study of the Role of Community Festivals and Events in Community Development*. Unpublished master's thesis. USA: Arcadia University.

Reason, P. & Bradbury, H. (Eds.). (2008). *The SAGE Handbook of Action Research Participative Inquiry and Practice* (2nd ed.). Los Angeles, London, New Delhi, Singapore: SAGE Publications.

Rigney, L.-I. (1999). Internationalization of an Indigenous anticolonial cultural critique of research methodologies: A guide to Indigenist research methodology and its principles. *Wicazo Sa Review*, 14(2), 109-121.

Ruhanen, L. & Whitford, M. (2012). Brisbane's annual sports and cultural festival: Connecting with community and culture through festivals. In Kleinert, S. A. (Ed.), *Urban Representations: Cultural Expression, Identity and Politics* (101–117). Acton, Australia: Australian Institute of Aboriginal and Torres Strait Islander Studies.

Satterthwait, L. & Heather, A. (1987). Determinants of earth circle site location in the Moreton region, southeast Queensland. *Queensland Archaeological Research, 4*, 5–53.

South Australian Tourism Commission. (1997). *Planning Special Events and Festivals*. Adelaide, SA: The Commission.

Whitford, M. & Dunn, A. (2014). Papua New Guinea's Indigenous cultural festivals: Cultural triumph or tragedy? *Event Management, 18*(3), 265–283.

Yugambeh Museum. (2016). *Yugambeh Mobo Festival*. Beenleigh, Australia: Yugambeh Museum Language & Heritage Research Centre.

Yunupingu, M., Langton, M. & Marett, A. (2002). *Garma Statement on Indigenous Music and Performance*. Available at: www.aboriginalartists.com.au/NRP_statement.htm Accessed 24/06/2018.

# PART IX

# Festival futures

# 40
# VIRTUAL REALITY
## The white knight of festival management education?

*Philipp Peltz, Olga Junek and Joel de Ross*

## Introduction

A substantial body of research suggests that cultural events and festivals play an important role in the economic and community development of destinations and regions. Impact studies have examined a variety of effects of cultural events and festivals at the local, regional, national and international levels (for a literature overview, see Getz 2010). The study of festival impacts is undoubtedly complex; effects can be both positive and negative, and span across a wide range of areas such as the economic, environmental, cultural, social and personal. Often, many conflicting objectives have to be balanced against each other (Reid & Arcodia 2002). Balancing the various interests of stakeholders to generate an overall positive outcome is a difficult task that requires a well-developed skill set of event managers.

Many events, in particular cultural festivals, often fail due to management issues. A recent example is the cancellation of the Maitreya Festival (scheduled to be held in Victoria, Australia in 2016). Despite an estimated injection of $2.5 million AUD into the Buloke Shire community, the council denied permission for the festival to go ahead, leaving festival organisers with lawsuits and disappointed fans and stakeholders (Griffith 2016). The Buloke Shire council reported that the organisers failed to provide documentation on insurance, security bonds, emergency contingency plans and agreements with Liquor Licensing and Ambulance Victoria (Moskowitch 2016). Getz (2002) has identified several causes of festival failures, of which the majority can be categorised as event management failures such as inadequate marketing or promotion, inadequate or unattractive venue, lack of uniqueness, incompetent event managers or staff, lack of corporate sponsorship and inadequate risk management plans and implementation.

To optimally prepare capable future festival and event managers, event management curricula should be constantly reviewed and updated to reflect market demands, trends and changes in the technological as well as in the economic, political and social environments. With the rapid advancement of information technology and related developments in teaching and learning in the 21st century, student learning experiences and learning outcomes have been significantly enhanced by these developments. One of the more recent developments has been the use of Virtual Reality (VR). Despite its appearance in the late 1970s (Guttentag 2010; Hedberg & Alexander 1994) it is only in the past decade that VR has come to the forefront of education in areas of business and leisure studies. In this chapter, we explore how new technology in the form of VR systems can be used to improve festival and event management education.

The chapter is structured as follows. First, we review the current state of festival and event management education and practices to identify weaknesses and possible areas of improvement. Subsequently, we look at the potential and limitations of VR used in teaching environments. Then, we evaluate how VR can be used specifically in the event management curriculum. In particular, we are interested in the question how VR can be implemented to improve the teaching of certain event management skills as well as the learning outcomes. The chapter concludes with a brief overview of the challenges and limitations of VR in event management education and implications for future research.

## Current state of event management education

As an industry, event and festival management has, over the past two decades, become more structured, professionalised and underpinned by research (Allen, O'Toole, McDonnell & Harris 2011; Barron & Ali-Knight 2017; Junek, Lockstone & Mair 2009; Mair 2009). However, events still exhibit a high rate of failure, particularly in the area of festivals (Getz 2002). This is partly due to the fact that many event organisers stumble into the events industry without being adequately prepared for the complexity of running a successful event (MacNeill 2017). However, this does not fully exculpate event management education from problems within the industry. Additionally, over the past two decades, events have grown in numbers substantially and also differ quite significantly in size and type. Event management programmes need to stay relevant to the changes within the industry as well to broader global changes and trends. Furthermore, they need to excite and motivate potential students to study the complex field of event management. For this purpose, event management course designers have to keep up-to-date with current developments in the market and incorporate new relevant technologies into the programmes. This will ensure the attractiveness and industry relevance of event management courses in order to hopefully decrease the number of incompetent event managers who enter the events industry without the appropriate training and education. In addition, event management courses have to develop the fundamental and necessary skill sets for future event organisers' abilities to plan and manage events and festivals.

Necessary skills include communication skills, numeracy and literacy, and operational hands-on skills. Graduates should be able to budget, plan for risks and crises, be project managers and computer experts, negotiate with performers and suppliers, be creative, be organised, manage staff including volunteers, and have an eye for detail as well as see the big picture of a festival (Allen et al. 2011; Jago & Deery 2010; Junek, Lockstone & Mair 2009; Mair 2009). Stadler, Fullagar and Reid (2014) see the creation, dissemination and management of knowledge as the differentiating factors between success and failure of festivals, whilst Robertson, Junek and Lockstone-Binney (2012) argue that creativity and innovation is one of the competencies seen as vital for a successful event management career. In a similar vein, it is the creative and conceptual aspects of design that pose the major challenge to event designers. Furthermore, the experience aspect of festivals and the added value gained from this has also been highlighted by Robertson, Yeoman, Smith and McMahon-Beattie (2015) as vital to the future of festivals, and in particular to music festivals.

One of the major challenges of event management education is to provide students with practical, hands-on learning experiences in addition to the theoretical foundation. Authentic learning is to bridge the gap between what is taught as the theoretical underpinnings of business courses and the practical aspects of the business world. Authentic learning aims to provide real-world practical experience within a safe and non-threatening learning environment (Brown, Collins & Duguid 1989). Similarly, experiential learning allows the participant to acquire skills and knowledge in a learning situation where he or she is actively involved. This involvement resulting in deep-learning (Fotiadis & Sigala 2015; King & Zhang 2017). To address the need for practical experiences outside of the formal business education, many higher education institutions offer, as part of their event management course, work-integrated learning (WIL). This could be an intensive period working in industry (between 3 and 12 months) or a required number of hours to be spent working at events in a paid or voluntary capacity. Despite the overwhelmingly positive results and pedagogical virtues, as documented in the literature on WIL, this approach is not without challenges (Barron & Ali-Knight 2017; Fanning, MacLeod & Vanzo 2017). Based on the authors' experiences in the events industry and their roles as event management lecturers and specialisation advisors, students are often, especially in the short-term form of WIL and as volunteers, thrust into working at events and festivals at short notice and without receiving an appropriate induction or explanation about the event's parameters. For many students, it can be an experience wrought with trepidation and the fear of making mistakes if students move from one event to the next without much understanding of the event.

Additionally, in the authors' experience as educators, creativity and innovation are areas where students are reluctant, self-conscious or uncertain as to how to be creative when designing events. *SketchUp* (SketchUp is a 3D modelling software often used in event management courses, see www.sketchup.com) and similar 3D design software can address this lack of creativity and innovation, but they are also limiting and often confronting for those who see themselves as not computer-savvy, beyond the usual suites of programmes students tend to use. VR can provide a risk-free environment where learners are allowed to practice and make mistakes without fear. In using VR, students can interact with and take part in real-world simulations (Guttentag 2010). VR can provide an environment that enables students to learn and practice requisite skills for their profession and can also include authentic assessment ensuring students are equipped with the 'skills and competencies needed to succeed in today's workplace' (Fook & Sidhu 2010, p. 154). Furthermore, employer input can be used to structure relevant activities and scenarios. Perhaps in the future, VR can also make use of avatars for simulation of communication and negotiation.

## Virtual reality and higher education

There are a number of definitions as to what VR is (Burdea & Coiffet 2003; Gutierrez, Vexo & Thalmann 2008; Vince 2004). For the purposes of this chapter, 'VR is defined as the use of a computer-generated 3D environment – called a 'virtual environment' (VE) – that one can navigate and possibly interact with, resulting in real-time simulation of one or more of the user's five senses' (Guttentag 2010, p. 638). In the education sector these are referred to as Virtual Reality Learning Environments (VRLE) (Huang, Rauch & Liaw 2010). The use of VR as a teaching and learning tool has gained importance in many of the technically based study areas such as medicine, engineering, construction and architecture. More recently, tourism has also adopted VR to plan and manage tourist destinations and attractions (Guttentag 2010).

The main characteristics of VR have been described as the $I^3$ which stands for *immersion*, *interactivity* and *imagination* (Burdea & Coiffet 2003). Immersion is defined as a state where the user is surrounded by another reality, to the exclusion of the 'real world' (Murray 1997).

In addition, VR is interactive, meaning the user is able to interact with virtual objects in real time (Dede 2009). As Wetzel, Radtke and Stern (1994) remark, full immersion can minimise external distractions and consequently reduce students' cognitive load. As a result, the VRLE can stimulate imagination and assist in the ability to conceptualise and facilitate deeper learning. Particularly interesting in the context of event management is that VR environments can improve one's ability to 'imagine, in a creative sense, non-existent things' (Huang, Rauch & Liaw 2010, p. 2). As will be elaborated on in the next section, the facilitation of imagination and visualisation can be very helpful in learning to design, plan and manage complex events. Similarly, Moreno and Mayer (2002) suggest that students participating in an immersive learning environment may learn more deeply than others who are observing or learning from the textbook.

## How VR can improve event management education

As outlined earlier, VR offers new learning opportunities for students in the 21st century, in particular for those areas of study where practical experience, in the form of simulation and immersion, is a valuable tool for learning and understanding (Janssen, Tummel, Richert & Isenhardt 2016). The following discussion addresses how VR can improve the learning and teaching of certain event management skills.

### *Event marketing and promotion*

As with other leisure business areas such as tourism, fashion, music and entertainment in general (Bolan 2015; Guttentag 2010; Saad 2015) VR will become an integral part of future event marketing and promotion campaigns. In this context, VR can function as an engaging pre-event promotion tool and also as an event capturing device to generate appealing content for future event marketing campaigns. For instance, in 2016 the music festival Coachella offered ticket buyers a VR headset which they could use with Coachella's official VR mobile application. The festival's website describes the added value as 'Before, during, and after the festival in April, fans from all over the world can be immersed in performances from top artists, experience 360-degree panoramic experiences from around the festival grounds, and watch VR experiences created by other festival-goers' (Coachella 2016). Interestingly, not only ticket buyers but also fans without tickets had selected access to the content. This shows how the organisers use VR as a marketing tool to establish its market position as an early technology adaptor who resonates with its target audience of technology affine young adults. The application also allowed users to upload their festival experiences and share it with the Coachella community. This way, Coachella enabled a high degree of involvement and instilled a community feel where fans become part of the Coachella brand.

To optimally prepare students for this changing environment, they need to develop digital literacy in VR technology. Inadequate marketing and promotion is, in the most cases, not a question of resources but a question of skills. An event organiser can spend a lot of time and money on marketing campaigns with a low level of efficacy. The future generation of event managers needs to be proficient in new technologies such as VR, and how these can be used in integrated event marketing campaigns. Event management courses in the higher education sector should not only adopt new technologies early but should also lead the change. This can only be realised if the change begins in the classroom to translate acquired skills and knowledge to the professional event industry.

## Venue selection

Venue selection is an important aspect of attendee quality perception as well as sponsor satisfaction (Michelini, Iasevoli & Theodoraki 2017). Learning how to select appropriate festival venues, indoor, outdoor and across multiple locations, is an important part of event management education but can be difficult to teach from a theoretical perspective. The needs of all stakeholders must be taken into account, such as risk factors, size, access and budget. Due to lack of experience, students often have difficulties matching venues with event types and audiences. When faced with selecting venues and spaces, students tend to choose safely, meaning the venues they know or have physically experienced. Selection of different or unusual venues is not often considered as it is difficult for the students to visualise the event faced with a two-dimensional representation and specifications. Problems arise when students try to bring together the multitude of considerations without being able to experience the venue or space in view of those consideration.

The visualisation of, and interaction with, spatial environments in a VRLE can help students in the selection, evaluation and design of adequate attractive venues. For instance, VR offers the possibility of showcasing multiple perspectives of the venue to spot potential problems and opportunities. Students can learn the optimal set-up and decoration of a venue by interacting with objects such as placements of sponsorship banners, seating arrangements, food trucks, stages and many other elements of event planning and implementation. These interactive, immersive virtual representations of real venues can stimulate experimentation and creative thinking, which can potentially lead to new and creative matches between venues and audiences.

## Event concept development

Bowen and Daniels (2005) suggest an event's success depends largely on the development of an innovative event concept. The authors write,

> Festival managers who rely on the music itself or a specific artist to draw large crowds may be sorely disappointed with their turnout. Equally important is creating a fun and festive atmosphere that offers ample opportunity to socialize and have new and non-musical experiences.
>
> *(Bowen & Daniels 2005, p. 162)*

The question, however, is how can students learn to create a fun and festive atmosphere that offers ample opportunity to socialise and have new and non-musical experiences on a piece of paper in the classroom? The creation of such festival experience requires a high level of creative thinking. A major challenge in developing innovative event concepts is to anticipate how the concept will translate into a real experience. What will a stakeholder's journey be like during event day? How will vision and sound be perceived from different locations on the floor? Is there enough space to socialise? Traditionally, students rely on a piece of paper or, in more advanced educational programmes, on software-based modelling platforms such as SketchUp. A VRLE offers a significantly enhanced simulation of festival experiences and can provide immediate feedback on how changes will affect the event. Bladen and Kennell (2014) see a big difference between 'doing' a design and 'learning a design' (p. 12). Through visualisation and interactivity students are immersed in the doing. Such a design environment enables an iterative design process. After the idea generation, a prototype is created and tested by users. The gathered data on how users experience the prototype will then be incorporated into a revised prototype, which after a number of iterations, will lead to the much-improved final product. Such an efficient design process is not feasible with traditional event design teaching methods as students are unable to experience how their concepts translate into experiences. A simulation of their event in a VRLE including sound, vision and interactive elements can approximate a real-world experience from different perspectives, such as an attendee, a performer, a sponsor or a staff member. This can help to test different concepts and solutions as well as identify shortcomings and build on strengths.

Another advantage of VR in the event concept design and development stage is to help students in understanding the financial and technical limitations of event concepts better. The next generation of integrated event management platforms such as *Metavents* (Metavents is an integrated festival-planning software featuring VR, see www.metavents.com) can provide integrated supply chain logistics disclosing market purchase and renting prices for event equipment such as PAs, stages, banners and stands. Hence, students receive immediate feedback about the incurring costs when designing events. This can help students to omit unrealistic event concepts in an early stage as they can observe how the costs of certain design concepts can quickly spiral out of control.

## *Induction and training of staff*

Events of all sizes and types rely heavily on the engagement of volunteers. However, tight budgets often prevent event organisers from providing adequate induction and training of volunteers. A number of authors suggest that volunteers often receive insufficient training (Dekker & Halman 2003; Flood, Gardner & Yarell 2006; Miller, Pauline & Donahue 2017) which can lead to volunteers not returning, thus resulting in a high turnover of volunteers. Here VR can be useful in tailoring training needs of different types of festivals. This can be done by setting up virtual scenarios that simulate emergencies, orientation issues, crowd control and marshalling. Trainers can also use simulations for assessment and problem solving. An additional benefit of digitalised virtual simulations lies in its location-independent nature. This can save significant costs for both volunteers and event producers in the form of travel and time savings.

## *Sponsorship acquisition and management*

Corporate sponsorship is one of the most important source of funding in today's festival industry. Sponsorship spending on music tours, festivals and venues shows robust growth over the last years, increasing by 4.8 per cent from 2016 to an expected $1.54 billion US in 2017 (IEG and ESP Properties 2017). Despite increasing spending from corporate sponsors, festival organisers report that a lack of sponsorship is a common cause of festival failure (Getz 2010). This shows that while some festival organisers successfully manage to secure corporate sponsorship, others struggle. In this context, finding, selecting and persuading suitable corporate sponsors is an important skill to develop for future event managers, and thus forms an important part of event management education. One of the biggest challenges for students in the creation of sponsorship pitches is to communicate complex event concepts in a persuasive way that clearly demonstrates the benefits to potential sponsors. Traditionally, a sponsorship pitch consists of text documents potentially including some visual components such as past event photos, sketches, graphs or logos. VR can significantly improve the presentation of event concepts for sponsorship pitches. In creating a simulation of certain event situations, potential sponsors can get a more realistic impression of the value they get in return for their engagement. Students can also experiment with the placement of sponsorship banners or the design and location of sponsorship stands. Sending a personalised event simulation where sponsors can experience how their brand will be perceived from different perspectives, can help event managers convince suitable sponsorship partners.

## *Risk management*

The past two decades have seen a much more stringent and regulatory approach to safety and risk management for festivals (Brown 2014). This has resulted in a more complex process involving a multitude of plans, permits, forms and going back and forth to councils with revised plans. The development of risk management plans involves numerous meetings with stakeholders often in different location over an extended period of time. If new risks arise during that time, the impacts of these need to be assessed and can take further time, effort and documentation. Failing to provide adequate risk and emergency plans to councils is a common cause of festival failure, including the previously mentioned Maitreya festival.

VR in the learning environment offers several advantages in the learning and teaching of risk management. Students can go through different scenarios and learn to analyse, evaluate and act appropriately on these scenarios in a VRLE. The simulation of incidents can provide students not only with the factual complexity of managing problematic situations but can also elicit an emotional response. Managing dangerous situations in the real world involves a high level of stress. Such stress situations can lead to decision-making based on emotions rather than rationality. Preparing future event managers by simulating stressful situations and decision-making under pressure can help make future festivals safer for all stakeholder involved. Another advantage of VR in the risk management domain is the ability to better communicate risk and emergency plans to stakeholders. Presenting festival simulations to stakeholders such as politicians or the local community, who may not be familiar with the details and complexity of such events, can reduce reservations about safety and risk, and potentially result in increased funding and positive perceptions about different types of festivals.

## Limitations of VR

Although we stress the benefits of VR in its ability to enhance event management education, a number of challenges and limitations need to be considered. First, teachers and tutors have to be trained and skilled in VR and its applications. Second, there is still an undeniable gap between experiencing real-world scenarios and virtual simulations of such scenarios. Hence, we see VR not as a replacement of other learning practices but rather as a complementary tool. The strengths of VR become apparent when it is used as an integral part of a larger events ecosystem. In this way, we see VR also in the classroom as a fundamental part of a broader teaching methodology.

## Conclusion

Learning by doing is crucial in event management education to prepare future event managers for a practical field such as event management. However, situating a student in relevant real-world environments often comes with insurmountable obstacles. VR allows students to be immersed in an interactive environment that simulates the planning and managing of festivals. We argue that this immersive, practice-orientated training can address many common mismanagement issues that often lead to festival failures. In this regard, VR can play an important role in the promotion of teaching effectiveness in event management programmes. With the rapid advancements of new technologies, especially after a mass market adaptation, in the words of Hedberg and Alexander (1994), we believe that VR can indeed be the 'white knight in the arsenal of event management education'.

## References

Allen, J., O'Toole, W., McDonnell, I. & Harris, R. (2011). *Festival and special event management* (5th ed.). Milton, Australia: Wiley.
Barron, P. & Ali-Knight, J. (2017). Aspirations and progression of event management graduates: A study of career development. *Journal of Hospitality and Tourism Management, 30*(March), 29–38.
Bladen, C. & Kennell, J. (2014). Educating the 21st century event management graduate: Pedagogy, practice, professionalism, and professionalization. *Event Management, 18*(1), 5–14.
Bolan, P. (2015). A perspective on the near future: Mobilizing events and social media. In Yeoman, I., Robertson, M., McMahon-Beattie, U., Backer, E. & Smith, K. A. (Eds.) *The Future of Events and Festivals* (pp. 201–208). London and New York: Routledge.
Bowen, H. E. & Daniels, M. J. (2005). Does the music matter? Motivations for attending a music festival. *Event Management, 9*(3) 155–164.
Brown, J. S., Collins, A. & Duguid, P. (1989). Situated cognition and the culture of learning. *Educational Researcher, 18*(1), 32–42.
Brown, S. (2014). Emerging professionalism in the event industry: A practitioner's perspective. *Event Management, 18*(1), 15–24.
Burdea, G. C. & Coiffet, P. (2003) *Virtual reality technology* (2nd ed.) Hoboken, NJ: Wiley-Interscience.Coachella. (2016). Welcome to the Coachella Virtual Reality App. Retrieved from www.coachella.vantage.tv/#/moreinfo. Accessed 27/11/2017.Dede, C. (2009). Immersive interfaces for engagement and learning. *Science, 323*(5910), 66–69.
Dekker, P. & Halman, L. (2003). *The values of volunteering: Cross-cultural perspectives*. New York, NY: Kluwer Academic/Plenum Publishers.
Fanning, C., Macleod, C. & Vanzo, L. (2017). The value of WIL in tourism and student perceptions of employability. In Beckendorff, P. and Zehrer, A. (Eds.) *Handbook of Teaching and Learning in Tourism* (pp. 246–258). Cheltenham, UK: Edward Elgar.
Flood, J. Gardner, E. & Yarell, K. (2006). Managing volunteers: Developing and implementing an effective program. Proceedings of the 2005 *Northeastern Recreation Research Symposium* (pp. 80–88). USDA Forest Service: Northeastern Station www.fs.usda.gov/treesearch/pubs/22260. Accessed 27/11/2017.
Fook, C. Y. & Sidhu, G. K. (2010). Authentic assessment and pedagogical strategies in higher education. *Journal of Social Sciences, 6*(2), 153–161.
Fotiadis, A. K. & Sigala, M. (2015). Developing a framework for designing an Events Management Training Simulation (EMTS). *Journal of Hospitality, Leisure, Sport & Tourism Education, 16*(June), 52–71.
Getz, D. (2002). Why festivals fail. *Event Management, 7*(4), 209–219.
Getz, D. (2010). The nature and scope of festival studies. *International Journal of Event Management Research, 5*(1), 1–47.
Griffith, N. (2016). Maitreya Fest promoters sued by ticketing company over missing money. Retrieved from www.themusic.com.au/news/all/2016/06/16/maitreya-fest-promoters-sued-by-ticketing-company-over-missing-money/. Accessed 27/11/2017.
Gutierrez, M., Vexo, F. & Thalmann, D. (2008). *Stepping into virtual reality*. London: Springer.
Guttentag, D. A. (2010). Virtual reality: Applications and implications for tourism. *Tourism Management, 31*(5), 637–651.
Hedberg, J. & Alexander, S. (1994). Virtual reality in education: Defining researchable issues. *Educational Media International, 31*(4), 214–219.
keHuang, H.-M., Rauch, U. & Liaw, S.-S. (2010). Investigating learners' attitudes towards virtual reality learning environments: Based on a constructivist approach. *Computers and Education, 55*(3), 1–12.

Jago, L. & Deery, M. (2010). *Delivering innovation, knowledge and performance: The role of business events*. New South Wales, Australia: Business Events Council of Australia.

Janssen, D., Tummel, C., Richert, A. & Isenhardt, I. (2016). Virtual environments in higher education – immersion as a key construct for Learning 4.0. *International Journal of Advanced Corporate Learning*, 20–26.

Junek, O., Lockstone, L. & Mair, J. (2009). Two perspectives on event management employment: Student and employer insights into the skills required to get the job done! *Journal of Hospitality and Tourism Management*, 16(1), 120–129.

IEG and ESP Properties. (2017). Sponsorship spending on music to total $1.54 billion in 2017. Retrieved from www.sponsorship.com/About/Press-Room/Sponsorship-Spending-On-Music-To-Total-$1-54-Billi.aspx. Accessed 27/11/2017.

King, B. & Zhang, H. Q. (2017). Experiential tourism and hospitality learning: Principles and practice. In Beckendorff, P. and Zehrer, A. (Eds.) *Handbook of Teaching and Learning in Tourism* (pp. 207–217). Cheltenham, UK: Edward Elgar.

MacNeill, K. (2017). Why have so many music festivals gone wrong this year? Retrieved from www.theguardian.com/music/musicblog/2017/aug/09/music-festivals-gone-wrong-fyre-hope-and-glory-y-not. Accessed 27/11/2017.

Mair, J. (2009). The events industry: the employment context. In Baum, T., Deery, M., Hanlon, C., Lockstone, L., & Smith, K. (Eds.) *People and work in events and conventions: a research perspective* (3–16) Ashgate, UK: Cabi.

Michelini, L., Iasevoli, G. & Theodoraki, E. (2017). Event venue satisfaction and its impact on sponsorship outcomes. *Event Management*, 21(3), 319–331.

Miller, J., Pauline, G. & Donahue, P. (2017). An investigation for safety training for triathlon events: Are volunteers prepared for emergencies? *Journal of Contemporary Athletics*, 11(2), 119–135.

Moreno, R. & Mayer, R. E. (2002). Learning science in virtual reality multimedia environments: Role of methods and media. *Journal of Educational Psychology*, 94(3), 598–610.

Moskowitch, G. (2016). Council row & paperwork gets Maitreya cancelled just days out. Retrieved from www.tonedeaf.com.au/maitreya-festival-cancelled/. Accessed 27/11/2017.Murray, J. (1997). *Hamlet on the Holodeck: The future of narrative in cyberspace*. Cambridge: MIT Press.

Reid, S. & Arcodia, C. (2002). Understanding the role of the stakeholder in event management. *Journal of Sport & Tourism*, 7(3), 20–22.

Robertson, M., Junek, O. & Lockstone-Binney, L. (2012). Is this for real? Authentic learning for the challenging events environment. *Journal of Teaching in Travel and Tourism*, 12(3), 225–241.

Robertson, M., Yeoman, I., Smith, K. A. & McMahon-Beattie, U. (2015). Technology, society, and visioning the future of music festivals. *Event Management*, 19(4), 567–587.

Saad, D. (2015). The future is virtual. In Yeoman, I., Robertson, M., McMahon-Beattie, U., Backer, E. & Smith, K. A. (Eds) *The Future of Events and Festivals* (pp. 209–218). London and New York: Routledge.

Stadler, R., Fullagar, S., & Reid, S. (2014). The professionalization of festival organizations: a relational approach to knowledge management. *Event Management*, 18(1), 39–52.

Vince, J. (2004). *Introduction to virtual reality*. New York, NY: Springer.

Wetzel, C. D., Radtke, P. H. & Stern, H. W. (1994). *Instructional effectiveness of video media*. Hillsdale, NJ: Lawrence Erlbaum Associates, Inc.

# 41

# INDUSTRY PERCEPTIONS OF POTENTIAL DIGITAL FUTURES FOR LIVE PERFORMANCE IN THE STAGING AND CONSUMPTION OF MUSIC FESTIVALS

*Adrian Bossey*

## Introduction

Festivals are an important expression of human activity that contribute much to our social and cultural life (Allen, O'Toole, Harris & McDonnell 2011, p. 15) and are also 'big business' (Webster & McKay 2016). Festivals form part of the growing events sector, and, as the Eventbrite Pulse Report noted in 2016, 'this is still an industry with many more opportunities than challenges' (Eventbrite 2017). Festivals may focus around various art forms or cultural activities but often have a particular association with music. For example, Shuker (2012, p. 130) defines a festival as 'a concert, usually outdoor, often held over several days … sites where commerce and popular ideology interact to produce historically significant musical meanings'. Music festivals are fluid environments, subject to change and reinvention, so that, for example, 'participative arts, audience theatricality and themed environments are increasingly popular within what may be described as the "boutique" festival sector' (Robinson, cited in McKay 2015, p. 177).

This chapter will look at those environments and will consider the current and potential future changes in technology, demand and innovation that are likely to impact the staging and consumption of live performances at music festivals.

## Literature review

The 'world of work' is changing rapidly so that machines are already undertaking tasks which were 'unthinkable – if not unimaginable – a decade ago' (Andy Haldane, Chief Economist, Bank of England 2015). Potentially this process could influence both the availability and the conceptualisation of 'leisure time', increasing demand for festival experiences and innovation in festival delivery. Following innovation around marketing, box office functionality and other event technology, industry experts have identified technology bringing 'digital audiences ever closer to the actual experience' as a consistent theme (Walker 2017). Furthermore, trends around festival audiences utilising mobile technology at festivals by, for instance, viewing performers through handheld devices whilst filming their live performance, could potentially influence their live experience. 'Technology is expanding the ways in which we make and experience culture; the digital dimension is becoming a "place" in itself' (DCMS, Culture White Paper 2017.

Commercial pressures to differentiate exist in an arguably oversupplied festival market (Robertson & Brown 2014). Furthermore, existing customers who have grown up with festivals are 'looking for something different' (Colegrave, writing in Access All Areas 2017); they realise 'the best festival experience wasn't the headline band but the quirky, thought provoking aspects'. Technology offers opportunities to improve ticket sales for early adopter festival organisers and could transform both objective and subjective leisure experience elements, enhancing the festival experience as a whole (Calvo-Soraluze & San Salvadore del Valle 2014, p. 175).

Currently, professional engagement with technology varies, so that 'social media continues to grow in popularity, as do event apps; while VR/ AR and big data/analytics are creeping towards wider adoption' (Eventbrite 2017, p. 4). Emerging digital event technologies may challenge festival organisers and audiences, in part because 'the sense of what is real and what is fantasy will become less profound [...] driving much event and festival experience into the realms of liminality' (Yeoman 2013, p. 257). Despite potentially positive digital futures, financial, technological and motivational barriers to engagement may exist, so the availability of technology does not necessarily mean it is being utilised evenly across live performance or festival contexts. As Steijn (2014, p. 141) notes, 'new technologies have seldom been used in connection with physical, spatial and aesthetic experiences in relation to live performances of classical music'.

Streaming of live content, defined by the Oxford English Dictionary (2017) as a live transmission of an event over the Internet, appears to be growing. Apple, Facebook, Google, Instagram and others all provide affordable live stream technology. For festivals, live-streaming of performances has occurred both directly from festivals and via media partnerships: for example entirely digitally with Red Bull at Demon Daze festival, www.redbull.tv/channel/festivals, and in a mixed terrestrial and digital format with the BBC and Glastonbury Festival, www.bbc.co.uk/events/ec584f. According to industry observers, this trend is growing and will have a major impact on the events industry in 2018 and beyond.

Audiences for communal screenings of live performances in secondary venues also appear to be rising. These events are referred to as 'livecasts' and originally emanated from the theatre arts sector, concentrated mainly in opera, theatre and (less so) ballet (Barker 2013). In particular, livecasting of theatrical content to cinemas has demonstrated significant growth with the National Theatre broadcasting to over 5.5 million people in over 2,000 venues around the world (Nationaltheatre.org.uk 2017). Furthermore, livecasting may have influenced broader music industry practice, with, for example, Billboard noting in 2013 that Robbie Williams's show at Estonia's Tallinn Song Festival 'will be filmed and beamed live into select theatres across 27 territories, including U.K. cinemas' (Kemp 2013). Conversely, the Elvis Presley/Symphony Orchestra 'The Wonder of You' tour in 2017 projected film footage of Elvis behind live musicians on stage. Thus, the potential for engaging communal audiences with 'mediatised' live content from festivals or incorporating 'as live' content in performances may be significant.

In an era of rapid technological change, the idea of networked performances is relatively old, with Gabrielli and Squartini (2015, p. 10) reporting an event in 1985 where musicians played simultaneously from two venues in NYC. Lazzaro and Wawrzynek (2001, p. 157) describe a Network Musical Performance occurring when 'a group of musicians, located at different physical locations, interact over a network to perform as they would if located in the same room'. Despite an evident challenge around achieving tolerable levels of latency, or time lag of the audio signal between different physical sites, networked performances have evolved to incorporate a variety of art forms and meanings.

Holograms, described by the Oxford English Dictionary as 'a photograph or an interference pattern which, when suitably illuminated, produces a three-dimensional image', have been used across the music sector for live and festival performances, including the Tupac Shakur 'performance' at Coachella in 2012 'with' Dr Dre. Despite this, the future for holographic technology at events remains unclear, with Eventbrite Pulse Report (2017, p. 20) describing them as 'a more futuristic technology [...] the least likely to be used at events in 2017, with only 4 per cent looking to definitely include it in the event experiences, and 78 per cent definitely not going to use it'.

Industry commentators are increasingly identifying potential immersive futures for events. The Eventbrite blog describes Virtual Reality (VR) and Augmented Reality (AR) as becoming increasingly mainstream. VR offers the chance to provide a richer event experience to those tuning in remotely, and AR lets organisers layer digital enhancements onto the immediate event environment, which can be shared out online. Magic Leap have developed AR eyewear, and such devices could potentially supplement visual information in a shared festival experience, providing users with a personalised view on a collective experience (Robertson 2017). However, there is an apparent 'time-lag' in implementing innovate practice, with Eventbrite reporting an evident 'gap' between awareness and deployment of VR and AR in 2017, with 31 per cent of organisers actively considering it for their events but just 7 per cent deciding to invest in it. Furthermore, VR and AR prompt questions around the achievability of communal interactions between audience members wearing individual headsets and performers. Robertson and Brown (2014) acknowledge the need for interaction of the audience member with the performance but note that there is limited acknowledgement of how it can be applied to the festival/live event environment.

Some commentators view the nature of festival audiences as being conducive to technological enhancements. According to Sadd (2014, p. 213), 'festivals will always be gatherings of people, yet these people are continually seeking ever more stimulating experiences and so technology is being used more and more to provide this'. Webster and McKay (2016) noted that festivals can be sites for musical experimentation and hybridity. Holograms may become more prevalent, and entirely virtual artists could potentially play festival shows to audiences sharing a celebratory experience. In Japan, Hatsune Miku (a humanoid persona/vocaloid, created and shared under creative commons to encourage fan-led content creation) is popular and has performed in holographic form to live audiences.

Robertson, Yeoman, Smith and McMahon-Beattie (2015) suggest that future technology will bring about a virtual experience trend, but audiences and festival promoters may relate to more a 'live' experience. This is because, as Van Es (2017, p. 161) points out, 'liveness matters to people because it promises them the experience of something (made to seem) relevant'. Liveness has been considered by academics with Baker (2013) identifying its five aspects as 'immediacy', 'intimacy', 'buzz', 'learning' and 'being'. Liveness itself represents a 'moving target', as new models for communicating are emerging in the media landscape, and as a result new forms of liveness are also likely to surface Van Es (2017).

Festivals have been ascribed the capacity to engender a sense of euphoria and even utopia: 'At the height of the festivity, we step out of our assigned roles and statuses – of gender, ethnicity, tribe and rank – and into a brief utopia defined by egalitarianism, creativity and mutual love' (Ehrenreich 2007, p. 253). Employing technology to enhance or generate performance-based content in ways which are sensitive to and supportive of liveness and capable of stimulating euphoria represents a significant challenge. Visions for the future vary, and the opportunity to act as pioneers in a 'brave new world' of digitised festivals may not appeal to all established professionals. Robertson et al. (2015) recognise that the notion that live performance takes place at a specific time and location and can be listened to only once will be challenged as technology allows live moments to be recorded and/or played elsewhere.

## Methodology

Primary research in the form of unstructured interviews was carried out with a sample group of five influential UK-based industry professionals with a range of roles in relation to festivals. These were Melvin Benn (Managing Director of Festival Republic), Paul Hutton (Director of Cross Town Concerts), Ian Biscoe (Producer, studiobiscoe.com), Steve Strange (booking agent, clients include Eminem and Coldplay and co-founder of X-Ray Touring) and Teresa Moore (Director of A Greener Festival).

Open questions were used to elucidate qualitative information around technological influences on marketing/sales for festivals in recent years; the value of streaming/filming of performances; Tupac Shakur's (holographic) performance at Coachella in 2012; perceptions of how festivals might develop streaming, holograms and networked performances; current programming which incorporates significant levels of additional digital content in some form; opinions on entirely virtual artistes; possible digital futures for existing (and/or new) festivals; and the concept of 'liveness'.

A range of ethical principles were considered including the author's professional relationship with the interviewees in relation to the researcher's responsibility to the academic community to remain objective. Interviewees gave informed consent to be named in this chapter.

The limitations of this case study include the small sample size and limited scope.

## Findings of the case study

### *Marketing and sales*

Technology and consumer attitudes are changing the way that live performances are being marketed and sold. As Melvin Benn highlighted,

> in the past, you could really only identify your audience [...] via relatively targeted music magazines; NME, Smash Hits or Kerrang [...]. Digital allows you to identify who your audience are and what they like and how much they like the acts that you've got on or the festivals that you run.

Paul Hutton agreed, noting that 'box office software is a huge change; everything is online... it changes everything because we can really get stuff out there effectively for nothing'. However, as Paul points out, this is not necessarily entirely a good thing: 'there's so much data going out, so it's very hard to analyse what part of your marketing strategy is working, because you can't be in control of other people's data flow'. This highlights one of the recognised difficulties of big data. However, social media can be used to promote positive messages – Teresa Moore suggests that festival organisers have an opportunity to influence behaviour:

On the social marketing or social media front, there is a lot more that could be done with audiences to persuade (them) to act more sustainably, to act greener, when they come on site. One of those is to try to encourage people not to bring as much stuff with them [...] You know you've got your audience's attention, when they buy a ticket.

## *On-stage screens*

The increased screening of live footage and other visuals on and adjacent to festival stages was commented on positively by two interviewees. Steve Strange suggests, 'Screens are an extension to the vibe that you are adding to the event [...] (they) create a more intimate atmosphere in such a big place'. According to Paul Hutton, screen usage is now normal: 'As a standard, I think that people expect it, if you put on a show anything above say, 15,000 people'. However, Paul suggests that the popularity of screen usage can prompt performers to take an alternative 'stripped down' approach by not using screens: 'Sometimes when people don't do anything that's almost like the new black and white; in a sense; they are trying to make some kind of point "we don't need all this"'.

The use of screens can alter the live experience by distracting audiences from the stage itself. Paul suggests,

> Quite often when you stand there you've got three lots of people; one looking at one side of the stage, one looking at the stage and the other looking at the other side. After a while you can't stop yourself looking at the screen and that's all you end up doing.

Screens could represent a gateway to increasingly digitised experiences; Ian Biscoe states,

> At festivals it's always just one or two big screens but I (like) the idea of positioning remote performers and taking people remotely who can't be there or from a location relevant to the performance and inserting them visually [...] to build up more complex worlds in physical environments.

## *Televising or streaming performances*

Televising festival content and streaming of performances has gained in popularity, facilitated in part, by content produced for on-site screens. Melvin Benn welcomes this as a promotional opportunity: 'Of course, I stream the shows and I broadcast them [...] and so relaying a live performance; there's a great merit to it'. Commenting on his previous work with the BBC, Melvin explains, 'Glastonbury is a sell-out show, it can't get any bigger, and I love the idea of shows being televised and of course, my principle aim is those that are buying tickets for the real performance'. However, Melvin disputes that televised content creates a virtual alternative to physically attending a major festival:

> People do (make an event of it at home) very much so, and that's great, but TV has always done that, it isn't about music; football matches do it, and big episodes of a soap opera do it. Nothing about that is related to a festival or a music audience per see, it's related to a television happening.

Nevertheless, Paul Hutton thinks Glastonbury is an exception to 'pretty much every rule that's out there'.

## Digital futures for live performance

> I don't think every festival could televise live content [...] if people knew that other festivals were going to be televised they might consider not buying tickets. A number of them have been televised before but generally it's a delayed broadcast.

Whilst some artists do not want to be filmed, Steve Strange identifies that

> most of them do these days. It becomes part and parcel of the overall profile and gains that you get from a festival. Rather than sitting in the press tent for three hours you get a hell of a lot more done by being filmed and screened, or filmed for later broadcast.

Steve values editorial control, 'just say there's some problem, it's good to be able to have the ability to say well we don't want to use that one'. Potentially, the increasingly mediatised environment at festivals may itself encourage official filming:

> Everyone's got the ability with mobile phones these days to film anything and when they put them up on YouTube they're there for ever anyway [...] I think given that option most people will obviously go for the big camera shoot.

Streaming can be a two-way process; Ian Biscoe described a three-day event in Falmouth:

> we ran a live stage with music and digital artists from different places jamming but we also had remote artists performing (including) musicians in London, Paris, Frankfurt, Scandinavia and New York, and a dancer (in Falmouth). The dancer was captured in motion capture and that data was sent to (the musicians) and they used that to modify the composition they were playing and then we streamed the resulting music, with video and projected it onto the façades of several buildings.

Finally, there may be potential environmental benefits to streaming; as Teresa Moore recognises, 'If you can stream the performance out to other locations to some extent you are ameliorating for example the $CO_2$ footprint of transport'. However, considering the 'intensely private experience' of downloading music more generally, Teresa suggests that

> what would seem to be a more sustainable way in terms of delivery of music actually had the opposite effect in that, if it's true, we've seen a huge growth in the live sector because people want to live the experience.

### *Livecasts*

Music industry recognition of the growth of commercial livecasts was confirmed by Steve Strange: 'There have been exclusive shows that have been sold to cinemas where people go to the cinema to watch a show because they can't be there'. Livecasting could unlock innovation in a festival environment. Paul Hutton speculated that a very big artiste might decide

> we are going to do a huge spectacular show on top of Machu Pichu [...] there won't be an audience there because you can't get there kids but we can, and we will do this show and we will film it (and) play to the world; this huge thing where everyone will watch it.

Paul also identified a specific opportunity: 'I'm amazed actually when you think about it, obviously U2 would be the prime suspects for this one, why they haven't done that [...] maybe I should take that idea to them!'

## *Networked performances*

Interviewees demonstrated limited awareness of networked performances, which Ian Biscoe defined as being 'about trying to get the same type of quality and immersion in a performance that involves performers in multiple places, and normally audiences in multiple places, that you would do in a single live venue'. According to Ian, they are potentially less logical, exploring 'new areas of what is real, what is virtual, what is remote what is physical, what is augmented, what is tangible'. Ian perceives that networked performances could be applied to festivals: 'It is possible to do this, it's having enough people who understand artistically and dramaturgically how to connect people in these contexts'.

## *Holograms*

Steve Strange attended a 'seminal' holographic performance:

> I was at Coachella and saw the Tupac thing, that was the first example I've ever seen and I was quite amazed by it. It looked so real, but at the same time it was part of a proper live, human show.

However, despite acknowledging some financial potential, Steve remains unconvinced: 'I know it sells, I can't argue with that, maybe for an older audience who are a bit more open minded about what they are going to see'. Paul Hutton is also unsure:

> It obviously has some merit because people are going to see it. I know there's talk of an Amy Winehouse one at some point. It's difficult I think [...] people like Elvis, who nobody in Britain ever saw play, that's as good as it's ever going to get.

A 'novelty factor' around holograms could positively influence a percentage of audiences according to Teresa Moore, who references a drive for 'authentic experiences': 'in a way using holograms to recreate stars from the past may not be viewed as an authentic experience, but it may be that the hologram experience itself is the thing that takes us into the future'. The complexity of holograms is currently self-limiting according to Ian Biscoe: 'it's very fixed so it's still kind of a screen, there's no such thing as the holographic projector which can move images about freely in space and time'. However, there could be 'traction' here, and further developments around holographic content at festivals may be expected.

## *Immersive futures*

The potential use of VR headsets at festivals was not popular. Melvin Benn stated, 'Virtual reality headsets isolate people ... you get an incredible experience when you are enjoying it, but it's in a very singular fashion'. Conversely, Melvin perceived Silent Discos, deployed to overcome noise restrictions, as being 'entirely the opposite; it is the most collective thing that you can possibly do, it's incredibly fun and people do that together, it is absolutely not an isolating experience'. Noise and the challenge of interactivity were also commented upon by Paul Hutton:

> If everybody had headphones on then we would never have any noise problems in that sense. (But) if you take that out to a whole festival based on that then there's no interaction between people, so then you've just got 20,000 people wandering aimlessly around haven't you!

As Ian Biscoe notes though, removing the need for headsets could alter things: 'There could be nothing worse than getting together with a group of people and then visually occluding them. I think augmented reality, which is the idea of projecting things into space, holographs, is more interesting'.

## *Working with an entirely virtual artiste*

The concept of programming or representing a virtual artiste also proved contentious with Melvin Benn commenting that it is 'absolutely not about, for me, providing a virtual performance in front of a live audience. I think people are trying to develop it for the sake of it, it's just not happening, and it becomes very problematic'. From an agency perspective, Steve Strange said that he is a 'rock and roll' person at heart and that 'I like things to be as real as they can. I'm a musician [...] and that chemistry thing is very important for me and I wouldn't personally want to represent something that wasn't real'. However, Paul Hutton was more amenable, stating,

> I don't think it's impossible... Look at silent disco; who would have thought that something that was 300 people wearing effectively headphones in the same room but listening to three different types of music would be having so much fun? Now you go to these things and there's 3000 people doing it, more sometimes. So, I guess it's like everything there will always be room for it, whether people want it or not, they will vote with their feet.

## *Possible digital futures*

Pioneers like Ian Biscoe feel the market for digital performances is already developing and the potential for innovation is significant: 'There are endless possibilities still, we've still seen very little of what's possible using networked performances and digital technology'. Teresa Moore believes that technology will change festivals in unforeseen ways: 'I do think that we are not going to step back from being technologically driven and there are new things coming on stream all the time'. However, Ian considers that the optimum conditions for innovation predominantly exist at festivals 'like Festival Number 6', who foster an artistic activity, that isn't just 'a bunch of headline acts'.

A potential reaction to technology from audiences who want an authentic, less technologically driven, 'stripped-down' experience is proposed by Teresa Moore: 'we've seen this in the record industry (with) a resurgence in vinyl and my own view is that we will see a resurgence in the traditional values of festivals'. Senior professionals appear firmly aligned to these 'traditional rock and roll' values, with Melvin Benn stating, 'A festival is a live activity, it is not a virtual activity and I'm not at all interested in anything being virtual'. This view is broadly shared by Steve Strange: 'I don't believe in a virtual festival experience, you can really only experience a festival by being there'. However, Steve does expect that the visual side of festivals will keep updating: 'Every artist these days wants to programme their set into a video wall'.

Steve also reiterated the competitive nature of the festival market place: 'there are a lot of festivals out there and every year one or two of them hit the wall because there's too much competition'. Paul Hutton agreed that Britain in particular is saturated with large-scale camping festivals, and that 'sales for some of these events are terrible [...] because there are just too many of them'. However, this 'churn' in the market may also create opportunities for new formats aimed at more technologically inclined festivalgoers.

## *Liveness*

Most interviewees championed a traditional sense of 'liveness'. Melvin Benn stated categorically that 'It's entirely about the live performance ... people go to a festival to see the live performances and to enjoy the community of people that also want to see the live performances'. This was supported by Paul Hutton, who commented,

> I often wonder why people do go to shows or keep coming back [...] they were part of a crowd, it was loud, you can feel the music, they were part of something that was happening, it was a shared experience. Whether you can replicate that in any other form I don't know and if you talk to 99 out of a 100 people that work in the live industry they probably give the same answer that you can't replicate a live concert. But you can do it sometimes, maybe.

However, Teresa Moore suggests that audience behaviours involving stepping back and channelling a live festival experience through a digital medium are a 'really interesting phenomenon'. She goes on: 'We may already be on our way there, that we are not really experiencing live anymore because we are so wrapped up in reporting it and photographing and channelling it through our phones, that already we are once removed'. This aligns with the findings of the DCMS White Paper around 'making and experiencing culture' and represents an interesting focus for future research.

## Conclusion

The narrative approach in this case study has provided useful reflections from generous expert commentators on a spectrum of potential technological developments and emerging digital formats for performative activities at festivals, and their potential impact on audiences. Interviewees concurred with Robertson and Brown's (2014) finding that the market for festivals is oversupplied; however, this may stimulate digital innovation as the digital arena opens up new opportunities across a range of artistic and operational processes.

Video walls and live streaming are well established amongst festivals and were, perhaps unsurprisingly, the least contentious of the formats under discussion. Most interviewees were relatively open to the concept of 'livecasts', but the music industry interviewees did not have personal experience of networked performances, perhaps evidencing the 'time lag' in adoption of new technologies identified by Eventbrite, or a lack of commercialised application to date. On balance, and despite their nascent 'traction' in the marketplace, even interviewees who had experienced holograms in a festival setting were less than enthusiastic about the incorporation of holographic elements into live performances. Virtual artists were unpopular amongst music industry professionals, who exhibited a clear passion for the purity of the traditional live 'rock and roll' experience, a festival model which celebrates a pure form of liveness and delivers a recognised commercial impact. However, the ubiquity of mobile device ownership amongst festival attendees, combined with an increased tendency for audiences on and off site to interact with festival performances using technology, may suggest that significant change is already underway.

Further research opportunities clearly arise around both 'liveness' in the making and receiving of festival content and potential applications of commercially available technologies in festival environments.

## References

Allen, J., O'Toole, W., Harris, R. & McDonnell, I. (2011). *Festival and Special Event Management*, 3rd ed., Milton: John Wiley & Sons.
Barker, M. (2013). *Live to Your Local Cinema: The Remarkable Rise of Livecasting*. London: Palgrave Macmillan.
Calvo-Soraluze, J. & San Salvadore del Valle, R. (2014). The transformation of leisure experiences in music festivals. In Richards, G., Marques, L. & Mein, K. (Eds.) *Event Design: Social Perspectives and Practices* (161–180). Oxford: Routledge.
Colegrave, S. (2017). Access all areas. Available at: https://view.joomag.com/access-all-areas-october-2017. Accessed 26/07/17.
DCMS (Department for Culture, Media & Sport) (2017). *The Culture White Paper*. London: Stationary Office.
Ehrenreich, B. (2007). *Dancing in the Streets: A History of Collective Joy*. London: Granta Books.
Eventbrite. (2017). Eventbrite Pulse Report 2017: All the Event Industry Statistics You Need to Know. Available at: www.eventbrite.co.uk/blog/event-industry-statistics-pulse-report-2017/. Accessed 26/07/17.
Gabrielli, L. & Squartini, S. (2015). *Wireless Networked Music Performance*. Singapore: Springer.
Haldane, A. (2015). *Labour's Share Speech*. London: Bank of England.
Kemp, S. (2013). Robbie Williams' Estonia concert to be beamed into cinemas. Billboard 7 October. Available at: www.billboard.com/articles/news/1569434/robbie-williams-estonia-concert-to-be-beamed-into-cinemas. Accessed 26/07/17.
Lazzaro, J. & Wawrzynek, J. (2001). *A case for network musical performance - NOSSDAV '01:* Proceedings of the 11th international workshop on Network and operating systems support for digital audio and video (157–166). New York. ACM Press.
McKay, G. (2015). *The Pop Festival: History, Music, Media, Culture*. London: Bloomsbury.
National Theatre Live. (2017). Who we are and what we do. Available at: http://ntlive.nationaltheatre.org.uk/about-us. Accessed 26/07/17.
Robertson, A. (2017) *Magic Leap finally unveils augmented reality goggles, says it's shipping next year*. Available at: www.theverge.com/2017/12/20/16800474/magic-leap-one-creator-edition-augmented-reality-goggles-announce. Accessed 03/01/18.
Robertson, M. & Brown, S. (2014). Leadership and visionary futures. In Yeoman, I., Robertson, M., McMahon-Beattie, U., Smith, K. and Backer, E. (Eds.) *The Future of Events and Festivals* (219–235). Oxford: Routledge.
Robertson, M., Yeoman, I., Smith, K. & McMahon-Beattie, U. (2015). Technology, society, and visioning: The future of music festivals. *Event Management*, 19(1), 567–587.
Sadd, D. (2014). The future is virtual. In Yeoman, I., Robertson., M., McMahon-Beattie, U., Smith, K. and Backer, E. (Eds.) *The Future of Events and Festivals* (209–219). Oxford: Routledge.
Shuker, R. (2012). *Popular Music Culture: The Key Concepts*. Oxford: Routledge.
Steijn, A. (2014). Classical music, liveness and digital technologies. In Richards, G. Marques, L. & Mein, K. (Eds.) *Event Design Social Perspectives and Practices* (137–160). London: Routledge.

Van Es, K. (2017). *The Future of Live*. Polity: Cambridge.
Walker, M. (2017). 5 Things to expect from the events industry in 2017. Available at: www.eventbrite.co.uk/blog/5-things-to-expect-from-the-event-industry-in-2017-ds00/. Accessed 26/07/17.
Webster, E. & McKay, G. (2016). *The Impact of British Music Festivals*. London: AHRC.
Yeoman, I. (2013). *A Futurist's Thoughts on Consumer Trends Shaping Future Festivals and Events*. Bingley: Emerald Group Publishing.

# 42

# UTOPIAN FUTURES

## Wellington on a Plate and the envisioning of a food festival in Tuscany

*Ian Yeoman, Sochea Nhem, Una McMahon-Beattie, Katherine Findlay, Sandra Goh and Sophea Tieng*

### An introduction: food festivals

With the growth and popularity of food tourism, in parallel we have seen the emergence of food-specific events and festivals (Getz, Robinson, Andersson & Vujicic 2014). Events have become an important element of the experience economy; they are often related to improvements to quality of life for communities and regions through their economic and social benefits (Yeoman, McMahon-Beattie, Fields, Albrecht & Meethan 2015). Food festivals provide an opportunity for society to socialise as by their nature, food festivals bring people together. As consumers search for real experiences rather than 'products', they seek new meaning and this has led to an increased importance of events and festivals in society (Yeoman, Robertson & Smith 2012). Fundamentally, food festivals and events are a representation of how the experience economy is at the epicentre of the changing nature of the tourism product (Getz et al. 2014). Unlike Italy, France or Spain, who have a strong history of food production and associated food tourism experiences, New Zealand is a country that is not considered a food tourism destination in its own right. Known as the youngest country in the world (Yeoman 2013), it does, however, offer a diversity of experiences and products. As part of the development of its varied experience economy, Wellington on a Plate (WOAP) is New Zealand's leading food festival. Focussing on utopian ideals, this chapter creates a vision of the future and outlines the actions to create that future. The vision is based on a scenario in Tuscany, La Natura food festival, and this vision assists the reader in considering possible implications for WOAP.

### Wellington on a Plate

WOAP began in 2009 with 43 participating restaurants, 30 events and approximately 400 tickets sold. In 2016, this had grown to 148 restaurants, 140 events and 9,070 tickets (Miekle 2017). The festival takes place in Wellington, the capital city of New Zealand. The event began with the realisation that there was a gap in the events calendar. Positively Wellington, the regional tourism organisation responsible for tourism management and destination planning for the city, brainstormed ideas in order to fill the gap and hence the birth of WOAP, a food festival for the city. From conception to the first event was only six weeks in all. However, the festival has established itself as a significant feature in the Wellington annual events calendar.

WOAP (www.visawoap.com) is held in the last two weeks of August, and it showcases the best of Wellington's food products and experiences. From farm to plate, it is a celebration of food and beverage through festival events, special menu offerings and industry activity. The festival incorporates a number of specially designed products and experiences including specific lunch and dinner menus for the festivals known as Dine Wellington. The festival organizes a best burger competition, featuring special and innovate ideas from participating restaurants. Events range from free public lectures, events for pets, competitions, cookery classes and night markets to a beer festival and much more. Award-winning events have included Rimutaka Prison Gate to Plate with celebrity chef Martin Bosley, who mentors inmates to create a fine dining experience at the local prison, thus taking on a social responsibility dimension. Another example is Dine with Monet, which is a dining experience based on the food found in Monet's paintings. The focus of WOAP is foodie experiences, innovation and excitement. Although the majority of events are focussed in Wellington, they spread into the hinterland as far north as Kapiti and the Wairapa in the East.

The festival is organised by Wellington Culinary Events Trust (WCET) with Sarah Miekle as Chief Executive and Festival Director since inception. The trust is a not-for-profit trust that sets out to work across consumer, industry and partner channels to showcase the very best of the Wellington culinary and hospitality community.

## Research brief

This chapter portrays one future from a wider scenario planning study about WOAP. The wider study was commissioned by WCET as it wanted to know (and understand) what the festival could look like in the future, the key drivers of change that are impacting on the festival, what an international comparator looks like, and what WOAP's future values and strategic directions might be. WCET wanted to create a range of scenarios that portrayed a set of culinary food festivals set in 2050 based upon different perspectives to stretch their understanding of food festivals. It sought to understand the implications of these scenarios for WOAP. Four scenarios were created as seen in Figure 42.1.

### *Future studies and scenario planning*

In future studies, plurality is dominant rather than a singular term to counter the notion of only one future (Dator 2014), the latter having conceptual and political limitations. This pluralism opens the choices of alternatives, stretching our understanding of the future. Thus, pluralism is dominant in the research and frameworks adopted in futures studies. In this context, the method that dominates futures studies is scenario planning (Ringland 2010; Slaughter 2002). Scenario comes from the Latin *scaena* meaning scene and was originally used in the context of the performing arts (Asselt, Klooster, Notten & Smits 2010; Bishop, Hines & Collins 2007), with the term being adopted because of the emphasis on storytelling. Kahn and Wiener (1967, p. 273) defined scenarios as 'hypothetical sequences of events constructed for the purpose of focusing attention on causal processes and decision points'.

*Utopian futures*

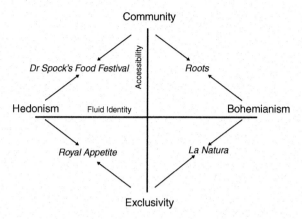

*Figure 42.1* Food festival scenarios

## The wider scenarios and project context

A scenario planning team was created for the WOAP project. The outcome was four scenarios using a 2 × 2 matrix framework (Van der Heijden, Bradfield, Burt, Cairns & Wright 2002). This framework approach adopts a perspective shaped by two dominant drivers, accessibility and fluid identity. In Figure 42.1, the vertical axis depicts accessibility, which is about how accessible the festival is for the masses (Lee 2014). On one end of the scale is community (Jepson & Clarke 2015), indicating a festival which is open to everyone. The opposite is exclusivity, which highlights a festival that is catering for only a few select people, focussing on luxury experiences and high-end consumers (Kapferer 2014; Yeoman & McMahon-Beattie 2014). The horizontal axis shows a scale of fluid identity. Fluid identity focusses on forms of tourist behaviour where tourists want individual experiences and novelty rather than specific activities (Yeoman, 2010). On one end of the scale, we have hedonism (Taquet, Quoidbach, de Montjoye, Desseilles & Gross 2016.), which can be defined as a state of luxury and indulgence in the pursuit of pleasure. At the other end, we have bohemianism (Huston, Wadley & Fitzpatrick 2015), which can be described as an alternative setting, focussing on originality and non-conformism.

The four scenarios are named Dr Spock's Food Festival, Roots, Royal Appetite and La Natura. Dr Spock's Food Festival is a science fiction future emphasising creativity, quantum leaps and science as a food experience. Roots is a predictive scenario based upon facts and statistical trends with a focus on community, the beach and fresh food. The Royal Appetite scenario is a prognosis scenario focussing on high value and exclusivity in a neo-liberal world. The final scenario, La Natura, creates a vision around tourism as a food paradise. This scenario is the focus of this chapter.

## Utopian futures: creating a vision

La Natura is a scenario that pictures a future food festival that is focussed on community, well-being and sustainable practice. The purpose of the scenario is to highlight a utopian future, of what a food festival should be. It is constructed within the context of Bergman and colleagues' (2010) ontological classification of the future and sets out to create a vision or desired state.

## The imperfections of Utopia

Utopia is a contentious and contradictory term, with a strong spatial component. It has been described as a perfect, good, happy place (*eutopia*) or as a 'no place' (*outopia*) that does not exist and may never exist (Brown 2009). Utopias generally represent both a critique and a proposal. Embedded in the context of their contemporary conditions, they entail a critique to current society and an ideal that provides tools to 'measure' it, inspiring a quest for the construction of a better alternative (Hedrén & Linnér 2009). Therefore, utopias offer an alternative for a good or at least relatively 'better' place; 'what should or could be'. This better place or situation is often located in the past. Such utopias rely on a certain sense of nostalgia (for childhood, a previous golden age or rural idyll), or it is seen as a state of becoming (Coyle & Fairweather 2005). It has been suggested that to explore the desires and ethical underpinnings of utopias, it is important to look at what aspects of society are being repressed, controlled or erased in proposed utopian alternatives (Levitas 2010). The term utopia has been avoided or even rejected by advocates of alternative ideas of society and places because it is often associated with unrealistic and unachievable ideals, making them appear naive and impossible.

According to Bell (1993), utopias are visions, ideal futures that are credible yet not really attainable. They include elements of fantasy or wishful thinking, and their purpose is about how to make the future possible or creating a pathway to it. This pathway is supported by Asselt et al. (2010) and Veenman (2013), who introduced the category of normative futures studies which favours a single image of a desirable future and the deployment of backcasting methodologies as reason to achieve that desirable future. Included in normative futures studies are critical futures which represent desires, values, cultural assumptions and world views. Thus, utopias are a desired position or are about idealism.

## Paradise and Utopia

Tourism is first and foremost an activity about difference and encounter, and its influence in the representation of places and societies is crucial (Yeoman et al. 2015). In geography, the notion of 'geographical imagination' refers precisely to the ways in which we represent and imagine the world, places and people, and the increasing role of tourism in shaping these imaginaries has been stressed (Mowforth & Munt 2009). Yeoman et al (2015) argue it would be hard to imagine the tourism without a gaze or image as in a certain context, tourism is a paradise, a place to get away from the everyday. The meaning of paradise is not universal and varies within different cultural or religious contexts. In the Western world, notions of paradise often refer to heaven or to an ideal or perfect place on earth (Chiu 2009). Costa (1998) suggests that it was first used by Homer, and later by other Greek and Roman writers and has been in use since approximately 3,000 years ago. They described paradise as a place of isolation, abundance and difference. Later, the Judeo-Christian tradition linked conceptualisations of heaven and the Garden of Eden to the concept of paradise. During the European Age of Discovery, paradise was related to the exotic and primitive, including the notion of the noble savage. In contemporary times, paradise is commonly understood as heaven outside the earthly domain while also acknowledging that paradise-like places exist on earth.

## The scenario: La Natura

*The landscape around Tuscany gives a food lover hope and vision for fresh, local and authentic cuisine. Surprisingly, the region itself has become one of the leading culinary delights on the organic food-tourism* trail and is acknowledged as the United Nations Educational, Scientific and Cultural Organisation (UNESCO) gastronomy festival in 2050. This is the best food festival in the world. The festivalgoer is demanding, will search out for the best ingredients, is concerned about the environment and advocates sustainable practices. Authenticity, community and provenance are key words. The food festival offers a range of exotic, innovative and exciting events for the foodie to the service of more basic humble dishes that represent the history of the region. The festival has a strong sense of pride with community, with political and industry support. The festival advocates a balance between nature and human, emphasising the role food can play in communities. Health and well-being are important ingredients in shaping the human capital elements during the festival. It runs for two weeks offering diversity of products and experiences, from educational courses on food and wine to expensive dining experiences with celebrity chefs. Prices and access range from free to the exclusive.

## Drivers

La Natura is a utopian scenario with the central proposition of how to create a food paradise and vision. Drivers are the key trends or propositions that are shaping the scenario's story.

### Driver 1: increased knowledge and education

Society is more knowledgeable and better educated (Muller 2015). This has been fuelled by expanding technologies that make information freely accessible (Yeoman 2012). In Italy, the proportion of students who are expected to graduate from university has increased remarkably from 19 per cent in 2000 to 36 per cent in 2016, and the upward trend will continue in the future (OECD 2017). In the similar vein, Yeoman (2008) suggested that affluent countries are expecting to see an increase in graduate-level qualified employees. The rising level of education enables consumers to be better informed about their health issues, and as a result, they are willing to make important and life-extending changes in lifestyle (Yeoman, McMahon-Beattie, Backer, Robertson & Smith 2014).

### Driver 2: health and wellness

In line with disposable income growth, consumers have become more concerned about what they are eating, and they tend to seek food that is local, organic and produced in a sustainable manner (Yeoman 2012). According the United Nations World Tourism Organisation (UNWTO 2012), food is playing a greater role in destination image and, as part of that image, it is portrayed local and with a provenance. This food is seen as pure and untainted, suggesting health benefits and a natural lifestyle. With ageing populations, tourists will seek out new ways to extend their years and slow down the ageing process; thus healthy food, exercise, Eastern medicines, yoga and herbal remedies will play a greater part in the future (Yeoman et al. 2015).

### Driver 3: scarcity of resources

Peak oil is an example of scarcity of resources. Peak oil will lead to uncertainty in the future over the availability of oil. The issues of the scarcity of resources can be related to the growth in world tourism and population. As the world's population grows and economies become more industrialised, non-renewable energy sources will become scarcer and more costly (Yeoman 2012). Currently, tourism is dependent on the availability of oil and is comparatively oil-intensive. While forecasts for future tourism growth are optimistic, there is also increasing evidence about the imminence of a peak oil production and the economic effects that this would cause (Yeoman 2012). According to Yeoman (2012), population estimates suggest that world population will reach 9.1 billion in 2050. As a result, the challenge of growing competition for resources is likely to be met by more efficient exploitation of existing resources.

### Driver 4: social demographic changes

An aging population will see more individuals having time to attend festivals. This living longer means we celebrate occasions more often, whether it is birthdays or events (Yeoman et al. 2014n). According to the United Nations (UN 2015), Italy's old-age dependency ratio is the highest in Europe. For every 100 working-age Italians there are 32.7 elderly Italians to care for. There are approximately 150 over-65s for every 100 people under 14. It is predicted this will rise to 263 elders for every 100 young people by 2050. Increasing aging population implies a growing demand for food and services catering to the elderly who seek to remain fit and active (Yeoman 2008).

### Driver 5: awareness of food knowledge

Due to issues such as climate change and greater education, people are more aware of what they are eating. Thus the future tourist will be more sophisticated, be aware and demanding. According to Yeoman (2008), the scale of communication and immediacy of knowledge will become a more global phenomena. Combined, the higher quality, variety and new experiences will dominate tourist food consumption (Yeoman et al. 2015).

## Implications for WCET and WOAP

Having examined the drivers of change in the future scenario for La Natura, it is now useful to consider how similar drivers may be relevant to WAOP in the future, and what actions may be needed to ensure the positive development of the festival under this scenario.

### Advocating organic and healthy food

In the world where people are more affluent and well educated, the demand for health and wellness is obvious. La Natura highlights the drivers and directions for the future. In this sense, one noticeable implication for WCET is to work more collaboratively with key stakeholders, especially producers, to offer more healthy, authentic and local produce so that it can add more value to exotic and unique dining experience they offer to their clients.

### Creating a vision of a food paradise

La Natura is a vision scenario, a perfect place where people want to be. Thus, under this scenario, WCET has to ensure that WAOP represents a mystery, a paradise and something that people desire. It needs to be attractive with a clear value system that advocates authenticity, provenance and community. At the same time, it needs to offer a variety of access points, maintaining an illusion of desire and excitement. WOAP has to be a food tourist's dream festival.

### Growing number of responsible businesses

La Natura stimulates interest in healthy and organic food. This scenario also illustrates to society and industry that demand for such food is increasing. Thus, WOAP needs a supplier and stakeholder system that advocates sustainable choices, practices, a focus on community and championing food in a responsible way.

### Encouraging more organic farming practices

La Natura goes beyond the tourism industry by recognising the holistic nature of the food supply chain from farm to fork. In such a scenario, WOAP and WCET are partners with local suppliers, producers and farmers advocating organic practices.

### Creating a polarised society driven by exclusivity

However, there is a risk with this utopian future: it should be recognised that an organic and provenance approach to food might be seen as a luxury for the rich and elite in society, thus alienating those in the lower socio-economic classes. WOAP doesn't want to be seen as a product for foodies and posh people. This dark side would create a polarised society (Yeoman et al. 2014) where only the top class would have access to such festival.

### Concluding thoughts: learning points for a future strategy

The purpose of investigating La Natura was to create an action plan in order to create the future that scenario portrays. Considering the elements of the scenario and the drivers of change, the actions required from WOAP and WCET are as follows.

### Action 1: create a food story and champion the cause

New Zealand most certainly has a food story, although this is the youngest country on earth, and its food culture is still evolving. It is about embracing its *turangawaewae*, New Zealand's place in the world and about having confidence in New Zealand itself. WOAP needs to present that story from a tourism perspective. The story must embrace the values, characteristics and actions that are seamless from farm to fork. It should be built around the themes of sustainable practice, provenance, excitement and an advocacy for the right path.

### Action 2: vision

A strong vision needs to be created for the WOAC, highlighting the world-class culinary experiences in Wellington that push out gastronomic boundaries. WOAP should be recognised as the festival that delivers the most original and innovative culinary event in the Oceania region so that it becomes a global benchmark.

### Action 3: be accessible

Food should be accessible, not exclusive, so that all New Zealanders can be proud of its food and beverage products and service showcased at WOAP. They should be celebrated, supported and consumed with pride.

## Action 4: values

WOAP should draw out the values portrayed in La Natura such as authenticity, anchoring the community, excellent collaboration and innovation. The experiences delivered should be authentic, genuine and real. This will ensure that they are talked about well after the festival. Food and beverage products and experiences are best shared, laying the foundations for a stronger and more connected community. Experiencing excellence in terms of the products, services and experience should be the norm for WOAP festivalgoers. The festival should be a collaboration of a wide variety of the people to deliver the WOAP experiences. Finally, the festival should aim to be innovation, making the food tourist wonder and dream.

## Action 5: be a winner

Wellington should aim to achieve UNESCO gastronomy city status in the near future.

## Conclusion

*La Natura* highlights the key trends shaped around health consciousness and at the same time, suggests that consumers are willing to pay more for food that is healthy, sustainable and local. This is a scenario about partnership in which WOAP becomes a gateway for responsible suppliers; thus those wanting to participate in WOAP would need to have similar values. The risk in this scenario is that a festival is created for the liberal, educated and informed in society, which alienates vast majority of locals. The knowledge gained from the use of this scenario should help WOAP establish itself as a sustainable food festival and a desirable food tourist experience. Overall, in the context of the scenario La Natura food festival, this chapter has explored a vision of the future of WOAP festival and has outlined a series of realistic actions to create that future. For the wider festivals community, the chapter demonstrates how communities and organisations can use scenario planning to create a direction, understand risk and create a debate about the future.

## References

Asselt, M., Klooster, S., Notten, P. & Smits, L. (2010). *Foresight in Action: Developing Policy-Oriented Scenarios*. London: Routledge.
Bell, W. (1993). *Foundations of Futures Studies: History, Purposes, Knowledge: Human Science for a New Era*. London: Transaction Publishers.
Bergman, A., Karlsson, J. C. & Axelsson, J. (2010). Truth claims and explanatory claims. An ontological typology of futures studies. *Futures*, 42(8), 857–865.
Bishop, P., Hines, A., & Collins, T. (2007). The current state of scenario development: An overview of techniques. *Foresight*, 9(1), 5–25.
Brown, G. (2009). Utopian cities. In Kitchin, R. & Thrift, N. (Eds.), *International Encyclopaedia of Human Geography* (pp. 125–130). Amsterdam: Elsevier Science.
Chiu, C. (2009). What's in the name "Tasmania"? A discourse analysis of Tasmania as a paradise for tourists of Chinese origin. *International Journal of Language, Society and Culture*, 28(1), 16–20.
Costa, J. A. (1998). Paradisal discourse: A critical analysis of marketing and consuming Hawaii. *Consumption Markets & Culture*, 1(4), 303–346.
Coyle, F. & Fairweather, J. (2005). Challenging a place myth: New Zealand's clean green image meets the biotechnology revolution. *Area*, 37(2), 148–158.
Dator, J. (2014). Four images of the future. *Set: Research Information for Teachers*, 61–63.
Getz, D., Robinson, R., Andersson, T. & Vujicic, S. (2014). *Foodies and Food Tourism*. Oxford: Goodfellow Publishers.

Hedrén, J. & Linnér, B.-O. (2009). Utopian thought and sustainable development. *Futures, 41*(4), 197–200.

Huston, S., Wadley, D. & Fitzpatrick, R. (2015). Bohemianism and urban regeneration. *Space and Culture, 18*(3), 311–323.

Jepson, A. D. & Clarke, A. (2015). *Exploring Community Festivals and Events*. New York: Routledge.

Kahn, H. & Wiener, A. J. (1967). *The Year 2000: A Framework for Speculation on the Next Thirty-Three Years*. New York: Macmillan.

Kapferer, J.-N. (2014). The future of luxury: Challenges and opportunities. *Journal of Brand Management, 21*(9), 716–726.

Lee, S. (2014). Music festivals and regional development in Australia. *Annals of Leisure Research, 17*(2), 243–244.

Levitas, R. (2010). *The Concept of Utopia*. Oxford: Peter Lang.

Miekle, S. (2017, 14th November 2017). *Personnel Communication* [Statistics for Wellington on a Plate].

Mowforth, M. & Munt. I. (2009). *Tourism and Sustainability: Development, Globalisation and New Tourism in the Third World* (3rd ed.). London, New York: Routledge.

Muller, J. (2015). The future of knowledge and skills in science and technology higher education. *Higher Education: The International Journal of Higher Education Research, 70*(3), 409–416.

OECD (2017). *Education at a Glance 2017*. Organisation for Economic Co-operation and Development Publishing.

Ringland, G. (2010). The role of scenarios in strategic foresight. *Technological Forecasting and Social Change, 77*(9), 1493–1498.

Slaughter, R. A. (2002). From forecasting and scenarios to social construction: Changing methodological paradigms in futures studies. *Foresight, 4*(3), 26–31.

Taquet, M., Quoidbach, J., de Montjoye, Y.-A., Desseilles, M. & Gross, J. J. (2016). Hedonism and the choice of everyday activities. *Proceedings of the National Academy of Sciences of the United States of America, 113*(35), 9769.

United Nations Statistical Division (2015). *World Statistics Pocketbook*. Retrieved from Geneva: http://data.un.org/CountryProfile.aspx?crName=ITALY. Accessed 16/12/2017.

UNWTO (2012). Global Report on Food Tourism. Retrieved from http://cf.cdn.unwto.org/sites/all/files/docpdf/amreports4-foodtourism.pdf. Accessed 16/12/2017.

Van der Heijden, K., Bradfield, R., Burt, G., Cairns, G. & Wright, G. (2002). *Sixth Sense Accelerating Organizational Learning with Scenarios*. Chichester: Wiley.

Veenman, S. A. (2013). Futures studies and uncertainty in public policy: A case study on the ageing population in the Netherlands. *Futures, 53*(September), 42–52.

Yeoman, I. (2008). *Tomorrow Tourist: Scenarios and Trends*. London: Elsevier Science.

Yeoman, I. (2010). Tomorrows tourist: Fluid and simple identities. *Journal of Globalization Studies, 1*(2), 118–127.

Yeoman, I. (2012). *2050: Tomorrow Tourism*. Bristol: Channel View Publications.

Yeoman, I. (2013). Tomorrow's tourist and New Zealand. In Leigh, J., Webster, C. & Ivanov, S. (Eds.), *Future Tourism* (pp. 161–188). London: Routledge.

Yeoman, I., Lennon, J. J., Blake, A., Galt, M., Greenwood, C. & McMahon-Beattie, U. (2007). Oil depletion: What does this mean for Scottish tourism? *Tourism Management, 28*(5), 1354–1365.

Yeoman, I. & McMahon-Beattie, U. (2014). Exclusivity: The future of luxury. *Journal of Revenue and Pricing Management, 13*(1), 12–22.

Yeoman, I., McMahon-Beattie, U. Backer, E., Robertson, M. & Smith, K. (Eds.) (2014). *The Future of Events and Festivals*. London: Routledge.

Yeoman, I., McMahon-Beattie, U., Fields, K., Albrecht, J. & Meethan, K. (2015). *The Future of Food Tourism: Foodies, Experiences, Exclusivity, Visions and Political Capital*. Bristol: Channel View Publications.

Yeoman, I., McMahon-Beattie, U. & Findlay, K. (2014). The future of urban spas: A trend analysis of the UK market. *Tourism Recreation Research, 39*(3), 397–413.

Yeoman, I., Robertson, M. & Smith, K. (2012). A futurist's view on the future of events. In Page, S. & Connell, J. (Eds.), *The Routledge Handbook of Events* (pp. 507–525). London: Routledge.

# INDEX

*Adekyem* Festival of Bechem, Ghana 352–354
*Apuor* Festival of Techiman, Ghana 349–351
Akaroa Harvest Festival 219–220
Akaroa Heritage Festival/French Fest 218–219
attendees 45; experiences 248, 341–342, 362–363; motivations 236–237

Barbaros Strawman Festival, İzmir 145–148
behaviour change 78

co-creation 108, 125, 163–165
*communitas* 177, 246, 258, 306–307
community 215–217, 264–265, 286–287
cost–benefit analysis 47–49
culture and heritage 152–154, 200–201, 300–301, 357–358, 390–391

destination branding 142–143, 143–144, 153–154, 186–187, 190–191

economic development 308–309, 370
economic impacts 27–28, 48; CGE modelling 46–67; direct expenditure 46; economic impact analysis 46–47; evaluation 44–45; I–O modelling 46
education 398–399
emotions 250, 270, 307–308
empowerment 278–279
environmental leadership 76
environmental management 72–73
environmental sustainability: definitions 28, 72; energy 74; transport 74–75; waste 74; water 75
event bundling 298–299
eventful cities 196–199
Exit Festival 187–191

families 235–236; activities 327–328; quality of life 237–238, 239–241
festival: definitions 4–5, 43–44, 246; product 346–348; types 14–15
*Festival Internacional Cervantino*, Mexico 154–160
festival research: approaches 19; methods 13, 16–17; priorities 19–20; religious/spiritual research 313–316; themes 3–4, 12; trends 17–18
festivalisation 317–318, 339–341
Fleadh Cheoil, Northern Ireland 177–182

Geelong Revival Motoring Festival 225–230
Guelaguetza, Mexico 359–363

heterotopia 376–377, 379–382
holism 32–33
holograms 412
hybrid festivals 103–104

ICT: gamification 260; influence on the attendee experience 258–259; Technology Acceptance Model 256; trends 259–230; types/use 255–256, 407–409
identity 290, 304–306
INH (I Need Helpers) 86–89
innovation: at festivals 113–114; definitions 111–113; diffusion of innovations theory 256
Izmir European Jazz Festival, Turkey 137–139
Izmir Festival, Turkey 137–139

*Laufskálarétt*, Iceland 337–342
leveraging 176–177
liminal/liminoid experiences 306–307, 377–378, 379–382
livecasts 411–412
live screens 410

## Index

Macau Arts Festival 115–119
meanings of festivals 32–38, 122–124, 264–265, 269
Mértola Islamic Festival, Portugal 266–270

nationalism/national identity 324–325
networks 122; network nanagement 125–127

online festivals 104–106
OMF (outdoor music festivals) 92–93; alcohol and drug abuse 93–94; harm minimisation/health promotion 94–95; health policy 96; Ottawa Charter 95–96

Peirce, C.S. 32–33
phenomenology 35–38
place 55–56
politics: politics of division 177–178; politics of feminism 277–278; politics of protest 206–210; politics in Serbia 187–189
portfolios 24
pride parade/s 207–208
protest 208–210

*Ramleela* of Patunda, India 368–372
religion/spirituality 316–317
resilience 215–217

Saussure, F. de 32–33
scenario planning 418–419
semiosis 32–33
senses 250, 307–308
social capital 54–55, 247–248
social inclusion 199–200

social media: attendee decision-making 165–166; attendee experience 166–168; definitions 103; festival marketing 168–170; user-generated festivals 106–107
social sustainability: definitions 56–58, 62–63; indicators 56–57
sociocultural capital 63, 387–390
socio-cultural impacts 63–64, 175–176, 289–290
sponsorship: marketing benefits 133–135; types 135–137
stakeholders 77, 97–98, 125, 205–206, 346
streaming 410–411
suppliers/supply chain 73–74
SWOT (strengths, weaknesses, opportunities and threats) 147–148

tourism and festivals 27, 152, 201, 295–298, 335–336, 361–362
triple bottom line 45

value: definitions 22–23; measurement 23; non-use value 25
virtual reality 103–104, 399–403, 412–413
volunteers: management 85–86; motivations 84; research 83–85

Wacken Open Air Festival 66–68
Water Festival of Kızılcahamam, Turkey 375–382
Wellington on a Plate 417–418, 422–424
willingness to pay 64
women in the festival space/feminism 275–276, 279–280

*Yugambeh Mobo* Festival 384–391